THE BOOK OF BOOKS

THE
BOOK OF BOOKS

Biblical Interpretation, Literary Culture, and the
Political Imagination from Erasmus to Milton

Thomas Fulton

Published in Cooperation with
Folger Shakespeare Library

PENN

UNIVERSITY OF PENNSYLVANIA PRESS

PHILADELPHIA

Published by
University of Pennsylvania Press
Philadelphia, Pennsylvania 19104-4112
www.upenn.edu/pennpress

Printed in the United States of America on acid-free paper
10 9 8 7 6 5 4 3 2 1

A catalogue record for this book is available
from the Library of Congress.
ISBN 978-0-8122-5266-8

For my parents

CONTENTS

A Note on Texts   ix

Introduction   1

Chapter 1. Erasmus's New Testament and the Politics of Historicism   24

Chapter 2. Tyndale's Literalism and the Laws of Moses   48

Chapter 3. A New Josiah and Bucer's Theocratic Utopia   83

Chapter 4. The Word in Exile: The Geneva Bible and Its Readers   110

Chapter 5. Battling Bibles and Spenser's Dragon   141

Chapter 6. *Measure for Measure* and the New King   174

Chapter 7. Milton's Bible and Revolutionary Psalm Culture   200

Chapter 8. Milton Contra Tyndale   232

Coda. Legitimating Power   249

Notes   259

Bibliography   303

Biblical Index   337

General Index   345

Acknowledgments   369

A NOTE ON TEXTS

I have struggled with whether to modernize texts or leave them in the original. Except for the titles of early books cited in the notes and bibliography and passages quoted in the notes, I have chosen to modernize spelling and (very occasionally) punctuation throughout the text. I have generally preserved the original irregularities of capitalization. When humanistic study seems under siege, there remain few compelling reasons to exclude nonspecialists or international readers, especially with the difficulties of early Tudor orthography. It also seems inconsistent to surround modernized texts such as Shakespeare's with the erratic spelling of his contemporaries. The one exception is Edmund Spenser, because modern editions of Spenser are left in original spelling, and because it seemed too big a task in a monograph with a broad scope to question that well-defended scholarly tradition. In some cases, where the original spelling of the word represents a somewhat different or particularly expressive word—as when Henry VIII articulates his scruples over scripture as a "scripulositie"—I have included the original with the transcription.

Introduction

After the Bible was Translated into *English*, every Man, nay every Boy
and Wench that could read *English*, thought they spoke with God
Almighty and understood what he said, when by a certain number
of Chapters a day they had read the Scriptures once or twice over, the
Reverence and Obedience due to the Reformed Church here, and
to the Bishops and Pastors therein, was cast off, and every Man became
the Judge of Religion, and the Interpreter of Scriptures to himself.

—Thomas Hobbes, *Behemoth: The History of the Causes of the
Civil Wars of England* (written ca. 1668)

Many years ago, in an effort to recover the experience of early modern readers, I
began the seemingly simple task of reading their Bibles. What started as explor-
atory and haphazard became more and more systematic as I sought to understand the Geneva version, an annotated Bible created by Protestant exiles during
the reign of Queen Mary. This was the Bible used by major figures and theologians of Elizabethan and Jacobean England, as well as a huge swath of its
reading population—it was the Bible of Queen Elizabeth, Aemilia Lanyer, William Shakespeare, Edmund Spenser, Richard Hooker, John Whitgift, and the
Earl of Oxford, Edward de Vere, among many others.[1] Because the Geneva
Bible grew to be immensely popular, with something like half a million copies
in well over 100 editions in sixty years, and because it had such extensive notes,
I realized that if I were to follow the course of study Hobbes observed in his
contemporaries—reading a certain number of chapters a day, as every boy and
girl did—I would gain a far more tangible sense of how readers accessed this

text, and how it shaped their access to others. Studying the popular Geneva text and its notes closely—and reading it comparatively with other Renaissance Bibles—seemed a first step (however belated) in understanding the interpretive habits and reading practices of early modern Britain.

The exercise also offered a way to reassess how Hobbes and others imagined the Bible as the premier text in the intellectual origins of the English Civil War. In the opening of *The Intellectual Origins of the English Revolution* (1965), for example, Christopher Hill asked whether "there were Montesquieus, Voltaires, and Diderots of the English Revolution," answering, "the Bible, especially the Geneva Bible with its highly political marginal notes, came near to being a revolutionists' handbook."[2] Given that royalists were also great readers of scripture, these causal assertions from Hobbes and Hill seemed slightly mythologizing, but it remained clear that there was far more to be understood about the social and political dimensions of the English Bible.[3] If the question of whether the text could be blamed (or celebrated) for the dissolution of political authority seemed unanswerable, the question of precisely how the ancient text worked its way into the social fabric—and how it became so readily applicable to contemporary politics—remained quite vital.

Considering this, I pursued a course of systematic reading that centered on a comparative study of England's two dominant vernacular Bibles: the Geneva text of 1560 with its extensive notes, and the 1611 Authorized Version, whose much sparser marginal notes serve only as cross-references, short philological glosses, and alternate readings. The stark paratextual differences between these key Renaissance Bibles originate in a remarkable moment in political and bibliographic history when James I, at a conference at Hampton Court in 1604, pronounced the notes of the Geneva text to be "very partial, untrue, seditious, and savoring too much, of dangerous, and traitorous conceits."[4] This fiery indictment, often seen as pervasively representative of courtly opinion, has profoundly colored the reception history of the Geneva text and, in turn, other vernacular Bibles. Yet relatively little work has been done to verify the reputed dangerousness of the notes or the actual social use—be it subversive, royalist, or puritan—of particular Bibles.[5] In undertaking a comparative reading of biblical versions and notes, I paused over central texts and their political use to trace the histories of interpretation and translation in older versions of the Bible. The biblical translations and annotations of Desiderius Erasmus and William Tyndale in particular provide a major point of origin for Tudor biblical translations and annotations, and also, like the later paratexts, they offer a remarkable site of commerce between translation and cultural reuse. Here, too, one could ask whether the early modern Bible and its paratext operated as a kind of polemic or political advice manual, and, contrariwise, whether and how much the political context shaped biblical interpretation. Not only offering correctives to long-held suppositions about the contents of the annotations, my systematic reading also vastly challenged assumptions I had held about the interpretive habits the notes represent and prepared me for the present investigation into their cultural and political role. The annotations in the Geneva Bible opened a world of readings and interpretive methods quite out of step with what I had understood to be the literal approach of the Protestants, as described by reformers such as Calvin or Tyndale. The annotators of these Bibles were motivated far less than they claimed by the humanistic recovery of the "historical" text or meaning. In fact, their reading habits proved much more medieval, more figuratively typological, and above all more anachronistically presentist than they had been described to be.

The book that has resulted examines the process of recovery, reinterpretation, and reuse of scripture in the early modern political imagination. It focuses in particular on the literary and cultural transformations of the biblical text for political purposes. It thereby attends to Hobbes' concern in *Behemoth* that independent scriptural reading led to the dissolution of authority by seeking to understand what role the Bible had in shaping early modern political thought. But most importantly, this study seeks to understand *how*, precisely, it played this role: what hermeneutic and practical procedures enabled early modern English readers to transform this supremely authoritative text for their use? How did certain imperatives in reading—such as literalism, or whatever we might call their actual method—shape or impede this transformation? To get at the most common, most everyday form of reading, and the most immediate transition from biblical text to cultural discourse, I am drawn in particular to the apparatus surrounding the text, the interpretive paratext and marginal annotations. Naomi Tadmor's *Social Universe of the English Bible* has attributed the extraordinary success of the English Bible to the degree to which the translated text Anglicized the ancient Hebrew and Greek, so that more than simply translated, the text was "slightly moulded" to conform to an English framework, and "rendered in terms that made sense to people at that time."[6] Biblical annotations take this process of molding still further, as they had far greater liberty than the translated text to draw a passage closer to a meaning and context germane to its readers. My interest here is not only in the content and function of biblical annotations, but also in what occurs in the space that they represent, an interface between the ancient code of biblical meaning and the currency of the early modern world.

Like Hobbes, though with more enthusiasm than anxiety, scholars have long felt that an intense interest in scripture profoundly shaped Renaissance culture, especially after the advent of the printed vernacular Bible and the reading imperatives that accompanied it. After the extensive dissemination of vernacular Bibles during Edward VI's reign, scripture quickly became the central object of study by every literate sector of society; the Bible and biblical primers were among the first things read, often systematically, by boys and girls.[7] The poet Katherine Philips, to cite one famous example, is reputed to have "read the Bible thorough before she was full four years old."[8] John Milton, possibly given the new King James Bible when he was five years old (his marked 1612 copy is preserved in the British Library), learned the vernacular Bible at a young age, but he also became acquainted with the text in its original languages: his earliest extant poems, purportedly composed at the age of fifteen, are Psalm translations; his earliest letter thanks his tutor, Thomas Young, for his gift of a Hebrew Bible.[9] Like other early modern students and scholars, Milton took a systematic approach to his reading—culling particular passages in a theological commonplace book for later reuse. As he writes retrospectively in the introduction to *De Doctrina Christiana*, a work of extensive biblical citation, "I began in my youth . . . to study assiduously the books of the Bible, both Testaments, in their original tongues; then go carefully through some of the shorter Systems of theologians, and, following their practice, to distinguish appropriate topic-headings, under each of which I would classify whatever passages of the Bible presented themselves for extracting, so that I could recover and use them when I needed to."[10] This method largely describes Milton's reading procedures in his extant commonplace book, as it follows deep-seated conventions of reading in early modernity: biblical passages are culled, set under topics, and stored for "use" and "extraction" in the event of a thematic, theological, or polemical need.[11]

Given an early modern culture of readers familiar with the Bible and preoccupied with problems of biblical interpretation, this project seeks to recover the shape and impact of this preoccupation on cultural discourse. On a certain level, the book's premise builds on foundational work such as Northrop Frye's *Great Code: The Bible and Literature* and Frank Kermode's *Genesis of Secrecy* among other studies that allow us now to take for granted the deep influence of the biblical text on the literary imagination. My specific interest, though, is the combination of the biblical text and the paratextual packaging of that text, which revolves around particular sites of social controversy as well as the larger, often dynastically oriented, conditions under which particular Bibles were created. Much of the literature of the English Renaissance grew out of a culture of interpretation bent on making the biblical text applicable to political use. Texts laden with biblical references, such as Erasmus's *Education of a Christian Prince*, the first book of Spenser's *Faerie Queene* (also called the *Legend of Holiness*), Shakespeare's *Measure for Measure*, Milton's 1648 Psalms or *Paradise Lost*, were in conversation not just with the biblical text itself, but with the rich interprctive structures around that text. The relationship between socially oriented biblical interpretation and literary production is much more complex than simply one of source and influence, in which the dominant biblical text impresses its shape on literary production. I have sought to understand how writers endeavor to mimic and participate in the interpretive enterprise—even to argue against it and re-shape it.

To further complicate the traditional top-down vision of the Bible's influence on literary texts, the collaboration between biblical interpretation and early modern political writing often took place within the work of a single figure. Interpreters and even translators of scripture were also writers and polemicists. Arguably true of Milton, at the end of the period, this is certainly true of earlier writers like Martin Bucer, who turned from an unfinished Latin Bible to help create *The Book of Common Prayer* (1549) and write his treatise of political advice *De Regno Christi* (1550), or William Whittingham and Anthony Gilby, who worked on the annotated Geneva Bible while authoring polemics on resistance.[12] The dual, even triple, roles of biblical translator, interpreter, and political writer were fully inhabited by the two towering figures in the history of the English Renaissance Bible, Erasmus and Tyndale. On the larger European map, a significant dichotomy is usually drawn between Erasmus and Luther, and one might expect Tyndale to represent the local English version of Luther as well as the local purveyor of Lutheran ideas. Yet unlike Luther, Tyndale never openly pitted himself against Erasmus in a sustained fashion. Instead, Tyndale started his translating career as a translator of Erasmus's *Enchiridion* (1522; manuscript discovered in 2015), and then translated Erasmus's annotated New Testament, both its Greek and sometimes Erasmus's Latin; Tyndale's English New Testament was subsequently published in diglot editions with Erasmus's Latin.[13] Tyndale's possibly apocryphal words, recorded by John Foxe, that "If God spare my life, ere many years I will cause a boy that driveth the plough shall know more of the scripture than thou dost,"[14] derive from Erasmus's *Paraclesis*, where Erasmus declares in a series of wistful subjunctives, "I would desire that all women should read the gospel and Paul's epistles, and I would to God they were translated in to the tongues of all men, so that they might not only be read, and known, of the Scots and Irishmen, but also of the Turks and Saracens. . . . I would to God the plowman would sing a text of the scripture at his plowbeam."[15] Stephen Greenblatt rightly points to the "vast difference between Erasmus's 'Would that' and Tyndale's 'I will cause,'"[16] yet this difference is in many ways bridged by Foxe's myth-making report, which reframes Erasmian aspiration as Tyndalean volition. Indeed, the 1529 translation of Erasmus's *Paraclesis* (quoted here) was used to preface Tyndale's New Testament in 1536. Here and elsewhere, Erasmus is paradoxically cast as a progenitor and even a figure of the English Reformation.

With one writing exclusively in Latin and the other in the vernacular, Erasmus and Tyndale set the stage early in the northern Renaissance as model scholars involved in translating and commenting on scripture as they wrote political advice books and works theorizing the application of scripture to the problems of the state. Erasmus undertook the project of annotating and retranslating the *Novum Instrumentum* (1516) at the same time that he developed rhetorical approaches for addressing princes in the *Education of a Christian Prince* (1516) among many other works. Tyndale was similarly occupied in such biblically inflected works as his *Obedience of a Christian Man and How Christian Rulers Ought to Govern* (1528), *The Practice of Prelates: Whether the King's Grace May be Separated from his Queen* (1530), and the polemical *Exposition of Matthew* (1533) while translating the New Testament and parts of the Hebrew Bible. Henry VIII had been outraged at what he called the "pestilent glosses in the margents"[17] of Tyndale's first New Testament—seemingly more scandalizing than the text itself—but he eventually found use for vernacular scripture as well as Tyndale's theory of obedience.

This book begins its history with Erasmus and Tyndale, and traces the connected problems of interpretation and application through several punctuated moments in the combined history of biblical production and political change: the crisis of religion at the moment of Henry's divorce, the biblical installment of Edward VI, the period of exile for Protestants during Mary's reign, tensions under Elizabeth, uncertainties surrounding the arrival of James from Scotland, and the dissolution of the monarchy in the 1640s. These moments occasioned Bibles and biblical texts that sought to cultivate particular views, including Tyndale's Pentateuch (1530), the Edwardian Bibles of Edmund Becke (1549, 1551), the Geneva Bibles created in exile (1557, 1560), the Bishops' Bible (1568), the Douay-Rheims Catholic Bible (1582, 1609) with its intense biblical "confutations" published as superannotated Bibles, and the King James Version (1611), radically shorn of explanatory notes.

Dynastic shifts often motivated biblical production, and these moments of revision are tied to problems in interpretation. In the case of what are often called "official" Bibles, such as the Bishops' Bible, monarchs and their bishops worked together to produce a new version; and, in the case of the unofficial Geneva Bible, exiled annotators inscribed the conditions of the "nation" under Catholic rule into the margins and then, on the death of Mary, prefaced the new Bible with a dedication to Elizabeth.[18] As I discuss further in Chapter 2, a complex scheme of Protestant royal iconography reinforced this connection between the monarch and the Bible in the Tudor era, often drawing on Hans Holbein's influential woodcut in the first complete printed English Bible of 1535. The same image of a Tudor monarch appears with the boy king Edward in Thomas Cranmer's *Catechism*, and then with Elizabeth in the place of her father in editions of the Bishops' Bible, though with significant changes in iconography.[19] (These images are discussed in chapters 2, 3, and 6.) Images participate in the interpretive paratextual structure surrounding the biblical text; working in coordination with the verbal components, they play a major role in sustaining a particular reading of the text. In 1539, Henry VIII issued an official "Great Bible"—"great" simply for its enormous pulpit size—and here the title page image depicts Henry with Bibles in each hand, inscribed with "VERBUM DEI," passing them to Thomas Cranmer and Thomas Cromwell.[20] In Edward's reign, though the project never came to being, Archbishop Cranmer invited German reformers to create a new Latin Bible—improving on Erasmus's work—that would originate in England. And in Elizabeth's reign, Matthew Parker and other bishops created the Bishops' Bible, which drew both notes and translation ideas (though revised) from the Geneva Bible.

The association between Bibles and monarchs was so strong that the Interregnum church historian Thomas Fuller, in his major work *The Church-History of Britain* (1655), enumerates the first four translations of the Bible, which he calls according to their royal sponsors—the "last and best" being the King James Version (Figure 1). The chart Fuller provides to illustrate these four translations is telling for its unconscious inaccuracies as well as its deliberate omissions, especially the omission of the Geneva Bible. Many of the inaccuracies are not in the least surprising, given how hard it would be to reconstruct such a complex bibliography—even a century later—without a *Short-Title Catalogue*, the specialized *Historical Catalogue of Printed Editions of the English Bible*, and the still-growing body of scholarship on the English Bible.[21] Yet the omissions in the list are more striking, especially because

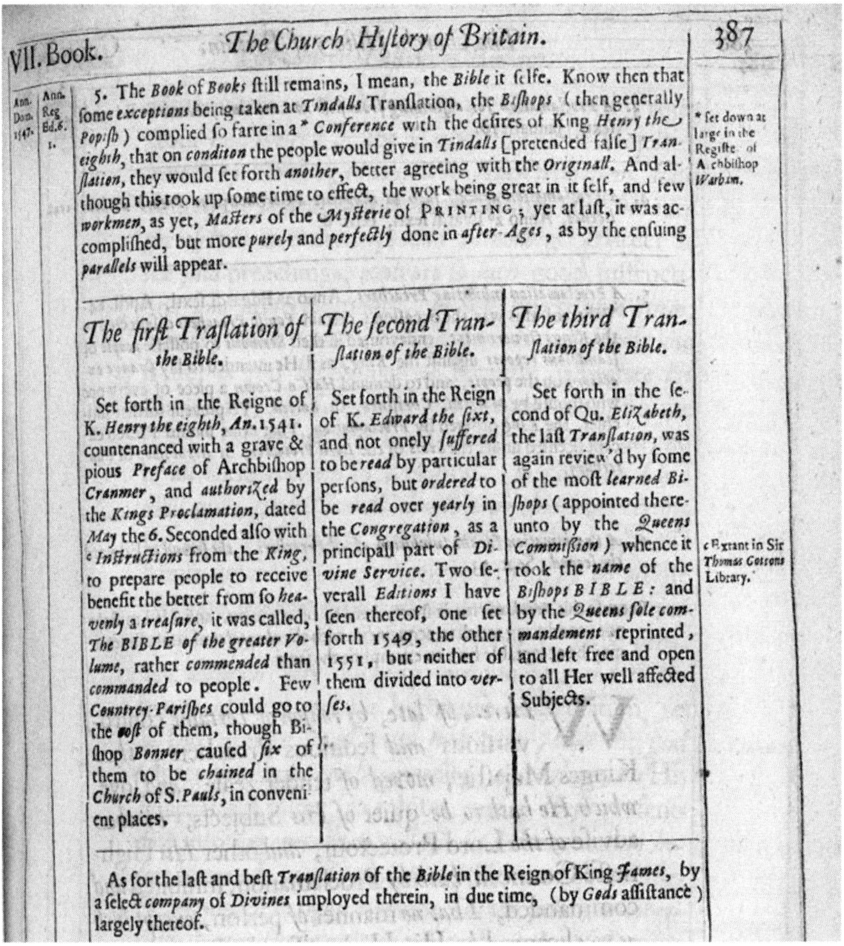

Ann. Dom. 1547. / Ann. Reg. Ed.6. 1.

5. The *Book* of *Books* still remains, I mean, the *Bible* it selfe. Know then that some *exceptions* being taken at *Tindalls* Translation, the *Bishops* (then generally *Popish*) complied so farre in a * *Conference* with the desires of King *Henry the eighth*, that on *conditon* the people would give in *Tindalls* [pretended false] *Translation*, they would set forth *another*, better agreeing with the *Originall*. And although this took up some time to effect, the work being great in it self, and few *workmen*, as yet, *Masters* of the *Mysterie* of PRINTING ; yet at last, it was accomplished, but more *purely* and *perfectly* done in *after-Ages*, as by the ensuing *parallels* will appear.

* set down at large in the Registe of Archbishop *Warham*.

The first Traslation of the Bible.	The second Translation of the Bible.	The third Translation of the Bible.
Set forth in the Reigne of K. *Henry the eighth*, *An.*1541. countenanced with a grave & pious *Preface* of Archbishop *Cranmer*, and *authorized* by the *Kings Proclamation*, dated *May* the 6. Seconded also with *Instructions* from the *King*, to prepare people to receive benefit the better from so *heavenly* a *treasure*, it was called, *The BIBLE of the greater Volume*, rather *commended* than *commanded* to people. Few *Countrey-Parishes* could go to the *cost* of them, though Bishop *Bonner* caused *six* of them to be *chained* in the *Church* of S.*Pauls*, in convenient places.	Set forth in the Reign of K. *Edward the sixt*, and not onely *suffered* to be *read* by particular persons, but *ordered* to be *read* over *yearly* in the *Congregation*, as a principall part of *Divine Service*. Two severall *Editions* I have seen thereof, one set forth 1549, the other 1551, but neither of them divided into *verses*.	Set forth in the second of Qu. *Elizabeth*, the last *Translation*, was again review'd by some of the most *learned Bishops* (appointed thereunto by the *Queens Commission*) whence it took the *name* of the *Bishops BIBLE*: and by the *Queens* sole *commandement* reprinted, and left free and open to all Her well affected Subjects.

c Extant in Sir *Thomas Cottons* Library.

As for the last and best *Translation* of the *Bible* in the Reign of King *James*, by a select *company* of *Divines* imployed therein, in due time, (by *Gods* assistance) largely thereof.

Figure 1. "The Book of Books" from Fuller's *Church-History of Britain* (1655). The first, second, third, and "the last and best Translation of the Bible"—the King James Version—each "set forth" in the reigns of Protestant monarchs. The Geneva Bible is notably omitted from the chart. Thomas Fuller, *Church-History of Britain* (London: Printed for John Williams, 1655), 387; Call number: 151–385f. Used by permission of the Folger Shakespeare Library.

Fuller knew the Geneva well (it receives more explanation in his text than any of the others).[22]

Also not given a place in the chart, Tyndale's translations nonetheless appear in the preliminaries as a "[pretended false] Translation," which had to be recalled and replaced with the Great Bible, supposedly "rather commended than commanded to people." The supposed "first" translation is, as Fuller describes the Great Bible, the authoritative correction to Tyndale, "Extant in Sir Thomas Cotton's library," which he incorrectly dates 1541. The first Great Bible was printed in 1539, but there were official and semiofficial Bibles before this, the earliest complete printed edition, the Coverdale Bible, having first appeared in 1535 or early 1536. Cranmer had urged Cromwell to obtain the king's "most Gracious License" for the 1537 Matthew Bible, so named after "Thomas Matthew," a pseudonym designed to cloak the extensive presence of Tyndale, killed the year before its appearance. The same license is given to the 1537 printing of the Coverdale Bible, which had (with Holbein's help) flatteringly portrayed the king.[23] As Fuller relates, the Great Bibles were chained in Saint Paul's Church in London, though many "*Country-Parishes*" could not afford them.[24] By Edward's reign, congregations systematically read the Great Bible throughout the year, and, according to the nutshell account in Fuller's "*Book of Books*" chart, Elizabeth's official Bishops' Bible (his so-called "third Translation") is "left free and open to all Her well affected Subjects."

Fuller describes each English Bible as originating from a Protestant monarch in association with the bishops and handed, in one way or another, down to the people. There is some truth to this, though Edward's reign saw only the repackaging of old translations in spite of the court's aspirations to create the great Protestant Latin translation and the similarly abortive efforts of John Cheke to create a vernacular New Testament.[25] Fuller's invented "second Translation" under Edward seems to originate from the profound branding power of visual and textual paratexts, especially the images of Tudor monarchs in Bibles issued in their reigns. For him, it is natural to assume that with each new Protestant monarch came a new translation, and that there are only four translations worthy of mention, one for each monarch, with the last and best belonging to James. In the case of the Edwardian Bible, Fuller probably here refers to Edmund Becke's editions published by John Day in 1549 and 1551. Although not a new translation, it is a newly edited edition of the Matthew Bible. Edmund Becke supervised these editions and wrote an important dedication to Edward VI that would have given Fuller the impression of another official translation. There were, in fact, many more than four English translations, and more of them

originated from exiles (both Protestant and Catholic) and private scholars than
from the commands of kings or the labor of bishops. By far the most read and
disseminated among these translations—unacknowledged in Fuller's chart—
was originally the product of exiles writing during the reign of a Catholic
Queen.

The occlusions and inaccuracies in Fuller's bibliographic presentation point
to a reality that may have been even stronger in perception: Bibles were highly
effective products for those in power. Engendering assent in large portions of
society, Bibles served as powerful expressions of national sovereignty. From a
cultural standpoint, therefore, translation, commentary, and paratext were often the province of the powerful even when created by the marginalized or exiled. Miles Coverdale, hiding on the continent to create what would essentially
become a royalist biblical production—issued just before Tyndale's execution—
serves as a case in point. Similarly, the Genevan exiles filled their translation
with subversive notes long before they had any idea that Queen Mary would die
in time for them to repackage the Bible of early 1560 into an influential statement of Elizabethan nationalism, proclaiming—and arguably helping to
shape—the new Queen as the "our Zerubbabel," the descendant of David who
would build the second Temple after the nation had been captured by idolaters.[26] The powerfully nationalist "Epistle to Elizabeth," one of the changes
made to turn the Marian text into an Elizabethan one, introduced Genevan and
London editions for the next twenty-two years.

Rethinking the Literal Sense

The "Letter to Can Grande" attributed to Dante connects literary criticism with
biblical hermeneutics and usefully encapsulates the layered forms of medieval
allegory that were common prior to the Reformation. The text is valuable not
only as a potential example of a writer considering biblical hermeneutics as a
reflection of his own modes of representation, but also as an illustration of the
differences between medieval and Renaissance forms of reading. Medieval
forms of reading had developed into several interpretive modes. Called the
Quadriga after the Roman chariot drawn by four horses, these were the literal,
the allegorical (often synonymous with typological), tropological (or moral),
and the anagogic (spiritual). In Dante's famous explanation of these layers of
meaning, he takes a passage from Psalm 114: "When Israel went out of Egypt,
the house of Jacob from a barbarous people, Judea was made his sanctuary, Is-

rael his dominion." As the text explains, the passage carries four senses: the literal, that the Israelites left Egypt in the time of Moses; the allegorical, that this represents redemption through Christ; the tropological, that this signifies the conversion of the soul from misery to the state of grace; and finally, the anagogical, that this relates the "departure of the sanctified soul from bondage to the corruption of this world into the freedom of eternal glory."[27] Protestant reformers sought an interpretative method less layered and less polysemous, insisting that scripture should have only one sense. "They divide the scripture into four senses," wrote Tyndale, "the literal, tropological, allegorical, anagogical. The literal sense is becoming nothing at all. For the Pope hath taken it clean away and hath made it his possession." He then makes what is perhaps his most famous statement, intoned in terms that resonate with the imperatives of the Ten Commandments: "Thou shalt understand therefore that the scripture hath but one sense which is the literal sense." Further, Tyndale denounces allegorical reading altogether: "The greatest cause of which captivity and the decay of the faith and this blindness wherein we now are, sprang first of allegories." To be sure, scripture offers allegories among other figures, but these must be subordinated to a literal reading: "that which the proverb, similitude, riddle or allegory signifieth is ever the literal sense which thou must seek out diligently." Thus, Tyndale in 1528 cautions against securing too much meaning in biblical books like Revelation, which rely heavily on allegory without a literal backing: "The Apocalypse or Revelations of John are allegories whose literal sense is hard to find in many places."[28]

In spite of such credos of simple literalism, close attention to the interpretative practices of Tyndale and other English Protestants reveals that they still read scripture on multiple levels. The contradiction raises two related concerns: first, that the interpretive habits of readers do not necessarily conform to the way they define these habits; and second, that the words they used to define their methods, such as "literal," have changed or narrowed since the early modern period, complicating our adoption of these terms. The persistence of medieval modes of reading—themselves far more nuanced than the critical parodies of the Protestants suggest—also stems simply from the weight of habit and tradition.[29] Centuries of habituated interpretation cannot change in a matter of a single year or decade even if a coherent plan for hermeneutic change were instituted. But many voices planned the Reformation—or Reformations, as Christopher Haigh has shown of England, and certainly such multiplicity existed outside of the island as well—and significant changes of mind occurred within individual careers and within the movements.[30]

Rather than relying on the reformers' self-defined methods of interpretation, therefore, this project endeavors to reconstruct methods of interpretation from the practices of interpreters, annotators, and readers, with particular attention to the margins of the biblical text—both the printed margins and paratexts, and, where possible, the valuable marks of readers. As I have discussed elsewhere with Kristen Poole, hermeneutics, a field of study we often relegate to the lofty world of theologians, was in fact so often the subject of sermons and commentaries that we can confidently speak of "popular hermeneutics": common readers were versed not only in the biblical texts themselves but in modes of interpreting them.[31] These interpretive cultures are shaped as much by habit, of course, as by self-conscious expressions of method. The explanatory notes in the Geneva Bible conform to several different categories of reading, many of which are, in fact, holdovers from medieval traditions in the Quadriga. Following the Quadriga, and drawing from it, these modes of reading exist in something like four categories:

1. Historicist reading, which falls into two related subcategories:
   a. Contextualist historicism, which seeks to explain a passage according to the conditions of the ancient past contemporary to the text. Historicist glosses sometimes include cross-references, or references to Josephus.
   b. Philological historicism, which seeks to recover the sense of words from their ancient lexical context. Although Erasmus simply intermixed these subcategories in his annotations, contextualism and philology began to be disaggregated in the Geneva annotations, so that sometimes philology appears in the explanatory notes, but more often in separate italicized notes set off by straight quotation marks rather than numbers. The explanatory note for the word "masons" in 1 Kings 5:18, for example, a passage describing the workers gathered by Solomon to build the Temple, is philological: "The Hebrew word is, Giblim, which some say, were excellent masons." A similar philological note appears in the margins of the King James Version (which ostensibly had no explanatory notes), since translators were clearly intrigued by this Hebrew word: "*Or, Giblites, as Ezek. 27:9,*" which enforces this group as the proper name of a people from Gebal. More often in the Geneva text philological notes appear separately, as in the one on "camel" in

Jesus's statement, "It is easier for a camel to go through the eye of a needle, then for a rich man to enter into the kingdom of God" (Matt. 19:24). The gloss, *"Or, cable rope"* derives from new research into the early Syriac translation, which helped determine ambiguities around Aramaic and Hebrew words for rope and camel. The reading offered in the margin functions more as an alternate reading than an embellishment, and the fact that it remained in the margins rather than the text should not imply a lesser status. In this case, the domesticated service animal associated with this passage since Wycliffe and Tyndale (and before in the Vulgate's *camelum*) had maintained enough cultural strength to retain the English word in the text even while a different signifier had emerged.[32] These alternate readings, often introduced by "or," became the dominant marginal paratext in the King James Version, as is discussed in chapter 7. The King James text often adopts the alternate reading of the Geneva, as if the passage of time had enabled a promotion of the marginal translation into the text. Here the KJV stayed with the traditional "camel" and did not offer an alternative.

2. Anachronistic reading, which falls into two subcategories:
   a. Typology, a medieval tradition readily adapted by Protestants, which reads a specific event or person in the Old Testament as a "figure" or "type" for an event or person in the New Testament, sometimes with cross-references.
   b. Presentist reading, which applies any event, symbol, or biblical personage to the early modern historical present. The most telling indication of this sort of reading is in the anachronistic vocabulary of the notes: words like "papist" or "tyrant" evoke the early modern present in the biblical past.

3. Universalist moralizing (a form of "tropological" interpretation): proverbial commonplaces on theology and human nature, such as a note on Lamentations 3:37: "He showeth that nothing is done without Gods providence." ("Gods providence" has a particularly Calvinistic resonance here, but otherwise it is simply a note geared toward reinforcing the moral lesson of the passage.)

4. Allegorical interpretation. In spite of Tyndale's explicit rejection of this mode of reading (especially when not subordinated to literalism), allegory persists. As I discuss in chapter 5, allegory powerfully

reenters the Protestant hermeneutic arena after the polemical power
of the Book of Revelation becomes apparent, mostly after 1530.
Signaling the ostensible Protestant aversion to the term, "allegory"
itself is exceedingly rare in the Geneva notes—I have found just
two instances, and significantly not in Revelation, where it most
belongs. It is used to explain the genre of the Song of Songs, which
begins with this description in the Argument: "In this Song,
Solomon by most sweet and comfortable allegories and parables
describeth the perfect love of Jesus Christ." Allegory is an established mode of reading the Song of Songs that many used, including Milton.[33] The rare term similarly appears in Galatians 4:22 and
following, where the headnote to the chapter explains that Paul
"confirmeth his argument with a strong example or allegory." This
is one of a few examples Tyndale provides to support his view that
allegorical reading must be supported by literal: "And (Galatians 4),
The spirit cometh by preaching of the faith etc. Thus doth the
literal sense prove the allegory and bear it, as the foundation
beareth the house."[34]

Outside of the Book of Revelation, which becomes increasingly important as a
separate entity, the most dominant modes of interpretation in the Geneva Bible's
notes are historicism and presentism (that is, 1a and 2b), with forms of typology
also playing an important role in readings of the Old Testament and informing
the allegorical approach to Revelation. Of course, these four modes of reading
frequently overlap.

The interrelatedness of different genres of annotation occurs in a gloss on
Lamentations 4:20 in the Geneva Bible, which I discuss in chapter 4, at a moment of lament by the vanquished Jews notable for its obscurity: "The breath of
our nostrils, the Anointed of the Lord was taken in their nets, of whom we said,
Under his shadow we shall be preserved alive among the heathen." The note attached to "breath of our nostrils" reads the phrase as a royal epithet, referring
implicitly to their King Zedekiah, the last of the kings before the fall of Judah.
But the English note explicitly attaches the epithet to an actual king that has a
specific English resonance: "Our King Josiah, in whom stood our hope of Gods
favor, and on whom depended our state & life, was slain whom he calleth
anointed, because he was a figure of Christ." The repetition of "our" in "our
king," "our hope," "our state" inferentially includes the reader, and draws on the
recent loss of "Our King Josiah"—that is, King Edward VI, the young king,

like Josiah, tragically lost and replaced by the persecuting Queen who is so much the subject of these glosses. This is a case of historical typology—where a biblical king stands in for an actual English king—a phenomenon closely studied by Kevin Killeen.[35] The Geneva margin is reluctant to go so far as to make the explicit connection, but it provides sufficient framework for the reader to do so. This suggestive historicist reading, perhaps too suggestive to withstand scrutiny, ultimately gives way to biblical typology: the anointed king is a figure of Christ. The paratext performs what many notes strive to do in converting a relatively obscure passage to useful applicability. It suggests that in spite of the frequent insistence on the simple sense of scripture, Protestant reading can be far more complex than it describes itself to be: more polysemous, often historical, more frequently allegorical, typological in a couple of ways, but always intent on transforming the ancient text for use in the early modern present.

Ostensibly, at least, Tyndale broke interpretive practices down into a simple binary, the literal versus the allegorical or figurative. The binary between literal and figurative was long imagined in terms of Paul's aphoristic statement in 2 Corinthians 3:6, "the letter killeth, but the Spirit giveth life," a passage that seemed for many medieval Catholics to celebrate allegorical reading and mandate against the literal sense. Tyndale's prose, which offers more exhortation than explanation, describes how the passage was mistakenly thought to condemn literalism: "Yea they are come unto such blindness that they not only say the literal sense profiteth not, but also that it is hurtful and noisome and killeth the soul. Which damnable doctrine they prove by a text of Paul (2 Corinthians 3) where he saith the letter killeth but the spirit giveth life. Lo say they the literal sense killeth and the spiritual sense giveth life."[36] Tyndale's emphatic endorsement of the literal sense may not be without its own paradoxical complexity, or precisely identical to the views of other reformers on the subject, but it is broadly representative of the teaching, if not always the practice, of Protestant reformers.

In an influential reading of the Pauline passage in *De Doctrina Christiana*, Augustine eschewed "blind adherence to the letter": "For he who follows the letter takes figurative words as if they were proper, and does not carry out what is indicated by a proper word into its secondary signification."[37] In a later work, *De Spiritu et Litera*, Augustine offers a revised interpretation, that Paul's words are not primarily about the literal and the figurative, but about the way that the letter or law may prescribe against sin, yet is unable in itself to provide a way to salvation.[38] Simple adherence to the outward formality of the law is, consequently, spirit killing. It is this interpretation that Luther and Calvin, among other reformers, embraced, denying the validity of the first.[39] As Calvin complains, "during several centuries, nothing was more commonly said, or more generally received, than this—that Paul here furnishes us with a key for expounding Scripture by allegories, while nothing is farther from his intention."[40]

From the knotty aftermath of the Protestant assault on medieval reading, an acute tension emerged between literal and nonliteral forms of interpretation. English literalism, as inaugurated by Tyndale, often took an extreme form that James Simpson, in a polemical and influential reassessment, has identified as fundamentalism.[41] I do not use this anachronistic term here, though the early moderns had no term for the strict interpretive tendency that emerged among Protestants, especially those of a puritanical slant. Following the tenets of *sola scriptura*, strict literalists embraced a way of reading bent on adhering to the prescriptive power of scripture, and to shorter, commandment-like statements, such as "touch not mine anointed" (1 Chron. 16:22; Ps. 105:15), or "honor thy father and thy mother" (Exod. 20:12) that could serve in a wider application than the biblical context might allow. The same interpretive tendency also sought to make scripture "the only rule to frame all our Actions by," as a polemical interpreter of the Psalms wrote, and the "only Law whereby to determine all our *Civil* Controversies."[42] The repeated words "only" and "all" are suggestive of the kind of intensive interpretive mode of this sort of literalism, as are the ways that scripture here becomes synonymous with "Law," even when law is only a generic subcategory of scripture. The passage is also suggestive of the way such readings emerge in political application. Literalism and its extreme form manifest themselves in the political realm largely in terms of reading biblical law, and accordingly they are closely allied with legalism. In Simpson's view, the "resistance to fundamentalism" that emerges in the early Tudor period comes from Catholics such as Thomas More. I argue that this oppositional model in fact describes a tension that exists within English Protestantism itself, which is deeply divided about how to read the biblical text and, in turn, how to apply textual interpretation to the ethics of daily life. The various reformations and counter-reformations in English religion do not create monolithic forms of reading, but rather reveal a profound tension within English interpretive culture between a strict literal approach and a nonliteral approach that is formed largely in response. It was against English Presbyterians in the mid-1640s, for example, that Milton turned to decry "the strictness" of "literal interpreting" that had distorted their thinking and caused illiberal marriage legislation as well as an irrational adherence to divine right.[43] The interpretive methods he proposed in turn—in his divorce tracts and in arguments about political sovereignty—allowed for far less stringent reliance on a singular, isolated biblical text. Even in the most seemingly Protestant of contexts, such as the work of Milton, English polemical and literary texts were constantly responding to, readjusting, and eroding Tyndale's foundational concept of the literal text.

The polarized paradigm of literalism versus anti-literalism provides a useful working framework, but it is also seriously complicated by the very fact that "literalism" remains incomplete as a hermeneutic label even for a figure like Tyndale. As my chapter on Tyndale argues, his core argument for political obedience, following Luther, relies on an embellished reading of the Mosaic law regarding the obedience of parents—a reading that is not, in fact, readily recognizable as literal, though it does follow an increasingly predominant hermeneutic pattern in social and political applications. The interest of this project, then, is to reconstruct a hermeneutic method that derives not from the self-proclaimed literalist method of Tyndale and other writers, but from the realities of their practice. A broad reading of the notes of Renaissance Bibles, and of manuscript annotations and other traces of readerly activity, enable both an expanded history of early modern reading and a revised history of interpretation, one that sees more connection between practice and theory. Combining hermeneutic histories with the history of reading, I build on scholarly research that has reconstructed the way that early modern readers processed and reused textual material.[44] This research has uncovered the degree to which early readers conceived of the activity of reading in highly utilitarian terms, describing themselves less as readers, which suggests passive reception of material, but as "users," reading for action.[45] This research in the history of reading, largely devoted to the use of secular and classical texts, deserves to be widened to consider religious texts, particularly the most read of texts, the Bible. Not surprisingly, the cultural propensity to transform classical reading material for current application also deeply characterizes the reading and interpretive procedures of early modern Bible users. Scriptural commentators constantly turned, even twisted (Erasmus used *detorquere*, "to twist") biblical verses to make them applicable to present circumstances. Thus, the habits of biblical readers and their interactions with biblical paratexts, their methods of interpreting and reusing the authoritative text, can be used to reconstruct a more accurate, if multifaceted, understanding of Renaissance biblical interpretation. I have ventured here to consider a predominant mode of socially and politically oriented reading as "applied literalism," not because it truly conforms to what we or Tyndale might consider to be literalism, but because it represents a practice closely associated with and sometimes falsely protected by the solid assurance of literal meaning.

This project shares interests with recent work on political theology such as that of Julia Lupton and Graham Hammill that approaches the combination of politics and theology from another theoretical position.[46] Much of their scholarship on these questions has focused respectively on the figures of Paul and Moses, who both play a major role in this study, since readings of Romans and the law in Exodus and Deuteronomy dominate Tudor political writing. This branch of criticism on biblical politics draws, however, from different paradigms, particularly in its use of the term "political theology." The term has been used in some of the most prominent work on politics and religion in early modern studies, though Carl Schmitt originally used it (in *Politische Theologie*, 1922) as a way of metaphorically understanding the nature of political authority emerging, as Victoria Kahn writes, either "as a symptom of or resistance to the new secular political order."[47] Drawing on Schmitt, Lupton and Hammill similarly theorize political theology as a phenomenon attached to the transition to early modernity: "We take it to name a form of questioning that arises precisely when religion is no longer a dominant explanatory or life mode."[48] Although this critical paradigm has been useful for the latter part of the early modern period, religion remains a dominant form of explanation for most of the period and for the authors covered in this book, where the conjunction of politics and theology are far different from what Schmitt imagined; indeed, since Schmitt did not concern himself directly with sixteenth-century politics and theology, it is not entirely fair or useful to gauge the truth value of his theory in this early context. Yet the seemingly unavoidable term has also pervaded very different critical perspectives. Not meaning to invoke Schmitt, "political theology" frequently describes that part of the theology of the Reformation that is political, as in Debora Shuger's *Political Theologies in Shakespeare's England*.[49] I have generally used less elegant terms to prevent confusion, though my book shares and builds upon Shuger's sense that early English political thought is largely a branch of theology. Since political theologies are constructed from the biblical text itself, my work focuses primarily on the interpretive procedures that enabled these points of contact between scripture, the political imagination, and literary discourse.

The revisionist historiographic movement of the last part of the twentieth century left an enduring critique of teleological notions of history. The revisionists were particularly sharp in their criticism of the progressivist tendency (as Blair Worden put it) to "congratulate the past on becoming more like the present."[50] Teleological cultural history tends to occlude elements in the past that do not fit the immediate concerns of the present, often leaving the sheer strangeness of the past eclipsed. Partially as a result of these historiographic shifts, early modern literary criticism has at the turn of the new millennium been far more localized, often confining its study to a single year or decade. Acknowledging the liabilities of doing so, I have sought here to widen the lens of inquiry, trying not to lapse into the old grand narrative by focusing on punctuated moments rather than moving quickly over a vast terrain. Progressivist interpretations of cultural and literary history have been particularly strong in studies of Reformation and Counter-Reformation culture, which brings me to a word about tone. I confess to admiration and even outright affection for my subject, among other things a cluster of extraordinary people, but I ardently seek not to be an apologist. We live in an age of denial—of science, of climate, even of earth's roundness—and it would seem profoundly untimely to write a book that knowingly overlooks self-contradiction, religious militancy, or any other misfortunes in human cultural history. In English scholarship there is a long history of Protestant self-congratulation, and while efforts to adjust this bias may also distort the past, triumphalist historiography still occludes other cultural and confessional histories, and draws teleological connections that do not exist. If my efforts to draw cultural history warts and all exposes more warts than were actually there, I will account myself less erring than if I airbrush them from the past.[51]

The first chapter, "Erasmus's New Testament and the Politics of Historicism," shows how Erasmus approached scripture as a literary historicist, framing its meaning within the specific circumstances from which the text arose. Erasmus's biblical readings became a vital model for his own rhetorical procedures. Investigating several Pauline verses, chapter 1 focuses in particular on a passage central to early modern politics and biblical interpretation, Paul's doctrine of obedience in Romans 13:1–7, which states that every soul must "submit himself unto the authority of the higher powers" because "there is no power but of God." Following the English educator John Colet, Erasmus proposed disarmingly that Paul meant the words only in a rhetorical sense. Paul cannot have literally meant that "magistrates are ministers of God," they argued, because the magistrates in this context—Claudius and Nero—were ungodly pagans. Reading Paul's letters and other scriptural texts as works of rhetorical ingenuity, Erasmus used them as literary models, especially in advice books to princes: Erasmus's concept of a "Christian prince" in *The Education of a Christian Prince* hinges on the very distinction between a Christian prince and the pagan magistrate in his reading of Romans 13.

The Bible of the Protestants owed much of its existence to the historicist textual recovery of Catholic humanists like Erasmus and Lorenzo Valla, but their interpretative methods were more text-bound and less flexible. In exercising the same philological attention to the Hebrew Bible as had been given the

New Testament, Tyndale and other Protestants not only interpreted Paul more rigidly, but they also supported their "literal" interpretation by way of a new emphasis on the laws of Moses, so that Paul's doctrine of obedience incorporated the support of Mosaic law. Chapter 2, "Tyndale's Literalism and the Laws of Moses," explores the relationship between Tyndale's translation and hermeneutic work and the formation of a new code of obedience. The chapter focuses on vital moments of exchange between biblical interpretation and polemic between 1525 and 1536, a period demarcated by the publication of Tyndale's first fragmentary New Testament, rich in polemical annotation and prefatory paratext, and the circulation of the Coverdale Bible in 1536, the year of Tyndale's death. These were remarkable years: in the late 1520s, Henry fell for Anne Boleyn and found himself questioning the papal dispensation that had allowed his marriage to Catherine of Aragon. This dispensation, he argued strenuously with the help of theologians, expressly contradicted laws in Leviticus and Deuteronomy. Responding to this interpretive crisis, Tyndale worked simultaneously on politics and annotated translation just as Erasmus had done. The interchange between this annotated Pentateuch and Tyndale's polemic shows the extent to which his particular form of literalism arose in a highly consequential context. The chapter ends by exploring the constructions of kingship—in particular, of Henry VIII—in early Tudor Bibles and in biblical texts owned by the king himself.

Chapter 3, "A New Josiah and Bucer's Theocratic Utopia," turns to the short reign (1547–1553) of Edward VI, in which applied literalism evolved into more extreme legalistic forms. When Edward took the throne, Archbishop Cranmer pronounced him "God's vice-gerent and Christ's vicar," invoking in exaggerated terms the "minister of God" in Romans 13. Cranmer then drew a near-typological comparison with the biblical king Josiah, who restored the southern kingdom of Judah through the rediscovery of the Book of Law (an early version of Deuteronomy), which Edwardians saw as analogous to their project of reform. Edward would, Cranmer prophesied at the coronation of Edward VI, with his "predecessor Josiah, [see] God truly worshipped, and idolatry destroyed . . . according to all the law of Moses."[52] The court's interest in Mosaic law appears in widely disseminated catechisms, in the new Edwardian Bibles, and in the major political treatise by Martin Bucer, *De Regno Christi*, given in manuscript to the king. Drawing inspiration from More's *Utopia*, this treatise prescribes a reformed English legal system based largely on Mosaic law.

Chapter 4, "The Word in Exile: The Geneva Bible and Its Readers," begins a series of chapters on the English Renaissance's most widely circulated Bible and arguably its most influential text. The Geneva text and paratext reflect the condition of its creators, the English Protestants exiled during the reign of Queen Mary I, who first produced an annotated New Testament in 1557 (the only English Bible in Mary's reign) and then the complete Bible soon after Elizabeth's accession. With something like half a million copies in circulation, the Geneva Bible and its complex marginal notes and other devices played a major role in shaping the early modern English reader. Two of its paratextual features are of particular importance: the enumeration of verses, facilitating the easy extraction and application of short passages, and extensive marginal annotations that further enable the application of biblical passages to social, religious, and often political situations. The notes were most influential in Elizabethan and Jacobean England, yet they reflect the condition of the exiled community, constructing a vision of the English "nation" as analogous to the Israelites after the destruction of the Temple by the Babylonians. This chapter focuses on the patterns of interpretation in the Geneva annotations and on connections between these and the resistance tracts of the exiles.

Chapter 5, "Battling Bibles and Spenser's Dragon," explores the first book of Spenser's *Faerie Queene* from the perspective of the Elizabethan biblical reader. Drawing from the evolving Geneva annotations to the Book of Revelation and related visual and textual paratexts, the chapter reads Spenser in the context of the cultural debates that developed after the appearance of the annotated English Catholic Bible of 1582. This production gave rise to a series of multilayered Protestant confutations that sharply defined the biblical and hermeneutic orientation of these religious differences. I then turn to the fascinating annotations of *The Faerie Queene* by a contemporary reader who supplied not only biblical verse numbers but also the annotations of the Geneva Bible in the margins of his *Faerie Queene*, demonstrating how much the Geneva annotations resonated for a contemporary reader with Spenser's text, and providing at the same time an example of a reader applying the annotations outside the biblical framework.

Drawing on a range of biblical and paratextual allusions in Shakespeare, chapter 6, "*Measure for Measure* and the New King," explores the relationship between Shakespeare's biblical play and its political context. At a conference at Hampton Court in January 1604, soon after his accession to the throne, King James called for a new edition of the Bible that would have "no marginal notes" like those of the Geneva edition. Like Henry VIII, outraged at the "pestilent glosses in the margents" of Tyndale's New Testament, James complained that the Geneva notes, which had now grown to some 300,000 words, were seditious, dangerous, and traitorous.[53] James's indictment reinforces the profound imbrication of biblical interpretation and the machinery of the state. In the context of the biblical investment of James, Shakespeare's *Measure for Measure* ironizes the rise of literalism and legalism as a problem connected to a strict reading of Paul's words about the magistrate as God's minister in Romans 13.

The final two chapters focus on both the material and immaterial evidence for Milton's deconstruction of Protestant literalism during the revolutionary years of the English Civil Wars. Milton, born twenty years after Hobbes and directly into the legacy of the King James Bible, had a very different readerly experience from those who grew up reading the annotated Geneva Bible. Although the new Bible was deprived of explanatory notes, it was filled instead with alternate readings, usually indicated with a word that predominates in Milton's *Paradise Lost*: "or." In chapter 7, "Milton's Bible and Revolutionary Psalm Culture," I explore an actual copy of the King James Version (1612) marked by Milton and an amanuensis, and draw connections between the physical evidence of how Milton read and the more intangible evidence of how he interpreted. The annotations in Milton's King James Bible suggest, in connection with his citation habits, that the poet imitates the alternate readings supplied in the margins in the paratext to his intensely political Psalm translations of April 1648, written at the nadir of the English Civil War. Milton designs these psalms, written in service meter, to look and perform like the text and paratext of the King James Bible, though they provide a radically different interpretation.

Chapter 8, "Milton Contra Tyndale," turns back to the fundamental question of biblical legalism that had haunted English theo-politics since Tyndale, becoming particularly strong in Edward's reign, especially in Bucer's *De Regno Christi*. Milton's political writing forms a fitting conclusion to this study, for, countering Tyndale, Milton's is the first attested use of the word *literalism* in English, and he is also the first to use *literalist* to describe the misguided, rigid readings of his opponents. Milton is thus arguably the first within the Protestant tradition to define his hermeneutics explicitly as anti-literal, identifying the problem as central to the Tyndalean tradition. The words occur in the divorce tracts, in a formative series of exegetical arguments against the rigid readings of his opponents. Paradoxically, one of these divorce tracts is an excerpt from *De Regno Christi*, and Milton's translation of this reveals some of the complications of his turn from the early Reformation. Milton's deviations from literalism offer a return to some of the historicist techniques of Erasmus, whose historicism and radical revisionism inform Milton's later political writing.

The following chapters thus cover a wide range of biblical texts and their use, from frontispieces to the illustrations of the Apocalypse, with special attention given to Mosaic law, some of the Davidic and non-Davidic psalms, parts of the histories and prophetic texts, the gospels, the letters of Paul, and the Book of Revelation. Many of these sections of the Bible were treated as distinct entities, and sometimes published separately, such as the "Book of Law" (the imagined Bible as it existed before King David, but also the Commandments), the Book of Psalms (the genre of poetry mastered by David), the Gospel (such as the fragment of Matthew that first circulated in print in 1525), and the Book of Revelation (available in separate editions and commentaries from Bale's 1545 *Image of Both Churches* through Francis Junius's immensely popular *Apocalypsis* in 1592). For readers interested in accessing discussions of particular biblical texts and their cultural intersections, a separate index is provided.

CHAPTER I

Erasmus's New Testament and the Politics of Historicism

I am Paul, because I imitate Paul.

—Lorenzo Valla, *On the Donation of Constantine* (1440)

The story of Renaissance biblical scholarship arguably begins long before the English Renaissance, with an Italian humanist whose textual criticism often took a polemical edge, Lorenzo Valla. Before composing his *Novum Testamentum ex diversorum utriusque linguae codicum collatione adnotationes* ("Annotations on the New Testament collated from diverse codices in each language"), a work that scandalously challenged the Vulgate, Valla exposed the Donation of Constantine, used for centuries to legitimate papal claims to secular authority. This scathing polemic, or *Declamatio* (1440), is often seen to epitomize an emerging consciousness of historical difference in the Renaissance, since its argument hinges largely on the anachronism of the text.[1] Valla debunked Constantine's supposed transfer of power to Pope Sylvester I by demonstrating that the language and context of the document betrayed its eighth-century origins. Valla's brazen act of criticism is also exemplary for what it attempts to accomplish politically. He used historicism to drive a wedge between those in power and the texts they used to legitimate their authority. In exposing this anachronism, Valla sought to divest the power of the church from its secular interests: "I can scarcely wait to see, particularly if it is carried out on my initiative," he concluded, "that the Pope is the vicar of Christ alone and not of Caesar as well."[2] The historicist criticism in Valla's tract spread with various editions through northern Europe and England, destroying, as it went, a major illusion of power.[3] Luther loved Valla's treatise, which was first published in Germany in the fateful year of 1517.[4]

The polemical energy behind Valla's historicist method reveals an inextricable relationship between ideological positions and methods of interpreting texts. Historicism revolutionized textual studies in ways that had profound implications for biblical interpretation and, in turn, for the ways scripture might be used by those in power. The work of historically recovering the biblical text was undertaken in various ways by a diverse group of humanists that included Valla himself, Jacques Lefèvre, John Colet, and Erasmus, whose massive project of annotating and retranslating the New Testament first appeared only a year before Luther posted his ninety-five theses in 1517. At the same time that humanists were developing hermeneutic and rhetorical approaches to scripture and other texts, they were also in conversation about effective political rhetoric. Erasmus's *Novum Testamentum*—first titled *Novum Instrumentum*—and its *Annotationes* were published in the same year as his *Education of a Christian Prince* (1516), as well as More's *Utopia*. Erasmus's *Panegyric* to Philip the Archduke of Austria, published in 1504, also drew heavily in its rhetorical formulations from what Erasmus gained in his close historicist analysis of Pauline scripture.[5]

This chapter explores connections between historicist interpretive methods and the development of early modern political rhetoric. Renaissance historicism was applied toward a vital concern in the early modern present: that of speaking truth to power. Erasmus and his contemporaries were preoccupied with the problem of giving efficacious advice to princes, which often entailed speaking the truth from behind a carefully constructed rhetorical curtain. Thomas More famously theorized such a curtain, first in *Richard III*, and then in the dialogue on counsel in *Utopia*. In both texts, More articulates a rhetorical strategy he calls the *obliquus ductus*, a method of giving counsel that assures the safety of the counselor. Rendered in the English version of *Richard III* as "touched a slope craftily," the method of *obliquus ductus* enables its user to avoid sovereign wrath.[6] More's *obliquus ductus* is an explicit expression of what Annabel Patterson described in Elizabethan and Jacobean England as "a highly sophisticated system of oblique communication, of unwritten rules whereby writers could communicate with readers or audiences . . . without producing a direct confrontation."[7] Although unwritten in the moment of use, in this early sixteenth-century coterie of humanists these rules were sometimes theorized in less overt places, such as correspondences, political writings, and biblical annotations. Whether they were hired or otherwise motivated to advise, instruct, and entertain in court circles, these writers habitually reached for ancient literary models analogous to their circumstances. More's *ductus* is associated with Quintilian's rhetorical method for criticizing power safely, *emphasis*, which is used "when it is not safe to speak openly."[8] Quintilian elaborates on this technique with the evocative image of the "hidden shaft" or the *telum occultum*, suggestively similar to More's *obliquus ductus*.

> You can speak as openly as you like against those tyrants I was talking
> about, and to good effect, as long as your words can be taken in a
> different way. You are trying to avoid personal danger (*periculum*),
> that's all. . . . If the danger can be dodged by some ambiguity of
> expression (*ambiguitate sententiae*), everyone will admire the cunning
> with which it is done (*nemo non illo furto favet*). . . . Sometimes the
> hidden shaft sticks, and because it cannot be seen on the surface it
> cannot be removed. But if you were to say the same thing openly, it
> can be defended and its existence demonstrated.[9]

Some genealogy of influence from Quintilian's *occultum telum* to the hidden ways of the humanists seems evident, though with an obvious difference in metaphor between a conduit of influence and the penal blow of a rhetorical projectile.

In *Utopia*, More draws an analogy pervasive in political advice books between Roman authors under Nero and the problematic role of an early modern advisor of kings. In the first book, More discusses the danger of addressing princes. "In the councils of kings," he writes ironically, "where great matters are debated with great authority, there is no room for true advice." He illustrates through analogy the conditions that distort true speech, imagining a scene from Plautus performed over the din of the household slaves' chatter. Suddenly an out-of-place philosopher intrudes: it is Seneca addressing Nero in *Octavia*, the autobiographical Senecan tragedy now considered spurious. As More suggests, the combination of dramatic voices is absurd: it makes a "hodgepodge of comedy and tragedy,"[10] and philosophers cannot function in the courts of kings. To compound the effect, More has chosen a passage—the dialogue between Seneca and Nero—that relentlessly illustrates the failure of counsel. Seneca vainly attempts to mitigate Nero's implacable tyranny, while Nero stands firm in the position that a prince cannot be advised, a position strangely close to the early modern ideology of divine right: "*Principem cogi nefas* [to urge a prince is sacrilege]."[11]

In forging their identities as advisors to princes, these humanists looked to the Roman imperial writers as literary models. Yet as I will argue, the method of *obliquus ductus* seems to come as much from emulation of Seneca's biblical contemporary Paul as it does from classical rhetoricians. Thanks largely to a popular (though spurious) epistolary correspondence between them, Paul had an especially close connection to Seneca in the medieval and early modern imagination, and a classicized version of Paul played a major role in forging the identity of a political writer. "I am Paul," wrote Valla in the polemical pages that open his oration on the Donation, "because I imitate Paul."[12] Even in the process of berating the dark ages for not distinguishing the present from the past, Valla seems here—and in a manner shared by both Colet and Erasmus—to lapse into a sort of medieval celebration of anachronism, in which Paul can be brought into the present day by a practice of *imitatio*. Valla saw himself as Paul because the apostle was an orator and a parrhesiast, one who speaks truth to power: "no one who knows how to speak well can be a considered a true orator unless he also dares to speak out. . . . A person who sins in public and who accepts no private counsel must be charged in public, *to frighten all the rest*. Did not Paul, whose words I have just used, reproach Peter to his face before the church . . . and leave this in writing for our instruction?"[13] Paul's rhetorical method was not just a necessary component for the interpretation of scripture; it also bore a saintly quality that pagan classical rhetoricians lacked. The rhetoric of Paul is explored in various places throughout the range of genres in Erasmus's corpus, but the *Annotations* on the New Testament are of particular significance, not only because they help define an important hermeneutic shift in the sixteenth century, but also because they provide a stamp of validity on what might in another context seem an ironic or half-hearted assertion of meaning.

Colet and Erasmus Interpret Romans 13

The greatest shift in biblical interpretation prior to the Reformation resulted from the philological recovery of the historical meaning of texts. Scholars such as Valla, whose manuscript annotations Erasmus "stumbled across"[14] and subsequently published as *Adnotationes* in 1504, and Lefèvre, whose translation of Paul's epistles in 1512 was among the first to supplant the Vulgate, share and influence Erasmus's philological methodology.[15] Brian Cummings has shown how the classical studies that informed humanist approaches to the Bible brought scholars like Erasmus even to the point, on occasion, of privileging the literary over the theological.[16] In an astonishing assertion of the value of the literary, Erasmus praised Valla in his annotations as "a man more concerned with

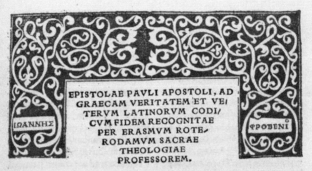

Figure 2. Letters of Paul in Erasmus's *Novum Instrumentum* (1516). Johann Froben's elegantly printed bilingual *Novum Instrumentum* (1516), shown at the start of Paul's epistles with rubricated ornamental headpiece and initials. In this copy, a reader has inscribed the verse numbers that emerged several decades later in Latin and vernacular Bibles, the first in English being the Geneva New Testament of 1557. *Novum Instrumentum Omne* (Basel: Froben, 1516), MLh691 +b516 Copy 2. By permission of the Beinecke Rare Book and Manuscript Library, Yale University.

literature than with theology"[17] in the enterprise of biblical scholarship.[18] Erasmus meant this with some customary irony: theology is, of course, a central goal in this kind of textual recovery and interpretation. But the tone here is also inflected by Erasmus's effort to distinguish his enterprise from the airy hairsplitting of the scholastics and even, as it would emerge later in their debates over free will, the kind of theological absolutism of Luther. A literary treatment of the text—rhetorical, philological, contextual, and *practical*—was for him the key to accurate recovery of meaning.

Recovering the biblical text in its historical form would have major consequences, not least in upsetting the stability of a text that had been sacrosanct for over a thousand years. Erasmus's work in establishing a better Greek text and translation involved making such momentous changes to the Vulgate as the omission of the so-called Johannine Comma, a line in 1 John 5:7 that asserted the unity of the Trinity—influential to Milton's anti-Trinitarian thinking—or the retranslation of Matthew 3:2 and 14:7 and other passages to suggest that the sacrament supported by the words "do penance" was unsupportable—readings used by Luther in his attack on Indulgences.[19] Erasmus feared that his rewording of Jerome's Vulgate might scandalize readers, and hid many controversial readings from the 1516 *Novum Instrumentum*, adding these in the increasingly extended notes of subsequent editions of the (now renamed) *Novum Testamentum* and *Annotations*—though in the case of the Johannine Comma, he conceded to critics and returned it in the third edition.[20] Johann Froben's magnificent publication included the Greek text facing the new Latin in one volume, with extensive glosses in a second volume, often bound with the first (Figure 2). In the four editions that would follow—the versions of 1519 and 1522, a three-columned text of 1527 (with the Greek, Erasmus's Latin, and the Vulgate), and the final version of 1535—Erasmus continued to revise and embellish the work.[21]

The pioneering humanist and pedagogue John Colet helped establish Erasmus's place in educating generations of students by including his work—and quite possibly More's *Utopia*—in the curriculum of St Paul's School.[22] Some seventeen years before Erasmus produced the *Novum Instrumentum*, and at a time when Greek scholarship was in a nascent stage, Erasmus, himself not yet competent in Greek, visited Colet at Oxford. Colet did not know Greek, nor would he go on to learn it, as Erasmus did, around the relatively late age of 30, convinced that it would be necessary to pursue an accurate reconstruction of meaning.[23] Justifiably, the long-standing and somewhat Anglocentric belief that Colet was the chief source for Erasmus's interpretive methods has been revised, especially around the issue of philology.[24] But although Colet worked with the Vulgate, and lacked the tools to do philological historicism, his contextual historicism proved innovative and influential, especially with regard to political readings of Paul. Colet lectured on Paul at Oxford in the late 1490s, and Erasmus heard him in 1499 (their mutual friend Thomas More, an Oxford student from 1492 to 1496, may also have been present). At around this time, Erasmus began a long commentary on Romans, which, though never published, fostered ideas for his annotated New Testament and subsequent *Paraphrases on the New Testament*. He wrote to Johann Popenruyter in 1501 that he had been "carefully preparing an interpretation of [Paul] for some time."[25] And in a letter to Colet in 1504 that accompanied a gift of the newly published *Enchiridion militis Christiani* or *Handbook of the Christian Soldier* (1503), Erasmus wrote that he was "astonished that none of your commentaries on Paul and the Gospels [have] yet been published," going on to speak of his own unpublished work: "Three years ago, indeed, I ventured to do something on Paul's Epistle to the Romans, and at one rush, as it were, finished four volumes."[26] His ongoing project accounts for the frequent references to Paul in his letters and the published work leading up to the publication of the *Annotationes* and the *Novum Instrumentum* in 1516. Although the project of the *Novum Instrumentum* was not fully conceived until Erasmus began collaborating with Froben during a fruitful move to Basel in 1514, Erasmus was well prepared for the close readings that characterize his annotations of Paul's letters.[27] In the *Enchiridion* alone, there are sixty examples drawn from 1 Corinthians and fifty from Romans.[28]

Colet's Oxford lectures provided a reading of Paul's language that took into account the historical circumstances from which the text arose.[29] He maintained that Paul's seeming support of divine right was provisional and rhetorical, framed in dangerous conditions that must be brought to bear on the interpretation of the text. Paul states in Romans 13 that all power derives from God, and that magistrates hold the power of vengeance in a sword seemingly authorized by heaven. The words demand obedience without exception. "Let every soul submit himself unto the authority of the higher powers," Tyndale's translation reads, "For there is no power but of God. The powers that be, are ordained of God. Whosoever therefore resisteth power, resisteth the ordinance of God. And they that resist, shall receive to themselves damnation." To urge or coerce a prince, as Nero said in *Octavia*, is sacrilege. Paul goes on to define the "ruler" to whom one owes obedience as a "minister of God": "For he is the minister of God, for thy wealth. . . . Wherefore ye must needs obey, not for fear of vengeance only: but also because of conscience. And even for this cause pay ye tribute."[30]

As I discuss in subsequent chapters, Tyndale and English Protestants after him interpreted this passage in an unflinchingly narrow literal manner: magistrates are ministers of God, and resistance is damnable.[31] Just prior to the Reformation, however, historicizing humanists like Colet saw Romans 13 in a very different manner. Using Suetonius and Roman history to help locate the precise moment of the epistle, Colet reconstructs the historical conditions surrounding Paul's text, which he considers to date from the reigns of Claudius and Nero. Colet notes that Paul "perished in the first persecution of the Christians that continued under Nero."[32] "I mention this," he continues,

> that St. Paul's great thoughtfulness and prudence may be remarked. For being aware that Claudius Caesar had succeeded to the throne; a man of changeable disposition, and bad principles, and sudden purposes; a man too who, as Suetonius writes in his Life, *banished the Jews from Rome, as they were in constant insurrection at the instigation of CHRESTUS* (on account of which insurrection I suppose St. Paul to have written this Epistle, and that what Suetonius meant to convey was, that the Jews had been banished by Claudius on account of their disputes about Christ);—St. Paul understanding, I say, that the Roman Emperor, as Suetonius also relates, was levying some *new and unheard of taxes*. (95–96)

Considering that Claudius, like Nero, fiercely opposed the new Christian sect, Colet poses a simple question: how can Paul really have meant that magistrates are "ministers of God"?

Paul's position, Colet proposes, must have been constructed for the early survival of the church. In such a state, it was "St. Paul's wish, while the Church is still as yet in its infancy, and especially in the case of those at Rome, under such wide control of heathens, that all things should be done discreetly" (91). That these magistrates were "heathen" made the precepts of Paul provisional, taking meaning from a situation that had long since elapsed: "St. Paul implies [that] God allows and suffers such [pagan] magistrates, and the power of the unbelieving, *for a time*" (92; emphasis added). Colet imagines that Paul bestowed divine approval on these magistrates as a peacemaking tactic, and one that might bring the magistrates "to grow gentle": "it follows readily that they must needs have been strongly induced to deal mercifully with the inoffensive Christians, and allow them to remain in the state without injury. This would follow, I mean, on their hearing that rulers were not to be objects of terror to the good, but to the bad; and that they were *the ministers of God*" (98). In Colet's reading, Paul's words should be read only as they *functioned* rhetorically, and as they were designed to function in that context—not in terms of their literal meaning. Phrases like "minister of God" are not meant to signify an actual quality in the magistrate, so much as to engender a desired one. By using this rhetorical ploy, Paul "covertly teaches (*latenter docet*) what sort of men the rulers of states ought to be" (97, 202).

Colet's historicist reading suggests that the apostle used rhetorical strategies analogous to More's *obliquus ductus*. The covert teaching, like the rhetorical obliquity of the *obliquus ductus*, is a self-protective method for correcting those in power. While Colet seeks an accurate historical reading of Paul's intentions, he also lapses into contemporary discourse on how to address kings. As Colet writes in diction rather more like Cicero's than Paul's in the Vulgate, Paul "relates the duties of the king and governor of the state (*officium principis et gubernatoris reipublicae*)" (97, 202). Romans 13 thus turns from being instructions addressed to subjects on their duties (the primary literal sense of the passage) to instructions to the magistrate on the duties of office.

Other than this presentist lapse, the bulk of Colet's interpretation remains historically specific, suggesting that Colet sees nothing in Romans 13 applicable to his present time. When Paul says that "every one must needs be subject to the higher powers," it is "the powers of the heathen (*paganorum*), that is, in whose hands all power in secular matters *then* lay" (97, 202; emphasis added). The separation from Colet's present is thus twofold: Paul's treatment of sovereignty is a rhetorical gesture that means something different from what it says, and that rhetorical gesture only functions properly in its historical context, in which the magistrate was pagan.

Colet presses his historical reading yet further with the suggestion that Paul had consciously designed his letter with the possibility that it "should make its way into Roman hands" (97). The purloined letter was a justifiably common feature of the humanist imagination. Erasmus's friend Busleyden wrote to Erasmus in 1511, for example, advising him to exercise more self-censorship, because letters can be intercepted, which "to [his] peril" he had "discovered" for himself: "I have given much thought to what you wrote in it at some length, and rather freely, about kings; and, since your sentiments are such as could more safely be confided in person to trusty ears than set down in a letter, I hope you will be discreet enough to moderate them in revising them for publication."[33] For Colet, Paul wrote with the possibility of epistolary interception in mind, which is why he "speaks in such a way of the Roman magistrates, as at once to instruct them, and win their favour for the Christians" (97). Paul's rhetoric assumes even greater utility upon the possibility of Roman magistrates finding the letter: "should they have ever chanced to read his Epistle, it follows readily that they must needs have been strongly induced to deal mercifully with the inoffensive Christians" (98).

Following Colet, Erasmus works subtly against the literal meaning of Romans 13 in the *Annotations*. He points out that "minister" does not mean anything other than "agent," and argues that "Paul was aware that some Christians, under the pretext of religion, were refusing the orders of their rulers, and that as a result the established order would be upset and all things thrown into disarray." It was these historical circumstances that brought Paul to teach that "they should obey any one at all entrusted with public authority—making exception for the interests of faith and piety."[34] Erasmus reads further than the passage allows, since Paul does not make exception here for the interests of faith and piety. He also softens the Vulgate in important ways, removing the threat of "damnation" (*damnationem acquirunt*) in 13:2, and replacing it with "judgment" (*iudicium accipient*)—an emendation retained by the translators of the Geneva Bible, though not the Bishops' or the King James Version. He also removes the "necessity" of obedience in 13:5—usually translated as "*must* be subject"— replacing it instead with a weaker expression of *ought*; hence the Vulgate's *ideoque necessitati subditi estote* "and so on this account be subject to necessity," becomes in Erasmus's Latin "wherefore you ought to be subject" [*quapropter oportet esse subditos*] (350). Tyndale and subsequent English translations stayed closer to the Vulgate, with "receive damnation" in 13:2, and "must needs obey" in 13:5.

In the annotations on this passage, Erasmus shares Colet's view that the words of Paul were meant to apply only to a pagan magistrate, though again he asserts this with subtle irony: "True," he wrote, "these very rulers are pagan (*ethnici*) and evil; but order is still good."[35] Erasmus continues to stress the same difference between pagan and Christian in his note to Romans 13:7–8: "Pay to everyone what is owed: tribute to whom tribute is owed . . . Owe no one anything": "It can be understood in such a way that the previous words [that is, 13:7, pay tribute] refer to magistrates who were pagan (*magistratus ethnicos*), as they all were at that time; what follows—[owe] no one anything etc.—refers to Christians: 'pay them [the magistrates] what you owe, but a Christian owes a

Christian nothing except mutual love.'"[36] These guarded ironic readings were probably concessions to his conservative critics, for whom Erasmus admitted making compromises in the interpretation of well-known passages; as he related, he was "well aware that certain biblical passages were too familiar to be changed without creating an uproar."[37]

In the *Institutio Principis Christiani* or *Education of a Christian Prince* (1516), however, published in the same year as the New Testament and Annotations, Erasmus emphasizes the full implications of Colet's distinction between pagan and Christian princes. Erasmus employs historicism with particular rigor in reading Romans 13, enabling the distinction implied in the title between a Christian and a pagan prince.[38] Pointing toward the well-known verse in Romans, Erasmus writes, "Do not let it escape you that what is said . . . about the need to endure masters, obey officials, do honour to the king . . . is to be taken as referring to pagan princes." That is, "A pagan prince requires to be honoured; Paul says honour is to be shown him. He levies a tax; Paul wants the tax to be paid. . . . For the Christian man is in no way diminished by these things. . . . But what does he go on to say about Christians? 'You ought not,' he says, 'to have any debts among yourselves, except to love one another'" [Romans 13:8]. The relationship of a Christian prince to his subjects must, according to Erasmus, be understood in a radically new light—and not by the doctrines set down by Paul in Romans 13, which does not pertain to them. "I hope," he continues, that "such thoughts as these will not occur to anyone":

> 'Why then do you take away the prince's own rights and attribute
> more to the pagan than to the Christian?' But I do not; I stand up for
> the rights of the Christian prince. It is the right of a pagan prince to
> oppress his people by fear . . . to plunder their goods and finally make
> martyrs of them: that is a pagan prince's right. You do not want the
> Christian Prince to have the same, do you?[39]

The repetition of "rights" underscores the close historical relationship between biblical and legal hermeneutics: these are rights determined by scripture, read by a socially authorized hermeneut such as Erasmus.[40] He concludes, suggesting that the claims about a prince's rights are contingent on the authority of this explication: "Or will his rightful power seem to be reduced if these things are denied him?" (236). The rights "denied him"—the "right" to absolute obedience—can only be denied by the assertions of an exegetical authority who argues that Paul does not give princes that right. Erasmus began the *Institutio Principis*

Christiani with a preface to Charles V using a distinction between himself and Isocrates: "he was a sophist, instructing some petty king or rather tyrant, and both were pagans; I am a theologian addressing a renowned and upright prince, Christians both of us."[41] Erasmus's special authority is that of a renowned scholar and theological interpreter, and the fact that they are both Christian changes the meaning and application of Paul.

Saintly Seneca and Political Paul

Treating Paul's collection of letters as another classical text had the effect of placing it conceptually close to other authors who operated fatally under Nero. The particular favorite, illustrated by More's anecdote in *Utopia*, was Seneca. The stoic philosopher and dramatist, as well as *consul, ac senator, & Neronis praeceptor*[42] as Erasmus described him in his 1515 edition of Seneca's works, shaped the way in which humanists framed their endeavors at court—with emphasis on Seneca's role as "praeceptor," or teacher, of the young Nero. "For Nero it was Seneca," Erasmus wrote hopefully to Henry VIII in 1513, indicating the relationship he hoped to cultivate with the young king, "and if Nero had obeyed his advice he would have reigned longer, and might have earned a place among the good emperors as well."[43] But soon after in the *Education of a Christian Prince* (which Erasmus sent to Henry), Erasmus wrote, "Nero's nature was so corrupt, that even that saintly teacher Seneca could not prevent his becoming a most pestilential ruler."[44] To be a bad king, or become one, was to become a Nero. In the rhetorical work *De Copia,* when speaking of the art of comparison, Erasmus instructed, "A good ruler should be compared with Trajan or Marcus Aurelius the philosopher-emperor, a bad one with Nero or Caligula."[45]

Just as Erasmus imagines Seneca as a "saintly teacher," he recasts Paul as a teacher and rhetorician operating in the Neronian context. Seneca has a familial connection with Paul even in canonical scripture, as Acts 18:12–17 mentions that his brother the proconsul of Achaea received Paul with clemency, a passage that helped draw the world of the New Testament close to the literary world of Imperial Rome.[46] Yet in medieval and early modern Europe, Seneca and Paul had a still more solid connection, one that astonishingly placed Senecan letters within conceptual world and even the corpus of the New Testament. For hundreds of years leading up to and even beyond the corrective of Renaissance historicism, Seneca the playwright and stoic philosopher and Paul the erstwhile persecutor turned Christian reformer were connected through a set of spurious letters.

These letters posit that, as Nero's advisor, Seneca hid his friendship with Paul and his Christian beliefs (conveniently lodging them in his stoicism) to avoid Nero's wrath and win the emperor over to the Christian side.[47] The forged letters would not ultimately survive the scrutiny of humanism, and they would eventually be dismissed as the Donation of Constantine had been on the grounds of implausibility and linguistic anachronism. But the correspondence had such a hold on the early modern imagination as to carry considerable force; indeed, many of Erasmus's contemporaries still adhered to its authenticity. The correspondence appears uncontested in editions of Paul by Lefèvre, whose 1512 edition of the Epistles of Paul with commentary offered the only printed Latin translation to supersede the Vulgate prior to Erasmus's complete edition, and Erasmus consulted it carefully.[48] Like Colet and Erasmus, Lefèvre read texts in terms of the political conditions under which they were formed. Lefèvre thought the correspondence to be authentic and set it beside Paul's letter to the Hebrews. Lefèvre explains how Seneca's pen or style (*stilus*) obscured and dissimulated (*adumbrasse & dissimulasse*), with an effort to conceal his Christian identity should the letters be found by Nero.[49] Other contemporaries, as Irena Backus has shown, "had no hesitations about using the *Seneca Correspondence* . . . to extend the Pauline corpus."[50]

Erasmus did not credit the correspondence, but he was obviously affected by the story. He claimed that Jerome wrongly used the correspondence "as a pretext for praising Seneca" while presuming that, as "a critic of keen discernment, Jerome well knew [the letters] were written by neither of them." This is untrue: there is nothing to suggest that Jerome's conviction was disingenuous. But for his own part, Erasmus possessed the same conflicted acceptance he sees in Jerome. For he embraces Jerome's sentiment which led him to include Seneca "alone among Gentiles . . . recorded in *The Catalogue of Illustrious Authors*," for Jerome "thought him the one writer who, while not a Christian, deserved to be read by Christians." "Nothing," Erasmus wrote, "sets a higher tone than his pronouncements. . . . Seneca alone calls the mind away to heavenly things."[51] Erasmus included the spurious correspondence in his edition of Seneca's works, published a year before the *Novum Instrumentum*, "for fear," he explained, "the reader might need something and not find it."[52] Perhaps it was his publication of the letters in Seneca's works in the previous year that kept them from appearing in Erasmus's New Testament. To prepare the edition of Seneca's works, Erasmus consulted the commentaries of Barzizza, who presents Seneca as a follower of Paul at Rome. For Erasmus, as the ensuing pages show, the rhetorical stratagems he admired in Paul became those that he himself used when advising princes.

The Pauline Rhetoric of Praise

Erasmus presented the *Panegyric for Archduke Philip of Austria* as a speech in January 1504 and put it into print soon after, and it was later reprinted alongside Erasmus's *Education of a Christian Prince* in 1516.[53] The panegyric speech was given, its longer title relates, to congratulate the Archduke "on his triumphal departure from Spain" and his "most joyful return to his country" (120). This hyperbolic language partly obscures the fact that Erasmus presented the *Panegyricus* at a tense political moment. Members of the Estates of Brabant were concerned that Philip would join his father Maximilian in an invasion of Guelders or Gelderland, a province bordering Germany to the east of Holland.[54] Erasmus's oratory before the Estates and members of Philip's council indirectly enforces, through fulsome praise, the lawfulness of Philip's contract with his Estates and the recklessness of military invasion.

Defending the adulatory language of his *Panegyricus*, Erasmus provided a sound lesson in rhetoric. "Those who believe panegyrics are nothing but flattery," he wrote in a letter published with the encomium, "seem to be unaware of the purpose and aim of the extremely far-sighted men who invented this kind of composition, which consists in presenting princes with a pattern of goodness"— and here italics are added to emphasize the letter's self-betraying function as a key to the text's meaning—"in such a way as to *reform bad rulers*, improve the good, educate the *boorish*, reprove the *erring*, arouse the *indolent*, and cause even the *hopelessly vicious* to feel some inward stirrings of shame."[55] (Erasmus probably gambled, here, that Philip would not read the published version.) He goes on, identifying the most important of these "far-sighted men": "Did not the apostle Paul himself often use this artifice (*artificio*)—a sort of pious adulation (*pia adulatione*)—of praising in order to amend?"[56] "Again," he goes on, weaving in a commonplace from Persius, "how can one reproach a wicked ruler for his cruelty more safely, yet more severely, than by proclaiming his mildness; or for his greed and violence and lust, then by celebrating his generosity, self-control, and chastity, 'that he may see fair virtue's face, and pine with grief that he has left her.'" Erasmus meaningfully omits some fiery words in the source, in which Persius excoriates tyrants before introducing the quoted sentence: "Great father of the gods, may you punish savage tyrants, when terrible desire dipped in fiery poison has affected their minds, exactly like this: that they may see virtue and pine with grief that they have left her."[57] Persius's sharp satire lurks under the comparatively placid veneer of Erasmus's letter, thus reenacting the rhetorical structure he advocates: a veneer of praise under which true speech can safely operate.

In the letter attached to the *Panegyricus*, Erasmus does not specify where Paul uses the "artifice" of "pious adulation." But the very phrase appears in Erasmus's own analysis of Romans, showing that he used Paul as a rhetorical model for his own work—or, in a circular way—that he read into Paul his own experience of advising princes. The artifice Erasmus attributes to Paul appears in the notes to Romans 1:11–12, where he annotates the words *simul consolari*, or comfort together, συμπαρακληθῆναι, from which "Paraclete," the "comforter," or "Holy Spirit" derives—hence Erasmus's title *Paraclesis*, the "summons" to his readers of the *Novum Instrumentum*.[58] Here Paul says to the Romans, "I am longing to see you so that I may share with you some spiritual gift to strengthen you—or rather so that we may be mutually comforted by each other's faith."[59] Erasmus notes that Paul "feared that he might offend the Romans, with their somewhat arrogant disposition. . . . Thus he explains this strengthening as their 'mutual comfort,' speaking, as usual, with the greatest modesty." Erasmus then describes, in a gloss that did not appear until the 1527 edition, how Paul "softened and tempered his speech":[60]

> For when he had said 'to be strengthened,' fearing that the arrogant Romans might reply, 'What? do we waver so that we have to be propped up by your tongue?' he softened this by changing the word 'strengthening' to 'comforting.' And not content with that he said, not παρακληθῆναι [comfort], but συμπαρακληθῆναι [to comfort together], as if he himself needed their comfort no less. . . . This is pious cunning and holy, if I may say, flattery.[61]

> Quum enim dixisset, confirmari, metuens ne Romani arrogantes dicerent, Quid? an vacillamus, ut tua lingua simus fulciendi: mitigavit hoc, & verbum confirmandi, vertit in consolandi. nec hoc contentus, non dixit παρακληθῆναι, sed συμπαρακληθῆναι: quasi non minus ipse egeret illorum consolatione. . . . Haec est pia vafricies, & sancta, ut ita dixerim, adulatio.[62]

No doubt Erasmus is on to something: why would Paul say one thing, "strengthened," and then correct himself, but leave that correction in his text? The somewhat arrogant Romans might not want to hear "strengthened"—not, at least, if there were not some mutual profit to be had. In the doubling of the phrases *pia vafrities* and *sancta adulatio*, Erasmus builds on the former notion of *pia adula-tio*, used to defend his own method of writing. It is pious, after all, because Paul uses it. Here it is worth pausing to distinguish another feature of Erasmus's an-notation that works differently from the extensively annotated Geneva Bible and later annotated Bibles in this study: his analysis of larger passages. After the breaking up of the text into verse numbers in English and Latin Bibles in the 1550s, literary analysis is naturally confined more to smaller clusters of words, since units of sense were demarcated with the enumerated verses. In this case, the verse break falls between "strengthened" and "comforted," which would not facilitate Erasmus's subtle reading. Another difference in Erasmus's contextual-ist approach lies in his effort to characterize the particular audience as well as authorial intent in any given speech act, thus requiring varied hermeneutic ap-proaches in different Pauline contexts—Roman, Corinthian, or Ephesian.

In the letter appended to the *Panegyricus* fashioning his adulatory rhetoric after Paul, Erasmus elaborates on the power and danger of disingenuous praise. "It does not matter under whose name a pattern of the good prince is publicly set forth, provided it is done cleverly, so that it may appear to men of intelligence that you were not currying favour but uttering a warning."[63] A complex dynamic characterizes the praise and blame of epideictic oratory, which strives toward a mode of praise that hints at blame, in which the mechanisms of recognition are crucial to the effect. If the element of blame goes unrecognized by the prince, the praise may misfire dangerously, stoking the fires of self-aggrandizement. Early in his career, Erasmus was, like More's Hythloday, concerned that the epideictic role had an ultimately corrupting influence. "I sang my songs to Midas," he wrote in a letter of 1499, citing his favorite exemplum of the corrupt king next to Nero, "and, paying too assiduous court to men of his kind, in the end all that I achieved was failure to please them, or scholars either."[64]

The dangers of false praise frequently loomed on the periphery, threatening to spoil the whole enterprise. Erasmus wrote to Colet that he was "reluctant to compose the *Panegyricus*" and did not "remember ever doing anything more unwillingly; for I saw that this kind of thing [or genre, *genus*] could not be handled without flattery."[65] Yet this reluctance ultimately seems rhetorical, since he continues more elatedly to speak of a *new* rhetorical strategy: "However, I employed a new stratagem [*novo artificio*]; I was completely frank while I flat-tered and also very flattering in my frankness."[66] The strange balance of misgiv-ing and resolution suggests a thin line between the right kind of flattery—the holy flattery of Paul—and one in which the hidden bitterness of correction be-comes lost in the thick icing of adulation. Erasmus's printed letter to Desmarez that was affixed to the *Panegyricus* attributed this *artificium* to Paul. But here in his very next dated letter, Erasmus proclaims to Colet that what he is doing represents something "new" (*novum artificium*); he has devised a new rhetorical technique. The changing authorship of the artifice from Paul to Erasmus in the two letters provokes the question whether Erasmus forgot he had just attributed the artifice to Paul when he claims it as his own. More likely, he seems to be admitting in this private letter to Colet that he projects his own rhetorical inventions on Paul. That Colet should have occasioned such self-revision seems particularly significant, since the two shared a five-year connection as fellow explicators of Paul. Not only confirming a genuine mutual enterprise of Pauline interpretation, the admission also implies that these readings produce new forms of expression that are not in scripture itself.

Erasmus had long since familiarized himself with the panegyric genre, and with the possibilities of a cunning form of criticism that functioned under the guise of flattery. In a remarkable letter of 1498 to the young Adolph, Prince of Veere, he defends the writing of panegyrics and explains his theory of an indirect approach. This letter became public in 1503, when it was affixed to the front of the *Oration on the Pursuit of Virtue*:

> When I consider the matter carefully I do not, as a rule, conclude that
> the ancients' habit of formally praising kings and emperors with
> panegyrics, even to their faces, was caused by a vicious tendency to
> obsequious toadying and flattery. Rather, my view is this: intelligent
> men who had an exceptional understanding of nature and of the
> human spirit gave up hope that any noble and lion-hearted king with
> fastidious ears would ever come to tolerate the moral authority of an
> adviser or the stern censure of a critic. So, acting out of a concern for
> the public interest (*utilitatis*), they changed their tack; they kept on
> towards the same goal, but took a more hidden route (*occultiore via*).[67]

This *occultiore via*, perhaps drawing from Quintilian's *occultum telum*, anticipates More's *obliquus ductus*, and underscores again the degree to which More's famous concept emerged from a highly developed exchange of ideas among humanists. "This practice," Erasmus continues, "was a concession made in times past to the violent temper of barbarian kings, not, I think, from some shameful motive, but from prudence."[68]

Erasmus's scriptural exegesis reveals Paul as the prime model from "times past." A fascinating example lies in his interpretation of the address to the Athenians in Acts 17:23–25, where Paul says, "ye men of Athens, in all things I perceive that ye are very religious, for as I passed along, and observed objects of your worship, I found also an altar with this inscription: To An Unknown God." Paul goes on to say, in the words from Erasmus's *Paraphrase* on Acts, "those who allege that I am introducing new and foreign gods are therefore mistaken. On the contrary I proclaim to you the very one whom you worship as unknown, as that inscription on the altar shows."[69] As in the note to Romans 1:11–12, Erasmus applauds Paul's pious cunning (*pia vafricie*), which Jerome apparently also noticed:

> *Unknown God*: Jerome points out that Paul used a certain pious
> cunning, because he changed something in the inscription; he
> omitted not a few things in order to twist the sense (*detorqueret*) more
> serviceably towards a ground (*exordium*, rhetorical beginning)
> through which to preach Christ.[70]

> *Ignoto Deo*) Et hic Hieronymus indicat Paulum pia quadam usum
> vafricie, quod nonnihil mutavit in titulo, non pauca omisit, quo
> commodius detorqueret ad exordium praedicandi Christum.[71]

The word *detorquere* might be translated more neutrally than "twist." But Erasmus's point is that Paul has cunningly shifted the meaning of the original. Indeed, Erasmus and his contemporaries usually use *detorquere* and *torquere* negatively, when their opponents have "twisted" the meaning of scripture.[72] He uses the word in the diatribe with Luther, where he describes how people "twist (*detorquent*) whatever they read in the Scriptures into an assertion of an opinion which they have embraced once for all."[73] Paul's usage is far more praiseworthy, though there must be a hint of irony in Erasmus's choice of word. In Acts 17, Paul has "twisted" the meaning of the inscription in order to insert Christ into the Athenians' minds. More than just reinterpreting, Paul left something out, changing "gods" to "God."

Erasmus goes on to explain how Paul transformed the original text:

> For the inscription thus had, by the author, in the manner cited
> from Jerome, *to the gods of Asia, and Europe, and Africa, and to the
> gods unknown and wandering*. Out of the "gods unknown" he made
> a "God unknown," and omitted the mention of the remaining
> ones.

> Titulus enim sic habebat, auctore, quem modo citavi Hieronymo, Diis
> Asiae, & Europae, & Africae, Dis ignotis & Peregrinis. Ex diis ignotis
> deum fecit ignotum, & mentionem caeterorum omisit.

This long gloss became even longer in the edition of 1519, in which Erasmus
added the daring commentary that would remain through 1535:

> In this manner indeed, I think there is truly an image of the state for
> those who seek to lead pagans—or princes, corrupted by bad
> upbringing—towards piety, lest they directly make reproaches, and
> exacerbate what they wish to remedy, but instead, while dissimulating
> many things, gradually lead them toward a better mind. And perhaps
> it ought not to be blamed, if good men act in this spirit in the courts
> of princes, and gradually steal into the mind of the prince, so long as
> they are not the doers of deeds that are openly wrong, although they
> may be permitted to overlook certain ones unwillingly.

> Quam equidem civilitatem imitamen arbitror iis, quibus studium est
> ethnicos, aut principes mala educatione depravatos, ad pietatem
> adducere, ne protinus convitiis rem agant & exacerbaent quibus
> mederi volunt, sed multa dissimulantes, paulatim illos adducant ad
> mentem meliorem. Et fortassis reprehendi non oporteat, si boni viri
> hoc animo in regum aulis agant, quo paulatim irrepant in principum
> affectus, modo ne sint auctores eorum quae palam sunt iniquia, licet
> ad quaedam conniveant inviti.[74]

Here a biblical gloss has been transformed into a commentary on the conditions
of speaking in court. From Paul's method of *detorquendi*, of shifting the meaning of the original text to apply to the immediate purpose of the reformer, Erasmus draws an example for the advisors of princes. The association between "lead
the pagan" and "lead princes" suggests a satiric correlation between the Pauline
role of converting pagans and Erasmus's role in reforming princes.

   Another elaborate biblical gloss on Pauline political rhetoric can be found
in Colossians 4:6: "Walk in wisdom toward them that are without, redeeming
the time. Let your speech be always with grace, seasoned with salt, that ye may
know how ye ought to answer each one." Here, the bracketed passages were
added to the 1527 edition:

Seasoned with salt: Ambrose read, "always with grace seasoned in salt" as if it stated, "Let your speech be salt, seasoned with grace." And yet the Greek commends a reading in this manner—as if you were to say, "let your speech always have grace and be seasoned with salt": so we might understand charm and modesty in the conversations [of the Christians] with the Pagans, but we may also understand that conjunction with wisdom. This can be turned (*detorqueret*) for our use, as when with magnates it needs to be done, lest by untimely maledictions and bitterness we provoke them, and render them even worse than they already are. We ought instead to lead them gradually toward the better with a moderated, prudent speech[, if they err in any way.]

Sale sit conditus) Ambrosius legit semper, in sale gratia sit conditus, quasi dictum sit. Sermo vester sit salsus, conditus gratia. Tametsi graeca perinde valent ac si dicas, Sermo vester semper habeat gratiam, sale conditus, ut intelligamus jucunditatem ac modestiam in collo-quiis [Christianorum cum] ethnicis, sed eam cum sapienta conjunc-tam. Hoc detorqueri potest ad nos, si quando cum magnatibus agendum est, ne intempestiva maledicentia & acerbitate provocemus eos reddamusque deteriores quam sunt, sed prudenti moderatione sermonis paulatim adducamus ad meliora[, si quid aberrant].[75]

As the bracketed passages show, Erasmus continued to develop the contrast between Christians and pagans in the later editions. The annotation makes use of *detorquere* to speak not so much of Paul's transformation, but of how we might further transform Paul's own text; that is, how we might use Paul as an "exortium through which to assert" our own view. Lessons learned from the historical association between the Christians and the pagans might be applied in reforming those who are more powerful. Like the "conversations of the Christians with the pagans," speech used to address magnates must be seasoned with salt (or grace). It is in this sense that Erasmus's mode of interpretation will carry the most influence in the early modern period: that biblical texts may be applied, sometimes forcibly, to fit the needs of the present.

The word I have translated as "charm," *jucunditas*, in "charm and modesty in the conversation between the Christians and the pagans" is a rhetorical device central to *The Praise of Folly*.[76] Although it is not a straightforward work of epideictic rhetoric, Erasmus's early turn from praise of princes to praise of Folly carries with it many of the tropes and inventions associated with his reconstructed Pauline rhetoric. This satiric inversion of the panegyric genre may have developed from frustration at the ineffectiveness of the *Panegyricus*, since, soon after its performance, Maximilian and Philip invaded Guelders, the very conquest Erasmus had sought to oppose. After this mishap, Erasmus moved to England, where he translated Lucian's satires of tyrants, conquerors, and ethically untenable pursuers of glory.[77] He then moved to Italy in 1506 to further his training in Greek for a yet undefined New Testament project, returning to England three years later to compose *The Praise of Folly* (1511, 1514).[78] In 1515 he looked back on the cluster of writings over the past fourteen years, aligning *The Praise of Folly* with the *Panegyricus* and the *Enchiridion*: "Nor was the end I had in view in my *Folly* different in any way from the purpose of my other works, though the means differed. In the *Enchiridion* I laid down quite simply the pattern of the subjects in which a prince should be brought up. In my *Panegyricus*, though under cover of praising a prince, I pursue indirectly [*oblique*] the same subject that I pursued openly in the earlier work."[79]

The Praise of Folly takes further some of the rhetorical methods reconstructed in the Pauline context. Folly expounds on how kings by nature shun wise men: "they are afraid that perhaps one of them might be so frank (*liberior*) as to say what is true rather than pleasant,"[80] reusing the same language he had used to tell Colet about a new artifice that allowed him to be flattering when frank, and frank (*libertate*) when flattering.[81] "Quite right," Folly continues, "kings do hate the truth. But my fools, on the other hand, have a marvelous faculty of giving pleasure (*jucunda*) not only when they speak the truth but even when they utter open reproaches, so that the very same statement which would have cost a wiseman his life causes unbelievable pleasure if spoken by a fool" (56; 116). In the same way that grace and salt may be mixed to moderate the bitterness of truth, playfulness and wisdom may be so combined that a statement becomes safe and efficacious which would, if baldly expressed, have provoked the wrath of a magnate. Folly also treats of the dangers of oratory in a speech initiated by the question of "what wisdom" caused Socrates "to be sentenced to drink hemlock." She describes Plato's vain attempts to "help his teacher in his hour of mortal danger," and then launches into an inquiry into the effects of "fear" on the orator's "fight" to maintain the state. "Quintilian," she goes on at length, "interprets this fear as the sign of a wise orator well aware of the dangers (*periculum*) of his task."[82] Folly probably had in mind the passage of Quintilian in which the rhetorician describes the technique of *emphasis*, which allows one to speak truth to power and avoid danger (*periculum*).[83] Folly's inquiry into the dangers of oratory continues until folly itself is proposed as the safe method for giving advice. "There are two main obstacles to gaining a knowledge of affairs: modesty, which throws the mind into confusion; and fear, which keeps people from undertaking noble exploits once the danger becomes apparent. But folly removes these hindrances in fine fashion" (42; *ASD*, 104). Here the context for Quintilian's "fear" becomes still more apparent: it is a fear of speaking directly in such a way, as More relates in *Richard III*, and Erasmus in *The Praise of Folly*, that could "cost a wiseman his life" (56). One cannot "speak all the truth," More wrote in *Richard III*, "for fear of [the king's] displeasure."[84]

An untimely death caused by an act of truth (or, in More's case, silence) was for these humanists a very real possibility, as it was for those imperial writers Seneca and Paul who, as Colet wrote, "perished under Nero." In a bitter epigram written on the death of More, Erasmus cast his friend as perhaps both Seneca and Paul: "If you want the praises of Henry to be summed up in one verse, combine Midas and Nero into one man."[85] Even his saintly teachers could not prevent Henry from becoming a "most pestilential ruler." Erasmus, Colet, and More developed their elaborate methods of rhetorical subterfuge with a keen sense of the danger of speaking truth to power. It is no wonder that in his commentary on Romans 13 Colet turned abruptly from mentioning Paul's death under Nero to explain Paul's "great thoughtfulness and prudence" in shaping his rhetoric in a way that could "secretly teach" the powerful and keep his flock out of danger.[86] Colet's historicist reading of Paul set a vital example for Erasmus, who developed rhetorical methods for reading the biblical text that he then appropriated—even twisted, *detorquere*—for present use in advising princes.

*   *   *

As northern Europe fragmented into Catholic and Protestant identities, Erasmus continued to be read. Readers of vernacular Bibles often show their study of Erasmus in the annotated margins and in other writings, in spite of the fact that many of his readings were not accepted by either side of the schism that occurred after 1517.[87] Protestants grappled with but often rejected or ignored Erasmus's liberal interpretive approach, even though new vernacular translations—such as those of Tyndale and Luther—were based on his text.[88] On the Catholic side of the schism, the Council of Trent repudiated Erasmian textual studies by determining that the Vulgate was an "authentic" replacement of the Greek original. Erasmus's major reconstruction of the past had thus a troubled legacy, one still reflected in the neglect of modern scholarship. But in spite of the differences between Erasmus and Continental reformers, Erasmus remained profoundly important to Tyndale and the newly formed Church of England, as we see turning to the next chapter.

In the series of Reformations that eventually turned most of early modern England Protestant, Erasmus's different approach to passages like Romans 13 quietly persisted in wide circulation. His interpretive method appeared in works explicitly devoted to hermeneutics, such as the *Annotationes* or *Ratio seu Methodus Verae Theologociae*, but also by example throughout texts like the *Enchiridion*, published in over fifty editions in Latin and more than ten in English before 1600, *The Praise of Folly*, and *The Education of a Christian Prince*. Erasmus's *Paraclesis* was anonymously translated as *An Exhortation to the Diligent Study of Scripture* (1529), and appended to versions of Tyndale's New Testament, further suggesting that the English reader saw continuity between Erasmian humanism and the English Reformation.[89] As late as 1550, Erasmus remained the dominant authority for the English New Testament, and the official Great Bible of that year advertised its translation as "according to the text of Erasmus, permitted and authorized by the king's majesty."[90] When an Edwardian mandate, reinstated by Elizabeth, placed the *Paraphrases on the New Testament* alongside the Bible in every church, Erasmus played a material role in the Church itself.[91] Prominent figures undertook the translation of this work in a collaboration that included the playwright and cleric Nicholas Udall, the Catholic princess Mary Tudor, and Katherine Parr, the dowager queen, who oversaw the project.[92] As can be imagined, the *Paraphrases*, rejected by Luther, contain Erasmus's validation of works and free will as means to redemption, and have been the focus of scholarship showing the continued presence of Erasmian method and theology in England.[93] Erasmus's sharpest contradictions to Protestant interpretation were seemingly ignored, waiting patiently for a time when they could force their way into the fissures of what would become a dominant Protestant culture.

Erasmus's opposition to Protestant ideas thus persisted even in his officially enforced corpus of writing. Gregory Dodd's important book *Exploiting Erasmus* argues that although "Erasmus did represent mainstream English Protestantism," his "legacy became a counterpoint to the emerging dominance of Calvinist theology within English religious culture" (3). Yet it is remarkable just how much the legacy of Erasmus originates in essentially the same place as mainstream and even puritanical English Protestantism. Both Tyndale and Coverdale translated the *Enchiridion* (Coverdale's is an abridged version), and even Erasmus's polemic against Luther, *De Libero Arbitrio* (1524) is marked approvingly by Cranmer, who as late as 1550 listed Erasmus as the only early modern author necessary for study in the Cathedral Library at Canterbury.[94] The English Church—born of compromise and hybridity—sustained through this connection with Erasmus a variety of largely unspoken contradictions. The following chapter begins in considering how some of these contradictions played out as Erasmian texts and annotations were translated and transformed by that early purveyor of reform in Tudor England, William Tyndale.

CHAPTER 2

Tyndale's Literalism and the Laws of Moses

For first he would make the people believe that we should believe
nothing but plain scripture in which point he teacheth a plain pestilent
heresy.

—Thomas More, on Tyndale

Tyndale deeply admired Erasmus, though—in spite of much mythmaking to
the contrary—he probably never had occasion to meet him.[1] Early in his career,
Tyndale translated Erasmus's *Enchiridion militis Christiani* (1501) and distributed it in manuscript—a fact long thought to be true from reported accounts,
but finally confirmed in 2015 with the discovery of Tyndale's 1523 manuscript of
Erasmus's work.[2] This remarkable late discovery marks the manuscript as the
first known translation of Erasmus into English, and vivifies numerous paradoxes concerning the place of Erasmus in Tyndale's thought and in English
Protestant culture more broadly. Titled "A Compendious Treatise of the Sowdear
[Soldier] of Christ" in manuscript, and in revised printed versions *The Manuel of
the Christian Knight* (1533) or *The Handsome Weapon of a Christian Knight* (1534),
these evolving English translations of Erasmus offer many contradictions to Tudor Protestantism. Tyndale's *Enchiridion*, for example, frequently uses the word
"Pope" (changed to "the Bishop of Rome" for late Henrician and Edwardian
printings and back again in Mary's reign). Tyndale's early translation of Erasmus also treats Peter as a "captain" of the Church in a way later rejected by him.
In addition, it dutifully follows Erasmus in performing the very allegorical readings that Tyndale would later disparage in *The Obedience of a Christian Man*.[3]
Most significantly, as Brian Cummings points out, a profound contradiction
arises between the *Enchiridion* and Tyndale's *Obedience of a Christian Man* con-

cerning the literal reading of scripture. "In the *Enchiridion* Erasmus states that for scripture we should choose those interpreters *qui a littera quammaxime recedunt*," which is translated by Tyndale as "the literal sense little regarded," and reinforced by a marginal note in the manuscript: "The mystery must be looked upon in all manner learning." In contrast, Tyndale famously intones in his own voice only five years later, "scripture hath but one sense which is the literal sense," a statement which, as Cummings observes, is "the very opposite of the lesson of the *Enchiridion*."[4]

Tyndale's work represents a decisive break from the past in both belief and interpretive method. Since belief was to be founded solely on the interpretation of scripture, a new articulation of method would provide a solid key to this new theology. Yet the break from the past is far more complicated than its proponents made it seem, and disparities in belief do not always hinge on their proclaimed hermeneutic differences. That Tyndale's treatise on obedience, which builds its claims on a reading of Romans 13 opposite to Erasmus's, should also contain this famous repudiation of medieval hermeneutics and an exaltation of the one true method, literalism, provides yet another puzzle. For the difference between the historicism that characterizes Erasmus's approach and Tyndale's literalism has little to do with the articulated break from medieval hermeneutics at the end of *The Obedience of a Christian Man*. Adding to this complexity is the fact that, in spite of the divergence in interpretive methods, the humanist practice of historicism nonetheless had a great deal in common with Protestant literalism; indeed, the historical or literal reading of the Protestants arguably derived from the humanist focus on the historical form of the text. Yet the so-called literalism of Tyndale differs sharply from the open-ended, rhetorically oriented historicism of Erasmus.

A more nuanced and less categorical way of describing early modern cultures of interpretation, based more on practice than on modern or early modern theory, will better enable us to discern interpretive tensions in English culture. These tensions are often understood as existing predominantly between the emerging Protestants and medieval Catholics, and scholars have traditionally used hermeneutic categories that derive from their own terms. This model has fallen under scrutiny in recent years; the work of Brian Cummings and Debora Shuger, among others, has helped blur the conventional view of a sharp division between the allegorical and literal that followed the Reformation.[5] The lasting models of Erasmian humanism, existing before and outside of Reformation methods, as well as the hermeneutic tensions that emerged within English religious culture, deserve still more attention. Tyndale's inversion of Erasmus's hermeneutics in the *Enchiridion*—demoting allegory and emphasizing literalism—by implication frames Erasmus's method as medieval and Catholic in a way that had its own rhetorical and polemical purpose. Tyndale knew full well that Erasmus had broken from the past, as did other early Protestants, and many of their new positions rested on Erasmus's historicist philological discoveries in re-translating the New Testament. The inversion of Erasmian language in 1528 may reflect the debate on free will between Erasmus and Luther in the mid-1520s, which solidified Erasmus's position as anti-Reformation and forced reformers to define themselves against Erasmus even when largely indebted to him.[6] This debate frequently hinged on hermeneutic differences: Luther went so far at one point to demand "a [biblical] text pure and simple," suggesting that the "contro-versy" between them was not even "about the text itself," but about the way it was interpreted.[7] Whereas Luther became vitriolic in his disappointed rejection of Erasmus, Tyndale acknowledged his indebtedness to Erasmus with strategic prominence, as at the end of the preface to *The Obedience of a Christian Man*, when he refers readers to Erasmus as an authority: "as thou mayest see in *Paraclesis* Erasmi and in his preface to the paraphrases of Matthew."[8] Erasmus functions here as a prop as well as a genuine point of reference; and Luther, by contrast, is invoked but only to be defended, deep in the book, not for his ideas but against charges of misconduct. Anne Richardson's formulation that Tyn-dale's "roughhewn Reformation classic begins aglow with Erasmophilia and concludes with a rejection of major Erasmian assumptions"[9] suggests a shift in thinking during the composition of *The Obedience of a Christian Man* that does not fully appreciate Tyndale's ability to sustain contradictions or his calculated consideration of English readers who trusted Erasmus. Although quietly in-formed by Luther, this early document of English Protestantism presents itself as Erasmian.

In the early 1520s, Tyndale had moved from translating the *Enchiridion* to translating from Erasmus's *Novum Testamentum*, using both its Greek and Latin in creating the earliest print edition of the New Testament in English. In this project he also translated and revised Luther, using Luther's 1522 New Testa-ment in concert with Erasmus's 1522 *Novum Testamentum*, and drawing heavily on Luther's notes and prefaces.[10] Tyndale's first effort was a quarto New Testa-ment with prologue and annotations, but only a fragment was produced before the printing was halted in Cologne in 1525.[11] Somehow this fragment, a hand-some pamphlet containing only the first twenty-two chapters of Matthew, man-aged to escape into circulation. Tyndale and his company fled to Worms, where in the following year they completed an octavo edition of the whole New Testament, shorn of notes. These two print runs met with immediate opposition, and remarkably, it is the fragmentary first edition with its prologue and notes that elicited the most vigorous response. Possibly the most contentious of all marginal glosses—and certainly the longest—explained a passage in Matthew that had been used to prove that Peter was the first pope, since Jesus calls him the rock upon which he would build his Church. To the horror of Thomas More, Tyndale amended the institutional term "Church" with a lowercase "congregation": "thou art Peter. And upon this rock I will build my congregation" (Matt. 16:18).[12] Tyndale's marginal note went still further, disabusing readers of the idea that Peter had any special authority besides being a true believer, and that this "rock" had anything to do with Rome or the papacy: "Peter in the Greek signifeth a stone in English. This confession is the rock. Now is Simon Barjona or Simon Jonas' son called Peter because of his confession. Whosoever then thiswise confesseth of Christ, the same is called Peter. Now is this confession come to all that are true Christian. Then is every Christian man & woman Peter. Read Bede, Austen [Augustine] & Hieron [Jerome], of the manner of loosing & binding and note how Hieron checketh the presumption of the Pharisees in his time, which yet had not so monstrous interpretations as our new gods have feined. Read Erasmus' Annotations."[13] In Tyndale's polemical reading, supported by Erasmus, Christ might have called anyone who had the "confession" of a true Christian "Peter": that is, punning on the Greek, a rock. The packed note continues, drawing a comparison between Jesus's clashes with the Pharisees and the true believers' conflicts with the Catholics. This was not just a translation of the New Testament into English, but a well-packaged piece of Protestant polemic.

Following Tyndale's career from its Erasmian origins, this chapter traces the relationship between his polemical literature and his biblical translations and annotations, which caused major controversy even from the very beginning. In 1527, Henry VIII decried Tyndale "for the translating of the New Testament in to English as well with many corruptions of that holy text as certain prefaces and other pestilent glosses in the margents."[14] Since the glosses belong to the fragmentary printing, the king's reaction suggests that Matthew alone was enough to stand for the whole New Testament. This is not surprising, since the Wycliffite Bible, still in use, circulated primarily in forms we now understand as fragmentary.[15] Also seeming to react to the fragmentary printing, Bishop Cuthbert Tunstall wrote that a maintainer of "Luther's sect" had "translated the New Testament into our English tongue, entermedling therewith many heretical articles and erroneous opinions."[16] The 1525 and 1526 printings were recalled, bought up by Church officials, and burned.[17] The king reported that, with the advice of Cardinal Wolsey, and his "tender zeal" toward his people, he would severely punish keepers and readers: "In the avoiding whereof, we of our especial tender zeal towards you, have with the deliberate advice of the most reverend father in God, Thomas Lord Cardinal . . . and other reverend fathers of the spirituality, determined the said corrupt and untrue translations to be brenned [burned], with further sharp correction & punishment against the keepers and readers of the same."[18] Few of these early New Testaments have survived: a fragment from 1525 and three copies of the 1526 printing.[19]

Tyndale followed Erasmus in writing political literature while engaging in biblical translation and interpretation, and his translations and glosses emerge from a deeply interactive context. These two sides of Tyndale—the translator and the polemicist—are seldom considered as integral, as if his biblical translation aspired to the permanence enshrined in the King James Version, where it famously constitutes some eighty percent of the whole, and his roughhewn polemics by contrast were tied to the vicissitudes of history, to be discarded with them. This reception history has occluded not only the importance of Tyndale's polemics, but also the polemical importance of his biblical production. Tyndale's polemics had an immediate impact on biblical translation and annotation, reinforcing the fact that translation itself is tied to history. In the 1970s Barbara Lewalski observed a phenomenon of Protestant culture that has since been more fully explored, in which biblical history was not merely "exemplary" but "actually recapitulated" in early modern lives.[20] By the same token, early modern life is sketched into the authoritative margins and occasionally even into the text of vernacular scripture.[21]

The close relationship between biblical translation, interpretation, and political argument continued through Tyndale's short but intense publishing career. Between his early New Testaments and the revised edition in 1534, Tyndale worked simultaneously at translating the first five books of the Old Testament and writing several tracts, including *The Obedience of a Christian Man* (1528), responses to the criticism of Thomas More in *An Answer unto Sir Thomas More's Dialogue* (1531), and *An Exposition upon the Fifth, Sixth, and Seventh Chapters of Matthew* (1533), among others. In what is arguably his most scandalizing polemic, *The Practice of Prelates: whether the King's grace may be separated from his Queen, because she was his brothers wife*, published in the same year as the Pentateuch (1530), Tyndale argues that Henry's divorce is not supported on Levitical or Deuteronomic grounds, even while he suggests that the king ought simply to ignore the Pope and his prelates, and publish his own case using scripture.[22] Tyndale became an enemy of the state not merely because he published parts of the English Bible just before the state was ready for it, but largely because he would not support the king's case for divorce on scriptural grounds, writing openly against the prelates who did support it. As history unfolded, England's most important Reformation martyr remained on the wrong side of an issue that paradoxically enabled its reformation—or, at least, its break from Rome. And from this break, and the divorce that forced it, the remarriage produced yet another problem of legitimacy: an heir to the throne, which happened to be Elizabeth, future queen for nearly half a century. If the divorce was illegitimate, she too would be. Passages on the divorce were accordingly excised from Edwardian single editions of *The Practice of Prelates* and from Elizabethan collections, in which the tract was renamed as *The Practice of Popish Prelates* to distinguish Tyndale from anti-prelatical puritans disputing the hierarchy of the Elizabethan Church.[23] The practice of casting Tyndale as proto-Anglican thus started early.

The fertile interactions between polemical writings and Tyndale's ongoing interpretive project follow an Erasmian model. Yet the differences between Tyndale and Erasmus remain profound—not just in method and belief, but also in their reception. The Dutch humanist held a position of broad authority that the younger Englishman would never enjoy. An early modern celebrity, Erasmus found himself frequently in the company of princes, advising many who entreated this honor even when his advice was stewed with stern instruction. He wrote poetic encomiums to Henry VII and to Prince Arthur and was first introduced to Prince Henry by Erasmus's pupil Baron Mountjoy in 1499, when the prince was eight years old. Erasmus continued to keep a solicitous eye on the Henrician court prior to the fall of Thomas More.[24] In 1517, Erasmus sent Henry a copy of *The Education of a Christian Prince*—one of a few literary gifts over the years.[25] Those advising the king often invoked the authority of Erasmus, as did Thomas Elyot in the advice manual *The Book Called the Governor* (1531), in which he wrote of Erasmus's monumental perpetuity in the English literary culture.[26] Erasmus's *Education of a Christian Prince*—among a great many other Erasmian titles—marked the height of value in early Tudor England. Elyot drew heavily on it for his advice book, yet in spite of his profound admiration, he does not revisit Erasmus's central conceit marking the difference between pagan and Christian princes that draws from a historicist reading of Romans 13. Erasmus's reading of that passage remained seemingly unrepeatable.

As England sorted out its religious identity over the course of the sixteenth century, its admiration of Erasmus remained undimmed by the reality that

Erasmus was emphatically not Protestant. The enthusiastic repetition of Erasmus's authorship testifies to the extraordinary marketability of this enigmatic figure. It is Erasmus's name—and rarely Tyndale's—credited on the title pages and in the preliminaries of Tudor vernacular Bibles. Early Tudor diglot Bibles that set Erasmus's Latin directly against Tyndale's English usually include only Erasmus's name, such as *The new Testament in English and in Latin according to the translation of doctor Erasmus of Rotterdam* (London, 1538).[27] Even during the heated reform movement under Edward, Tyndale is not credited with the English translation in such diglot Bibles, but Erasmus's name is stressed repeatedly, as in the introduction of a 1550 bilingual New Testament, which advertises "the translation of the most noble and famous Clerk Erasmus," and repeats his name on the title page without any mention of Tyndale.[28] These omissions suggest a persistent aura of scandal associated with Tyndale in early Protestant England that is not fully expunged until Foxe's history, although he begins to receive more credit for his work in later Edwardian Bibles, as we shall see.

In the 1520s and early 1530s Tyndale could only achieve currency with a tinge of scandal; his outlawed books circulated dangerously among general readers and stole their way into court. Paradoxically, Tyndale's advice to princes was far less critical than Erasmus's; whereas Erasmus sought to limit the terms of obedience and dissociate secular power from the divine, Tyndale advocated a new form of obedience in which the authority once vested in the pope could be shifted to the king—a theory of obedience that would, remarkably, become part of the new political language in Tudor England.[29] Tyndale advocates this position most powerfully in *The Obedience of a Christian Man, and how Christen rulers ought to govern*, built on a reading of the commandment to obey parents in Exodus 20:12, and confirmed in particular by Romans 13:1–7, which plays a dominant role in Tyndale's theory of obedience.

This chapter investigates the reciprocal relationship between Tyndale's biblical interpretation and the political context. Tracing Tyndale's unfolding career as translator, interpreter, and polemicist, I turn to his major theory of obedience in the *Obedience of a Christian Man* (1528) and then to his scandalous *Practice of Prelates* (1530). The complex interactions among text, paratext, and polemic appears vividly in annotations in Tyndale's Pentateuch that mirror arguments in *The Practice of Prelates*, both published in 1530. The parallel with Erasmus's coterminous writing and annotating provides valuable comparisons: Erasmus's *Education of a Christian Prince* (1516) and the annotated *Novum Instrumentum* (1516), written at the same time, develop a contingent reading of Paul in the same way that Tyndale's readings of Mosaic law, both in polemic and in annotated scripture, develop in immediate, applied practice. These close synchronic intersections help delineate a larger pattern of cultural interchange. Tyndale's polemics turn from Erasmus's historicist interpretation toward a literal reading of Romans 13 that is heavily inflected by Mosaic conceptions of political obedience.[30] The new emphasis on Mosaic law was partly engendered by the increased study of Hebrew, and by the fact that the Pentateuch remained, for five years before the appearance of the Coverdale Bible, the only printed English translation of the Old Testament besides a handful of less significant individual books.[31]

But the Mosaic orientation of English politics also grew out of the particular dynamics of Tudor history. Because of the double effect of biblical humanism and the Levitical and Deuteronomic origins of the king's great scruple concerning Catherine of Aragon, English politics became deeply oriented in biblical law. One of the major players defining the new biblicist politics was the king himself, not yet Protestant but certainly humanist, circulating throughout his court, arguing for particular readings of Leviticus and Deuteronomy. The intensity of the debate over biblical law that happened to accompany the birth of English Protestantism helped characterize the king as a divine lawgiver: a Moses but more often a David, and like David (the connection followed) a flawed but great king, an adulterer divinely punished with the loss of a child in infancy—echoing God's curse in Leviticus—but who would nonetheless be forgiven and elevated, made the father of a line of monarchs and temple builders.

The emergence of new habits of interpretation—Tyndale's form of "literalism"—must therefore be explored in relation with the particular areas of scripture that become culturally dominant. In this case, the practice of "literalism" emerges appropriately at the same time that Mosaic law—the Pentateuch, or Torah—assumes a position of dominance. The most iconic of these laws were those inscribed by God and borne from the mountain. All subsequent law, often repeated or revised in Deuteronomy, Leviticus, and Numbers at different stages of biblical history, was built on this foundational moment in Exodus when God physically provided Moses with law written in stone.[32] The Ten Commandments had a profound impact on Tudor English culture, as Jonathan Willis writes in an important book on the subject:

> The English reformation catapulted the Decalogue from a relatively
> low value card in the medieval confessor's deck—far less important
> than the Seven Deadly Sins, and on a par with the commandments of
> the Church . . . to the single most visible and important scriptural text

in the whole of Christian religion. The Commandments were to be recited from the pulpit regularly—more frequently than the other two principal pedagogic texts, the Creed and the Lord's Prayer—and taught as part of the catechism alongside the *Pater Noster*, the "Belief," and the sacraments. They were the first text ordered to be displayed publically in churches, painted directly onto the walls or on highly decorated boards. The Decalogue was integrated into the liturgy, and was also versified and included not once but twice in the runaway musical success that was the Sternhold and Hopkins *Whole Booke of Psalmes.*[33]

Major handbooks of church instruction such as a book termed "the King's Book," issued by the new Church of England, *A Necessary Doctrine and Erudition for Any Christian Man, Set Forth by the Kings Majesty of England* (1543), provided the Ten Commandments among a handful of other essential points of doctrine, and offered explications that were inflected by Tyndale's readings.

Thus the new culture of interpretation, self-defined as a simple, stripped down mode of literal reading, emerged at a moment of intensified interest in scriptural law. As the ensuing pages show, this socially focused interpretive practice became intensely presentist and utilitarian in ways that were neither precisely nor exclusively literal, even when we expand our sense of this term to accommodate the sixteenth-century meaning. During this same early Tudor period, the English Bible moved quickly from being an outlawed object to an object of kingly importance, royally controlled and promulgated.[34] At the end of this chapter, I turn to look at the ways that biblical paratexts of later Henrician Bibles sought to frame the king as reader, and in turn how the king himself—intent on applying the biblical text to the conditions of kingship—left traces of his readership in vernacular Bibles. In the manner of Tyndale and Erasmus, Henry demonstrates modes of applying scripture to the political present.

Literalism and Politics: *The Obedience of a Christian Man*

Anne Boleyn's copy of Tyndale's New Testament has survived, but the survival of another of her reputed Tyndale volumes, *The Obedience of a Christian Man*, is devoutly to be wished.[35] The uncorroborated story of her possession of this book has profoundly shaped posterity's perception of how the renegade reformer helped to underwrite the new Protestant state. The story comes from two seemingly independent sources, transmitted orally and transcribed decades later: a manuscript account from John Louth collected by John Foxe, and a late sixteenth-century biography by George Wyatt, grandson of the poet Thomas Wyatt.[36] The different accounts abound in tantalizing rich detail, as when Boleyn highlights passages with her fingernails for the king to read.[37] According to the tale, Boleyn lent her copy of *The Obedience of a Christian Man* to a friend, and Cardinal Wolsey confiscated it. Boleyn went successfully to the king to have her book restored, beseeching her future husband, as Louth's account relates, "most tenderly to read the book. The king read and delighted in the book, 'For, (sayth he), this book is for me and all kings to read.'"[38] These widely credited words are found only in Louth's account; Wyatt's version continues to play out the idea that Boleyn identified particular passages for the king: she "showed him of the points that she had noted with her finger," and "the notes the queen had made, all turned the more to hasten [Wolsey's] ruin, which was also furthered on all sides."[39] Both narratives portray a king easily persuaded, his actual agency in Protestantism's rise thereby diminished, and a Boleyn—mother of the queen for these authors—who emerges contrastingly as a hero, bringing about the English Reformation and the new Henrician supremacy through her interpretation of Tyndale's writings.

For better or worse, the conflated accounts have informed subsequent historiography. With the framework of these legends it has been argued, largely on the basis of royal manuscripts with questionable dates, that Tyndale's *Obedience of a Christian Man* influenced Henry VIII's decision to become head of the Church of England in decreeing the Act of Supremacy (1534).[40] This surprising dependence in the historiography on Boleyn's alleged intervention has been variously challenged. Clare Costley King'oo and Susan Felch have questioned the king's "delight" in reading Tyndale's theory of kingship, and even whether he and Anne would have owned or sifted through folksy polemical literature.[41] And in a rigorous reconsideration of misdated manuscripts and early Tudor political tracts, Richard Rex has shown that the "adoption of Tyndalean obedience doctrine did not so much precipitate as follow the espousal of the royal supremacy."[42] Luther's concepts of obedience, through Tyndale's treatise, became "an integral part of this network of new ideas" that formed Henrician political discourse.[43] With both *The Practice of Prelates* and *The Obedience of a Christian Man*, Tyndale's representative practices of reading emerged from the dynamic interactions of biblical interpretation and polemical writing.

The role of Tyndale's *Obedience of a Christian Man* in the history of political thought has been influentially cast by David Daniell as a "central document" in the emergence of "modern political thought."[44] This assessment deserves a brief reconsideration at the outset of a discussion of Tyndale's work, since it mischaracterizes Tyndale in a manner consistent with an enduring view of early modernity. In this view, Tyndale figures as part of a wave of new thinking that topples benighted modes of medieval thought and sets the stage for modernity. No doubt it is useful to place Tyndale and other Protestant political writers in the context of the philosophical discourse we term "political thought," such as that of Aristotle, Hobbes, Harrington, or Locke. Yet there are dangers in this categorical alliance, since theology tends to be prescriptive rather than descriptive, focused on divine rather than natural laws. One solution has been to change the category, and use "political theology" rather than "political thought," though this has been complicated by the fact that "political theology" had already been used by Carl Schmitt, not to describe the merger of politics and theology in early modernity, but the appropriation of a form of "theology" by absolutists in a later secular context.[45] In this earlier context, theology is certainly applicable in its true sense, since politics for Tyndale belongs in the field of theology. His *Obedience of a Christian Man* fits into a genre of political writing that emerged in the early years of the Reformation, such as Luther's *Open Letter to the Christian Nobility* (1520), which had an intensely monarchist position that hardened still further after the German Peasants' War (1524–1525), which (from Luther's perspective) threatened to associate the Protestant movement with rebellion. Luther wrote the *Admonition to Peace* (1525) and *Against the Murderous, Thieving Hordes of Peasants* (1525) to counter this insurgency and the impression it made, and both works are authoritarian in their application of biblical passages such as the commandment to obey parents in Exodus 20:12 and Deuteronomy 5:1, and especially the injunction to obey rulers in Romans 13:1–7. Later in England, after Kett's Rebellion and the Prayer Book Rebellion of 1549, John Cheke's *Hurt of Sedition* (1549) and Martin Bucer's masterwork, *De Regno Christi* (1550), discussed in the next chapter, can be seen in the same vein. The new movement was eager to show that it was not the Protestants but "the bloody doctrine of the Pope," as Tyndale asserted in *The Obedience of a Christian Man*, which "causeth disobedience, rebellion and insurrection."[46] But more than merely appeasing authorities, these defenses made obedience a central theological value. In this way, Protestants moved politics further into the realm of belief.

Daniell's claim then about Tyndale's role in the emergence of "modern political thought" is simply not tenable. It draws from a triumphalist conception of Protestantism and liberalism as inexorably intertwined, and risks tracing cultural history along the lines of religious prejudice. "Modern" these writings are not. Enlightenment political thinking moves in a different direction from the political theology of the Reformation. It is more secular and scientific, with an interest in finding the best form of government using propositions drawn from justice and laws of nature. Nor is there in Tyndale a glimmer of the tolerationist thinking associated with modernity.[47] Using a method that is prescriptive rather than descriptive, and using scripture alone rather than human reason, Tyndale asserts the rules of obedience and the rights of the monarchy—and monarchy, importantly, is the only form of government under consideration. The traditional view of a shift toward modernity at the Reformation is also belied by the fact that Tyndalian and Lutheran political theology can be distinguished from pre-Reformation humanism, with the latter seeming paradoxically more modern. Catholic humanists like Erasmus and More were quite capable, drawing on classical models and Italian examples, of considering "the best form of government, a monarchy or republic," or engaging in utopianism and cultural relativity, or even raising Brutus above Caesar.[48] The exaltation of Brutus would occur in some Protestant resistance tracts in the later sixteenth century, but not in Tyndale or Bucer.[49]

The intensely biblical orientation of the Reformation demanded that political arrangements were to be understood as part of the new theology grounded in scripture. Although it defined itself as the inevitable result of *sola scriptura*, Protestant theology focused on obedience and subordination, interpreting scripture in its own image. "God (and not the common people) chooseth the prince," Tyndale explained, reading and quoting Deuteronomy 17:14–15: "When thou shalt come unto the land which the Lord thy God giveth thee, and shalt possess it, and dwell therein, if thou say, I will set a King over me, like as all the nations that are about me, then thou shalt make him King over thee, whom the Lord thy God shall choose: from among they brethren shalt thou make a King over thee: thou shalt not set a stranger over thee, which is not thy brother." For Tyndale these Deuteronomic lines mean that humans had no role in the institution of the monarchy. The lack of human volition was commensurate with Reformation theology, and a break from Italian and Erasmian humanism. "God," he wrote, is "the chief chooser and setter up of [rulers], and so must he be the chief putter down of them again, so that without his special commandment, they may not be put down again."[50] Deuteronomy 17 was often read in connection with the moment when the Israelites actually drew on it, centuries later, when they begged the prophet Samuel for a king as other nations had. Samuel confronted God, who suggested that he let the people have their folly, and (in a moment of weakness) they made the poor choice of Saul, the first king of Israel.

The annotators of the Geneva Bible, as I discuss subsequently, see this moment very differently, as does Milton, who saw the biblical element of choice in support of the human right to choose a form of government.[51] These later writers show there are non-monarchist strains in scripture, but such strains find no place in Tyndale's readings.

For Tyndale, biblical meaning does not exist in the abstract, but as an applied reinforcement of social function. The first biblical passage read within the framework of Tyndale's *Obedience of a Christian Man*—after the prefatory matter—is the commandment to honor parents in Exodus 20:12, which Tyndale interprets as enabling a series of interconnected hierarchies: "The obedience of wives unto their husbands," bolstered by Genesis 3:16 ("he shall rule over thee") and Pauline texts, also "The obedience of servants unto their masters," and finally "The obedience of subjects unto kings, princes and rulers," a subheading under which Romans 13:1–7 is simply quoted in full, and then explicated for a dozen or more pages.[52] A series of Mosaic commandments thus funnel into and enhance a literalist reading of Romans 13. The layout in the original (Figure 3) makes clearer that the Pauline text has simply been inserted in the place of Tyndale's voice at this crucial moment in the text. It provides the first major illustration in the book outside of its title page, a large inhabited first letter for Romans 13, depicting an armored king with the divinely bestowed sword and the *globus cruciger*, or the "sovereign's orb," suggesting a union of the spiritual and secular.

The passage lifts the first half of Romans 13 from Tyndale's 1526 translation in the *Obedience*:

> The thirteenth Chapter of Paul (Romans): Let every soul submit
> himself unto the authority of the higher powers. There is no power but
> of God. The powers that be are ordained of God. Whosoever therefore
> resisteth the power resisteth the ordinance of God. They that resist,
> shall receive to them self damnation. For rulers are not to be feared for
> good works but for evil. Wilt thou be without fear of the power? Do
> well then and so shalt thou be praised of the same. For he is the
> minister of God, for thy wealth. But and if thou do evil, then fear. For
> he beareth not a sword for naught. For he is the minister of God, to
> take vengeance on them that do evil. Wherefore ye must needs obey
> not for fear of vengeance only, but also because of conscience. Even
> for this cause pay ye tribute. For they are God's ministers, serving for
> the same purpose.[53]

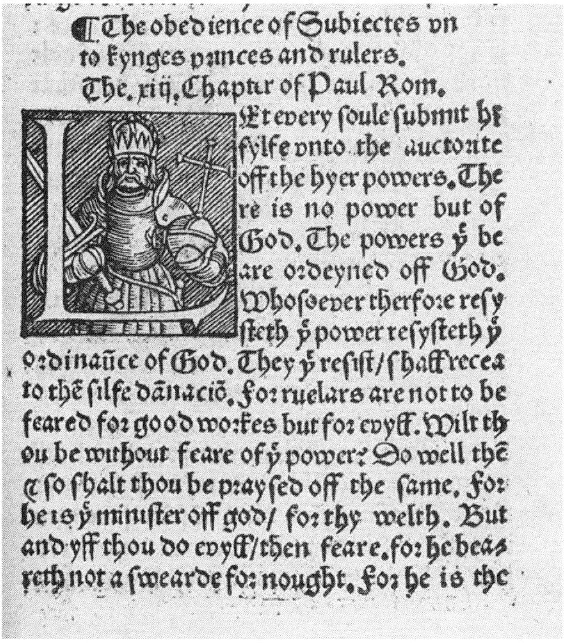

¶ The obedience of Subiectes vn
to kynges princes and rulers.
The. xiij. Chaptar of Paul Rom.

Et every soule submit hy
sylfe vnto the auctorite
off the hyer powers. The
re is no power but of
God. The powers p̃ be
are ordeyned off God.
Whosoever therfore resy
steth p̃ power resysteth p̃
ordinaūce of God. They p̃ resist/ shall recea
to thē silfe dānaciō. For ruelars are not to be
feared for good workes but for evyff. Wilt th
ou be without feare of p̃ power? So well the
q̃ so shalt thou be prayfed off the same. For
he is p̃ minister off god/ for thy welth. But
and yff thou do evyff/then feare. For he bea̅
reth not a swearde for nought. For he is the

Figure 3. Romans 13 set into Tyndale's *Obedience of a Christian Man.*
An inhabited "L" figures the sovereign with the *globus cruciger* and the sword
of power. The subheading, "the obedience of Subjects unto kings, princes,
and rulers," reinforces Tyndale's monarchist reading of Paul's *archontes,*
or "magistrates." Beinecke Mhc5 T976 Ob4, fol. xxix^r. By permission
of the Beinecke Rare Book and Manuscript Library, Yale University:
Rare Book and Manuscript Library, Yale University.

Seldom is such a long passage excerpted in polemical literature, and nowhere
else in *The Obedience of a Christian Man.* It works effectively as a whole, unlike
the short Mosaic commandment that precedes the Pauline text and partly gov-
erns its meaning. Tyndale's translation enforces monarchical authority as much
as possible, restoring the Vulgate's threat of "damnation" from which Erasmus
had deviated when he changed *damnationem acquirunt* to *iudicium accipient,* an
emendation recovered in the Geneva Bible. The monarchist quality of this reading is all the more apparent when viewed in comparison with other major Bibles
discussed in this study. The term "rulers" or Greek *archontes,* chief magistrates,
in Romans 13:3, "For rulers are not to be feared for good works" goes through
several English revisions—the 1557 Geneva text follows Tyndale almost exactly, but
archontes becomes "princes" in the 1560 Geneva text, perhaps as an affirmation

of Elizabeth, and then radically "Magistrates" in the "Geneva-Tomson" text produced after 1576, following Calvin and Erasmus, to return to Tyndale's "rulers" in the King James Version. Following Erasmus's emendation of the Vulgate's *principes* to *magistratus* in Romans 13:3, Calvin uses the term *magistratus* in rendering Romans 13, allowing the occasional right of high magistrates to depose tyrants.[54] The radical potential of Calvin's reading operated in tension throughout early modern England with Tyndale's more authoritarian interpretation adopted by the English Church.[55] And, to look forward momentarily to the very end of the period covered here, Milton overturns both Calvin and Tyndale in *The Tenure of Kings and Magistrates*, a title that draws from this interpretive history of Romans 13.[56] Thus, although he had Erasmus's *Novum Testamentum* and its annotations open while translating and writing polemics, Tyndale does not accept either Erasmus's translation or interpretive reading. Although Erasmus's translation of these vital lines would persist in informing the more radical positions of the Calvinists, few if any Protestants—until Milton—adopted Erasmus's historicist interpretation.

For Tyndale, Pauline obedience relies heavily on its Old Testament derivation, even when that derivation must be constructed and patched together. One commandment, Exodus 20:12, seems to have a more powerful status here than Paul, although it is shorter and less pertinent. The Old Testament—where Erasmus ventured far less—thus emerges in Tyndale to assure a reading opposed to Erasmus. Tyndale never makes completely clear how a political sense derives from "Honor thy father and thy mother, that thy days may be long in the land which the Lord thy God giveth thee," as he first translated it in 1530, and as it essentially remained in later English versions, often employing his readings in their margins.[57] But a strong political sense emerges from the commandment to honor parents in Exodus 20:12, and while not explicitly about obeying monarchs, it came to have that function. In this way the core text of *The Obedience of a Christian Man* derives its meaning from a reading that is not, in fact, literal.

In spite of the dominance of the fifth commandment in political discourse, efforts to read a political sense into it seldom approached careful exegesis. The hermeneutics around this crucial passage were insistent and rhetorical. In a colorful moment just before the section on the "obedience of subjects unto kings," Tyndale draws the fifth commandment into a cluster of relationships of obedience, and then into a comical rant against Catholics: "O how sore differeth the doctrine of Christ and his apostles from the doctrine of the Pope and of his apostles. For if any man will obey neither father nor mother, neither lord nor master, neither king nor prince, the same needeth but only to take the mark of

the beast, that is, to shave himself a monk, a friar or a priest, and is then immediately free and exempted from all service and obedience unto man."[58] The irony
is brought out in the margins: "If thy master please thee not, shave thyself a
monk a friar or a priest," one snide note reads. Another comments, "To obey no
man is a spiritual thing," alluding to the fact that the commandment to honor
parents was applied to spiritual "fathers" in medieval exegesis. As Richard Rex
has pointed out, prior to the Reformation, "spiritual interpretation applied the
commandment to 'spiritual' as well as natural parents," and thus "the over-
whelming tendency of medieval exposition was to inculcate obedience to the
church, rather than to the state." To distinguish the new Protestant emphasis,
which rejected the spiritual mode of interpretation, Rex tentatively considers
Tyndale and Luther's reading as what "one might call an expanded literal interpretation."[59] Allowing an element of understatement, the term "expanded" may
still be too generous, given just how expanded it is. The reformers took the
Catholic spiritual application and redirected it to secular authorities: *political*
rather than spiritual interpretation might be more on the mark. Yet these reformers are driven by still more than a political reorientation. Their so-called
literalism is political and presentist, *applied* in a present social and political
sphere.

 In the case of reading the commandment to honor parents as an injunction
to obey kings, Tyndale's applied literalism is also shaped by a desire to harmonize Romans 13 with Old Testament law. In a passage in *The Practice of Prelates*,
Tyndale revealingly weaves the language of Exodus and Romans 13 intricately
together, enfolding the Pauline keywords "obey" and "powers" into the Mosaic
phrasing, and substituting obedience for honor: "he that so loveth God cannot
disobey father and mother, in which two names are contained all high powers."[60] Once "honor" is broadened to mean "obey," the substituted word enables
such a merger. The applied literal approach to the commandment gathers force
in Tyndale's later work. In *An Exposition upon the Fifth, Sixth, and Seventh
Chapters of Matthew*, he glossed the commandment in fiery political terms: "by
father and mother is understood all rulers; which if thou obey, thy blessing shall
be long life; and contrary, if thou disobey, short life, and shalt either perish by
the sword, or by some other plague, and that shortly."[61] The passive expression
"is understood," adopted in early biblical annotations, suggests a kind of built-in
clarity of signification, though one that depends on a small gloss. In spite of the
fact that scripture hath but "one sense, which is the literal sense," Tyndale's
reading implies that either scripture hath two senses, or that we are to take both
the text and his gloss literally. The same use of "is understood" occurs in "The

King's Book," a propagandistic document of Henrician doctrine. After listing
the Ten Commandments, the volume provides an "exposition" on each. For the
fifth commandment it explains both how "honor" means "obey," and "mother
and father" means a larger collection of authorities: "In this commandment, by
these words, *father and mother*, is understood not only the natural father and
mother, which did carnally beget us, and brought us up, but also princes and all
other governors, rulers, and pastors, under whom we be nourished and brought
up, ordered, & guided. And by this word *honor*, in this command . . . is not
only meant a reverence, and lowliness in words and outward gesture, which
children and inferiors ought to exhibit unto their parents and superiors, but also
a prompt and a ready obedience to their lawful commandments."[62]

After the Act of Supremacy, the political use of the fifth commandment
pervaded Tudor discourse. The Geneva Bible glosses the phrase "Honor thy
father and thy mother" with a marginal note that expands and applies in the
manner of Tyndale: "By the parents also is meant all that have authority over us"
(Exod. 20:12). Tyndale and Genevan translators like Anthony Gilby share an
interpretive insistence, as if no opportunities for applicable meanings, however
tangential, should be overlooked. The gloss, necessary even in the world of *sola
scriptura*, insists on its reading as though it inhered in the text: by parents "is
meant" rulers, echoing Tyndale's passive construction "is understood." The
shared insistence is especially surprising given that Tyndale and the Genevan
translators are exilic annotators, and the Genevan writers were often far less
monarchist than Tyndale—yet not so here. And in spite of his exilic status—
outcast, banned, executed with strangulation, stake and fire—Tyndale's textual
corpus was nonetheless used to create the magisterial doctrine of Henry, now
Supreme Head of the Church. In a series of propagandistic documents issued in
and around 1536, writers went so far as to take the Mosaic commandment to
obey father and mother to require no gloss in its application for kingly obedience. Richard Morison, for example, a humanist scholar and propagandist
under Thomas Cromwell, enjoined his audience: "which of all the commandments is more necessary for us than this, 'Obey ye your king.'"[63] The gloss becomes the text, and the fifth commandment is Romans 13.

In another royalist tract written in 1536, the *Remedy for Sedition*, Morison
again echoes Tyndale, converting the fifth commandment into a "Law" of political obedience: "God maketh kings, specially where they reign by succession.
God took away prince Arthur, & would king Henry the eight, to be our head,
and governor. Will we be wiser than God? Will we take upon us, to know who
ought to govern us, better than God? God made him king, and made also this

law, Obey your king."[64] Morison's debt to Tyndale is especially clear in his calling "obedience" the badge of the "Christian man": "How can ye say, you fight in a good cause, which in one act offend so many of God's commandments? Who is he that very nature hath not taught, to be obeisant to his sovereign lord the king? Peter, Paul, Christ, finally all say, that say well, Obey thy prince. I am sorry, that Turks heathen creatures, men cast away, if Truth say truth, I am sorry that they should so far excel us, in a thing that only pertaineth unto us, and little or nothing to them, Obedience is the badge of a true Christian man."[65]

The shift from a spiritual reading of the commandment to honor parents to an applied political reading enabled the investment of power in a single sovereign. The shift from spiritual reading to an applied political one allowed the disempowerment of popes and prelates, the subject of Tyndale's next polemic: "Kings were ordained then, as I before said, and the sword put in their hands to take vengeance of evil doers, that others might fear, and were not ordained to fight one against another or to rise against the Emperor to defend the false authority of the Pope that very Antichrist."[66] The implication of a true literal reading of Romans 13, here, is that prelates will be disempowered: "Bishops, they can only minister the temporal sword, their office the preaching of God's word laid apart, which they will neither do nor suffer any man to do, but slay with the temporal sword (which they have gotten out of the hand of all princes) them that would."[67] In railing against the practices of prelates, the subject of his next work, Tyndale writes of the misuse of the sword, which belongs in the King's hands: "whether in the scripture or in your own traditions or in the pope's law, that ye compel the lay people to observe violently, threatening them with your excommunications & curses, that they shall be damned both body and soul if they keep them not. And if that help you not, then ye murther them mercilessly with the sword of the temporal powers whom ye have made so blind that they be ready to slay whom ye command, and will not yet hear his cause examined nor give him room to answer for himself."[68] In *The Practice of Prelates*, to which I now turn, Tyndale writes still more urgently about the particular practices of Cardinal Wolsey and others surrounding the king.

The King's Great Matter in Tyndale's Pentateuch and *The Practice of Prelates*

Even before the Reformation came to assert scripture above other authorities, England's politics became immersed in a biblical problem that would reshape the use of scripture on the public stage. The king's divorce from Catherine of Aragon began with a royal scruple over a biblical text that sent much of Europe into debate over Levitical and Deuteronomic meanings. As the king reported, the revelation that he was in the wrong marriage began as a "pricking" of "conscience" over a text in Leviticus, phrasing richly exploited by Shakespeare and Fletcher in *Henry VIII*, where the keywords "conscience" and "prick" are revisited in both psycho-religious and sexual registers. Modern historiography has largely followed the playwrights' lead in probing the question of whether Henry's prick of conscience was really the sincere experience of a "God-fearing man and proto-Protestant monarch," as Michael Davies writes, or the groin-orientation of a "nascent tyrant and philandering crook."[69] Henry's personal report occurs during the divorce case in 1529, looking back to a moment in 1527: "it was a certain Scripulositie [scrupulosity] that pricked my conscience upon diverse words that were spoken at a certain time by the Bishop of Biean [Tarbes] the French King's Ambassador, who had lain here long upon the debating for the conclusion of the marriage between the princess our daughter Mary and the Duke of Orliaunce [Orléans]."[70] As Scarisbrick wrote, it is hard to imagine that an ambassador would have had the audacity to question the legitimacy of a princess, and apparently English ambassadors were later told to drop this part of the story.[71] The case lay, however, on readings of Leviticus and Deuteronomy, and how these readings had first entered the king's and then the public's minds has long been disputed. The Levitical reading may have come from Anne Boleyn, as Reginald Pole claimed, or from Wolsey, as Catherine claimed, or from the "many theologians" with whom the king studied, or perhaps, as has been argued by G. W. Bernard, from Henry's despairing search of scripture after several infant deaths and stillbirths.[72] Whatever the origin, the king became so well studied in biblical interpretation that he was widely reputed to know "more than a great theologian and jurist."[73] Henry personally went about to win people over to his argument, as Thomas More reported, "laid the Bible open before me and there showed me the words that moved his highness and diverse other erudite persons so to think."[74] According to Leviticus, first available in English in the very year that Tyndale wrote his tract, "Thou shalt not unhele [uncover] the secrets of thy brother's wife, for they are thy brother's secrets"[75] (Lev. 18:16), using an ancient Hebrew euphemism for sex. The prohibition is repeated a couple chapters later but given the additional force of divine punishment: such unions would be "childless" (Lev. 20:21). It was largely this childlessness—his lack of an heir—that made this Levitical line seem predictive of Henry's condition.

Tyndale's was the first English translation of the Pentateuch from the Hebrew, and it emerged just in time for a multitude of English interactions with Mosaic law. Tyndale's polemical writing in *The Practice of Prelates* drew from his translation and its glosses in vital ways. An early biographer, Robert Demaus, observed astutely that "the marginal glosses on his Pentateuch" were woven "into an elaborate parable" in *The Practice of Prelates*; more recently, Mark Rankin has written about how Tyndale weaves images from his translation of the Book of Revelation into the tract.[76] Here I would like to look specifically at the ways that Tyndale confronts the use of Leviticus and Deuteronomy in contemporary political discourse, shaping his glosses and even the wording of his and subsequent English Bibles around the king's great matter.

Henry's case for divorce—while he strove to obtain papal approval—focused partly on nullifying the dispensation granted Catherine. Henry had married her in 1509 with a dispensation obtained from Julius II in 1503 that allowed an exception to the rule against affinity or interfamilial marriage. Although Catherine had protested that her marriage with Henry's brother Arthur had not been consummated before he died (and thus true affinity had not been obtained), papal dispensation still seemed a necessary precaution. But as the case came to trial, the very existence of the dispensation unfortunately implied the guilt of affinity. And here lay Henry's case against the pope, one that would resonate in retrospect with scriptocentric Protestants: Pope Julius had somehow thought he could override Leviticus.[77] For the first years of negotiation with the papacy, it was incumbent on Henry, with the help of Wolsey, to convince the pope—now Clement VII—that the dispensation was a mistake. Henry had unwittingly broken a law of Moses.

Of course, to maintain the argument, Mosaic law would need to seem violated. That Catherine had consummated her first marriage to Arthur was only one piece of supporting evidence—and it was highly contestable. But there was other evidence that seemed to corroborate the Mosaic prohibition: Henry's inability to produce a male heir confirmed for him the curse of childlessness for those who broke God's law. Yet the king was not, opponents argued, *childless*: there was Mary, of course, and there had been other children, even boys, who died after a struggle. In Tyndale's translation, the phrasing is "If a man take his brother's wife, it is an unclean thing, he had uncovered his brother's secrets, they shall be childless therefore" (Lev. 20:21). Tyndale embellished "childless" with a marginal note: "They shall dye immediately and not tarry the birth, as Judah would have burnt Tamar being great with child."[78] On the surface the gloss might appear harmless, and indeed the part about Tamar—though not the part about dying immediately—appears in subsequent marginal glosses. The marginal note was designed, however, as a double reinforcement against the argument that the threat concerned only male children: even if "childless" might mean "boyless," as Henry's theologians helped him to argue, the boy would still need to "die immediately," and not last (as one prince had) for fifty-one excruciatingly long days in 1514. That, for Tyndale, was no Levitical curse. Tyndale's Leviticus was the only one available in print in English, and Tyndale thereby ensured that any reader consulting this passage—and especially the king, to whom it was most applicable—would find that it flatly refuted the royal argument. Astonishingly, Tyndale incorporated the same gloss into his discussion of the biblical text in arguing against the king's divorce in *The Practice of Prelates*: "And this doth the xxth chapter of the said Leviticus prove, where Moses saith, If a man lie with his brother's wife, they shall die immediately, and not tarry the birth: as Judah would have burnt Tamar, his daughter-in-law being yet great with child."[79] Moses does not say this about Tamar here—Tyndale lifts this from a story in Genesis. Yet for Tyndale the loose connection to Genesis 38 creates a gloss so true to the original, so much a part of the original text, that it can be cited as if it were the original. From the earliest printed English Bibles—even for those who created them—glosses took on the authority of the text itself.

Henry's supporters had glossed that text differently. Robert Wakefield, a pioneering Hebraist who published a case for the uncorrupted purity of the Hebrew text in his *Syntagma* of 1534, helped the king by substituting "'filiis' (sons) for 'liberis' (children), and then, further, translating 'filiis' as 'heirs,'" and Cranmer even suggested "male heirs."[80] The king and Wakefield, at the time a lecturer in Hebrew at Cambridge, drafted a series of "books" in manuscript, many in debate with John Fisher, Bishop of Rochester. A "king's book" was presented to the pope in 1527, proclaiming itself "by the king's labour and study written."[81] Henry relates that he had "acted out of ignorance" in marrying Catherine, and "had not been as skilled in languages nor as familiar with scripture as he now was."[82] Drawing from a close study of scripture in the original languages (and using this to argue against the pope), the king may begin to seem Protestant, but this moment must not be read retrospectively: that Henry argued for particular interpretations against papal authority would only happen to fit, and retrospectively reinforce, the religion his state would adopt. The more important historical development here is not in the content of the debate, since the scriptural readings were not generally accepted by posterity, but the manner of it: the assertion of a scriptural reading by a king and his theological supporters as the highest authority, logically higher than papal authority. None of these propagandistic efforts at rephrasing the Vulgate's "liberis" made it into subsequent English translations of the Old Testament: neither the Coverdale Bible nor the Great Bible (nor any others) deviate from Tyndale in their translation of Leviticus. If these reformers had been willing to differ publicly from Tyndale, "childless" would surely have taken a masculine form in scripture, as it did in court circulation and in the trial. Whereas the king's books, and his address to court in 1529 silently substitutes "sons" for "children"[83] in Leviticus 20:21, printed versions that appeared in subsequent years followed Tyndale's "childless" or "without children."[84]

Added to the problems of deciphering Leviticus, Deuteronomy 25:5 threatened to close down the whole controversy. Moses rules here that brothers must marry sisters-in-law who are left as widows without children: "When brethren dwell together and one of them die and have no child, the wife of the dead shall not be given out unto a stranger: but her brotherlaw shall go in unto her and take her to wife and marry her." The margins of Tyndale's Pentateuch supply a polemical gloss: "It were hard to prove this a ceremony."[85] The gloss, written at the same time as *The Practice of Prelates*, counters the argument of Henry and his supporters that this levirate marriage was "ceremonial," in that this law applied only to Jews, not Christians. Ceremonial law concerns that part of Mosaic law, like circumcision, that once had a special sign or significance, putting "either of the benefits of God done already" or "signs of the promise and appointment made between God and man." This category of Mosaic law, Tyndale goes on to explain, "ceased as soon as Christ had offered up the sacrifice of his body and blood for us; and instead of them came . . . our signs which we call sacraments."[86] The ceremonial laws ceased only as required action; they never became sinful—an act like circumcision was "an indifferent thing." Moreover, there would be no sinfulness in marrying a deceased brother's wife in the absence of children, nor would there be contradiction between this passage and Leviticus, because (for Tyndale) the prohibition in Leviticus pertained to living brothers. Bolstering his argument still further, Tyndale argued that levirate marriages were not ceremonial: "for it be a ceremony, then it is a sign, and must have a signification."[87] And even if this levirate marriage were "a ceremony," as Henry and his agents wrongly claimed, "how happeneth it that this one ceremony is unlawful among all other?"[88] Tyndale's gloss in the Pentateuch, "it were hard to prove this a ceremony," gestures wryly toward the debate and perhaps his own belabored repudiation.

The effort to prove that this Deuteronomic passage was no longer applicable was, in fact, arduous. Henry's agents went so far as to find a rabbi in Venice, among other Italian Jews, to attest that the practice no longer applied even to Jews, let alone Christians.[89] Henry's opponents, meanwhile, pointed to a recent case of a Jew in Rome who "had been compelled by Jewish law to marry the widow of his brother"—although, as Bernard points out, "the event may have been specially staged."[90] The incidents betray the immense international effort that went into the glossing of a few lines of Moses.

Unlike the prohibitions in Leviticus found in Tudor Bibles, which did not adopt "male heir" to support the king's cause, Deuteronomy found some room for appeasement. In glossing and translating Deuteronomy, later English Bibles favored Henry's case by dissociating the two passages and denying the obligation of levirate marriage. In the Coverdale Bible of 1535, Coverdale revises the phrasing of Tyndale and the Vulgate, changing Tyndale's "brotherlaw" (or brother-in-law) and the Vulgate's *frater* (*Ah* in the Hebrew) to the less literally correct "kinsman," nullifying the applicability of this passage to Henry's case.[91] The imperial ambassador Eustice Chapuys commented that in the new translation, "texts that favor the queen, especially Deuteronomy 19, have been translated in the opposite sense."[92] Chapuys must have been thinking of Deuteronomy 25. This change, adopted by the Geneva Bible of 1560, is reinforced in a note explaining that this is about "kinsmen," translating Deuteronomy 25:5 as "If brethren dwell together, and one of them die & have no child, the wife of the dead shall not marry without: that is, unto a stranger, but his [d]kinsman shall go in unto her, and take her to wife, and do the kinsman's office to her." The note at "kinsman" curiously acknowledges that the Hebrew actually "signifieth a brother," but excuses its less-than-literal (but more politically expedient) translation with the explanation: "Because the Hebrew word signifieth not the natural brother, & the word, that signifieth a brother, is taken also for a kinsman: it seemeth that it is not meant that the natural brother should marry his brother's wife, but some other of the kindred, that was in that degree which might marry."[93] Thus the Elizabethan world was relieved of obligatory marriage, and the marriage to Anne Boleyn and the lineage of Elizabeth were thereby legitimated.

Tyndale's *Practice of Prelates* has been vastly underrated and misunderstood— largely because the text does not support the triumphalist theory that Protestantism (and not merely the will of Henry) won the case against the pope. Tyndale's position has been apologetically presented by scholars such as Daniell as being out of step with that of other "reformers": "Writing for English readers, he knows that reformers like Latimer argue that it was no marriage at all, and ought to be broken."[94] This is not Tyndale's thinking. His knowledge of Latimer's views back in England, if it exists at all, is not relevant at this moment; the position of secret English reformers only became clear after Wolsey's efforts to reverse the dispensation had failed, and when a break from the pope became conceivable. At this moment, the divorce is very much Cardinal Wolsey's cause—not the Protestants'. Gervase Duffield wrote similarly that Tyndale "differs from nearly every other Reformer" and then explained that "later editions [of *The Practice of Prelates*] omitted the passages about divorce where Tyndale was at variance with other Reformers."[95] This too misrepresents history: Tyndale is at variance with Wolsey and the prelates in this tract, and only at variance with the political history that would follow; for, after the marriage to Anne Boleyn and the break from Rome, no sensible publisher would print these arguments.[96] In composing *The Practice of Prelates*, Tyndale was not intervening in a debate among reformers. Until his fall in late 1529, Wolsey was the main architect of the king's divorce, designed indeed to keep England Catholic, and the book is mainly a rejection of Wolsey. The point of Wolsey's and Henry's efforts at the time was to convince the papacy of the legitimacy of his reading in order to secure the pope's approval for the divorce. Tyndale's tract rejecting these readings thus stands at the very cusp—and concerning the very issue—of England's break from Rome.[97]

As Rankin has shown, the tract was immediately respected even by Tyndale's opponents; Chapuys, for example, praised its "masterly and most complete manner" of treating the divorce in his letter to Charles V, and thought it "tells the truth too plainly to please the king."[98] This comment may help shed light on the question of whether Tyndale's writings—as in the case of *The Obedience of a Christian Man*—made it into the king's hands; it suggests that the court had an expectation that he would read Tyndale. We have a report of such reading, in a 1531 letter from Cromwell to Stephen Vaughan, thanking him for sending "that part of Tyndale's book, enclosed in leather, which ye, with your letters, directed to the King's Highness." The king, Cromwell reported, "nothing liked the said book, being filled with seditious slanderous lies, and fantastical opinions, showing therein neither learning nor truth."[99] The Milanese ambassador reported 3,000 copies in circulation in early autumn 1530, soon after Wolsey had fallen from grace. In November, a book burning was staged, and possessors and distributors of the book were forced to parade through London with a sign of repentance about their necks for sinning against the king.[100]

Yet Tyndale and King Henry came to agree on a matter that was more important than any particular interpretation of Leviticus: Henry's right to interpret scripture and to promulgate his interpretation as the law of the land. As

Tyndale glosses his argument: "The pope hath no authority against God." "If the king's most noble grace will needs have another wife," Tyndale advises before suggesting his own interpretation of the passages, "then let him search the laws of God, whether it be lawful or not. . . . If the law of God suffer it, then let his grace put forth a little treatise in print, and even in the English tongue, that all men may see it, for his excuse and the defense of his deed, and say, 'Lo, by the authority of God's word do I this.'"[101] Of course, implicit in Tyndale's very publication is his own equal right to promulgate an interpretation of scripture, a higher authority than the king. The king and subsequent Protestant monarchs follow this mode of operation, in which the biblical text now legitimated royal authority without intervention from the pope. Powerful iconography aided the monarchist interpretive positions in the first complete English Bibles to appear in print.

Royal Bibles and Royal Readers

In 1535, a book known as the Coverdale Bible appeared in an anonymous city in northern Europe.[102] Although the text was furtively produced by exiles, its publication was coordinated by authorities in the English court, and facilitated by James Nicolson, a printer in Southwark, who furnished copies sent from the Continent with the dedicatory epistle to the king and other preliminaries.[103] The dedication validates Henry's second marriage on the first page: "your dearest just wife, and most virtuous Princess, Queen Anne"—soon "Queen Jane," whom the king married before the 1537 edition.[104] The book opens to a title page woodcut by Hans Holbein (Figure 4) showing the king surrounded by the English court and leading churchmen. Seated on a throne, Henry holds a sword in one hand and a Bible in the other. He is flanked on one side by nobles and on the other by bishops, to whom he appears to be handing the Bible. In niches on either side stand Paul, with a sword, and David, with a harp. In Holbein's image the bishops seem to receive the divine word as a gift from the king, though it looks equally as though the bishops, as interpreters of the word, hand the Bible up to the king as a way of conferring divine power.[105] As Kevin Sharpe and Greg Walker have shown, this depiction of English bishops, arranged in consultation with Cromwell, himself apparently portrayed in bishops' garb, is prescriptive of a relationship that *will* occur, a "persuasive rather than celebratory image" that "seeks to 'sell' the Coverdale text to Henry." The "principal intended audience for the image was not," as Walker argues, "a popular readership but precisely the

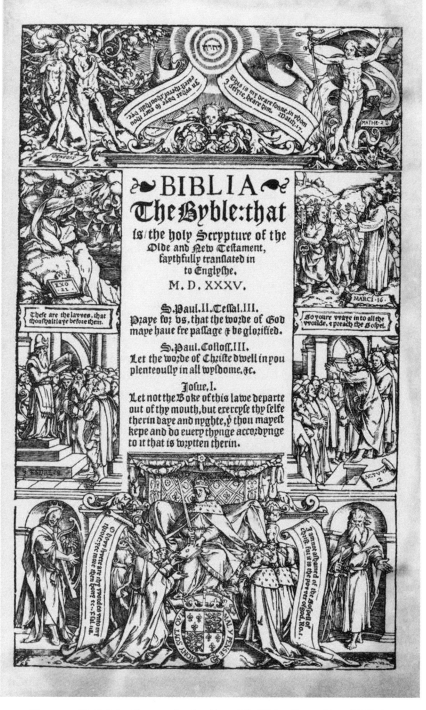

Figure 4. Holbein's title page for the Coverdale Bible of 1535. Hans Holbein the Younger created this woodcut showing Henry VIII with sword and Bible in hand, flanked by his churchmen, his court, King David, and Paul. By permission of the Beinecke Rare Book and Manuscript Library, Yale University.

king himself."[106] This important observation should be borne in mind in relation to many other Tudor biblical publications, such as a collection of King Solomon's writings and King David's psalms, both seemingly packaged for a royal reader, and both successful in attracting one. Entries in the Stationers' Register show "delivered to the king's highness the vi day of January [1541/2] a psalter in English and Latin covered with crimson satin," and "delivered the same time a psalter/the proverbs of Solomon, and other small books bound together."[107]

Holbein's woodcut thus folds the king into a history that has not yet occurred: Henry had not yet been ceremoniously handed an English Bible by his bishops and courtiers, nor, certainly, had he handed one down to them, as the image more prominently suggests. But although this Bible was not a royal production, Nicolson and Coverdale had the text and the preliminaries vetted by the king and his bishops prior to its publication.[108] And although the book in the image is unnamed, this woodcut likely depicts the very Bible in which it appears, inaugurating the royal proprietorship of biblical production and affixing the Bible at the center of the new Protestant state.

The Bible and the sword in Henry's hands work together as symbols of divinely ordained power. The sword derives from the new Protestant reading of Romans 13, in which God has given the prince a sword that entitles him to act as "God's minister": "But if thou do evil, then fear, for he [the prince] beareth not the sword for naught."[109] Coverdale glosses these words in his preface to the same Bible, seeming to glance back at Holbein's portrait of the King: "[The Bible] declareth most abundantly that the office, auctorite [authority] and power given of God unto kings, is in earth above all other powers: let them call themselves Popes, Cardinals, or what so ever they will, the word of God declareth them (yea and commandeth them under pain of damnation) to be obedient unto the temporal sword."[110] Coverdale's reading reflects Tyndale's implication that the king's power supersedes the prelates of the Catholic Church: the mention of "Cardinals" points toward Wolsey, who had recently fallen from an office that was not sustained.

In Holbein's image, Paul is not paired with Peter, as was traditional, for Peter was by this time too closely associated with the papacy. Peter's place is taken instead by a new royal favorite, David.[111] Holbein depicts King David with a harp, the instrument of the psalmist; Henry and Paul both hold the sword. Like many images in early Bibles, this woodcut bears scriptural tags partly designed to justify the circulation of scripture: "Pray for us, that the word of God may have free passage and be Glorified" (2 Thess. 3:1), and "Let not the

book of this Law depart out of thy mouth" (Josh. 1:8). The latter is Joshua's resolution as the Israelites entered the Promised Land after years of wandering and
enslavement in Egypt, which would take on contemporary resonance in the
reign of King Edward VI. Henry was still most often associated with David: as
king, sinning but repentant, victorious and favored by God.

A remarkable biblical text once owned by Henry VIII is the sumptuous
manuscript edition of the psalms from the Vulgate version, the most heavily annotated of Henry's books. This royal manuscript seems to have been produced
with its single recipient in mind, and in this way it is profoundly different from
a printed text for a wide audience.[112] Yet the manuscript shares with printed literature an association of King Henry with the biblical King David. One image
shows the king in his bedchamber reading the psalms—like Holbein's woodcut,
an image within the book of the king holding the book.[113] Two other sumptuously bound books lie on the floor. In another chamber (Figure 5), the king
holds David's harp, and is joined by his fool William Sommers to illustrate the
line in Psalm 52:1 (Psalm 53:1 in the Hebrew numbering), "The fool says in his

Figure 5. Henry VIII as David in the Henry VIII Psalter. Detail
of image of the King as David with his Fool, Will Sommers,
illustrating Psalm 52 in a Latin manuscript Psalter, London, ca. 1540,
British Library Royal 2 A. xvi, f. 63v. © The British Library Board.

heart, 'there is no God.'"[114] In Psalm 68, David as Henry has a vision of the angel of God.[115]

But the king possessed cruder biblical printed books that nonetheless seem designed to be royal possessions. The works of King Solomon are published by Miles Coverdale in a volume containing several books, entitled, *The Books of Solomon, Namely: Proverbia. Ecclesiastes. Sapientia, and Ecclestiasticus, or Jesus the Son of Sirach* (1542–5?). Although the markings in these books are relatively simple, they show the king as a keen reader of the vernacular text, with a particular interest in identifying passages that concern kingship. George Joye's *Psalter of David in English Truly Translated out of [Bucer's] Latin* (1544?) was printed with an erotic fantasy woodcut of 2 Samuel 11:2–4, featuring a contented Bathsheba, receiving the king's messenger even without her Tudor bathrobe, while the king, looking like he had just stepped out of the more dignified occasion in Holbein's woodcut in the Coverdale Bible, directs from aloft (Figure 6).[116] David's adultery with Bathsheba had been dramatized in writers like Wyatt,

Figure 6. David, looking again like Henry VIII, watches Bathsheba bathe.
George Joye, *The Psalter of Dauid in english truly translated out of Latyn*
([London]: By Edwarde Whytchurch, [1544?]), vi^v after title page.
BL C.25.b.4.(2.), first published in 1530, although without this suggestive image.
© The British Library Board.

whose expanded Penitential Psalms detailed the biblical king's unfolding adulterous relationship. But neither Bathsheba' receptiveness nor the letter presented by the messenger (a medieval tradition) occurs in the biblical text. This opening image casts the whole volume of psalms as pertaining to David's adultery.

The king marked the vernacular text in red ink, leaving a signature squiggle and three dots demarcating passages of interest—these have been variously understood as the King's own markings, or a doting scribe copying from the king's other psalter.[117] Among other things, the annotations call attention to the applicability of passages to kingship. The end of Psalm 20 reads, "Now they are thrust down and all fallen: but we stand and are made fast. / The Lord preserved us, he is our king and answereth us when we call upon him" (fol. 15ʳ; Figure 7). The king's marking—"pro rege oratio"—speech or perhaps prayer concerning (or on behalf of) the king—gives us only a glimpse into what he might have been thinking. The impulse behind the marking, following the humanist practice articulated by Erasmus among others, seems to be an interest in collecting passages pertinent to particular subjects.[118] In this case, the king may also be commenting that the verse is actually about kings, rather than about God, an ambiguity in the translation that would lend support to sentiments of sacerdotal kingship. The psalm is a prayer for battle victory of the king, and the marked line "The Lord preserved us, he is our king" might be more clearly translated, as it is on the cover of *The Necessary Doctrine* (1543), as "Lorde preserve the King, and hear us when we call upon thee," or, in the King James Version, "Save, Lord: let the king hear us when we call."

As suggested by the tags on *The Necessary Doctrine*, the psalms provided a trove of short royalist sayings. The king finds another passage concerning kingship at the end of Psalm 63, this one a prayer or "song" of David during the "time he was banished into the desert of Judah," as the biblical headnote explains. More Tudor paratext is added, explaining that this was the time that Saul persecuted David, providing the context for the story in 1 Kings 22. Henry writes several marginal symbols, and then marks the last line "de rege" (Figure 8), where the text reads: "But the king shall rejoice in God, and he shall glory that sweareth by him, for their mouths [s]halbe stopped." The line suggests that King David shall rejoice in God, and those others who swear by him (God, rather than king) shall also glory, because (by this rendering) their mouths are stopped—suggesting some kind of divine despotism.

As Pamela Tudor-Craig wrote of this cluster of marked texts, "David, and his equally glorious son, Solomon, were Henry's new mentors. By 1543, Henry,

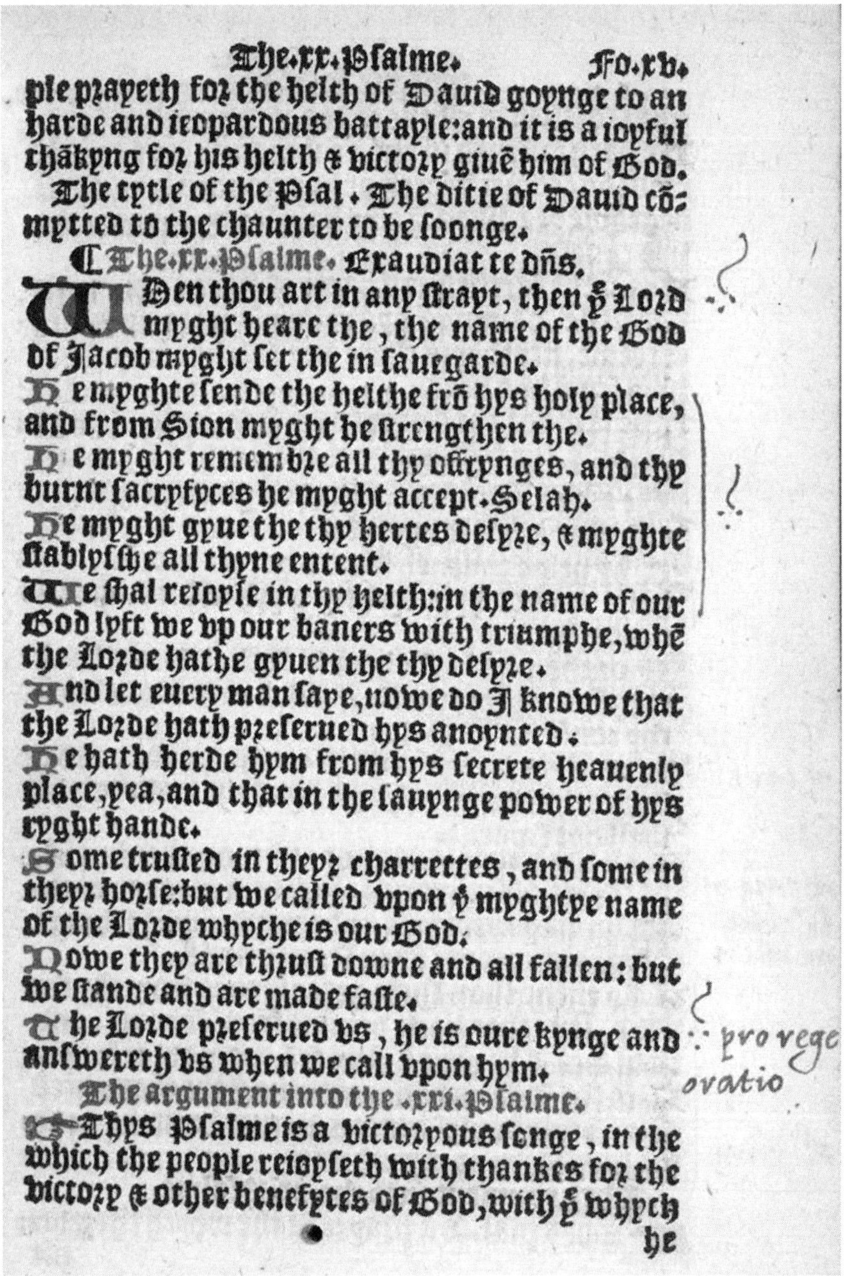

ple prayeth for the helth of Dauid goynge to an
harde and ieopardous battayle: and it is a ioyful
thākyng for his helth & victory giuē him of God.

The tytle of the Psal. The ditie of Dauid cō=
mytted to the chaunter to be soonge.

C The .xx. Psalme. Exaudiat te dñs.

W Den thou art in any strayt, then ý Lord
myght heare the, the name of the God
of Jacob myght set the in sauegarde.

H e myghte sende the helthe frō hys holy place,
and from Sion myght he strengthen the.

H e myght remembre all thy offrynges, and thy
burnt sacryfyces he myght accept. Selah.

He myght gyue the thy hertes desyre, & myghte
stablysshe all thyne entent.

W e shal resoyse in thy helth: in the name of our
God lyft we vp our baners with triumphe, whē
the Lorde hathe gyuen the thy desyre.

And let euery man saye, nowe do J knowe that
the Lorde hath preserued hys anoynted.

He hath herde hym from hys secrete heauenly
place, yea, and that in the sauynge power of hys
ryght hande.

S ome trusted in theyr charrettes, and some in
theyr horse: but we called vpon ý myghtye name
of the Lorde whyche is our God.

Nowe they are thrust downe and all fallen: but
we stande and are made faste.

T he Lorde preserued vs, he is oure kynge and
answereth vs when we call vpon hym.

The argument into the .xxi. Psalme.

C Thys Psalme is a victoryous songe, in the
which the people reioyseth with thankes for the
victory & other benefytes of God, with ý whych

•

he

[marginal annotations: "pro vege ovatio"]

Figure 7. Henry VIII's annotations of Psalm 20. George Joye, *The Psalter of
Dauid in english truly translated out of Latyn* ([London]: By Edwarde
Whytchurch, [1544?]), C.25.b.4. (2.), fol. 15ʳ. Joye's translation of Bucer's Latin
psalms first appeared in 1530. © The British Library Board.

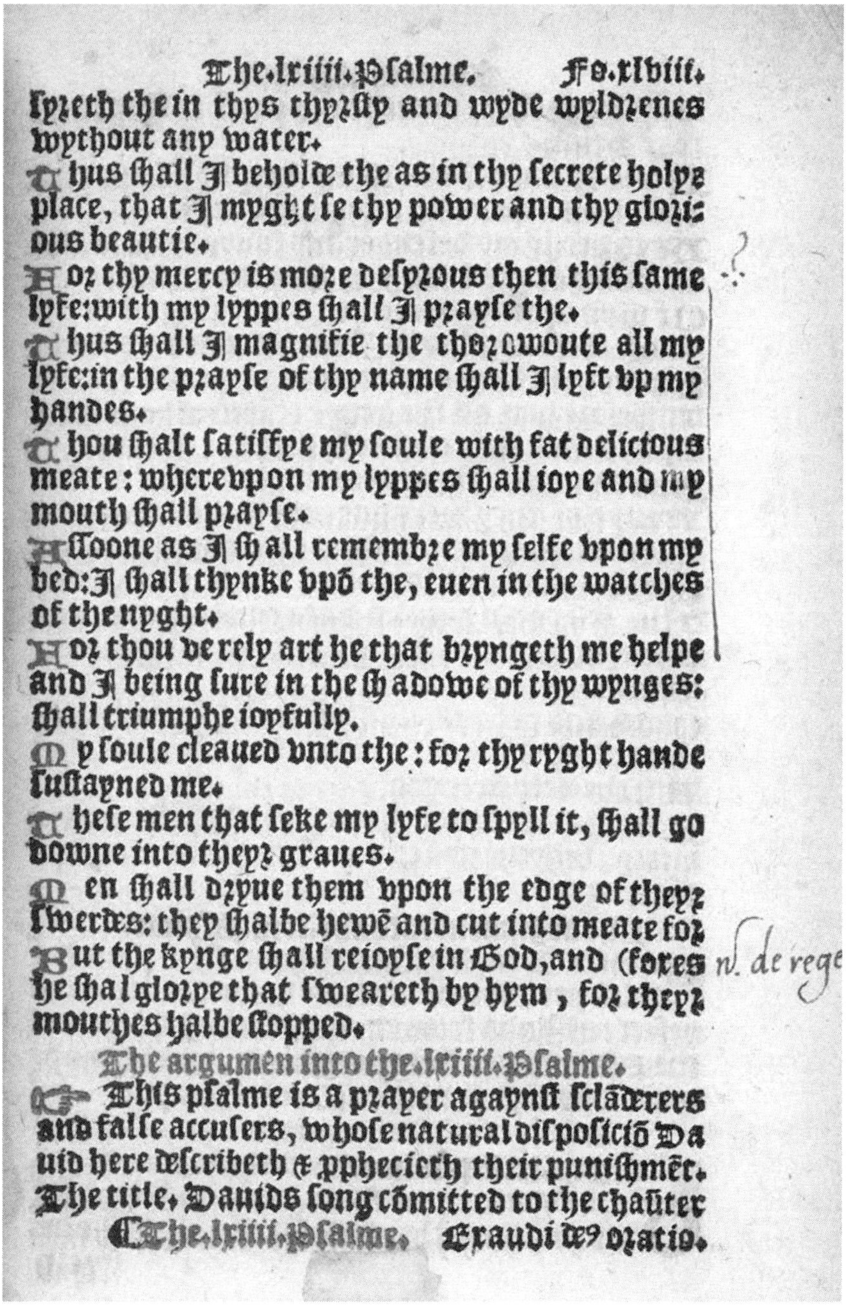

spreth the in thys thyrsty and wyde wyldrenes
wythout any water.

☞ hus shall J beholde the as in thy secrete holye
place, that J myght se thy power and thy glori=
ous beautie.

Hor thy mercy is more delyrous then this same
lyfe:with my lyppes shall J prayse the.

☞ hus shall J magnifie the thorowoute all my
lyfe:in the prayse of thy name shall J lyft vp my
handes.

☞ hou shalt satisfye my soule with fat delictous
meate: wherevpon my lyppes shall ioye and my
mouth shall prayse.

Assoone as J shall remembre my selfe vpon my
bed:J shall thynke vpō the, euen in the watches
of the nyght.

Hor thou verely art he that bryngeth me helpe
and J being sure in the shadowe of thy wynges:
shall triumphe ioyfully.

My soule cleaued vnto the: for thy ryght hande
sustayned me.

☞ hese men that seke my lyfe to spyll it, shall go
downe into theyr graues.

Men shall dryue them vpon the edge of theyr
swerdes: they shalbe hewē and cut into meate for

But the kynge shall reioyse in God,and (foxes
he shal glorye that sweareth by hym , for theyr
mouthes shalbe stopped.

w. de rege

The argumēn into the.lriiii.Psalme.

☞ This psalme is a prayer agaynst sclaterers
and false accusers, whose natural disposiciō Da
uid here describeth ⁊ pphecieth their punishmēt.
The title. Dauids song cōmitted to the chaūter
☞ The.lriiii.Psalme.   Exaudi deꝰ oratio.

Figure 8. Henry VIII's annotations of Psalm 63. Joye, *The Psalter of Dauid in english truly translated out of Latyn* ([London]: By Edwarde Whytchurch, [1544?]), C.25.b.4.(2.), fol. xlviii. © The British Library Board.

like David, but unlike Arthur, had his own young Solomon beside him."[119] The volume of Solomon's writings attached to the English Psalter, *The Books of Solomon*, is marked in places that reflect an interest in patriarchal advice, as Proverbs 3:1–6: "My son, forget not my law, but see that thine heart keep my commandments." One of Edward's tutors reported to the king in 1545 that "Every day in the mass time he readeth a portion of Solomon's Proverbs, for the exercise of his reading, wherein he delighteth much; and learneth there how good it is to give ear unto discipline, to fear God, to keep God's commandments . . . to be obedient to father and mother."[120] The wisdom of Solomon stands in here even for the Commandments, which would become under Edward—king only two years after this—the central text for the instruction of the young.

∗   ∗   ∗

In the familiar but still baffling story, Tyndale was executed for heresy in October 1536, at about the same time the first complete English Bible was finished by Miles Coverdale and printed abroad in 1535 and in London in 1537 "with the Kings most gracious license," as the title page advertises. The Great Bible of 1539, the officially endorsed Church Bible, depended heavily on Tyndale, though it made many emendations. Bible production slowed considerably after a burst of activity in the mid-1530s; as Christopher Haigh put bluntly, "On 16 November 1538 Henry VIII stopped the Reformation dead."[121] Biblical production slowed at times to a halt. From 1540 to the accession of Edward VI in January 1547, only the official Great Bible appeared, with a five-year gap after 1541. This is the longest gap in biblical production after Tyndale's first effort in 1525—never to be exceeded, not even in the five and a half year period of Mary's reign, which saw the production of an English New Testament by Genevan exiles in 1557, and in which the production of a Catholic vernacular Bible was planned but never executed by Cardinal Reginald Pole.[122] In the uncertain period toward the end of Henry's long reign, reformers were burned at the stake, as were evangelical texts such as the biblical translations of Tyndale.[123] Thus the source of biblical production, reflected in the iconography and packaging of these books, moved from exiled outlaw to ordained head of state, but was then held uncertainly. Meanwhile, the same exiled outlaw contributed to the content and method of biblical politics adopted by the state.

The new habits of biblical reading immediately shaped literary production. The shift from spiritual readings of scripture to applied political readings is reflected in the biblical plays of the period, which are "dominated by Old Testament stories,"[124] unlike the predominantly New Testament focus of earlier plays. In the 1530s, Thomas Cromwell patronized playwrights writing biblical plays for civic purposes. This program is described in a remarkable manuscript by his protégé Richard Morison, who advises that the "plays of Robin Hood, Maid Marian, Friar Tuck," full of "lewdness and rebawdry [ribaldry] [and] disobedience," must be replaced with plays that "declare and open to them the obedience that your subjects by God's and man's laws owe unto your majesty."[125] The most important playwright patronized in this effort was John Bale, who follows these marching orders in plays such as *Three Laws of Nature, Moses, and Christ*, which stresses the unity of these laws as deriving from the "commandments," a term that dominates the legalistic roles of Nature, Christ, and Moses. At the close of the morality play, the audience is enjoined to "obey your king":

> For he in his life   that Lord doth represent
> The safeguard of the just   and sinner's punishment.
> See that ye regard   such laws as he doth make,
> For they are of God   as Solomon doth report.[126]

Bale's reinforcement of the doctrine of obedience draws from now familiar Tyndalean biblical sources throughout the play, with Romans 13 playing a central role: the Lord "doth represent" the King, who bears the sword to punish sinners and safeguard the just. The intensely scriptural play draws largely on the laws of Moses and "Christ," yet here again Solomon is given a significant voice, drawing from the proverb that reports from God's perspective, "Through me, kings reign, through me, princes make just laws" (Prov. 8:15).[127]

Henry's long reign is followed by two short reigns before Elizabeth assumes the throne for nearly half a century. Each of these had a defining impact on English biblical culture: the first, Edward, a Solomon allowed to build the Temple, but even more a Josiah, the boy king whose priests discovered the book of Law in a painfully truncated period of utopic Protestantism; and the second (after the nine-day "reign" of Lady Jane Grey), Mary, the daughter of Catherine of Aragon: Catholic, married to a Spaniard, reverser of court religion. Protestants went into hiding and exile, and on the continent they produced an astonishing body of biblical and polemical literature. In Geneva, English Bibles and psalters would once again be inflected by the conditions of exile and persecution. Like Tyndale's Bibles and notes, the Genevan exiles' interpretations worked their way into their political writings, which in turn informed their Bibles. The ensuing chapters will investigate how much the increasingly extensive paratexts of English Bibles continue to carry out the methods of reading already present in Tyndale's intensely utilitarian method of reading, to which I give the working label "applied literalism." In the meantime, the short reign of Edward, to which we now turn, continued to build on the Mosaic legalism of Henry's reign. The final biblical slogan on the Coverdale Bible's title page, a resolution to follow the book of law from Joshua, took on major cultural significance: "Let not the Book of this law depart out of thy mouth, but exercise thy self therein day and night, that thou mayest keep and do everything according to it that is written therein." This is Joshua, having just ministered to the death of Moses, bringing the book of law into the Promised Land. In a passage added to *King Johan* after its 1538 appearance, Bale reads Joshua as a type for Henry, drawing on the use of this passage as a way of describing the Henrician Reformation:

> Till that duke Joshua,   which was our late King Henry,
> Clearly brought us out in   to the land of milk and honey.[128]

Joshua is read as a "duke," and in later Edwardian applications he stands in for a king, although the first true king of Israel was the poorly chosen Saul, replaced by the divinely sanctioned King David. The image of Joshua bearing the book of law into the Promised Land frequently appears in the reign of Edward, not only because the interest in biblical law continued, but also because the biblical context seemed to correspond perfectly with the Tudor context: the nation was finally delivered to the Promised Land after years of servitude and wandering.

CHAPTER 3

A New Josiah and Bucer's Theocratic Utopia

> If you could forget your law, . . . and specially the Canon law which
> purposely corrupteth the truth of Gods word, you should be much
> more apt to understand and receave the secrets of holy scripture.
> —Thomas Cranmer to Stephen Gardiner

At Edward VI's accession to the throne, major players in Reformation history were repositioned like chess pieces at the start of a new game. Hugh Latimer, who had been imprisoned in the Tower of London for refusing Catholic doctrine in the Six Articles of 1539, reassumed his position as bishop, and Archbishop Cranmer finally felt enabled, after ten years of frustrated efforts, to move forward in a program of Protestant reform.[1] The term "Protestant" itself had remained virtually a foreign word, used (as Diarmaid MacCulloch writes) "to describe the doings of foreigners, even among those who felt enthusiastic about their opinions."[2] As it happened, German reformers sought to relocate due to the Schmalkaldic War; and Cranmer, hoping to establish England as the international center of the Reformation, provided university positions to several major figures: Immanuel Tremellius, Peter Martyr Vermigli, Paul Fagius, and Martin Bucer. Martyr taught at Oxford, while Bucer and Fagius were given the Regius professorships of Divinity and Hebrew (respectively) at Cambridge. Tremellius also emigrated from Germany, staying with Cranmer at Lambeth Place, becoming the third Regius Chair of Hebrew after the death of Fagius.[3] For this short period, future "Elizabethan bishops and their earliest opponents," as Patrick Collinson observed, "sat at Bucer's feet in Cambridge and with Peter Martyr Vermigli in Oxford."[4] Collinson actually echoes Milton, another English

Reformation historian: "once the learnedest of England thought it no disparagement to sit at [Bucer's] feet!"[5]

With the help of these continental theologians, Cranmer aspired to rebuild the church and produce a new Latin Bible that would help position England as an international leader in the movement. Such a Bible would also serve, as Bruce Gordon has shown, "as the foundation for a new English Bible to be used by the clergy and people."[6] Fagius and Bucer were well qualified for the assigned task of creating the Latin Bible. Fagius had established the first Hebrew press in Germany and collaborated on such projects as the Yiddish-Hebrew-Latin-German dictionary, *Shemot Devarim*.[7] Bucer had been with the German Reformation essentially from the very beginning; after being transported by Erasmus's *Novum Testamentum* in 1516 as a member of the Dominican order, he fell under Luther's influence in 1518 and disavowed his monkhood.[8] His Latin Psalms and commentary had been translated by George Joye in 1530, being the first printed English Psalter, and the paratexts of these psalms were then imported into the Matthew Bible.[9] The ambition to produce a new Latin Bible, though, like other projects in Edward's truncated reign, fell by the wayside after Fagius died of the plague in 1549. A project for a new vernacular New Testament foundered as well; the renowned Greek scholar John Cheke, tutor to Edward VI and princess Elizabeth, began a translation that was never finished. Rumors of his work somehow gave birth to a New Testament that "trafficked under the name of Sir John Cheke,"[10] but was really a revised version of Tyndale. Later repackaged with the same paratext, "Master Cheekes [supposed] translation"[11] became the most popular New Testament of Elizabethan England, though, well into the 1590s, it still bore a portrait of Elizabeth's princely half brother.[12] Even after fifty years, Edward's image carried immense cultural value as a symbol of Protestant nationalism and the mythic purity of the English Church.

The child-king's reign lasted six and a half years, just a year longer than the subsequent reign of Mary that is sometimes seen to have erased Edwardian innovations. Yet this is hardly the case. The framework of church government, the nature of the liturgy, and major theological positions of the Elizabethan and Jacobean Church were largely drafted in this short period.[13] The truncated reign also became the stuff of legend, a brief moment when the church moved toward perfection, and from which all that followed, for puritans in particular, was a narrative of decline. As long as a century later, writers such as Milton harkened back nostalgically to Edwardian figures in making the case that the current "Reformation" fell short of this original.[14] Milton wrote in *Tetrachordon* (1645) that he would defend "not only Martin Bucer, and all the choicest and holiest of our Reformers, but the whole Parliament and Church of England in those best and purest times of Edward the sixth."[15] European Protestants are here included among "our Reformers," and even the national "Church of England" paradoxically functioned as an object of puritan veneration. Milton's bitter sonnet "On the detraction which followed upon my writing certain treatises" reflects wistfully its last three lines on the learned Tudors (and tutors) of Edwardian England: "Thy age, like ours, O soul of Sir John Cheke, / Hated not learning worse than toad or asp; / When thou taught'st Cambridge, and King Edward Greek."[16] There is doubtless good reason for nostalgia, here, as Edward's education is impressive even by Miltonic standards.[17] But "learning" is only part of the many points of comparison with Edwardian England, and Milton's rosy hindsight overlooks the reality that some of the lasting achievements of the Edwardian church, such as *The Book of Common Prayer*, were under siege by his own puritan cohort. Yet his nostalgic mythologizing illustrates the extent to which the memory of Edward VI could be invoked by English Protestants of almost any stripe to shame others for not being sufficiently educated, English, or Protestant.

Sermons supporting Edward's accession and subsequent political literature fortified Tyndale's literal reading of Romans 13 and reinforced cultural preoccupations with the laws of Moses, the subject of this chapter. The legalist strain in Tyndale flourished and hardened in the new reign. When Edward took the throne at the feeble age of nine, Cranmer's coronation speech addressed the anointed king as "God's vice-gerent and Christ's vicar within your own dominions." The same view informs an early sermon of Bishop Latimer, preaching before King Edward: "Consider the presence of the King's majesty, God's high Vicar in earth . . . and consider that he is God's high minister. . . . Long we have been servants and in bondage, serving the Pope in Egypt." Latimer and Cranmer's shared reading of Romans 13:4–6—in which the king is not just God's "minister," but his "high minister," "vice-gerent," "vicar," and "high Vicar"—underscores their enthusiasm for the sacred merger of religious and secular power. Seasoned by his imprisonment, Latimer's contention that they had "long" been servants of the pope suggests that the later years under Henry, though officially broken from the papacy, were tainted by papist tendencies, and that Edward constitutes the true break. In addition to the intensely applied literalist reading of Romans 13, Cranmer stressed a near-typological connection with biblical history that would permeate Edwardian political culture: Edward would become a new Josiah. He would "see, with your predecessor Josiah, God truly worshipped, and idolatry destroyed, the tyranny of the bishops of Rome banished from your

subjects, and images removed. These acts be signs of a second Josiah, who reformed the church of God in his days. You are to reward virtue, to revenge
sin, to justify the innocent, to relieve the poor, to procure peace, to repress violence, and to execute justice throughout your realms." Cranmer continued his
comparison with Josiah by quoting from the book of Kings: "Like unto him
there was no king before him that turned to the Lord with all his heart, according
to all the law of Moses" (2 Kings 23:25).[18]

The allusion to the young king as Josiah evoked a biblical king of a comparable age, and it also cast the English present as replaying the rediscovery, as told
in 2 Kings, of the Book of Law by a high priest. The book discovered by Josiah's
priest Hilkiah during this ancient reform movement was then thought (as it still
is) to have been some early form of Deuteronomy.[19] In the spirit of evangelical
optimism under the new king, the correspondences between the biblical narrative and contemporary England seemed undeniable and profound: the similar
age of the pious new king, the rediscovery of scripture occasioning repentance
for the idolatry of the past, and the fact that Mosaic law was recovered precisely
at a time when England needed a new law book to replace papal canon law.[20]
The printed introduction to Latimer's sermon before Edward casts the king as
Josiah and Latimer as Hilkiah the priest: "Josiah received never the book of
God's will at the hands of Hilkiah the high priest, or that admonition of Huldah that prophetess, with a more perfect and godly fear, then our most noble
King doth most faithfully, give credit unto the words of good father Latimer."[21]
The Book of Law is discovered when Josiah comes of age, and Josiah reads it
publicly as an act of reestablishing the state of Israel. The headnote to the passage invoked by Cranmer at 2 Kings 23 (4 Kings in the Bible of 1551) explains:
"Josiah readeth Deuteronomy before the people. He putteth down the Idols,
after he had killed the Priests thereof." The notes in the Matthew Bible (1537),
revised and reprinted by Edmund Becke in 1549 and 1551, had already marked
the struggle between true religionists and idolaters in ancient Judah in contemporary terms: a marginal gloss that "Camarim signifieth, smoked or burnt,
or black monks of Baal: and so do the Jews call them" at 2 Kings 23:2–4 anachronistically dresses the heathen Camarites in a Roman Catholic habit.[22] The
passage disturbingly suggests the burning of Catholic heretics, enacted by a
present-day Josiah.

Cranmer had Holbein's image from the Coverdale Bible recast in the frontispiece of a 1548 Catechism, a vital genre for the circulation of the new religious
program (Figure 9). The new version of Holbein's image represents the new king

in the same posture as the old, though in Holbein's original, the book, presumed to be the Bible, has no title. In the reimagined Edwardian version, the
boy king holds "BIBLIA," the Latin title actually used for the Coverdale Bible,
a title unique to this first English printed Bible: "*BIBLIA, The Bible: that is.*" The
titulus underneath the image cites Joshua and Deuteronomy in recommending
close attention to "the book of this law."

The emphasis on the "book of this law" along with this depiction of the
king and a specific Bible suggests a synecdochic relationship between the Bible
and the book of law. As is often the case with synecdoche, "BIBLIA" does
more than simply stand in for the Book of Law celebrated by Joshua and rediscovered later by Josiah's priests; in this combination of image and biblical
text, the Bible in the center of the picture *becomes* the book of law. When
Hilkiah the priest rediscovered the Book of Law and Josiah read it publicly, just
as Joshua had "read all the words of the Law" upon reaching the Promised Land
(Josh. 8:34), the Book of Law was all that the Bible was. The Book of Law came
in the form of this very publication, as Cranmer's text features a series of lessons
on the Ten Commandments.[23] "Surely there can be no greater hope of any kind
of persons," Cranmer addressed the young king in the preface, "to be more apt
to set forth and maintain all Godliness and true religion, than of such as have
been from childhood nourished and fed with the sweet milk, and as it were the
pap of God's holy word, and bridled and kept in awe with his holy commandments."[24] In advocating the "bridle" of the commandments in the education of
youth, Cranmer puts into practice a view he had expressed in his critique of
Stephen Gardiner, poorly raised on canon law: "If you could forget your law,
which hath been your chief profession and study from your youth, and specially
the Canon law which purposely corrupteth the truth of God's word, you should
be much more apt to understand and receive the secrets of holy scripture."[25]
Scripture, and particularly the commandments of Mosaic law, would thus replace the ecclesiastical law of the past.[26]

In Cranmer's early catechism, the commandment "Honour thy father and
thy mother that thou mayest lead a long life in the land which the lord God
shall give unto thee," is read (following Tyndale) as it had been in Henry's King's
Book, as pertaining to parents and rulers: "this commandment speaketh of the
most excellent and most dear personages unto us that live upon the earth, as of
our parents and rulers of the commonwealth, and it teacheth how we should
order our selves towards them, that is to say, to honor and dread them. . . .
Wherefore good children listen to it diligently, that you may know the true

meaning thereof."[27] "Parents and rulers" should be honored (obeyed) and feared: by adding "dread" (or fear) and "ruler," Cranmer interweaves Romans 13 and the fifth commandment.

At the same time that catechisms, sermons, Bibles, and other widely disseminated vernacular texts reinforced the political applications of Mosaic law, so too did the most elite political advice books. The theo-political treatise in 1550, Bucer's *De Regno Christi* (*On the Kingdom of Christ*), given to Cheke in a presentation manuscript copy—a "book of law"—for the king.[28] These two texts, the widely disseminated catechism and *De Regno Christi*, together represent a movement to animate scripture as a social and political instruction manual. Indeed, Bucer's "First Law" in the extensive list of political proposals in *De Regno Christi* is that "Children must be catechized and educated for God."[29] These two documents, *De Regno Christi* and Cranmer's catechism, from the most exclusive form of circulation to the lowest and most broadly disseminated, stress the use of Mosiac law in shaping the new Protestant nation.

This chapter will first look at the repackaging of the Matthew Bible by Edmund Becke, a text and paratext revealing the intensified legalism of Edwardian England. Turning to Bucer's *De Regno Christi*, the chapter then turns from considering the biblical paratext and its cultural interface to the cultural interface itself: how the increasingly codified use of Mosaic law in the construction of the new polity operated, and how it is built on a holistic concept of scripture as a template. Bucer's form of political hermeneutics represents a strain of legalism among English Protestants that is found in the prominent paratexts of Edwardian Bibles. In fact, a work like *De Regno Christi*, like Erasmus's *Institutio Principis Christiani* (1516), might be considered a form of extended biblical paratext, as it draws and highlights biblical passages pertinent to this advice book and weaves them together, with annotations or readings, into a new whole.

Edmund Becke's Bibles

In 1549, the publisher John Day, then "the most innovative and industrious popularizer of the Bible,"[30] with William Seres engaged the minor theologian Edmund Becke to revise John Rogers's compilation of Tyndale's and Coverdale's work in the pseudonymous "Matthew Bible," first issued in 1537. Little is known about Becke's biography or his connections to court, though he is ordained deacon by the Bishop of London, Nicholas Ridley, in 1551, possibly as a reward for his biblical work. After the extraordinary solo achievements in translation by early scholars like Tyndale, biblical production in England continued largely as a process of collaborative revision and accretion. This revised Matthew Bible of 1549 represents an effort to preserve Tyndale's text, notes, and prefaces, with added text by Coverdale and notes by John Rogers. In the 1549 edition, Tyndale is mostly unacknowledged, perhaps reflecting a taint of scandal held over from the Henrician era, but then in 1551 the printer frequently inserts on what is otherwise a virtually identical page, "made by William Tyndale" to such para-texts as the "Prologue to the second boke of Moses called Exodus."[31] The identity of Tyndale is sometimes implicit in the writing, as in the prologue to Exodus, when he enjoins the reader to search out the meaning and beware of allegories as he had entreated in *The Obedience of a Christian Man*, even using the first person pronoun: "endeavor thy self to search out the meaning of all that is described therein, and the true sense of all manner of speakings of the scripture, of proverbs, similitudes, & borrowed speech, whereof I entreated in the end of the obedience, and beware of subtle allegories."[32] All of the notes—either from Tyndale, John Rogers, or an anonymous source, are revised from the Henrician Bibles by Becke, who repackages them to suit the new Edwardian context, making the Bible appear freshly annotated (even when that is only sometimes the case), and adding a lengthy address to Edward.[33]

The title advertises the Bible ambiguously as "truly and purely translated into English and now lately with great industry and diligence recognized." "Recognized" is to be taken in its Latin sense of "revised," and Becke's title surely derives closely from the Latin phrasing in Erasmus' *Novum Instrumentum Omne, diligenter ab Erasmo Rot. recognitum et emendatum*, "diligently . . . revised and corrected." The notes are relatively slight compared to those in the Geneva Bible, the next major revision, but they still suggest vital aspects of Edwardian theo-political culture. They occur most frequently in the Book of Revelation, which incorporates the readings of Bale's recently published *Image of Both Churches* (1545), including images depicting John of Patmos's visions with accompanying rhyming couplets. Becke's Bible has borne the moniker "wife-beater's Bible" because of a crude note to the verse in 1 Peter "to dwell with a wife according to knowledge" (1 Pet. 3:7), "And if she be not obedient and help-ful unto him, endeavoreth to beat the fear of God into her head, that thereby she may be compelled to learn her duty and do it."[34] This gloss's misogynistic severity can only be loosely associated with the legalist vehemence and militant sectarianism of more political notes, but the tone remains similar, and domestic and political spheres overlap considerably. As in many of the publications of this period, the vulnerability of the nascent evangelical state is expressed in fierce, preservationist terms.

Becke's Bible opens with "An exhortation to the study of Holy Scripture, gathered out of the Bible," containing a collection of biblical verses that reinforce the importance of reading the text. Primary among them is the quintessential Edwardian text, entitled "The Lord unto Joshua": "Let not the book of this law depart out of thy mouth: But accord therein day and night, that thou mayest be circumspect to do according to all that is written therein." The passage reinforces the synecdochical relation between the early Mosaic lawbook represented in the passage and the Edwardian reuse of it to represent the whole of scripture. In the address to King Edward that follows, Becke enlists this central passage twice as a mandate for the new king. Entitled "To the most puissant and mighty prince Edward the sixth," the address enjoins the king to see himself as a divine lawmaker. Becke begins with a gesture of patronage toward the king as among the few appropriate dedicatees of Bibles: "To what other person in earth doth the tuition and patronage of God's book so justly appertain, as to kinges, princes, and high magistrate, whom the scripture vouchsafe to nominate and call Gods (Exodus 22)." The use of Exodus to support divine kingship is strained in a way consistent with this Bible's magisterial politics and its focus on the Pentateuch. Kings are called Gods because this passage from Exodus perplexingly uses "gods" in the plural in a syntactic alignment with rulers: "Thou shalt not rail upon the gods, neither curse the ruler of thy people" (Exod. 22:28). Although this translation and interpretation might have given pause—why, among other things, would the jealous God of the Hebrews have sought to protect other gods?—the syntactic alignment nonetheless implies an equivalence between gods and rulers for some early readers. (The Geneva text of 1560 changed the plural "gods"—Heb., *elohim*—to "judges," however, alleviating both the problem of sanctioned polytheism and the equated divinity of rulers.) The King James Version, which often prefers a more literal and a more traditional translation, retains "gods" but offers the Geneva reading "Or, *Judges*" in the margin, suggesting that "gods" should be understood as judges. In the unfettered magisterial biblicism of the Edwardian context, however, the passage nominates and calls princes only "Gods."

Becke's address to the king reinforces the institution of kingship as it is laid out in Deuteronomy 17:14–20, where the nation of Israel is instructed to set a king over themselves, "whom the Lord thy God shall choose." The king then must copy out the book of Deuteronomy (called "this second law" in this translation, from the literal sense of *Deuteronomy*):

> Their interest and title herein, dependeth not only upon prescription
> of time or stablished by politique statutes, laws, and ordinances of mu-
> table men, but it is ratified & confirmed by the infallible word of God,
> as it appeareth evidently in the xvii of Deuteronomy, where the
> institution of a king is described, and immediately upon his institu-
> tion these Godly words ensuing are inferred.

A modern text would end here with a colon followed by quotation marks, since Becke then quotes directly from Deuteronomy 17:18–20:

> When the king is set upon the seat of this kingdom, he shall write
> him forth this second law, in a book, taking a copy of the priests and
> the Levites, and it shalbe with him, and he shall read therein all the
> days of his life, that he may learn to fear the Lord his God, to keep all
> the words of this law and these ordinances, to do them, that his heart
> arise not above his brethren, and that he turn not from the command-
> ment, either to the right hand or to the left that both he and his
> children may prolong their days in his kingdom in Israel.

Becke's application of this Deuteronomic narrative to King Edward is striking. In spite of its obvious foreignness (there are of course no Levites in Edward's court), Becke nonetheless seriously recommends something very near this practice, if one imagines the priests and Levites to represent such theologians as Cranmer and Bucer. A simultaneity of different activities is suggested in "writing forth" and "taking a copy of" the law, in which the king is on the one hand writing out the law himself, and on the other hand provided with a copy. The ambiguity is explained a bit more in a note to the 1560 Geneva text, though only to point out that the Hebrew remained confusing, and the scholars involved would not resolve whether the king or the priests do the writing, leaving it open to either reading, as their note reinforces: "He [the king] shall cause it to be writ by them, or, he shall write it by their example." The King James translators decided to make the king the writer of the law, adding a few italicized English words to help with the complicated syntax: "he shall write him a copy of this Law in a book, out of *that which is* before the Priests the Levites." (Modern translations, such as the Revised Standard Version, have demoted the king, reading a priestly agency in the production of Deuteronomy: "When he has taken the throne of his kingdom, he shall have a copy of this law written for him in the presence of the levitical priests."[35]) This moment in Deuteronomy represents a powerfully monarchist vision—oddly far from the actual kings in the Old Testament, though Deuteronomy was probably written or revised during the period of kings by royal scribes.[36] In Deuteronomy 17 two copies of the Book of Law are maintained: one to be kept and daily studied by the king, and the other to be placed beside the ark of the covenant (Deut. 31:26), where it was eventually rediscovered in the temple by Hilkiah (2 Kings 22:8). It is both monarchist and utopic, in that the king is meant to be profoundly educated in the law that he administers, and thus perfectly fitting for Edward and the Tudor version of the Book of Law. The English fixation on this passage in Deuteronomy 17, and on the moments in the biblical text that seem to ritualistically realize it—when Joshua reads the law to the people, and then when Josiah does the same—reflect the awkward fact that, with the possible exception of these exploitable ambiguous passages, for the Israelites, the law does not belong to the king, but to God. As Michael Walzer writes: "Israel's law is God's alone; it has no other possessive modifier. Above all, and in contrast to other Near Eastern codes, it isn't the king's law."[37] Tudor interpreters sought to have the law both ways, as the king's and as God's. They reshaped these exceptional moments in the Hebrew Bible, making the law seem to emanate from the king, making kings seemingly equated with God(s) in Exodus, and reading Joshua as royal—all in ways that construed an imagined monarchist significance.

The anachronism of Becke's choice to set this scene in the English context in his address to Edward is all the more complicated by the fact that the early book of law (something short enough to be copied even by a king) partly stands in for the bulk of the complete early modern Bible, reproduced by print technology. That the king might "take a copy from the priests" *or* "write him forth this law" is illustrated by a small woodcut in 1551 of Becke handing King Edward the Bible (Figure 10). In the indeterminate fashion of Holbein's illustration in the 1535 Bible, Becke may be providing the king with a copy—but it may also represent the king, having "written forth" the book, now handing it down. The image of Edward holding the book of the law in the catechism of Figure 10 explicitly cites the biblical passage in Deuteronomy, but even that leaves open the question of whether the king or the priests write the law. A copy of Becke's 1549 Bible in the Yale Divinity School Library marked by a contemporary hand reinforces the basic legalism of the passage in Deuteronomy. At "[the king] shall

Figure 10. Edmund Becke presenting the Bible to Edward VI. Following
Holbein's image in the Coverdale Bible, this historiated letter shows the author
presenting the Bible to (or receiving it from) the king. *The Byble, that is to say,
al the holy Scripture conteined in the olde & newe Testament, faythfully set furth
according to y[e] coppy of Thomas Mathewes trauslacio[n]* (London: John Day,
1551), iii^r, Yale Divinity School Special Collections, 939082.
By permission of the Yale Divinity School Library.

write him out this second law in a book taking a copy of the priests and Levites,"
the reader has emphasized that the king is not above the law: "Kings ought to
hearken the Law of God."[38]

From this Deuteronomic passage on the institution of kings, Becke immediately draws a connection to Joshua. The same connection is illustrated on the
cover of Cranmer's 1548 Catechism (Figure 9), which quotes and cites the passage from Joshua, but then simply cites "Deut xviid" as it is (for these readers)
the biblical foundation for Joshua's actions. According to Becke's narrative,
Joshua was precisely following the directive to kings in Deuteronomy:

> That puissant prince, that valiant and doughty Joshua, which succeed-
> ing next unto Moses, had the salve [safe] conducting of God's people,
> was by express words commanded of God himself to study God's
> book to meditate and peruse the same day and night. Let not the book

of this law depart out of thy mouth, but study therein day and night, that thou mayest perform and keep all that is written therein.[39]

Joshua in later depictions is not a prince or king, but a leader and companion of Moses, a "ruler and governor over his people."[40] The origin of kings was often understood (as from the Geneva Bible forward) to be the later moment when the Israelites ask Samuel for a king in 1 Samuel 8, and choose Saul. But for Edwardian readers, Joshua is arguably a prince for three reasons: because he follows the ritualistic reading prescribed in Deuteronomy 17, because he finalizes the journey out of the wilderness to the Promised Land, and because it suits the focus on the Book of Law in Edwardian England. The biblical reading is formed by its immediate context. Five sentences later, Becke quotes the same passage insistently to reinforce the king's duty: "It lieth not now in a king's choice to study or not study in God's book. He must not let the book of this law depart out of his mouth, but study in it day and night." Scripture—not just Deuteronomy—now stands as the best source to establish a new legal code, as Becke concludes:

> We therefore that profess Christ, in stablishing and devising of our
> laws, must not counsel only with worldly wisdom and policy (for that
> is too fearful and cast is too many perils) but we must rather cleave
> fast to the counsel of God's book, and ground our laws thereupon.

Grounding laws upon God's book would be precisely the project undertaken by Bucer. Becke explains the need for the Bible as a source for law in the new realm, one that had recently cast off an erroneous legal system:

> The late experience [that is, the rupture from the papacy] hath learned
> us, that over worldly wise laws be not long lasting. Such semblable
> laws were made by the bishops of Rome, without the counsel of this
> book, and violently obtruded to us your loving subjects, but thanks be
> to God, your highness by the advice of your honorable counsel, hath
> dissolved and utterly abrogated and discharged the same because they
> swerved from the perfect laws of this boke which threateneth the ruin
> and rotting out of them.

Becke's address to Edward suggests that the highest role the biblical text will play is as a source of *true* law, distinguished especially from the canon law of the "bishops of Rome." Bucer's manuscript advice book to the king, *De Regno Christi*, to which we now turn, is built on the same presupposition: the biblical text has in it a legal code that can be extracted and applied in the political world.

Bucer's *De Regno Christi* and Protestant Utopianism

In Cranmer's efforts to establish reformist ideas under the new king, he implored Bucer to come to England, "where the seeds of true doctrine are happily sown," to be "a labourer in the harvest of the Lord."[41] To what extent Cranmer and even Edward might have redirected Bucer from the translation project to write this major advice book, or whether it was an unassigned undertaking, remains unclear. It is often thought that Bucer had written some parts of the treatise, especially the more abstract and less topical sections such as those on divorce, before leaving Germany.[42] (This section was later extracted and translated into a separate divorce tract by Milton; it is disproportionately larger than the other sections, a fact Milton exploits to argue for its centrality.) Yet the urgency of the advice, Bucer's deference to his frequently invoked royal audience, and his stated sense of duty throughout the text suggest considerable integration of the English context into his prescriptions. Bucer had already published on marriage and divorce while in Strasbourg and had been asked in 1531 to join other German Reformers in writing on the legitimacy of Henry's proposed divorce of Catherine of Aragon. Unlike a few of the others, such as Simon Grynaeus (who saw it as an opportunity to win England over to the Protestant cause), Bucer would not sanction Henry's divorce in spite of his support of divorce in some cases. Sharing some of the reasons Tyndale had given in the *Practice of Prelates* (1530), Bucer felt that the king's party misread the edict against marrying one's brother's wife in Leviticus 18:16, since Arthur was no longer alive. Instead, he suggested polygamy, since this was not prohibited by divine law and practiced by biblical kings like David. In connection to this unheeded solution to Henry's problem, Philip of Hesse, a German prince who supported Protestantism, approached Bucer and Luther with a request to legitimate his bigamy.[43] The theologians, called upon again to interpret biblical law for a prince, begrudgingly found biblical precedent, but Luther wrote in a letter signed also by Bucer and Melanchthon that "we cannot advise that any should make a public introduction, that is, a law, that it is allowable to marry more than one wife."[44]

This legitimation of a prince's bigamy was an aberration, to be sure. But it illustrates how the rupture from established customs and canon laws of the

Roman Church had in a sense erased the rulebook, allowing for a wild range of invention and disagreement among the early reformers. Many of the new rules proffered in these nascent years—such as the Davidic legitimacy of bigamy, supported in Deuteronomy 21:15—never made it into the mainstream. Yet the novelty of this moment—the possibility of an entirely new understanding of biblical law—is inflected in Bucer's late masterwork.

Bucer's method is based on a particular way of understanding *sola scriptura*. "God's law is perfect and entire," he observes in his collected commonplaces, "and its teaching enables us to conform the whole of life to the will of God." "Wherefore Scripture is bound to contain oracles to deal definitely, though not in precise detail, with every aspect of public or private life."[45] Again, "God's Law" and "scripture" are treated synonymously, as if the whole of the biblical text were composed of precepts or laws that must be conformed to, and these extractable laws can be reassembled. The Reformation scholar Wilhelm Pauck wrote of Bucer's biblicism that it departed from Luther's "distinction between the law and the gospel," and "regarded the Old Testament and the New Testament as a unity."[46] This difference must partly rest on another division between Bucer and Luther, Bucer's idiosyncratic reading of Romans 2:13, "doers of the Law will be justified," in a way that reconciled it with Romans 3:20 and 3:28, which for Luther stressed uncompromisingly that justification occurred by faith alone apart from the works of law.[47] Recent scholarship on Bucer's distinct doctrine of justification further shows how Bucer's theology was less uncompromising, and reinforces the extent to which we must be extremely cautious in speaking of "Reformation theology" as if there is one sweeping doctrine, agreed upon unanimously by the major reformers.[48] The divisions between the early reformers also emerged between Luther and Zwingli over the Eucharist, which Bucer, often seen as an Erasmian mediator—irenic and less uncompromising—tried in vain to reconcile.[49] Especially in these formative years, Reformation theology was a new frontier, and the different positions sketched out by different figures left lasting tensions. In line with his positive conception of biblical law, Bucer sought in the Pentateuch a prescriptive code that would provide direction for all moral and political questions.[50]

Bucer begins *De Regno Christi* thanking the king for the twenty pounds that enabled him to furnish himself with a stove beside which he was able to "warm [his] frail body" and compose the treatise. Since, he wrote, "literary [*Lit[t]erarium*] composition is expected" of him (suggesting some degree of assignment, if also artistry), he produced "a work giving counsel" that would "please and prove useful to Your Majesty."[51] The two volume presentation copy now in the British Library (Royal MS. 8 B. VII) is bound with a Continental binding in leather with biblical inscriptions in Latin, Greek, and Hebrew, including the Greek of Romans 13 in gold on the front.[52] Other quotations on the cover point to Edward as the new Josiah, such as the quotation from Ecclesiasticus 49:3, on the memory of Josiah: "In the days of the lawless he strengthened piety."[53] The presentation manuscript is "extremely fine and striking in appearance"—so lavish that it seems to have contributed to Bucer's financial distress—and it must have made a distinct impression of importance on its young recipient.[54] Bucer's conception of this work as "Literarium" raises the question of what kind of genre or level of imagination he wishes to operate: although this is far from the irony and ambiguity of the *Utopia* (1516), and lacking the allusive range of something like *The Education of a Christian Prince* (1516), Bucer is deeply conscious of both works, and shares the Platonism of both. His treatise bears many of the hallmarks of utopian literature, including a chapter on how "those who have no aptitude for honorable skills should be reduced to manual labor and humble tasks," and prescriptions for what kind of literature should be created and disseminated.[55]

A few other manuscript copies were produced at this time, and in the Marian exile at least one copy made its way to the continent and was printed in Basel in 1557, two different French translations appeared in Geneva and Lausanne in 1558, and *De Regno Christi* appeared in print again in Basel in 1577 in a memorial volume entitled *Scripta Anglicana* that included encomia of some seventy-seven scholars.[56] In spite of this solid publication history, given Bucer's sharp criticism of Edward's ministers and the urgency of his advice, it is unlikely that the presentation copy given to the king as a New Year's gift was meant for immediate print circulation.[57] Direct counsel often occurs amid otherwise more abstract theorizing, creating a generic hybridity between public treatise and private advice, and suggesting perhaps that the prolix reformer sought to recraft a preexisting and idealistic plan for the particular concerns facing England. In the opening of book two, for example, Bucer suggests that the English Reformation is hampered by traditionalist bishops in the majority who must be overruled by Edward. Some long sentences reflect in their convolutions the uncertain decorum of telling a young king his ministers are incompetent, as in this sentence from the beginning of the second book: "Your Royal Highness, I have no doubt that Your Majesty himself sees that the reformation of the Kingdom of Christ which we require, rather, which the salvation of all of us requires, cannot really be expected from the bishops while there are so few among them who are fully aware of the power of this Kingdom and their own official responsibilities but so many who by all possible means which they dare employ either oppose, postpone, or delay this reformation."[58] The mid-sentence corrective clause, from "we require [*requirimus*]" to the collective "rather, the salvation of all of us requires [*imo quam requirit salus omnium nostrum*]," reveals something about the source of Bucer's timidity: no, the correction seems to suggest, this is not a sagacious Protestant "we" that implicitly includes Bucer and Cranmer requiring reformation of a young king, but rather the collective salvation of the nation that compels this royal action.

Having arrived from a Germany that he perceives as irredeemably fragmented, Bucer prescribes a plan for England in *De Regno Christi* that is intensely disciplinary—indeed, his prescription may be one of the sources (reinforced by the younger reformer, Calvin) for the central concept of "discipline" in the later puritanical language of reform. On his deathbed in the year after the presentation of the manuscript, Bucer expressed a hope that England would not follow Germany in falling asunder, and identified that hope as the reason for writing of church discipline [*de disciplina Ecclesia*][59] and prescribing it to England's monarchy. The earliest puritan pamphlets, such as the Presbyterian *Admonition to the Parliament* (1572), reputedly written in part by Anthony Gilby, who worked on the Geneva Bible, echoed this imperative of "ecclesiastical discipline," which, the pamphlet demands, means "correction of faults severely."[60] Bucer's theo-political system is, like Plato's *Republic* and *Laws*, a structure of discipline, and one that sees rulers as having a spiritual role—like David, Josiah, or Hezekiah—in guiding and protecting their citizens, and effecting their salvation. Mosaic law played a major role in Henry's case for divorce and in Tyndale's polemics, and it becomes still more articulated in Bucer than in previous political theologies. With surprising independence, Bucer's devised a program for disciplined social, political, and religious life that merges, as Shuger has shown, Mosaic legal code (such as that in Deuteronomy) with the utopian thought of Plato, particularly from *The Laws* and *The Republic*. As Shuger writes, "*De regno Christi* lays out both the earliest and fullest exposition of what would become the Puritan social programme for the next 75 years. The Puritan hallmarks are all present: English '*Rezeption*' of the Mosaic penal code, and capital punishment for adultery and 'rape,' which for Bucer includes consensual clandestine marriage."[61] Moreover, Moses and Plato supply not only a body of laws, but—in a strange combination—a penal code. "When they [malfeasants] have done their impious misdeeds openly, and will not change their ways when corrected, it is proper to remove them from the commonwealth, as Plato indicates in his *Politics*," writes Bucer. Embracing Mosaic law in its literalist form meant the severest punishment for transgressions like adultery, idolatry, and various other heresies. "For the Lord," Bucer continues right after invoking the Greek philosopher, almost seeming to confuse Plato with the deity, "has commanded his people quite strictly that they are to drive criminal and incorrigible men from their midst, and to burn them with fire, and thus to wipe out their offensiveness as completely as possible." This singeing is backed up by a series of references to Deuteronomy, which usually suggests that the righteous "stone" the established transgressors "with stones, till they die" (Deut. 17:6), a punishment prescribed for adamant disobedience, riotousness, and drunkenness (Deut. 21:18–22), and for women who lie about their virginity entering marriage (Deut. 22:21), and even thievery (Deut. 24:7), all invoked by Bucer as guidelines for a reformed state.[62]

Later in the treatise, in the discussion of the modification of penalties, he insists that the biblical text be followed in administering capital punishment for those laws provided by Moses:

> Accordingly, in every state sanctified to God capital punishment must be ordered for all who have dared to injure religion, either by introducing a false and impious doctrine about the worship of God or by calling people away from the true worship of God (Deut. 13:6–10 and 17:2–5); for all who blaspheme the name of God and his solemn services (Lev. 24:15–16); who violate the Sabbath (Exod. 31:14–15, and 35:2; Num. 15:32–36); who rebelliously despise the authority of parents and live their own life wickedly (Deut. 21:18–21); who are unwilling to submit to the sentence of a supreme tribunal (Deut. 17:8–12); who have committed bloodshed (Exod. 21:12; Lev. 24:17; Deut. 19:11–13), adultery (Lev. 20:10), rape (Deut. 22:20–25), kidnapping (Deut. 24:7); who have given false testimony in a capital case (Deut. 19:16–21).[63]

In his own life in Strasbourg, Bucer apparently "offered to let himself be stoned to death in true Mosaic style if his life and teaching were proved to be heretical."[64] However, Bucer's concern is not with the precise method of punishment so much as its severity: "all the sons of God must exert their utmost concern and all their strength to purify the commonwealth of such pests as soon as possible, according to the Word of the Lord: 'You shall exterminate' (indeed, the Hebrew word is 'burn out') 'evil from your midst' (Deut. 13:5)."[65] Such punishments were also reinforced in Becke's notes in the 1549 Bible, which explains the stoning to death "unto the gates" of those who have served strange Gods: "Here is to be noted, that such as have deserved to suffer death, ought to be brought to open execution and not to suffer in prison, nor to be there tormented or caused to swear against themselves, or to foreswear themselves."

Bucer's political theology is exclusively monarchist. The treatise operates on a profound analogic comparison between the monarchic structure and the kingdom of heaven, with the idea that the closest approximation of the kingdom of heaven on earth—with the rules provided by scripture—best enables the salvation of the kingdom's political body. The very language of "kingdom" in scripture is used to identify the similarity of political forms between the divine and earthly realms. The utopian idea of maximizing the common good or the happiness of individuals within the state is thus Christianized; it is not earthly, but eternal happiness that motivates Bucer's political system. There is little doubt that Bucer has been influenced by Thomas More's *Utopia*, which he had acquired during his life as a monk.[66] The philosopher king in this utopia— though Bucer does not use those specific terms—is the Christian prince, advised by a master theologian like Bucer, but ultimately endowed with a divine right to rule over the bishops and theologians, as well as the moral obligation to help shepherd his people toward salvation.

In contrast to the Pauline orientation of Erasmus, Bucer conceives of kingship as if he were Hilkiah advising Josiah, reinforcing these rules from the Book of Law: "it will be the duty of Your Royal Majesty to sanction this covenant with holy laws and just provisions against its violators, and to preserve this most vigilantly and constantly. He [ie., you] will then zealously sanction, indeed, restore among his subjects the laws that that Almighty God established concerning the care and preservation of Christ's religion (Num. 15:40; Deut. 13:4–18 and 17:2–3)."[67] In support of the preservation of "Christ's religion," Bucer here and throughout the treatise draws on distinctly Mosaic legal passages, asserting that the Reformation of the state lies in implanting and reinforcing Old Testament prescriptions. The passages listed here, frequently invoked in Bucer, reinforce the commandments, and reinforce putting the false prophet or "dreamer of dreams" to death, because "he hath spoken to turn you away from the Lord your God which brought you out of the land of Egypt, & delivered you out of the house of bondage" (Deut. 13:1–5). Deuteronomy 17 recommends stoning those who have "wrought wickedness in the sight of the Lord thy God, that they have gone beyond his appointment, so that they have gone & served strange Gods and worshipped them" (the Geneva text, which otherwise follows this wording verbatim, changes "gone beyond his appointment" to "transgressing his covenant," and "strange Gods" to "other gods") (Deut. 17:2–3).[68] In a series of recommendations to follow the commandments and punish them with death,

Bucer stresses the value of the fifth commandment, particularly as it pertains to obedience to kings: "There should therefore be no toleration among Christians of those who are openly opposed to this Fifth Commandment of God, which enjoins that parents should be honored and obeyed (Exod. 20:12), and which, therefore, is especially applicable to rulers and magistrates of the commonwealth" (380). The Latin is "Nullo igitur modo tolerari inter Christianos debent, & qui quinto Dei praecepto palam adversantur: quod est datum, de audiendis honorandisque; parentibus, ac ideo cum primis de Principibus Reip. & magistratibus."[69] The word "obeyed"—*audiendis*—is not in Exodus, and used to emphasize the connection to Romans 13, though neither Erasmus nor the Vulgate use precisely this term; Tyndale and others translate "subita sit," either literally as "be subject to," or "obey." Bucer's emphatic but unargued "therefore" or "and so" [*ac ideo*] and "*especially applicable [cum primis]* to rulers and magistrates" exposes the hermeneutics of political urgency, an interpretative method that I have been calling applied literalism. The commandment that parents be honored cannot really make it *especially* applicable to the obedience of kings, but Bucer's insistence overweighs the lack of inherent meaning.

Bucer urges the young king to empower himself by the divine entitlement offered in Romans 13, which he renders to fit this application, using neither the Vulgate nor Erasmus, but seemingly rephrasing in his own Latin, interweaving text and commentary: "omnemque animam suo imperio subjectam, etiam Episcoporum, & Cleri universi,"[70] or "every soul was made subject to his royal authority, including the souls of bishops and all the clergy (Rom. 13:1)." The reading follows Tyndale closely, in that the supremacy implied in Paul must be exercised over churchmen—that the king, as minister of God, rules over actual ministers of God. Bucer then draws from a series of Old Testament examples of kings:

> Worthy of Your Majesty's consideration and conscientious imitation
> are the examples of men like David, Solomon, Asa, Hezekiah, Josiah,
> and Nehemiah, whom the Scriptures praise resoundingly for their
> piety and the sound administration of their kingdoms. When true
> religion had seriously fallen apart in their times and the priesthood
> was perniciously corrupted, these men personally undertook the task
> of the renewal of religion as a matter of royal right and duty. For this
> holy and difficult purpose, they gathered around them as advisers and
> assistants some priests, prophets, and other devout men, who, they
> thought, gave promise in their knowledge of God and in their zeal of

accomplishing very much indeed. They then took care before all else that the law of God was very energetically declared and explained to the people. The next step was to persuade all, after they had professed obedience to the law, once more wholeheartedly to accept and truly to reverence the Lord's covenant. Then, finally, they reorganized and renewed the estate and ministry of priests and Levites and the entire administration of religion, according to the law of God.[71]

This passage demonstrates how vital Old Testament narratives of kings reasserting the law were to present-day England. "The law of God" implies the Book of Law that constituted the biblical text for much of the history of the Old Testament. Its role in the Edwardian cultural imagination was both typological and practical—even literal: the law book served as a source for legal content and practice, and the biblical narratives about it served as a model for the reformation of the present state. Bucer's desire for Edward to model his reform on exemplary kings of Israel and Judah is more than merely literary analogy. The very legal code that these kings returned to, the "Law of God" invoked twice in this passage, is the law that Bucer believes should be instated in England for reform to take root.

The turn from Romans 13 as the New Testament proof text to the Mosaic legal texts or the histories that involve them, such as that of Josiah, follows a common pattern. Romans 13 is the dominant biblical text in *De Regno Christi*, as it is in Tyndale's *Obedience of a Christian Man*. As in Tyndale, there is incoherence between the sacred kingship enabled by Romans 13 and the blunt possibility that even tyrants must be obeyed, since they, too, are somehow ministers of God: "Christ our King . . . wills that his own also should obey from the heart not only the true kings and just princes of this world, but also very iniquitous lords and terrible tyrants to whom public power has been given (I Peter 2:13–17), not only to pay legitimate taxes, but to observe their edicts with a patient spirit, acquiesce to their unjust judgments, and studiously meet all personal obligations to the State. This is what the Holy Spirit commanded in the thirteenth chapter of the letter to the Romans (1ff): 'Let every soul be subject unto the powers that are above them'" (186). Where Erasmus would have attended to Paul as an idiosyncratic author, operating in a particular context and with a particular character, Bucer has erased authorship, in a sense homogenizing the biblical text as issued from the "Holy Spirit." This integration may have further enabled Bucer to turn quickly from Pauline obedience to "laws": princes can deduce that "all their power is from God alone and that he has appointed them shepherds of this people, govern and guard those subject to them according to his judgment, and take care lest any one of those entrusted to them by God . . . should weaken in faith or abuse his laws." And thus from Paul, the text immediately turns to Moses: "Hence it is with a truly merciful judgment that God sanctioned in his law the stoning by all the people of anyone who had spoken blasphemy against him (Lev. 24.16), of those who had violated the Sabbath (Exod. 31:14, and 35:2), of those who had embraced a false religion or attempted to introduce one to others, and had deliberately transgressed his laws (Deut. 13:1–10 and 17:2–5; Num. 15: 30–36)" (189). Following the pattern in Tyndale, the text largely oscillates between Pauline obedience and Mosaic legal practice.

Bucer's heavy use of Mosaic law occasionally reflects some of the contradiction implicit in this use to the theologians around him who argue for the abrogation of the law.[72] When the reformers were asked to advise Henry about his divorce after the fall of Wolsey, Luther told Henry VIII, "Moses is nothing to us."[73] While this "us" did not include Bucer, who took Mosaic marriage laws seriously, there are also times when even he recognizes that not all laws of Moses apply in the Christian context. As Milton translates the portion of this text devoted to divorce law, deep into the second part of the treatise: "I confess that we being free in Christ are not bound to the civil Laws of Moses in every circumstance, yet seeing no laws can be more honest, just, and wholesome, then those which God himself gave, who is eternal wisdom & goodness, I see not why Christians, in things which no less appertain to them, ought not to follow the laws of God, rather than of any men." A distinction is drawn, but the passage still ultimately recommends a return to Mosaic law. The fact that such a defense—and one that is a bit more tentative than the ostensibly earlier parts of the treatise— should appear so late in the text supports the sense that this later section on divorce may have been written earlier. Bucer's reasoning here follows a kind of Pascalian logic: we may not be necessarily compelled at all times by Mosaic law (especially where it obviously does not apply), but since these are the best laws we can know (because they came from God), ought we not to comply when we can know no better? Bucer goes on: "We are not to use circumcision, sacrifice, and those bodily washings prescrib'd to the Jews; yet by these things we may rightly learn, with what purity and devotion both Baptism and the Lord's Supper should be administered and received. How much more is it our duty to observe diligently what the Lord hath commanded, and taught by the examples of his people concerning marriage; whereof we have the use no less then they."[74]

Bucer asserts the need for biblical law from every angle: it is God's law and therefore perfect; even if and when imperfect, it is the closest thing we have to

God's law; and we need it because throwing off the papacy (which had long subordinated civil powers) requires that we turn to find authoritative law in scripture. In Milton's translation, Bucer writes: "The Antichrists of Rome, to get the imperial power into their own hands, first by fraudulent persuasion, afterwards by force drew to themselves the whole authority of determining and judging as well. . . . Therefore it hath been long believed, that the care and government thereof doth not belong to the civil Magistrate. Yet where the Gospel of Christ is receav'd, the laws of Antichrist should be rejected." And thus, Bucer makes the case from a pragmatic standpoint, having to do with the recent rejection of canon law: "Since we have need of civil laws and the power of punishing, it will be wisest not to contemn those giv'n by Moses; but seriously rather to consider what the meaning of God was in them, what he chiefly requir'd, and how much it might be to the good of every Nation, if they would borrow thence their manner of governing the Common-wealth; yet freely all things and with the Spirit of Christ." Furthermore, no one "could make better laws than God." "Many Magistrates at this day do not enough acknowledge the kingdom of Christ, though they would seem most Christian, in that they govern their States by laws so diverse from those of Moses." Here Bucer quotes his own earlier commentary on the Gospels, *Martini Buceri Enarrationes Perpetuae in Sacra Quatuor Evangelia*, first published in the late 1520s. In that context, as in *De Regno Christi*, he is headed to the assertion that "our Saviour . . . came to fulfill, and not to dissolve, did not only permit, but also command; for by him the only Mediator was the whole law of God giv'n. But that by this law of God marriage was permitted after any divorce is certain by *Deut.* 24:1."[75] In other words, as Milton himself would later argue, though with different emphasis and method, Christ cannot be overturning Moses's law permitting divorce.

In keeping with utopian literature and its Platonic roots, and in direct opposition to Milton, whose *Areopagitica* is published just a few months after his translation of *De Regno Christi*, Bucer advocates the supervised production of pious literature as well as its strict regulation. Like the program of literary reform instigated under Cromwell by Richard Morison, the focus is on drama— what Bucer calls "holy comedies" and tragedies from "pious poets" (351), based on Aristotelian aesthetic models (reversal, verisimilitude), but largely drawing from Old Testament narratives. "The Scriptures everywhere offer an abundant supply of material for tragedies, in almost all the stories of the holy patriarchs, kings, prophets, and apostles, from the time of Adam, the first parent of mankind" (351). Yet, as Bucer writes, there must be a censor as well: "In order that the people of Christ may receive this enjoyment from holy comedies and tragedies, men must be put in charge of this matter who have a singular understanding of poetry as well as a known and constant zeal for the Kingdom of Christ so that no comedy or tragedy is enacted which these persons have not seen and decreed fit for performance" (352). Platonic utopianism is a natural development for Protestant biblicism, and one that Milton appropriately identifies in his rejection of Presbyterian ideology and legislation in *Areopagitica*, as is discussed in Chapter 8. Somehow, in spite of the rejection of the works of law in Lutheran theology, an intense literalist embrace of *sola scriptura* paradoxically led some of the strictest Protestants toward a way of thinking about political life that was solely directed by scripture, turning scripture into law, emphasizing the value of scripture *as* law, and also stressing the value of scriptural law.

English Bucerians in and after the Exile

As Patrick Collinson has observed, among the Continental Protestants, "the echo of Bucer's voice resounded longest" in England.[76] "Echo" is an appropriate term: Bucer's voice bounced from one side of England's divided confessional body to another. The Anglican theologian John Bramhall during the English Civil War, for example, uses Bucer to argue against the puritans, first establishing Bucer's credentials as an English near-martyr: the "Learned Bucer" was "employed in the first Reformation of this Church" and "was so opposite to Popery, that after his Death, his very bones were taken out of his Grave and burned by the Papists."[77] This was the case with Bucer's and Paul Fagius's bones, as well, and Matthew Parker and Walter Haddon sought to undo their desecration in a public ceremony in 1560.[78] "He is full in many places," Bramhall goes on, citing *De Regno Christi*, of "the very Apostles themselves, we see that it seemed good to the Holy Ghost, that among the Ministers, to whom the charge of the Church was especially committed, one should undergo a singular care of the Churches and the whole Minister, and in that care and solicitude was before all the rest: for which cause the name of a Bishop was peculiarly attributed to these highest Procurators of the Church."[79] Bramhall was not wrong, and he scored a significant point against the anti-Prelaticals: bishops had a valuable role in the Church, as they seemed to in the ancient Christian world.

In contrast, Presbyterians saw in Bucer the roots of the real English reform movement. Robert Greville, commenting in 1641 on "the long expected Reformation" (as his title proclaimed) wrote that "Bucer most Rational," argued that the "Work of the whole Church, who are to Elect, to testify also and seal their

Election by Laying on their hands: And the Presbytery are but the Churches servants in This Act." He finishes this statement by saying, "I could heartily wish It were reduced to This again"[80]—as if suggesting that England once had a Presbyterian church government under Bucer. It did not, but the myth remains as palpable as the uncertain truth. Milton's *Of Reformation touching Church-Discipline in England* (1641) was part of this same movement of puritans casting the Reformation as something that had begun to take root in Edwardian England and needed to be restored.

Collinson illuminated the importance of Bucer to both sides of Elizabethan Protestantism, in letters written by the Elizabethan puritan Thomas Sampson and by Edmund Grindal, both Marian exiles, in a case that provides a valuable segue to the next chapter on the exilic experience. Sampson, nephew to Hugh Latimer, was a fellow at Pembroke College, Cambridge, when Bucer and Fagius joined the faculty. He escaped arrest when Mary came to power in 1553 and fled to the continent "apparently in the company of Edmund Grindal,"[81] future Elizabethan Archbishop, both devoted students of Bucer. While Sampson studied with Tremellius, he was probably not one of the translators of the Geneva Bible, as is often claimed (including in some of my own work), since his preserved letters suggest he was not in Geneva for long enough or at the right time.[82] After returning from an itinerant life in exile, Sampson found positions in the Church, but was too obstinate for preferment. In 1565, in a landmark moment in the building tensions of Elizabethan Protestantism, Sampson became the first minister of the Church of England to be deprived of his post for nonconformity.[83] In letters to Lord Treasurer Burley in 1573, Sampson draws on the authority and theory of *De Regno Christi*, even providing Burley with extended excerpts, which may have derived from the 1557 Basel edition or translated from the French edition that appeared when he was in Lausanne. Dissociating himself from the more radical authors of the *Admonition*, Sampson nonetheless draws heavily on Bucer's authority as a great Edwardian professor, recalling how many famous Elizabethans had attended him at Cambridge, such as the future Archbishop of York, Edmund Grindal, the future Archbishop of Canterbury, Matthew Parker, and future Bishop of London, Edwin Sandys, among other figures known to Burley.[84] (Collinson also makes a compelling case for Elizabethan Bishop John Whitgift, discussed in Chapter 6, who had been a student at Pembroke and later refers regularly to Bucer in his writings.[85]) Yet Sampson uses Bucer for a puritan cause: that "True and diligent ministers of the word . . . are means to make God a holy people, and to the queen's majesty, good subjects"; they are not, "as Bucer sufficiently confuted," aiming to "taketh away the authority of Christian magistrates."[86]

Collinson has sought to restore an appreciation of Bucer's impact on the Elizabethan Church, especially in the way that pastoral care is conceived in *De Regno Christi*, which, he writes, was "very much as Bucer had conceived of it, active in the episcopal leadership of the Elizabethan Church."[87] As I have sought to illustrate in this chapter, another aspect of Bucer's thinking, which came out of an intensely biblicist reading culture in early Tudor England, has also been given too little attention. Bucer argued explicitly and forcefully that the Book of Law, the biblical text of Old Testament kings, and even the severest punishments that this law enforced, should become the law of the present state of England. This aspect of Bucer's thinking—indicative of a broader culture—would characterize the social and political positions of Elizabethan and Stuart nonconformists.

*   *   *

The Marian exiles' enthusiasm for Bucer, and its possible role in shaping the Geneva Bible, remains uncharted. Certainly, the practice of reinforcing Pauline obedience with Old Testament law continues to occur, as for example in the arguments against the rule of women, which was the main language of resistance when Mary came into power. These too impose Mosaic (and hence divine) legal sentiment where the original Pauline language bears a much weaker mandate. One conspicuous instance occurs in Christopher Goodman's resistance tract *How Superior Powers Oght to be Obeyd of their Subjects* (Geneva, 1558), designed to unseat the Catholic queen Mary I. It supports its political misogyny in citations such as 1 Corinthians 14:34, taken from William Whittingham's freshly published New Testament (1557), "Let your women keep silence in the congregations: for it is not permitted unto them to speak, but *they are commanded* to be under obedience, as also the Law saith."[88] The phrase "they are commanded" is italicized because the English words are added here to the translated Greek, conjuring a connection with the Ten Commandments that does not exist in the original, though it builds on Paul's use of "Law." Tyndale had the milder phrase "let them be under obedience" (1534), and in this case Whittingham added the Mosaic language of commandment to the Pauline language of obedience, since the two were now made to operate in concert, especially when they could be used against Mary. Paul's use of "Law" gestures back to God's curse after the Fall in Genesis 3:16 that (according to Goodman) "the woman be in subjection to her husband" and thus is forbidden to be "Ruler of a Realm or nation."[89] Whittingham's 1557 phrasing was modified for the 1560 Geneva Bible that appeared soon after Queen Elizabeth ascended the throne. For the 1560 translation, 1 Corinthians is less absolute: "*ought* to be subject," rather than *commanded*, which is more sympathetic to Elizabeth and more faithful to the Greek.

Some interest in using Mosaic law in contemporary politics also appears in the Geneva Bible's marginal notes. A note for Deuteronomy 16:20, "That which is right and just shalt thou follow," reads, for example, "The magistrate must constantly follow the tenor of the Law, and in nothing decline from justice." As is often the case, the Geneva note adds the word "magistrate" when it may only mildly inhere in the text, turning the combined text and paratext into a mirror for magistrates (the title of another bestseller that appeared in 1559). Yet this and other notes on law by the Geneva annotators mostly do not represent the kind of historicism turned presentism found in Becke's and Bucer's conversions of the Book of Law for Edward, or their insistent determination to apply it in the contemporary world; rather, they represent the universalist moralizing that derives from medieval tropological interpretation, in which proverbial commonplaces reinforce a general message, with a specific interest in inculcating good behavior in magistrates.

The Geneva Bible, as the subsequent chapters make clear, frequently reads like an advice book to magistrates, converting intensely applied historical readings to present political use in the margins. Yet the focus and strength of the legalistic readings in Edwardian Bibles and texts, as well as the magisterial use of Romans 13, wane considerably in the readings of the exiles (though legalism itself returns, as is discussed in Chapters 6 and 8). The address to Elizabeth in the preliminaries of the 1560 Geneva Bible gestures once toward the moment when Josiah "put to death the false prophets and sorcerers, to perform the words of the Law of God," and that God "blessed him wonderfully, so long as he made Gods word his line and rule to follow,"[90] but neither the fixation on the "Book of Law," nor its insistent application to Tudor politics, are present here. Joshua and the reading of the Book of Law is not invoked in the Geneva preface, nor are they given special attention in the notes; when Josiah is invoked the narrative alludes to the tragic loss of Edward, the second Josiah, rather than to his applicable rediscovery of the Book of Law. When biblical commentators no longer speak in concert with the national center of power, the tenor of their commentary shifts, as do the central passages of interest. The Geneva annotations speak largely from a position of defeat rather than triumph. Instead of the book or books of law, history and prophecy take on a much higher value, while commentary on the psalms and on the Book of Revelation continue to evolve.

CHAPTER 4

The Word in Exile

The Geneva Bible and Its Readers

What need any exposition to apply this unto England?
—Anthony Gilby, *An Admonition to England and Scotland*
(Geneva, 1558)

For Thomas Hobbes, eighty years old and looking back to Tudor England for the causes of the English Civil War, the Marian exiles who created the Geneva Bible bore a singularly heavy responsibility.[1] Born in 1588, Hobbes had the unusual perspective of having lived through a vast portion of the tumultuous period from the Spanish Armada through the Restoration. In *Behemoth, the History of the Causes of the Civil Wars of England* (written in 1668), Hobbes explains the significance of the Marian exile to biblical interpretation and to politics: "Those persons that fled for Religion in the time of Queen *Mary*, resided, for the most part, in places where the Reformed Religion was profess'd, and governed by an Assembly of Ministers, who also were not a little made use of (for want of better States-men) in Points of Civil Government, which pleased so much the *English* and *Scotch* Protestants that lived amongst them, that at their return they wished there were the same Honour and Reverence given to the Ministry in their own Countries." Although the exiles succeeded at these efforts in Scotland, Hobbes continues, they "could never effect" such changes in England "till this last Rebellion." But soon after Presbyterianism rose to power in the Civil War period, "they were defeated again by the other Sects, which, by the preaching of the Presbyterians, and private Interpretation of Scripture, were grown numerous."[2] For Hobbes, private rather than state-authorized interpretation was to blame for the dissolution of the monarchy, and all of this started with the exiles under Mary I.

Modern historians have drawn a similar teleology, though with different motives. Perhaps the most prominent among them is Christopher Hill, who followed Hobbes in connecting the Genevan exiles to seventeenth-century sectarianism and in setting the Bible above all other texts in the history of English revolutionary thought. In *The Intellectual Origins of the English Revolution* (1965), Hill states that "The Bible, especially the Geneva Bible with its highly political marginal notes, came near to being a revolutionists' handbook."[3] When Hill returned to the question three decades later in a book on the Bible's role in the revolution, he reemphasized the importance of the Geneva text in setting the stage for social change in Tudor England. "Radical protestants made a special point of publishing cheap editions of the Bible," he wrote. "In Edward VI's reign the Bible and the Apocrypha were issued in six octavo parts. The Geneva Bible was usually printed in italic [that is, roman font], not old-style black letter. It was cheap, relatively small and pocketable; failure to produce cheap editions of the Bishops' Bible of 1568 helped to make the Geneva Bible the Bible of the people."[4] As valuable as this scholarship is, the small points supporting this claim are not correct: the Geneva Bible was printed in European roman font when it was printed in Geneva, but it was more commonly printed in black letter—which was *not* old-style for Elizabethans—from English presses. Efforts to produce cheap Bibles predated the Geneva Bible. Fundamentally, it was not the Bible of the people, but the Bible of virtually everyone.

Important though it is, the scholarship of Hill and others has led to the unfortunate impression that the Geneva Bible was favored even in Elizabethan England by a radicalized "puritan" readership, and that it was a persistent thorn in the side of worried royalists. The scholarly bias stems not only from Civil War historiography, but also from a special interest in the King James Bible, whose oppositional relationship to the Geneva Bible has profoundly influenced the earlier Bible's Elizabethan reception history. In 1604, calling for a new translation, King James took exception to the Geneva notes as "seditious, and savoring too much, of dangerous, and traitorous conceits," a blustery comment that has incorrectly characterized the general reception of this text.[5] Histories of these Bibles often project James's criticism of the Geneva Bible back onto Elizabeth, suggesting that she, too, disapproved of the text. One account claims that "Elizabeth, as well as her successor, James I, expressed strong reservations regarding the Geneva Bible and its annotations."[6] Another asserts that "[the Geneva Bible] was not fated to gain [Elizabeth's] support."[7] The spurious notion of Elizabeth's opposition carries such strong presumptive power that it is frequently adduced without citation. In a history of the King James Bible, Alister McGrath echoes the established view that "official opposition to the Geneva Bible could not prevent it from becoming the most widely read Bible of the Elizabethan, and subsequently the Jacobean, era." Given the supposed Elizabethan opposition, McGrath argues that it is natural that "Shakespeare, in penning his dramas, should make use of the Geneva Bible, rather than the official translations urged on the English people by church authorities."[8] It has also been suggested that Shakespeare, influenced by French Protestant neighbors in London, "bought a Huguenot Bible [i.e., a Geneva Bible] sometime around 1596 and read it seriously."[9]

These presumptions about the Geneva Bible—that it was preferred by radicals and pre-revolutionary puritans and was officially opposed from the moment Elizabeth took the throne—must be revised. There is little solid evidence for official opposition to the Geneva Bible before James, nor is there any indication that readers, even those as astute as Shakespeare, would have approached bookshops equipped with political or doctrinal prejudices about which translation of the Bible to choose.[10] The Geneva Bible was not associated with Elizabethan readers of a particular party line but was preferred indiscriminately by the English public, both high- and low-brow, high church and low church. It was a translation used by Lancelot Andrewes, Richard Hooker, Archbishops Whitgift and Laud, Spenser, Shakespeare, Aemilia Lanyer, the Earl of Oxford (Edward de Vere), Queen Elizabeth, and most likely, King James himself, since he oversaw its establishment as the official Bible of Scotland, and—despite the story of having just received it from an "English Lady"—his sharp examples from the notes indicate that he knew it well.[11] Although influenced by French contexts and translations, as discussed below, the Geneva Bible was not a Huguenot Bible, nor would it have been perceived as such. It is instead a powerful expression of English nationalism and Tudor mythmaking—so powerful as perhaps to have cloaked some of its inherent radicalism.

The idea of official opposition to the Geneva Bible, pervasive in scholarly literature, has further implications: courtly readers and monarchists, it might follow, would have gravitated toward safer "official" versions of the Bible, such as the Bishops' Bible (1568) or the King James Bible (1611). In contrast, nonconformists like Milton, it is often assumed against ample contrary evidence, "would have used the Geneva Bible."[12] But in fact Milton quotes extensively from the King James Version throughout his prose, and he owned and annotated an understudied 1612 copy that is now in the British Library—arguably neglected because of an unfounded bias about its politics.[13] The Geneva Bible is allowed an almost unbelievable social significance, but for all of its purported strength and character, the language of its text and paratext has paradoxically received little close scrutiny.[14] There is no doubt that this Bible—perhaps "the most widely distributed book in the English Renaissance"[15]—had a major cultural significance, but the received view of its oppositional status in Tudor England is not only misleading, it is also polarized in a way that occludes a more accurate history.[16]

The findings of this chapter and the two following derive from a comprehensive study of the text and annotations of the first two English Bibles created in Geneva: the 1557 New Testament, the only English Bible to be printed during Mary's reign; and the 1560 complete Bible, issued about a year and a half after Elizabeth succeeded to the throne. The so-called Geneva version went through important changes later in Elizabeth's reign, especially in added notes to the New Testament starting in 1576 (Geneva-Tomson) and then in the replacement of the notes to the Book of Revelation in 1603 (Geneva-Tomson-Junius)—Bibles that really begin to have a separate identity. While these and other alterations tell their own important stories of Elizabethan markets and readers (as subsequent chapters indicate), the purpose here is to understand the Marian and early Elizabethan moment of the first Geneva Bibles, at a time of relative scarcity in English Bible markets, and to recover their early impact on readers. The Geneva Bible of 1560 constitutes the base form of a Bible that would be revised and repackaged throughout Elizabethan and early Stuart England, starting almost immediately in 1562 and again in 1570 in Geneva (Edward de Vere's Bible), and then with increasing intensity from 1575 onward in London, in new printings that coexisted with the later revisions. The translation and annotations influenced those of the Bishops' Bible, which first appeared in 1568. In my view, the Geneva annotations deserve far greater attention, not just for their ubiquity in Elizabethan culture, but also for the ways that this scaffolding around the biblical text enabled a mode of exchange between the ancient text and the early modern world.

Particularly striking in these extensive marginal annotations is the hermeneutic tendencies they demonstrate and, of course, inculcate in their readers. The commentary is more social than theological in its orientation, and the hermeneutic habits or methods represented in the notes are not usefully categorized as "literalism," the predominant term defining Reformation hermeneutics. Nor are they bent on the historicist recovery of original meaning, as might be expected—though these methods are certainly present and often enough the ostensible mode of reading. Instead of aiming for literalism and historicism, the Geneva annotators seek to transform biblical passages for use in the early modern present, a present that sometimes becomes very specific to the national and political uncertainty of the exiles. The annotator and polemicist Anthony Gilby's statement cited in the epigraph, "what need any exposition to apply this unto England?" encapsulates the urgent presumptiveness of the annotators: "literal" for them means that the meaning is transparent, needing no exposition, and the purpose is "to apply" passages to the current conditions of the nation.[17]

Literary scholars in recent years have shed a great deal of light on the ways that paratexts conditioned the perception of readers.[18] This scholarship has revealed how much a text's packaging shaped readers' constructions of meaning and their subsequent reuse of reading material.[19] The unmediated scripture that reformers aspired to eschewed "false glosses," as Tyndale wrote in 1536. For him, the church had "nailed a veil of false glosses on Moses's face, to corrupt the true understanding of his law."[20] Reformation writers like Tyndale would have been responding to a glossed Bible like the *Glossa Ordinaria*, the "most widely used edition of the Bible in the later middle ages and well into the sixteenth century," in which the biblical text was surrounded by a scholastic explanatory apparatus.[21] Increasingly, however, after theologians started taking degrees from Protestant universities and establishing a new hierarchy of instruction, and after "heresies" like Anabaptism (discouraged in the Geneva notes) emerged from unsupervised lay readership, Protestants returned to a similarly enclosed biblical text, though with the implicit claim that the text was still unmediated because the notes facilitated the transparency of literal meaning.[22] Yet the marginal notes are in fact up to something much more transformative than the illumination of literal meaning. Rather than being aids to self-evident meaning, they represent modes of interpretation that work in close relation to their immediate social and discursive context.

To recover the hermeneutic implications of these annotations, this chapter will unfold in three parts with three related aims: first, to reassess the entrenched reception history of the Geneva notes, making way for new approaches; second, in turning to the initial Marian context of the Bible, to explore the relationship between the vocabulary of margins and that of the text itself (focusing on the infamous word *tyrant*); and third, to turn from vocabulary to methods of reading and interpreting and to the ways these reading habits develop in relation to the biblically inflected literature of the Genevan exiles. Rather than thinking of the defining mode for Protestant reading as literalism, a term promulgated by the reformers themselves, I propose that we find a more capacious and yet more precise way to define the cultures of reading in the post-

Reformation period, derived from the texts and paratexts of this popular vernacular Bible.

Paratexts in Exile and the Elizabethan Reader

Mary Tudor took the throne after the brief July reign of Jane Grey, the Protestant whose relative lack of support demonstrated the residual strength of Catholic sentiment in the nobility and English people.[23] Committed Protestants faced either exile or punishment, and under Mary I's reign nearly three hundred English Protestants were reputedly executed or burned at the stake, leaving others scared and angry. Approximately a thousand exiles fled the country and settled throughout Germany and Switzerland—a relatively small group, but a very prolific one, including figures like John Bale, John Foxe, and the translator of Calvin and possible sonneteer Anne Vaughan Lock.[24] Geneva was the industrial center for both biblical scholarship and publication, with Latin and several vernacular texts in process in the same few years. The Bibles produced there derived a great deal from the latest scholarship of continental theologians, and particularly Calvin, whose commentaries are woven into the arguments and notes. The English Bible is particularly indebted to a French Bible that was in production at the same time, *La Bible, Qui Est Toute La Saincte Escriture* (Geneva: Nicolas Barbier and Thomas Courteau, 1559), and I endeavor here to compare the English notes with the French to see what is particular to the English readings. Shared wording and even woodcuts between the two reveal physical as well as intellectual collaboration; the residual French in such woodcuts allows us to imagine workers running from one press to the other bearing a borrowed woodcut block. The biblical printing industry—with many Genevan presses producing large volumes in several languages—would have supported hundreds of workers, intellectual and mechanical, of different nationalities. Like the King James Version, the Geneva Bible stems from collaborative work, though who served what role is far less clear; indeed, unlike the trove of archival evidence around the King James Bible, there are no known remaining notes from any Genevan translator.[25] Translators included the Hebraist Anthony Gilby, and possibly Thomas Cole, with the resistance theorists Christopher Goodman and John Knox in close association, and sometimes included in the list.[26] William Whittingham translated and annotated the 1557 New Testament and was undoubtedly involved with other aspects of the 1560 edition.[27] The Bible bears the marks of their experiences as political exiles: the keywords *tyrant* and *persecution* frequently appear in its paratextual scaffolding.[28] The 1560 letter to the reader shares this focus on *persecution*, observing "the time [after Mary came to the throne] was most dangerous and the persecution sharp and furious."[29]

Given the cast of characters associated with this Bible's production, their status as exiles and the tenor of their annotations, there is little surprise that it has been assumed to carry (and deliver) radical views. No doubt it did. The bigger surprise is that the view James famously expressed at Hampton Court is unrepresented in the forty-seven years before the event. Hardly a shred of evidence suggests that anyone before James felt that the Geneva Bible or its notes were "seditious," "traitorous," or "dangerous"—an astonishing fact, given the strength of those words and the corresponding political energy in the margins. The Elizabethan bishops Matthew Parker and Edmund Grindal express themselves as staunch supporters in a letter addressed to Elizabeth's Secretary of State, William Cecil, seeking a twelve-year extension of privileges to print the Geneva Bible. In 1565–1566, the bishops wrote that "we think so well of the first impression, and review of those which have sithence [since] travailed therein, that we wish it would please you to be a mean that twelve years longer term may be by special privilege granted him [Bodley], in consideration of the charges by him and his associates in the first impression, and the review sithence sustained." The bishops go on to relate plans to create a Bible themselves: "For though one other special Bible for the churches be meant by us to be set forth, as convenient time and leisure hereafter will permit: yet shall it nothing hinder, but rather do much good, to have diversity of translations and readings."[30] The enthusiasm of the bishops for a coexistence of translations reflects a reformist doctrine affirming multiple readings, but there are investment risks in introducing a Bible in a competitive market. As Aaron Pratt has pointed out, the Archbishop worries about the publisher becoming a "great Loser" (quoting Parker) if sales "suffered as the result of competition."[31] While this particular concern is not about the Geneva Bible, it reinforces the reality that market interests need to be protected, which may inform Parker's later characterizations of the Geneva translation. In a letter to the queen, presenting the new Bishops' Bible in 1568, Parker wrote that "in certain places [i.e., churches] be publicly used some translations which have not been Labored in your Realm having insperded [interspersed] diverse prejudicial notes which might have been also well spared."[32] Parker also gives instruction that the forthcoming Bible would have "no bitter notes upon any text, or yet to set down any determination in places of controversy."[33] What Parker means here remains uncertain, but he is not calling for empty margins, nor does he seem concerned with seditiousness as James was, as is clear from the similar political notes in the Bishops' Bible.[34] "Prejudicial" and "bitter" suggest doctrinal leanings and unnecessary tone, rather than the political strength of "seditious" or "traitorous."

The sudden singularity of the new king's forceful words therefore remains something of a mystery, but it may rest largely on the very newness of the Stuart reign. The Geneva Bible is a deeply Tudor document, intricately tied to the uneasy birth of English Protestantism during the reign of Henry VIII, and to the tumultuous shifts from Edward to Mary, and from Mary to Elizabeth. These shifts, especially the fallen hope of Edward, the rupture of exile, and the troubled reign of Philip and Mary, are written into the margins of the Bible. It also seems quite likely, as Patrick Collinson has argued concerning the role of the Geneva annotations in the trial of Mary, Queen of Scots, that James was personally offended by the notes' connection to the execution of his mother.[35] At any rate, an Elizabethan would have been far less prone to call the paratext "seditious" because it is strongly tied to the Tudor dynasty and to the destiny of the English nation under the Tudors. As the prefatory letter of the 1560 edition exclaims, "God hath made" Elizabeth "our Zerubbabel," the descendant of David who would build the second Temple after the Babylonian captivity: she would erect "this most excellent Temple" and "plant and maintain his holy word to the advancement of his glory."[36] Parts of the Geneva Bible seem thus to have been revised after Mary's death in 1558 in order to depict Elizabeth I as fulfilling biblical typology.[37]

It is unclear, however, just how much of the text and notes could have been revised after Mary's death on November 17, 1558, given that the prefatory letters are dated April 10, 1560. Indeed, a key question in understanding the immediate context of the Geneva Bible is just how much of the text and notes could have been revised after Elizabeth became queen. Even in the first year of her reign, before the Religious Settlement of April 1559, in which Parliament passed the Acts of Uniformity and Supremacy, there remained considerable uncertainty as to which direction the church would take. The physical production of the book would have taken months; it is not just a hefty volume of more than 1,200 pages, but it also features complex marginal annotations and other paratextual features, many woodcuts (some with the borrowed French still on them, suggesting haste), and five maps printed on separate leaves—all of which would have left little time for changes. Both Gilby and Whittingham remain in Geneva until 1560 (as does Cole), suggesting that they saw the production through to the end.[38] Although most of the 1557 Marian glosses remain in what ultimately becomes an Elizabethan context in 1560, some important changes to the 1557 text suggest last minute rewording, as in the alteration of the contentious word *congregation* in 1557 to *church* in 1560—that is, changing from Tyndale's more controversial wording to a potentially safer word, though also, as I suggest in the next chapter, a word that has lost its institutional resonance after John Bale's reading of Revelation in *Image of Both Churches* (ca. 1545).[39] The 1557 translation of Romans 13:3 takes Tyndale's broader word *ruler* in the significant political passage, "For rulers are not to be feared for good works, but for evil," but the 1560 Geneva text uses the safer, narrower, and more royal "princes" (to be replaced again in 1576 with Calvin's broadly governmental "magistrates," full of radical potential.[40]) But mainstays of Marian Protestant literature such as *persecution*, or the exilic conditions implied in such words as *stranger* or *strange country*, reinforced the margins of the 1557 version and would remain in 1560.

The language of the Genevan text and notes is thus poised at a profound moment of cultural change, one that would radically transform the resonances for English readers of such common words as *true religion, persecution, idolater, heretic, tyrant, captivity, stranger,* and *nation.* What these words meant for the exiles writing in 1556–1558 would take on different senses for Elizabethan Protestant readers, whose actual nation was no longer in the hands of idolaters. The exiles' history becomes mythologized, then, as they depict themselves as persecuted fugitives devoted to protecting the Word, like the Israelites during the Babylonian exile. Parallels between the ancient text and the experiences of its sixteenth-century annotators are written into the interpretive structure of the Bible itself. The state of the Protestant "nation" under Mary I and Philip II of Spain is constantly reinforced in the notes, as when Moses's injunction "Thou shalt not set a stranger over thee" (Deut. 17:15) is glossed "who is not of thy nation, lest he change true religion into idolatry, and bring thee to slavery"— phrasing not at all found in the French, nor in the notes of prior English Bibles such as Becke's.[41] All of these notions—"nation," "true religion," even "idolatry"—are imported into the biblical text from without, each with sharply changing resonances for writers and readers around the years 1557–1560. Similarly, at Mark 10:30, where Jesus speaks of the rewards that will come for those facing "persecution," a 1557 gloss, maintained in 1560 (and which does not derive from the French), continues in a way designed to comfort English Protestant readers at that moment: "We must not measure these promises by our own covetous desires, but refer the accomplishment to God's will, who even in our persecutions and afflictions performeth the same so far as they be expedient. Let us therefore learn to have enough and to want, that being tried, we may enjoy our treasures in heaven."[42] This is the wisdom of *King Lear*, also born of extremity, and possibly from these very margins: "Let . . . each man have enough" (4.1.66–70). The Genevan annotator's frequent use of the first person plural—"us" and "we"—reinforces a sense that the textual apparatus served as an expressive voice for a particular collectivity united by uncertainty and affliction, a collectivity that is then transferred to the reader.[43]

Traces of the exilic experience left in the margins seem to have been influential to the Bible's readers, as is detectable even in their marginalia. A 1577 printing of the Geneva Bible now at the Bodleian Library has a marginal reading of Revelation 18:24 pertaining to the Whore of Babylon: "And in her," the biblical verse reads, "was found the blood of the Prophets, and of the Saints, and of all that were slain upon the earth." Following the annotators' reading of Babylon as Catholic Rome, and taking it further, the Elizabethan reader notes, "Rome and her heads have shed the blood of the saints of God, as in all ages is manifest especially in the Marian times" (Figure 11).[44] Given how subtly and yet persistently the Geneva notes draw connections to the Marian present, a reader might have been compelled to make such a connection without necessarily recognizing that it was implicit in the notes.

For the exiled Protestants composing the Geneva Bible's notes and text, not knowing when or if their nation would return to Protestantism, these readings

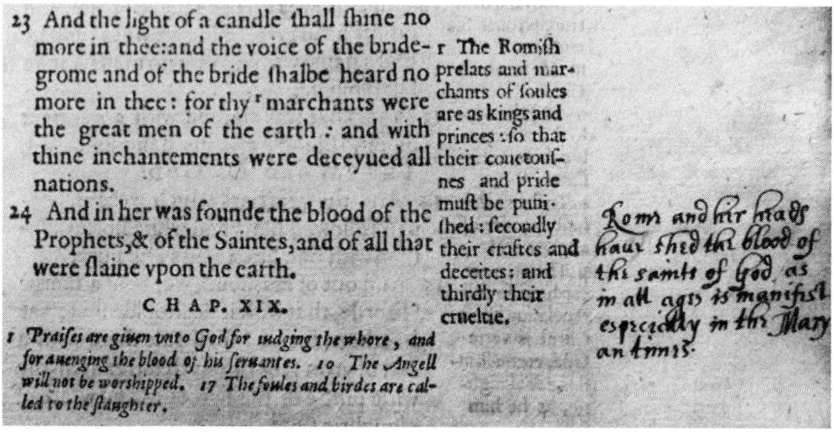
23 And the light of a candle ſhall ſhine no more in thee: and the voice of the bridegrome and of the bride ſhalbe heard no more in thee: for thy r marchants were the great men of the earth: and with thine inchantements were deceyued all nations.
24 And in her was founde the blood of the Prophets, & of the Saintes, and of all that were ſlaine vpon the earth.

CHAP. XIX.

1 Praiſes are giuen vnto God for iudging the whore, and for auenging the blood of his ſeruantes. 10 The Angell will not be worſhipped. 17 The foules and birdes are called to the ſlaughter.

r The Romiſh prelats and marchants of ſoules are as kings and princes: ſo that their couetouſnes and pride muſt be puniſhed: ſecondly their craftes and deceites: and thirdly their crueltie.

Rome and her heads haue shed the blood of the saints of God as in all ages is manifest especially in the Maryan times.

Figure 11. An annotation in a 1577 Geneva Bible at Revelation 18. "Rome and her heads have shed the blood of the saints of God, as in all ages is manifest especially in the Maryan times." A manuscript gloss enlarging on the printed gloss of Revelation 18:24. *The Bible, that is, the Holy Scriptures* (London: Christopher Barker, 1577), pressmark BOD Bib. Eng. 1577 d.1. By permission of the Bodleian Library, University of Oxford.

had a conditional quality, a desire and even expectation that they would, like the exiled Israelites, return to their nation, but the constant repetition of "nation" only worked *if* the body comprising the nation could return to its identified land. The shift away from exile and loss toward nation and delivery is powerfully reflected in the woodcut on the title page, clearly one of the quick paratextual changes made to convert what the 1560 Bible might have been had Mary still reigned to a Bible that would usher in the new monarchy of Elizabeth (Figure 12). Three biblical tags surround this image from Exodus where Moses leads the Israelites to the edge of the Red Sea, with the Egyptians in pursuit. The top reads, "Feare ye not, stand still, and behold the salvation of the Lord, which he will show to you this day" (Exod. 14:13), with the next line from Exodus at the base of the woodcut, "The Lord shall fight for you: therefore hold you your peace" (Exod. 14:14). The vertical tag is from Psalms: "Great are the troubles of the righteous, but the Lord delivereth them out of all" (34:19). The exiled Protestants may now return to the Promised Land, across the sea, and reestablish their nation. The woodcut, actually reused from its place in Exodus, and used again at the title of the New Testament, is one of many paratexts that draw a connection between the struggling Protestant nation and the nation of Israel.

The paratexts of the Geneva Bible thus reflect, with startling detail, the hopes and fears of the community of Marian exiles that produced them. Yet the exiles' creative interpretations of scripture were facilitated not only by conventions of biblical annotation, but also by their novel approach to organizing the text. Whittingham's New Testament of 1557 introduced the innovation, for English Bibles, of numbering verses.[45] For detractors like John Locke, leaving the biblical text "chopped and minced" by breaking it paratextually into a series of numbered verses meant that "the common people take the verses usually for distinct aphorisms."[46] A series of markers point to corresponding philological explanations, cross-references, and detailed annotations. "Where the place is not greatly hard," Whittingham explains, "I have noted with this mark "[that is, a quotation mark], that which may serve to the edification of the Reader: adding also such commonplaces, as may cause him better to take heed to the doctrine."[47] This is an early instance of a practice in which printers sought to anticipate the marginal annotations of readers, aiding them in identifying appropriate passages to copy in commonplace books. Further, the text italicizes English words not found in the Greek, "which lacking would have made the sense obscure," a practice continued in the King James Version.[48] Lowercase letters point to marginal notation explaining difficult verses (especially those that have been

Figure 12. Moses leading the Jews out of Egypt in the Geneva Bible (1560).
The woodcut is used three times in the Bible, both to illustrate the passage in
Exodus and to furnish the title pages of the two testaments with a topical
image of the delivery of an exiled nation. *The Bible and Holy Scriptures*
(Geneva: Rouland Hall, 1560). By permission of the Beinecke Rare Book
and Manuscript Library, Yale University.

"falsely expounded by some, or else absurdly applied by others").[49] Here again
the annotators use the language of "application"—in which their gloss tries to
fix an absurd application of a biblical text from past commentaries. The categories then receive a set of differing marks: the straight quotation marks for easier
passages, commonplaces that seem to form a separate category of marginal comment, curvy quotation marks for places where the Greek originals or copies offer
different words, and asterisks for when the Greek copies differ in entire sentences

Figure 13. The 1570 crimson velvet Geneva Bible of the Earl of Oxford, Edward de Vere, furnished with silver gilt clasps and corners, and an armorial plate bearing the crest of the Earl. *The Bible* (Geneva: John Crispin, 1570). STC 2106. By permission of the Folger Shakespeare Library.

(happily, this system is simplified for the 1560 edition). "Last of all," Whitting-ham writes after nearly two pages of explanation, "remain the arguments."[50] He and the printer squeezed a great deal into a concise frame, which for all of its apparatus manages to leave space for manuscript annotation.

Geneva Bibles frequently show signs of readers' use that engages both the text and the paratext. The 1570 quarto copy belonging to de Vere, refashioned with an armorial binding for an aristocrat (Figure 13), shows a reader in action, and also provides an example of how mixed Elizabethan readership could be. The Earl of Oxford was a minor poet, dissolute courtier, in and out of favor with the Queen, Knight of the Garter, patron of writers and performers, and at times a Catholic sympathizer.[51] His marked Geneva Bible, the third printing of the complete Bible, shows signs of the earl gathering advice and reinforcement from the text and paratext, as if to add notes to his commonplace book.[52] It is bound in crimson velvet with a heraldic engraved crest and silver clasps, as sumptuous as Redcrosse Knight's ornamental gift to Prince Arthur in *The Faerie Queene*, "A booke, wherein his Saveours testament / Was writ with golden letters rich and brave."[53] Crimson or scarlet velvet symbolizes wealth, and the wearing of it was enforced in Tudor England by sumptuary laws that forbade it to anyone under the "the Estate of a Duke, Marquise, Earl or their children."[54] While Bibles were manufactured as books, they were often bound, as Alexandra Walsham has written, "to function as fashion accessories and insignia of social status."[55] In fact outfitted for all classes of readership, the usual description of the Geneva Bible as the "Bible of the people" is anachronistic.[56] In spite of its extraordinary history, this Bible must be understood as broadly representative of Elizabethan views and reading habits.

The Earl of Oxford wrote commonplace topics in the margins of his Geneva Bible, words such as "Mercy," "Usury," "Servant," "Poor," "Works," "Swearing," "Sin," and "Alms," often with accompanying marks such as flowers (a sign of florilegia, to be picked and collected together) and manicules indicating a particularly extractable sentiment.[57] These themes—appropriate to this spendthrift courtier—also motivate frequent underlining. The clusters of interest around atonement through good works potentially indicate a Catholic proclivity. From a young age, under the wardship of William Cecil, the Queen's Principal Secretary and Master of Wards, the unruly earl was groomed close to the center of power, but was also involved in dangerous activities, even reckoned among those friendly to the Ridolfi plot to supplant Queen Elizabeth with Mary, Queen of Scots.[58] De Vere marked many passages in red and black ink in Book of Ecclesiasticus, canonical for Catholics. The earl may also have been attracted to this book for its extractable value, where single sentences aspire to contain

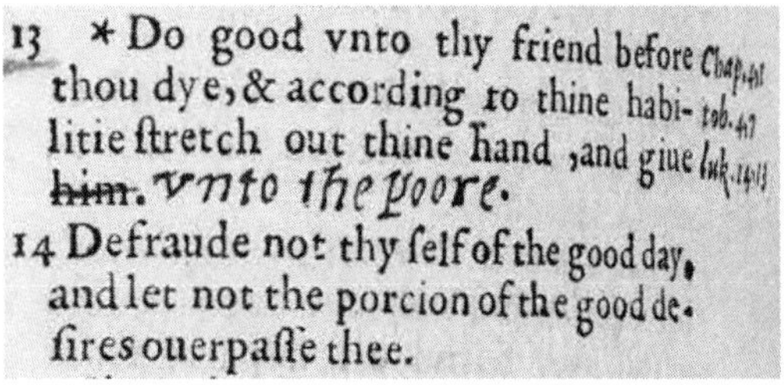
13 *Do good vnto thy friend before
thou dye, & according to thine habi-
litie ſtretch out thine hand, and giue
~~him.~~ vnto the poore.
14 Defraude not thy ſelf of the good day,
and let not the porcion of the good de-
ſires ouerpaſſe thee.

Figure 14. A correction in Edward de Vere's Geneva Bible in the apocryphal book of Ecclesiasticus, one of his most marked biblical books (Ecclesiasticus 14:13). The red line used under verse 13 frequently marks passages having to do with money. *The Bible* (Geneva: John Crispin, 1570). STC 2106. Printed with permission of the Folger Shakespeare Library.

complete formulas for self-improvement, as in verse 40:24, underlined in red: "Friends and help are good in time of trouble, but alms shall deliver more than both." At one point the Geneva wording is corrected, a phenomenon that also occurs in Milton's King James Bible, suggesting a reader's participation in the process of translation. In de Vere's case the correction conforms to what would become the accepted Catholic English translation, though it is also used in the Bishops' Bible: where the Geneva wording at Ecclesiasticus 14:13 is "Do good unto thy friend before thou die, & according to thine ability stretch out thine hand, and give him." De Vere emends this to "and give unto the poor" (Figure 14).[59] De Vere has probably been guided to this correction either by a church service to which he brought his Geneva Bible, or by a private study session in which a chaplain or priest brought attention to passages supporting the donation of alms, and offered the correction. The correction reinforces how vernacular translation remained unfixed, open to participation by the reader.

A method of citing by verse numbers encourages using short, separable units, with the liability that the units will lose their original meaning when taken out of context. Indeed, one short but highly important biblical phrase illustrates how the original meaning of a scriptural excerpt could be transformed by glossators with specific political agendas. The phrase "touch not mine anointed" comes from the full verse "Touch not mine anointed, and do my Prophets no harm" (1 Chron. 16:22; Ps. 105:15). Early moderns often cited this phrase—quite contrary to its original context, as we shall see—to support the divine right of kings.[60] At an ironic moment in *Richard III*, for example, when the tyrant king is approached by his mother among other critics, Shakespeare has Richard invoke Psalm 105:15, saying "let not the heavens hear these tell-tale women / Rail on the Lord's anointed" (4.4.154–155). Psalm 105 was hotly debated in the early stages of the English Civil War, but in Tudor and Stuart literature about kings, the meaning was usually based on its sense out of context.[61]

Tyndale seems to have been one of the first to interpret the phrase as pertaining to kings. In a passage mentioned previously in Chapter 2, Tyndale argues "God (and not the common people) chooseth the prince," in a combined reading of Psalm 105 and Deuteronomy 17:14–15: "When thou shalt come unto the land which the Lord thy God giveth thee, and shalt possess it, and dwell therein, if thou say, I will set a King over me, like as all the nations that are about me, Then thou shalt make him King over thee, whom the Lord thy God shall choose: from among thy brethren shalt thou make a King over thee: thou shalt not set a stranger over thee, which is not thy brother." Tyndale interpreted these lines to mean that humans had no role in the institution of monarchs. "God," he wrote, is "the chief chooser and setter up of [rulers], and so must he be the chief putter down of them again, so that without his special commandment, they may not be put down again." Thus, Tyndale writes, invoking Psalm 105, "when we have anointed a king over us at his commandment, he sayeth, Touch not mine anointed."[62]

Given how deeply Tyndale knew scripture, it is a surprise that he has taken the phrase from Psalm 105:15 quite out of context, especially when, in the unusual case of this psalm, it also appears in a historical narrative in 1 Chronicles 16:1–22, which tells us how David, surrounded by musicians and holy men, recites the psalm ceremonially before the Ark of the Covenant. It is a psalm that looks back on the kindness of God in the distant past. The pithy phrase is not about kings; in fact, in its context it is from a non-monarchical time in the history of the Israelites. The psalm looks back to a past time before Saul, when there were no kings in Israel: "Albeit they were few in number, *yea*, a very few, & strangers in the land, And walked about from nation to nation, and from *one* kingdom to another people, Yet suffered he [God] no man to do them wrong, but reproved Kings for their sakes, *saying*, Touch not mine anointed, and do my Prophets no harm" (Ps. 105:12–15). The passage in fact makes a claim opposite to Tyndale's use: here it is the kings who should not touch (or harm) the anointed people of Israel.

The Geneva note on Psalm 105:15 corrects Tyndale's reading and its usefulness for divine right theology and emphasizes what is clear in the biblical context: the line refers to God's special people. It is not about kings; in fact, in its context it is from a pre-monarchical moment in Jewish history. "Mine elect people & them whom I have sanctified," the note in 1 Chronicles 16:22 tells us, or, as the note in Psalms relates: "Those whom I have sanctified to be my people."

The note in Psalms goes on to elaborate on "Prophets": "Meaning the old fathers, to whom God showeth himself plainly, and who were setters forth of his word." It is impossible to say whether the Geneva annotators make this correction because they are better historicists or Hebraists, or because their historicism in this case at once fits their present situation as exiles while also allowing them to push back against divine right theology. Yet the revision of Tyndalean political theology is pervasive in both the notes and the translation of the Geneva version.

Modern biblical scholarship, after the movement of Higher Criticism, has recognized monarchical and non-monarchical strands in the Bible's ancient editorial history. Though antedating this scholarship, the Geneva Bible's different annotators draw out some of the conflicts about monarchy inherent in the original text. In the prefatory argument to 1 Samuel, the annotators refer precisely to the moment in Deuteronomy that Tyndale and Milton read very differently: the accession of Saul is what "God had ordained Deut. 17:14," write the Genevan annotators, taking a more Miltonic than Tyndalean angle, showing how Saul, the first king of Israel, was chosen by a discontented populace, a people that, "not contented with that order [a non-monarchy], which God had for a time appointed for the government of his Church, demanded a King, to the intent they might be as other nations . . . not because they might the better thereby serve God." To punish them for this poor choice, "Therefore he gave them a tyrant"—a phrase underlined by a reader of the 1570 Geneva copy, who, with de Vere, took great interest in this Argument—"and an hypocrite to rule over them, that they might learn, that the person of a King is not sufficient to defend them, except God by his power preserve and keep them."[63] The glossator's claims that Saul is a "tyrant" and a "hypocrite" are distinctly imported into the margins of the text by the Genevan exiles, since they are not used in the biblical text itself. The conclusion they draw as to the moral of 1 Samuel (a book that depicts Saul's downfall and replacement by David) likewise reveals the glossator's political interests. The notes conclude that this story should teach us that kings are not sufficient to defend them, and that David is so only because he is "the true figure of the Messiah, placed in his stead, whose patience, modesty, constancy, persecution by open enemies, feigned friends, and dissembling flatterers are left to the Church and to every member of the same, as a pattern and example to behold their state and vocation." The glossators add all of this language—"tyrant," "hypocrite," "dissembling flatterers," "persecution," and "Church"—to the biblical account, enabling the Davidic story to become a sixteenth-century power struggle between Protestants and Catholics fostered by corrupt courtiers and bad policy.[64]

Two basic observations should be made at this juncture about the dynamic interaction between the ancient text and the Renaissance paratext. First, not unlike students using present-day annotated editions of Spenser, early modern readers conflated the notes and the text into a singular conglomerate, if not necessarily a textual unity, even though the text and notes are often starkly different, in terms of both language and meaning. Many words in the notes rarely occur in the text, and a true disparity between text and paratext occurs with words like *Gospel* and *grace* in the Old Testament, as well as the frequent terms *idolatry* and *idolators* and a rarer term that these are subtly meant to signify, *papists*. Furthermore, many of the notes insist on the confusion between text and paratext, as if the gloss exists not to add embellishments or modernized terms but to fill in aspects of the narrative that are missing. Such conflation was also facilitated by the fact that the translation itself depends on interpretation, and therefore the marginal interpretation of the text sometimes informs the text itself, as when the Geneva text lets interpretation shape translation in its anachronistic use of *Christ* in the Hebrew Bible. Philologically, Christ (from the Greek *khristos, the anointed one*) should not be in the text of the Hebrew Bible (the word never occurs there in the King James Version), but in one moment the Christian enthusiasm of the notes creeps into the text of Psalm 2:2, which the Geneva Bible translates, "The Kings of the earth band them selves, and the princes are assembled together against the Lord, and against his Christ." A philological note *"Or, anointed"* provides the alternate translation, which the King James Version adopts as text.

The second observation is that the Geneva notes perform an interpretive function that departs sharply from the practice of literalism commonly associated with Protestant reading. This investigation will turn now to explore first the lexical dimension of the relationship between text and notes, focusing on the word *tyrant*, the most infamous keyword in this Bible, and one that demonstrates both the sharp differences but also (for readers) the strange cohesion between paratext and text. From the lexical and philological differences between text and notes, I then move to the conceptual, using as examples a few representative moments in which the annotators project their present context onto the ancient biblical past.

Four Hundred Tyrants from Geneva

Readers often gauge the politics of the Geneva Bible according to the number of times the word *tyrant* appears, since this word was foundational in resistance theories. Adam Nicholson, for example, claims that "the word 'tyrant,' . . . which is not to be found in the King James Bible, occurs over 400 times in the Geneva text."[65] This remarkable word count may be the most compelling argument concerning the different tenor of these Bibles. Sadly, despite the increased ease of quantification that comes with digital data mining, it is not a number that is easy to replicate (at the time of my writing), in part because the notes were largely illegible to the transcriber, and words that become broken and hyphenated to fit in a marginal space often remain unavailable to digital searching. By my hand-count, the number in the 1560 Geneva Bible—tallying both *tyrant(s)* and *tyranny*—is 124.[66] Moreover, like many others, Nicholson has misleadingly described the large number, for where he writes "text," he should write "paratext," as only nine instances occur in the language of the Bible itself (Job 3:17, 6:23, 15:20, 27:13; Ps. 54:3; Isa. 13:11, 49:25; Jer. 15:21; James 2:6).[67] Here the English version also departs from the French; the only instances in which English *tyranny/tyrant* derives from French *tyrannie/tyran* are Job 6:23 and Job 27:13.

But these occurrences in the texts of Job, Psalms, Isaiah, Jeremiah, and James are relatively innocuous; the Geneva notes also do not highlight them in any way, with the exception of Psalm 54:3, in which the note calls attention to Saul as the tyrant in question. At Job 15:20, for example, "The wicked man is continually as one that travaileth of child, and the number of years is hid from the tyrant" (translated "oppressor" in the KJV); or Isaiah 13:11, "I will cause the arrogancy of the proud to cease, and will cast down the pride of tyrants" ("pride of the terrible" in the KJV); or Isaiah 49:25, "But thus saith the Lord, Even the captivity of the mighty shalbe taken away: & the prey of the tyrant shalbe delivered" ("prey of the terrible" in the KJV). None of these Old Testament uses is played up or echoed in the notes. In fact, the uses of the word in the Revised Standard Version returned to the Geneva's rendering of *tyrant* in Isaiah 13:11, and twice in Isaiah 49:24–25, where the Hebrew word "עָרִיץ" (*aritz*, "the mighty") is rendered *tyrant*.[68] The only other instances of *tyrant* or *tyranny* in the Geneva and the King James Version are in the books of Maccabees in the Apocrypha (using the Greek *tyrannos*), where there are two occurrences of "cruel tyrant" in the second book (4:25 and 7:27). The remaining 115 occurrences of the word *tyrant* in the Geneva Bible occur in the notes or other paratextual elements. These occurrences are partly concentrated in particular biblical books, perhaps having to do with which annotator was assigned a particular book: Psalms taking a large portion (about 20 percent), and Isaiah taking about 15 percent; with 1 Samuel taking eight instances, and 2 Samuel merely one.

In what is perhaps the most striking gauge of difference between text and paratext—as well as a further complication in the cultural confusion of the two—

the word *tyrant* in the margin never corresponds to the word *tyrant* in the text. Occasionally, it even serves as an alternate reading, as in the surprising introduction of giants in the early days of humanity, a line that caught the fancy of the *Beowulf* poet.[69] "There were *gyantes in the earth in those days" (Genesis 6:4) is provided an alternate marginal reading, not supported by the Hebrew *nephilim*, which is never elsewhere given such a gloss: "*Or, tyrants." The alternate suggestion would seem almost whimsical—even whimsically *sonic*, in the similarity between "gyant" and "tyrant"—except that the marginal reading of this tonally heroic biblical verse continues to hold a consistent course as it glosses further: "yea," the biblical narrator goes on, "and after that the sons of God came unto the daughters of men, and they had borne them children, these were mighty men, which in old time were men of ᶠrenown." With a marginal note keyed to the alphabetical superscript on "renown," the annotators respond, seemingly eager to represent fully the evil of those heroic days: "Which usurped authority over others & did degenerate from the simplicity, wherein their fathers lived." Here the annotators take a morally neutral passage and transform it into an ethics lesson, in which *tyrant* becomes a reading of the events within the text rather than something that originates from it. The notes are interested in tyrants and other political problems, enabling the reader to consider the material in the text in a much more politicized manner.

Of course, everyone knows that Pharaoh is a tyrant—and Herod, Nimrod, Nebuchadnezzar, Pilate, and Nero. But the translators of the actual text were much more sensitive to the original language when they could be more liberated in the notes. The biblical text itself is fully self-aware in representing despicable royal behavior—kings do "evil in the sight of the Lord," as the refrain in the Book of Kings has it—but they are not referred to as *tyrants* or as exhibiting *tyranny*. The Geneva notes, in contrast, do sometimes use this word to describe bad rulers, including the *mighty* Nimrod, who is glossed as "a cruel oppressor & tyrant" (Genesis 10:8), or to describe the edict of Pharaoh to slay the male Hebrew babes: "When tyrants can not prevail by craft, they brast [burst] forth into open rage" (Exodus 1:22). Other words current in early modern politics, such as *flatterer* or *flattery*, which may derive from Erasmus's biblical glosses, similarly appear in the notes but not the text.[70] Yet the word *tyrant* makes its way into glosses of anecdotes that seem to have little to do with kings or politics. For example, after wrestling with God, the patriarch Jacob returns to his family to reunite with his wronged brother Esau, which he does with great rejoicing. But the humble posture of Jacob's family is described in the margin as being "the image of the Church under the yoke of tyrants" (at Genesis 33:6), a line that evokes John Bale's influential reading of Revelation, *The Image of Both Churches* (1545), which looks back on the Old Testament as a history of the true church. While Jacob and his family are not under threat of tyrants in this instance, the image of the Church under the yoke of tyrants is such a common refrain that it appears in cases where it may not inhere in the text. In every use of the word *tyrant*, the vocabulary of the Renaissance margin is in dynamic tension with the ancient text it surrounds. In each case, too, the guiding principles of interpretation are not really literalist and historicist, but opportunistic and presentist. The running headnotes perform a similarly transformative function, even when they purport to serve merely as a mnemonic aid and index to the main themes. "Tyrants are bridled" runs the marginal headnote to Isaiah 37:20–38, atop a page that contains neither of these terms. The word "bridled" may recall Calvin's similar usage in the *locus classicus* of resistance theory at the end of the *Institutes of Christian Religion*: "The correcting of unbridled government by the revengement of the Lord."[71] Facilitated by proximity, paratext and text can be elided in the popular imagination.

Modern-day readers like Nicholson are not the only ones to have confused the biblical text with its glosses. In what appears to be the first printed misconception of the Genevan *tyrants*, Sir Robert Filmer—a late Stuart royalist concerned with the political history of biblical translation—observed that the word had been amended by the King James translators. This occurs in a work of royalist political theory, *The Anarchy* (1648), in which Filmer rebuts the anti-absolutist Philip Hunton, and digressively fulminates about corrupt biblical translation and radicalized readers:

> It is a bold speech, to condemn all the Kings of Judah for tyrants, or to say all their subjects were slaves. But certainly the man doth not know either what a tyrant is, or what a slave is: indeed the words are frequent enough in every man's mouth, and our old English translation of the Bible useth sometimes the word tyrant; but the authors of our new translation have been so careful, as not once to use the word, but only for the proper name of a man, Acts xix, 9, because they find no Hebrew word in the scripture to signify a tyrant or a slave.[72]

In an odd slip, Filmer omits the fact that *tyrant* derives not from the Hebrew but from the Greek, and that Hebrew is not the only biblical language. His reference to "our old translation" gestures back to the Geneva Bible, but the accusation only partly fits, as there are a negligible number of tyrants in either translation. The real reason *tyrant* rarely appears in the King James Bible is simply its paucity of explanatory notes. Like Nicholson, Filmer has mistakenly conflated text and paratext. The scaffolding has become the building itself.

Filmer's is a later Stuart reflection, one that reinforces the ways in which what had become normal in Elizabethan England might verge on "seditious" or "dangerous" in Stuart England. For the sake of understanding the Marian context of the Geneva Bible, we would need to consider what *tyrant* meant to a translator like Anthony Gilby, who had helped make it a household word in late Tudor England. Born in 1510, and thus well into adulthood by the time of the Henrician Reformation, Gilby was a fierce critic of Henry, who (he believed) initiated the English Reformation on false and personal grounds, and of Mary, who employed some of her father's agents to oust Gilby and his friends when Edward died. Greg Walker has pointed out that "novel and savage legislation" in the latter half of Henry VIII's reign made it a "specific capital offence" for anyone to call the king a tyrant.[73] The Treasons Act, passed in 1534, just after the first Act of Supremacy, made it a capital offense to "wish, will or desire, by words or in writing," injury against the "king's most royal person, the queen's or the heirs apparent," or to deprive the king of his titles or to call him "heretic, schismatic, tyrant, infidel or usurper of the crown."[74] The 115 *tyrants* in the paratextual scaffolding of the Bible provide for the possibility of an extended comparison between the actions of biblical rulers and those of early moderns. Gilby, closely associated with the translation and annotation, was simultaneously at work on a powerful admonition to the people of England and Scotland in which he calls both Henry VIII and Mary tyrants in terms that derive from his biblical work, as they also feed into it: "There was no reformation," wrote Gilby, "but a deformation in the time of that tyrant and lecherous monster. The boar I grant was busy rooting and digging in the earth, and all his pigs, that followed him." After calling Henry a tyrant, retrospectively violating the Treasons Act, Gilby turns back to the Act of Supremacy: "This monstrous boar for all this must needs be called the head of the Church in pain of treason, displacing Christ our only head, who ought alone to have this title."[75]

The political conditions of these exiles inflect the biblical notes and the resistance theories written in the Marian context. Goodman's *How Superior Powers Ought to be Obeyed of Their Subjects* (Geneva, 1558) is designed to undermine women in power, as is Knox's *First Blast of the Trumpet against the Monstrous Regimen of Women* ([Geneva], 1558). On June 6, 1558, soon after the appearance of Goodman's book, Mary I issued a proclamation decreeing that anyone found with it would be put to death.[76] Whittingham introduced Goodman, stressing

that the printing of this extended biblical exegesis is for "not only we here present"—in other words the exilic community in Geneva—but so that "our brethren in England and other places might be persuaded in the truth of that doctrine
concerning obedience to the magistrate."[77] Goodman's book and a cluster of
1558 tracts aimed to discredit the legitimacy of Catholic queens in England and
Scotland. But they were timed poorly, as Mary died prematurely within months
of their appearance, and they served instead to insult the new queen.[78]

Gilby's thunderous *Admonition to England and Scotland to Call Them to
Repentance* was bound with Knox's *Appellation of John Knox from the Cruel and
Most Unjust Sentence Pronounced against Him* (Geneva, 1558) in a small volume
that includes a powerful letter from Knox promising a "second blast," and an incendiary metrical adaptation of Psalm 94 by William Kethe, with calls to arms
such as: "who now will up and rise with me / against this wicked band?"[79] Like
the other tracts by Genevan exiles clustered in this period, this cluster pamphlet
loudly advocated the deposition of Mary. Gilby's *Admonition* performs a sustained reading of the parable of the vineyard in Isaiah 5 in the vein of Jeremiah
or the Lamentations. Gilby looks back to the failed Reformation under Henry
that left ground for weeds like Gardiner to return:

> And one crafty Gardener, whose name was Stephen now, having
> wolf-like conditions, did maintain many a wolf, did sow wicked seed
> in the garden, and cherished many weeks to deface the vineyard. And
> his maid Marie, who after was his mistress, now married to Philip,
> wanting no will to wickedness when she was at the weakest nor
> stomach to do evil, when she gat that mastery did cherish many
> weeds. Those two I say have so broken the hedges of the same vine-
> yard [Isaiah 5:5], (God so punishing the sins of those, that ought to
> have made better provision for the same) that the husbandmen are
> hanged up, the diggers, dressers, and planters are banished, prisoned
> and burned. Such havoc is made, that all wild beasts have power to
> pollute the sanctuary of the Lord. O heavens behold her cruelty, oh
> earth cry for vengeance, oh seas, and desert mountains witnesses of
> her wickedness, break forth against this monster of England. But
> whether do I run by the bitterness of my grief?

Gilby here appropriates the tone of prophetic "admonition," which is another
word used in the notes (but not the text) to describe the genre of prophets—
King Asa, for example, "disdained the admonition of the Prophet, and punished

him, as the wicked do when they be told of their faults" (note at 2 Chron. 16:10). Amidst the close reading of Isaiah, Gilby works the condition of England into the parable and then the parable of Isaiah with other biblical pieces into the condition of England. Mary becomes, for example, a Jezebel—as would Mary, Queen of Scots, in her trial:

> And of the time of Mary what should I write? England is now so miserable, that no pen can paint it. It ceaseth to be in the number of children, because it openly despiteth God the father. It hath cast off the truth known and confessed, and followeth lies and errors, which once it detested. It buildeth the building, which it once destroyed, it raiseth up the idols, which once were there confounded: it murthereth the saints, it maintaineth Baal's prophets by the commandment of Jezebel.

Jezebel, in turn, is understood in the notes of the Geneva Bible to maintain "strange religion and exercised cruelty against the servants of God" (Rev. 2:20).[80] For Knox, as for Gilby, Goodman, and Whittingham, the identification of biblical tyrants with real figures enabled political action commensurate with one of four rules given in Knox's "Letter" of 1558: "Neither can oath nor promise bind any such people to obey and maintain tyrants against God and against his truth known."[81]

In addition to *tyrant*, then, many other words such as "admonition," "flattery," and "nation" in the Geneva paratext represent a religio-political lexicon for Tudor culture, and work to transform the ancient language for early modern use. In the next section, I ask what sort of interpretive methods enabled annotators to transform a biblical text into an early modern context, and how literalism and historicism work in these contexts.

At the Door of the Temple

Protestant hermeneutics are by Tyndale's and Luther's accounts simple: forget the Quadriga of medieval reading and its polysemous methods and layers and focus only on the single literal sense. Yet this hermeneutic credo must be understood as an effort of redirecting and reemphasis, not always as theoretically self-conscious or as rigorous as it itself suggests. Protestant reading was still polysemous, and the margins were replete with many genres of annotation. The

Renaissance interest in historical context, added to the engrained habit of reading typologically, allowed for a rich transferability from past to present. Simultaneously operating genres of annotation might be seen in a gloss on Lamentations 4:20, occurring at a moment of general lament by the vanquished Jews after the Babylonian conquest; the line before this, more famous and more clear, describes the strength of the vanquisher: "Our persecutors are swifter than the eagles of the heaven: they pursued us upon the mountains, they laid wait for us in the wilderness" (4:19). Then 4:20, notable for its obscurity: "The breath of our nostrils, the Anointed of the Lord was taken in their nets, of whom we said, Under his shadow we shall be preserved alive among the heathen." The Geneva note attached to "breath of our nostrils" reads this line as modern annotators do, as a royal epithet, referring implicitly to their King Zedekiah, the last of the kings before the fall of Judah.[82] But the note explicitly attaches the epithet to an actual king, a narrative, and adds a bit of typology: "Our King Josiah, in whom stood our hope of God's favor, and on whom depended our state & life, was slain whom he calleth anointed, because he was a figure of Christ." The repetition of "our" in "our king," "our hope," "our state" emphatically echoes the biblical narrative, adding to it as it ventriloquizes. The note draws from the French notes in the 1559 Barbier & Courteau edition closely, but the English annotators add "our," and "state" and "hope."[83] In addition to the standard dangers of paraphrase, new content is added through annotation, which is then inseparable from the text itself. Paraphrase like this occurs especially in historical explanations, though there is a strong presentist potential in "our king," "our hope," "our state," given that "our" inferentially includes the reader. The French note begins the process of projecting the Reformation into biblical history, and the English translators transform the French still further to apply specifically to themselves.

The notes read this king as Josiah, who has a special resonance for Tudor Protestants. Archbishop Cranmer had pronounced Edward to be a "second Josiah," and this attribution was frequently reinforced in the late 1540s and 1550s, and carried into Elizabethan England.[84] As the *Homily against Disobedience* states, God "taketh away a good prince for the sins of the people: as in our memory he toke away our good Josiah King Edward in his young and good years for our wickedness."[85] A topically resonant attribution of Josiah—which occurs elsewhere in the notes—is also suggested in the fact that the Geneva gloss strains history considerably, since Josiah reigned long before the Babylonian captivity.[86] Zedekiah was too inconsistent to be a useful model for an early modern Protestant, and, at any rate, he was not the king before the *English* exile, already identified as Josiah. Such annotations rewrite the biblical account, like a Shakespearean history collapsing time, to fit the biblical narrative into the English present, furthering the degree to which the glosses function as conduits between ancient and contemporary worlds. This historicist reading, perhaps too suggestive to withstand scrutiny, ultimately gives way to the service of biblical typology: the anointed king is a figure of Christ. The paratext performs what many notes strive to do: it converts a relatively obscure passage to useful applicability. The gloss facilitates multiple senses simultaneously: the king may be Josiah, a figure through which "our state" and "hope" could be projected, and a figure of Christ.

The vernacular annotations of the Geneva Bible and their history of use tell a more accurate story of the habits of readers than do the explanations of Tyndale and other reformers. Early vernacular Bibles of all sorts included some kind of instructions to the reader, often starting with the sentence that seemed more than anything else to support Protestant reading habits: "Search the scripture" (John 5:39). While there were no other English scriptures as extensively annotated as the Geneva Bible at the time, this injunction—as is true in the quarto and octavo editions of the Bishops' Bible in 1569 and after—could be applied as well to the paratextual structure that helped define scripture's meaning: the notes. Indeed, these words from John 5 were printed on the cover of Bishops' Bibles, and they served both as an injunction to readers and as a self-validation for providing readers the means to do so, a vestigial scripture-based defense of the vernacular text, and one of the central arguments for the *sola scriptura* method of building the Reformed church.[87] But "*search* the scripture" also points to an activity more purposefully invested than simply *reading*. Historians of reading stress the degree early modern readers thought of themselves as "users" rather than "readers."[88] Jardine and Grafton's seminal article shows Gabriel Harvey and others reading for "action"—preparing themselves and their patrons for leadership by outfitting them with well-chosen sentences, with the idea that what matters is the proper application of textual material.[89] There is a close connection between these practices of active reading—"searching"—and practices of interpreting. Scriptural commentators constantly turned—and even twisted, following Erasmus's *detorquere*—biblical verses to make them applicable to the present.

To reinforce this point, it is worth turning back to the epigraph to this chapter. In a vital moment in his reading of the parable of the vineyard in Isaiah 5:1–7, Gilby turns to his reader (perhaps originally his congregation), and asks, "What need any exposition to apply this unto England?"[90] Such application represents the steadfast aim of annotation and interpretation: since good readers are literalists, the text needs no exposition (even though one is provided) to be applied to the present: it is—and even must be—applied to England. Indeed, applicability is so vital, so urgently necessary, that where passages seem less applicable or usable, as in the example from Lamentations on "our king," "state," and "hope," they must be transformed for use. Utility is ultimately more important than historical meaning.

A set of Geneva annotations from the book of Isaiah demonstrates the extraordinary degree to which the annotations transform the ancient text for contemporary use. The text of Isaiah was of particular value to Protestants for its opening invectives against the empty performance of ritual—"ceremonies," as the Geneva annotators note, echoing the Protestant keyword *faith*, "void of faith and mercy." "The Prophet first condemned their superstition and idolatry," one note reads, "next their covetousness, and thirdly, their vain trust in worldly means."[91] The projection of Protestant values onto an ancient Jewish text may not be entirely surprising, given that much of the Hebrew Bible is appropriated by Christian readers toward their doctrinal ends. Yet the annotations present Isaiah as a Reformation figure in more than merely shared ideas: his actions and behavior too suggest a European reformer. Early in the book, God instructs the prophet: "Take thee a great roll, and write in it with a man's pen, Make speed to the spoil: haste to the prey" (Isa. 8:1). Translations of this passage have changed considerably since the Geneva and earlier versions: "roll" (French *rolle*)[92] is now usually read as a "tablet," the "man's pen," reads metaphorically as "in common characters," and the words that God told Isaiah to write—following the revision of the KJV—generally retain the Hebrew for effect, since it is a name: "Belonging to Maher-shalal-hash-baz" (meaning "make speed to the spoil; haste to the prey").[93] God told Isaiah to give his newborn son this long and bitter name, and before the child could speak, Israel would be taken away by the Assyrians, the son's name heralding the destruction of the northern kingdom. The Genevan annotators took a particular interest in the "witnesses" Isaiah calls upon. "Because the thing was of great importance," the margin explains, "he took these to witness, which were of credit with the people, when he set this up upon the door of the temple."

But—and here is the most surprising addition—the door of the temple appears nowhere in the text. In spite of the notion of *sola scriptura*, whereby scripture was said to be self-authenticating, scriptural texts were not often left to speak for themselves. This gloss does far more than intepret the text—it adds to it; *sola scriptura* has been entirely set aside, replaced by another mode of reading with very different motives. The annotators here draw on a Commentary on Isaiah by Calvin, which had been dedicated to Edward VI in 1551, and again (in a revised edition) to Elizabeth in 1559.[94] Calvin's reading, however, is speculative rather than assertive: "I think this prophecy was fixed to the doors of the Temple."[95] His reading becomes assertive when annotated in the French Geneva Bible, which draws almost word for word from Calvin's Commentary on Isaiah, without the qualification *dicam tamen sentio*, and this becomes the source for the English translators.[96] In both cases, the narrative about the door of the Temple partly compensates for the paucity of information in scripture about how prophets operated, beyond what they said. The textual apparatus goes further, however, than simply explaining how Isaiah spread the word. It portrays a prophet who operated as Luther did when in 1517 he affixed his message to a church door in the precise moment of Protestantism's origin.[97] It is, in fact, on a "Temple" in Wittenberg, as the first English account of the story has it, that Luther first shook the world: Luther, the account relates, "having his heart earnestly bent with ardent desire to maintain true religion, published certain propositions of Indulgences, which are in the first Tome of his works, and fixed them openly on the Temple that joineth to the Castle of Wittenberg, the morrow after the feast of all Saints, the year, 1517."[98]

The "argument" introducing the book of Isaiah explains the prophetic action of door-posting further, embellishing the specific moment in the text, in a passage that draws closely from the French: the "most principal points contained in this book [of Isaiah]" were combined with a "gathering of his sermons that he preached," and left to "stand upon the Temple door (for the manner of the Prophets was to set up the sum of their doctrine for certain days that the people might the better mark it, as Isa. 8:1, Habak 2:2)." These verse numbers may seem authoritative, but they are nothing but the false buttressing of an imagined claim. Neither of these passages supports the supposed practice of door-posting, which the headnote continues to embellish: "The priests took [the roll] down and reserved it among their registers: and so by Gods providence these books were preserved as a monument to the Church forever."[99] The translators' choice of "roll" (or *rolle* in French) rather than "tablet" also enables a Lutheran reading, since it is easier to affix a roll than a tablet to a door.

According to this marginal account of provenance and transmission, the rolls tacked to the temple door were then collected, edited, and eventually assembled into the Old and New Testaments as they are presented in these early printed texts. Starting with the higher critical scholarship of the late eighteenth century, biblical scholars would come to see that the book of Isaiah was composed at different moments in biblical history, having a plurality of parts in different voices that span before and after the Babylonian exile, when much of the Hebrew Bible is now thought to have been written and edited. Early modern readers, had only just begun the kind of speculation that led to this later historicism, nor of course would they know yet of the reconstruction occasioned by the 1947 discovery of the Dead Sea Scrolls, which had more Isaiah than any other biblical book.[100] Renaissance humanists were, however, drawn to the problems of textual recovery. The explanatory notes of the Geneva Bible frequently speculate on the frailty of the preserved record, especially when writings are recounted in the text. When Solomon is described as having "spake three thousand proverbs: and his songs were a thousand and five," the note explains that these "are thought to have perished in the captivity of Babylon."[101] This comment could be from Gilby, since he wrote of his own writings, that they, "by the rage of persecution, partly perished."[102] Readers are frequently reminded that the biblical text they have is only part of what they might have had.

While textual instability and lacunae may help authorize some embellishment in reconstruction, the liberties taken in Isaiah are motivated by stronger, more contemporary concerns. Building on a habit of appropriation common to all Christianized readings of the Old Testament, Isaiah functioned as a model Protestant, such as Luther, but also one who spoke to the particular condition of the English-speaking audience. The broadly typological reading is facilitated by the text's oracular obscurity, a frequent condition of prophetic literature. After the parable of the vineyard, Isaiah goes on with a series of admonitions, and in one oracle prophesies a dark but altogether uncertain futurity: "Then shall the lambs feed after their manner, and the strangers shall eat the desolate places of the fat" (5:17). The English annotators, quite likely Gilby, decode the oracular text, mixing the words up like pieces of a puzzle and reassembling them so that the words perform new functions in the new syntax: "God comforteth the poor lambs of his Church, which had been strangers in other countries, promising that they should dwell in those places again, whereof they had been deprived by the fat, and cruel tyrants." The gloss, seemingly based on the boorish "cruel" "tyrant" in Gilby's reading of Isaiah 5 in the *Admonition*, puns on the text itself: "fat" moves from a description of unsavory animal tissue in the text to an epithet of gluttonous tyranny in the note. Nor is the gloss about the Israelites at this moment, as they are not yet exiles living among strangers. Instead, in the mode of reading for usefulness, the gloss reconceives the text to concern God's comfort of a displaced (English) church persecuted by tyrants (Queen Mary and Philip). Although it masquerades as a kind of contextualist reading, the historicism is so distorted as to function as a form of presentism. Applicability has again overturned historicism and true literalism. Of course, anachronism is a constant in early modern readings of the Hebrew Bible, since the book was seen as heavily prescriptive of a Christian future; the words *Christ* and *Church* appear some 86 and 129 times respectively in the rich scaffolding of marginal annotations in Isaiah, though never in the text itself.[103] Yet this reconstruction of Isaiah goes further forward in history than just Christ; its transformative typology applies to the exiled community of Protestants annotating the Bible, living among strangers in other countries, deprived of their own by what they saw as the cruel tyranny of Mary. The completed past tense in the phrase "had been strangers" confirms that the prophecy had already been fulfilled and that they had returned to live in England again, as part of a cyclical pattern of exile and deliverance faced by the collective entity of the Church.

The early modern experience is thus written into the history of the Israelites. Isaiah becomes an advisor to those in power and a champion of the people ("the Church") when power has turned tyrannous. The Genevan reading of Isaiah as a reformer speaking to a persecuted English audience performs a transformative function that pervades both the marginal scaffolding and Reformation culture. Reformers such as Bullinger sought to frame their endeavors as advisors to princes "after the pattern of the Old Testament prophets admonishing the kings of ancient Israel."[104] Knox wrote that Isaiah "the Prophet called the Magistrates of *Jerusalem* in his time, companions to thieves, Princes of *Sodom*, bribe-takers, and murtherers," and so too would Knox call the magistrates of his time from Geneva, with other exiles involved in producing the Bible.[105] When Gilby wanted to rail against the injustice of Mary Tudor and Mary Queen of Scots, both the first queens of these nations and both Catholic, he invoked Isaiah: "reckon this also as the extremity of all plagues for the wickedness of the people to have women raised up to rule over you?" (Isa. 3:12).[106] In an important emendation presumably made soon after Elizabeth's accession, the Geneva notes took corrective pains to read this passage as not about queens per se, but about effeminacy in rule. Two verses later, in a series of hard-hitting invectives, Isaiah states that "The Lord shall enter into judgment with the Ancients of his people and the princes thereof: for ye have eaten up the vineyard: the spoil of the poor *is* in your houses" (3:14). The annotators gloss the term "Ancients" in a way that maps the English experience onto the text, and then projects the text as a warning to nations and magistrates: "Meaning, that the rulers and governors had destroyed his Church, & not preserved it, according to their duty." As well as being an admonition to its readers, the people of England

and Scotland, the Geneva Bible with its notes functions as a Renaissance advice book to princes, whose duty is prescribed by Protestant prophets and scribes.

* * *

In his majestic history of the English Church published in 1655, Thomas Fuller anticipates Hobbes in tracing the origins of the seventeenth-century political crisis to the Marian exilic experience. Fuller comments that the relatively small differences among the "banished exiles," some of them caused by their need to conform to foreign forms of church government, were "the pen-knives of that age," that "are grown into the swords in ours, and their writings laid the foundations of the fightings now adays."[107] Literally used at the time to trim quills for writing (Latin *penna*, feather), the penknife is an apt metaphor: an ubiquitous household instrument with an almost unrecognized potential for violence by its Elizabethan users. Fuller's penknives refer more to the biblically informed resistance theories and writings on church government than to the correspondent biblical annotations of the household Geneva Bible, though the Bible was more widespread and more read than virtually any other text. Yet for Elizabethan users, more important than the penknives that may have lurked in the margins is the question of how this Bible and its notes taught readers to use the biblical text. As I have sought to suggest, this was not so much the hermeneutic of literalism often associated with the Reformation, although this and the historical sense governed the rhetoric of the annotators. Heavily geared toward questions of national identity and destiny, the notes enforce an urgent presentist deployment of the biblical text. The intensive application of the biblical text was enabled largely through a paratextual structure that facilitated the translation of the ancient text into an early modern vocabulary and transformed—even to a degree of distortion—the text's meaning for the needs of the present. Drawing from Gilby's insistence that the text needs no explication to be applied to England, we may consider this reading habit as "applied literalism," an approach bent on making the text constantly applicable and historically present. In chapter 5, I consider the extraordinarily rich applied readings of the Book of Revelation, and in particular how Spenser engages these in the first book of *The Faerie Queene*.

Battling Bibles and Spenser's Dragon

—a fiction of our Queen Eliz: the maintainer of the gospel of Christ, to be by god himself betrouthed unto Christ, though by K[ing]:P[hilip]: and R[oman]C[atholics]: for: 6: years it was debarred.

—Marginal Annotation of *The Faerie Queene* (1590)
by John Dixon, ca. 1597

This chapter attempts to reconstruct how readers trained by Elizabethan Bibles confronted the first book of the *Faerie Queene* and other Spenserian texts.[1] One of the many differences between the Geneva Bible's paratextual world and the biblical text it surrounds is the marginal story of the "Church," the collective entity which winds its way from the beginning of time, through the settling of Israel, the exile in Babylon, the post-exilic experience, and even to the end of time. The invisible entity has a strange omnipresence in the Geneva Old Testament. Virtually every part of the Old Testament operates allegorically as the story of Christ's church, in which characters remain unaware of the role they play. "Church" is by far the most frequent anachronistic word in the margins, with "Christ" in second place. This Christian lexicon appears thousands of times in the marginal commentary of the Old Testament but almost never in the text itself—except for one small slip of an overeager translator, where the King James Version, more philologically fastidious, prefers Tyndale's once contentious "congregation."[2] The slip occurs in the beginning of Lamentations, the book that relates the tribulations of exiled Jews in Babylon. Personified as a woman, Jerusalem is described as defiled by the enemy: "The enemy hath stretched out his hand upon all her pleasant things: for she hath seen the heathen enter unto her Sanctuary, whom thou didst command, that they should not enter into thy

Church" (Lam. 1:10). Luther's *Babylonian Captivity of the Church* (1520) drew an influential parallel between the captivity of the exiled Jews and the condition of the church under papal rule, making this passage meaningful not only as a history of a church unknown to its participants, but also as an analogy for the conditions of the present, in which the "true church" had been held captive by Rome. In this moment in the Geneva version of Lamentations, commentary has crept into translation, and the ancient Jews hear a word they are not supposed to know. The reader, however, is constantly reminded by the marginal paratext of the biblical characters' ignorance of their own identity.

From Adam and Eve to the Apocalypse, the margins of the Geneva Bible taught readers to understand biblical history as a narrative tracing the destiny of the "Church," a collective that had institutional, conceptual, and national implications. This church, of course, constitutes the central allegorical association for Spenser's Una, daughter of the "most mighty king of *Eden* fayre" (I.xii.26), herself (like the church in the Bible) on an arduous journey with an incomplete sense of self-identity. In addition to "Church" and "Christ"—and "Antichrist," which appears almost entirely in the margins of Revelation—the paratext also traces the metaphoric and literal instantiations of "God's word," a marginal concept manifested in the veiled tabernacle of the Ark, or the rediscovered Book of Law in Josiah's reign, or the word (*verbum, sermo*) that was there at the beginning (John 1:1). The term signifies the biblical word itself, the Book protected by the Israelites and by the proponents of *sola scriptura*. This extensive apparatus inculcated readers in a Protestant allegorical reading that reinforced the history of the true church and the protectors of the word as extending far back before the invention of the Catholic Church. Woven intricately into the Bible's margins, this polemical narrative profoundly shaped Elizabethan visual and literary cultures.

This chapter's investigation of nationalist politics in readings of Revelation—or "the Apocalypse," as it was interchangeably called—is founded on two related propositions: first, that from his earliest works, Spenser sought to recreate the experience of reading the dominant English Bible; and second, that this experience of reading in turn informed the structures of analogy in the first book of *The Faerie Queene*.[3] The earliest known marked copy of *The Faerie Queene*, by a reader named John Dixon, to which I turn at the end of the chapter, provides a stunning example of a reader trained by the Geneva notes.[4] Dixon supplies both biblical references and topical readings, and in some remarkable instances, the very glosses from the margins of the Apocalypse, as if Spenser's own text need only be glossed as if it were the Geneva Bible. For this early reader, the field of allusion applies as much to the notes as it does to the text itself, affirming the power of the biblical paratext in asserting scriptural meaning.

Apart from the specific references to the Book of Revelation, so comprehensive in the first book as to make it almost an extended biblical gloss, Spenser's allegory in *The Faerie Queene* is deeply structured by the presentation of church destiny in the notes of Protestant Bibles, which convey church history in its Old Testament past, its New Testament present, and its prophesied future in the final book of the Bible. Spenser drew intensely from the end of the Bible: there are more than 140 allusions to the Book of Revelation in *The Faerie Queene* (far more than to any other biblical book), and Spenser's allusions adhere as much to the annotations as they do to the text of the Bible.[5] The reading of the Book of Revelation in the marginal annotations itself relied upon, and deeply colored, the glosses leading up to that point: the Old Testament Babylon read through the lens of Luther, for instance, shapes and reinforces a reading of "Babylon" as Rome at the end of the New Testament.[6] The Reformation reading of Revelation, which emerged as a highly invigorated afterthought well after 1517, focused in particular on two female visions, the Woman clothed in the Sun in Revelation 12 and the Whore of Babylon in Revelation 17, both types for the Spenserian characters Una and Duessa. For Protestant biblical annotators, the Woman clothed in the sun, bearing a child, was not, as Catholics had traditionally held, the Virgin Mary, but the true church itself, pregnant for a very long time: "The Church ever with a most fervent desire longed that Christ should be born," the Geneva note explains. The short text at Revelation 12:1–17 describing the allegory of the birth of Christ from the true church (rather than Mary), his protection by God while the "church" was persecuted by "the great dragon, that old serpent [in Genesis], called the devil and Satan" (12:9), was perhaps the single most consequential passage in Protestant England. Increasingly central to the self-definition of English Protestants, readings of Revelation paradoxically depended more heavily on annotation than any other biblical book. As the perceived threat of Roman Catholicism heightened, readings of Revelation in sermons, pamphlets, and literary texts, including Spenser's poetry, asserted themselves with increasing intensity in spite of—or perhaps because of—the destabilizing fact that these readings were not explicit or even implicit in the original text. Interpretations of Revelation were often about as far from the solid ground of literalism or *sola scriptura* as hermeneutics could get.[7]

The annotations to the Book of Revelation perform a thoroughly presentist function, as they tell the future of Christian history through the Catholic middle ages to the sixteenth-century present, reflecting back on the divided plight of the church. This view defended Protestantism against the charge that it was a new phenomenon, revealing the "true church" to be older than the papacy, already written into the Bible itself—or at least its margins—all the way back to Adam and Eve. The description of Una at the outset of *The Faerie Queene* as deriving from "Royall lynage" who held "all the world in their subjection" (I.i.5) to the later disclosure of her as the child of the "king of *Eden* fayre" (I.xii.26) would have required little annotation for contemporary readers, especially when Una is understood in contrast to Duessa, the "sole daughter of an Emperour, / He that the wide West under his rule has, / And high hath set his throne, where Tiberis doth pas" (I.ii.22)—that is, the Church of Rome. In fact, the title "king of *Eden* fayre" is from Duessa's letter, a moment interpreted by Dixon as depicting Mary Queen of Scots, concerning "the religion by her maintained to be the truth." Other contemporaries, such as Ben Jonson, also spoke of the Queen of Scots as Duessa.[8] Spenser's readers would have had little trouble, in contrast to modern readers, with the idea that the true (Protestant) church already existed, though hidden, deep in the early middle ages, and that the last book of the Bible actually addresses current and near current events. The Protestant reading of Revelation provided the perfect ground for a quest narrative, and one that is structurally self-aware that the very key to that reading lay in the future, even in Wycliffe's England, itself to be discovered.

At the same time that England could be seen as a point of origin for the true church, it conceived itself as the eschatological vision of New Jerusalem in Revelation 21. As Beatrice Groves writes, "early modern biblical interpretation, which foregrounded the typological importance of the present time, had begun to identify London with the new Jerusalem."[9] The liberation of this city from the violence of Catholicism, allegorized as Revelation's dragon, is the goal of Redcrosse Knight's quest. New Jerusalem forms a fitting contrast to the actual city of Jerusalem at the center of the earlier Catholic epic romance, Tasso's *Gerusalemme Liberata* (1581), since Spenser is involved in the polemic reappropriation of Revelation as a Protestant prophetic text.[10] In serving Una, Redcrosse is led to and enters the city to provide Una with the physical security to establish herself in this location (England, or near, at least, the other locations of Faery Land, such as *Cleopolis*, which he then names in contrast):

> From thence, far off he [Contemplation] vnto him did shew
> A litle path, that was both steepe and long,
> Which to a goodly Citty led his vew;
> Whose wals and towres were builded high and strong

Of perle and precious stone, that earthly tong
Cannot describe, nor wit of man can tell;
Too high a ditty for my simple song;
The Citie of the great king hight it well,
Wherein eternall peace and happinesse doth dwell. (I.x.55).

This vision of New Jerusalem in Revelation 21:10–21 is also described in Sonnet 15 of *The Theatre for Worldlings* (1568), a book containing visions from Revelation translated by Spenser. Here in the *Faerie Queene*, Spenser draws descriptive language directly from the Geneva version of Revelation. Redcrosse is shown by Contemplation this vision of New Jerusalem toward the end of the first book, just as John of Patmos is shown in the penultimate chapter of the Bible the same "great city" with a "great wall and high . . . garnished with all manner of precious stones" (Revelation 21:10–11). After this, Redcrosse, to become "Saint George of mery England" (I.x.61—his name finally revealed), will fight the Dragon from Revelation who threatened the Woman clothed in the sun. In addition to representing this figure, and hence the ancient true church, Una is also associated with another keyword in the marginal scaffolding, the "Word." As James Nohrnberg has pointed out, "Una's frequent quotation of Scripture and the veil that in part identifies her with the ark of the testimony make her, among other things, the Word of God that Redcrosse properly champions."[11] While Una transcends time, the historical landscape of Spenser's sixth-century Arthurian Britain is already Protestant and Catholic, although the characters, like those in the biblical text from Adam forward, are to varying degrees unaware of the true and false church.[12]

Militant Reformation readings of Revelation and Counter-Reformation reinterpretations constitute one of the most unfortunate chapters in the history of Renaissance hermeneutics, and it is little wonder that some of the best work in the field has ignored them altogether.[13] Yet this aspect of early modern interpretive culture is ignored at some peril, not only of potentially whitewashing the past, but also of undervaluing a central example of the intricate web of dependence between hermeneutic variation and social pressures, as well as the role of literature in negotiating between these realms. The enthusiasm for the apocalyptic prophetic mode enabled much of Spenser's poetics, which participate with biblical commentaries in asserting a presentist allegorical reading of Revelation. Yet Spenser is not precisely writing polemic, nor is his allegory, with its multifarious and polysemous modes of signification, prone to the same doctrinal fixities as the standard annotations of Revelation. At the same time, as I discuss below, the

Book of Revelation was peculiarly prone to a wide range of interpretive lassitude that likely contributed to a similarly wide range of possibility in Spenserian representation.

In an effort to reconstruct the interpretive cultures surrounding the Apocalypse in Spenser's England, this chapter briefly traces the history of reading Revelation from Erasmus forward. Surprisingly different views of the canonicity of the Book of Revelation contribute to the hermeneutic instability around this biblical text. The chapter then turns to the wide range of interpretations available in English Bibles, which went through considerable changes in late Elizabethan England. The debates that developed after the appearance of the English Catholic Bible in 1582 shed valuable light on what was at stake culturally in the years leading to the first edition of *The Faerie Queene* in 1590.[14] Since the illegitimacy of the Catholic Church—for Protestants—hinged largely on ways of reading the Apocalypse, the English Protestant position hardened in defense of its idiosyncratic reading.

Divergent Apocalypses and Propagandistic Hermeneutics

Revelation arguably became the most important and most influential biblical book in the West, but not without a rocky start. Of all the books of the Bible, this one has the most uneven Renaissance reception history, moving quickly from being a discredited text to one that formed the cornerstone of Protestant self-definition. Erasmus challenged the canonicity of the book in the 1516 *Annotations* by asserting that it could not have been written by John the Evangelist for stylistic reasons related partly to the author's anomalous use of allegory. He allowed that the dubious book might have some value for "illustrations and ornament," but it should never be used to "support a serious proposition" lest it lead to theological harm.[15] These objections were fortified in the expanded edition of the *Annotations* in 1522, and Erasmus was then criticized by the Catholic Church for casting doubt on its authority to determine the canon. He was censored in 1526, and Catholic authorities reasserted the authorship of John the Evangelist in the Council of Trent. At first, Protestant reformers followed Erasmus: Luther denounced Revelation in 1522, seeing it as incapable of teaching or conveying Christ; Zwingli also dismissed Revelation as unbiblical; Oecolampadius and Calvin expressed reservations; and Martin Bucer and Peter Martyr were "noticeably silent."[16] Tyndale reflects this uncertainty in the *Obedience of a Christian Man*: "The Apocalypse or revelations of John are allegories whose literal sense is hard to find in many places"—and since for Tyndale allegories should not stand without some other clear literal expression of meaning, he did not find it a text worth building a serious position on.[17]

Had the reformers stayed with Erasmus and continued to play down the book's authenticity, or stuck more firmly to their concerns about its lack of literal clarity, Protestant theology, literary culture, and perhaps history itself would have taken a different shape.[18] The polemical power of the Protestant allegorical reading may have started, in fact, with Lucas Cranach's whimsical illustration of Revelation 17, in Luther's *Septembertestament* in 1522, of a triple papal tiara cocked on the head of the Whore of Babylon. The Duke of Saxony took such offense at the image that the tiara was cut out of the subsequent printing in December, trimming it down to a cloudy crown. Yet Cranach might have opened the door to propagandistic hermeneutics. The image of the Whore of Babylon with a papal tiara would be repeated hundreds of times in subsequent Bibles and other publications. An interpretive history followed in the 1530s and 1540s, when a reading of the Apocalypse emerged that supported a militant Protestant position against the Catholic Church. Luther's reconsideration of his former opinion came about by way of a reference to a rediscovered passage from Wycliffe—buried in the annals of pre-Reformation England!—who once made an exploitable analogy between the monster of Babylon and the papacy.[19] Wycliffe's role as the original Protestant arises repeatedly, as in *The Theatre for Worldlings* which prophesies that "Kings and other temporal Magistrates . . . shall chase, pursue, and hunt the Babylonish whore of *Rome,* with the clear trumpet of Gods holy word. . . . Call to remembrance what God hath wrought by his servants, *John Wycliffe, John Hus, Martin Luther, Oecolampadie* [Oecolampadius], *Zwingli, Melanchthon, Capito, Bucer, Calvin, Theodore de Beza, Viret, Peter Martyr, Bullinger, Alasco* [Jan Łaski, another Edwardian emigrant], *Brentius, Regius,* and other more."[20] The visions in Revelation are not merely prophecies, but incentivizing directives to magistrates to take action. The distinguished list of champions of the Reformation is all the more astonishing when so many of them had initially dismissed the Book of Revelation.

What is particularly unusual about Reformation readings of Revelation, beyond the quick about-face in its fundamental reception, is an ongoing lack of interpretive consensus. The Apocalypse's initial lack of fixity in the Renaissance biblical canon gave its later reception a peculiar level of interpretive free rein. The reappropriation of allegory may have encouraged this confusing level of interpretive license. Readings of Revelation's allegories depended on the application-focused, presentist mode of reading that had been cultivated for other parts of the Bible. Readers allowed themselves a surprising degree of freedom; John Foxe, in a reading of the time of the "beast" given "power" for "two and forty months" in Revelation 13:5, offers an innovative reading that dates events to the very moment of Wycliffe: "And thus much of the persecution in the primitive church, which agreeth with the time of the Apocalypse, taking every month for a Sabbath of years: *42* Months, that make up just the time from Christ's death, to the last year of persecution by *Maxentius,* which were *294* & six years under *Licinius* in Asia: in all *300* years, reckoning from the death of *John Baptist,* to the end of *Maxentius* and *Licinius:* all which time Satan from the time of *Licinius* till *John Wickliffe* was bound up."[21] Wycliffe is a proto-Protestant in this retrospective reading, and also the one holding the very key to unlock the meaning of Revelation. It is an acrobatic bit of numerology, and one that shows how much effort was spent mapping national destiny onto an obscure system of prophecies. And unlike readings of Old Testament prophecies—as when the Geneva annotators map "our hope," "our King Josiah" onto the obscure oracle in Lamentations 4:20 discussed in the previous chapter—the Book of Revelation allowed for more than a merely analogic correlation. Its readers claimed a prophetic correspondence in which the biblical text addressed actual figures in recent English history: Wycliffe, Mary Tudor, and Mary Queen of Scots. There was no firmly established orthodoxy about the interpretation of allegories in Revelation, fostering a wide range of interpretive claims and endeavors. Even among major theologians, Irena Backus concluded, there is no "single Protestant approach to the Apocalypse," but "varying social, linguistic, and political conditions determined the way that different writers read the text."[22] The indeterminate interpretive culture enabled Spenser to recast the visions of Revelation into polyvalent topical allegories.

Like the Continental readings, English interpretation of this text was determined by varying social and political conditions, emerging with special intensity at hot button moments like the excommunication of Elizabeth, the Spanish Armada, or the Gun Powder Plot. Within the profound range of printed Protestant readings of the text, there is some consensus in interpretations that correlate the pope and Antichrist from Bale and Foxe and the Geneva Bible into the Stuart era. The complexity of the initial debates defining Protestantism—the philological precision behind arguments over free will and predestination, the biblical support for the sacraments, or the debates concerning the doctrine of works versus *sola fide*—all seem by comparison at once more substantiated and yet quaintly insignificant next to the commanding urgency of the Protestant visions of Apocalypse. As George Downame, Bishop of Derry, wrote in 1603, this one text allows for the resolution of all other disputes: the Apocalypse was "the chief of all controversies betwixt us and the Papists, and of the greatest consequence." Downame then goes on, perhaps unwittingly, to make an astonishing admission, that the biblical reading with the "greatest consequence" is in fact provisional, imaginable in other terms: "For if all this were once thoroughly cleared, all others would easily be decided." Yet the reading hardly needs to be "thoroughly cleared" for Downame to use it to powerful effect. Ignoring this "if" enabled Protestants to argue that Catholic doctrine was not merely in theological error, but evil itself; John of Patmos had foretold a monstrous Roman Antichrist, a satanic force that held the true church captive for centuries. Since the pope was the Antichrist, "it followeth necessarily, that Christian princes are not to tolerate either the religion of papists or their persons within their dominions."[23] A later clergyman instructed magistrates that Revelation 18:6 ("reward her even as she hath rewarded you") and 17:16 ("burn her with fire") authorized militant action against Catholics: "so far from being persecution, that it is a very glorious service unto the Majesty of the God of heaven."[24]

The first English version of what would become a dominant reading of Revelation was John Bale's *Image of Both Churches after the most wonderful and heavenly Revelation of Saint John the Evangelist* (1545?), perhaps first printed in Antwerp. After a couple of printings in Edwardian London, Bale's work appeared again in 1570, probably in response to the papal bull excommunicating Elizabeth in that year. The words "most wonderful" in Bale's frequently reprinted title appear in a letter of Gabriel Harvey to Spenser, describing Revelation as the "most wonderful Prophetical, or Poetical Vision."[25] Bale's polemic put two of Revelation's most evocative allegories in opposition: the allegory of the Woman clothed with the sun in Revelation 12:1–6 (Figure 15) and the Whore of Babylon in Revelation 17 (Figure 16). The two female images stood for the true and false church. The woodcut in Bale has a surprising image of God the father and the son (Rev. 12:5), later omitted from Bibles for fear of idolatry, in which God receives the son in heaven while the true church defends herself against the seven-headed dragon, attacked by Michael and his angels (Rev. 12:9). The Woman clothed with the sun bears here a "crown of twelve stars" [Rev. 12:1] that mirrors the tiara on the Whore of Babylon. The two visions supply the foundations for the characterizations of Una and Duessa as well as Lucifera in the Legend of Holiness.

Bale's *Image of Both Churches* provides a paraphrase of the Apocalypse that embellishes the biblical text, which is often followed by the annotators of the first Geneva Bible of 1560. There were, of course, more than two "churches" before and during the Reformation, such as in the Byzantine Empire and beyond.

Figure 15. Woman clothed with the sun in Bale's *Image of Both Churches*. An illustration of Revelation 12 that becomes frequent in biblical texts, in which the son is taken up by the father while the woman is pursued by the dragon. John Bale, *The Image of Both Churches* (London: Thomas East, ca. 1580), STC 1301, fol. 29ᵛ. By permission of the Folger Shakespeare Library.

But Bale's Eurocentric polarization excluded such complexities, placing the Catholic and the Protestant on an axis of evil and good, in which the papacy was represented by the Whore of Babylon, and the true church—which had existed before the earthly incarnation of Christ—was in a sense always allegorical, beyond the absolute reach of those who sought to approximate it.

Apocalyptic Hermeneutics in English Bibles

The Book of Revelation in Geneva Bibles and others has a different marginal vocabulary from the other books—addressing topics such as "Pope," "Papacy," and "Rome" that seldom if ever appear in the rest of the Bible. In revised printings of the Geneva Bible, major changes occur in the Book of Revelation; the 1602 version advertises its inclusion of "the Annotations of Fr[ancis] Junius upon the Revelation of S. John," creating the most extensively annotated biblical margins of the Tudor period, with the paratextual words far outnumbering those in the text. These draw from Junius's *Apocalypsis* (1592), the English translation of a Latin commentary on Revelation published in 1589.[26] Junius's version of Revelation became arguably the most influential in English.[27]

The prophetical readings of Revelation inflected the marginal apparatus of the entire Bible. Bale's conception of both "churches," ingested into the appara-

Figure 16. The Whore of Babylon, "which is the second kingdom of Rome." Revelation 17 in a late Edwardian New Testament revised and printed by Richard Jugge, which would become the most popular Elizabethan New Testament. *Newe Testament* (London: Jugge, 1552?), Beinecke MLm605 525p. By permission of the Beinecke Rare Book and Manuscript Library, Yale University.

tus of the Geneva Bible of 1560, shaped not just the Book of Revelation, but the use and sense of the word "church" in the margins of the Old Testament. Bale's book also seems to have revitalized the term as an acceptable translation of *ecclesia*, restoring it from Tyndale's "congregation." Like Spenserian characters, the true church in the Old Testament is unaware of its identity, even as the followers of God are unaware of a present though yet-unborn "Christ." When King David says at his death, for example, "For the pangs of death have compassed me; the floods of ungodliness have made me afraid" (2 Sam. 22:5), the margins explain David's *pangs*: "As David (who was the figure of Christ) was by God's power

delivered from all dangers: so Christ and his Church shall overcome most griev-
ous dangers, tyranny and death." David is a "figure" who supplies the language
of analogy: *so* Christ and his church *shall* overcome. Yet the church is not just a
future event, foretold by typological figures like David, but also an ever-present
condition, as when Elisha tells a king confidently not to rend his clothes, and
that "there is a Prophet in Israel" (2 Kings 5:8), the note assures that God "would
not leave his Church destitute of a Prophet, whose prayers he would hear, and to
whom other[s] should have recourse for comfort." Unbeknown to themselves,
the chosen in Israel are the church.

The Geneva notes relate a history of the church with characters who exist in
an unrealized state of self-consciousness about their own identities. Given that
the struggle of the church continues for the entirety of the Old Testament, it
exists unknown for an immensely long period. The church emerges physically
in the text shortly after the birth of Christ; but in the gospels it is still almost
entirely marginal with the exception of Jesus's statement to Peter, contentiously
translated by Tyndale as "thou art Peter. And upon this rocke I will build my
congregation" (Matt. 16:18). This reading persisted in the 1557 Geneva New Testament, but it is amended to "Church" in the 1560 Bible—either as a concession,
or more likely because the use of "Church" in the annotated Old Testament
became so extensive that its sense changed. After the Gospels, the church as
an institutional entity becomes increasingly central in the text. Paul's instructions were a constant source of interest, as in a passage widely understood to be
crucial to Reformation ideas around biblical annotation and, indeed, to Spenser:
"He that prophesieth edifieth the Church. I would that ye all spake strange languages, but rather that ye prophesied: for greater is he that prophesieth, then he
that speaketh divers tongues, except he expound it, that the Church may receive
edification" (1 Cor. 14:2–5). By the end of the Bible, in the prophetic allegories of
the Revelation of John of Patmos, the "Church" emerges as a futurity, attacked
by dragons, Satan, and a devious whore from Babylon. The backward-looking
Protestant interpretation of this book draws the whole history of the Bible together, explaining the role of Satan, who has a surprisingly tiny role in scripture
up to that point, but even more so explaining the plight of the true church
against an imposter "Church," signified by the Whore of Babylon—which, as in
Luther's *Babylonian Captivity of the Church*, is understood to be Rome—this
time not as an analogy, but as a prophetic meaning.

Mirroring the layered and vastly shifting reception history of Revelation
over the initial decades, habits of interpreting Revelation are particular to this
biblical book, wherein the dubious allowance of Erasmus's "ornament," Tyn-

dale's uncertainty, and the later polemical fierceness of Protestant prophecy all seem mutually present. Following Erasmus's concern about the book as a weak foundation for theology, no crucial theological issues hinge on readings of Revelation, even while the text became the major site for the repudiation of the papacy. English annotations are speculative and assertive at the same time, insisting on associations that cannot be concrete. The different readings are also reflected in differences between Geneva Bibles, where the later edition offers more comprehensive annotations translated from those of Junius, with differences showing the variety of possible Protestant readings. In the 1560 text, for example, the vision of the fifth Angel, influential to Milton's Sin in *Paradise Lost*, "blew the trumpet," and John "saw a star fall from heaven unto the earth, and to him was given the key of the bottomless pit" (Rev. 9:1). "A star" is glossed as having a plurality of possibilities, though each rather forcefully asserted: "That is, the Bishops and ministers, which forsake the word of God, & so fall out of heaven, & become Angels of darkness." But then the "key," belonging to the gatekeeper of the bottomless pit, is glossed, "This authority chiefly is committed to the Pope in sign whereof he beareth the keys in his arms." The annotation lurks somewhere between comically satiric (like Cranach's tiara) and dead serious, and by such authority Protestant readers may know the source in Revelation of the pope's keys. (In response, the English Catholic New Testament (1582) glosses "star": "The fall of an Arch heretic, as Arius, Luther, Calvin, out of the Church of God, which have the key of Hell to open & bring forth al the old condemned heresies buried before in the depth."[28]) In the later Junius translation, a vastly different reading is provided, in which the falling star is an "Angel of God glittering with glory"—"Whether thou take him for Christ, who hath the keys of Hell of himself . . . or some inferior Angel"—he is in any case to be taken as quite different from the fallen guard of the Genevan exiles.

The foundation of the allegorical reading of church history lay in understanding the biblical city of Babylon *as* Rome. Like the word "pope," "Rome" does not have much of a place in the biblical margins until the Apocalypse.[29] The notes in Revelation establish the historical context at the outset—glossing John's address to the "tribulation" of his audience in Revelation 2:9 as "the persecution under the emperor Domitian"—and this period (CE 81–96) is still accepted as the time when John wrote.[30] For readers like Bale, himself exiled, this context explains why John the Evangelist was on Patmos. As Bale writes in a bit of historicism equally loaded with presentist anachronism, "he was of the emperor Domitian exiled for his preaching into the isle of Patmos, at the cruel complaints of the idolatrous priests and bishops."[31] After John's address to the early churches, the interpretive glosses in the Geneva Bible no longer attend to the present context of the writer, but to the future meaning of the prophetic text. The annotations thus shift the context of signification to medieval European history, casting Rome itself in a particular national character that continued from the reigns of Domitian and Nero as the seat of tyrants and misleaders. For Hugh Broughton, Rome needed still further blame.[32] His *Concent of Scripture* (1588), an effort to establish an exact chronology of world history using both biblical prophecy and history, states that "Rome for killing of Christ, is the only cursed city of the world," and cites "Apocal. 17," the vision of the Whore of Babylon, as his proof text.[33] The text features an image of the Whore of Babylon on a cityscape with seven hills above the caption, "The empire of Rome, that crucified our Lord and serveth Satan in might and hypocrisy, is pictured thus in Gods word" (Figure 17). That these Roman Catholic things are "pictured in God's word" suggests that this is not an interpretation or a reading of the text, but simply a representation of what the word already pictures. The papal tiara such as that originated in Lucas Cranach's whimsical illustration in Luther's *Septembertestament* in 1522 now appears without irony or caprice. The connection between the Romans who killed Christ and the Rome of the papacy, not made in the Geneva paratext, represents an advancement of the defensive Protestant position. The seven-headed dragon from Revelation 12 "the great dragon, that old serpent, called the devil and Satan" (Rev. 12:9), is labeled in Figure 17 along with all the other symbols not labeled in the Bible: "Rome," the Whore of Babylon; "Empire," the beast she rides; the "Pope," a beast emerging from another part of the allegories, and the "belly God Clergy," a locust from yet another of John's visions (Rev. 9). The image shows just how variable—though asserted with great certainty—these readings can be.

The geographical framework for the battleground of the church by implication suggests other national sites that would work in a polar relation: if Rome is the source of tyrannical corruption, then other European centers might in contrast be connected to a true church. In this way, the allegorical reading shifts the axis of tension between Jerusalem and Babylon to a tension between the true church (ultimately New Jerusalem) and Rome. Babylon frequently figures in John's account, but it is always glossed to signify another city. "And there followed another Angel," he reports in Revelation 14:8, "saying, It is fallen, it is fallen, Babylon the great city: for she made all nations to drink of the wine of the wrath of her fornication." Two glosses show how both the geography and the type of sin (wrath of fornication) stand for something else: Babylon, the note explains, is "Signifying Rome, for as much as the vices which were in Babylon,

The empire of Rome, that crucified our Lorde and serueth Satan in might and hypocrisi, is pictured thus in Gods worde.

Figure 17. The Whore of Babylon in Broughton's *Concent of Scripture*. Image attributed to Jodocus Hondius the Elder. Printed on vellum, this copy was probably a presentation copy to the Queen. *A Concent of Scripture* (London: Gabriel Simson and William White?, 1590?), Folger STC 3851 copy 1. By permission of the Folger Shakespeare Library.

are found in Rome in greater abundance, as persecution of the Church of God, oppression & slavery with destruction of the people of God, confusion, superstition, idolatry, impiety, and as Babylon the first Monarchy was destroyed, so shall this wicked kingdom of Antichrist have a miserable ruin, though it be great & seemeth to extend throughout all Europa." The "wrath" of her fornication means more than mere sexual sin: "By the which fornication God is provoked to wrath: so that he suffereth many to walk in the way of the Romish doctrine to their destruction." The ancient text contrives a direct challenge to "Romish doctrine." While the annotators were less bold to provide a location for the New Jerusalem, cultural interfaces with this text and paratext were increasingly ready to do so.

English interpreters seldom shy away from topical usefulness, but topicality in the margins is usually more cautious—allowing readers, for example, to think that Isaiah prefigures a Protestant reformer like Luther without saying it outright. Apocalyptic hermeneutics belong in their own category, in which many of the rules and restraints guiding the interpretation of the former books were dissolved. The difference is most obvious in the way that a nonbiblical vocabulary brings new, contemporary concepts into the biblical meaning. References to "papacy" or "papists" sometimes appear in annotations throughout the Geneva Bible, but they appear with great intensity in the margins of Revelation. In the earlier biblical books, anachronistic uses of "papacy" occur almost universally as asides, rather than readings, as in a note on "sin" in Amos that glosses the sin specifically as idolatry: "For the idolaters did use to swear by their idols, which here he calleth their sin, as the papists yet do by theirs" (Amos 8:14). But here correspondence with the present is largely tangential. In the Apocalypse, the annotations unabashedly draw a direct correspondence between text and current controversy, and a new word, "pope," becomes dominant: "Such as may be understood by man's reason," the Geneva note explains the number of the beast 666 in Revelation 13:18, "for about 666 years after this revelation, the Pope or Antichrist began to be manifest in the world." The digressive explanation, one of many that illuminates the Pope as the prophesied Antichrist, illustrates how fanciful Apocalyptic hermeneutics could be.

Spenser and the Bibles of 1576–1589

Before composing *The Faerie Queene*, Spenser had explored the dynamic relationship between biblical text and paratext in early poetic translations and *The*

Shepheardes Calender (1579). In an evidently formative moment in his career, Spenser worked translating a volume of verse that drew from a culture shaped by the Geneva Bible's apocalyptic beasts, whores, and dragons. At only about fifteen or sixteen, he published anonymous verse translations of Du Bellay and four sonnets as a preface to Jan van der Noot's *The Theatre for Worldlings* (1569), an intensely polemical Protestant reading of Revelation.[34] The polemical poems first appeared in Dutch and then French in 1568 and in English (from the French) the following year, combining writers of different nationalities focused on anti-papal interpretations of Revelation.[35] Echoing the woodcut images that accompany John's visions in Bibles, each sonnet is accompanied by a woodcut. The sequence of fifteen sonnets is an edited cluster of Du Bellay's "visions," as Spenser later calls them, with four removed from the original, and four added at the end by Van der Noot, almost certainly also anonymously translated by Spenser. These are unusual sonnets, all without a solid rhyme scheme, and all—like emblems, but also like John's visions in Bibles—accompanying an image.[36] Since the poems were not republished in the *Complaints* (1591), we can perhaps hope that the young "Spenser was never so bad a poet as was the translator of the 'Sonets' from the Apocalypse,"[37] but it seems far more likely, given that they are uniform renditions within a poetic sequence, that the teenaged poet sought to provide something serviceable that he later had little reason to reprint; the Du Bellay poems undergo quite significant revision and further composition to comprise the "visions of Bellay" in Spenser's *Complaints* of 1591.[38] However we understand the history, Spenser was intimately involved with these apocalyptic sonnets whose emblematic biblical pageants inform his later work. The Van der Noot poems, from which Figure 18 is taken (the English version is cruder), are versified constructions of John's visions. The thirteenth sonnet, on the Whore of Babylon in Revelation 17, essentially translates and encapsulates the biblical text, throwing in a conclusion provided by the Angel in Revelation 18:2, that "Babylon the great city . . . is fallen."

> *I saw a Woman sitting on a beast*
> *Before mine eyes, of Orange color hew:*
> *Horror and dreadful name of blasphemy*
> *Filled her with pride. And seven heads I saw,*
> *Ten horns also the stately beast did bear.*
> *She seemed with glory of the scarlet faire,*
> *And with fine pearl and gold pufft up in heart.*
> *The wine of whoredom in a cup she bare.*

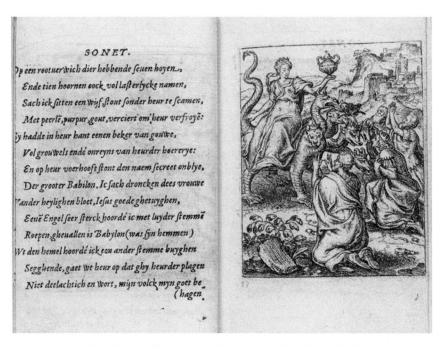

Figure 18. The Whore of Babylon in *The Theater of Worldlings*. The Babylonian
figure from Revelation 17 worshiped in an etching by Marcus Gheeraerts the
Elder in the elegant original Dutch language edition, one of the three
languages of this poetry printed in London. Jan van der Noot, *Het theatre oft
toon-neel* ([London]: [John Day], [1568]), Folger STC 18601.
By permission of the Folger Shakespeare Library.

The name of Mystery writ in her face.
The blood of Martyrs dear were her delight.
Most fierce and fell this woman seemed to me.
An Angell then descending down from Heaven,
With thundering voice cried out aloud, and said,
Now for a truth great Babylon is fallen.[39]

Spenser's probable translation closely follows the French, which roughly translates a detailed Dutch poem. The Dutch original draws closely from the Dutch
biblical wording, as does the woodcut, also nearly identical to that in English
Bibles.[40] The emblematic art form thus excerpts a visual biblical paratext and
provides an accompanying interpretive biblical poem. The poem patches to-

gether bits of Revelation, emphasizing the Foxean (and biblical) detail of the "blood of Martyrs" to affirm the Whore of Babylon as a specifically Roman Catholic monster in a contemporary northern European setting.

In the pastoral *Shepheardes Calender,* rich in glosses from the constructed annotator E. K., Spenser sought to replicate the biblical reading experience. As Catherine Nicholson has written, "the similarities between the presentation of the Geneva Bible and that of *The Shepheardes Calender*—the prefatory essays, prose arguments, marginal annotations and glosses, and woodcut illustrations— suggest that Spenser's pastoral is designed to elicit a reading practice like that promoted by the authors of the English Bibles, in which the value of accessibility is in constant, productive tension with the value of alienation."[41] Like the English printings of the Geneva Bible, Spenser's work was in "English" black letter, with the notes in Roman font.[42] Spenser's poem was published by Hugh Singleton, who had recently printed a brief catechism designed for "the simple sort," with black letter in the main text and roman type for marginal notes.[43] Spenser's negotiation of the problems of biblical interpretation and the state of the English Church in this pastoral poem invite comparison with his later epic. As Kearney has shown, the annotations in *The Shepheardes Calender* "illustrate the ways in which E. K.'s strange exegetical dance asks his readers to consider the vexed issues of interpretation and consensus in early modern England," teaching readers to "fend off a pernicious confidence in the ability of the authoritative note to resolve the problems of textual difficulty."[44] The 1570s and early 1580s were intensely productive for English editions of the Geneva Bible, which had only appeared in a few editions since 1560, and only in Geneva. But from 1576 to 1583, the period of Grindal's Archbishopric of Canterbury (between Parker and Whitgift), "eighteen editions of the complete Geneva Bible and thirteen of the Geneva New Testament were printed in England."[45] England became inundated with annotated Bibles and among these is a 1578 folio edition adorned to appear like an official English Bible: black letter, an almanac, calendar, and material from the Book of Common Prayer, with the introduction from Cranmer taken from the Great Bible of 1540. This reprinting of the Book of Common Prayer changed the official wording of the English Prayer Book, substituting "minister" for "priest," and making other significant omissions.[46]

At the same time that Spenser's pastoral poem replicates some of the experience of the biblical reader, it participates in a debate around individual interpretive practice within the English Church. In the May and July eclogues and in the character Algrind (an anagram for Grindal, then fallen archbishop), the poem subtly supports a figure who had himself supported a more continental reformist position, and had sought to resolve differences and bring puritan ministers under the umbrella of the English Church.[47] Grindal was sequestered by Elizabeth for fostering a series of learned discussions on the interpretation of scripture called "prophesying," after Paul's advice to pastors in 1 Corinthians 14, mentioned earlier, by means of a method of mutually arriving at an interpretive consensus. As the 1560 Geneva note explains: Paul speaks of prophecy "to expound the word of God to the edification of the Church." In his letter to the queen defending the practice, Grindal explicated this passage, but the queen remained firm that such interpretive groups would create "dangerous opinions" and a "breach of common order."[48]

Exploring the idea that the black letter edition of 1578 was designed for the "common- and conforming-protestants," and the "Geneva-Tomson for the Presbyterians,"[49] Kearney has argued that the "textual manifestation of the chronic tension within the Elizabethan Settlement . . . is the Geneva Bibles printed in the 1570s."[50] There is no question that some of these Bibles were shaped by Elizabethans with particular interests; indeed, it has been cogently argued that the 1578 black letter Bible, with modifications to the Book of Common Prayer, is also a puritan Bible in Church of England clothing.[51] As these Geneva Bibles were flooding the market from 1576 through the 1580s, another major biblical event occurred, with cultural aftermath pertinent to the biblical orientation of *The Faerie Queene*: the publication of the English Catholic New Testament, by Gregory Martin and English exiles in Rheims, in 1582.[52] In true Counter-Reformation form, the long awaited Catholic vernacular Bible is highly reactive, frequently countering Protestant readings in its marginal notes and annotations: "Protestants take it in their commentaries,"[53] the Rheims New Testament frequently intones. A powerful expression of Counter-Reformation belief and a systematic assault on Protestant reading, the annotated New Testament provoked a strong reaction from English Protestants. William Fulke, an advocate of puritan reform in the early 1570s, but increasingly more mainstream, responded immediately with a substantial *Defense of the Sincere and True Translations of the Holie Scriptures* (1583), which took on Martin's *Discoverie of the Manifold Corruptions of the Holy Scripture by the Heretikes of Our Daies* (1582). Financed by the great Bible publisher Christopher Barker, who provided two assistants for nine months, Fulke subsequently published a highly popular biblical "confutation," which took on the Rheims translation with extensive animadversions attending to "the controversies of these days."[54] Spenser may have known Fulke: supported by Leister's patronage, he became Master of Pembroke College at Cambridge in 1578 just after Spenser received his MA there, and had made a name for himself engaging in public debates with recusants like Edmund Campion before his execution in 1581.[55] In assuming the position of Master of Pembroke, Fulke replaced John Young, who moved from his post as Master to become Bishop of Rochester, and employed Spenser to serve as his secretary. Spenser portrayed him as Roffy in *The Shepheardes Calender*.[56] Spenser thus played an actual role in the English Church, even as he cast its members in literary roles.

Fulke's initial attack on the Catholic New Testament contains a letter to Queen Elizabeth that describes how Catholics use translation and annotation as polemic. For Fulke, the most dangerous part of the Rheims translation was the annotations, which could turn hearts away from true obedience to the queen. He wrote her that the Rheims text is "pestered with so many annotations, both false and undutiful, by which, under color of the authority of holy scriptures, they seek to infect the minds of the credulous readers with heretical and superstitious opinions, and to alienate their hearts from yielding due obedience to your Majesty, and your most Christian laws concerning true Religion established."[57] Fulke seems to take for granted that "credulous readers" instead of committed Catholics will read the imported publication, and devotes the rest of his life to the biblical and paratextual enormity created with Barker, though the layout of the text is probably the work of Barker, who had experience with dual texts.[58] Like Erasmus's columns of Greek and two Latin translations, Barker produced a split page New Testament, the image of both church Bibles, with the "Translation of Rhemes" on the left column, and the "Translation of the Church of England" on the right, the first in roman type, the second in italic. In this part of the presentation, there is no obvious bias; the size of each text is the same, and the side margins are each filled faithfully with cross-references in each Bible, enabling the kind of comparison allowed by Erasmus's columned New Testament publications, or by the diglot Latin and English Bibles printed in late Henrician and Edwardian London. The upper part of the page faithfully preserves both the Catholic and Protestant New Testaments, and the bottom of each chapter contains a running set of animadversions: the Catholic annotation and Fulke's rebuttal, labeled "*Rhem.*" and "*Fulke*," respectively. The very New Testament smuggled from Rheims that might alone have incriminated its owner was now available in a popular Protestant production.[59]

The multilayered paratext brought sharper definition to the biblical orientation of these religious differences, and it also brought a nationalist reading to the ancient "Church" represented in the biblical text. *The Image of Both Churches* was increasingly becoming, for English readers, the images of the Roman against the English Church. As Fulke writes in the "Dedication to Elizabeth," an oracle in Revelation links the true church to the Church of England:

> Thus hath the infinite goodness of our savior, not only given grace
> unto your Majestie, according to the heavenly oracle, Apoc. 18:4 to
> lead the people of God with you out of Babylon: but also sufficient
> power and just cause to render unto her as she hath rendered unto us,
> and to reward her double according to her works.

The preface to this Bible looks back to the preface of the Geneva Bible, in which the exiles had called Elizabeth "our Zerubbabel," the descendant of David who had "led the people of God . . . out of Babylon." Fulke sees himself called upon by the divine to defend the "faithful Church" (English), against "Antichrist," who has gone "against the Lord, his word, his Church, and your Majesty his anointed . . . by confuting these annotations."[60] Suitably, the annotations and the confutations are by far the most extensive in the book of Revelation.

A nationalistic polarity between the two churches emerges in *The Faerie Queene* at various points. After Una's and Redcrosse Knight's courses have parted for several cantos, and Redcrosse is thrown in the giant's dungeon, the two are finally reunited through the help of the young Arthur. The two meetings, first between Arthur and Una, and then between the two knights, occasion a set of exchanges that draw elaborate connections between national sovereignty and the English Church. One of these is Redcrosse's gift to Arthur of "his Saveours testament":

> A booke, wherein his Saveours testament
> Was writt with golden letters rich and brave
> A work of wondrous grace, and able soules to save.   (I.ix.19)

Critical discussion of this sumptuously decorated "testament" has generally presumed it to be the New Testament, based both on the categories of biblical production in Spenser's own time, and on the contrast with the Old Testament reading and doctrine introduced by Despaire in the trial of Redcrosse that follows.[61] As Maureen Quilligan has suggested, Redcrosse may have given away the very text that he needed to fight against the "law" offered him by Despaire, thus "dis-pairing" one part of the Bible from another.[62] Fidelia (or Faith) finally restores Redcrosse with New Testament doctrine from the "sacred Booke, with blood ywritt" (I.x.19), seeming to reconstruct the wholeness of the biblical text.

Yet the illuminated "Saveours testament" may connote a still more particular section of the Bible than simply the New Testament. In this moment, the phrase "Saveours testament" also plays on the concept of the "testament" that Christ himself offers in the Eucharistic moment at the Last Supper. Passing the wine, he states, "For this is my blood of the new Testament, that is shed for many for the remission of sins" (Matt. 26:28). This is the testament that is able to save souls, and indeed Spenser seems to be invoking the salvific power of this ritual act that is reinforced in the note, where "blood" is glossed: "The wine signifieth that our souls are refreshed and satisfied with the blood of Christ, so that without him, we have no nourishment." In this sense, the "Saveours testament" that is able "soules to save" might refer to both the Eucharistic sacrament and to the moment of sacrifice that it also represents. The "work of wondrous grace," then, is not so much a literary text, but an act recorded within that text. As with "New Testament" in Matthew, both the title of the book but also a moment of Eucharistic refreshment, so too does Spenser's sense play on both a single salvific event and a bibliographic object. Yet the specificity of the testament here belonging to Christ—"Saveours testament"—may suggest that this is not the New Testament in its entirety, but the gospel account alone. The material history of the biblical text confirms this possibility, as the gospels often appeared alone in medieval forms—and this description with its "golden letters" recalls an illuminated manuscript.

Spenser would certainly have known the medieval forms of the book that inform this description. The most important of such medieval gospels, and one probably known to Spenser and many of the readers in his circles, was the legendary Gospel brought by St. Augustine of Canterbury to England along with Christianity in 597. In the sixteenth century, this Gospel was owned by Matthew Parker and donated to Corpus Christi College, Cambridge, with Parker's immense library at his death in 1575. Spenser's connection to Parker's extraordinary library has been traced by Andrew Hadfield and Jennifer Summit. Summit shows that Parker's library, the product of a group of scholars, churchmen, and writers associated with Spenser, exerted a profound influence on the poet's imagination.[63] She describes *The Faerie Queene* in bibliographic terms: "Spenser's allegory of Protestant nationhood meditates on the post-Reformation transformation of the library and its broader implications for literary history and practice."[64] What has not yet been fully considered is the cultural significance of the volume at the very center of Parker's library—its greatest treasure, and the motivating force behind antiquarian efforts to recover England's most important medieval books. St. Augustine brought the manuscript to Britain to support his mission from Gregory the Great to convert Ethelbert and the English. In the course of that mission, he founded the Cathedral of Canterbury and inaugurated an unbroken line of archbishops leading to Parker, the seventieth. Parker obtained the St. Augustine gospel—perhaps *the* book of books for the English Church—as a result of the dissolution of the monasteries, and it became the core exhibit in the Archbishopric's effort to collect items confirming the independence of the English Church. Parker believed that the Church of England had been independent of Rome in the Saxon period, before the corruption of the Norman Conquest.[65] For Parker and other English Protestants, St. Augustine's pre-Reformation gospelbook represented a true relic of the original English Church, operating as a kind of quest object.

Given that this object is roughly contemporaneous with Spenser's sixth-century narrative, it is worth placing the two in dialogue, and considering what role this actual medieval testament might have played in the cultural imagination of Spenser's contemporaries. Hadfield has shown that Spenser had access to Parker's library, and would also have been conversant with its contents from many possible sources: he was under the employment of Bishop Young, Parker's associate, and he probably also knew Stephen Bateman, Parker's librarian, the author of *The Travailed Pilgrim* (1569), a probable source for *The Faerie Queene*, especially Book 1.[66] As Anne Lake Prescott pointed out, Bateman's poem is "England's only significant non-dramatic Protestant quest allegory before Spenser."[67] This cluster of Protestant theologians and allegorists were also involved in a bibliographic quest that would help establish the foundations of the English Church. Seeking a uniquely English Christian history, Bateman like Parker "searched the monastic libraries and gathered large collections of medieval books following the dissolution."[68] It therefore seems highly likely that any number of these potential contacts and their associations would have brought Spenser into contact with this sixth-century Protestant relic. Even if the St. Augustine Gospel itself eluded Spenser's gaze, the case shows that Spenser's contemporaries treated a sumptuous medieval gospel as a relic of the English Church.[69]

This "Saveours testament" is, however, incomplete—lacking Paul's letters, and lacking the Revelation of John, texts that could supply the theological tools through which Fidelia can fully prepare Redcrosse. When Fidelia reads to Redcrosse from her "sacred Booke, with blood ywritt" it seems infused with Pauline language and imagery from Revelation, as is the entirety of the visit to the House of Holiness in Canto X, with Fidelia, Speranza and Charissa representing the three central Pauline virtues Faith, Hope, and Charity (1 Cor. 13:13). Just before the description of the "sacred Book" that Fidelia takes out, Una requests

Fidelia to teach her knight "words divine," which she granted, and "daught" him "celestiall discipline / And opened his dull eyes, that light mote in them shine" (1.x.18). The Alexandrine is a citation from Paul's description of his conversion experience, when he is instructed by Christ to "open their eyes, that they may turn from darkness to light" (Acts 26:18). The instruction from Fidelia is of a particularly Pauline nature, and at the end of Canto x, Redcrosse is lead to the "higest Mount" (I.x.53; Rev. 21:10) from which he is shown "new Hierusalem" (Rev. 21:2), and thus brought through the latter part of the New Testament.

In addition to the "Saveour's testament," Spenser's Arthur owns other objects that represent original English national identity. When we first meet prince Arthur, still unnamed and described only as "the goodly knight," the future king's chivalric implements—his shield, armor, and sword—are endowed with a force that is both biblical and national:

> It Merlin was, which whylome did excell
> All living wightes in might of magicke spell:
> Both shield, and sword, and armour all he wrought
> For this young Prince, when first to armes he fell;
> But when he dyde, the Faery Queene it brought
> To Faerie lond, where yet it may be seene, if sought.   (I.vii.36)

In the Letter to Raleigh, Spenser associates the Armor of Redcrosse with the armor of the Christian man in the influential passage in Ephesians 6:11–17 that had served as the basis for Erasmus's "Christian Knight" in the *Enchiridion*. Spenser wrote to Raleigh that Redcrosse bore "the armour of a Christian man specified by Saint Paul v. Ephesians."[70] Paul wrote metaphorically of the equipment needed to defend faith: "take unto you the whole armour of God, that ye may be able to resist in the evil day . . . Stand therefore, and your loins gird about with verity, & having on the breast plate of righteousness. . . . Above all, take the shield of faith, wherewith ye may quench all the fiery darts of the wicked, And take the helmet of salvation, and the sword of the Spirit, which is the word of God" (Eph. 6:13–17). In this description, Arthur's magic shield, sword, and armor are emblematic sources of true religion and sovereignty in England. It is hard not to read a touch of irony in this last line, that these relics *may* be found in England, even though they are not immediately apparent or often "sought."

A few stanzas later, Una tells Prince Arthur her story, echoing the language of the Geneva notes throughout the Book of Revelation. As she explains in a complex chronological overlay of both Spenser's narrative and the Book of Revelation, she sped to the court of Gloriane in an allegorical London (Cleopolis):

> Forthwith to court of Gloriane I sped
> Gloriane great Queene of glory bright,
> Whose Kingdomes seat Cleopolis is red,
> There to obtaine some such redoubted knight,
> The Parents deare from tyrant's powre deliver might.   (I.vii.45)

The tyrant who captured Una's parents is the monster of Revelation, read by the Geneva notes as an allegory of "the church miserably defaced with idolatry and . . . tyrants" (note to Rev. 6:12)—which annotators and readers of the Geneva Bible applied to Mary and Philip, as noted by the annotations in a Bodleian copy of the Geneva Bible discussed in chapter 4. As the notes read, "God hath limited the time of Antichrists tyranny" (Rev. 11:2) over the church. When John in Revelation sees "a beast rise out of the sea, having seven heads" in Rev. 13:1, the note explains that this is a "description of the Roman empire which standeth in cruelty and tyranny," "first governed by seven Kings or Emperors after Nero," and then by the tyranny of the Roman Catholic Church. The Catholic annotators read the "seven heads" as "seven kings: five before Christ, one present, and one to come," which Fulke grants, adding that "These seven kings are the seven principal heads of government of the Roman Empire, whereof five were abolished before Christ, one, (which was of the heathen Emperors) was present, and the seventh then to come is the Pope, which is Antichrist. They that worship Antichrist, worship the devil, not in their intent (for Antichrist boasteth himself to be God) but because they worship him who hath his power of the devil."[71] These marginal readings are far from the language of the biblical text, yet they became standardized in the early modern imagination, where allusion points both to the text and to the gloss.[72]

Spenser's Redcrosse and Una occupy a landscape fraught with the same interpretive and national concerns as the text and paratext of the English Bible. Spenser's allegory demonstrates a culturally legitimated mode of interpretation. Informed by and participating in biblical annotation, *The Faerie Queene* asserts a nationalist reading of Revelation's allegories in a world where many different readings vied for ascendancy. By far the most important allegory for Spenser in Revelation is John's vision of the Woman clothed by the sun, which is the source for Una, in Revelation 12. It is in this passage, and again with the same phrasing in Revelation 20:2, that the serpent of the story of Genesis is connected with astonishing tangentiality to the Satan of Christian history. The revelation of the identity of Satan as the Serpent from the beginning of the Bible fittingly occurs at its very end: "And the great dragon, that old serpent, called the devil and Satan, was cast out, which deceiveth all the world" (Geneva, Revelation 12:9). The phrase "*that* old serpent"—probably gesturing back to the Serpent in Genesis, and certainly thought to be by tradition—is the only biblical validation of the reading of Serpent as Satan. Spenser evokes the wording in his summary argument of Book 1, Canto xi: "The knight with that old Dragon fights / Two days insessantly." The crucial question for readers of Revelation was how to interpret the devil (a single entity, or a conglomerate enemy?) and his release and reign (for a short period, or long, and for what purpose?) and finally, embellished in Revelation 20, his imprisonment (for a thousand years?).

In this vision, John sees a "great wonder in heaven: A Woman clothed with the sun, & the moon *was* under her feet, and upon her head a crown of twelve stars" (Rev. 12:1). The woman, bearing a child, is the "Church," according to the Geneva marginal apparatus, then "persecuted by Antichrist." The moon she stands over signifies mutability, and the twelve stars "God and his word." After her child (Christ) was taken up into "God and to his throne" (12:5), the church (or the woman) "fled into the wilderness where she hath a place prepared of God, that they should feed her a thousand, two hundredth and threescore days. And there was a battle in heaven. Michael & his Angels fought against the dragon, and the dragon fought & his Angels" (12:6–7). The reading that enables the Protestant reading of the Papacy as Antichrist stretches the measurement of time: the devil, we are told in Revelation 12 will reign for three and a half years, which was seen by readers as early as the fourth century as standing for 350 years.[73]

The Catholics at Rheims dismissed this possibility. The Rheims Catholic translation reads, "And after the dragon saw that he was thrown into the earth, he persecuted the woman which brought forth the man-childe: and there were given to the woman two wings of a great eagle, that she might fly into the desert unto her place, where she is nourished for *a time & times, & half a time, from the face of the serpent." This three and a half, seemingly the same as that figured in days earlier, is glossed by the English Catholics, "*This often insinuation that Antichrist's reign shall be but three years & a half (Dan. 7:25. Apoc. 11:23 . . .) proveth that the heretics be exceedingly blinded with malice that hold the Pope to be Antichrist, who hath ruled so many ages."[74] Fulke argues in response that "the persecution of Antichrist should be three hundred and fifty year. And indeed from the time of the chasing away of the Church into desert places, when the Pope by cruel wars and tyranny banished the faithful whom he persecuted by the names of Waldenses . . . unto the time that the Gospel began again to be openly professed by Wyckliffe and others, it is about the time of 350 years."[75] That John's prophecies of medieval Europe and England were not hitherto known should not seem surprising, since the meaning of prophecy is not manifest until its fulfillment: "this book containeth a prophecy of the state of the church until the end of the world, so it is no marvel if many things seemed obscure to the ancient fathers, before they were fulfilled, which are now clear and evident to us, after they be accomplished" (849). Fulke's observation may seem belated after decades of reading Revelation as pertaining to the recent past, but perhaps it is precisely because it *is* a hardly credible "marvel" that this near-presentist reading needs constant defense.

A Biblical Reader's Marked *Faerie Queene* (1590)

Like the Bible, Spenser's *Faerie Queene* inspired manuscript annotation from its readers.[76] A remarkable copy of the 1611 edition brought to light by Stephen Orgel and further illuminated by James Kearney shows a puritanical reader full of disdain for Spenser's seemingly Catholic forms of representation.[77] Fittingly, 1611 is the year of the King James Bible, and this reader may have also been a reader of the new Bible, shorn of explanatory notes that would provide context and illumination for Spenser's allegories and medievalism. The unknown Stuart reader took particular umbrage at Redcrosse, whom (as St. George) he reviles as a "popish saint, de-vised by idle Monks."[78] When Spenser introduces the knight at the very outset of Book 1, "But on his brest a bloudie Crosse he bore, / The deare remembrance of his dying Lord, / For whose sweete sake that glorious badge he wore" (I.ii.1–3), the scolding Protestant remarks, "This is not the way to adore him."[79] Spenser's imagery is both medieval and Erasmian; he draws on the tradition of the Christian soldier conceived by Paul. The Pauline passage informs Erasmus's *Manuel of a Christen Knight* (1533), and for Spenser as for Erasmus, the "cross" is part of the "badge" of the Christian soldier. "For what intent was the sign of the cross printed in thy forehead but that as long as thou livest thou shouldst fight under his standard,"[80] Erasmus wrote; "The Badges of Christ be come to all men, & the most honorable which be the cross, the crown of thorn . . . the signs or tokens which Paul rejoiceth to bear in his body."[81] As Kearney notes, the use of such symbols represented for this early reader "an unholy hybrid of the Catholic and the Protestant,"[82] and suggests less simple Protestant militancy in Spenser than is often understood.

An earlier reader named John Dixon, who signed his 1590 *Faerie Queene* in 1597, provides quite a different set of readings, though similarly polarized by religious zeal. Little is known about Dixon beyond evidence that he was a middle-aged Kentish man of considerable substance.[83] He is certainly a reader of the Geneva Bible, which dominates his field of reference. Rather than pausing over the icons of medieval Catholicism, Dixon reads Book I as an allegory of England's Reformation and its Counter-Reformation opponents. He has "little interest in the narrative line,"[84] as is clear from the mistakes (he confuses Sansfoy with Archimago, for example). But he has a keen interest in discovering hidden references, as if Spenser's first book—where all the biblical references are for this reader—provoked a desire for marginal annotation. While such a reader's reactions cannot be taken to indicate Spenser's intentions, they provide insight into how both *The Faerie Queene* and the Bible were read—and read together—by an Elizabethan reader. Both Spenser and his reader demonstrate a profound reliance on the paratextual packaging of the biblical text.

Dixon's markings reveal a reader trained by the Geneva Bible to interpret Spenser in a particular way. In parallel with the annotations of the Geneva Bible, the two most common nouns used in Dixon's marginal notes are "Church" and "Christ" ("Christ" being the second most common keyword in the Old Testament notes). The third most common manuscript annotation is "Antichrist," which similarly follows the proportion in the Geneva Bible's annotations to the Book of Revelation—in short, this early reader is so accustomed to the vocabulary of the biblical margins that he instinctively fills the margins of Spenser's text with the printed marginal vocabulary of Spenser's Bible, even though neither the Bible nor Spenser introduce these topics in the text.[85] When Fradubio, metamorphosed into a tree in the Wandering Wood, describes the witch who transformed him as "one Duessa a *false sorceress* / That many errant knights hath broght to wretchednesse" (I.ii.34), Dixon writes in terms that are both biblical and early modern: "Is Antichrist Compared to a harlot whose beauty only standeth in outward pomp and impudency." A few stanzas later, when Fradubio describes when he "chaunced to see in her proper hew . . . a filthy foule old woman I did vew" (I.ii.40), Dixon writes, "a covert description of Antichrist," which also draws from the margins of Revelation, suggesting that the multivalent representations of Antichrist in Revelation enable further allegorizing in literary representation. When the narrator relates at the opening of Canto viii that Redcrosse is still "Thrall to that Gyants hatefull tyranny" (I.viii.2), Dixon simply writes *"Antichrist."* Even beyond Dragons, the monsters of romance are easily transferable to those of the Apocalypse.

Dixon sees *The Faerie Queene* not as an "idle fiction,"[86] as the later Stuart reader did but as *"a fiction of our Queen Eliz: the maintainer of the gospel of Christe, to be by god himself betrothed unto Christ, though by K[ing]:P[hilip]: and R[oman]C[atholics]: for: 6: years it was debarred,"* a marginal gloss written at the argument for the final canto of Book I: "Fair Una to the Redcrosse knight / Betrothed is with Joy." The reading is astonishing on several accounts. As an Elizabethan reader would read the ancient text of Revelation to be about the present or near present condition—for example, the Woman clothed in the sun's wilderness exile being the captivity of the church before Wycliffe—Spenser is read as a medieval fiction pertaining to a period of captivity in the near present. Like the Elizabethan reader of the Geneva Bible who saw a passage in Revelation 18 as pertaining "especially in the Marian times"[87] (Figure 11), this Spenserian reader also takes the *Faerie Queene* to point to the Marian exile, a formative chapter in English national identity made all the more significant by the exilic Bible that taught both Spenser and his reader. At the argument to Canto xi, with its echoes of "that old Serpent" in Revelation, "The knight with that old *Dragon* fights," the Elizabethan reader annotates: "Antichristian religion over thrown, and the maintainer their of Q ma: by death victored." Queen Mary again signifies Mary Tudor, maintainer of "rc," as above, who was "victored," perhaps by some divine means, by her untimely death in 1558. Dixon's annotation, like that of the late Elizabethan reader who remarked on the "Marian times" in the margins of Revelation, shows that the Marian exile formed more than the context for the notes of the popular Elizabethan Bible: it was a chapter in English national history that was figured in the text itself.

Dixon reads both Spenser and the Bible itself as a nationalist defense of the English Church, using the Geneva text and annotations to help him understand both texts as nationalist documents. The reader connects Una's wanderings with those of the Woman clothed in the sun, the true church wandering in the wilderness. "And *Una* wandering in woods and forests" (I.ii.9) is annotated: "daughter and heir to a Persian king, but is rightly to be understood the daughter of Israel or the true Church, which was led by the wilderness 140 years." The time, like Una's confused heritage, seems problematic: the figure in the Bible is "a thousand, two hundreth and threescore days" (Rev. 12:6) or something like three and a half years. Duessa, in contrast, is described in *The Faerie Queene* as "Born the sole daughter of an *Emperor*" (I.ii.22); Dixon reads this again in terms drawn from the notes in Revelation, even without citation: "Antichrist taketh on her the name of Truth, feigned to be the daughter of a Persian king: but truth is only meant. to our Sovereign Eliz. Christ and his gospel." Una is often seen as correspondent to Elizabeth, as when the narrator states, "For fairest *Unas* sake, of whom I sing" (I.iii.2), Dixon marks simply: "Eliza." Spenser encouraged this reading in several ways, including the dedication after the title page of the 1590 edition, which states, "TO THE MOST MIGHTIE AND MAGNIFICENT EMPRESSE ELIZA-BETH, BY THE GRACE OF GOD QUEENE OF ENGLAND, FRANCE, AND IRELAND AND DEFENDER OF THE FAITH," the last title given Henry VIII by the pope when he wrote against Luther, and retained with some irony by the Protestants. The author thus sings for his heroine of the true church, one who, like Una, is often figured as the woman in Revelation 12.

Like some readers of *Paradise Lost*, who provide biblical chapter and verse numbers in the margins, Dixon frequently gives line and verse, particularly from Revelation, which look like cross-references within the biblical text. Some of these references correspond with annotations in modern editions of Spenser (such as A. C. Hamilton's), and some seem rather farfetched. At the description of the "darksome hole" (1.i.14) Redcrosse enters to fight Error, for example, Dixon's gloss reads "the lake which burneth with fire and brimstone, for the utter destruction of such as love The worlds vanities Revela: 21." When Error vomits up "bookes and paper" with "loathly frogs," Dixon correctly cites "reve: 16:13," which describes a vision of "unclean spirits like frogs" that came "out of the mouth of the dragon, and out of the mouth of the beast, and out of the mouth of the false prophet." The Geneva gloss to these unclean spirits reads this in as "the Pope's ambassadors which are ever crying and croaking like frogs and come out of Antichrists mouth, because they should speak nothing but lies and use all manner of crafty deceit." This gloss concerning the Pope's ambassadors continues to inform the next line in Revelation, "For they are spirits[n] of devils, working miracles, to go unto the °Kings of the earth, and of the whole world, to gather them to the battle of that great day of God Almighty" (Rev. 16:14). This line, embroidered with glosses, is roughly transcribed in the margins of Dixon's *Faerie Queene* to elaborate Archimago's conjuration of two spirits: "Of those he chose out *two*, the falsest two" (I.i.38) is glossed: "spirits of devils to work miracles on the kings of ye earth which are false profits to hinder the kingdom of Christ Rev: 16:14." Dixon's words thoroughly interweave text and paratext, drawing bits of Revelation 16:14 together with the "false prophets" of 16:13, and interlarding bits from the margins. The phrase "hinder the kingdom of Christ" derives from the gloss to "Kings": "For in all Kings courts the Pope hath had his ambassadors to hinder the kingdom of Christ." The glossing suggests that text and paratext were essentially interchangeable for this reader.

But in addition to the frequent citations to biblical verses in Revelation and other texts, Dixon cites the Geneva annotations themselves. As Austen Saunders writes, "Dixon clearly knew the Geneva version of Revelation extremely well as he quotes extensively from both text and notes, with and without attribution, and at times cites chapter and verse to provide a reference not to the biblical text itself, but to the accompanying note."[88] At one moment, for example, Dixon annotated Spenser's epic from the annotation to Revelation 2:8, as if annotating Spenser only meant transferring the biblical annotation from the Geneva margins to *The Faerie Queene*: "The eternal divinity of Jesus Christ is here most plainly declared with his manhood and victory over death."[89] This glosses lines spoken by the disguised Archimago as he falsely reports Redcrosse's death to Una: "Ah dearest dame (qd. hee) how might I see / The thing, that might not be and yet was donne?" (I.vi.39). The very same words annotate Revelation 2:8 in the Geneva Bible, "And unto the Angel of the Church of the Smyrnians write, These things saith he that is first, and last, Which was dead and is a live." This common gloss connects Redcrosse with Christ, as both are alive, though reported dead. But it also connects the *Faerie Queene* with the sacred text of the Geneva Bible, suggesting that the two texts foster the same kinds of nationalist, presentist, polemical interpretations.

*   *   *

The scaffolding of the Geneva Bible is thus drawn into Spenser's *Faerie Queene*, to be drawn out again by readers like Dixon, who added a marginal paratext that asserted, among other things, that the true Church is in England. Dixon reads the Geneva notes through the historical conditions of the Marian exiles who wrote them. Its specifically English triumphalism seems partly to derive from the fact Mary was "by death victored," and that the Bible essentially arrived with Elizabeth. The Book of Revelation provides what is at once the most militant, most uncertain, and most propagandistic prophetic text against the Roman Catholic Church. The text produced its own modes of interpretation that were associated only with this book—forms of reading that deviated profoundly from Tyndale's professed literalism to embrace a wildly propagandistic allegorical form. Still, the opportunistic roots of such readings were to some extent grounded in the habits of applied literalism actually practiced by Tyndale and other English readers, in which biblical passages are pressed to useful service in the present. Yet, as I have noted above, in spite of the settled multinational place of the Apocalypse in Protestant polemical literature, the book has a mixed reception history. Figures as prominent as John Overall, the Regius Professor of Divinity at Cambridge, provoked the opposition of other College

Heads in 1599 when he "opposed as too extreme the thesis that the pope alone was the Antichrist." Instead, "he demonstrated that all the notes of Antichrist might as easily pertain to Mohammed and the Turks, and suggested that it was most likely that the pope and the Turk together constituted 'that Antichrist' foretold in Scripture."[90]

Poets and playwrights responded to the complicated legacy of Revelation from both sides. Thomas Dekker, for instance, depicted the Whore of Babylon as his eponymous subject in his post-Gunpowder Plot drama that pits "that Purple whore of Rome" against a figure drawn from both Shakespeare and Spenser, "Titania the Fairy Queen: under whom is figured our late Queen Elizabeth."[91] Dekker appropriates figures from both Shakespeare and Spenser for his nationalist allegory, but the propagandistic tenor of his drama is far more indebted to Spenser and to modes of reading Revelation notably absent in Shakespeare. For, in spite of Dekker's allusion to *Midsummer Night's Dream*, the militant reading of Revelation was largely ignored by Shakespeare, the subject of the next chapter. In stark contrast to the work of his older contemporary, there are almost no overt references in the Shakespearean corpus to the confessionally charged reading of the Apocalypse, with a remarkable yet ambivalent exception in *Henry V*.[92] In the scene in which Falstaff's comrades reminisce after his death, the Boy recalls that Falstaff once said that "the dev'l would have him about women," and the Hostess responds that he "did in some sort, indeed, handle women; but then he was rheumatic, and talk'd of the whore of Babylon" (2.3.35–39). This is usually glossed as invoking the "common Protestant name for the Roman Catholic Church"[93] in Revelation 17:3–6, but the scene's treatment of such "rheumatic" (or fanatic) talk is comically dismissive, suggesting rather a critique of the fanatical use of this biblical image. The next chapter follows this critique in an unusually allegorical moment in Shakespeare's career, the highly biblical play *Measure for Measure,* whose representations draw on medieval forms while they ironize Protestant habits of political reading. The play is performed before a king who had only recently pronounced England's favorite Bible to be seditious and dangerous, laying the ground for the King James Bible.

CHAPTER 6

Measure for Measure and the New King

It is now disputed at every table, whether the magistrate be of necessity
bound to the judicials of Moses.
—Archbishop Whitgift, in a sermon before Queen Elizabeth

The creation of the most influential book in English, the King James Bible,
seems almost to have begun by accident. Some eight months after James VI of
Scotland became King James I of England, in a highly anticipated conference at
Hampton Court in January 1604, a puritan named John Reynolds called for a
new translation of the Bible. Reynolds urged "his Majesty, that there might be a
new *translation* of the *Bible*, because, those which were allowed in the reigns of
Henry the eight, and Edward the sixt, were corrupt and not answerable to the
truth of the Original."[1] Reynolds's presentation of evidence is strangely flawed:
other Bibles, both official and unofficial, had long since replaced those of Henry
VIII and Edward VI, and the three passages that he goes on to cite as examples
of corrupt translations come from the Great Bible (1539).[2] Since two of his suggested revisions come not from the Bishops' Bible but from the Geneva translation, it seems possible that Reynolds had hoped to give the Geneva Bible official
status. Evidently ready for such a project, James announced that a new Bible
must replace the old, not only because of inaccurate translations, but also
because of the notes in what had become England and Scotland's dominant
Bible, originally created in Geneva.

There are many accounts of the Hampton Court Conference from perspectives that usually bear an obvious bias toward either the puritans' or the bishops'
cause, but none as well circulated as William Barlow's semiofficial account, first
published in August 1604, and designed in part to refute other reports.[3] According

to Barlow, James "gave this caveat . . . that no marginal notes should be added [to the proposed new Authorized Version], having found in them, which are annexed to the *Geneva* translation . . . some notes very partial, untrue, seditious, and savoring, too much, of dangerous, and traitorous conceits."[4] James's scathing objections are politically rather than doctrinally focused, shown in suggestive and detailed citations: "As for example, Exod. 1:19 where the marginal note alloweth *disobedience to Kings*," and "2 Chron. 15:16. [where] the note taxeth Asa for deposing his mother, only, and not killing her."[5] The king's objection to the note at Exodus 1:19 puts him in an uncomfortable alliance with Pharaoh, who had ordered the midwives to kill all the Hebrew boys. The offending note provides a mixed assessment of the midwives' scheming efforts to save the boys: "their disobedience herein was lawful, but their dissembling evil."[6] The same explanation is roughly repeated in Bishops' Bibles, and is, in fact, not particularly unorthodox, since it derives from Peter's words in Acts 5:29 that "we ought rather to obey God then men"—that is, as the note goes on to specify, "when they command or forbid us anything contrary to the word of God." The problem of Asa and his idolatrous mother Maacah, whom he deposed, however, was far more personal for James, since this was a biblical passage that had been used to argue for his mother the Queen of Scots' execution by Elizabethan bishops and statesmen in 1572 and 1584.[7] The offending note, copied word for word though slightly abridged in the quarto edition of the Bishops' Bible, possibly by former exile Bishop Sandys, reads, "herein he showed that he lacked zeal: for she ought to have died both by the covenant, and by the Law of God."[8]

James's denunciation is usually seen as representative rather than exceptional, fitting in a long history of royal and episcopal opposition to biblical annotations that started with Henry VIII's rage at Tyndale's "pestilent glosses in the margents."[9] With the supposed opposition to Geneva Bibles by Elizabethan authorities, these statements are often charted on a grid that seems to illustrate the self-evident course of history. But these moments, valuable in themselves as cultural indicators, are open to far less interconnected explanations. While many have echoed in one way or another James's assessment of the potency of the Geneva notes—by 1604 reaching around 300,000 words in some versions, nearly half the word count of the biblical text[10]—the notes he objects to are essentially the same as those in the official Bishops' Bibles, which drew from the popular Geneva paratext, as for example in the note supporting the execution of Asa's idolatrous mother. The fact that some of the same offending glosses existed in versions of the Bishops' Bible further erodes the narrative that Elizabethan authorities, like James, opposed the Geneva Bible. The Bishops' glossing of

Exodus 1:19, to which James objected, is also hardly different from the Geneva: Exodus 1:15 "King of Egypt" is glossed "Tyrants try divers ways to oppress the Church."[11] Tyrants had not escaped the Bishops' Bible; indeed, the very passage that had offended James in the Geneva Bible is here glossed in the same manner, alluding to words of Peter and the Apostles in Acts 5:29: "It was better to obey God then man," and "He rewardeth their constancy, and not their lying."[12]

Hampton Court was newly frequented by Shakespeare's company "The King's Men," who probably attended the conference, as they had attended the king in red livery on his arrival in London.[13] The first recorded performance of *Measure for Measure* was almost a year later at Whitehall on December 26, 1604, near the beginning of Shakespeare's second season at court, though the first year had been considerably hampered in London by the plague.[14] The ravages of the plague added to the strong religious current in the work of poets who sought patronage under the new king, who had himself written religious verses as well as scripturally informed prose.[15] The Elizabethan courtier and poet John Harington closely watched the rise of King James VI/I and sought to realign his own poetry to suit the new king's interests. In about 1601 he dedicated his manuscript translation of the psalms to James, and in 1602 he sent the king a lantern inscribed with the words originally spoken to Christ on the cross: "Lord, remember me when thou comest into thy kingdom."[16] In April 1603, when James finally had come into his kingdom, Harington was ready to transform his writing for the new king, eschewing his former "sweet wanton" verse: "List he to write or study sacred writ . . . What he commands, I'le act without excuse, / That's full resolved: farewell, sweet wanton Muse!"[17] With similarly religious motivations, Michael Drayton sought laureateship with his *Moses in a Map of his Miracles* (1603), a long poem that uses the life of Moses to reinforce the new king's authority. Many of these poets, like Drayton, responded to James's own expressions of juridical authority in two books on government that circulated prior to his arrival: *The True Law of Free Monarchies* and the *Basilikon Doron*.[18] Shakespeare's biblical play—the first new Shakespearean play before the new king—is thus one of many religiously oriented texts produced in the beginning of James's reign. In addition to new works with religious themes, religiously oriented plays were revived, such as *The Merchant of Venice*, an older play preoccupied by biblical legalism, which was twice performed at Whitehall soon after the court performance of *Measure for Measure*. Each play was performed at significant moments in the liturgical calendar, the new play as part of the Christmas revels, and the older play on Shrove Sunday and then "again commanded by the Kings majesty" on Shrove Tuesday.[19] *Henry V,* an old play that undertakes a lengthy critique of contemporary readings of Romans 13, was also revived for court performance.[20]

The particularly biblical quality of *Measure for Measure*, with a title drawn from scripture and its frequent dramatization of scriptural readings, suggests a more specific orientation than the broadly religious vein of works inaugurating James's kingship. It seems likely, given the chronological proximity, the play's royal audience, and its richly ironic biblical content, that the play responds to James's famous indictment of the Geneva Bible.[21] The cultural response to James's indictment is surprisingly illegible, but it seems hardly possible that its ripple effects are not in effect here and elsewhere. Andrew Fleck has suggested that Aemelia Lanyer's use of the Geneva Bible in *Salve Deus Rex Judaeorum*, published in the same year as the King James Bible but composed in this interim period, is also inflected by anxieties stemming from James's pronouncements.[22] Like Lanyer and most Elizabethans, Shakespeare referred to the Geneva version more than to any other, both in the particular wording of his biblical references, and in his allusions to its accompanying glosses.[23] James's severe words could hardly avoid giving some impression that danger might befall the ubiquitous Bible and perhaps those who possessed it, given Tudor history; fundamentally, the royal pronouncement that the Bible was "seditious," "traitorous," and "dangerous" might have translated into an order to discontinue printing. Yet both the cultural and political effects of James's pronouncements are hard to gauge— there seems to have been smoke without much fire. In 1604 and well after the appearance of the new translation in 1611, Geneva Bibles continued to be produced by the very publisher assigned to the job of printing the King James Version. And though there is record of Archbishop Laud suppressing publication much later, production in the early seventeenth century seems to have decreased according to market demand rather than royal order.[24]

Measure for Measure contains more biblical allusions than any other Shakespearean play, beginning with the eponymous reference to the Sermon on the Mount, and continuing with numerous references that link the events in Shakespeare's Vienna to problems in scriptural interpretation. The play's allusions engage a trend of applied literalism and legalism, in which legislative proposals for the death penalty for adultery—shot down in Parliament in 1584 and 1604— were only part of a larger movement described as "the rise of Protestant legalism."[25] As has been noted in Chapter 3 on Edwardian politics, legalism had already been part of Tudor Protestantism, so that these instances represent more a *return* than a rise, prompted partly in this case by the hopeful puritans (or Presbyterians) at the outset of a Scottish king's reign. Beyond the potential prosecution of sexual crimes such as those dramatized in the play, another grave consequence of the legalistic movement was the promotion of Mosaic law allowing the death penalty for idolatry—represented in the summary execution of several Catholics for heresy at the beginning of James's reign.[26] In a manner of applying biblical code to early modern politics that stems back to Bucer's proposals to Edward VI, puritanical literalists sought to replace English with Mosaic law. As Archbishop Whitgift complained in a sermon before the queen in 1574, "It is now disputed at every table, whether the magistrate be of necessity bound to the judicials of Moses."[27]

A series of scriptural allusions in *Measure for Measure* seems to challenge contemporary hermeneutic habits concerning the application of divine law in a temporal universe. With its many complex biblical references and its fixation on interpreting and administering the law, the play is preoccupied with ways of reading and using the Bible. James was a new Solomon, who, in his popular book *Basilikon Doron*, promoted the office of the monarch as the "administration of justice."[28] As even his use of the title-verse from the Sermon on the Mount indicates, Shakespeare approaches the hermeneutic issues involving the administration of justice on a profoundly scriptural level, often dramatizing the act of biblical citation and interpretation on the stage. In studies of allusion in *The Merchant of Venice* and Marlowe's *Jew of Malta*, Barbara Lewalski and G. K. Hunter have shown the two playwrights to employ (in the words of Lewalski) "patterns of Biblical allusion and imagery so precise and pervasive as to be patently deliberate."[29] Shakespeare's later play exhibits a similarly deliberate effort, with an allusive richness that involves not just the Geneva Bible itself, but also (in at least one instance) its glosses, which, like Marlowe, he employs so as to expose "the fallacy in [the annotator's] handling of the argument."[30]

Studies of the biblical allusions in Shakespeare's plays have listed over thirty in *Measure for Measure*.[31] These references are often subtle and satiric, with a frequently Pauline quality, as in Elbow's satiric echo of Ephesians 5:2–5, "But fornication, & all uncleanness, . . . whoremonger," in his list of crimes: "Fornication, adultery, and all uncleanliness . . . be a whoremonger" (the only use of "whoremonger" in Shakespeare). This chapter will focus on a selection of these allusions, starting with the defense of divine right in Romans 13, central to the structure of the play and to Protestant political theology, in which magistrates are "ministers of God" who "bear not the sword for naught."[32] Unsurprisingly, Romans 13:1–7 is the most commonly referenced biblical passage of this length in all of Shakespeare.[33] The most frequently cited single lines are Matthew 5:44 ("Love your enemies") and Genesis 3:19 ("thou art dust, and to dust shalt thou return"), but this longer section at Romans 13:1–7 appears onstage at least twenty-six times in Shakespeare's dramatic corpus, and it is deeply structural to *Measure for Measure*. Quoted fully in chapters 1 and 2, Paul here claims that all power is "ordained of God," and "Whosoever therefore resisteth the power, resisteth the ordinance of God; and they that resist, shall receive to themselves condemnation." The magistrate or king is "a minister of God to take vengeance on him that doeth evil" (Rom. 13:1–4). This divinely endorsed potential for vengeance has a paradoxical relation to the play's eponymous verse on mercy: "With what measure ye mete, it shall bee measured unto you" (Mark 4:24), one of many of Jesus's teachings that uses chiasmus, a rhetorical figure that dominates Shakespeare's language and even plotting in this play, often with echoes of the so-called Golden Rule: "and as ye would that men should doe to you, so doe ye to them likewise"(Luke 6:31).[34] The play maintains a complex interplay between these lines and Mosaic law in Exodus ("Thou shalt not commit adultery") and the verse paradoxically close to the play's title, the so-called *lex talionis* of Exodus 21:24 ("an eye for an eye"), revoked in Matthew 5:38–42, but nonetheless ever-present in the language of justice. The play connects these passages thematically to two Pauline texts, Romans 9:15–17 and Romans 11:6, central to Reformation explanations of the arbitrary nature of divine mercy. Together, these allusions converge on the issue of how to balance justice and mercy in both temporal and divine applications. They also concern the differences between old and new religion, not just as they appear in the Bible, but as the old and new "religions" that coexisted as a result of recent convulsions in English religious history.

Coordinate with the controversy over legalism evinced in Whitgift's concern about the "judicials of Moses," the word "law" appears far more often in *Measure for Measure* than in any other Shakespearean play. (*The Merchant of Venice*, a distant second, records sixteen instances of "law" to *Measure for Measure*'s twenty-five.)[35] The word is usually used in theologically charged instances, as when the Duke pronounces against Angelo toward the end, "the very mercy of the Law cries out ... death for death ... and *Measure* still for *Measure*" (F 83; 5.1.407–411).[36] But word counts hardly reflect the full extent of legal language in the play, for the subject of law is often addressed without the word, as when Lucio speaks offhandedly of "the Ten Commandments" (1.2.8). Lucio's banter about razing the commandment "thou shalt not steal" (1.2.10), is echoed later in the play when the "fantastical" clownish character says to the Duke-as-Friar a little too presciently that "it was a mad fantastical trick of him to steal from State, and usurp the beggary he was never borne to" (3.2.93–94) in donning the trappings of holiness. "Minister of God," the ironic moment suggests, should only be taken so far. "Steal" suggests "sneak off" as well as break the eighth commandment, and "usurp the beggary" plays ironically on the propriety of the magistrate's appropriation of divinity. The eighth commandment was used in political discourse around questions of a subject's protection from the marauding arms of power, perhaps signified in Angelo's Lucrece-like victim.[37] Like Tarquin in Shakespeare's *Rape of Lucrece*, frequently called a "thief," Angelo becomes an "adulterous thief" (5.1.42), a simultaneous breaker of the commandments he sought to enforce.[38] The extensive treatment of the law in the play registers a cultural anxiety over forms of legalism that reemerged with the uncertainties surrounding the religious settlement at the Stuart accession. As I argue, Shakespeare's ironic treatment of strict literalism and Tyndalean political theology corresponds to the more explicit criticisms of Erasmian contemporaries like Richard Hooker.

Romans 13: Jacobean Readers and Medieval Genres

The centrality of Romans 13 to Tudor and Stuart political thought cannot easily be overstated.[39] Here Paul bids that every "soul be subject unto . . . the powers that bee," and characterizes a civil magistrate as a "minister of God": "For he is the minister of God to take vengeance on him that doeth evil" (13:1–4). King James's own reading of this verse appears centrally in *The True Law of Free Monarchies*. James sets out in *The True Law* "to build" the "true grounds" of government "out of the Scriptures." The king's "office," he writes in a paragraph with fourteen biblical citations in the margin, is "to minister justice and judgment to the people . . . to be the Minister of God . . . and as the minister of God, to take vengeance upon them that do evil [cf. Romans 13]." "And finally," James continues, likening himself to an ecclesiastical leader, "As a good Pastor, to go out and in before his people."[40] In a reading of Romans 13, James points out that the king, "whom *Paul* bids the *Romans Obey* and serve *for conscience sake*, was *Nero* that bloody tyrant, an infamy to his age, and a monster to the world, being also an Idolatrous persecutor." Since such a horrid tyrant "hindered not the spirit of God to command his people under all highest pain to give them all due and hearty obedience for conscience sake" we too must not disobey or resist the rule of even wicked kings.[41] As I have discussed in previous chapters, there was disagreement as to the extent and conditions of obedience. Yet James's politically advantageous reading—what I have been terming "applied literalism," in which present utility overrides the literal and historical—derives from established Protestant traditions.[42]

The nature of James's hermeneutics is central to the larger cultural concern of *Measure for Measure*. Using habits of reading that stem from Tyndale, James applies biblical verses to the contemporary political structure in a way that undergirds his authority. In his reading of Romans 13, the king fuses literalism and historicism, depriving historicism of its power to illuminate the alterity of the past.[43] As discussed in Chapter 2, Erasmus's contextualist historical reading rendered Romans 13 nearly unavailable to early modern Christian princes. Eramus's reading actually had some traction among English Catholics; the English annotator of the Rheims New Testament follows Erasmus in historicizing these verses, arguing that the princes of Paul's time were heathens, and thus the passage should be read differently.[44] Catholic readers, of course, had a more divided allegiance, serving God through obedience to the magistrate and the pope. The merger of holy minister and magistrate in the English Protestant world produced a frequently used image, placed in the front of Tudor Bibles and elsewhere, of the monarch holding the Bible in one hand, as the head of the church, and the "sword of heaven" from Romans 13:4 in the other.[45] This image, used first by Holbein in the Coverdale Bible of 1535 and reused in Foxe and in Edwardian versions, took on a somewhat different form under Elizabeth. The image used in Elizabethan Bibles—especially smaller editions of the Bishops' Bible—placed the two central accoutrements of the sword and the Bible in the hands of allegorical figures that flanked the monarch, rather than having these symbolic implements borne directly as they were by Tudor kings: the sword in the hand of "Justice," and the Bible in hands of "Mercy," with both figures holding the crown over Elizabeth's head (Figure 19). The flanking figures not only freed Elizabeth to hold the orb and scepter, but also placed some distance between her and the instruments of power conferred on her, in the same way that her father's title of "Supreme Head" of the Church of England became "Governor."

Perhaps the most conspicuous use of Romans 13:4 in *Measure for Measure* occurs when the Duke, still dressed as Friar but as himself alone on the stage, alludes to the biblical passage in a preachy soliloquy: "He who the sword of Heaven will bear / Should be as holy as severe" (3.2.261–262). Yet holiness for the Duke exists in opposition to severity. He seems incapable of condemning or of actually using the sword, with the possible exception of the condemnation of Angelo himself, which we will come to. In this monologue before the audience, the Duke's lines play on the theocratic investment in the monarch that had developed since the early stages of the English Church, as when Hugh Latimer

Figure 19. A Bishops' Bible from Queen Elizabeth's household. Signed, "Ann Mashart Russell, her book 1574," and filled in with color, this quarto edition of the Bishops' Bible bears an original armorial binding with Royal Arms. *The Holie Bible* (London: Richard Jugge, 1573), title page, STC 2108. By permission of the Folger Shakespeare Library.

preached that the king was "God's high Vicar in earth," replacing the position formerly held by the Pope: "Long we have been servants and in bondage, serving the Pope in Egypt."[46] The Reformation supported both a literalist approach and a view of civil authority that gave Romans 13 new meaning and emphasis, helped by Tyndale's uncompromising assertion that "scripture hath but one sense which is the literal sense."[47] Still, for Tyndale, allegory was often to be subsumed within a literalist approach: "that which . . . allegory signifieth is ever the literal sense" (156). Particularly when it came to politically oriented hermeneutics, literalism combined with the merger of secular and divine power often lent itself paradoxically to a form of substitution and even allegory, where one thing stands for another, as when Tyndale argues concerning the commandment to obey father and mother: "by father and mother is understood all rulers; which . . . if thou disobey, short life, and shalt either perish by the sword, or by some other plague, and that shortly."[48] To modern readers, Tyndale's scripture in fact has two senses, one of which is a kind of allegory or substitution: "by father and mother" we must understand "all rulers."

In Tudor and Stuart ideology, even scripture not specifically related to civil matters was often co-opted to reinforce civil obedience in an applied hermeneutic gesture like Tyndale's. Such a reading occurs in the *Homilie against Disobedience*, for example: "We read in the Book of Deuteronomy," the homily preaches in one instance, "that all punishment pertaineth to God by this sentence: Vengeance is mine, and I will reward (Deut. 32:35)." When the homily interprets this verse, it seems even to contradict itself in asserting a divine exclusivity that pertains also to monarchs. "*All* punishment pertaineth to God," it insists, but at the same time "we must understand" the verse "to pertain also to the magistrates, which do exercise God's room in judgment."[49] Like Tyndale's "is understood," the homily insists on a clarity that is not entirely evident. The homily reverses the exclusivity of the Bible: even though "*all* punishment pertaineth to God," readers and auditors are to add an assumed meaning: God, *and the magistrates*. The homily's contention that "magistrates exercise God's room in judgment" reinforces the degree to which placing the king at the head of the church effects the exclusion of magistrates from the dictum "judge not" in the gospel.

Shakespeare's enigmatic drama questions the problem of appropriation suggested in James's reading of Romans 13 and in the literal-but-allegorical mode of political hermeneutics, exposing the contradictions between literalist claims and allegorical practices in Protestant political theology. The play's allegorical form, combined with its ironic scriptural allusiveness, registers a systemic problem with the way English culture sought to legitimate not only its forms of domination but also its legal and moral strictures. In the same way that Latimer layered the new Protestant theocratic state over an older form of allegiance—king over pope— Shakespeare layers a Protestant political problem over the plot structure of an older allegorical genre, the morality play; indeed, "moral" plays are listed among the more modern genres in the royal warrant given Shakespeare's company soon after James's arrival in London,[50] and *Everyman*, the only printed medieval morality play, defines itself as a "moral play" in its introduction.[51]

Many scholars have explored Shakespeare's relationship with the drama of the late middle ages, showing that Shakespearean playgoers would have been sensitive to homiletic modes of expression from this still active form of representation.[52] The protagonist's experience of facing death with pastoral assistance in *Measure for Measure* follows the plot structure of the morality play, such as *Mankind* and many similar soteriological narratives in medieval art and literature. *Everyman* was one of the most available of such narratives, as it was reprinted at least four times in the sixteenth century. *Measure for Measure* follows the medieval plot structure, in which a man faces the prospect of death and is confronted in that journey by priestly characters, friends, and malfeasants. In addition to the plot structure, the allegorical characters and occasionally the language bear a close resemblance. The Duke-as-Friar's "thou art death's fool" speech to Claudio while he awaits death invokes the Catholic genre as it provocatively interrogates the Protestant magistrate-as-minister. The irony of a friar who is actually a ruler telling a condemned man who is not actually condemned to "be absolute for death" seems to vex the English Church's merger of minister and monarch.[53] The scene evokes the priestly visitation before death, which formally would involve the rite of absolution, ironically hinted at in the advice that Claudio "be absolute." The Duke-as-Friar's speech features a personified Death, and encapsulates the morality's plot structure: "For him [Death] thou labour'st by thy flight to shun, / And yet runn'st toward him still" (3.1.11–12). In the guise of a friar, the Duke tells the condemned man, "Thou bearest thy heavy riches but a journey, / And death unloads thee; Friend hast thou none" (3.1.27–28). The description uses a set of allegorized concepts (Death, Riches, and Friend) that follow the very progress in the "journey" of *Everyman*, which frequently uses the term "journey" to represent the pilgrimage to death. Later, in another visitation, the disguised Duke-as-Friar insists that the condemned Barnardine—Claudio's comic foil—"must die" in language and metrical cadences that evoke the homiletic genre: "therefore I beseech you / Look forward on the journey you shall go" (4.3.57–58). "Haste thee lightly that you were gone the journey," says Death to Everyman, "And prove thy friends if thou can."

Shakespeare transposes the morality genre to question the Jacobean connection of divine and earthly law. Instead of God, a "Duke," God-like, both in his "power divine" and in his power over the plot, sends his messenger "Angelo" to condemn men for the same reason as God does in the earlier morality play, and in the same language: his "law" is no longer "feared." The allegorical name Angelo—an Angel or deputy of God—shows a debt to the morality tradition. Shakespeare's language echoes that of *Everyman* in this deputizing moment between the lord and his substitute, using the same key words "law" and "fear," and "rod." God reflects before calling his deputy Death in the early play, "They fear not my rightwiseness, the sharp rod. / My law that I showed" (*Everyman*, 28–29), and the Duke sends for Angelo to "enforce, or qualify the Laws" (F 61; 1.1.65), because the "rod" has become "more mock'd" than "fear'd" (F 63; 1.3.26–27). The medieval genre is conspicuously Protestantized in the way it construes "works of the law," which structured the theodicy of this Catholic genre.

As the God-like Duke confers authority upon his surrogate, he acknowledges the theatrical nature of his kingship, complaining:

> I love the people,
> But doe not like to stage me to their eyes:
> Though it doe well, I do not relish well
> Their loud applause, and Aves vehement. (1.1.67–70)

Although he protests being put on "stage" and dislikes "applause," the Duke views the role of ruler as an actor in a performance of statecraft. As J. W. Lever has pointed out, the Duke's self-presentation echoes a description of James in his entry into London by Gilbert Dugdale, a collaborator with Shakespeare's Clown Robert Armin, in a pamphlet that also mentions that the "Kings actors" attended him. This pamphlet insists on the King's "love" to the people, even when he wishes for their silence.[54] Shakespeare thus seems to mirror personal aspects of James's rule in his depictions of leadership in this play. Earlier in the same speech, the Duke deputizes his power to Angelo in terms that derive from culturally reinforced biblical language. He tells Angelo:

> In our remove, be thou at full, our self.
> Mortality and Mercy in *Vienna*
> Live in thy tongue, and heart.   (F 61; 1.1.43–45)

The opposition of "Mortality" and "Mercy," capitalized in the original, neatly corresponds to the opposed accoutrements of the sword and Bible, or of Justice and Mercy, in such paratexts as the Queen's image in the Bishops' Bibles. The ruler functions like God, and as a staged or—in Angelo's case—*substitute* God, and like the character of God in an allegorical play. The Duke's high-handed declaration that he "elected him [i.e., Angelo] our absence to supply," evokes the Calvinist language of predestination central to the theology of both the Church of England and nonconformists in 1604.[55] The Duke imagines his political play generically as a morality play, organized around questions of judgment and the threat of death, and yet many of the lessons of the medieval play are no longer possible. Indeed, a stark contrast from Catholic interpretations of Romans 13 occurs in a passage in *Everyman* that could never have been performed before a Protestant monarch: "there is no Emperor, King, Duke, ne Baron, / That of God hath commission, / As hath the least priest in the world being" (*Everyman*, 713–715).

Shakespeare's generic layering occasions many deliberate dissonances, such as the constant irony of the friar who is actually a ruler usurping the beggary he was never born to. But the dissonances register on a deeper, more structural level, in which the allegorical form of the homiletic tradition is used to expose the problem of divine substitution and, by extension, the problem of scriptural appropriation that permeated Protestant political theology. Angelo is an allegorical figure who fails to live up to his name; he is only "Angel on the outward side" (F 74; 3.2.265). The allegorical substitute borrows the garment of divinity itself; he obtains power just as a monarch receives power from God: the Duke has "lent" the substitute "our terror" (cf. Rom. 13:3–5), "drest him with our love" (F 61; 1.1.19). This exchange reenacts not just the substitution of one man's place for another, but the substitution of one system of belief (religious) for another (political).

In its numerous instances of verbal, biblical, and character substitutions, Shakespeare's play criticizes a central problem that arises from the appropriative hermeneutics of English political theology. *Measure for Measure*, which uses the word "substitute" more than any other Shakespearean drama, is a play of substitutes, whose very abundance allegorizes the hermeneutics of substitution, provoking audiences to ask whether the monarch really is "heaven's substitute," as Gaunt calls Richard II, "his deputy anointed in his sight," or is inappropriately and even deleteriously held so.[56] The play's many substitutions—Angelo for the Duke, the Duke for the Friar, Mariana for Isabella, Barnardine for Claudio, "death for death," and measure for measure—question the appropriateness of substitution itself, as well as the procrustean hermeneutics that follow from a monarch's claim to be heaven's substitute.

Here it is worth pausing for a moment to consider the strangeness of the play's ironic criticism of Jacobean political theology (at least as I am arguing), given especially that this is an early play for the new king. Shakespeare's career had undergone a major promotion when he became the playwright for the King's Men, but becoming a "patronage dramatist" does not necessarily mean that he consigned himself to suiting the ideological needs of the court.[57] The King's Men had already been involved in a confrontational court production in 1603, *Sejanus, His Fall*, which led to Ben Jonson's appearance before the Privy Council on charges of "popperie and treason."[58] The tonal similarities between these two plays' treatment of political authority is reinforced by the fact that they are products of the same repertory, with Shakespeare even listed among the actors that performed *Sejanus*.[59] Another play, *Sir Thomas More*, might be considered in this context, since it is self-conscious about medieval literary history and similar in Shakespeare's use of Romans 13, a passage that pervades and structures *Measure for Measure*; the old play was arguably revised by Shakespeare and others—after being censored a decade before—around 1603.[60] The ironic treatment of politics in other plays performed in or around 1604, such as George Chapman's *Bussy D'Ambois* and Samuel Daniel's *Philotas*—which brought Daniel before the Privy Council—illustrate how much darkly ironic, confrontational theater was in vogue in the year after the king's accession.[61]

Romans 9–11: Predestination and the Law of the "Demy-god"

The substitution of divine for earthly justice becomes particularly problematic in the predestined universe of Shakespeare's Protestant England. For if a magistrate is really a resemblance of God, then how would civil condemnation and punishment correspond to the inexplicable justice of heaven? The complex picture of predestination in *Measure for Measure* may respond to an increased debate at the time. It was at the Hampton Court conference that anti-Calvinism and the question of predestination first received "an airing on a national level,"[62] though it had previously been more subtly disputed.[63] As Lake has demonstrated, the ostensible uniformity of opinion in part derives from "an effective system of censorship" that "prevented the appearance of anti-Calvinist opinions" in the 1590s.[64] Perhaps the most important allusion in the play to the Pauline chapters "On Predestination" occurs in a long speech on the arbitrary nature of authority by the newly condemned. In his first appearance on stage, Claudio, who is not at least in spirit guilty of the wrong the law has charged him with, is by a "special charge" of Angelo led by chains through the streets to prison. After he inveighs briefly against the injustice of his condition, he observes,

> Thus can the demy-god (Authority)
> Make us pay down, for our offense, by weight
> The words of heaven: on whom it will, it will,
> On whom it will not (so) yet still 'tis just.   (F 62; 1.2.120–123)

Like Isabella, who speaks frequently about "Authority" in the abstract, Claudio levels his protest not merely at Angelo, but at Authority itself, and especially its culturally legitimated deification. The Arden notes suggest that "no sarcasm need be inferred" in Claudio's words: "'Demi-god' . . . follows the Elizabethan commonplace . . . that rulers and judges had the attributes of gods."[65] But the passage needs to be understood in precisely the opposite fashion, especially as Claudio goes on to suggest this "Authority" is tyrannical and possibly fraudulent (1.2.158–164). This description of secular authority as a "Demy-god" does not passively reflect a dominant political discourse, but subtly registers its hypocrisy.

The irony of this passage works in even more subtle ways, for, in describing authority, Claudio alludes to a biblical verse on the nature of divine justice. Many editions, such as the Oxford, erroneously emend the original text's "words of heaven" to "bonds of heaven,"[66] a correction that overlooks the fact that Claudio is literally referring to "words of heaven" in the Bible, God's words to Moses in Exodus 33:19, which Paul interprets in Romans 9:15–17: "For he saith to Moses, I will have mercy on him, to whom I will show mercy: and will have compassion on him, on whom I have compassion. So it is not in him that willeth, nor in him that runneth, but in God that showeth mercy." As Brian Cummings has shown, Romans 9:15–17 is a central proof text for Protestants wishing to confirm Luther's predestinarian theology behind the *sola fida* reading of Paul. Paul is arguing here that justification "depends not on man's will or exertion, but upon God's mercy" (Rom. 9:16), and yet this still should not dissuade believers from the notation of a just God.[67] Claudio's words "On whom it will, it will" meaningfully omit the key word "mercy" from two biblical passages in a way that draws attention to its absence, suggesting that the Demy-god, secular authority, shows mercy (or, in this case, only punishment) to his subjects for reasons hidden to human understanding. Claudio's parody of political appropriation of scripture is particularly significant because the verse describes for

Calvinists a predestinarian God. For Reformation theologians, the words "it is not in him that willeth" meant that no active will could earn God's favor. The connection of this theology to secular authority, however, suggests a logical flaw in political theology.[68] For when this model of God's justice, in which the distribution of mercy does not conform to the ordinary logic of ethics, is transplanted onto the political world, then secular justice is also incapable of being influenced or explained.[69] The dubious justice of an arbitrary demigod is suggested in Claudio's ironic words of resignation: "yet still 'tis just."

Claudio's ironic resignation seems to allude, in fact, to an attempt by Genevan annotators to assert that God's arbitrary mercy *is* still just, though it may seem otherwise. For Luther and Calvin, Paul's words, "so it is not in him that willeth" invalidated the Catholic doctrine of free will.[70] A clear view of the "controversy" over these verses may be found in the "confutations" of the Rheims Bible, whose note on Romans 9:16 reads, "we may not with Heretickes inferre, that man hath not free will, or that, our will worketh nothing in our conversion or comming to God."[71] Romans 9:15–18 supported the idea of the arbitrary nature of God's gift of grace—apparent in the words "I will have mercy on him to whom I will." For Calvinists, God's decision was immutable: some are saved and others not. Yet the Reformation's popularizers, such as the Geneva annotators, did not want this arbitrary God to seem unjust. The annotations labor voluminously to defend the "just" though arbitrary distribution of God's mercy. Thus, Claudio's biblical words "on whom it will [show mercy], it will," are glossed:

> [Paul] answereth first touching them which are chosen to salvation: in the choosing of whom he denieth that God *may seem unjust*, although he choose and predestinate to salvation them that are not yet born, without any respect of worthiness: because he bringeth not the chosen to the appointed end, but by the means of his mercy, which is a cause next under predestination. . . . Now all these things orderly following the purpose of God, do clearly prove that he can by no means *seem unjust* in loving and saving his.[72]

The annotator's insistence without argument that that the words of heaven "do clearly prove that he can by no means seem unjust" betrays an inability to show how the arbitrary gift of mercy is, as Claudio says, "still just." Claudio's words subtly mock this enigmatic theology, but indict even more strongly its troublesome application to the arbitrary ways of secular authority. His earnest but allusive confusion parodies Protestant political theology and the appropriative hermeneutics of applied literalism. According to the logic of this common hermeneutic trend, justice on earth (like that in heaven) must be administered by demigods. If the likeness between God and king is taken too far, Claudio's irony suggests, a magistrate's judgments may have little or no relation to a subject's actual moral behavior.

Claudio's allusion to Romans 9:15 comes from a larger set of chapters, Romans 9–11, which are given the title "Of Predestination" in the 1602 Geneva Bible, showing their importance to Reformation theology. Some of the instability of belief can be seen in the wildly differing interpretations of a set of biblical verses in *Measure for Measure* among English readers. Annotations in the Catholic Rheims translation affirm the wickedness of this interpretive position with annotations on "*The heretikes writings of Predestination*" (Rom. 11).[73] Lucio alludes to this section of Romans after he invokes the Ten Commandments in the second scene, where he makes a provocative statement about religious "controversy." His statement, "Grace, is Grace, despite of all controversy" (F 62; 1.2.24–25), responds to the Gentleman's rejoinder, "in any Religion" (1.2.23)—by which is surely implied forms of Christianity, the "three religions," as one polemicist put it, "known commonly in England": "Protestants, Puritans, and Papists."[74] Reaching beyond context and character, Lucio's comment voices the ecumenical contention—shared, in fact, by Hooker—that grace might be found in "any Religion."[75]

What is still more remarkable about this passage is its complex use of biblical allusion to drive home the point. "Grace is grace" alludes to the arbitrary distribution of grace in Romans 11:6: "And if [Election] be of grace it is no more of works: or else were grace no more grace." Beyond the divisiveness of religious "controversy," rejected in Lucio's insistence that grace is grace, the controversy about this line lies in the question of just how Paul meant to value works, suggested in the Calvinist bias of the Geneva note: "election of grace is, not whereby men chose grace, but whereby God chose us of his grace and goodness." Lucio's words can be read as a mildly dismissive allusion to one of the verses upon which Reformation theology based its claim to an exclusive grace, earned without good works. The "controversy" in these lines is richly recorded in the annotations to the Rheims Bible, and in the aforementioned "confutations" to these same annotations, which demonstrate the vitality of hermeneutic dispute in English culture. As noted in the previous chapter, the English Catholic translation sparked a series of detailed attacks by William Fulke, George Wither, and Thomas Cartwright.[76] Fulke and Cartwright produced extraordinary Bibles with multilayered annotations and counter-annotations (Catholic notes and

Protestant confutations). "Take heed here of the Heretics exposition," the Catholic notes advise, "that untruly exclude Christian men's works." One refuter replies, "The apostle speaketh of the election by grace by which all are saved, therefore he excludeth the merit of all works."[77] Lucio's dismissive "Grace, is Grace" may be seen in this light, as it undermines the attempts of English Calvinism to make grace dependent on only one biblical reading, or on only one salvific model.[78] The two critical allusions to Romans 11 and Romans 9 in Lucio's and Claudio's speeches, respectively, also help to affirm Lake's tentative suggestion that *Measure for Measure* is not merely anti-puritan but more broadly skeptical of the Calvinism that had dominated the English Church.[79]

The Paradoxes of Biblical Legalism

A passing comment by Muriel Bradbrook offers unexpected insight into *Measure for Measure*'s relationship to late-medieval allegorical drama. According to Bradbrook, the play resembles "the late medieval Morality. It might be named The Contention between Justice and Mercy, or False Authority unmasked by Truth and Humility."[80] Bradbrook's imagined titles pinpoint the play's central homiletic concerns. But the play's actual title more subtly reveals Shakespeare's perspective on the relation of justice and mercy, as derived from biblical precepts and precedents. The irony in Shakespeare's use of the biblical verse in its title is seldom fully appreciated. One reader who takes it into account is Harold Bloom, who offers another alternative title, "Shakespeare should have called the play *Like for Like*, but he chose not to forgo his hidden blasphemy of the Sermon of the Mount, just sufficiently veiled to escape his own regime's frightening version of the law of the talion."[81] Although Shakespeare's evident irony supports Bloom's view of the playwright's fundamental skepticism, it seems more probable that the blasphemy lies not with the playwright but with those he criticizes. The phrase "measure for measure," though it echoes the so-called *lex talionis* (an eye for an eye) derives from the doctrine of mercy in the New Testament that sought, at least in its own representation, to supersede that law. The reciprocity intended in the New Testament phrase is of giving, rather than taking away: "Be ye therefore merciful, as your father also is merciful . . . condemn not and ye shall not be condemned: forgive, and ye shall be forgiven. Give, and it shall be given unto you: a good measure, pressed down, shaken together and running over shall men give into your bosom: for with what measure ye mete, with the same shall men mete to you again" (Luke 6:36–38).

The phrase "measure for measure" was alive in a proverbial usage whose re-taliatory sense may not always have been conscious of its irony.[82] Shakespeare, however, deliberately evokes an ironic dissonance between the proverbial retal-iatory sense and the biblical doctrine of mercy.[83] Indeed, his use of the phrase "measure for measure" in his new Jacobean play seems a retrospective glance toward the biblical distortions of one of his earliest villains, Richard III, who would clothe his "naked villainy / With odd old ends, stol'n forth of Holy Writ" (*Richard III*, F 179; 1.3.335–336), and who, "with a piece of Scripture," convinced the world that "God bids us do good for evil" (1.3.333–334). In *3 Henry VI*, the very words "measure for measure" are used to confound, rather than support, the doctrine of mercy. "Revoke that doom of mercy," says Richard ironically on the battlefield, a sword paused in an uncertain moment of clemency. "For 'tis *Clifford*," and Clifford took the life of "our Princely Father." Warwick agrees. Clifford's life must be taken: in a literal exchange of head for head, "Measure for measure, must be answered" (F 157; 2.6.46, 55). As Richard boasts, "piece[s] of scripture" are used here for purposes counter to their intended meaning: the doc-trine of mercy is invoked perversely to support the practice of revenge.

When the Duke invokes the same loose wording of Luke some years after its appearance in *3 Henry VI*, he employs the dark irony of Richard and War-wick, and thus in this brief moment in *Measure for Measure*, the Duke's politics are associated with the Machiavellian Bible-stealing of these early villains. His stilted invocation presents "measure for measure" not as a *revoked* doom of mercy but the "very mercy of the Law." Yet there is no "mercy" in the Duke's law. Like Richard and Warwick, he invokes the biblical injunction against con-demnation to support his condemnation of a man:

> The very mercy of the Law cries out
> Most audible, even from his proper tongue.
> An *Angelo* for *Claudio*, death for death:
> Haste still pays haste, and leisure, answers leisure;
> Like doth quit like, and *Measure* still for *Measure*
> . . .
> We doe condemn thee . . .   (F 83; 5.1.407–414)

The Duke's pronouncement against Angelo, "We do condemn thee," draws on the biblical passage in which Jesus forbids precisely that: "condemn not." The irony is that this is not the law of mercy, or even the "very mercy of the Law," but a law of requital. At this late point in the drama, the title's troubled relationship to mercy underscores a recurrent issue: something is wrong with the way the Bible is used. The character of the Duke—who until now has been unable to condemn even the condemned—reverses the law of mercy even as he invokes it. The Duke's usurping of the holy text places his moral authority into a doubt that is allayed only by the larger dramatic irony, the audience's knowledge that Claudio is not actually dead. His misuse of scripture is driven home by Mariana's and Isabella's entreaties for true mercy that follow, which make his pronouncements seem a mere exercise in retributive justice. A deliberately distorted form of New Testament language on mercy paradoxically expresses the spirit of revenge. "Measure for measure" is a distortion of a proverb from a culture that seems partially aware of its incapacity to absorb supposed doctrine. The Duke's pronouncement of this misread biblical text as the "Law" suggests, with the other dramatized moments of biblical appropriation, a fundamental misuse of biblical law in the construction of political theology.

The strained hermeneutic habits of Shakespeare's contemporaries derive in part from the literalist inclinations of Protestantism that paradoxically work against its very anti-legalistic roots. In many ways, Protestantism defined itself as a movement against legalism. Luther's doctrine of justification by faith alone denied the importance of law; he added the word *allein* (making the phrase "justification by faith *alone*") to Romans 3:28 because he felt that German could not capture the meaning of the Greek without it: "we hold that a person is justified by faith [alone] apart from works prescribed by the law."[84] The anti-legalism of Protestantism had its political applications, as well. Luther reputedly advised Henry VIII, for example, that "Moses is nothing to us."[85] James counsels his son in *Basilikon Doron*—apropos of "measure for measure"—not to be involved in a duel, for in such a private exchange of deaths "there is no warrant in the Scripture, since the abrogating of the old Law."[86]

It is precisely on this score that the most central irony of *Measure for Measure* has a timely cultural significance, for English Calvinists who should in theory have abrogated the law at times became almost obsessed with it, as the play's ironic merger of the so-called *lex talionis* with the doctrine of mercy suggests.[87] The characters on death row for sexual crimes are prosecuted, significantly, by the "precise" Angelo (F 63; 1.3.50), "precise" being a term used to describe puritans.[88] Bishop Whitgift had complained that Cartwright "bindeth the civil Magistrate to the observing of the judicial law of Moses, and condemneth this state . . . of manifest impiety," when the laws of Moses were abrogated, or simply not applicable in the early modern political world. Yet stricter Protestants and puritans like Thomas Cartwright argued in contrast that it is absurd to use such passages as "our Savior's refusal to condemn this woman taken in Adultery" to argue against this and other Mosaic laws, such as those against "thieves": "the Adulterer ought of necessity to be put to death." This is why the "Apostle [in Romans 13] putteth a sword in the hand of the Magistrate."[89] It was not Calvin and Luther, but the north-going reformers, such as Bucer, that pushed for a Mosaic legal system. Much of the Church hegemony followed Calvin in thinking that Mosaic political rule was not merely contrary to New Testament doctrine, but "most absurd," "perilous," "seditious," "false" and "stupid."[90] Yet, following the logic of *sola scriptura* and applied literalism still further than other Protestants, many English puritans sought to make English law harmonize with Mosaic law. As Whitgift complained, Cartwright "bindeth the civil magistrate to the observing of the judicial laws of Moses" in a way that is "most absurd, and contrary to all those places of scripture that teach us the abrogation of the law."[91] So, in spite of a flat dismissal of legalism among some Protestants, among the more rigorously literalist (perhaps tending toward fundamentalist) it came to represent the very meaning of reform.

The attempt to make Mosaic law commensurate with the law of a Christian state stemmed, in part, from the *sola scriptura* method of searching for biblical precedent—of purifying tradition with scripture—that is central to Protestantism. But paradoxically scripture *alone* leads easily to scripture extended and even allegorized, for when a culture seeks to put scripture into the service of the state, it must mean more than it intends literally. Tyndale, though not a full-blown legalist like Bucer, employs the Ten Commandments to a political end. Tyndale's seemingly strained appropriation of Mosaic law in "by father and mother is understood all rulers" combines hermeneutic trends and political theology that coexist in a normative though difficult relationship. As shown in Chapter 2, the Fifth Commandment was often used to substantiate the law of obedience, and it is one of many ways Mosaic law is figured in political discourse.[92] This appropriation of scripture derives from a hermeneutics bent on making scripture—and scripture alone—provide the rules for living. The construction of a legal and political system on the bedrock of scripture follows the Protestant practice of searching the scripture to replace what were felt to be false belief systems created by tradition or invention. "God's law is perfect and entire," as Bucer wrote in a passage cited in Chapter 3, "and its teaching enables us to conform the whole of life to the will of God. Wherefore Scripture is bound to contain oracles to deal definitely . . . with every aspect of public or private life."[93] For many theologians and political writers, scripture functioned as a necessary proof text for all social and political codes.

As Simpson's work on English fundamentalism in early Tudor England has shown, deep rifts emerged in English habits of reading and the theology that derived from them.[94] The rigorous literalism in Elizabethan England evoked a similar opposition. In *The Laws of Ecclesiastical Polity* (1594–1597), for example, Hooker is perhaps even more concerned with ways of reading than he is with belief itself. Hooker's work frames itself against the strict Genevan Calvinism found in Cartwright. "Because ye suppose," Hooker writes, "the laws for which ye strive are found in scripture; but those not, against which ye strive; and upon this surmise are drawn to hold it as the very main pillar of your whole cause, that *scripture ought to be the only rule of all our actions.*"[95] Instead, Hooker radically suggests, "Precepts comprehended in the law of nature, may be otherwise known then only by scripture" (188)—in short, *sola scriptura* must not be taken too far or too literally. Significantly, Hooker is essentially taking Thomas More's argument against Tyndale—or indeed Erasmus's position against the Protestants. More wrote against Tyndale, a bit less gently, ""For first he would make the people believe that we should believe nothing but plain scripture in which point he teacheth a plain pestilent heresy."[96] For Hooker, the hermeneutics of strict adherence may limit the scope of moral understanding. Not all laws, even laws concerning church government, can be found in scripture.[97] In offering a different hermeneutic method, Lake observes, "Hooker was attempting to lead his opponents step by step to a position rather different from the austere biblicalism with which they had entered the debate," and, in doing so, "he was attacking more than the epistemological underpinning of presbyterianism."[98] From different angles, Shakespeare and Hooker represent a larger concern with the problems of strict biblicalism. Considering the longer view of this project, it is worth considering the tensions between Tyndalean literalism and Erasmianism at play here. As Dodds has pointed out, "Erasmus remains the most complete antecedent to Hooker's thought."[99] Erasmus continued to enable, through a major (though not always representative) theologian of the English Church, a critique of strict and strictly applied Protestant literalism.

Early in *Measure for Measure* the idea of law is introduced in both juridical and biblical registers. In the opening of scene one, Angelo is commissioned "to enforce, or qualify the Laws / As to [his] soul seems good" (1.1.65–66), which addresses juridical administration in conspicuously religious language. The Duke's instructions engage a central concern of Protestant theology: that the interpretation of law must correspond to the stirring of the soul. A more specific religious use of the law appears in the comic scene that follows, when Lucio, who often speaks beyond character and context, bursts out, apropos of nothing, "thou conclud'st like the Sanctimonious Pirate, that went to sea with the ten Commandments" (F 62; 1.2.7–8). The formal opening assigning Angelo to enforce the law, followed by comic banter—"'twas a commandment, to command" (1.2.12)—helps to establish a sustained inquiry into the nature of the application of divine law to the mercy and justice of the temporal universe.

The problem of enforcing the law expresses itself most grossly when Angelo tries to force himself upon Isabella, where he proposes that she could through extorted sex "fetch your Brother from the Manacles / Of the all-building-Law" (F 69; 2.4.93–94), which editors emend to avoid the mixed metaphor, following Johnson, to "all-binding law." This is a difficult textual crux, and certainly "binding" makes sense as an emendation, in part because the Latin sense of "strict" as "bound" still inhered in legal discourse; "binding" was thus frequently used in relation to law and Mosaic law. Yet Shakespeare was hardly averse to mixed metaphor, especially when a character is in a heightened emotional condition (Hamlet's "taking arms against a sea of troubles"), and the mixed metaphor would still carry the meaning of a "binding" law through "manacles." Since *Measure for Measure* happens to be an exceptionally clean text in the original, there may be good reasons to yield to the editorial principle that prefers the *difficilior lectio*, the more difficult reading in the text itself, and explore the possibilities of the Folio wording. Some obvious care was taken in representing this phrase typographically with hyphenated connectors and capital letters, and the change from "building" to "binding" isn't just one of flipping a letter and letter order, but also adding a letter.

The mixed metaphor may attempt to represent Angelo's contorted adherence to law in both juridical and scriptural registers. As Donne wrote, "The Holy Ghost seems to have delighted in the Metaphore of *Building*."[100] In Galatians 2:16–19, Paul explains the idea of living by faith instead of by the letter of the law: "Know that man is not justified by works of the Law. . . . For if I build again the things that I have destroyed, I make myself a trespasser. For I through the Law am dead to the Law." Paul uses "building" in the sense of building the law back again that has been destroyed through the gospel: building the law is thus to misuse it, to become a literalist. William Perkins, a widely read English theologian, wrote in a *Commentary on the Galatians* in 1604 that "By *things destroyed*, Paul means the works, or the justice of the law," and thus, "He that builds the justice of the law which he hath destroyed, is a Minister of sin, or makes himself a sinner."[101] Angelo's "all-building-Law," in a play in which Shakespeare makes several fraught allusions to this theological problem, describes the way in which Angelo is embracing precisely what he ought not to embrace. He has kept the law alive: "The Law hath not bin dead, though it hath slept" (F 67; 2.2.91); he is unable to be guided through living merely by the law, and he is unable to resist his own inward corruption.

Whether it is "building" or "binding," Angelo's obsession with the Law touches distinctly on the contemporary controversy concerning Mosaic legalism. As suggested, not just between Protestantism and Catholicism, but among various Protestantisms were there vastly divergent ways of treating the law. Edwin Sandys told Bullinger, for example, that "the judicial laws of Moses are binding upon Christian princes, and they ought not in the slightest degree to depart from them." Yet, as Whitgift complained, the question was still debated at "every table." Part of the cause for these conflicting opinions lay in the problem of interpreting the mandate of *sola scriptura*: whether to emphasize Mosaic law or the Pauline emphasis on abrogated law. In light of these conflicting opinions, Angelo's "all-binding" or "all-Building-Law," in a play in which Shakespeare makes several fraught allusions to this theological problem, reveals a man too focused on, and corrupted by, outward adherence to the law.

In a sense, the play is preoccupied with hermeneutics even more, perhaps, than it is with ethics. It is a play about the misuse of the Bible, but also about the role of the biblical text in determining questions of social and political justice. The central problem in this play revolves around the supposed sexual crime of Claudio and Juliet, committed in the gray area between a private "true contract" and the public "denunciation" of "outward order" (1.2.134, 139). Similar sexual crimes work as foils, including the true crime that Angelo does or thinks he does in having sex with Mariana, Lucio's getting of "wench with child," and the act committed by Elbow's wife, who was "respected with him before he married with her" (2.1.169). These adulterous acts set Claudio's sexual "crime" in relief, lending even greater uncertainty to the question of what constitutes a sexual crime in the eyes of heaven or in the eyes of the law. And if the outward sacrament of marriage (in whatever form) were in itself sufficient to patch up the crime of sex (wanted or unwanted), then Isabella might simply agree to marry the man who proposes to her, as does her counterpart Cassandra in the source play.

Shakespeare's ironic allegorical play grapples with the paradox of legalism in a world in which some held tenaciously to the law, even when a central argument in Luther's protest lay in privileging faith to the exclusion of law. In this play about judgment, a play that formally borrows from its medieval predecessors, Shakespeare affirms that no legal system can substitute for what is in spirit good. The play's theological vocabulary cannot be easily appropriated by the recent view of Shakespeare as an adherent of the Old Faith.[102] Although there is much hidden here in the elusive recesses of theologically well-informed language and allusion, what is hidden does not seem to carry a Catholic doctrinal commitment or a recusant agenda. At the same time, a deep ecumenical skepticism seems to motivate the play's ironic representations of the habits of Protestant hermeneutics. On a general level, the new king's England is portrayed as a culture of self-contradiction, where one can refer to the law of mercy and yet stand for *lex talionis*. More specifically, *Measure for Measure* seems intent on exposing the structural contradictions in English biblical culture, which on the one hand invokes the power of the spirit over the law, while on the other hand it seeks the institution of Mosaic law as a "property of Government." This treatment of legalism may, as Lake has argued, operate as an "exercise in anti-puritanism"[103] in the early days of the new reign when the nature of the Jacobean religious settlement remained unclear. Yet the play's biblical paradoxes also suggest a broader concern with the appropriating and even allegorizing tendencies of Protestant hermeneutics, particularly with the more orthodox style of applied literalism involved in legitimating political authority.

*   *   *

After King James had declared that there should be a new Bible, it took some seven years to produce it, and several more before the same publisher stopped producing the Geneva Bible at the same time. But by the time Milton began using the King James Bible in the mid-seventeenth century, it had established dominance. Unlike the "Geneva Bible," which seems to have been called such early—one sermonizer speaks affectionately of "our Geneva *Bible*,"[104] for example, in 1608—the King James Version or King James Bible is a modern way to refer to what was simply termed things like "our New Translation"—if it was termed anything other than the Bible—in the mid-seventeenth century. Milton treats the KJV translation as if it is what everyone is reading; when he takes issue with a particular translation, for example, it is never in reference to another established version—as is true of readers like Donne, Hobbes, or Filmer, the generation that lived through the transition.[105] As I discuss in the following chapters, Milton expects readers to know that whatever quibble he has with *the* English translation is a quibble with the King James Version.[106] In the Civil War period, puritans did take an interest in the Geneva notes, even going so far at the outbreak of the Civil War as to create a King James Bible with Geneva notes in Amsterdam, a strange hybrid recreated in London after Charles's execution.[107]

Yet the King James Version was not only widely acknowledged as "the best translation in the world,"[108] in the words of Milton's admired older contemporary John Selden, but a market success as both a reading Bible and a church Bible.

Source studies have traditionally asked the question *what*—what did Shakespeare, or, as we turn to him, Milton, really read? In thinking about the early modern reception of the Bible, it is of course vital that we consider what they read, or what parts of the Bible they read with particular attention, or indeed, as I have sought to suggest in this book, what social controversies brought particular biblical readings into the sphere of cultural discourse. But it is also as vital that we ask *how* they read; that is, not just asking whether Shakespeare or Milton read one Bible or another, with particular interest in certain passages, but rather how, in what ways, and with what culturally reinforced habits and practices, did these writers read? As with so many topics, Shakespeare seems more elusive than either Spenser before him or Milton after him—perhaps with that *"Negative Capability"*[109] that Keats observed, he seems more intent on exposing the hypocrisy of his literalist contemporaries than asserting a particular reading. But as we turn to Milton, the picture becomes clearer, in part because we have an unusually large archive of material attesting to the many different forms of scripture that Milton read, and we also have an exceptional archive for understanding *how* Milton read. This archive includes not only his descriptions of reading and of his own practice, but also his own King James Bible, marked and extensively used, which is still extant.

CHAPTER 7

Milton's Bible and
Revolutionary Psalm Culture

[The King] borrows *Davids* Psalmes, . . .

Had he borrow'd *Davids* heart, it had bin much the holier
theft. For such kind of borrowing as this, if it be not better'd by the
borrower, among good Authors is accounted *Plagiarie.*

—J. M., *Eikonoklastes* (1649)

Over the course of the seventeenth century, readers increasingly confronted an
English Bible shorn of explanatory notes. In the long shift from the Geneva and
Bishops' Bibles to the King James Version, the annotations—extensive, helpful,
but arguably obtrusive—were stripped away, leaving in the margins only cross
references, philological notes about the original, and another feature less dominant in Geneva Bibles, the alternate reading. These brief notes, which total 8,422,
were either initiated by an abbreviation such as "*Heb,*" signaling a more literal
version of the Hebrew, or "*Or,*" signaling an alternate phrasing offered where the
original meaning was uncertain, contested, or simply open to various translations.[1]
Very rarely they supplied notes on facts like the value of currency. Compared to
the extensive annotations of Geneva Bibles, particularly in late Elizabethan editions, the margins of the King James were remarkably open. The cultural effect of
this shift has not been fully considered; it is no doubt significant, as Sir Robert
Filmer and others pointed out, that the word "tyrant" was removed from the text
and especially the paratext, but this change is miniscule next to removal of thousands of instances of "Church" and "Christ" from the margins and even the text
of the Old Testament. These two words are at the top of a long list of frequent

Christian terms such as "Antichrist," "idolators," "God's providence," "true religion," "justified by faith," "figure of Christ," "outward ceremonies," and "papists," that fill the margins of the Old Testament. The removal of New Testament language from the Old Testament in the King James Bible allowed the Old Testament to function more historically than allegorically, and it allowed readers to see it as something more like the Hebrew Bible than as a prognosticator of unfulfilled meaning. To point to a consequence particular to this study, the paratextual shift deprived readers of a guide to interpreting Spenser.

The shift to the open margins of the King James Bible is often viewed as politically motivated, since the Geneva notes were decried in King James's tirade: "very partial, untrue, seditious, and savoring too much, of dangerous, and traitorous conceits"—and, consequently, "no marginal notes" should appear in the proposed new version.[2] No doubt James's political charge was a determining factor. But when the Bible appeared seven years after this statement, the translators provided a distinctly different rationale for not including explanatory notes, one that drew from other traditions concerning annotation. Speaking for the translators in the preface to the new Bible, Miles Smith stressed the advantages of having margins that do not secure meanings: "doth not a margin do well to admonish the Reader to seek further, and not to conclude or dogmatize upon this or that peremptorily?" Instead, a more open interpretive posture is enabled by the alternate readings: "Some peradventure would have no variety of senses to be set in the margin, lest the authority of the Scriptures for deciding of controversies by that show of uncertainty, should somewhat be shaken."[3] Smith endorsed multiple senses over the false assurance of a single translation when there is disagreement—"controversy"—about meaning. As Jeffrey Miller points out in his scholarship on the drafting of the King James Bible, often these alternate readings represent rather deep cruxes in biblical scholarship.[4] Sometimes they resulted from disagreements among the translators, and in many cases, staid, more conventional phrasing remained in the text, making the alternate marginal reading actually the better, if more daring rendition of the original. The translators thus hoped to enable multiple interpretations; as Smith asserts, the "diversity of signification and sense in the margin, where the text is not so clear, must needs do good, yea, is necessary, as we are persuaded."[5] Explanatory notes such as those in the Geneva Bible may determine a meaning that does not necessarily inhere in the original. The alternate readings, in contrast, help readers to consider the variety of possible senses.[6]

The alternate possibilities in the King James Version played a significant role in Milton's experience as a reader, and, as I will argue, in what he sought to recreate for his readers. The alternate readings in the Bible may even inform one of the most common words in *Paradise Lost*: "or."[7] The first occurrence of "or" in the epic has a particularly biblical significance, since Milton invokes the same muse that inspired Moses on the mountain: "Sing heavenly Muse, that on the secret top / Of Oreb, or of Sinai, didst inspire / That Shepard, who first taught the chosen seed." The "persistent doubleness of the invocation," as this embedded alternate reading has been glossed, is reinforced by biblical uncertainties about which mountain—Horeb or Sinai—God revealed the Law to Moses, or, more likely, given different oral traditions, what the mountain was called.[8] Reformation scholars chose to resolve the geographical puzzle by attributing these different names to the same mountain, so that glosses in such Bibles as the Geneva Bible explain at the mention of "Horeb" at Exodus 3:1, "Called also Sinai," and a gloss on Moses's "Mount" in the margin of Deuteronomy 9:21 almost exactly anticipates Milton: "Horeb, or Sinai."[9]

A number of critics have drawn connections between Milton's hermeneutic and textual theories and his experiments in poetic representation.[10] My interest here is to consider the material practices of reading as part of this relationship. While we cannot yet say how much the "persistent doubleness" in *Paradise Lost* derives from the English Bible's paratextual use of "or," we can trace Milton's use of the alternate readings as a reader and a writer in relation to his 1648 psalm translations. I would like to claim that Milton's alternate meanings and adaptive readings were shaped by the paratext of the King James Bible, and, conversely, that Milton recreated the experience of reading the Renaissance biblical text, with its many paratextual intrusions, as a way of constructing a plausible (if radical) interpretation of the psalms. Although psalm translations constitute a relatively small part of Milton's poetic corpus, they reveal a great deal about his efforts to reuse biblical material for political and literary effect. As Mary Ann Radzinowicz has shown, the psalms more than any other biblical book undergird the poetic imagery and allusions in his late masterpieces.[11] Psalm translations span a large portion of Milton's career—from those that rank among his earliest poems, written at the age of fifteen, to these mid-career psalms written in a dark moment in English revolutionary history, to the translations written at precise dates after his blindness. Milton's 1648 Psalm translations—shrouded in uncertainties about their context and authorial purpose—deserve far greater attention, not only for how they demarcate the intersections of psalm adaptation and Civil War culture, but also for what they reveal about how political urgency reshapes what is permissible in the interpretation, translation, and adaptation of scripture.

Milton's psalm translations of 1648—Psalms 80–88—participate in an intensely rich moment in English psalm culture. They are often seen as "private and personal,"[12] and therefore not meant to be circulated like his polemical prose, but I would like to suggest that these psalms are in fact designed to have a vital public role. Psalm production intensified in the late 1640s partly in response to Westminster Assembly's efforts to replace the old Sternhold and Hopkins psalter with a fitting Presbyterian alternative. At the same time, psalm adaptation flourished as a royalist activity. In addition to artistic and church service productions, biblical scholarship on the psalms—inflected by wartime conditions—was peddled by booksellers and government agents: in July 1647, as I discuss below, Edmund Calamy issued a commentary on some psalms that happened to treat a third of Milton's nine. In the following year two important royalist Psalm collections were produced using poetic "paraphrases" by George Sandys, set to music by Milton's old friend and musical collaborator Henry Lawes. Charles had been imprisoned at Carisbrooke Castle on the Isle of Wight since late 1647, where he was reputed to take comfort in the psalms.[13] The Folger Shakespeare Library possesses a tiny copy of Sternhold and Hopkins embroidered in purple with gold and pearl that is catalogued as "once the property of Charles I" (Figure 20), a pocket edition that might have been among his royal accoutrements in prison.

The misfortunes of the king weigh heavily in Lawes's dedication in *Choice Psalms*: "I was easily drawn to this presumption [in publishing the book] by Your Majesty's known particular affection to *David*'s Psalms, both because the Psalter is held by all Divines one of the most excellent parts of holy Scripture; as also in regard much of Your Majesty's present condition, is lively described by King *David*'s pen."[14] The cult of Charles as David is preserved in many artifacts, one of which at the Bodleian is an elaborately embroidered cover of the New Testament featuring an image of Charles as David that was reputed to have come from one of the king's waistcoats.[15]

Where Milton's psalms fit in this moment remains obscured by long-standing conceptions of Davidic authorship. The well-established history of English monarchs associating themselves with David, such as that of Henry VIII discussed in chapter 2, helped support, as Achsah Guibbory has shown, a royalist appropriation of the psalms in Stuart England.[16] Yet the loose attribution of the psalms to King David has distorted modern reception histories. Radzinowicz wrote, for example, that Milton "attributed none" of the psalms "to any poet other than David," a presumption about David's authorship that still shapes much of the scholarship on early modern psalm culture.[17] Such prejudices

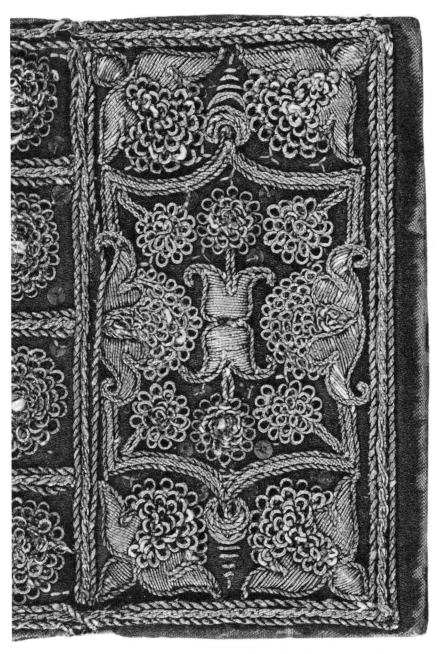

Figure 20. The embroidered purple velvet psalter of Charles I. *The Whole Book of Psalms* (London: Company of Stationers, 1624), embroidered with seed pearl, silver spangles, and gold and silver knot work. STC 2588. By permission of the Folger Shakespeare Library.

extend beyond English literary studies; biblical scholarship is often dismissive of the "pre-critical" period of textual interpretation, as if only after the historical-critical work of the modern era would readers have challenged the compositional unity of any given biblical book.[18] Either causally or simply in shared assumption, these prejudices shape literary and cultural histories. Even Kevin Killeen's valuable book on the political Bible states that the psalms are "presumed to be by David"[19] by early modern readers and writers.

The presumption that the psalms were uniformly Davidic, and generally the province of royalists, has occluded vital developments in early modern biblical scholarship and psalm culture. A significant number of the psalms were in fact placed in non-monarchic and even anti-monarchic settings. Although the earliest Tudor translations seem uninterested in drawing distinctions about authorship and context, by the time of the Genevan exiles, the non-Davidic context of many of the psalms became increasingly interesting to scholars, readers, and poets. In Calvin's influential publication of the psalms with a commentary, translated into English in 1571 by Arthur Golding (who offers his own new translation of the psalms), Calvin seeks to recover the historical context of each of the psalms. Entitled *The Psalms of David and Others*, the text and much of the paratext is shared by the Geneva Bible of 1560, which still uses the more conventional title, *The Psalms of David,* but both collections begin with precisely the same headnote to the first psalm: "Whither it were Esdras or some other man that gathered the Psalms into one volume, he seemeth to have placed this psalm in the beginning, instead of a preface"[20] This is a reference to Ezra the scribe, who returned from Babylon to Israel in around 450 BCE to edit the Bible. Calvin's uncertainty about the identity of the compiler further complicates questions of authorship. Once it is understood that the psalms developed as a compilation that was created hundreds of years after the first composition, and then continuously added to, it then follows that the titles given to the psalms were themselves provided much later—possibly without knowing precisely which "Prophet," as Calvin called the psalmist, composed the psalm. While Ezra seems the likely compiler, Calvin also speculates that some psalms were written not only after the ruin of the First Temple (after 597 BCE), but as late as the desecration of the Temple by Antiochus (ca. 167 BCE), suggesting that even after the psalms were first collected during and after the exile, they were added onto, necessitating a further process of compilation. The historicizing of the psalms, now almost a century after Calvin's *Psalms of David and Others*, had become part of the fabric of English psalm culture.

The most obvious biblical hint that some psalms are not by David is in Psalm 137, when the psalmists weep by the waters of Babylon, referred to by Jesus in *Paradise Regain'd*, "our Psalms with artful terms inscrib'd, / Our Hebrew Songs and Harps in Babylon / That pleas'd so well our Victor's ear" (4.335–337). The choice seems to touch poignantly on Milton's compositional history: Jesus associates himself with the wartime psalms, even those written in defeat, yet they are "with artful terms inscrib'd," while they speak as Psalm 137 does of the destruction of Babylon. "Artful" suggests "cunning" (*OED*), picked up in the line of the psalm, "O Jerusalem, let not my right hand forget her cunning" (137:5)—"artful" thus suggests a kind of *obliquus ductus*, an expression of defiance that somehow pleased the victor's ear. Outside of this explicit reference to the Babylonian context in Psalm 137, the question of authorial attribution largely rests, both for modernity and early modernity, on the manner of the psalm's titles, which serve as a kind of paratext within the biblical text itself. The Hebrew expression "To/for David," often read as "of David," occurs in the titles of some seventy-three psalms, and in thirteen instances the title provides some information pertaining to an incident in the life of David; in short, about half of the psalms are roughly associated with David.[21] There are also other psalm titles, such as the "Sons of Korah," containing several of those Milton translated (Pss. 42–49, 84, 85, 87, 88), and an Asaph collection that contains a few more of the psalms in Milton's cluster (Pss. 50, 73–83). One of Milton's nine psalms has an ambiguous biblical attribution to David, and the others remain unattributed in the compiled biblical text.

The Genevan exiles—who fashioned themselves as Babylonian exiles—had already used the psalms as texts of resistance. William Kethe's powerful translation of Psalm 94, which radicalized Calvin's already presentist interpretation, shows how historical contextualization worked both in poetry and in biblical scholarship. Kethe's incendiary metrical translation is appended to polemics by Anthony Gilby and John Knox in 1558, urging readers, "Who *now* will up and rise with me / Against this wicked band?" [italics added].[22] The word "now," added six times in Kethe's translation, reinforces the link between the biblical past and the urgent present. Calvin had written in 1557 that the psalmist "calleth upon God for help against the wicked and violent persons that oppressed the Saints tyrannously & cruelly."[23] Calvin applies the psalm to the present condition of the Church: "Now seeing that the reprobates have executed so great tyranny in the church of old time, and God hath not redressed it out of hand: let us not marvel if the Church at this day also lie long time oppressed, neither let us think it to be utterly forsaken of God."[24] The words "throne of iniquity" in line 20 are glossed, "He blameth not the common cut throats . . . but inveigheth against the tyrants that oppressed Gods church under self pretense of the law."

Milton's psalms, as is also true of his prose tracts at the time—*The Tenure of Kings and Magistrates* and *Eikonoklastes* in particular—react strongly against the royalist appropriation of the psalms, and the misuse of David as a representative of royal ideology, even if and when we can be confident of Davidic authorship.[25] *Eikonoklastes* reacts explicitly against the associations of Charles with David in *Eikon Basilike*, and in one wild occasion, Milton accuses the king of plagiarizing David, not because he copied David, but because he copied David *badly*: "[The King] borrows *David's* Psalms, as he charges the *Assembly of Divines* . . . Had he borrow'd *David's* heart, it had been much the holier theft. For such kind of borrowing as this, if it be not better'd by the borrower, among good Authors is accounted *Plagiary*."[26] The passage seems infused with self-referential irony, in which the poet (among good Authors), having in recent months "borrowed" (and perhaps bettered?) the psalms, acquits himself of the literary abuse he sees in the king and elsewhere among royalists.

The misuse of the Davidic corpus preoccupies much of Milton's writing during the king's trial as well. In *The Tenure of Kings and Magistrates*, published only weeks after the king's death, "David" appears a dozen times in the forty-two pages of the first edition, frequently with an explicit attack on a wrongful reading of a psalm, as "Yet some would persuade us that this absurd opinion [of divine right] was King *David's*, because in the 51 Psalm he cries out to God, *Against thee only have I sin'd*; as if David had imagin'd that to murder Uriah and adulterate his Wife, had been no sin against his Neighbour."[27] Indeed, the example Radzinowicz used to argue that Milton attributed the psalms exclusively to David occurs when Milton suggests in *The Tenure of Kings and Magistrates* that David is "likeliest to be Author of the *Psalm 94:20*," *"Shall the throne of iniquity have fellowship with thee?"* (*CPW* vol. 3, 211), yet this is a case where Milton posits David's possible authorship for rhetorical purposes, to make a stronger case against the fallacy of the royalist position, and against the misuse of David. The passage also shows that Milton was quite ready to consider some psalms outside the Davidic canon. Psalm 94 is, in fact, Kethe's psalm, and the line that Calvin glosses, "he inveigheth against the tyrants that oppressed God's church under false pretense of the law."[28] In the slightly expanded edition of *The Tenure of Kings and Magistrates*, Milton refers to the resistance tract by Knox and Gilby that includes Kethe's psalm, suggesting he was energized by Kethe's exilic adaptation of the psalms in his rebuke of Charles, and also influenced by Kethe in his own incendiary psalm translations several months prior.[29]

Instead of translating conspicuously Davidic psalms in 1648, in vogue among royalists, Milton chose a set of psalms that are largely post-Davidic, and even post-monarchical, though at least one is also understood by Calvin and others to concern "such a time as Saul persecuted [David], and thus also concerning tyranny."[30] According to contemporary readings fully available to Milton, some of these psalms were attributed to Israelites after the Babylonian captivity, or (in some readings) to a moment after the desecration of the Temple by Antiochus, when the Jews were preparing for the Maccabean revolt. These psalms are wartime poems that call for repentance, recovery, and liberation—and even more so in Milton's rewriting. These translations are written in service meter, meaning that—unlike the musically complex elite productions of Lawes and Sandys, which also included music—Milton's were arguably *less* literary, as they were in standard meter and could be sung to well-known psalter music. Looking at Milton's psalm translations in conversation with those of his contemporaries, I read the "April 1648" Psalms as urgently connected to the tense impasse that led finally to the execution of the king. Milton's translation decisions are in dialogue with both the old Sternhold and Hopkins psalter and a Presbyterian alternative, and they are supported by a biblical paratext that he creates to mimic the King James Bible. Milton's own marked Bible contains evidence of how he read the text and paratext, and even some possible evidence of the revolutionary context of the psalms.

Milton's Marked King James Bible

It is still widely presumed that Milton preferred the Geneva Bible. This bias is partially due to Christopher Hill, who incorrectly claimed that Milton preferred the Geneva Bible, but that "some of his amanuenses used the AV."[31] Milton used a Latin Bible that was closely associated with the later Genevan Bibles (they both had notes of Beza and translations by Junius), and his third wife Elizabeth Minshull owned a 1588 Geneva Bible that she had in their house after they married in 1663, but these seem the closest connections that can be drawn to the Geneva text.[32] The King James Version thoroughly pervades Milton's writing. Milton's use is especially clear in his English prose, in which large biblical passages are often lifted directly from the King James Version. Milton's exegetical procedure in these cases often included correcting—or offering corrections—to the English Bible's wording, treating the text as if he presumed his audience would be using the same version. At one point in *The Doctrine and Discipline of*

Divorce, for example, Milton takes issue with the word "odious" in the KJV, though without providing reference to it, as if it would be obvious that he referred to this official and ubiquitous version: "And this law the Spirit of God by the mouth *Solomon*, Prov. 30:21, 23, testifies to be a good and necessary Law; by granting it that *a hated woman* (for so the Hebrew word signifies, rather than odious, though it come all to one)."[33] Older Bibles were still used in the seventeenth century, of course, but by the 1640s the King James Version reached a particularly broad audience, both inside and outside the Church of England.

In addition to marginal variant readings, the King James followed the Geneva Bible in italicizing English words that lacked an exact correspondence with the Hebrew or Greek but were needed to capture the sense of the original; as in Genesis 1:30: "And to every beast of the earth, and to every soul of the air, and to every thing that creepeth upon the earth, wherein there *is* life, *I have given* every green herb for meat: and it was so." Milton's psalms use this paratextual feature liberally, as he explains in the headnote to the text, mimicking the biblical text: "all but what is in a different Character, are the very words of the Text, translated from the Original" (Figure 21).[34]

Milton's relationship with the paratext of the King James Version is demonstrated in a few other bodies of evidence, including his frequent use of alternate readings in allusions, the imitation of these as well as the italics in his psalm translations, and in the manuscript annotations in his Bible. Milton's King James Bible is the only one of Milton's Bibles known to have survived, and one of only ten titles in eight volumes known to be extant from his library, though the number may be growing, given the discovery of Milton's possible markings in a Shakespeare Folio in 2019.[35] The allusions in his Latin and English prose show that the poet had several Bibles representing both the original languages and modern translations: his Hebrew Bible, a Greek New Testament, at least one scholarly Latin edition, which had Latin translations of the Greek and the Syriac versions of the New Testament side by side in parallel columns, as well as Erasmus's *Annotationes* on the New Testament, and Diodati's *Pious Annotations upon the Holy Bible*.[36] Milton worked with at least four editions in at least four different languages, and even after he lost his sight, he kept up with new developments in biblical translation and scholarship. At what is the most contentious point in Milton's theology—the denial of the Trinity—he turns to the "Arabic and Ethiopic" translations to amass evidence that early versions of 1 John 5 did not contain the so-called "Johannine Comma" at 5:7–8, calling the "Father, Son, and Holy Ghost" one entity; for access to these versions, the blind writer and assistants would have consulted Walton's new *Biblia sacra polyglotta* of

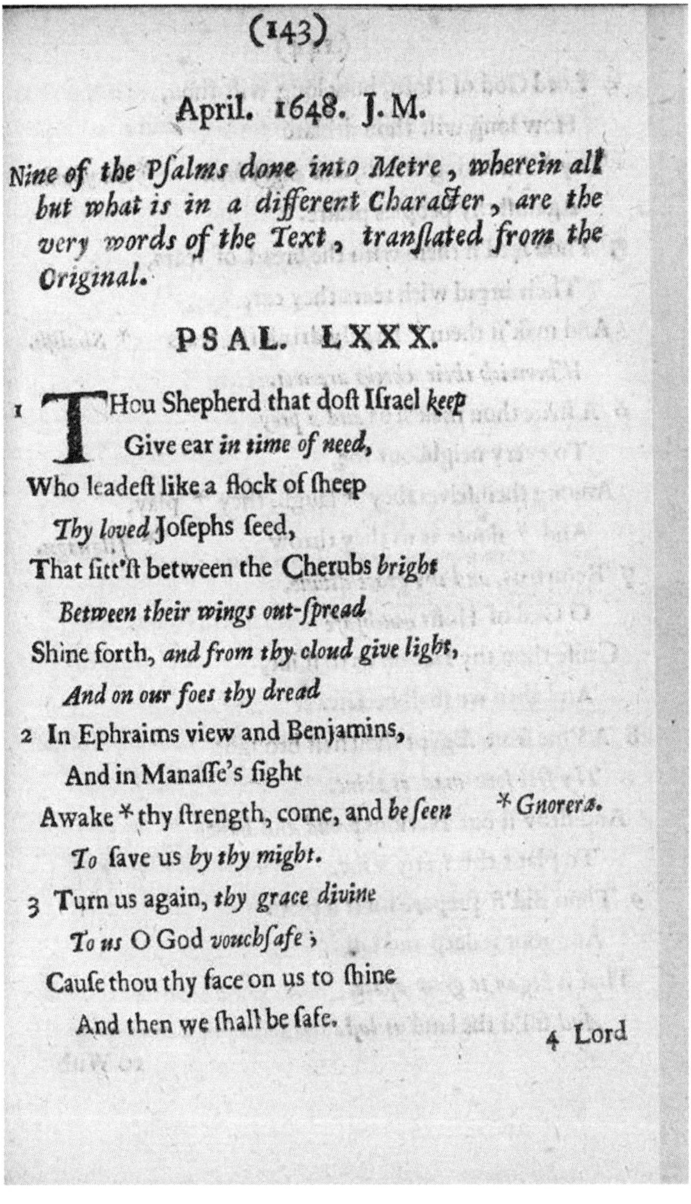

April. 1648. J. M.

Nine of the Pfalms done into Metre, wherein all but what is in a different Chara&er, are the very words of the Text, tranflated from the Original.

PSAL. LXXX.

1 THou Shepherd that doft Ifrael *keep*
    Give ear *in time of need,*
Who leadeft like a flock of fheep
    Thy loved Jofephs feed,
That fitt'ft between the Cherubs *bright*
    Between their wings out-fpread
Shine forth, *and from thy cloud give light,*
    And on our foes thy dread

2 In Ephraims view and Benjamins,
    And in Manaffe's fight
Awake * thy ftrength, come, and *be feen*   * *Gnorera.*
    To fave us *by thy might.*

3 Turn us again, *thy grace divine*
    To us O God *vouchfafe* ;
Caufe thou thy face on us to fhine
    And then we fhall be fafe.
                   4 Lord

Figure 21. Milton's translation of Psalms 80–88 in his *Poems* (1673). The occurrence of "J. M.," unique to the volume, suggests the compositor drew from a manuscript designed for circulation. Milton's instructions, that "all but what is in a different Character, are the very words of the Text," followed the practice of the King James translators. Milton's *Poems, &c. upon Several Occasions* (London, Tho. Dring, 1673), 143, Beinecke Ij M642 C645c. By permission of the Beinecke Rare Book and Manuscript Library, Yale University.

1655.[37] As Milton also knew, this controversy like so many others began with Erasmus's 1516 edition of the *New Testament*, which scandalized the world by not including the comma.

Milton was obviously devoted to philological study, but it is a mistake to presume that English translation is simply "convenient," or that "it was the Bible in its originals that was important to him, not the versions."[38] The idea of translation for convenience is an anachronistic way of understanding an early modern Protestant's relationship with the vernacular. Milton's profound understanding of the history of English translation inflects his poetry in vital moments, as at the end of *Paradise Lost* when Adam and Eve prepare to leave Eden, and the archangel Michael instructs them in a series of virtues, among them "Love, / By name to come called Charity, the soul / Of all the rest." In "Charity" and "Love," Michael alludes to the controversy that would erupt in the sixteenth century when Tyndale translated the Pauline term *agape* as "love."[39] The angel's explanation that "love" would come to be called "charity" reverses the actual lexical history, suggesting—in spite of the trenchant objections of Thomas More—that Tyndale's "love" was so true to the theological idea as to precede even English itself. In his validation of Tyndale's "love" over the less ancient, Latinate "charity," Milton disputes the now dominant English translation of the Bible, whose translators in this case had sided with Thomas More, making Paul's triad of virtues faith, hope, and charity. Milton's recognition of the weight carried by a single translation also plays an important role in the sonnet "On the New Forcers of Conscience under the Long Parliament," which concludes: "New *Presbyter* is but old *Priest* writ large." Tyndale controversially translated *presbyteros* as "elder," rather than "priest" or "bishop." The name "Presbyterian" celebrates this lexical distinction and its ecclesiastical implications, although as Milton suggests, the only real distinction for these "New Forcers" may have been the length of the word.

Closer study of Milton's acts of translation, such as Jason Rosenblatt's work on Milton's psalms, shows that Milton's act of translating the biblical Hebrew into English poetry has a profound, even competitive relationship with the King James Version. Rosenblatt characterizes Milton's relationship with the KJV as one in which Milton would hold the original Hebrew in one hand and the English Bible in another, waiting "for the word or phrase that will give him a (limited) opportunity to express himself by improving or correcting" what John Selden had termed, "'the best translation in the world.'"[40] In Harris Fletcher's analysis of Milton's extensive use of the King James Version in his prose, Milton used its wording some 80 percent after his blindness, and 48 percent

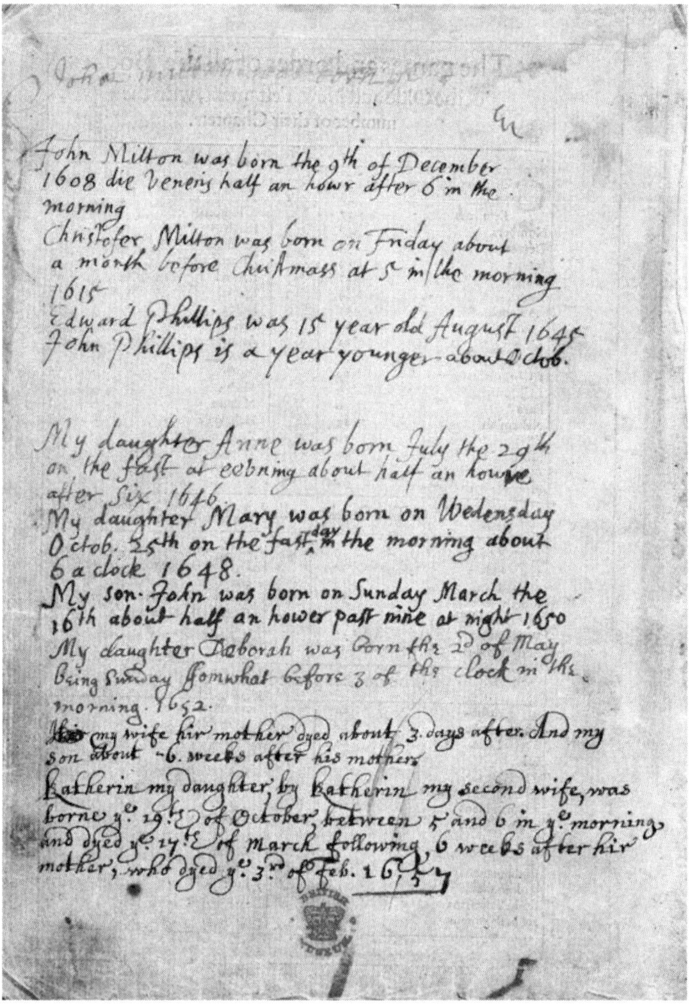

John Milton was born the 9th of December
1608 die Veneris half an howr after 6 in the
morning
Christofer Milton was born on Friday about
a month before Christmass at 5 in the morning
1615
Edward Phillips was 15 year old August 1645
John Phillips is a year younger about Octob.

My daughter Anne was born July the 29th
on the fast at eevning about half an howre
after six 1646
My daughter Mary was born on Wednesday
Octob. 25th on the fast day in the morning about
6 a clock 1648.
My son John was born on Sunday March the
16th about half an hower past nine at night 1650
My daughter Deborah was born the 2d of May
being Sunday somwhat before 3 of the clock in the
morning. 1652.
my wife hir mother dyed about 3 days after. And my
son about 6 weeks after his mother
Katherin my daughter, by Katherin my second wife, was
borne ye 19th of October, between 5 and 6 in ye morning,
and dyed ye 17th of March following, 6 weeks after hir
mother, who dyed ye 3rd of Feb. 1657

Figure 22. The family history of John Milton in his King James Bible (1612). "John Milton was born" is written in Milton's hand, suggesting that he copied the information. The family genealogy continues in Milton's hand, with Jeremie Picard filling in entries after his blindness. BL MS Additional 32310, a quarto edition of the *Holy Bible* (London: Robert Barker, 1612). STC 2220. © The British Library Board.

before his blindness when it seems he often revised the common vernacular translation after consulting the original or the scholarly Latin and multilingual versions of Beza and Tremellius.[41]

The careworn 1612 copy of the King James Version, now in the manuscript collection at the British Library, has been mined for its record of family history—starting with Milton's birth, written in his own hand (Figure 22).[42] William Riley Parker speculated that the Bible was a gift from Milton's parents when he was four years old (when the Bible would have then been hot off the press).[43] There is no real way of knowing, of course, but this reconstruction makes sense because the book is treated as Milton's own family Bible. The fact that he records his own birth (the main record for this event) at around the same time he records his brother's birth and the ages of two nephews who came to live with him *might* suggest that he acquired or inherited the Bible later in life, except that the place where this information is recorded is abnormally far into the Bible, after many pages of preliminaries.[44] This likely occurred because the earlier preliminaries, now lost, had already become too worn and unusable, as is indicated by a hitherto unnoticed bit of evidence tucked into the Bible, a scrap of the backside of Jasper Isaac's engraved title page, which is a rendition of Cornelis Boel's famous title page engraving in the 1611 folio edition (Figure 23).[45] On the rear-side of Aaron's shoulder, the tantalizing words "my," "day," and the first four letters of "night" are inscribed—all suggesting this is a fragment of an original genealogical history; indeed, these words occur in Milton's genealogy. This fragment implies that Milton's later record of his birth in his own hand is a copy from this scrapped genealogy, which may itself have been copied from another family Bible containing the record of Milton's birth in 1608.

Milton's Bible is astonishingly heavily used, as if with intense but messy utility: it is food stained, ink stained, inadvertently fingerprinted, pinned together, full of tears and burn holes suggesting that its user or users brought food and lamp oil and other flammables to light their way through increasingly tattered pages (Figure 24). The most distinctive example of Milton's own hand, outside of the genealogy, occurs in a correction to Proverbs 4:5, in which he crosses out "youth" and writes the correct word "mouth" (Figure 25), possibly because he was checking the Hebrew as he read (his reading often involved collation), or heard the correction in a church setting.[46]

But like many marked books, Milton's Bible provokes at least as many questions as it answers. Reading marks are often tantalizingly obscure: several marked passages are given the cryptic initials "KT" long thought to be KJ, possibly because KJ at least made sense to modern interpreters as the initials denoting the Bible

Figure 23. Fragment of Aaron's shoulder and a lost genealogy. Milton's Bible
has a genealogy that was written in later, and the remains of a genealogy on
the backside of Jasper Isaac's original frontispiece. The left side shows the
fragment of the title page, and the right its reverse. BL MS Additional 32310.
Holy Bible (London: Robert Barker, 1612). © The British Library Board.

itself, "King James," and this has shaped some readings of these passages in a
Jacobean context.[47] KT, sadly, is far more elusive. Nor do all of the marked passages have a precise correspondence with Milton's heavy patterns of use in his
writing. There are about 149 passages with deliberate marks, Milton's characteristic
"x" (sometimes looking like a "+"), Hebrew letters at the acrostic psalms, underlines, or words, but there are hundreds more that contain the stains of a vagrant
pen or bottle of ink.[48] Moments where we hope to find some comment or correction bear a less measurable record of use. Romans 13, for example, a passage used to
support the divine right of kings, which Milton refers to directly at least thirty-
two times, with countless indirect allusions, has no marginal markings at all,

Figure 24. A single page from Proverbs in Milton's Bible. In addition to having many intelligible markings of readership, as this single page shows, the Bible is pinned together, food stained, fingerprinted, torn, spilled on by oils, liquids, and inks. Other pages are burned through, many patched with the lost words written in by hand. BL MS Additional 32310. *Holy Bible* (London: Robert Barker, 1612). © The British Library Board.

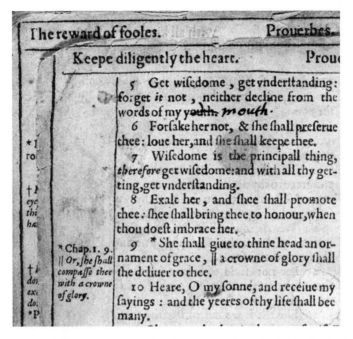

The reward of fooles.   Prouerbes.

Keepe diligently the heart.   Prou

5 Get wisedome, get vnderstanding: forget *it* not, neither decline from the words of my ~~youth~~ *mouth*.

6 Forsake her not, & she shall preserue thee: loue her, and she shall keepe thee.

7 Wisedome is the principall thing, *therefore* get wisedome: and with all thy getting, get vnderstanding.

8 Exalt her, and shee shall promote thee: shee shall bring thee to honour, when thou doest imbrace her.

*Chap.1. 9. || Or, *she shall compasse thee with a crowne of glory.*

9 *She shall giue to thine head an ornament of grace, || a crowne of glory shall she deliuer to thee.

10 Heare, O my sonne, and receiue my sayings: and the yeeres of thy life shall bee many.

Figure 25. Milton corrects the phrasing in Proverbs in his Bible. Similar in style to the correction in De Vere's Bible (Figure 14), although in this case the correction is for a mistake in Proverbs 4:5, rather than a preferred reading. BL MS Additional 32310 BL MS Additional 32310. *Holy Bible* (London: Robert Barker, 1612). © The British Library Board.

but the print is so worn from the page that letters had to be filled back in by pen (see chapter 8, Figure 29). This is in itself extraordinary, yet it tells us little more than that Milton pored over this passage so frequently that he wore out the print. This book may have received less specific annotation than Milton's others because it was in continuous use—constantly open on the desk, rather than consumed in a relatively short period. He may also have valued the translators' reasons for omitting marginal explanation.

The most revealing annotation is not by Milton precisely but by his amanuensis, Jeremie Picard, though it was likely made under Milton's supervision. Picard worked with Milton in the late 1650s on transcribing polemics, poetry, and *De Doctrina Christiana*. He also made entries in Milton's Commonplace Book and recorded Milton's wife Mary's death, and the death of his second wife Katherine, and a daughter, in February 1657/1658.[49] In a rare moment at Romans

15:6, Milton and his amanuensis enlist themselves as additional translators of the King James Version, perhaps not correcting the printed wording of the passage in the way that Milton does when he cancels the wording altogether, but retaining the original in correction, even adding an alternate possibility. The Romans 15:6 amendment seems to come from Milton's work on *De Doctrina Christiana*, where he and Picard were amassing proof texts from Milton's Latin Bible. The only time Romans 15:6 comes into play in a recognizable moment of exegesis in Milton's corpus is in chapter 5 of the *De Doctrina Christiana*, "Of the Son of God," in which Milton and Picard, writing in Latin, cite the line from the Latin edition they used, the Beza version, reading at Romans 15:6, "Ut concorditer uno ore glorificetis Deum ac Patrem Domini nostri Jesu Christi," or (in the KJV), "That ye may with one mind and one mouth glorify God, even the Father of our Lord Jesus Christ."[50] For Milton and Picard, the Greek original word for "ac" or "and," *kai*, functions in "Deum ac Patrem" as a simple conjunction, so that the KJV's emphatic expression "God, even the Father" is a less accurate rendering. From the English words supplied in the margins of Milton's KJV, Milton would translate "ac Patrem" not in the emphatic sense of "even the father," but with an inclusive *and* as well as a definitive article *the* God and Father, thus recognizing the individual relationship of these two entities, and that Jesus is, as Milton writes in *De Doctrina Christiana*, "by nature less than" and "subject to" the "God and the Father" (243). Thus, in the midst of asserting in *De Doctrina Christiana* that "Christ himself ascribes all divine attributes to God alone," Milton and Picard seem to have turned to the vernacular text, and instead of correcting the wording, offered an alternate reading (Figure 26).

This invaluable if statistically limited record of direct physical interaction with the biblical text provides some sense of the role and importance of marginal readings. Fletcher's figure that citations to the KJV in Milton's prose rise in precision after his blindness from 48 percent to 80 percent suggest in part the diminishing level of collation with Greek and Hebrew possible with a scribal helper. While Milton would have known many of the vernacular passages by heart, he would have needed scribes' help in citing chapter and verse, and in evaluating marginal alternative readings. Yet the prose Milton wrote while he could see used alternative marginal readings of biblical passages, and this tendency continued even after blindness.[51] The habitual use of the marginal readings suggests a reading process that constantly weighs alternate words or phrases (as the translators advised) to choose one reading or the other. Milton's late pamphlet, *A Treatise of Civil Power in Ecclesiastical Causes* (1659), provides a telling example. "What I argue," Milton states at the outset, "shall be drawn from

Figure 26. Romans 15:6 in Milton's 1612 King James Bible, showing
Milton's and Jeremie Picard's preferred reading "the God and father."
BL MS Additional 32310. *Holy Bible* (London: Robert Barker, 1612)
© The British Library Board.

the scripture only; and therin from true fundamental principles of the gospel."[52]
The extensiveness of citation suggests a correspondence between this English
polemic and *De Doctrina Christiana*, and it seems likely that Picard assisted
Milton with both. An entry in Milton's Commonplace Book by Picard corresponds to an addition in the reprint of *Pro Populo Anglicano Defensio* in 1658,
showing that Picard had worked with Milton in updating the citations to this
polemic.[53] When writing the late tolerationist polemic probably just before it
was printed in February 1659, *A Treatise of Civil Power*, Milton and his amanuensis occasionally drew from alternate readings, as when Milton strips "heresy"
of its special institutional significance by showing how Paul uses the word.[54] He
writes, "Where it is mentioned with blame, it seems to differ little from schism,"
as in "1 *Cor.* 11:18, 19. *I hear that there be schisms among you* &c. *for there must also
heresies be among you* &c."[55] But the text of the King James Bible itself has "I
hear that there be ||divisions among you," with "|| *Or, schisms*" added in the
margin. When citing a passage from Luke 7 in *A Treatise of Civil Power*, Milton
and his scribe choose the marginal "frustrated" over "rejected," to provide a
more dynamic and more applicable reading of the line "*they frustrated the counsel
of God*" (Luke 7:30).

Milton makes use of the marginal alternate readings in his poetry, too, and
particularly in the psalms, which draw on and create a variety of readings. In
the King James Version's Psalm 82, the verse "They know not, neither will they
understand; they walk on in darkness: all the foundations of the earth are † out

of course" supplies the alternate reading: "†Heb. *moved.*" In his rendition of the psalm in 1648, Milton uses the KJV's marginal "moved" as well as the "out of" from the KJV, thus bringing both readings into his verse, though he alters the phrase slightly to be "out of order" rather than "out of course." Thus, he works both readings into his verse, glossing his own work by simply giving the Hebrew itself in the margin:

> The Earths foundations all are * mov'd
> And * out of order gone.   * *Jimmotu.*

In another instance, Milton takes a single Hebrew word and translates it two ways, leaving both alternatives in the verses, and simply explaining in the margin that the Hebrew bears both meanings:

> Thy wrath from which no shelter saves
>   Full sore doth press on me;   *The Hebrew bears
> * Thou break'st upon me all thy waves,   both
>   * And all thy waves break me.

As the Hebrew bears both possible (though somewhat contrasting) meanings, Milton works both into his verse.

Psalms 80–88 of April 1648

The neglect of Milton's translations of Psalms 80–88 is due in part to their mysteriously specific date of April 1648, some 25 years previous to their appearance in print.[56] Their abab rhyme scheme has seemed out of line with Milton's late work, and his rendering of the Hebrew has to some readers seemed fraught with strange inaccuracies. The odd grouping as nine sequential psalms leave the impression of an unfinished sequence, or of an exercise in translation rather than autonomous artistic vision. Without other explanations, Milton's choice of Psalm 80 as a starting place seems connected to the Westminster Assembly's review of metrical psalms for use in churches; Psalm 80 happened to be the beginning of one of the four divisions sent to a committee for review.[57] The coincidence of Milton's starting point has advanced the impression that the psalms were meant for such an institutional review. As a result, the particular context of April 1648—in spite of the date provided—has seemed less relevant.

There are major problems with this established position, which has, I believe, confused and occluded Milton's project. Beyond the simple fact that Milton's psalms are not mentioned among those reviewed, the psalm review process
had been long underway, with the psalter so divided since November 1643.
Moreover, the date of April 1648 was hardly an occasion in this long process. In
this month, the review committee happened to convene in Edinburgh.[58] Yet at
this time, Milton could not have been more opposed to the Presbyterians or the
Scots, who had sided against the New Model Army and colluded with Charles.
While it seems quite possible that Milton at one point in the early 1640s had
studied these psalms for a revision to the service psalter, at the moment of their
scribal context in April 1648, they would have had a very different use, with revisions to fit the current moment. The choice of this sequence of Psalms, moreover, can be better explained by their appropriateness to the immediate situation
of England. Milton's psalm translations are written with a sense of urgency in
every respect—following Kethe's "now," Milton adds the word "now" eleven
times where no other translation uses it. Milton's "April 1648" is *now*, and the
psalms are designed to have an urgent temporal connection to the twists and
turns of political history.

In addition to the date at the top of the page, Milton's psalms also bear the
initials J. M. (Figure 21), which must be an unedited holdover from the manuscript; his initials occur nowhere else in the printed volume. The signed initials
"J. M.," oddly retained in this publication, were the same used to indicate the
authorship of his polemical prose, such as *The Tenure of Kings and Magistrates*.
The initials suggest that they came from a separate manuscript formatted for
circulation in 1648, and they are placed after the English poems in the printed
volume, after all the other occasional poems and psalm translations written
after these, suggesting a rushed addition to the 1673 volume. In this way the
added psalms might mirror the publication process of the "Omissa" appended at
the end of *Samson Agonistes* (1671), possibly inserted late in the printing to cir-
cumvent inspection by the licenser, which contain that poem's "most urgent and
violent images for the revitalization of the Good Old Cause."[59] However the
collection of nine psalms got into print, the evidence suggests that it existed in
separate manuscript unit, one that would have functioned as a scribal publication
like the sonnet he sent to Henry Lawes in 1645 (initialed "J. M." in the Trinity
MS), or the poem written by a scribe to the librarian John Rouse, sent in 1647 to
the Bodleian where it still rests, or the sonnet "On the Lord Gen. Fairfax at the
siege of Colchester," written in August 1648, at the decisive victory at the end of
the Second Civil War, and designed to be delivered to Fairfax, as were a number

of Milton's occasional poems addressed to particular recipients.[60] The April manuscript of the psalms, also written at a decisive moment in the civil wars, was surely designed for wartime use.

Where he may have sent copies of the manuscript—or if he sent it, of course—cannot yet be determined, but we should, I think, steer away from the sense that these are private meditations, especially given the urgency of their contents. The fact that the psalms are designed to be sung, like those set to music by Milton's father in the 1620s, has been read by some scholars as designed for Church review, yet this overlooks how much the singing of psalms occurred outside of church.[61] In Thomas Ravenscroft's musical publication of the Sternhold and Hopkins Psalter with Milton's father's compositions, instructions are given on which psalms to sing under particular conditions such as hardship or dejection. During the Civil War, psalms were sung by soldiers; at one point during an engagement in Scotland, for example, Cromwell "halted his pursuing horsemen for a few moments to sing Psalm 117."[62] The most plausible application for these psalms, at this decisive moment in Civil War history, was a meeting of the New Model Army at Windsor where the Army Council prayed and debated for several days in late April 1648.[63] This compelling idea, once put forward by Margaret Boddy, deserves further consideration.[64]

The psalms have a powerful regicidal energy, which would be all the more powerful in their biblical format: "But ye shall die like men, and fall / As other Princes *die*" (82:7). In Psalm 83, the psalmist gestures back to enemy chieftains killed by Gideon in Judges 8 in anger against the present oppressors of Israel: "As Zeba, and Zalmunna bled / So let their Princes *bleed*" (83:11). No other translation of these lines has the immediate and specific applicability of these lines: "ye shall die" and "fall / As other Princes *die*," for example, significantly transforms the King James's weaker phrasing, "like other princes," to make the death of *this* prince like other princes who *die*—a word Milton has also added to emphasize the necessary though unseemly action for political closure. The self-recrimination and military resolve of these rewritten psalms mirror the recorded somber mood of Army leaders. Marchamont Nedham's satirical weekly periodical, *Mercurius Pragmaticus*, characterized the meeting as "their *Saviours*" having "had a day of *Humiliation* lately at *Windsor*, it being high time to betake themselves to their *Sackcloth* and *Ashes*."[65] Oliver Cromwell and William Goffe, future signer of Charles's death warrant, attended. The prayer meeting of the Army Council mixed military deliberation with biblical meditations, and proved a decisive turning point. As an account of this event recalls, the army agonized over what direction to take, meditating on biblical texts, such as a line from Proverbs: "And at this time, and on this occasion, did the then Major *Goffe* (as I remember was his title) make use of that good word, *Prov.* 1:23, *Turn you at my reproof, &c [behold, I will pour out my spirit unto you, I will make known my words unto you.].* which (we having found out our sin) he urged as our duty from those words, and the Lord so accompanied by his Spirit, that it had a kindly effect, like a word of his, upon most of our hearts that were then present." After intense and tearful soul-searching, the Army concluded "that it was our duty, if ever the Lord brought us back again in peace, to call *Charles Stuart,* that man of blood, to an account, for that blood he had shed, and mischief he had done."[66] The biblical source for this language of blood reckoning begins with Genesis 9:6, which is elaborated in Numbers 35:33, and 2 Samuel 16:7–8; all used by Independents against the king prior to the Windsor meeting.[67] The use of "blood" in gauging the crimes of Charles and the account he must consequently face is encouraged in Milton's adaptive translation, which adds both "bled" and "*bleed*" to the wording of Psalm 82:11. If Milton wrote for this occasion, as would also have been true for the sonnet to Fairfax at the siege of Colchester later in the summer, or *The Tenure of Kings and Magistrates*, written during the trial of the king, the poet would have needed to work under tight time constraints, which could also explain the rushed borrowing of Sternhold and Hopkins.

In what is either a statistically incredible coincidence or some sort of marginal carbon copy of the historical context, the words "Windsor"—for the Army meeting at Windsor?—and "John"—part of the author's name?—are written by a scribe in the margins of Milton's Bible near the end of Psalm 88, the very psalm ending Milton's own translation (Figure 27). The words fall into the margins in the way that many proper names end up in Bibles, either as graffiti, or as stray words meant for another document, possibly resulting from an overlay of documents on a dimly lit desk. Until a positive match is made, this evidence can only help us imagine the conditions of scribal composition for the Psalms of 1648. The now lost manuscript copy imitated this print paratext, changing between roman and italic fonts, and Milton may have worked closely with the scribe, as he did with Picard. The copy of Milton's Bible might then have been open to this page either for the purposes of translation and composition—as Rosenblatt has reconstructed, with the Hebrew text open as well—but Milton's Bible would also have been needed for more material formatting purposes, providing reference to the paratextual devices shared in Milton's psalms: the line numbers, the italics, the philological notes, and the alternate readings.

Whether or not the psalms reached the audience they seem constructed for, these psalms do not support the reclusive portrait of Milton retreating after his

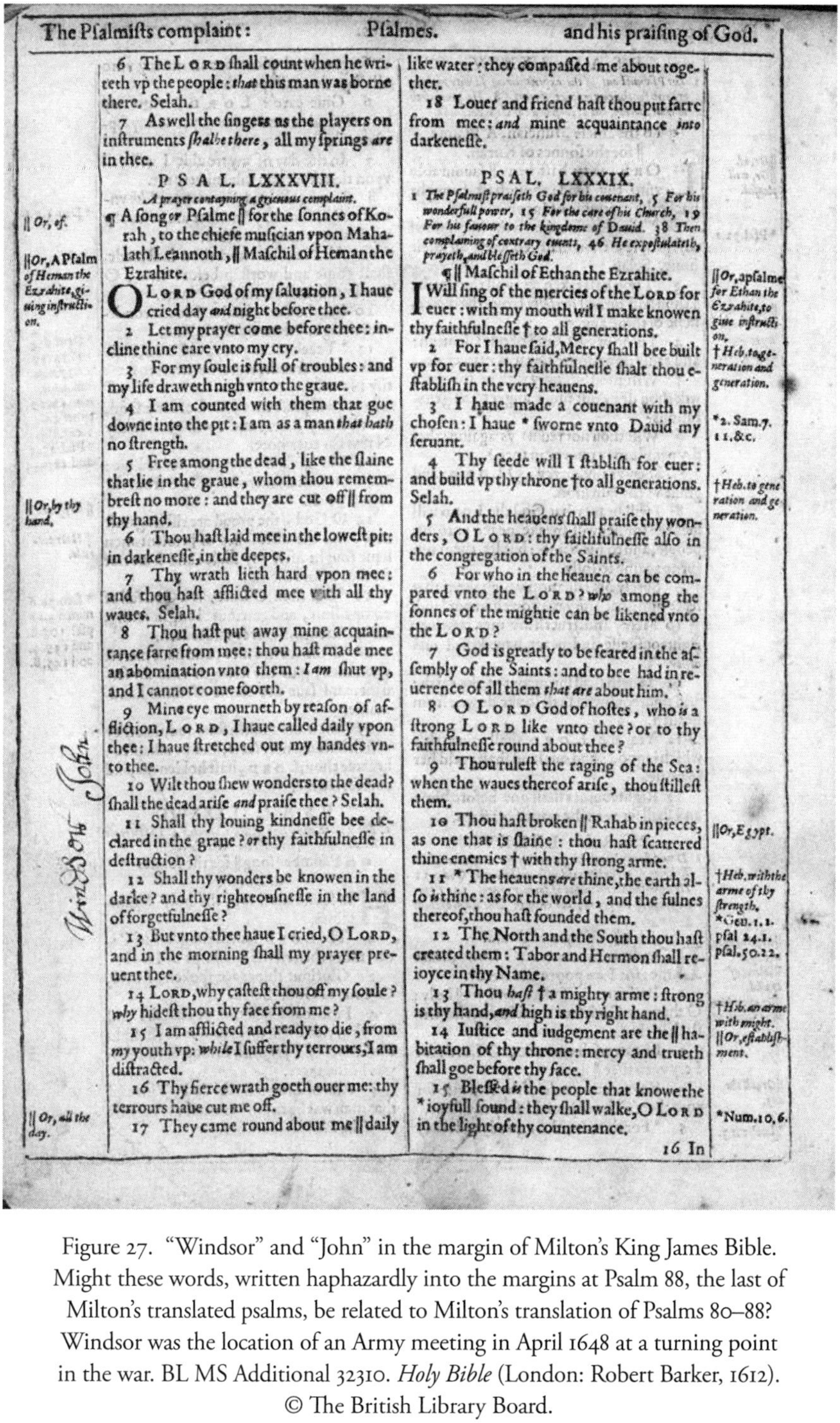

6. The Lord shall count when he writeth vp the people: *that* this man was borne there. Selah.

7. As well the singers *as* the players on instruments *shalbe there*, all my springs *are* in thee.

PSAL. LXXXVIII.

A prayer contayning a grieuous complaint.

¶ A song *or* Psalme || for the sonnes of Korah, to the chiefe musician vpon Mahalath Leannoth, || Maschil of Heman the Ezrahite.

O Lord God of my saluation, I haue cried day *and* night before thee.

2. Let my prayer come before thee: incline thine eare vnto my cry.

3. For my soule is full of troubles: and my life draweth nigh vnto the graue.

4. I am counted with them that goe downe into the pit: I am as a man *that hath* no strength.

5. Free among the dead, like the slaine that lie in the graue, whom thou remembrest no more: and they are cut off || from thy hand.

6. Thou hast laid mee in the lowest pit: in darkenesse, in the deepes.

7. Thy wrath lieth hard vpon mee: and thou hast afflicted mee with all thy waues. Selah.

8. Thou hast put away mine acquaintance farre from mee: thou hast made mee an abomination vnto them: *I am* shut vp, and I cannot come foorth.

9. Mine eye mourneth by reason of affliction, Lord, I haue called daily vpon thee: I haue stretched out my handes vnto thee.

10. Wilt thou shew wonders to the dead? shall the dead arise *and* praise thee? Selah.

11. Shall thy louing kindnesse bee declared in the graue? *or* thy faithfulnesse in destruction?

12. Shall thy wonders be knowen in the darke? and thy righteousnesse in the land of forgetfulnesse?

13. But vnto thee haue I cried, O Lord, and in the morning shall my prayer preuent thee.

14. Lord, why castest thou off my soule? *why* hidest thou thy face from me?

15. I am afflicted and ready to die, from my youth vp: *while* I suffer thy terrours, I am distracted.

16. Thy fierce wrath goeth ouer me: thy terrours haue cut me off.

17. They came round about me || daily like water: they compassed me about together.

18. Louer and friend hast thou put farre from mee: *and* mine acquaintance *into* darkenesse.

PSAL. LXXXIX.

1 *The Psalmist praiseth God for his couenant,* 5 *For his wonderfull power,* 15 *For the care of his Church,* 19 *For his fauour to the kingdome of Dauid.* 38 *Then complaining of contrary euents,* 46 *He expostulateth, prayeth, and blesseth God.*

¶ || Maschil of Ethan the Ezrahite.

I Will sing of the mercies of the Lord for euer: with my mouth wil I make knowen thy faithfulnesse † to all generations.

2. For I haue said, Mercy shall bee built vp for euer: thy faithfulnesse shalt thou establish in the very heauens.

3. I haue made a couenant with my chosen: I haue * sworne vnto Dauid my seruant.

4. Thy seede will I stablish for euer: and build vp thy throne † to all generations. Selah.

5. And the heauens shall praise thy wonders, O Lord: thy faithfulnesse also in the congregation of the Saints.

6. For who in the heauen can be compared vnto the Lord? *who* among the sonnes of the mightie can be likened vnto the Lord?

7. God is greatly to be feared in the assembly of the Saints: and to bee had in reuerence of all them *that are* about him.

8. O Lord God of hostes, who *is* a strong Lord like vnto thee? or to thy faithfulnesse round about thee?

9. Thou rulest the raging of the Sea: when the waues thereof arise, thou stillest them.

10. Thou hast broken || Rahab in pieces, as one that is slaine: thou hast scattered thine enemies † with thy strong arme.

11. * The heauens *are* thine, the earth also *is* thine: as for the world, and the fulnes thereof, thou hast founded them.

12. The North and the South thou hast created them: Tabor and Hermon shall reioyce in thy Name.

13. Thou *hast* † a mighty arme: strong is thy hand, *and* high is thy right hand.

14. Iustice and iudgement are the || habitation of thy throne: mercy and trueth shall goe before thy face.

15. Blessed *is* the people that knowe the * ioyfull sound: they shall walke, O Lord, in the light of thy countenance.

16 In

Marginal notes (left column):
|| *Or, of.*
||*Or,* A Psalme of Heman the Ezrahite, giuing instruction.
||*Or, by thy hand.*
||*Or, all the day.*

Marginal notes (right column):
||*Or, a psalme for Ethan the Ezrahite, to giue instruction.*
†*Heb. to generation and generation.*
2. Sam.7. 11. &c.
†*Heb. to generation and generation.*
||*Or, Egypt.*
†*Heb. with the arme of thy strength.*
Gen.1.1. psal 24.1. psal.50.22.
†*Heb. an arme with might.*
||*Or, establishment.*
Num.10.6.

Figure 27. "Windsor" and "John" in the margin of Milton's King James Bible. Might these words, written haphazardly into the margins at Psalm 88, the last of Milton's translated psalms, be related to Milton's translation of Psalms 80–88? Windsor was the location of an Army meeting in April 1648 at a turning point in the war. BL MS Additional 32310. *Holy Bible* (London: Robert Barker, 1612). © The British Library Board.

final divorce tract and the publication of an elegant volume of poetry with Humphrey Moseley in early 1646 to a contemplative life from which he awoke only late in 1648, when Colonel Pride purged Parliament on December 6, to compose *The Tenure of Kings and Magistrates*.[68] Throughout 1648, Milton is composing interventionist wartime literature: the Psalms in April, the Sonnet to Fairfax, and (as I have elsewhere argued) the "Digression" to the *History of Britain*.[69] Milton's psalms place him in ongoing conversation with a rich context of psalm production. Francis Rous, whose modified metrical psalms appeared in London during the Civil War, now had the honor of having his psalms considered as a possible official replacement. An MP by this time, Rous had wanted to avoid making poetic concessions to the meaning, and thus reduced the rigidity of the rhyme scheme while maintaining the meter. He writes that he decided not to invent a "form wholly new" as it "would not please many who are fastened to things usual and accustomed (though if Psalms of a new Form be read before they be sung, there is no hindrance but that they may be presently used; and after a little use will grow familiar.)" He "assayed only to change some pieces of the usual version, even such as seemed to call aloud, and as it were undeniably for a Change." The old psalter was crying out for a change, as it agreed "less with the New Translation [that is, the King James Version], yea, with the Original itself."[70]

During these uncertain years, psalms had become a form of public political expression. In July 1647, the same month that a new psalter was to be reviewed by the Westminster Assembly, former Smectymnuuan Edmund Calamy helped to issue a posthumous commentary by Thomas Pierson entitled *Excellent Encouragements against Afflictions, or, Expositions of Four Select Psalms*. As mentioned, these were Psalms 27, 84, 85, and 87—three of Milton's nine. As Calamy explains in the letter to the reader, he felt he had to do the author "this right, not only to give an *Imprimatur* to this *Commentary* of his upon some *Psalms,* but also to signify to the Reader, the *Piety, Learning,* and *Worth* of the *Author,* and to commend these his *Sermons* to every good Christian, as holding out many *Orthodox and savory Truths,* and by obedience to which *Truths,* many souls went to Heaven, without entangling themselves in the many *un-edifying janglings* of these sad divided times."[71] As with so many early modern readings, this commentary stresses the applicability of the biblical text to the vexed conditions of the present, an application enabled by historical reading. In the case of the psalms, historicism challenged the notion of a wholly Davidic authorship. Pierson's commentary on the first lines of Psalm 85 reads, "Compare the three first verses with the 4, and 5, which will well agree, either, to the times of *Ezra* and

Nehemiah, when, notwithstanding their return from *Babylon,* the people were in great distress at *Jerusalem:* as *Nehem.* 1:3. or, to the more heavy times, when *Antiochus Epiphanes* did tyrannize over them, as the book of *Maccabees* shows more at large, 1 *Maccab.* 1:25, 36. &c. Like unto this is Psal. 44:1. &c. *We have heard with our ears, O God, our fathers have told us, what works thou didst in their days, in the times of old, &c. Thou hast saved us from our enemies, and put them to shame that hated us, verse 7. But thou hast cast off, and put us to shame: and goest not forth with our armies. verse 9.*[72] This reading of Psalm 85 is entitled, again following Calvin, "The Church's Exercise under Affliction." "I have chosen to entreat of this Psalm," the prefatory remarks explain, "as containing fitting matter unto our times and occasions."[73]

Soon after this Presbyterian commentary on the psalms, Milton's old friend and musical collaborator Lawes presented to Charles I his *Choice Psalms put into Music* (1648) in a thoroughly royalist production, published by a figure connected to both Lawes and Milton, Humphrey Moseley. Charles had been imprisoned since late 1647 and tried unsuccessfully to escape in late March amid negotiations among the Scots, Presbyterians, and Royalists to restore him. In these uncertain circumstances, Lawes's volume appeared, with Milton himself as the author of a commendatory sonnet, though it had been sent to Lawes two years earlier for a delayed volume of airs.[74] In this volume Lawes also preserves the work of his brother, who died "in these unnatural Wars; yet lies in the Bed of Honour, and expir'd in the Service and Defense of the King his Master."[75]

Whether *Choice Psalms* appeared before Milton's own Psalms in April 1648 remains uncertain; Milton would, in either case, have been painfully aware of the public appearance of his sonnet, and of the use of George Sandys's versified psalms to express Lawes's hope that the sacred king would be restored. *Choice Psalms* may have been presented as part of the commemorative celebrations on the anniversary of Charles's coronation in March.[76] Sandys's "paraphrased" psalms appeared in a more complete volume in the same year, stating in his dedication to Charles, "Since none but Princes durst aspire / To sing unto the Hebrew Lyre; / Sweet Prince, who then your self more fit / To read, what sacred Princes Writ?"[77] Milton's own feelings could not have been more opposed, and yet in the moment of his composition of the psalms in April, it looked as though the king might, after years of war, be restored.[78]

In the first psalm of his collection, Milton invokes both the old Sternhold and Hopkins translation and the Rous by retaining complete lines from his rivals in his translation. This correspondence suggests some interaction with the public debate about the psalter, even as it also might indicate either a hurried

process of composition, or a deliberate process of composing through collation.[79] Unlike his rivals, Milton provides a paratextual packaging that imitates
the King James translation, replicating the formatting of the biblical page—the
numbers, the italics, and the marginal alternative readings and philological
notes. Thus, Milton's psalms pose as being responsibly correspondent to the Hebrew, yet they are rich in inserted phrases that bear more resemblance to a par-
tisan marginal gloss applying the biblical text to the English present. This set of
insertions is craftily derived from the practice of adding italics where an English
word is needed to supply the sense of the Hebrew. From the very beginning of
the collection, the italicized additions work to reinforce the present urgency of
these psalms:

> Thou Shepherd that dost Israel *keep*,
> Give ear *in time of need*

This "time of need" added to the first lines is echoed in the word "now," which
is conspicuously added six times in italic phrases that are not in the Hebrew, and
the five remaining instances also do not appear in any other editions. The *now-
ness* of Milton's translation overlaps with Milton's present in more than just urgent temporality. When God speaks in Psalm 81, it is with a sense that the
enemies of the godly exert a present danger:

> Then would I soon bring down their foes
> *That now so proudly rise*   (81:14)

The added words bring considerably new meaning to the text, which is much
more attentive to the English present than the King James Version's "I should
have subdued their enemies, and turned my hand against their adversaries" or
Hopkins's hypothetical "How soon would I confound their foes, / and bring
them down full low: / And turn thy head upon all those, / that would them
overthrow?"[80]—or, indeed, any of the other translations at this time.

The opening of Psalm 83 stresses the urgent present, the military threat of
the enemy, and the emotional condition of the godly:

> Be not thou silent *now at length*
> O God hold not thy peace,
> Sit not thou still O God of *strength*
> *We cry and do not cease.*

> For lo thy furious foes *now* *swell   *Jehemajun
>   And *storm outrageously,
> And they that hate thee *proud and fell*
>   Exalt their heads full high.   (83:1–2)

At times the added words reinforce the potential violence against princes:

> *For they amidst their pride* have said
>   By right now shall we seize
> Gods houses, and *will now invade*
> † Their stately Palaces.   (83:12)

Milton's re-use of the psalm has transformed it for action: "now" we shall seize God's houses and *now invade* the stately palaces (Figure 28). Milton adds a note suggesting that he has created an alternate reading here: the Hebrew, he argues, bears both meanings, though in this case he does not provide both meanings, but simply the *other* meaning. This passage in Psalm 83 is invoked in an abridged edition of the Remonstrance of the Army, printed in late December 1648 to support the overthrow of the King.[81]

Psalm 82:6 was frequently used to denote sacerdotal kingship, as in King James's declaration "Kings are called *Gods* by the prophetical King *David*,"[82] which is glossed with this Psalm. James provides a cluster of biblically based assertions about divine right, with a series of marginal citations that include Romans 13. A similar cluster of texts occurs in a royalist publication put out in mid-March of 1648 for the imprisoned king's inauguration day celebration with the gambler's title, *Great Britain's Vote: or, God save King Charles*. Here, like the early Stuart text, the assertion "they are called Gods"[83] is supported with a marginal note to Psalm 82:6. The royalist application of Psalm 82:6 appropriates a short line from a larger biblical passage whose support of this interpretation is far less clear. The psalm imagines a heavenly court that may not be applicable to earthly courts. God addresses a "congregation of the mighty; he judgeth among the gods" (KJV 82:1), and thus it seems God's charges to them about earthly injustice are charges to imagined members of a divine council. The turn at the end of the psalm seems to threaten the members of this council because of their failure to administer justice on earth: "I have said, Ye *are* gods; and all of you *are* children of the most High. But ye shall die like men, and fall like one of the princes" (KJV 82:6–7). An early reading of this passage occurs in John, when Jesus is stoned by unbelieving Jews, and states "Is it not written in your law, I

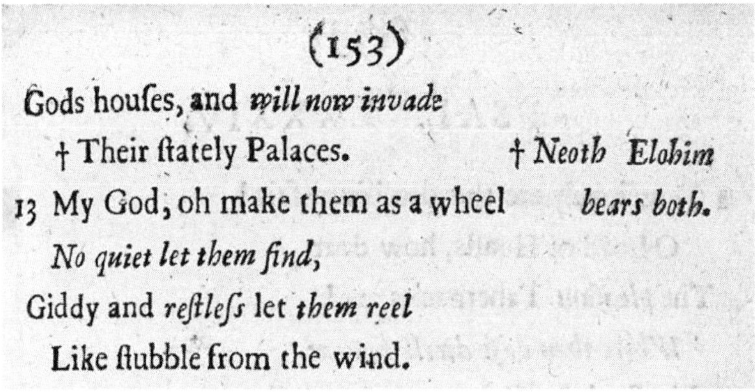

(153)

Gods houſes, and *will now invade*

  † Their ſtately Palaces.   † *Neoth Elohim*

13 My God, oh make them as a wheel   *bears both.*

  No quiet let them find,

  Giddy and *reſtleſs* let *them reel*

  Like ſtubble from the wind.

Figure 28. Alternate readings and italics in Psalm 83 in Milton's *Poems*. "*Will now invade* / Their stately Palaces." The italicized words are added to the original, an addition partly explained with a note on the Hebrew. *Poems, &c. upon Several Occasions* (London: Tho. Dring, 1673), 153. By permission of the Beinecke Rare Book and Manuscript Library, Yale University

said, ye are Gods," and goes on to argue that he cannot then be accused of blaspheme for saying "I am the Son of God" (John 10:34, 36). The moment seems to destabilize the Old Testament meaning by suggesting that "ye" implies earthly prophets, rather than a heavenly council.[84] On the highest authority, then, English royalists interpreted this line as pertaining to kings.

Milton resolves some of the confusion between the translation and the cultural reception of the psalm by providing for both a divine council and earthly kings at the beginning, adding the phrase "of Kings and lordly States":

God in the * great * assembly stands
  Of Kings and lordly States,   * *Bagnadath-el.* [*assembly of gods*]
† Among the gods † on both his hands   † *Bekerev.* [*in the midst of*]
  He judges and debates.   (82:1)

At the closure of Milton's Psalm, the expression universally translated in the present tense, "Ye *are* Gods,"—although importantly weakened by the King James Version's italics—is changed. Here the passage is clearly addressed to the "Kings" rather than the heavenly council, and Milton changes the expression to the past tense, as if a historical change has occurred as a consequence of God's judgment:

I said that ye were Gods, yea all
    The Sons of God most high;
But ye shall die like men, and fall
    As other Princes *die*.   (82:6–7)

God's final statement emphatically suggests that the death of Princes—or the death of *a* Prince, once called a god—will be part of an effort to restore earthly justice. The phrasing "As other Princes," rather than the King James Version's "like one of the Princes" has been seen to suggest Milton's weak grasp of the similar Hebrew words for "one" and "other."[85] But this is unlikely—"other" is workable enough, and Milton is not aiming for precision as much as he aims for present utility. His phrasing drives home the increasingly personal and singular connotations of "Ye." Milton's phrasing "Sons of God," usually translated as "sons of the most High," echoes Jesus's later reuse of the Psalm. Thus, the phrase frequently used to support divine right in Milton's Stuart context is dismissed as something God might once have said: kings *were* Gods, comparable to all "sons of God," but such a dictum would not prevent the full administration of justice.[86]

Scholarly literature on these psalms has often agonized over the liberties Milton takes, as if he is either in error as a Hebraist, or in some way in need of apology or defense in his translation choices.[87] But I think we need to see the paratextual display as being much more emblematic of Milton's engagement with scripture, particularly in the creative and polemical setting of his vernacular poetry and prose. We see in this series of examples a reader whose attention to the literal text is at times hair-splittingly precise, even while, at others, the text seems malleable to the needs—and present conditions—of the interpreter. Milton, like many of his contemporaries, can be rigorously attentive to the original meaning when it is suitable to be so, but he also deviates—sometimes with a gesture of disclosure, italic or otherwise—from the original in order to refashion it for the urgent English present.

*   *   *

Tyndale's oft-quoted injunction that "scripture hath but one sense, which is the literal sense"[88] is a flat renunciation of the complex figurative modes of reading in medieval Christianity, which Dante—or a text attributed to Dante—once used to describe his own methods of representation, drawing perhaps the most frequently cited connection between literary representation and biblical hermeneutics. The key example attributed to Dante explains the polysemous layers of reading for Psalm 114:1–2, "When Israel went out of Egypt, the house of Jacob from a barbarous people, Judea was made his sanctuary, Israel his dominion,"[89] as not only about the Israelites leaving Egypt, but also allegorically about the redemption of Christ. For Tyndale, it was not only vital that the literal sense replaced the polysemous layers of medieval hermeneutics, but that scripture have just *one* sense. This singularity of sense—perhaps more than literalism per se— continued to be reinforced in the seventeenth century. William Ames's popular theological manual *The Marrow of Sacred Divinity*, for example, reinforces Tyndale's dictum, though omitting entirely the idea of the "literal": "there is only one sense of one place of Scripture (*Hinc etiam unius loci Scripturae unicus est sensus*): because otherwise the sense of the scripture should be not only not clear and certain, but none at all: for that which doth not signify one thing, signifieth certainly nothing."[90] Ames's treatise had a profound structural influence on Milton's *De Doctrina Christiana*, although Milton often used this structure as a point of departure rather than agreement. In a chapter of *De Doctrina Christiana* bearing the same title as the corresponding chapter in Ames, "De Scriptura Sacra,"[91] Milton also asserts that "The sense of each scriptural passage is single (*Sensus cuiusque scripturae unicus est*),"[92] thus crediting the unassailable single sense of Reformation theology. Yet Milton goes on to explain how there is often duplicity in this singularity: "In the Old Testament, though, it is often a compound of the historical and typological (*compositus ex historia et typo*)."[93] Using an example from Hosea 11.1, "out of Egypt I called my son," Milton then points an example where such a "double sense" can be established in a way similar to Dante's example from Psalm 114—a psalm translated by Milton at 15—concerning the Israelites' deliverance from Egypt.[94]

In addition to Milton's complication of the Tyndalean "single sense" in his hermeneutics, Milton's textual analysis also draws attention to the problem that the written text is ambiguous, and not always by design. The New Testament, though far less ancient than the Old, suffered from less careful stewardship, leaving contradictions and textual instability. Summarizing the Renaissance recovery of the New Testament and collation from "diverse handwritten codices," by such "learned men" as Erasmus and Beza, Milton reflects that "God's providence (*providentia Dei*) . . . committed the contents of the New Testament to such wayward and uncertain guardians . . . so that this very fact might convince us that the Spirit which is given to us is a more certain guide than scripture, and that we ought to follow it."[95] Thus, "particularly under the gospel," there is a "double" or "twofold scripture"[96]—an internal scripture and an external scripture. The theoretical arguments behind Milton's practices of interpretation share a common ground with the material aspects of his psalm translations, particularly in the alternative readings, which allow for alternate, and even overlapping interpretations. The next and final chapter turns to these theological (or theoretical) grounds, and explores another way that Milton confronts the hermeneutics of literalism in the polemical debates of the English Civil War. Rather than focusing on the particular moment in April 1648, the following chapter surveys Milton's hermeneutic development throughout the period of the civil wars and leading up to the Restoration of Charles II in several punctuated moments in his polemical prose.

CHAPTER 8

Milton Contra Tyndale

I forbid not to read, I forbid to reason.
—Archbishop Cranmer, Preface to the Great Bible, 1540

Milton is credited by the *Oxford English Dictionary* with the first use of the term *literalism* in English and the second use of *literalist*, and in both cases the term is used in a derogatory manner, calling down the reading practices of his political opponents. In using the terms *literal, literalist,* and *literalism* with sudden and recurring intensity in his polemics against the Presbyterians in the mid-1640s, I would like to argue, Milton consciously identifies a culturally dominant interpretive habit that stems from Tyndalean origins. His critiques of his contemporaries' interpretations are therefore attacks, not just on the substance of their readings, but also on the method that brought them to adhere to these positions. These hermeneutic criticisms occurred during a crucial shift in Milton's career that coincided with the fragmentation of Protestant sects after the first phases of the civil wars. After his interventionist poems and psalm adaptations of 1648, Milton reenters the print polemical debate to legitimate the overthrow of Parliament and the deposition of the king in early 1649, employing the same inventive hermeneutics as he had in the divorce tracts to refute the Presbyterians' and royalists' interpretation of Romans 13, though pushing his methods a step further.

Yet the story of Milton's extraordinary breaks from theological and hermeneutic conventions begins when he was a more conventional—or at least *seemed* a more conventional—Calvinist in the period building up to the Civil Wars. After a failed "Short" parliamentary meeting that had ended more than a decade of rule without Parliament (a period variously termed "Personal Rule" or "Eleven Years' Tyranny"), the king called the "Long Parliament" in November 1640 to raise funds for a religious war with Scotland. The engagement (known as the Bishops' Wars) would be an important prologue to the English Civil War, since the king sought to impose English Episcopal uniformity on the Presbyterian kirk of Scotland.[1] The Scottish rebellions were instigated in the late 1630s by the English imposition of a Book of Canons to replace John Knox's *Book of Discipline* and then a new *Book of Common Prayer* in 1637.[2] Between the first meeting of the Long Parliament and the outbreak of the English Civil War in August 1642, Milton wrote some five tracts to influence the course of parliamentary reform against the episcopal structure of the English Church: *Of Reformation, Of Prelatical Episcopacy, Animadversions, The Reason of Church Government,* and *Apology against a Pamphlet.* In these "anti-prelatical" prose tracts, Milton allied himself with the Presbyterian opponents of the Church of England and took on much of the puritanical language that aspired to maintain the Reformation in its (supposed) original form. At this early point, the cause was essentially divided between the puritan Roundheads in Parliament and the Royalist Cavaliers who supported the divine right of Charles.

Milton's anti-prelatical work shares with the Presbyterians a rigidly scripture-based hermeneutic that pits itself—as Cartwright had done in opposition to Hooker—against human reason. In these early tracts, Milton sought to construct the correct "discipline," to use their common term, according to what God prescribed. Crying out against his royalist opponents in *The Reason of Church Government* (1642), "Let them chant while they will of prerogatives," Milton countered: "we shall tell them of Scripture [until] the mighty weakness of the Gospel throw down the weak mightiness of mans reasoning."[3] In these arguments, including *Of Reformation,* Milton follows the extreme forms of *sola scriptura* practiced by such reformers as Tyndale, Luther, and Bucer. As Luther proudly conceded in his debate with Erasmus, human reason and predestinarian theology were separated by a vast abyss: "it gives the greatest possible offense to common sense or natural reason that God by his own sheer will should abandon, harden, and damn men as if he enjoyed the sins and the vast eternal torments of his wretched creatures."[4] Reformation theology often relied on and defined itself in terms of its opposition to rational explanation, which made adherence to the rules of scripture—and indeed, to law—all the more appropriate.[5] Cranmer's cautious words in the preface to the Great Bible of 1540, "I forbid not to read, I forbid to reason" represents part of this tradition: read scripture, but do not reason beyond its immediate meaning. Yet soon after the ascendency of the Presbyterians in 1643, Milton took a radical shift and turned against their biblicism and against Reformation theology more broadly. The turn coincides not only with a rising movement of "Independents" amid other splinter groups during the heady years of the civil war period, but also with the new direction of Milton's thinking, particularly on divorce, that was working to alienate him from dominant Presbyterians in Parliament. This concluding chapter thus seeks to trace the hermeneutic tensions that accompanied Milton's radical shifts in thinking at crucial points in the Civil War.

Milton is an especially useful figure with which to conclude, not only because he embodies in one career the three intersecting arenas of inquiry central to this study—as theologian, political polemicist, and biblical author—but also because he is himself an historian of the English Reformation. His first piece of published prose formatively sought to argue how the twists and turns of English history had hindered the progress of Reformation. *Of Reformation touching Church-Discipline in England: and the Causes that Hitherto Have Hindered It* (1641) seeks to understand "how it should come to pass that England (having had this grace and honour from God to bee the first that should set up a Standard for the recovery of lost Truth, and blow the first Evangelic Trumpet to the Nations . . .) should now be the last." The "first" to plant the flag of Reformation in England is John Wycliffe, the mythological originator in England of Protestantism, and Milton's tract traces a history of how "true Discipline" began to be planted again in England under "that godly and Royall Childe," Edward VI by such figures as Latimer and Cranmer, but met with a series of ill-chances, dynastic changes, and the machinations of bad churchmen and compromising monarchs.[6] Following a central argument throughout the reform movement, "Reformation" for Milton and his near contemporaries (including Bale and Spenser) was a process of recovery rather than innovation, of finding something that had legitimately existed already, lost or thwarted in its progress by corrupt and papish agents. Yet, in Milton's case, it is also through telling this history of the Reformation—and even, in the case of his use of Bucer—of *translating* significant works from that history—that Milton came to diverge significantly from the hermeneutics and theology of the past. In the midst of retelling this history, Milton came to conceive of Reformation instead as an evolving, forward-moving phenomenon. In a sense, Milton writes and rewrites Reformation history only to turn it in a different direction.

This chapter thus briefly returns to the central texts and reading methods of major protagonists at the beginning of this story—Erasmus, Tyndale, and Bucer—as they are seen and reframed through a succession of transformations in Milton's thinking. I begin in the divorce tracts and *Areopagitica* (1644), where Milton formatively breaks from the Calvinist Presbyterians and begins to formulate an anti-predestinarian theology, attacking at the same time his contemporaries' hermeneutics. I then turn to the crisis of sovereignty at the overthrow of Parliament in December 1648, and to the trial of Charles I, when Milton wrote *The Tenure of Kings and Magistrates* (1649), a tract defending the deposition of the king that is titled after different traditions of reading Romans 13. Milton's readings of Romans 13 and other biblical passages used by the royalists and Presbyterians attack the literalism that bound them to a strict reading of this passage. In the final section of the chapter, I describe how Milton seems to discover Erasmus's radical historicist reading of Romans 13 in the *Annotations* on the New Testament during his use of Erasmus's annotations in his research for *De Doctrina Christiana*, which explains why Erasmus's annotations appear for the first time in his polemical prose in a tract written just before the restoration of Charles II, *A Treatise of Civil Power* (1659). Although a number of Milton's deviations from Tyndalean Protestantism are Erasmian, this marks a fairly explicit moment.

Hermeneutic Invention in the Divorce Tracts

Milton's critique of literalism arrives with concentrated intensity in the divorce tracts, which appeared like the anti-prelatical tracts in a sudden flood of productivity, in five tracts—including a substantially revised republication. Milton's first work on divorce, *The Doctrine and Discipline of Divorce*, was published in August 1643 and again six months later in a "revis'd and much augmented" form in February 1644 (events moved so quickly at this time that months and even days are sometimes needed to chart changes in position). The expanded version of *The Doctrine and Discipline of Divorce* is addressed "to the Parliament of England with the Assembly" because this tract is partly prompted by debates about marriage in the Westminster Assembly, a council of theologians and parliamentary members appointed in 1643 to restructure the English Church.[7] Milton announced in the long title of his first tract that he intended this "restored" doctrine would liberate England "from the bondage of Canon Law," just as Bucer and Cranmer had sought to reform ecclesiastical law from its Catholic canon law origins, a fact that Milton uses in his translation of Bucer six months later.[8] In the meantime, Herbert Palmer, a member of the Westminster Assembly, declared in a sermon before Parliament that Milton's *Doctrine and Discipline of Divorce* was "a *wicked book* . . . abroad and *uncensured* [*uncensored*], though *deserving to be burnt*."[9] The printed sermon would have been perceived as a serious threat in a world that increasingly sought to punish heresy. This strenuous opposition marked Milton's last effort to address the Westminster Assembly, and hardened his counterattacks. *The*

Judgement of Martin Bucer concerning Divorce, Written to Edward the sixt . . . Wherein a Late Book restoring the Doctrine and Discipline of Divorce is here Confirm'd and Justify'd by the authority of Martin Bucer, was addressed only to Parliament, and *Areopagitica; A Speech of Mr. John Milton for the Liberty of Printing, to the Parliament of England,* deeply connected to the challenges represented by Palmer, appeared three months later in November. The final two tracts, ending for several years Milton's industrious output of print polemic, are further defenses of his established position in *The Doctrine and Discipline of Divorce*: first, *Tetrachordon: Expositions upon the Four Chief Places in Scripture, which treat of Marriage,* for which Milton digs up (and promulgates on his title page) "an intended Act of the Parliament and Church of England in the last year of Edward the sixth"—still the sainted prince of Reformation; and second, *Colasterion*, "a reply to a Nameless Answer against *The Doctrine and Discipline of Divorce.*" Both were published in 1645 and neither addressed to the Parliament or the Assembly. After publishing his *Poems* in early 1646, Milton turns away, ceasing for a time his polemical interventions—until perhaps the April 1648 manuscript of Psalms 80–88.

Milton's work on divorce breaks from the modes of interpretation that supported his opponents' positions. It is here in 1643–45 that he identifies "literalism" as the source of the problem, using the word for the first time in *The Doctrine and Discipline of Divorce*. It occurs some four times as such and in several different extended forms in this polemical prose, as Milton decries the misguided "extreme literalist" or the "obstinate literality" of bad interpreters.[10] In the 1644 edition of *The Doctrine and Discipline of Divorce*, he seems even to coin the term "literalism," again repudiating the narrow interpretive habits of his opponents, here cast as a hypothetical third person singular: "none of these considerations . . . can avail to the dispossessing him of his precious literalism." In *The Judgement of Martin Bucer* the buzzword turned slur appears again when Milton addresses the Parliament at the outset, suggesting that the current views of divorce derive from the "canonical tyranny of stupid and malicious Monks" and (painting literalism as a medieval Catholic mode of reading) an "abrupt and Papistical way of a literal apprehension against the direct analogy of sense, reason, law, and Gospel."[11] "Literal" occurs seven more times in *Tetrachordon* (1645), the tract that focuses most on exegesis, among these criticizing "the fury of his literal expounding," the dangers of "literal rigidity," and the problems of "Literal bondage" for those who are "still the servants of a literal indictment," and obey any "literal Law in the vigor of severity."[12]

Milton is not the first Protestant to worry about overly literal readings, but his sustained critique in this debate sharply demarcates a larger cultural division in which the interpretive habits of a group of reform-minded Protestants are distinctly associated with their incapacity for actual reform. In the process Milton argues for a different, much less narrowly focused hermeneutic approach, and at the same time advocates—like Hooker against Cartwright—the use of "reason" in determining an interpretation in a way that counters Reformation traditions. Both of these methods are then extended to his reading of Romans 13 at the crisis of sovereignty in 1649.

The major biblical verses under stress in the divorce tracts are Christ's seeming renunciation in Matthew 5:31–32 of the Mosaic allowance for divorce in Deuteronomy 24:1–2, the "writ of divorcement." The central scriptural restriction to divorce occurs in Matthew 5:32: "that anyone who divorces his wife causes her to commit adultery." But for Milton, the sole focus on Christ's words in Matthew amounts to an overly strict literalist reading. In *The Doctrine and Discipline of Divorce*, Milton combats "the strictness" of "literal interpreting," arguing that "we are not to repose all upon the literal terms of so many words, many instances will teach us: Wherein we may plainly discover how Christ meant not to be taken word for word."[13] Milton argues against the bondage to a single verse of scripture by harmonizing the text with other parts of scripture, while treating each individual part in its context: the posture and context of Christ's words here, in comparison to the genres and contexts of other points of scripture. As he explains in the preface to the translation of Bucer, Milton's method (though not Bucer's), is to "expound the words of our Saviour . . . duly by comparing other places, as they needs must do in the resolving of a hundred other Scriptures."[14] The main other places of scripture, expounded more fully in *Tetrachordon*, are God's words about the bonds of marriage in Genesis 2:18, "It *is* not good that the man should be alone: I will make him an help meet for him"; Moses's allowance of divorce; and Paul's words about marriage, especially in 1 Corinthians 7, "let not the husband put away his wife" (1 Cor. 7:11).

At the same time that the divorce tracts develop a broadly comparative and contextualist method of reading scripture, they are informed by the new methodology of political philosophers like John Selden and Hugo Grotius. Milton cites a title of Selden's in his text "that noble volume written by our learned *Selden, Of the law of nature & of Nations*" (the *De Jure Naturali et Gentium*), and refers to Grotius ten times (ten of the eleven times in his English prose) in the divorce tracts.[15] In concert with these and other seventeenth-century philosophers, Milton is drawn to make his argument accord with the rules of "natural reason," but also with a charitable reading of scripture that takes character, tone, context, and author into account. In looking at God's self-presentation in Genesis, for example, when God decides that it is "not good for man to be alone" (Gen. 2:18), Milton circumnavigates the idea that this should be read as an imperative charge of marriage. His contextualist hermeneutics involve "natural reason": God "presents himself like to a man deliberating; both to show us that the matter is of high consequence, and that he intended to found it according to natural reason, not impulsive command, but that the duty should arise from the reason of it, not the reason be swallow'd up in a reasonless duty."[16] Imbedded here is a critique of reading scripture for law, or precept—an argument that looks surprisingly similar to Satan's view, after overhearing God's edict concerning the tree of knowledge, that it is "reasonless": "can it be sin to know?"(PL 4.516–7). Milton suggests that God's posture of speculation should bring us to conclude that God meant to instill in us the freedom to use our own "natural reason."[17] The text of the Bible itself thus encourages the use of reason by its calculated textual richness and indeterminacies, and, indeed, by other means—the speculative posturing of a narrator—that would be reborn, perhaps, in Raphael or the other narrators of Paradise Lost.

When Milton begins to formulate a theory of reason in Areopagitica, he does it in a way that challenges the legalist political utopianism and theology of predestination that had been central to Reformation thought. His critique of utopianism, both Edenic and Platonic, follows in immediate sequence and less than four months after the publication of his translation from Bucer's De Regno Christi, the central work of Protestant utopianism and legalism of the Reformation. In Areopagitica, Milton makes a forceful case against utopianism and its related Presbyterian legalism: "To sequester out of the world into Atlantic and Utopian polities, which never can be drawn to use, will not mend our condition; but to ordain wisely as in this world of evil, in the midst whereof God hath plac't us unavoidably."[18] The terms of this explicit rejection of utopianism suggest that Milton views the Presbyterians' legalistic prohibitions on publishing—and their efforts at suppressing heresy—as a part of a longer tradition of legalism.

Milton also takes a very different position from Bucer in interpreting the Ten Commandments. "It is," he writes, in De Doctrina Christiana, "conformity with faith, not with the ten commandments, which must be considered as the form of good works. Thus if I keep the Sabbath, in accordance with the ten commandments, when my faith prompts me to do otherwise, my precise compliance with the commandments will be counted as sin and as . . . unlawful behavior. It is faith that justifies, not compliance with the commandments; and only that which justifies can make any work good."[19] For Milton, conformity to the will of God is really only properly a conformity with faith that happens also to be the will of God, a common Reformation argument. But Milton goes one step further to suggest that that faith may tell us to do something other than what God seems to command. Milton's stress on individual freedom brings him so far as to suggest that even the Ten Commandments might in some circumstances be broken. As Samson says, realizing that what is required for revelation is freedom, "Commands are no constraints. If I obey them, / I do it freely."[20] In *De Doctrina Christiana* and other works, Milton formulates this individual, cognitive authority in the language of both faith and reason. He states, for example, that "God of his wisdom determined to create men and angels reasonable beings, and therefore free agents"[21]—suggesting the same essential freedom indicated in Samson's words.

In the case for "free reasoning" in *Areopagitica*, a great deal hinged on the prescriptive quality of scripture as it was valued by many Protestants and especially puritans, who had—following figures like Bucer and Cartwright—come to treat scripture as a source of prescriptive rules: "the only rule to frame all our Actions by," as one anonymous civil war theologian wrote, and the "only Law whereby to determine all our *Civil* Controversies."[22] Milton's critique of this posture emanates from *Areopagitica*, emerging in a reading of the conditions of humanity: "God uses not to captivate under a perpetual childhood of prescription, but trusts him with the gift of reason to be his own chooser."[23] "Prescription" captures Law in a broad sense that includes both scriptural and political legalism, and ultimately gestures toward the "childhood of prescription" in Eden, which set youthful humanity under a single prohibition concerning the Tree of the Knowledge of Good and Evil. In *Areopagitica*, Milton is making an epistemological claim as well as a political one, condemning laws that would prohibit the free press, but also speaking against the oppression of Protestant legalism more generally. He takes this idea up again in reinforcing a reading of the Fall as a fortunate event: "Many there be that complain of divine Providence for suffering Adam to transgress, foolish tongues! When God gave him reason, he gave him freedom to choose, for reason is but choosing" (527). Choice is necessary for reason, and under the Edenic prohibition Adam and Eve cannot really know without the knowledge of both good and evil. In this reconsideration of the fall in *Areopagitica*, Milton makes the "free reasoning"[24] espoused in *The Doctrine and Discipline of Divorce* part of his core argument behind the freedom of the will essential to the acquisition of knowledge in a republic. The argument represents a major break from Reformation theology, since it was largely on the grounds of the Anglican slippage and embrace of the Arminian (and Erasmian) doctrine of free will that the Presbyterians based their theological charge.[25]

William Prynne argued that the Arminian doctrine of "free will [was a] total and final apostasy from the state of grace,"[26] and in his own anti-prelatical tracts, Milton had also suggested that the Arminian position was untenable, though not as fiercely.[27] Yet he does not make his position explicit until he restates the same argument in *Paradise Lost*. "Reason also is choice," argues God in *Paradise Lost*, and "when Will and Reason" are "made passive," as in Reformation theology, humanity serves "necessity / not me" (*PL* 3.108–10). The theology of predestination, once built on the bedrock of scripture, is now refuted on rational rather than scriptural grounds.

Defending the Regicide

While the imprisoned king read psalms and waited for resolution in 1648, the forces of power now divided between the Parliament and the Army were held in a tense stalemate. The Parliament, represented by Presbyterians like William Prynne, favored reconciliation with the king following the end of the second Civil War. This was an unexpected turn for republicans like Milton, because the same Presbyterian advocates for the maintenance of the Stuart monarchy had originally sided against the Royalists. Prynne, now famous for complaining in the margins of his *Histrio-Mastix* (1633) that "Shakespeare's Plays are printed in the best Crown paper, far better than most Bibles," and for having his ears cropped for seditious libel, had been a major puritan advocate against the king.[28] Prynne's multivolume parliamentarian work at the outset of the war, for example, *The Sovereign Power of Parliaments and Kingdoms* (1643)—which Milton's title, *The Tenure of Kings and Magistrates* may deliberately echo—bore in its longer title a justification for Parliament's "necessary defensive war against the Kings offensive malignant, popish forces."[29] The seminal work, frequently referred to in 1648 in an effort to convince parliament that revolution had always been the objective,[30] had made the case that "The Parliament being the Highest Power, the King Himself ought to submit thereto, and to be ruled and advised thereby."[31] The argument was based largely on a Calvinist reading of Romans 13: if Paul says to "be subject unto the higher powers," and Parliament is the highest power, then the king must submit. Prynne even makes the remarkable historicist argument that "In Paul's time, the highest Powers in Rome, were not the Roman Emperours, as ignorant Doctors make the unlearned world believe, but the Roman Senate, who had full power, not only to elect and command, but censure, and depose their Emperours, and adjudge them unto death" (106).

However, when Prynne and other MPs in parliament had the king under their power, and Charles had, it seemed, submitted at least to some demands, the same passage in Romans—with others adduced—prevented them from touching further the Lord's anointed. Thus, when to the horror of Prynne and other strict Calvinists, Colonel Pride and the New Model Army forcibly purged Parliament of those who opposed the king's deposition, a new and better interpretation of Romans 13 would be needed to legitimate the deposition of both kings and magistrates. Using some of the same hermeneutic tools employed in the divorce tracts, Milton quickly advanced a powerful reading.

The position established by Calvin, and translated and reprinted in the *Institutes of the Christian Religion*, held that while lower magistrates could lawfully depose monarchs in some cases, it was not lawful for a "private" person like Thomas Pride. Milton states his case against the Calvinist position in the extended title of *The Tenure of Kings and Magistrates,* "proving that it is Lawful . . . for *any*, who have the Power, to call to account a Tyrant, or wicked KING, and after due conviction, to depose, and put him to death; if the ordinary MAGISTRATE have neglected or deny'd to do it."[32] "Any," which I italicize here, points to the private persons—such as Pride and his troops—who have pushed aside "Magistrates" who have neglected to do what they should have done. The question of KING or MAGISTRATE had hinged to a large extent on how the Greek word *archontes*, αρχοντες, *chief magistrates*, is translated in Romans 13:3 ("For rulers (*archontes*), are not to be feared for good works"). As with so many readings, the difference is rooted in Erasmus's rewording of the Vulgate, in which *archon* had been rendered as *princeps* (*prince*, even *emperor*, as it was adopted by Augustus). Erasmus chose *magistratus*, which made it easier for the text to imply any high official.[33] Calvin's reading follows Erasmus, as do later editions of the Geneva Bible. This translation allowed Calvin and his followers to make the distinction that God gives not just monarchs the ordained sword, but high magistrates, who can in rare and divinely motivated cases use the sword against the monarch.[34] Editions of Calvin's *Institutes of the Christian Religion* (1561), Englished at the beginning of Elizabeth's reign by the parliamentarian playwright Thomas Norton, glossed Calvin's "magistrates" in English terms, marking "Parliament" in the margin of the passage lest readers miss the implications of Calvin's "magistrate" in an extraordinary passage:

> Let Princes hear and be afraid. . . . For though the correcting of
> unbridled government be the revengement of the Lord, let us not by
> and by think that it is committed to us, to whom there is given no

other commandment but to obey and suffer. I speak always of private
men. For if there be at this time any Magistrates for the behalf of the
people, (such as in old time were the Ephori, that were set against the
kings of Lacedemonia, or the Tribunes of the people, against the
Roman Consuls: or the Demarchi, against the Senate of Athens: and
the same power also which peradventure, as things are now, the three
estates have in every Realm, when they hold their principal assemblies)
I do so not forbid them according to their office to withstand the
outraging licentiousness of kings: that I affirm that if they wink at
kings willfully ranging over and treading down the poor communality,
their dissembling is not without wicked breach of faith, because they
deceitfully betray the liberty of the people, whereof they know
themselves to be appointed protectors by the ordinance of God.[35]

English translators of Calvin placed the word "Parliaments" conspicuously in
the margin next to "according to their office, making clear that Parliament had the
right to resist tyranny." Calvin's position was already radical resistance theory:
most English political theologies simply argued that it was never permissible ac-
tively to resist a sovereign. For Calvin, and for the Calvinist tradition of reading
Romans 13 in England, Parliament had the right to depose only when a revenging
God called them as agents. No doubt, this was in itself a conflicting message,
since it was no easy task to determine whether God had made such a choice. Ty-
rannicide was sometimes permissible, but only when high magistrates were enacting God's will, since the "wicked ruler" is itself "a judgment of God," and
obedience to wicked rulers is also "required in scripture." Only if magistrates are
"sent by God's lawful calling to carry out such acts, of taking up arms against
kings"[36] might a deposition be sanctified. This indeed was Prynne's warning in
the *Brief Memento to this Unparliamentary Juncto*, published several times in late
1648, and cited in Milton's tract: "be subject to Kings and the Higher Powers,
and to submit unto them," he intoned, enforcing the same passage in several
other pamphlets in the year, including his charge at the very end of one in 1647
that "any officers or soldiers in the Army" had better not "openly oppose or enforce without this guilt of Treason and Rebellion; the breach of Rom. 13:1,2,3."[37]

Milton's task was to reread Romans 13, and as in the divorce tracts, he uses
other biblical texts to harmonize with and ultimately alter the literal sense of the
passage. Also following the hermeneutic strategies of the divorce tracts, he invokes natural reason. The tract appeals to reason in its very first clause: "If men
within themselves would be govern'd by reason."[38] Unlike many of the biblical

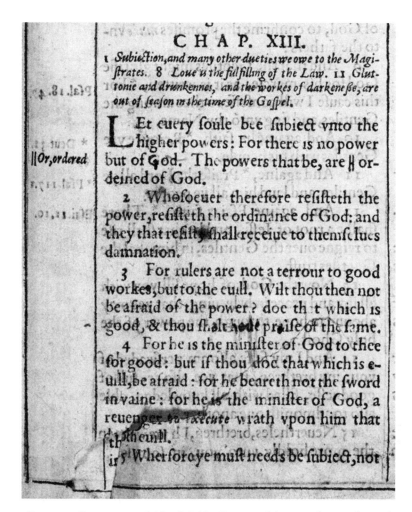

CHAP. XIII.

1 *Subiection, and many other dueties we owe to the Magi-*
strates. 8 *Loue is the fulfilling of the Law.* 11 *Glut-*
tonie and drunkennes, and the workes of darkenesse, are
out of season in the time of the Gospel.

Et euery soule bee subiect vnto the
higher powers: For there is no power
but of God. The powers that be, are ‖ or-
deined of God.

2 Whosoeuer therefore resisteth the
power, resisteth the ordinance of God: and
they that resist shall receiue to themselues
damnation.

3 For rulers are not a terrour to good
workes, but to the euill. Wilt thou then not
be afraid of the power? doe that which is
good, & thou shalt hede praise of the same.

4 For he is the minister of God to thee
for good: but if thou doe that which is e-
uill, be afraid: for he beareth not the sword
in vaine: for he is the minister of God, a
reuenger to execute wrath vpon him that
doeth euill.

5 Wherfore ye must needs be subiect, not

citations in the text, Milton's reconsideration of Paul's supposed doctrine of obedience alludes without citation, his exegesis becoming at times artfully incorporated into his prose: "all men naturally were born free, being the image and resemblance of God himself, and were, by privilege above all the creatures, born to command, and not to obey." The passage orients readers in the beginning of Genesis, and then pits the notion that humans were given dominion (Gen. 1:26) against Pauline obedience—"ye must needs obey" in Tyndale's wording or from Calvin's words above, that the Lord has given "no other commandment but to obey and suffer."[39] Milton takes bits and pieces of Romans 13:1–6 and reworks them into a new formulation: "For if all human power to execute, not accidentally but intendedly, the wrath of God upon evil doers [Rom. 13:4, "he is a minister of God, a revenger *to execute* wrath upon him that doeth evil"] without exception, be of God; then that power, whether ordinary, or if that fail, extraordinary so executing that intent of God, is lawful, and not to be resisted [Rom. 13:2]."[40] As mentioned in the previous chapter, the print of this passage in Milton's own copy of the King James Bible is worn out, replaced in a few places with handwritten letters, and the page is torn (Figure 29). These signs of use imply that he returned to it again and again, a supposition reinforced by the many times it is woven, with and without reference, into his texts. As was true of Shakespeare, this cluster of verses is almost certainly the most referenced in Milton's corpus.[41] Here he weaves the text into his prose in a way that shows how it might be read as a proof text for popular sovereignty. The tone is bold, even with an edge of irony, as if Milton is partly asserting a powerful, liberating reading of the passage in the adaptive manner of his psalm translations of 1648, and partly exposing the liabilities of using mere fragments of the biblical text to establish meaning. Milton's brazen line "not to be resisted," inverts the Pauline text about obedience to power, "They that resist, shall receive to themselves damnation" (Rom. 13:2), and adds to the general subversion of Calvin's political theology: resistance must be willful, an act of "human power," not the "accident" of Calvinist theology. It is unlawful, Milton suggests, in an ironic twist of conventional exegesis, to resist the just course of action.

When Milton explicitly approaches Romans 13, later in the tract, he has already prepared readers for interpretative eccentricity. The direct citations, however, require a more formal explication. Here, as Milton had done in the divorce tracts, Milton ascertains meaning through a process of "comparison of one text with another,"[42] as he instructs in *De Doctrina Christiana*, to make sure there is no contradiction, since, as he writes in *Tetrachordon*, "God cannot contradict himself."[43] To compare or harmonize one biblical text with others, Milton first invokes a scene of a king and advisors from the Hebrew Bible, the "wise Coun-selors whom *Rehoboam* first advis'd with [1 Kings 12:6–11] spake no such thing, as our gray headed Flatterers now are wont, stand upon your birth-right, scorn to capitulate, you hold of God, not of them. . . . Therefore Kingdom and Mag-istracy . . . is call'd a *human ordinance*, 1 Pet. 2:13. &c. which we are there taught is the will of God we should [alike] submit to, so far as for the punishment of evil doers, and the encouragement of them that doe well. *Submit* saith he, *as free men*."[44] Placed in the context of Rehoboam, the passages from 1 Peter are then applied for comparison to the language of Romans 13: "*There is no power but of God*, saith *Paul, Rom.* 13. As much as to say God put it into man's heart to find out that way at first for common peace and preservation, approving the exercise thereof; else it contradicts *Peter* who calls the same authority an Ordinance of man."[45] There is a hint of Erasmian quietism here in the chronology implied by "at first for common peace and preservation," yet this primacy is not historicist—placing it in the Pauline context—so much as a kind of anthropology, suggest-ing where God *first* planted the concept of ordained power. Yet Paul's concept of "authority" cannot, according to Milton, finally mean this, since it would *con-tradict* Peter, who makes it a human ordinance.[46]

Having invalidated the central biblical text on which English monarchic authority constructed itself, Milton proceeds to build an argument on the an-thropological grounds of natural philosophy, rather than on biblical grounds:

And because no faith in all was found sufficiently binding, they [i.e., early humans] saw it needful to ordain some authority, that might restrain by force and punishment what was violated against peace and common right. This authority and power of self-defense and preserva-tion being originally and naturally in every one of them, and unitedly in them all, for ease, for order, and least [i.e., lest] each man should be his own partial Judge, they communicated and deriv'd either to one, whom for the eminence of his wisdom and integrity they chose above the rest, or to more than one whom they thought of equal deserving: the first was call'd a King; the other Magistrates . . . to be their Deputies and Commissioners, to execute, by virtue of their entrusted power, that justice which else every man by the bond of nature and of Cov'nant must have executed for himself, and for one another. And to him that shall consider well why among free Persons, one man by civil right should bear authority and jurisdiction over another, *no other end or reason* can be imaginable.[47]

No biblical quotation has entered this argument, and by the words at the end, no proof text imaginable could challenge these reasons for civil right: Milton is legitimating political authority by other means. Martin Dzelzainis observed that "Milton here committed himself to the view—without precedent in any vernacular work of political theory—that, in a state of nature, each and every individual can punish offenders against the law of nature, and that, in executing justice, the civil magistrate was exercising no new right but one which had initially been possessed by all pre-political individuals."[48] And from the point of view of hermeneutic method, Milton here goes further than the divorce tracts, in making the case for an extra-biblical mode of argumentation without confirmation by the biblical text.

Milton's turn to an argument from natural reason no doubt represents a turning point in the history of political argument. Milton's engagement with scripture in this tract has two distinct modes, one that offers a different interpretive method to counter the literalism of his opponents, and one that uses natural reason as both an affirmation of exegesis, but also as a method of legitimation independent of scriptural exegesis. Milton illustrates this independence in drawing on the actions of Jehu, the ninth-century king called by the prophet of God, who, after he poured oil over Jehu's head and anointed him, bid him to "smite the house of Ahab thy master, that I may avenge the blood of my servants the Prophets" (2 Kings 9:7). This provided the godly with a Calvinistic example of God enacting his revenge, and was invoked by revolutionaries as an exemplar.[49] Milton invokes the scriptural example to credit it as a good one *if* one wanted to be Calvinist, though, he asserts, natural reason could provide better validation: "And whereas *Jehu* had special command to slay *Jehoram* a successive and hereditary Tyrant, it seems not the less imitable for that; and where a thing grounded so much on natural reason hath the addition of a command from God, what does it but establish the lawfulness of such an act."[50] Like the endorsement of reason found in *Areopagitica* and the divorce tracts, this tract presents scripture not as the source for moral law, but as the confirmation of laws produced by "natural reason."[51]

Erasmus Arrives Late

Milton's first Latin *Defense of the People of England*, the *Pro Populo Anglicano Defensio*, published in 1651 in response to the French Protestant theologian Salmasius, contains some extensive interpretations of Romans 13 and comes close to arguing that the heathen context might occasion a radically different interpretation. Instead, it simply ridicules Salmasius's absolutist interpretation that "since the very king whom they were ordered to obey was Nero, then tyrant at Rome," therefore "we too must submit to tyrants."[52] James I had used the same argument, as discussed above in chapter 6: he argues that the king, "whom *Paul* bids the *Romans Obey* and serve *for conscience sake*, was *Nero* that bloody tyrant, an infamy to his age, and a monster to the world," but this "hindered not the spirit of God to command his people under all highest pain to give them al due and hearty obedience for conscience sake."[53] Milton undermines Salmasius's claim merely by suggesting that it was not Nero, but Claudius (or perhaps in the "good" part of Nero's reign), and by suggesting that Paul would never have meant obedience to tyranny. Paul's letter "was in fact composed under Claudius, an honest ruler and a decent man . . . and even Nero had five excellent years, so that oft-repeated argument is as false as it is common, namely that a tyrant must be obeyed because Paul told the Romans to obey Nero."[54] Here, Milton comes close to Colet's and Erasmus's argument, at least in the sense of arguing that the context of Paul's letter dictates the precise meaning, yet his conclusion is not that Paul was being rhetorically ingenious or that the words do not apply in a Christian setting, but simply—and somewhat satirically—that Paul would never have made such a statement had he known how bad tyranny could be.

Remarkably, it is not until *A Treatise of Civil Power in Ecclesiastical Causes* (1659), one of a collection of late vernacular tracts written to try to restructure the commonwealth after the death of Cromwell, that Milton finally makes the case made by Erasmus, the case that fully disarms the application of Romans 13. Here Milton also explicitly turns away from many of the core positions of Reformation theology, even those he had sometimes endorsed throughout the 1640s, such as the theocratic intermingling of church and state that was central to Bucer's vision in *De Regno Christi*.[55]

In the earlier anti-monarchist polemics, Milton does not employ Erasmus's historicist reading, which effectively disarms Romans 13 of its application in divine right ideology, possibly because it has become unavailable to him. But in a sustained eight-page close reading of "this most wrested and vexed place of scripture" in *A Treatise of Civil Power*, Milton employs the historicist reading in the same place when he invokes Erasmus to support his claim, and while it is an annotation to a different verse (Gal. 5:12), Erasmus seems also behind Milton's forceful reading of Paul in Romans 13. In this unique moment in his English polemics, Milton cites Erasmus as taking the same position in terms of separating spiritual and secular power: "Whom *Erasmus* and others in their notes on the New Testament have cited to interpret."[56] Milton then argues that the case for a theocratic state stands on a reading of Romans 13, maintained by those who "cannot long subsist but in a bodily fear," and "for want of other proof will needs wrest that place of S. Paul Rom. 13 to set up civil inquisition, and give power to the magistrate both of civil judgment and punishment in causes ecclesiastical." For Milton, Romans 13 thus supported two tendencies in English politics: the wrongful elevation of the magistrate to a position above legal accountability, and the wrongful binding of church and state under one theocratic head.

> But let us see with what strength of argument. *Let every soul be subject to the higher powers.* First, how they that the apostle means other powers *then such as they whom he writes were then under*; who meddled not at all in ecclesiastical causes, unless as tyrants and persecutors; and from them, I hope, they will not derive either the right of magistrates to judge in spiritual things, or the duty of such our obedience.[57]
> [italics added]

The "tyrants and persecutors," he goes on to insist, were "heathen," thus drawing the distinction between "heathen" and "Christian" essential to Erasmus's reading: "to the shame of those Christians and especially those churchmen, who . . . never cease calling on the civil magistrate to interpose his fleshly force; an argument that all true ministerial and spiritual power is dead within them: who think the gospel, which both began and spread over the whole world for above three hundred years under heathen and persecuting emperors, cannot stand or continue, supported by the same divine presence and protection to the worlds end, much easier under the defensive favor only of a Christian magistrate."[58] Milton's early radical arguments for the separation of the church and state necessarily focus on the theocratic reading of Romans 13 that had dominated English Protestantism. Here in this late treatise, he turns finally to Erasmus's historicist argument that Paul's words about obedience apply only to the "heathen" magistrate of Paul's context. The view of Romans 13 that had dominated Protestant political theology had finally been dismantled from a Miltonic, rational, and an Erasmian historicist perspective.

Legitimating Power

The thunderous little book *Vindiciae Contra Tyrannos* (1579), produced by a Huguenot during the French religious wars, explains its purpose in its longer title as *de principis in populum legitimata potestate*, or, in the French translation issued in Geneva, "De la Puissance legitime du prince sur le people." This title might be translated into English with a little chiastic addition as "*Concerning the Legitimate Power of a Prince over the People, and of the People over a Prince,*" as it was during the English Civil War—reputedly by the executioner of King Charles himself, and published by Milton's printer, Matthew Simmons.[1] The influential treatise has gained attention for its republican elements, conspicuously expressed in the pseudonym of the author ("Stephanus Junius Brutus") and in lapidary capitals at the end of some editions: *BRUTE, MAGISTER ERAS* ("O BRUTUS, YOU WERE MY TEACHER").[2] Yet this tract, an attempt to define the terms by which power is given legitimacy, is not most accurately described along an axis from republicanism to absolutism. In fact, the classical features of this treatise, like many in the early modern period, pale by comparison to its biblical orientation: it is an attempt to legitimate power and its overthrow in chiefly biblical terms. The text is largely focused, in fact, on the question of how to interpret Romans 13, entrusting the sword to the lower magistrates in a way that builds on Calvin's reading of that passage.[3]

This project has understood the central problem of political legitimacy from the Erasmian pre-Reformation to the execution of Charles as fundamentally hermeneutical, in which the major questions of theo-political legitimacy rest not only on biblical texts, but on the way those biblical texts were read. Claims to political legitimacy are predominantly worked out, challenged, and explained through some kind of interpretation of the biblical text. "Legitimation," the "action of making or declaring something lawful" (*OED*) reminds us that "law" (*lex, legis*) is *that which is read* (*legere, legit*), a fundamental, even ritualistic act of validation that is represented in the ancient world of the Israelites as the moment in which the king, with his priests, reads from a copy of the book of law (Deut. 17:18–19).[4] The infamous monarchomach who wrote the *Vindiciae* constructs "legitimation" in a way that anticipates Habermas, who in *Legitimation Crisis* describes a moment in which a governing body holds power but is no longer able to demonstrate to those governed the moral grounds by which it claims sovereignty.[5] The story does not quite end, of course, in 1649. When Charles II returned to England and landed in Dover in 1660, the mayor presented him with "a very rich Bible . . . which he took and said it was the thing that he loved above all things in the world."[6] This pageantry replays something like the presentation of the Bible to Elizabeth in 1558, and even the scene depicted by Holbein on the title page of the first complete Bible printed in 1535. Yet the legitimation crisis of the English monarchy in the mid-seventeenth century began a process that would forever change English political discourse, and political beliefs would seldom again—especially after Locke's refutation of Filmer's *Patriarcha* in *The Two Treatises on Government* (1689)—hinge so completely and resolutely on biblical texts. This is not to say that biblical passages no longer shape political discourse—at the time of this writing, the Attorney General of the United States has invoked Romans 13 to defend its immigration law enforcement; it has also been invoked by a twenty-first-century Supreme Court Justice to legitimate capital punishment.[7] But as shaping as the biblical text still is to contemporary politics, it has not had as broad and dominant a grip on English political culture since the Renaissance.

This book has focused on the struggle of the English monarchy—and the culture itself—to explain the legitimacy of its political system even while English religion was in a constant state of flux, destabilized by competing systems of belief: Catholicism, puritanism, and the Church of England. In exploring this history, I have sought to scrutinize punctuated moments in the history of political legitimation, chiefly moments of transition or instability that often occur at the accession of a new monarch: the Henrician crises of legitimacy around secular obedience and dynastic lineage, the biblical installment of Edward VI, the reversion to Catholic rule in Mary's reign, the accession of Elizabeth and the challenges of confessional orientation during her reign, the arrival of James from Scotland, and the political crisis of the 1640s. These moments were accompanied by outpourings of theologically oriented political literature and, often, by the publication of a new biblical text.

Within these punctuated moments, this project has explored the intersections of three discursive fields: the biblical text, the paratext surrounding that text, and the political world occupied by readers and writers, who digest the interpreted and translated text and reframe it in biblically inflected literature. In some cases, the relationship of text and paratext of particular Bibles are recreated in a literary context. Spenser recreated the experience of an Elizabethan reader of the Geneva Bible, for example, in his polemical interpretation of the Book of Revelation, in both *The Theatre for Worldlings* and the Legend of Holiness in *The Faerie Queene*, just as he arguably sought to recreate the biblical reader in the *Shepheardes Calender* and his sonnet sequence *Amoretti*, which follows the liturgical calendar of scriptural readings.[8] In the cases of Spenser's use of Revelation, not just the paratextual words but also the woodcuts in the illustrated Book of Revelation were crucial to literary images in both publications. As I have also suggested in chapter 6, Shakespeare's *Measure for Measure* opens with language and imagery that seems to draw from one of the most vital biblical paratexts in Tudor England, the image of the monarch on the title page, deriving power from God, with "mercy" in one hand and "mortality" in the other. Milton recreates the reader's experience of the King James Bible in his polemical 1648 rewriting of the psalms, using its italics within the text to signify where the English has departed from the Hebrew, supplying verse numbers, and imitating its philological notes and alternate readings. In this case the surviving Bible of the author, a 1612 King James Bible, provides additional evidence to reconstruct a history of reading practices and illuminates the relationship between Milton's reading experience and that which he seeks to recreate.

In these cases, the biblical paratext has a vital role in shaping the reader's perception of the text. Indeed, it can hardly be a coincidence that the first words Milton chose for both *Paradise Lost* and *Paradise Regained* essentially repeat the first words of the King James Bible. Just after the title page and at the beginning of the genealogy, these words drawn from Romans 5:19 are inscribed on a panel within an image of Adam and Eve, standing over death in the garden: "As by one man's disobedience many were made sinners, so by the obedience of one shall many be made righteous" (Figure 30). Milton's *Paradise Lost* begins on this very note. The famous words "Of Mans First Disobedience and the Fruit / Of that Forbidden Tree, whose mortal taste / Brought Death"—at the foot of Adam and Eve—"into the World, and all our woe, / With loss of Eden, till one greater Man / Restore us"[9] recapture the physical opening of Milton's most used book. The scholarly focus on Milton's classical heritage has taught us that the first few lines of *Paradise Regain'd* rely, as did Spenser's *Faerie Queene*, on the reader's

Figure 30. "As by one man's disobedience": the beginning of Milton's Bible. The opening paratext found in the 1612 King James Bible, such as that which Milton owned, in the first page of the biblical genealogy (this page in Milton's actual Bible is now missing). The opening of the Bible mirrors the opening lines of Milton's two biblical epics. *Holy Bible* (London: Robert Barker, 1612). Folger STC 2220. By permission of the Folger Shakespeare Library.

knowledge of the first lines of Virgil's *Aeneid* included in early modern editions but now considered inauthentic, in which the Roman poet introduced himself as "he who once tuned my song on a slender reed."[10] It has not been noted that Milton's *Paradise Regain'd* interweaves the first lines of the Renaissance *Aeneid* with the first lines of this Renaissance Bible: "I who erewhile the happy Garden sung / By one mans disobedience lost, now sing" echoes the very words of the biblical paratext: "by one mans disobedience."[11] In this case, unlike the *deliberate* reuse of the biblical paratext in his 1648 psalms, the now blind poet may be unconscious in recapturing the quotation that so prominently begins the King James Bible in the opening of his epics—although his memory of it is surely as vivid as it is of the pseudo-Virgil. Yet whether conscious or not, Milton's echo of the biblical paratext, here and in the psalm translations, reinforces how profoundly important the packaging and apparatus of a book could be in shaping the reader's perceptions of the text. The slippage between gloss and text from Tyndale to the translators, annotators, and readers of the Geneva Bible suggests that the anachronistic distinction between text and paratext was much less defined in early modernity.[12] The paratext played a far less ancillary and far more energized role than it does for modern readers. Even the sparse but highly important marginal and typographic devices of the King James Bible shaped the practices and citations of a writer like Milton. In many instances the King James Bible's margins offer what is a superior alternate reading—"Judges" rather than "Gods," for example, when the text of Exodus reads "thou shalt not revile the Gods, nor curse the ruler of thy people" (Exod. 22:28). This kind of interpretative substance in the margins indicates that readers were expected to value these margins on a level that their omission from modern editions belies.

The instances of paratextual play in Spenser and Milton, so bound to the material conditions of reading Renaissance Bibles that much is lost for modern readers by the absence of originals, are admittedly extraordinary. Yet they speak to a more pervasive interaction between literature texts and biblical texts and paratexts, one that this project has sought to trace forward from the interactive relationships between Erasmus's annotations and his advice books and Tyndale's translations, glosses and polemics. One of the great incongruities of history is that so much of the Reformation Bible is built on Erasmus's major textual work on the New Testament, yet in many cases, Reformation readers drew vastly different conclusions and approached the text with very different interpretive practices. This is nowhere more paradoxical than in England, wherein Erasmus's six years or so of cumulative visits somehow left a profound legacy, even leading James McConica to argue influentially that the English Reformation was fundamentally Erasmian, an idea that was often maintained throughout the Renaissance: Thomas Bodley, for example, included Erasmus in historical friezes in the Oxford library among the figures who established the Protestant Reformation in England, and the late seventeenth-century Latitudinarian, Edward Stillingfleet wrote that "to this day, *Erasmus* is in far greater esteem among the Divines of our Church, than either *Luther*, or *Calvin*."[13] If we agree with the majority of current scholarship that Erasmus is not quite Protestant doctrinally, he had a strange authority in England, nowhere more evident than in the mandate that *The Paraphrases on the New Testament* be included with the Bible in every English church by Edward VI and again by Elizabeth in 1559, and also that it be part of the education of the clergy.[14] The theologically flexible Nicholas Udall and the other Protestant and Catholic translators of the *Paraphrases* show that the origins of this translated work already bore something of the ecumenical *via media* that Gregory Dodds describes.[15] Yet the translation of Erasmus in England originated from still more stridently Protestant sources than Udall and the court. Tyndale began his career translating Erasmus: first the *Enchiridion*, and then the New Testament (1525), where his most controversial annotation, on Peter as "rock" (and not the first pope) in Matthew 16:18, calls on Erasmus's authority. Bucer's *De Regno Christi*, for all of its hard-nosed legalism and literal readings, draws from the Platonic advice book *Institutio Principis Christi* of Erasmus and the *Utopia* of Thomas More, a fierce critic of the reform movement and later treated as a Catholic martyr.

In spite of their debts to Erasmus, Tyndale and Bucer represent a mode of reading that diverges profoundly from Erasmus's literary and rhetorical approach to the New Testament. Their form of literalism is practiced widely by English Protestants, and especially by those of a puritanical slant, such as Thomas Cartwright, or Shakespeare's Angelo, or the heresy-hunting contemporaries of Milton. This form of literalism claims to adhere powerfully and exclusively to the literal meaning of the biblical text and finds particular strength in the legal codes of Moses. Indeed, the exclusive and even hyperbolic term "all," as in Angelo's "all-building-Law," frequently occurs in the hermeneutic asseverations of "precise" Protestants. The use of "all" appears in this manner in Cartwright's arguments about how to apply scripture, refuted in Erasmian terms by Hooker: "These as the very main pillar of your whole cause, that *scripture ought to be the only rule of all our actions*."[16] Scripture is "the only rule to frame all our Actions by," wrote a polemical interpreter during the civil wars, and (repeating "all" and "only") the "only Law whereby to determine all our *Civil* Controversies."[17] The packed formulation repeats a series of clichés among strict Protestants: the interchangeability of "scripture" and "law," as if all of scripture can be read as law and applied as such; the exclusive operation of *sola scriptura* as the *only* mode of apprehension; and the *application* of this mode of reading to politics, to *"all* our *Civil* Controversies."

The particular penchant for application of scripture to civil controversies supported a mode of reading that I have labeled "applied literalism," which extends especially back to Tyndale and Bucer. Bucer similarly treated scripture as if it might be reduced to the Book of Law, and read as if it were law: "God's Law is perfect and entire. . . . Wherefore Scripture is bound to contain oracles to deal definitely . . . with every aspect of public or private life."[18] "Scripture," with all of its tonal variety and modes of representation—and for all of the characteristic diversity of authors like Paul, Moses, or John of Patmos—is yet interchangeable with "Law," a mode of representation that is not only prescriptive and absolute, but also necessarily reduceable to shorter, often sentence-length clusters of words. Scripture is "bound" to "deal definitely" with all aspects of "public or private life." This applicability may be obvious in cases like Moses's law concerning adultery, but is much less so in the application of the commandment to honor parents to "all rulers,"[19] as Tyndale argued, and as Bucer wrote, the "Fifth Commandment of God, which enjoins that parents should be honored and obeyed (Exod. 20:12) . . . is especially applicable to rulers and magistrates of the commonwealth."[20] There is, of course, no real ground for this single line of scripture to be *especially* applicable to rulers except the intense desire for such application, and a habit of reading scripture that enables it. The urgency behind these applied readings is suggested in Richard Morison's conversion of gloss to text when he asks "which of all the commandments is more necessary for us than this, 'Obey ye your king'?"[21]

The Book of Books has thus explored two related trends in the relationship between political literature and biblical interpretation: one interpretive trend that masquerades as a kind of Protestant literalism but loses its true literalist quality in its zeal for contemporary application, and one that more truly adheres to the literalist sense of the text, with a penchant for turning the text into legalistic sentences. The first of these trends, the often creative reconstruction of the text for practical application, was practiced and encouraged by Erasmus, who notably advocated, even in his *Annotations* on the New Testament, the purposeful appropriation of scripture. Observing Paul's manner of turning particular phrases for his own use, Erasmus averred that scripture itself might in the same manner "be turned (*detorqueret*) for our use, as when with magnates it needs to be done."[22] This mode of application often takes the form of brief phrases, sentences, or precepts, such as "touch not thine anointed" (Ps. 105:15), or even the counterintuitive "measure for measure" of Shakespeare's text, and follows the widespread practice, also advocated by Erasmus, of excerpting and reusing passages.[23] This manner of application occurs especially with short passages, facilitated by the numbering of verses, but also occur in the application of parables from the gospel—the context for Gilby's "what need any exposition to apply this unto England?"[24]—and the allegories in the Book of Revelation, applied to the divided condition of the church.

But the second of these habits of legalistic biblical reading, the literalist movement that Milton criticizes using this very term, has no real roots in Erasmian humanism beyond the historical focus on the text. Erasmian theology and hermeneutics lurked just beneath and often at the surface of early modern English culture, as Dodds has also shown in other respects, to serve "as a *counterpoint* in English religious thought as first Protestantism and then Calvinism came to dominate English religion."[25] Dodds has shown how Erasmianism emerged in such figures as Hooker in his efforts to curtail predestination theology and the Calvinist church model, and also among the Great Tew intellectuals who were still more forthright in their adaptation of Arminian free will and anti-literalism.[26] Erasmus's *Annotations* on the New Testament were influential even for Milton, one among those later seventeenth-century figures whose positions were strengthened by the Erasmian legacy.

Literature itself cannot exist in a purely literalist world, and it is not surprising that texts like Shakespeare's *Measure for Measure*, characters like the "Puritan" Malvolio, or a poet-theologian like Milton complicate and satirize Protestant literalism.[27] Literature in post-Reformation England became a major if somewhat surprising medium for theological ideas, inquiry, and debate. I have hoped to add to an ongoing scholarly conversation about how literary texts engage the habits of biblical readers and interpreters in particular.[28] If there were more space in this survey to focus on relationships between literature and political interpretation at every stage, I would have wished to spend still more time in the early Tudor period when Protestantism is first established, an area deserving further exploration.[29] Bucer himself, perhaps trying to mimic the obvious literary qualities of More's *Utopia* and even Erasmus's *Education of a Christian Prince*, saw himself in *De Regno Christi* as creating "literary composition," a "work giving counsel" (as was fashionable) that would "please and prove useful to Your Majesty."[30] Yet it is largely the literalist tone of this work that forbids its modern categorization outside the realms of theology and politics, in spite of the author's efforts. And in contrast, it is in part because Erasmus saw scripture as literature that his writings that derive from it bear that quality. As English Protestantism became increasingly established in Elizabethan England, it was also old enough to be subjected to increasingly complex literary interrogations. Elizabethan and Stuart writers turned into fictive forms the biblically inflected advice books of the previous generation, as if Protestant culture had grown comfortable enough with its assumptions to subject them to further and more imaginative interrogations. The biblically oriented literature of the period relied on increasing tensions in English culture, not only between the poles of Protestant and Catholic, but between the Erasmian and the Tyndalian, and between members of the English Church and the Presbyterians—and, once Milton came along—among the Presbyterians, their Independent and Separatist critics, and the Church of England.

NOTES

INTRODUCTION

1. Concerning Elizabeth's Geneva Bible, see King and Pratt, "Bibles as Books," 84; on Whitgift and Hooker, among others, see Shaheen, "Misconceptions about the Geneva Bible," 156–158; on Laud, see Stallybrass, "Books and Scrolls," 52; on Lanyer, see Fleck, "To Write of Him," 545–560.

2. Hill, *Intellectual Origins*, 3–4; Hill, *English Bible*, 58, passim; Betteridge, "Bitter Notes," 41–62; Greaves, "Traditionalism," 94–109; Craig, "Geneva Bible," 40–49. Hobbes was born in 1588, and like other readers of his generation who lived long enough, such as Donne, Hobbes switched from the Geneva Bible to the King James Version. McCullough, "Andrewes and Donne," 66–88. On one occasion in *The Leviathan*, Hobbes compares the two; Hobbes, *Leviathan*, 281. Hill's words are echoed even in the standard bibliography of Bibles, where the Geneva Bible is accounted as having notes that "endeared it especially to the Puritans, and for three generations it maintained its supremacy as the Bible of the people"; Herbert, *Historical Catalogue of Printed Bibles*, 61. For a more sceptical reading, see Furniss, "Reading the Geneva Bible" 1–21.

3. On Hill's claims and royalist biblicism, see Killeen, *Political Bible*, 6–7.

4. Barlow, *Svmme and Substance*, 47.

5. For a study of paratextual content and readership from a marketing perspective, see Pratt, "The Trouble with Translation," 33–48; see also Furniss, "Reading the Geneva Bible," 1–21.

6. Tadmor, *Social Universe*, 17, passim.

7. Tadmor, *Social Universe*, 10; Fox, "Religion and Popular," 266–282; Spufford, "'I bought me a primer,'" 72–85; Spufford, "First Steps," 407–435; Cressy, *Literacy and Social Order*, 1–61.

8. Aubrey, *Brief Lives*, 249. Spufford accounts for similar abilities in less privileged children; "First Steps in Literacy," 411.

9. *Epistolae Familiares* (1674), 9; dated 1625. Rosenblatt, "Milton, Anxiety, and the King James Bible," 181.

10. Hale and Cullington, *Complete Works of John Milton*, vol 8, part 1, 5. Campbell has argued that the "Index Theologicus" cross-referenced in the extant Commonplace Book was created for polemical purposes; Campbell, "Milton's *Index Theologicus*," 12–16.

11. Fulton, *Historical Milton*, esp. 38–81.

12. Whittingham introduces Goodman, *Superior Powers* (Geneva: John Crispin, 1558).

13. As is discussed in chapter two; see Cummings, "William Tyndale and Erasmus" (2018), 29–52; Rankin, "Tyndale, Erasmus," 135–170. For discussion of the diglot *New Testament in English after the Greeke translation annexed with the translation of Erasmus in Latin* (London, 1550), see Fulton, "English Bibles and their Readers," 420–421.

14. Foxe, *Acts and Monuments*, 1563; quoted in Daniell, *William Tyndale*, 79.

15. Erasmus, *Exhortation to the Diligent*, a5v–6r. See Rankin, "Tyndale, Erasmus," 135–170.

16. Greenblatt, *Renaissance Self-Fashioning*, 106.

17. Henry VIII, *A Copy of the Letters, wherin the most redouted [and] mighty pri[n]ce, our souerayne lorde kyng Henry the eight* (1527), STC 13086, sig. A5ᵛ.

18. *The Bible and Holy Scriptures* (Geneva, 1560), sig. ***iiʳ.

19. Cranmer, *Catechismus* (1548), frontispiece, BL G.11830. Images of Elizabeth with Bible and sword were used in smaller editions of the Bishops' Bible; see *The Holi Bible* (1569), STC 2105.

20. *Byble in English* (London, 1539), title page; Kastan, "'Noyse of the New Bible,'" 56–62.

21. Pollard and Redgrave, *Short-Title Catalogue*; Herbert, Darlow, and Moule, *Historical Catalogue*; Westbrook, *Long Travail*; Pratt, "Trouble with Translation," 33–48.

22. Fuller, *Church-History of Britain*, third book, 387. I've benefited from conversation with Alexander Hardie-Forsyth; see Hardie-Forsyth, "Towards a Marginal History," 1–16.

23. Kastan, "'Noyse of the New Bible,'" 51–52.

24. More evidence of parish hardship is discussed in Kastan, "'Noyse of the New Bible,'" 54.

25. On the Latin Bible proposed by Cramner, see Gordon, "Authority of Antiquity," 7; on Cheke's New Testament, see Davies, "Sir John Cheke," 1–12; Pratt, "Trouble with Translation," 33–48.

26. *The Bible and Holy Scriptures* (Geneva, 1560), ***iiʳ. Ezra. 4:[6]; Esdra. 2:16 in the margin.

27. Dante (attributed), "Letter to Can Grande," in *Literary Criticism of Dante Alighieri*, 99; see also "The Four Levels of Interpretation," 112–114.

28. Tyndale, *Obedience*, 156, 160, 156, 157. For discussions of the literal sense, see for example Brownlee, *Biblical Readings*, 10, 47–48, passim; Luxon, *Literal Figures*, esp. ix–x, 1–33; Shuger, "Isaiah 63 and the Literal Senses of Scripture," 149–163.

29. Smalley, *Bible in the Middle Ages*; Alastair Minnis, *Medieval Theory of Authorship*, esp. ix–xxv, which offers a summary of the bibliography; see also McDermott, *Tropologies*.

30. Haigh, *English Reformations*.

31. Fulton and Poole, "Popular Hermeneutics in Shakespeare's London," in *Bible on the Shakespearean Stage*, 1–16.

32. Also in Mark 10:25 and Luke 18:25. For the extensive critical tradition around the translation of "camel," see Cummings, *Mortal Thoughts*, 191–195; Bishop, "Discontented Harmonies," 103–117, esp. 107–117.

33. Milton, *Complete Prose Works*, vol. 2, 251; see Flicker, *Song of Songs*, 149; Brownlee, *Biblical Readings*, 113–142.

34. Tyndale, *Obedience*, 159.

35. Killeen, *Political Bible*, passim.

36. Tyndale, *Obedience*, 160.

37. Augustine, *On Christian Doctrine*, in *The Works of Aurelius Augustine*, vol. 9, 86; MacCallum, "Milton and Figurative Interpretation," 63.

38. Augustine, *Later Works*, 199. MacCallum, "Milton and Figurative Interpretation," 63.

39. Luther, *Luther's Correspondence*, vol. 1, 43–44; MacCallum, "Milton and Figurative Interpretation," 63.

40. Calvin, *Commentary on Corinthians*, vol. 2, 172; MacCallum, "Milton and Figurative Interpretation," 63–64.

41. Simpson, *Burning to Read*; see more recently Simpson's related book, *Permanent Revolution*.

42. *A Discourse Presented to Those Who Seek the Reformation of the Church of England . . . with a short exposition upon some of Davids Psalmes, pertinent to these times of sedition* (London, 1642), 5.

43. Milton, *Doctrine and Discipline of Divorce*, 5.

44. See Fulton, *Historical Milton*, esp. 15–81; Jardine and Grafton, "'Studied for Action,'" 30–78; Hackel, *Reading Material*, 69–136; Sharpe, *Reading Revolutions*; Sherman, *Used Books*; and Zwicker, "Reading the Margins," 101–115; Zwicker "What Every Literate Man once Knew," 75–90.

45. Sherman, *Used Books*, and Grafton and Jardine, "'Studied for Action.'"

46. Hammill, *Mosaic Constitution*; Lupton, *Citizen-Saints*. Political theology is discussed in greater detail in Fulton, "Political Theology from the Pulpit and the Stage," 204–221.

47. Kahn, *Future of Illusion*, 12.

48. Hammill and Lupton, eds., *Political Theology and Early Modernity*, 1.

49. Shuger, *Political Theologies*.

50. Worden, "Toleration and the Cromwellian Protectorate," 199. On revisionist historiography and literary criticism, see Coiro and Fulton, "Old, New, Now," 5–8.

51. I wrote this in allusion to Cromwell's warts before discovering a similar note in Walzer, *In God's Shadow*, x.

52. Cranmer, *Miscellaneous Writings*, 127.

53. Barlow, *Svmme and Substance*, 47; Lupton, *History of the Geneva Bible*; vol 5, 133; Greaves, "Traditionalism," 94.

1. ERASMUS'S NEW TESTAMENT AND THE POLITICS OF HISTORICISM

1. Burke, *Renaissance Sense of the Past*, 55–59; Struever, *Language of History*, 71–74; Ginsburg, *History, Rhetoric, and Proof*, 54–70; Grafton, *Forgers and Critics*, 29–30; see also Hiatt, *The Making of Medieval Forgeries*, 136–155.

2. Valla, *Donation of Constantine*, 79–80. I have modified the last few words to reflect the original: "non etiam Caesaris." Valla, *Treatise of Lorenzo Valla*, 182.

3. See Valla, *Donation of Constantine*, vii–xiv. On the political dimensions of Valla's oration, see Camporeale, "Lorenzo Valla's 'Oratio'," 9–26.

4. Whitford, "The Papal Antichrist," 28; Whitford notes that Luther read Valla in 1520, as his thinking about the Pope as Antichrist started to crystalize.

5. Lupton's *Citizen-Saints* has illustrated how Paul played a central role in the construction of the political self in Shakespearean England.

6. More, *Complete Works of St. Thomas More*, vol. 2, 59.

7. Patterson, *Censorship and Interpretation*, 53.

8. Quintilian, *Institutio Oratoria*, vol. 4, 74 (9.2.65–66). More's inventive rhetorical terminology—the *obliquus ductus*—likely derives from classical rhetoricians and from the fifth-century theorists Fortunatianus and Martianus Capella, rediscovered in the Renaissance by George of Trebizond. Cox, "Rhetoric and Humanism," 657–658. See also Montefusco, "*Ductus and Color*," 113–132.

9. Quintilian, *Institutio Oratoria* vol. 4, 74–79 (9.2.67–75). This translation derives from Ahl, who discusses this trope in the context of Imperial Roman authors in *Lucan*, 32.

10. More, *Complete Works of St. Thomas More*, vol. 4, 98–99. I have slightly modified the translation.

11. *Octavia,* line 582, in Seneca, *Tragedies,* vol. 2, 568. My translation. See Crossett, "More and Seneca," 577–580.

12. "Immo Paulus sum, qui Paulum imitor." Valla, *Treatise of Lorenzo Valla,* 24–25. See Camporeale, "Lorenzo Valla's 'Oratio'," 11.

13. Valla, *Donation of Constantine,* 2.

14. Bentley, *Humanists and Holy Writ,* 35.

15. Valla's philological notes inform many of Erasmus's glosses, though they are not crucial to the readings explored here. For representative instances, see Rummel, *Erasmus' Annotations,* 85–88; also Bentley, "Biblical Philology," 8–28. Valla's annotations, like Lefèvre's, are short philological notes rather than discursive commentaries. Erasmus published this work, written in 1442–1457, as *Adnotationes in Novum Testamentum* in 1505; it is reprinted in Valla, *Opera Omnia,* vol. 1, 803–895.

16. Cummings, *Literary Culture of the Reformation,* 146; also Rummel, *Erasmus' Annotations,* 14–15. On the classical and rhetorical origins of Erasmus's hermeneutics, see Eden, *Hermeneutics and the Rhetorical Tradition,* esp. 64–78.

17. Epistle 337; *The Collected Works of Erasmus,* vol. 3, 137; hereafter cited as *CWE.*

18. Trapp, *Erasmus, Colet and More,* 5–6.

19. Valla was the source for the reading of penance in Matthew. On Valla's inclusion of the comma in his *Adnotations* even though it is "likely that not a single Greek manuscript included the comma," see Bentley, *Humanists and Holy Writ,* 44–45. As Bentley points out, Valla's other writing has suggested "affinities between Valla and the anti-Trinitarian heretics of the sixteenth century" (44). Whitford, "Yielding to the Prejudices," 19–40. King'oo, *Miserere Mei,* 82–94.

20. See Whitford, "Yielding to the Preludices," esp. 21, 35, 39. Cummings, *Literary Culture of the Reformation,* 102n1. See Metzger and Ehrman, *Text of the New Testament,* 142–149.

21. For a fascinating study of how the changes correspond to Erasmus's debate with Luther, see Kroeker, *Erasmus in the Footsteps of Paul.* Comparison of the changing versions of Erasmus's *Annotations* is made easy with the annotated facsimiles in Reeve and Screech, eds., *Annotations on the New Testament,* 3 vols.

22. See Jardine, *Erasmus, Man of Letters,* 175–80.

23. Gleason, *John Colet,* 58–59. See Cunningham, *Anatomical Renaissance,* 212–215.

24. Gleason, *John Colet,* esp. 93–132. See also Kroeker, *Erasmus in the Footsteps of Paul,* 9–10. Gleason rightly revises the traditional view that Erasmus was a "disciple" of Colet, but he may go too far, as I argue here, in suggesting there was little indebtedness. To reinforce this view, he suggests that Erasmus showed no interest in 1500 or 1501 in pursuing theology or in "planning an edition of the Greek New Testament"—that his interest in Greek was initially literary, and "not any awakening of religious interests" (113), but evidence shows that Erasmus had turned at this point to his own commentary on Paul. For Colet's influence on Erasmus see also Rummel, *Erasmus' Annotations,* 10–12; and Jarrott, "Erasmus' Annotations and Colet's Commentaries," 125–144. Gleason also argues that Colet's historicism is suspect, since "most of the 'history' is taken by Colet from a document now known as the pseudo-Clementine *Recognitions*" (127). But the authenticity of the source has little bearing on the method of criticism—Colet is clearly practicing historicism, and at any rate, Erasmus himself thought the *Recognitions* were genuine. Finally this source is not the only historical text—Suetonius being another—that Colet turned to. See also Rabil, *Erasmus and the New Testament,* 37–52, 129–132. For a chronicle of Erasmus's intervals in England, see Schoeck, "Erasmus in England, 1499–1517," 269–283, esp. 276–279. For general influence, see Adams, *The Better Part of Valor,* and Kaufman, *Augustinian Piety and Catholic Reform.*

25. Epistle 164; *CWE*, vol. 2, 53; Erasmus, *Opus Epistolarum*, vol. 1, 375.

26. *CWE*, vol. 2, 86; *Opus Epistolarum*, vol. 1, 404. See Payne, "Erasmus and Lefèvre," 54–83; at 56; and Payne, "Erasmus: Interpreter of Romans," vol. 2, 4ff.

27. Vessey, "Basel 1514," 3–26.

28. See Anne O'Donnell's analysis in *Erasmus, Enchiridion Militis Christiani*, xxi.

29. On Colet's lectures, see Gleason, *John Colet,* esp. 67–184; and on the manuscript dates, see 67–92. The lectures on Romans are preserved in a manuscript that dates from approximately 1499–1505, thus representing a revised set of views, but since Erasmus pesters Colet about not publishing them, we have some evidence that he had read as well as seen the lectures. See also Adams, *The Better Part of Valor*, 21, and Seebohm, *The Oxford Reformers*. According to Erasmus, Colet lectured on all of Paul's letters at Oxford. *Opus Epistolarum*, vol. 4, Epistle 1211; Epistle 181. Payne, "Erasmus and Lefèvre," 55.

30. Tyndale, *Tyndale's New Testament*, 238.

31. See Tyndale, *Obedience*, 36–49; 54.

32. Colet, *An Exposition of St. Paul's Epistle to the Romans*, 95. Subsequent citations are given parenthetically within the text; the Latin is in the second half of the book.

33. *CWE*, vol. 2, 203. The concern has a famous classical analogue in Cicero, who claims in his letters to Atticus that he must shroud his meaning in allegory in case the letters are found. *Ad Atticum* 2.20; see Ahl, *Lucan*, 27; Bishop, *Seneca's Daggered Stylus*, 12–14.

34. *CWE* vol. 56, 347.

35. *CWE* vol. 56, 347; original in Erasmus, *Annotationes in Novum Instrumentum* (1516), 448.

36. *CWE*, vol. 56, 352–53; the original is Erasmus, *Novum Instrumentum* (1516), 448–449.

37. *Desiderii Erasmi Roterodami Opera Omnia*, Jean Leclerc, ed. (Leiden, 1705), vol. 6, 223f. Hereafter cited as LB. See Rummel, "St Paul in Plain Latin," 309–318; at 310. Rummel shows that his New Testament was "combated with undiminished fervor by conservative theologians" (309).

38. For a discussion of Erasmus's lesson in historicism, see Eden, "Equity and the Origins," 137–145; at 137. Eden notes that Erasmus "uses historicism as a tool of dissent" (138).

39. *CWE*, vol. 27, 235–236; the Latin may be found in *Opera Omnia Des. Erasmi Roterodami*, vol. 4, part 1, 166. Hereafter cited as *ASD*.

40. See Eden, *Hermeneutics and the Rhetorical Tradition*, 2, 12–17.

41. Erasmus, *Education of a Christian Prince*, 4.

42. Seneca, *Senecae Opera*, ed. Erasmus (Basel, 1515), 6.

43. *CWE*, vol. 2, 251. Epistle 272.

44. *CWE*, vol. 27, 238.

45. *CWE,* vol. 24, 625.

46. This is L. Junius Gallio, the proconsul of Achaea; see Lupton, *Citizen-Saints*, 26.

47. See Panizza, "Gasparino Barzizza's Commentaries," 297–358.

48. The editor of the correspondence overlooked Lefèvre's edition. See Barlow, ed. *Epistolae Senecae*. On Lefèvre and Erasmus, see de Jonge, "Relationship of Erasmus' Translation," 2–7; Payne, "Erasmus and Lefèvre," 54–83; Steenbeek, "Conceptual Background of the Controversy," 935–945; Rummel, *Erasmus' Annotations*, 12–15.

49. Lefèvre, *Epistolae Viri Pauli Apostoli*, 226.

50. Backus, "Renaissance Attitudes," 1184.

51. *CWE*, vol. 3, 66.

52. Epistle 325, *CWE*, vol. 3, 64.

53. Erasmus, *Education of a Christian Prince*, 112.

54. Tracy, *Politics of Erasmus*, 13, and *Holland under Habsburg Rule*, 20–21.

55. *CWE*, vol. 2, 81. Epistle 180.

56. *Opus Epistolarum*, vol. 1, 400.

57. Persius, *Satura*, 3.35–38, in *Juvenal and Persius*, 76–77.

58. Cummings, *Literary Culture of the Reformation*, 105.

59. Metzger and Murphy, eds., *The New Oxford Annotated Bible*.

60. *CWE*, vol. 56, 36.

61. This translation is based on Sider, *CWE*, vol. 56, 37. For discussion of this passage, see Sider, "Erasmus on the Epistle to the Romans," esp. 131.

62. Erasmus, *Novum Testamentum Omne* (Basel, 1535), 344.

63. *CWE,* vol. 2, 82. Epistle 180.

64. *CWE*, vol. 1, 222.

65. *CWE*, vol. 2, 87. Epistle 181.

66. Modified from *CWE*, vol. 2, 87. The full Latin: "A Panegyrico sic abhorrebam ut non meminerim quicquam fecisse me magis reluctante animo. Videbam enim genus hoc citra adulationem tractari non posse. Ego tamen nouo sum usus artificio, ut et in adulando sim liberrimus et in libertate adulantissimus." *Opus Epistolarum*, vol. 1, 405.

67. *CWE*, vol. 29, 3. For the Latin see LB, vol. 5, 65. On Erasmus and More, see Hexter's notes on *Utopia* in *Complete Works of St. Thomas More*, vol. 4, 373–374.

68. *CWE*, vol. 29, 3.

69. *CWE*, vol. 50, 108.

70. My translation. Unless otherwise marked, translations are my own.

71. Erasmus, *Novum Instrumentum Omne* (1516), 393.

72. *Detorquere* functions for Erasmus as a rhetorical trope: "Erasmus likes to use the verb *detorquere* to show how the genuine meaning of a biblical text is twisted into an alien meaning." Hoffmann, *Rhetoric and Theology*, 265 n148. See for example, *CWE*, vol. 56, 351; Erasmus, *Novum Testamentum* (Basel, 1535), 417. See also Rummel, *Erasmus' Annotations*, 58. For More's use, see *Complete Works of St. Thomas More*, vol. 5, 288. Cummings cites a moment when Erasmus accuses Luther of being "uncontrollably attached"—*assertive*, and like someone in love—as one who twists (*detorqueat*) the meaning (Cummings, *Literary Culture of the Reformation*, 155). Jarrott, "Erasmus' Biblical Humanism," 351–382; Rummel, "God and Solecism," 54–72.

73. Rupp and Watson, eds., *Luther and Erasmus*, 37; LB, vol. 9, 1215.

74. From the 1519, *Novum Testamentum Omne*, vol. 2, 224. My translation. This is not in the 1516 edition (vol. 2, 393), but it remains in the 1522 edition (vol. 2, 259) and the 1535 edition (vol. 2, 311). LB vol. 6, 501. The Folger 1535 Copy, 160–246f, owned by a reader who carefully crosses out troublesome interpretations, and here carefully underlines the passage, highlighting "usum vafricie, and from "irrepant in principum affectus" to "inviti" (311).

75. Erasmus, *Novum Instrumentum Omne* (Basel, 1516), 550; Erasmus, *Novum Instrumentum Omne* (1522), 510.

76. See Hoffmann, *Rhetoric and Theology*, 52, 53, 187–190; *passim*; Lausberg, *Handbook of Literary Rhetoric*, 244, (no. 540); 467, (no. 1072).

77. Adams, *The Better Part of Valor*, 27. Thompson, *Translations of Lucian*.

78. Halkin, *Erasmus*, 65.

79. The Latin for the sentence on the *Panegyrics* runs, "in Panegyrico sub laudis praetextu hoc ipsum tamen agimus oblique lusus quam actum est in Enchiridio." Ep. 337 To Maarten van Dorp, Antwerp, [end of May] 1515. *CWE*, vol. 3, 111. *Opus Epistolarum*, vol. 2, 93.

80. Erasmus, *Praise of Folly*, 56; original Latin in *ASD*, vol. 4, part 3, 116.

81. *Opus Epistolarum*, vol. 1, 405.

82. Erasmus, *Praise of Folly*, 37. *ASD*, vol. 4, part 3, 98.

83. Erasmus's familiarity with this passage may be assumed from his knowledge of Quintilian, as well as from distinct references to *emphasis*. See Hoffmann, *Rhetoric and Theology*, 36, 51, 185–186; see also Chomarat, *Grammaire et Rhetorique chez Erasme*, vol. 2, 803–815.

84. More, *Complete Works of St. Thomas More*, vol. 2, 59.

85. "Henrici Lardes vis versu claudier ono, / Eeque Muida facias eque Nerone virum." Attribution uncertain, but its authenticity seems evident in the personalized vocabulary denoting bad kings as Nero or Midas, terms also used included in early letters to Henry himself. *CWE*, vol. 85, 143–144.

86. Colet, *Exposition of St. Paul's Epistle*, 95. On the traditions of explaining Paul's death, see Lupton, *Citizen-Saints*, 30.

87. Rummel, *Erasmus' Annotations on the New Testament*, 17, 26–31, 33, 123–170; Cummings, *Literary Culture of the Reformation,* 147–156. Erasmus's work was popularized in such publications as *The New Testament in Englishe after the Greeke translation Annexed wyth the Translation of Erasmus in Latin* (London, 1550); Parker, ed., *William Royle's An Exhortation to the Diligent Studye of Scripture,* esp. 51–54; Lesse, *The Censure and Judgement of the Famous Clark Erasmus of Roterodam* (London, [1550?]).

88. See Juhàsz, "Antwerp Bible translations," 110–112; and Simpson, *Burning to Read*, 55.

89. See Cummings, "William Tyndale and Erasmus," 44.

90. Bible, title page (STC 2861).

91. Frere and Kennedy, eds., *Visitation Articles*, vol. 2, 117–118. Dodds, *Exploiting Erasmus*, 5.

92. The Englishing of the *Paraphrases* are discussed in Dodds, *Exploiting Erasmus*, xi, xix–xx, 3–59. Mary Tudor began a translation of the Paraphrase on John under the direction of her Catholic chaplain, Francis Malet, who translated an unknown portion of the gospel (Dodds, *Exploiting Erasmus*, 11).

93. Erasmus, *The First Tome or Volume of the Paraphrase of Erasmus vpon the Newe Testament* (1548; STC 2854). The copy at the Folger library has at the 25th Chapter of Matthew—"Good Works" written here in the margin (Fol. xcviʳ). The most significant scholarship on this topic is Dodds, *Exploiting Erasmus*, and on the *Paraphrases* in particular, see 8–59; on Luther and the *Paraphrases*, see 9.

94. Dodds, *Exploiting Erasmus*, 8–9. On Coverdale's translation of the Enchiridion and his views of Erasmus, see Parker, "Religious Polemics," 94–107.

2. TYNDALE'S LITERALISM AND THE LAWS OF MOSES

1. The elaborate history of this mythmaking is recounted in Rankin, "Tyndale, Erasmus," 135–170.

2. Cummings, "William Tyndale and Erasmus," 29–52; Parker, "English *Enchiridion militis Christiani*," 16–21; Devereux, "Some Lost Translations of Erasmus," 255–259; for a digital edition, *British Library (Additional MS 89149, f. 1r)*. For a representative treatment of the uncertain connection before the manuscript's discovery, see Greenblatt, *Renaissance Self-Fashioning*, 87.

3. "Peter a capteyn of the churche"—1533 *Enchiridion* 16th rule of chapter 25 image 145; see Erasmus, *Erasmus, Enchiridion militis Christiani: An English Version*, xxxvii–xxxviii.

4. Cummings, "William Tyndale and Erasmus," 49.

5. See, for example, Cummings, "Protestant Allegory," 177–190; Shuger, "Isaiah 63," 149–163; Zysk, "John 6, *Measure for Measure*," 51–68; Simpson, "Tyndale as Promoter," 48; Kearney, *Incarnate Text*, 78; Luxon, *Literal Figures*, passim.

6. Tyndale's reaction to Erasmus's antagonism to Protestants appears in a few small comments, as in an autobiographical passage in his preface to the Pentateuch (1530), parenthetically dismissing Erasmus's praise of Cuthbert Tunstall; Daniell, *Tyndale*, 73, 83.

7. Rupp and Watson, eds., *Luther and Erasmus*, 220.

8. Tyndale, *Obedience*, 25. On Tyndale's relationship with Erasmus, see Rankin, "Tyndale, Erasmus"; Cummings, "William Tyndale and Erasmus," 29–52; Richardson, "Tyndale's Quarrel with Erasmus," 46–65; McDiarmid, "Defense of Tyndale, 1528–1533," 56–68.

9. Richardson, "Tyndale's Quarrel with Erasmus," 46.

10. Arblaster, Juhász, and Latré, eds., *Tyndale's Testament*; on Tyndale's use of the 1522 edition of Erasmus, rather than the 1519 as is often argued, see Rankin, "Tyndale, Erasmus," 140; McDonald, "Erasmus and the Johannine Comma (1 John 5:7–8)," 42–55; and McDonald, *Biblical Criticism*, chapter 1; Cummings, "William Tyndale and Erasmus"; Juhász, *Translating Resurrection*, 287–288.

11. Juhász, *Translating Resurrection*, 14. See Herbert, Darlow and Moule, eds., *Historical Catalogue*, 1. Herbert draws on Johann Dobneck, *Commentaria de Actis et Scriptis Martini Lutheri* (1549), 132f, who claims that 3,000 copies were distributed. The marginal comments of this Bible were significant; one scholar has counted ninety glosses, fifty-two of which are directly indebted to Luther; see Demaus, *William Tyndale, A Biography*, 131. On the print history of Tyndale's New Testament, see Kastan, "'The Noyse of the New Bible'," 46–51. On Tyndale's use of Erasmus, see Daniell, *William Tyndale*, 115.

12. More, *The co[n]futacyon of Tyndales answere*, cxxviii. For a discussion of "congregation" in Erasmus's New Testament and in the debate between More and Tyndale, see Ferguson, "Faith in the Language," 1001.

13. Tyndale, *New Testament* (1525), fol. xviii^v–xix^r.

14. Henry VIII, *A Copy of the Letters* (1527), STC 13086, sig. A5^v.

15. On the circulation of Middle English Bibles, see Raschko, "Taking Apart the Wycliffite Bible," 459–486; and on a remarkable Edwardian copy, see Rankin, "Royal Provenance," 587–597.

16. Pollard, *Records of the English Bible*, 133; see Simpson, *Burning to Read*, 35.

17. Daniell, *The Bible in English*, 144–146; 189–191. The evidence around these burnings remains unclear; see Felch and King'oo, "Reading Tyndale's *Obedience*," esp. 98.

18. Henry VIII, *A Copy of the Letters* (1527), STC 13086, sig. A6r.

19. *New Testament: A Facsimile of the 1526 Edition*, unpaginated introduction.

20. Lewalski, *Protestant Poetics*, 131; for a sustained study of this phenomenon, see Killeen, *Political Bible*, and the work on Jerusalem by Groves, such as "England's Jerusalem," 88.

21. See Tadmor, "Social and Cultural Translation," 175–187.

22. Discussed in Warner, *Henry VIII's Divorce*, 38–39.

23. First produced in Antwerp in 1530, *Practyse of Prelates* was printed in altered forms in London in 1548 and 1549, and then in *The Whole Workes of W. Tyndall* (1573), where Tyndale's work is retitled.

24. Starkey, *Six Wives*, 107.

25. Erasmus, *Education of a Christian Prince*, xii; Walker, *Writing Under Tyranny*, 7.

26. "It wolde nat be forgotten, that the lytle boke of the most excellent doctour Erasmus Roterodame (which he wrate to Charles, nowe beynge emperour, and than prince of Castile)

which booke is intituled the Institution of a christen prince, would be as familyare alway with gentlemen at all tymes and in every age, as was Homer with the great king Alexander, or Xenophon with Scipio . . . there was never boke written in latine, that in so lytle a portion, contayned of sentence, eloquence, and vertuous exhortation, a more compendious abundance." Elyot, *The Boke Named the Gouernour* (1531), fol. 42^r.

27. For discussion, see Fulton, "English Bibles and their Readers, 1400–1700," 418–423. Notable cases of prominent titles include *The Newe Testament yet once agayne corrected whearevunto is added an exhortacio to the same Erasmus Rot* (London, 1542); *The Newe Testament in Englyshe and in Latin of Erasmus* (London, 1549); *The New Testament in Englishe after the Greeke Translation Annexed wyth the Translation of Erasmus in Latin* (London, 1550). As Aaron Pratt points out, the "English New Testament published by Richard Grafton and Edward Whitchurch in 1540 advertises that it follows 'the texte of master Erasmus." *The newe testament in Englyshe* (1540; STC 2846), *1^r; Pratt, "The Trouble with Translation," in Fulton and Poole, eds., *The Bible on the Shakespearean Stage*, 33.

28. *The New Testament in Englishe after the Greeke Translation Annexed wyth the Translation of Erasmus in Latin* (1550), STC 2822.

29. Rex, "Crisis of Obedience," 863–894, and further discussion.

30. Graham Hammill has argued that "the Mosaic constitution had an integral role to play in the emergence of early modern concepts of the state"; Hammill, *Mosaic Constitution*, 2. Eric Nelson writes of how the study of Hebrew contributed to new forms of political thought in *The Hebrew Republic*; see also Schochet, Oz-Salzberger, and Jones, eds., *Political Hebraism*, and for more bibliography on English Hebrew studies, see 67n9.

31. Tyndale's Book of Jonah, the books of Isaiah, Jeremiah, Lamentations, and George Joye's translation of Martin Bucer's Psalms—and only Tyndale's came directly from the Hebrew.

32. On the formation of biblical law, see Walzer, *In God's Shadow* 16–35.

33. Willis, *Reformation of the Decalogue*, 3–4. The phenomenon stemmed from both Reformation and Counter-Reformation movements: "Reformers had indeed universally adopted the Decalogue, with some misgivings in Luther's case," John Bossy wrote in a pioneering essay, "but so had the Church of Rome in the *Catechism of the Council of Trent*," published in 1566. Bossy, "Moral Arithmetic," 217. Lander, "Maimed Rites," 197.

34. For a valuable discussion of this, see Kastan, "'Noyse of the New Bible'," 46–68.

35. Her copy of Tyndale's 1534 New Testament is extant. British Library C.23.a.8. As the holdings notes record, the book "has her arms emblazoned on the second titlepage" and "the words 'Anna Regina Angliæ' painted on the gilt edges of the leaves."

36. Nichols, ed., *Narrative*, 52–57.

37. Wyatt, *Extracts*, 438.

38. Nichols, ed., *Narrative*, 56. See Felch and King'oo, "Reading Tyndale's *Obedience*," 87. As Felch and King'oo point out, this line is often misquoted; see Daniell, *William Tyndale*, 244–247; Daniell in Tyndale, *Obedience*, xxiv.

39. Wyatt, *Extracts*, 440, 441. Wyatt has the chronology jumbled; he has Wolsey on the historical stage in 1533 when Elizabeth is born. At the time of its publication, only Boleyn would have been sympathetic to Tyndale's religious views, and Wolsey, whose decline and fall began in the summer of 1529 and ended with arrest in November, about a year after Tyndale's book had been produced in Antwerp, thus leaving a tight (though possible) window for the domestic tussle over the book.

40. The positions are summarized in Felch and King'oo, "Reading Tyndale's *Obedience*," 89.

41. Felch and King'oo, "Reading Tyndale's *Obedience*," 103. Tyndale writes in a vernacular that is underrepresented in the surviving records of the king's and queen's books; see Carley, *Books of King Henry VIII.*

42. Rex, "Crisis of Obedience," 871.

43. Rex, "Crisis of Obedience," 864. King'oo and Felch have pointed out that Tyndale divided the temporal from the spiritual or ecclesiastical in ways that are not precisely prescriptive of the monarch as supreme head of the church. Felch and King'oo, "Reading Tyndale's *Obedience*," 102–103. See also Bernard, *Anne Boleyn*, 54–56; Boehrer, "Tyndale's *The Practyse of Prelates*," 257–276.

44. Daniell in Tyndale, *Obedience*, xxv.

45. Fulton, "Political Theology," 204–221.

46. Tyndale, *Obedience*, 29.

47. As Greenblatt once described it, Tyndale's is a "violent obedience." *Renaissance Self-Fashioning*, 89.

48. More's Epigram 198, which was also used as part of the preliminaries to the *Utopia*. *Complete Works of St. Thomas More*, vol. 3, part 2, 228–231; see Curtis, "Best State," 106. On *Utopia* and civic humanism, see Peltonen, *Classical Humanism*, 7–11. See especially Erasmus's cry, "O extinct line of Brutus!" in Phillips, *Erasmus on His Times*, 144. Adage 2.8.65 in *CWE*, vol. 34, which Erasmus wrote around the time of *Utopia* and implored More to read it; see *CWE*, vol. 5, 402. Tracy, *Politics of Erasmus*, 35, 150. See also Erasmus's manuscript epigram against Pope Julius, which ends stating that only one thing would make him a "complete Julius: that some / Brutus should turn up for you"; *CWE*, vol. 85, 339.

49. A positive use of Brutus (Lucius Junius) occurs at the end of the *Vindiciae Contra Tyrannos* (1579).

50. Tyndale, *An Exposycyon vpon the V.Vi.Vii. Chapters of Mathewe* (1536), G4ᵛ–G5ʳ.

51. The implications of these verses on republican thought are explored in Nelson, *Hebrew Republic*, 3, 23–46. See Lim, *John Milton*, 15, 23, 48; Charnaik, "Biblical Republicanism," 147–160.

52. Daniell, ed., *Obedience*, 34–48.

53. This is exactly the same as the wording in Tyndale's New Testaments except for a small "yᵉ" before "power," which is incorrectly transcribed in Tyndale, *Obedience*, 36, as "that power." The 1526 wording is exactly the same—minus an introductory "And"—as the 1534 wording of Romans 13, where Tyndale makes marginal cross references to "God's commandment," in Exod. 20. c. and Deut. 5. b. See Daniell, ed., *Tyndale's New Testament*, 238.

54. In the *Institution of Christian Religion*, Calvin translates Romans 13:3 with "magistratui"; Calvin, *Institutio Christianae Religionis* (1609), fol. 308ᵛ. (Book 4, chapter 20, 19).

55. Certain forms of civil disobedience are permitted in Tyndale; see Felch and King'oo, "Reading Tyndale's *Obedience*," 95 (and n35), 99 (and n51).

56. See Fulton, *Historical Milton*, 143–173; and chapter eight in this book.

57. [The Pentateuch] (1530), fol. 35ʳ.

58. Tyndale, *Obedience*, 35–36.

59. Rex, "Crisis of Obedience," 867–868.

60. Tyndale, *Work of William Tyndale*, ed. Duffield, 385.

61. Tyndale, *Work of William Tyndale*, ed. Duffield, 287; *An Exposycyon vpon the V.Vi.Vii. Chapters of Mathewe* (1536), M3v. Then Tyndale adds the rule for rulers, epitomizing the turn from the Christian man to the ruler in the earlier book's structure: "And even so shal the ruler, if he rule not as God hath commanded."

62. *A Necessary Doctrine and Erudition for Any Christen Man* (1543), sig. S1^r. See Rex, "Crisis of Obedience," 892.

63. Morison, *A Lamentation* (1536), sig. A3^r; quoted from Rex, "Crisis of Obedience," 883. See also Morison, *An Exhortation* (1539), sig. B2^r.

64. [Morison,] *A Remedy* ([1536]), Biii^r.

65. Morison, *A Lamentation* (1536), sig. Aii^v–Aiii^r.

66. Tyndale, *Obedience*, 46–47. Tyndale associates the Pope with the "great idol the whore of Babylon, Antichrist of Rome," an interpretation of Revelation 17:1–5 discussed in Chapter 5; Tyndale, *Obedience*, 48, 51.

67. Tyndale, *Obedience*, 47.

68. *Practyse of Prelates* (1530), sigs. A4^r.

69. Davies, "Converting Henry," 262.

70. Cavendish, *Life and Death of Cardinal Wolsey*, 83.

71. See Scarisbrick, *Henry VIII*, 153.

72. Bernard, *King's Reformation*, 1–9; Scarisbrick, *Henry VIII*, 154.

73. Bernard, *King's Reformation*, 16.

74. More, *Correspondence of Thomas More*, 496–97; quoted in Bernard, *King's Reformation*, 17.

75. *Practice of Prelates*, in Duffield, ed., *Work of William Tyndale*, 383. On the king's interest in this passage, see Starkey, *Six Wives*, 203.

76. Demaus, *William Tyndale*, 294; see Rankin, "John Foxe (1530)," 175–176.

77. Scarisbrick, *Henry VIII*, 152. See also 400, on how Luther and Melanchthon agreed with Tyndale.

78. [The Pentateuch] (1530), fol. 37^r.

79. Tyndale, *Expositions and Notes*, 329.

80. Bernard, *King's Reformation*, 17. On Wakefield and the study of Hebrew among humanists, see Grafton, "Some Early Citizens," 6–28; Rex, "Earliest Use of Hebrew," 522–523.

81. Murphy, "Literature and Propaganda," 144. Quoting BL Microfilm, M 485/52, Hatfield MS 198, fol. 31v. *Henricus Octauus* MS survives as Trinity College, Cambridge, MS B.15.19.

82. Murphy, "Literature and Propaganda," 139.

83. Murphy, "Literature and Propaganda," 149.

84. This is also true of the Taverner edition of 1539; *The Most Sacred Bible, whiche is the Holy Scripture* (1539).

85. [The Pentateuch] (1530), fol. 43^v.

86. Tyndale, *Work of William Tyndale,* ed. Duffield, 384.

87. Tyndale, *Work of William Tyndale,* ed. Duffield, 386.

88. Tyndale, *Work of William Tyndale,* ed. Duffield, 387.

89. Bernard, *King's Reformation*, 18.

90. Bernard, *King's Reformation*, 18.

91. See Rosenblatt, *Renaissance England's Chief Rabbi*, 24.

92. Brewer, ed., *Letters and Papers, Foreign and Domestic, of the Reign of Henry VIII*, vol. 10, 352, 698; quoted in Mozley, *Coverdale and His Bibles*, 115–116.

93. See the discussion of this in Rosenblatt, *Renaissance England's Chief Rabbi*, 23–25.

94. Daniell, *William Tyndale*, 203.

95. Tyndale, *Work of William Tyndale,* ed. Duffield, 381.

96. Rankin discusses these omissions in Rankin, "John Foxe," 182.

97. Warner, *Henry VIII's Divorce*, 38; McDiarmid, *"Practice of Prelates,"* 40–47. After the fall of Wolsey, the divorce precipitously fell into the domain of the secretly or not-so-secretly Protestant. Edward Foxe, for example, working for Wolsey and Henry, but also a friend of Latimer and advised by Cramner to appeal to universities, helped to craft a vital piece of print propaganda on the legitimacy of the divorce. Foxe, *Determinations of the Moste Famous*, 1531, fol.2ᵛ.

98. de Gayangos ed., *Calendar of Letter*, vol. 4.1., no. 539; quoted from Rankin, "John Foxe," 158.

99. Cromwell and the king also become convinced that Vaughan was falling under Tyndale's influence and begged him to stay clear. Anderson, *Annals of the English Bible*, vol. 1, 275. See Rankin, "John Foxe," 159. Henry VIII read and marked another polemic against the divorce that still survives in Lambeth Place Library; the author was executed in 1540; see Christie-Miller, "Henry VIII and British Library, Royal MS. 2 A. XVI," 4.

100. Rankin, "John Foxe," 159.

101. Tyndale, *Work of William Tyndale*, ed. Duffield, 383.

102. Despite its attribution to Marburg and Antwerp by Sheppard and Latré, respectively, the location of the Coverdale Bible's printing remains unclear. Blayney has critiqued both scholars for perpetuating historical inaccuracies: Sheppard for attributing overmuch the movement of one of the alleged printers to Marburg a month after the Coverdale Bible's completion; Latré for the historical gymnastics on which his argument for the printing's location in Antwerp relies. However, Blayney's argument that Cologne was the printing location of the Coverdale Bible does, in part, rely on Sheppard's assertion that the repeated use of woodcut initials in the book indicates that the printers were Eucharius Cervicornus and Johannes Soter, both of Cologne. Blayney, *The Stationers' Company*, 1.344–347; Hope, "Antwerp Origins," 39–54. See also Kastan, "'Noyse of the New Bible'," 52–54.

103. *Biblia, the Byble, that is, the Holy Scrypture of the Olde and New Testament* ([Southwark?, J. Nycolson], 1535); The preliminaries only—and of most copies—seem to have been produced at first by Nycolson. Mozley, *Coverdale and His Bibles*, 65–71; 110–122. A letter from Nycolson to Cromwell, in which Cromwell is shown materials before printing, suggests some previous endorsement from Cromwell, though Mozley argues that Cromwell is just "asked to enlist the royal support"(112).

104. *Biblia, the Byble, that is, the Holy Scrypture of the Olde and New Testament* ([Southwark?, J. Nycolson], 1535), ✠ii^r.

105. John King argues that the portrait is "a rendering of royal approval for the free circulation of the English Bible." King, *Tudor Royal Iconography*, 60; see Walker, *Persuasive Fictions*, 85; Tudor-Craig, "Henry VIII and King David," 193.

106. Walker, *Persuasive Fictions*, 87, 86; see Sharpe, *Selling the Tudor Monarchy*, 140–144.

107. *Stationers' Register*, vol. 2, 50–60; quoted from Hattaway, "Marginalia By Henry VIII," 166–170; 166; see Tudor-Craig, "Henry VIII and King David," 193–194; see also Carley, *Libraries*, 202, 230.

108. King, *Tudor Royal Iconography*, 60, passim. Mozley, *Coverdale and His Bibles*, 110.

109. *Biblia, the Byble, that is, the Holy Scrypture of the Olde and New Testament* ([Cologne?], 1535), Romans 13a.

110. *Biblia, the Byble* (1535), sig. *2ᵛ. Fulton, "Political Theology," 204–221.

111. See the full discussion in Tudor-Craig, "Henry VIII and King David," 192–194. For discussion of Henry as a "new David" in the Great Bible's imagery, see Kastan, "'Noyse of the New Bible'," 56.

112. King, "Henry VIII as David," 78–92.

113. British Library Royal 2 A. xvi, f. 3.

114. Christie-Miller, "Henry VIII and British Library, Royal MS. 2 A. XVI," 1–19. See also Carley, *Books of King Henry VIII*, 58. The manuscript is digitally available from the British Library.

115. Royal 2 A XVI, f. 79. This image and others are discussed in White, "Psalms, War, and Royal Iconography," 556–562, 570–573.

116. This image (and its origins and later uses and permutations) is discussed in King'oo, *Miserere Mei*, Ch. 1.

117. There is debate in the scholarly literature about whether it really was the king who made these markings, or, as Micheline White suggests, "Henry's annotations later became a kind of prized 'text' unto themselves, as someone paid a scribe to recopy them in red ink into a printed English Psalter"; White, "Psalms, War, and Royal Iconography," 558; Tudor-Craig also attributes these penned markings to a scribe, 195. Some evidence may challenges this narrative. Not all the markings in the manuscript psalter have been transcribed, and the pattern of difference suggests simultaneity rather than later transcription (see Christie-Miller, "Henry VIII and the British Library," 15–16). The markings extend also to the collection of Solomon's Proverbs, bound with the psalter, and the king may have acquired both of these books together; see Hattaway, "Marginalia By Henry VIII," 166. Blots of red ink in the manuscript psalter show that the printed psalter and the manuscript were consulted together; Christie-Miller suggests "that it was Henry himself who copied the markings and who spilled the red ink," adducing new evidence in the "marked similarity of the only manicule in Whytchurch to those other manicules (shown below) attributed to Henry" (8). In the end, it does not matter for these purposes if the king or a scribe copied the markings, since these are still his reading responses; the more important evidence is that these vernacular texts were the king's, as the king marks the Solomonic literature.

118. Erasmus, *On Copia of Words and Ideas*, 2. See White's reading of Psalm 20 in this context, "Psalms, War, and Royal Iconography," 554–574.

119. Tudor-Craig, "Henry VIII and King David," 191.

120. Potts, ed., *King Edward the Sixth on the Supremacy*, xvi; quoted from Hattaway, "Marginalia," 169.

121. Haigh, *English Reformations*, 152.

122. Walsham, "Unclasping the Book?" 150.

123. MacCulloch, *Thomas Cranmer*, 359.

124. Carpenter, "Reforming the Scriptures," 24.

125. Anglo, "Early Tudor Programme," 179.

126. Bale, *Complete Plays of John Bale*, vol 2., 68, 119–120.

127. *Biblia, the Byble, that is* (1535), fol. xxxix^v.

128. Bale, *Complete Plays of John Bale*, vol 1., 58.

3. A NEW JOSIAH AND BUCER'S THEOCRATIC UTOPIA

1. Henry VIII turned sympathetically toward the Reformation in the last year of his reign, helping to establish the stability of Edward's court. This was in part thanks to "two extraordinary strokes of luck for the evangelical party," when the most powerful conservative nobleman, the Duke of Norfolk, and the most prominent conservative bishop (Gardiner) enraged the king.

MacCulloch, *Thomas Cranmer*, 359. Setbacks in reform in late Henrician England are discussed in Haigh, *English Reformations*, 152–167.

2. MacCulloch, *Tudor Church Militant*, 2; MacCulloch, *Thomas Cranmer*, 2. See also Simpson, *Burning to Read*, 8–9. MacCulloch and Simpson prefer "evangelical," which may have an unnecessarily strong contemporary resonance for American readers. It should be stressed that the word "Protestant" is not wholly unused; it seems to emerge around 1539 (see *OED*, which reminds us that "Protestant" and "Reformed" often implied "Lutheran" and "Calvinist," respectively), and in the earliest cases it is used to describe foreigners. But some uses are more native: Miles Coverdale records an agreement between the two: "catholike sorte must kepe the olde religion: and the estates of the protestantes must holde them vnto it," *The Supplicacion* (1542), sig. C1ʳ. See also Gilby, *A commentarye vpon the prophet Mycha* (1551), sig. Diʳ.

3. Austin, *From Judaism to Calvinism*, 63–75; Austin, "Epitome of the Old Testament," 217–235. Tremellius' 1569 edition and translation of the Syriac New Testament was dedicated to Elizabeth. Wilkinson, "Immanuel Tremellius'," 9–25.

4. Collinson, *Godly People*, 27.

5. Milton, *Judgement of Martin Bucer* (1644), sig. B4ʳ; see Loewenstein, "Milton and the Creation of England's Long Reformation," passim.

6. Gordon, "Authority of Antiquity," 7; Greschat, *Martin Bucer*, 233; all that now remains is a fragment of Matthew with commentary.

7. Gordon, "Fagius, Paul," *Oxford Dictionary of National Biography* (2004).

8. In 1523 he was excommunicated for preaching the Bible as the only source for religious practice. Eells, *Attitude of Martin Bucer*, 5, 14. Lugioyo, *Martin Bucer's Doctrine*, 18.

9. Duffield, "First Psalter," 291–293. *The Psalter of Dauid in Englishe purely a[n]d faithfully tra[n]slated aftir the texte of Feline [ie., Bucer]* (1530).

10. Pratt, "Trouble with Translation," 39; Davies, "Sir John Cheke," 1–12.

11. Jackson, ed., *Records of the Court*, 20. Pratt, "Trouble with Translation," 39.

12. MacCulloch, *Tudor Church Militant*, 222.

13. On the resolution of Eucharistic theology through the debate between Cranmer and Stephen Gardiner in 1550–1551, see Allen, *Eucharistic Debate in Tudor England*; Anderson, "Language and History," 20–51. On the general issues of Church theology and liturgy, see MacCulloch, *Tudor Church Militant*, 11–12; see also Alford, *Kingship and Politics*, passim.

14. On Cranmer, see Milton, *Complete Prose Works* (abbreviated as *CPW*) vol. 1, 531; 533; 535; 974; *CPW* vol. 2, 716 (below). Milton credits the idea the Edward was poisoned by his "fals Protector" (*Eikonoklastes, CPW* vol. 3, 438).

15. *Tetrachordon* (1645), A3ʳ; *CPW* vol. 2, 581. Milton digs into a moment key to his argument about the unfinished Reformation in *Tetrachordon*: "in those times which are on record for the purest and sincerest that ever shon yet on the reformation of this Iland, the time of Edward the 6ᵗʰ. That worthy Prince having utterly abolisht the Canon Law out of his Dominions, as his father did before him, appointed by full vote of Parlament, a Commotty of two and thirty chosen men, Divines and Lawyers, of whom *Cranmer* the Archbishop, *Peter Martyr*, and *Walter Haddon*, (not without the assistance of *Sir John Cheeke* the Kings Tutor, a man at that time counted the learnedest of Englishmen, & for piety not inferior) were the chief, to frame anew some Ecclesiastical Laws, that might be in stead of what was abrogated. The work with great diligence was finisht, and with as great aprobation of that reforming age was receav'd; and had bin doubtlesse, as the learned Preface thereof testifies, establish by act of Parlament, had not the good Kings death so soon ensuing, arrested the furder growth of Religion also, from that season to this"

(*CPW* vol. 2, 716–717). See Loewenstein, "Milton and the Creation of England's Long Reformation," 169–173.

16. Milton, *Complete Shorter Poems*, 309. The title comes from the Trinity Manuscript.

17. John King observes how the ideas of Erasmus in the *Institutio Principis Christiani* (1516) are followed in the appointment of tutors for Edward; *English Reformation Literature*, 171. MacCulloch, *Tudor Church Militant*, 15–23.

18. Cranmer, *Miscellaneous Writings and Letters*, vol. 16, 127.

19. This is a widely accepted position; Collins, *Introduction to the Hebrew Bible*, 14.

20. Bucer's sentiment is perhaps best represented in Milton's translation: "where the Gospel of Christ is receiv'd, the laws of Antichrist should be rejected"; *CPW* vol. 2, 442. See Cranmer, *An Aunsvvere by the Reuerend Father* (1580), 29; Gilby also inveighs against Gardiner's adherence to canon law in *An Ansvver to the Deuillish Detection* (London, 1548), fol. Clxxxxii^v. See also Williams, *Radical Reformation*, 1193.

21. Latimer, *Fyrste Sermon of Mayster Hughe Latimer* (1549), epistolary letter.

22. The original has it at "4 Kings," because the books of Samuel were then counted as Kings. Matthews Bible (1537), Folger call number 2066, sig. 6^r–v; also in the 1551 printing [Beinecke z84 0126]; the Becke Bibles are *The Byble, that is to say all the Holy Scripture* (London: Day and Seres, 1549), fol. Lxiiii^v, and *The Byble, that is to say al the Holy Scripture* (London: Jhon Day, 1551), fol. ixviii^v. See Simpson, *Burning to Read*, 13.

23. Ian Green persuasively argues that the catechism became the most effective tool for the dissemination of the new faith. Green, *The Christian's ABC*.

24. Cranmer, *Catechismus* (1548).

25. Cranmer, *Aunsvvere by the Reuerend Father* (1580), 29.

26. The book reprinting Cranmer's debate with Gardiner also points out that Henry's great matter—the divorce—was a formative moment in which scripture supplanted canon law: "The kynges matter remoued from the popes Canon law, to the triall of the Scriptures." *Aunsvvere by the Reuerend Father* (1580), sig. Aii^r.

27. Cranmer, *Catechismus* (1548), fol. 38^v–39^r.

28. Pohl and Tether, "Books Fit for a King," 1–35.

29. This is the heading of Chapter IX of the Second Book in to *De Regno Christi*, in *Melanchthon and Bucer*, 280.

30. King, *English Reformation Literature*, 128.

31. *The Byble, that is to say all the Holy Scripture* (1549), fol. xxi^r, and *The Byble, that is to sall all the Holy Scripture* (1551), fol. xxii^r. The same is true for the "Prologue shewing the use of the scripture, in fol i^r; the prologue to Leviticus, though, is acknowledged in the 1549 edition with "W.T." fol. x^r.

32. *The Byble, That Is to Say All the Holy Scripture* (1549), fol. xxii.

33. The changes are analyzed in Westbrook, *Long Travail and Great Paynes*, 113–126.

34. Westbrook, *Long Travail and Great Paynes*, 113–114.

35. *The New Oxford Annotated Bible* (RSV), 241.

36. Weinfeld, *Deuteronomy and the Deuteronomic School*, 179–189; Walzer, *In God's Shadow*, 20.

37. Walzer, *In God's Shadow*, 22.

38. The reader signs the Bible at the end, "This is Johan Gentwaye Byble." fol cxxi^r.

39. *The Byble, That Is to Say All the Holy Scripture* (1549), sig. A5^r–v.

40. Argument to the Book of Joshua, 1560 Geneva Bible, fol. 96^v.

41. Cranmer, *Writings of the Rev. Dr. Thomas Cranmer*, 268.

42. Arnold Williams draws a solid connection with Bucer's earlier tract, *In Sacra Quatuor Evangelica, Enarrationes* (Basel, 1536)—a reprint from book first published in the 1520s—in *CPW* vol. 2, 444.

43. Eells, *Attitude of Martin Bucer*, 9–10, 13–15, 29, 36–43; passim. Luther also supported this bigamy; see Faulkner, "Luther and the Bigamous Marriage of Philip of Hesse," 206–231.

44. Faulkner, "Luther and the Bigamous Marriage," 213.

45. Bucer, *Common Places of Martin Bucer*, 303; Avis, "Moses and the Magistrate," 13.

46. *Melanchthon and Bucer*, 156, 165.

47. Fink, "Doers of The Law," 520: "For Calvin, Luther, and most other Protestant theologians, good works become the by-products of this *gratia gratum faciens*; for Bucer, however, works of the law occupy a more significant position as the means by which God has chosen to materialize the righteousness first granted at the *initium fidei*." See Lugioyo, *Martin Bucer's Doctrine of Justification*, 69–77.

48. Lugioyo, *Martin Bucer's Doctrine of Justification*, 69–77, passim.

49. On Bucer's Erasmianism, see for example, de Kroon, "Martin Bucer," 157–168.

50. As Wilhelm Pauck points out, Bucer "regarded the Reformation as a movement through which the Christianization of all human life was to be accomplished. The Bible was for him the source and pattern of all legislation required to this end. This view was far different from that of Luther, because it did not agree with the latter's distinction between the law and the gospel." *Melanchthon and Bucer*, 156. Pauck, "Butzer and Calvin," 85–99.

51. Bucer, *Melanchthon and Bucer*, 175. Original: "Literarium enim, & de loco aliquo religionis nostrae admonens munusculum requiri a me, facile intelligo: sed tale, quod S.T.M vel aliquam adferat cum iucudam, tum non inutilem admonitionem." *De Regno Christi* (1557), 2.

52. Pohl and Tether, "Books Fit for a King," 12, 14.

53. Harding, "Authorial and Editorial Influence," 132–133.

54. Pohl and Tether, "Books Fit for a King," 15.

55. *Melanchthon and Bucer*, 345–346; on the regulation of poems and songs, see 346–352.

56. Pohl and Tether, "Books Fit for a King," 13.

57. Early printings of Bucer's work appeared as *De regno Christi Iesu seruatoris nostri, libri II. Ad Eduardum VI Angliae regem, annis abhinc sex scripti . . . de coniugio & divortio, etc* (Basileae, 1557); it appeared in French in 1558 as *Deux Liures de Royaume de Iesus Christ nostre sauueur, composez par M. Bucer peu de temps auant sa mort, & dediez a Édouard VI. Roy d'Angleterre . . . Nouuellement traduits de Latin en François* ([Lausanne?], 1558) and in Geneva as *Du Royavme De Iesus Christ Nostre Savvevr* (Geneva, 1558), and then in the commemorative volume *Martini Bvceri Scripta Anglicana fere omnia* (Basel, 1577); see Collinson, *Godly People*, 34. Grindal contributed through Hubert to *Scripta Anglicana*; 35. Books and manuscripts were commonly given as New Year's gifts; see Pohl and Tether, "Books fit for a King," 2–9.

58. Bucer, *Melanchthon and Bucer*, 266. The Latin is "Primum haud dubito, Serenissime Rex, M. T. ipsam videre hanc, quam requirimus, imo quam requirit salus ominium nostrum, Regni CHRISTI restitutionem, ab Episcopis nullo modo esse expectandam, dum adeo pauci inter eos sunt, qui vim huius regni & propria munia, plane ipsi cognoscant: plerique autem eorum illud etiam quibus possunt, & audent modis, vel oppugnent, vel different atque renorentur." *De Regno Christi* (1557), 83.

59. Bucer, *Martini Buceri Scripta Anglicana* (1577), 875.

60. *Admonition to the Parliament* (1572), A1ʳ.

61. Shuger, *Political Theologies*, 11; for discussions of Platonic legal codes, see 9–13, 39–47; Bucer, *Melanchthon and Bucer*, 164–65, 181, 183.

62. Bucer, *Melanchthon and Bucer*, 181; the modernized references to Deuteronomy are 13:5ff, 17:2–5, 19:11–21, 21:18–21, 22:13–28, and 24:7.

63. Bucer, *Melanchthon and Bucer*, 378–379.

64. Eells, *Attitude of Martin Bucer*, 7.

65. Bucer, *Melanchthon and Bucer*, 380.

66. See Greschat, *Martin Bucer*, 227; see examples in *Melanchthon and Bucer*, 339, 341, 354, 382, some pointed out by Pauck; see also his dicussion on in *Melanchthon and Bucer*, 164.

67. Pauck, ed., *Melanchthon and Bucer*, 279–280.

68. Becke, ed., *The Byble* (London, 1549), and Becke, 1551. Geneva text of 1561, *Bible and Holy Scriptures conteyned* (Geneva, 1561), fols. 85r, 86r.

69. *Martini Bvceri Scripta Anglicana* (1577), 162.

70. *Martini Bvceri Scripta Anglicana* (1577), 56.

71. *Melanchthon and Bucer*, 266–267. Further citations are paranthetically noted within the text.

72. This is discussed in Chapter 6.

73. Eells, *Attitude of Martin Bucer*, 35; 211.

74. *Judgement of Martin Bucer* (1644), 2–3; *CPW* vol. 2, 443. For the original in *Scripta Anglicana* (Basel, 1577), see *CPW* vol. 2, 88.

75. *Judgement of Martin Bucer* (1644), 2–3; *CPW* vol. 2, 442–444, 454.

76. Collinson, *Godly People*, 25.

77. Bramhall, *Serpent Salve* (1643), 207.

78. *Scripta Anglicana* (Basel, 1577), 935ff; cited in *Melancthon and Bucer*, 160. See *A Briefe Treatise concerning the Burnynge of Bucer and Phagius* (1562).

79. Bramhall, *Serpent Salve* (1643), 207–208; citing *De Regno Christi*, cap. 13.

80. Brooke, *Discovrse Opening the Natvre* (London, 1641), 74–75.

81. Collinson, *Godly People*, 30; Alec Ryrie, "Sampson, Thomas," *Dictionary of National Biography*.

82. There is a great deal we do not know about how the community of translators and annotators operated; while in these letters he discusses other translation work, particularly of Gaulter's *Antichrist*, he never mentions biblical translation. Sampson's letters are in Robinson, ed., *Original Letters*, vol 1., 170–183, and these originate from Swiss and French locations outside of Geneva, suggesting that he could not have been at least a very industrious member of the team. On Gaulter's *Antichrist*, see 174 and 176. See also Alec Ryrie, "Sampson, Thomas," *Oxford Dictionary of National Biography*. I regret following previous scholarship in listing Sampson as a translator in "Toward a New Cultural History of the Geneva Bible," 491.

83. Ryrie, "Sampson, Thomas" *Oxford Dictionary of National Bibliography*; For the record of his deprivation in 1565, see Styrpe, *Annals of the Reformation*, vol. 1, 476–477.

84. Collinson, *Godly People*, 30.

85. Collinson, *Godly People*, 32.

86. Collinson, *Godly People*, 30.

87. Collinson, *Godly People*, 44.

88. *The Nevve Testament of our Lord Iesus Christ* (Geneva, 1557), 1 Corinthians 14.34.

89. Goodman, *Superior Powers* (Geneva, 1558), 52.

90. *Bible and Holy Scriptures* (Geneva, 1560), sig. ***iiʳ.

4. THE WORD IN EXILE

1. Like most Elizabethans before him, Hobbes was himself a reader of the Geneva Bible, though on some occasions he refers to the King James Bible, even comparing the two in *Leviathan*, ed. Tuck, 281. On Hobbes and the Geneva Bible, see Somos, *"Mare Clausum, Leviathan,* and *Oceana,"* 103.

2. Hobbes, *Behemoth* (1682), 36–37.

3. Hill, *Intellectual Origins,* 3–4. For similar views, see Greaves, "Traditionalism," 94–109; Craig, "Geneva Bible," 40. Hill's words seem echoed even in the standard bibliography of Bibles, where in Herbert, Darlow and Moule, *Historical Catalogue,* the Geneva Bible is accounted as having notes that "endeared it especially to the Puritans, and for three generations it maintained its supremacy as the Bible of the people" (61). See also Furniss, "Reading the English Bible" 1–21. The output of the exiles is catalogued in Baskerville, *Chronological Bibliography.*

4. Hill, *English Bible,* 18; see also Hill, *Antichrist in Seventeenth-Century England,* 3–4.

5. Barlow, *Svmme and Substance,* 46–47.

6. Sheppard, ed., *Geneva Bible,* 6.

7. Betteridge, "Bitter Notes," 42. See also Greaves, "Traditionalism," 94–109; and Greaves, "Nature and Intellectual Milieu," 233–249.

8. McGrath, *In the Beginning,* 127–129.

9. Velz, "Shakespeare and the Geneva Bible," 117.

10. For Shakespeare and the Geneva Bible, see Shaheen, *Biblical References in Shakespeare's Plays*; Kastan, *A Will to Believe,* 26; Mowat, "Shakespeare Reads the Geneva Bible," 25–39; Groves, "Shakespeare's Sonnets," 114–128; Hamlin, *Shakespeare and the Bible*; Harris, "Written in the Margent," 301–304; Fulton and Poole, *Bible on the Shakespearean Stage,* 1–14, passim.

11. Barlow, *Svmme and Substance* (1604), 47. The Geneva Bible was the only Bible printed in Scotland; the first Bible printed in Scotland was a 1579 Geneva Bible, STC 2125, with a long dedication to King James. In the same year it was ordered by the General Assembly that every parish in Scotland subscribe to purchase the Bible, and an Act in the Scots Parliament ordered every householder worth a certain amount to have a vernacular text. Herbert and Darlow, *Historical Catalogue,* 88–89. On the Scottish Bible and James, see Hall, "Genevan Version," 125. On Elizabeth's Geneva Bible, see King and Pratt, "Bibles as Books," 84. On Whitgift and Hooker, see Shaheen, "Misconceptions about the Geneva Bible," 156–158. On Laud, see Stallybrass, "Books and Scrolls," 52. On Lanyer, see Fleck, "'To Write of Him and Pardon Crave'," 545–560.

12. Milton, *Divorce Tracts of John Milton,* ix; discussed in Fulton, review of *Divorce Tracts of John Milton,* 196–199.

13. The presumption of Milton's puritan readership remains pervasive; a biblically annotated edition of *Paradise Lost* is available, a major scholarly undertaking, with glosses extensively supplied from the 1560 Geneva Bible, produced over 100 years prior to Milton's epic. Milton, *Paradise Lost, The Biblically Annotated Edition.*

14. Excellent recent work includes that of Femke Molekamp, "Genevan Legacies," 38–53; Molekamp, "Using a Collection," 1–13.

15. Sherman, *Used Books,* 71. More than 140 editions and over half a million copies were produced.

16. Among the reiterated views of the Geneva Bible's special populism is that it was small, readable, and cheap; Betteridge, "Bitter Notes," 42. Its size ranged from tiny editions to folios, but this proved a virtue to the well-to-do as well; Elizabeth I had a small sextodecimo copy that

she annotated (see King and Pratt, "Bibles as Books," 84; the Bible is STC 2881.5 (c. 1580), Bodl. Arch. G e.48). Nor is the Geneva Bible the first cheap or frequently published Bible: the six-year reign of Edward saw more intensive biblical production than the first six years of Elizabeth's reign by a ratio of nearly four to one. Not until the late 1570s and 1580s does biblical production resume what it had been thirty years before. See Herbert, Darlow and Moule, *Historical Catalogue*, 60. It is surely anachronistic to assume that black letter was seen as "old-style." The first Geneva Bible was produced at a Genevan press that used roman fonts for its French, Latin, and Italian Bibles. *La Bibia* (F. Durone, 1562), made for Italian Protestant refugees, is astonishingly similar in type and *mise en page* to the English, and, like the French edition of 1560, it shares many woodblocks with the English version. The first quarto editions printed in England in 1579 were black letter, and, as King and Pratt have pointed out, "In quarto and folio format [. . .] forty-one extant black-letter editions outnumber twenty-two extant roman editions by nearly two to one." King and Pratt, 81. See also Shaheen, "Misconceptions about the Geneva Bible," 156–158.

17. Gilby, *Admonition to England*, appended to Knox, *Appellation of John Knoxe* (1558), fol. 72r.

18. The foundational work on paratexts is Genette, *Paratexts*, see esp. 1–15. On early modern paratexts, see Hackel, *Reading Material*, 69–136. See also Smith and Wilson, eds., *Renaissance Paratexts*; Sherman, *Used Books*; Slights, "Edifying Margins," 682–716; Slights, "Marginal Nots," 255–278; Tribble, *Margins and Marginality*.

19. For discussions of this point and further bibliography, see Fulton, *Historical Milton*; Sharpe, *Reading Revolutions*.

20. Tyndale, *A Path Way i[n]to the Holy Scripture* ([1536?]), sig. D4v; Tribble, *Margins and Marginality*, 11–12.

21. McDermott, "Ordinary Gloss on Jonah," 424.

22. See Scribner, "Heterodoxy, Literacy, and Print," 274–278. On "Anabaptism" in the Geneva notes, see for example 1560, Revelation 2:24.

23. See Haigh, *English Reformations*, 203–234.

24. On the census of Marian exiles, see Pettegree, *Marian Protestantism*, 3–4. See also Kirby, *Zurich Connection*, 1. On Lock in Geneva, see Lock, *Collected Works*, xxiii–xxx. Lock came at the urging of Knox, and did so in 1557, returning in 1559. Lock's authorship of the sonnets has been questioned in May, "Anne Lock," 793–819.

25. Van Kampen, "Translator's Notes" 290–302.

26. Molekamp, "Genevan Legacies," 40–41; Johnson, "Marginal at Best," 244. Sometimes John Pullian and Miles Coverdale are included in this list, but they were not frequently in Geneva during this period; the main translators seem to be Gilby and Whittingham. See Danner, "Contribution of the Geneva Bible," 5.

27. Danner, "Calvin and Puritanism," 152.

28. See the examples in Craig, "Geneva Bible as Political Document," 44, such as a note on 2 Chronicles 23:21: "For where a tyrant and an idolator reigneth, there can be no quietness."

29. *The Bible and Holy Scriptures* (1560), sig. 3*4ʳ.

30. Parker, *Correspondence of Matthew Parker*, 261–262. For reasons that remain unclear, the London edition was not printed until 1575, just after Parker's death, which may suggest that there was an unrecorded decision changing this stated allowance. Perhaps more important in 1575 is the appointment of Edmund Grindal as Archbishop.

31. Pratt, "Trouble with Translation," 35; *Calendar of Patent Rolls*, vol 3, 227; Blayney, *Stationers' Company*, vol. 2, 732.

32. Archbishop Parker to Queen Elizabeth, Pollard, *Records of the English Bible*, 295.

33. Parker, *Correspondence of Matthew Parker*, 336. Pollard, *Records of the English Bible*, 297; Greaves, "Traditionalism," 94.

34. Collinson, "Monarchical Republic," 410. Bishops' Bibles have notes, and they are in some printings so much like the notes that James objected to as to belie specific connection between the two incidents. The glossing of Exodus 1:19, to which James objected, is hardly different from the Geneva: "King of Egypt" in 1:15 is glossed "Tyrantes trye divers ways to oppresse the Church." And just below this is the marginal note: "God for his names sake wyl deliver his Churche from the affliction of tirants." STC 2114 (1575) also has a longer note on Exodus 1:21 that does not differ in substance from the note in the 1568 and 1572 folios. This longer version appears in the quarto edition of 1569 (STC 2105). Tyrants had not escaped the Bishops' Bible.

35. Collinson, "Elizabethan Exclusion Crisis," 83; see also Collinson, "Monarchical Republic," 407–413. A vital moment for the use of the Geneva Bible was during the parliament of 1572, which debated executing Mary or barring her from succession.

36. *The Bible and Holy Scriptures* (1560), sig. 3*2ʳ, with marginal citations of Ezra 4:{6} and 1 Esdras 2:16, which mark the beginning of two accounts of the Persian King Artaxerxes who obstructed the building of the Temple, representing the contrary forces that Elizabeth must withstand.

37. On history and typology, see Killeen, *Political Bible*, 33–42.

38. See Danner, *Pilgrimage to Puritanism*. Gilby was "one of the last refugees to leave" (36); Whittingham "remained in Geneva until it was finished" (44); Danner also places William Cole among the translators, who "doubtless saw the Geneva Bible to its completion" (82).

39. The 1557 New Testament has the important line from Matthew 16:18, "And I say also unto thee, that thou art Peter, and upon this rock I will build my congregation (*ekklesia*)." "Congregation" also occurs in Matthew 18:17. *The Newe Testament of Our Lord Iesus Christ* (1557), sig. d4ᵛ.

40. See Fulton, *Historical Milton*, 149–153; Fulton, "Political Theology on the Pulpit," 204–221.

41. *La Bible* (1559).

42. *The Newe Testament of Our Lord Jesus Christ* (1557), sig. 2*3ʳ.

43. Clare Costley King'oo observes a similar phenomenon in "Elizabeth's Prayerbook" (1569); see *Miserere Mei*, 132–144; the prayerbook reproduces the Geneva Bible psalm prefaces (137).

44. *The Bible* (1577), Bodleian Library pressmark BOD Bib. Eng. 1577 d.1. I am grateful to Beatrice Groves for this reference; see her discussion in "England's Jerusalem in Shakespeare's Henriad," 87–102.

45. The first New Testament to be broken into individual verses was Robert Estienne's 1551 edition.

46. Locke, *Paraphrase and Notes* (1671); vii, quoted from Norton, *A History of the English Bible as Literature* (2000), 87.

47. *New Testament* (1557), sig. **.iiiʳ.

48. *New Testament* (1557), sig**.iiᵛ.

49. *New Testament* (1557), sig**.iiivʳ.

50. *New Testament* (1557), sig.*.iii.

51. Nelson, *Monstrous Adversary*, 1, 55, 68, see later discussion; on the notes in the Geneva Bible (at 1 Corinthians 6:9–20) and their possible correspondence to biograpy, see 53, 214–5.

52. It is sometimes thought that the earlier Geneva copies were not read. Folger 2105.8 has more academic markings with references to Zwinglii (fol. 25ʳ; 285ʳ) and other markings; 32ʳ, 72ʳ,

72ᵛ, 121ʳ, 156ᵛ, 199ʳ⁻ᵛ, 200ʳ, 210ʳ, etc., 285ᵛ "Marriage the covenant of god"—this reader is more text than paratext; but see underlining at Hehemiah, 223ʳ. and at Jeremiah 10, 328ᵛ. Folger 2105.9 has red lines added throughout (a common addition), and occasional reader annotations that again seem more scholarly than de Vere's; as in the back of the figures inset at Leviticus 18; this one has less marking.

53. Edward de Vere's marked 1570 copy at the Folger Shakespeare Library, STC 2106. Another red velvet Bible is the Bishops' Bible doubtfully attributed to Elizabeth, Folger STC 2099 copy 3. There are only two de Vere books extant, both at the Folger; the copy of Guicciardini's *La historia d'Italia* (1565) has the same crest of the boar, but embossed in the leather. Similarly sumptuous Bibles include Anne Boleyn's gold painted and apparently vellum *newe Testament, dylygently corrected and compared with the Greke by Wyllyam Tindale* (Anwerp [sic], 1534) (BL C.23.a.8) and gold-bound copy of the *Penitential Psalms and other Psalms, in English verse* [by John Croke], BL MS Stowe 956. *Faerie Queene,* I. 9. 19; discussed in Kearney, "Rewriting the Letter," 119–123.

54. See the Lamentation upon the destruction of Jerusalem, "they that were broght up in skarlet, embrase the dongue" (4.5). Luders et al., eds., *Statutes of the Realm,* vol. 3, 430; see Monnas, *Renaissance Velvets,* 23–38.

55. On the ways that "elaborately bound books could function as fashion accessories and insignia of social status," see Walsham, "Jewels for Gentlewomen," 126.

56. This description originates in the bibliography of English Bibles, Herbert and Darlow, *Historical Catalogue,* 61, and is repeated in Hill, *English Bible,* 18.

57. The neat italic hand in the margins of de Vere's Bible is consistent with other witnesses; see for example the early letter in French, BL Lansdow. 6/25, fol. 79; 23 August 1563 (especially "usant" like "usuary"); Cecil Papers 8/24; 17–18 March 1575; Lansdowe 11/53, the "p," "v" and long "s"; Lansdowne 14/84, Cecil Papers 8/12 is pertinent to the question of Usury, concerning the "greatnes of my dett, & gredines of my crediters." Lansdowne 38/62; Lansdowne 42/39. Thanks to the advice of Alan Nelson, who deposited a major collection of facsimiles of de Vere's letters at the Folger Shakespeare Library.

58. Nelson, *Monstrous Adversary,* 68; this is in 1571, just after he acquired the Bible; for other evidence of his strong Catholic sympathy, see the account of his friendship with Thomas Howard, whose thoughts of marrying the Queen of Scots entangled him in the Rising of the Northern Earls, *Monstrous Adversary,* 55; see also 1.

59. Bishops' Bible (1568), *The Second Tome of the Holie Bible Faithfully Translated into English* (1610), 393.

60. See Marks, *English Bible,* 1064 (note on Ps. 105); Hill, *English Bible,* 60–61.

61. The civil war witnessed a pamphlet battle devoted to this line, in Prynne's *Vindication of Psalme 105:15* (1642). [Anon.], *The Soveraignty of kings, or, An absolute answer and confutation of that groundlesse vindication of Psalme 105.15* (1642), [Anon.], *A Revindication of Psalme 105.15.* (1643). See also John Knox, *Historie of the Reformation* (1644), sig. f2ᵛ.

62. Tyndale, *An Exposycyon vpon the V.Vi.Vii. Chapters of Mathewe* (1536), sigs. G4ᵛ–5ʳ.

63. The underlined material is from the Folger Shakespeare Library's 1570 copy of the Geneva Bible, shelfmark 2105.9, fol. 127ʳ.

64. On this point, see Prescott, "Exploiting King Saul," 178–194.

65. Nicholson, *God's Secretaries,* 58.

66. This is revised from my 2017 article "Toward a New Cultural History," in which I had missed two.

67. There are also a few in the Apocrypha, which translates the Greek as it is: Wisdom of Solomon: 12:14 "There dare nether Kyng nor tyrant in thy sight require accountes of them whom thou hast punished." The word occurs again in 2 Maccabees 4:25, 7:27.

68. Whitaker et al., *Eerdmans Analytical Concordance*, 1148. Brown, *Hebrew and English Lexicon*.

69. Genesis 6:4; see *Beowulf*, (ll. 1557–1559): "Then he saw a blade that boded well, / a sword in her armory, an ancient heirloom / from the days of the giants, an ideal weapon," (Heaney translation of: "Geseah ða on searwum sige-eadig bil, / eald-sweord eotenisc ecgum þyhtig, / wigena weorð-mynd.") At the Old English prose Hexateuch, Genesis 6.4, the noun for "giant" used by the Old English writer is "ent" (the plural given is "entas") and the line translates in the same way it is in the Geneva Bible. The *Beowulf* poet uses three different words for giant in the poem: "eoten," "gigant," and "ent," the same word used by the prose biblical translator. The word "ent" appears three times in Beowulf: lines 1679, 2717, and 2774; and then once as an adjective "entisc" (line 2979; "made by giants"). On Giants, Genesis, and *Beowulf*, see Neidorf, "Cain, Cam, Jutes, Giants," 610–611; Emerson, "Legends of Cain," 888–894.

70. The passage of 1 Kings which relates how the succession of the monarchy from David to Solomon is challenged by a pretender, Adoniiah, who has gained support in the court, is annotated with the detailed explanation, not in the text: "The King [David] being worne with age, could not attend to the affairs of the realme, & also Adoniiah had many flatterers which kept it from the king" (1 Kings 1:18).

71. Calvin, *Institutes* (1561), fol. 170ᵛ. Similarly in the KJV: "The tyrants fall," above Isaiah 14.

72. Filmer, *Anarchy* ([London], 1648), 16.

73. Walker, *Writing under Tyranny*, 1.

74. The Treasons Act was repealed in the first year of Edward's reign, though reinstated in Elizabeth's. Brewer and Gairdner, eds., *Letters and Papers*, vol. 8, 1105, cited in Starkey, *Six Wives*, 523.

75. Gilby, *Admonition to England and Scotland* (1558), fol. 69ᵛ–70ʳ.

76. Steele, *Tudor and Stuart Proclamations*, No. 488; lxxxv.

77. Goodman, *How Superior Powers Oght to be Obeyd* (1558), 4.

78. Danner, *Pilgrimage to Puritanism*, 42. Goodman's tract was printed in Geneva by John Crispin, who printed later editions of the Geneva Bible and the popular *Forme of Prayer and Ministration of the Sacraments* (Geneva, 1556), which went through at least ten editions. See Danner, "Calvin and Puritanism," 160. On Knox's tract, see Felch, "Rhetoric of Biblical Authority," 805–822; Richards, "To Promote a Woman to Beare Rule," 101–121. Healey et al., "Waiting for Deborah," 371–386.

79. Knox, *Appellation of John Knoxe*, fol. 79ʳ; the Geneva translation has "against the wicked." Psalm 94:16.

80. Gilby, *Admonition to England*, fols. 71ᵛ–72ʳ.

81. Knox, *Appellation of John Knoxe*, fol. 78.

82. See the explanations in Marks, *English Bible*, 1427; and the NRSV, 1055.

83. The note from Barbier & Courteau, *La Bible* (1559): "C'estoit Josias leur roy, qu'ils disens estre l'esprit de leur narines: c'est a dire leur vie a cause qu'ils anendoyent une vie pleine de paix & de repos par le moyen d'iceluy. Ce roy figuroit Christ le vrai oinct, duquel seul procede la vie, paix et vray repos & lequel est tombé ès daqs des iniques." Or "It was Josiah their king, whom they say to be the spirit/breath of their nostrils: that is, their life because they redeemed/repaired a life full

of peace and calm by means of him. This king figured Christ the true anointed, from whom alone proceeds life, peace, and true repose and who was felled by blows of the wicked." fol. 330ʳ.

84. Cranmer, *Miscellaneous Writings and Letters*, 127; Williams, *Radical Reformation*, 1192–1193; Simpson, *Burning to Read*, 10–11; Gordon, "Authority of Antiquity," 9; and Bradshaw, "David or Josiah?" vol. 2, 778–790.

85. Anon., *Homilie against Disobedience and Wylfull Rebellion* [1570], sig. B2ʳ⁻ᵛ.

86. See for example the headnote "Argument" to Jeremiah, and the note to Ezekiel 1:1.

87. See Tyndale, in his letter to the Reader in *The Obedience of A Christian Man*, ed. Daniel, 17; Tyndale, *An Exposycyon vpon the V.Vi.Vii. Chapters of Mathewe* (1536), fol. lxxxivʳ. Beza, *Ane Answer Made* (1561), sig. Diiiiᵛ; Beza, *Master Bezaes Sermons* (1587), 150.

88. This is the central claim of Sherman's *Used Books*.

89. Grafton and Jardine, "'Studied for Action'," 30–78.

90. Gilby, *Admonition to England* (1558), fol. 72ʳ.

91. Note on Isaiah 2:7; it is unique to the English version; not in *La Bible* (1559).

92. *La Bible* (1559), fol. 283ʳ.

93. *New Oxford Annotated Bible*.

94. Calvin, *Commentarii in Isaiam prophetam* (1551); Calvin, *Commentarii in Isaiam* (1559); the 1583 edition contains both dedications to Edward VI and Elizabeth.

95. The quotation here is taken from the later English translation; Calvin, *Commentary upon the Prophecie of Isaiah* (London, 1609), 87; the Latin is *Commentarii in Isaiam prophetam* (1551), 4–5; see also *Commentarii in Isaiam* (1583), 75.

96. The first note to Isaiah 8:1 in Barbier and Courteau, *La Bible* (the first phrase of which the English annotators translate in their own note b. to Isaiah 8:1) reads, "A la façon commune. Le Seigneur commande que ceste prophecie soit escrite & publie en la maniere qu'il est dit en l'argument de ce livre." The English annotators' note to the verse 8:2 is a rendering of the reminder given at this point in the French. *La Bible* (1559), fol. 283ʳ.

97. Melanchthon's report of Luther's posting of the Ninety-five Theses was given in his funeral oration in 1546; it was expanded in *Historia de vita et actis Lutheri* in 1548; a French translation was made in 1549; and an English translation was made by Henry Bennet, *Famous and Godly History* (1561), which was adapted by Foxe in *Actes and Monuments*. See Cummings, *Literary Culture of the Reformation*, 15–16, n.2. See also Marius, *Martin Luther*, 137–139.

98. Melanchthon, *A famous and godly history* (1561), sig. C1ʳ⁻ᵛ.

99. The argument to Isaiah in Barbier and Courteau in *La Bible*—which translates directly from Calvin's commentary—is very similar: "Car la coustume estoit entre les Prophetes (apres avoir exposè & declare au people la doctrine & la volonte de Dieu) de regider en vu brief sommaire leur predictions, & de l'afficher aux portes du temple, afin que nul ne peust ignorer leur prophecie. Et certains jours apres cedit sommaire estoit arrachè des portes susdites, puis mis et reserve au thresors par les ministers du temple, pour en perpetuer la memoire, ainsi que l'on peut colliger du 2. chap. D'Abacuc, & du 8. de ce livre." *La Bible* (1559), fol. 280ʳ.

100. For an assessment of the implications of the scrolls for textual criticism, see Collins, *Dead Sea Scrolls*, 185–212; on the complexities of Isaiah, 187. A seminal work is Cross, *Ancient Library of Qumran*; for the list of texts see Tov, "List of the Texts from the Judaean Desert," 196–199; the psalms are a close second, and would vie for first place were it not for the complete Isaiah scroll.

101. 1 Kings 4:32. Later in 1 Kings, the writer asks, "Are thei not written in the boke of the actes of Solomon?" (11:41), and the marginal note similarly indicates the loss of this book during

captivity. The chronicles mentioned throughout the Books of Kings as a source similarly "perished in the captivitie" (1 Kings 4:29), and the books of Nathan and Gad the prophets mentioned in 1 Chronicles 29:29 are also "thought to have been lost in captivitie"; in Joshua 10:13 a book is mentioned that the note argues, against a reading of the "Chalde texte," is "now lost."

102. This is Gilby's own reflection on his *Commentarye upon the Prophet Malaky* (1553?); see Gilby, *Briefe Treatice of Election, and Reprobation* ([1575?]), sig. A2ʳ.

103. Remarkably the two Christian words do actually appear, though very rarely, in the Geneva Old Testament—never in the KJV—in cases where the marginal interpretation seems so weighty as to enter the vocabulary of the translated text.

104. Kirby, *Zurich Connection*, 28–29. On Isaiah as a model scholar-prophet, see Gordon, "Bibliander's Oration on Isaiah," 107–141. As Gordon writes, "In Bibliander's mind . . . the true prophet is a Christian humanist, like Isaiah," 120. Bullinger's advice on magistrates, see *Decades of Henry Bullinger*, 298–435.

105. Knox, *Historie of the Reformation*, 180.

106. Gilby, *Admonition to England*, fols. 60ᵛ–61ʳ.

107. Fuller, *Church-History of Britain*, bk. 8, 27.

5. BATTLING BIBLES AND SPENSER'S DRAGON

1. This chapter deviates from the large body of scholarship drawing connections between the Book of Revelation and *The Faerie Queene* (*FQ*, hereafter) in attempting to understand this relationship within the Elizabethan reader's whole experience of the Bible. See Bennet, *Evolution of The Faerie Queene*, 110–122; Hankins, *Source and Meaning in Spenser's Allegory*; Stillman, *Spenser's Elect England*; Wittreich, *Visionary Poetics*, 59–78, and Wittreich, "Apocalypse," 46–48; for a closely related study of *FQ* Book V and the "Post-Armada Apocalyptic Disourse," see Mallette, *Spenser and the Discourses*, 143–168; Kearney, *Incarnate Text*, 85–139.

2. "Church" occurs many times in the Douay Old Testament; see Stock, *Complete Concordance*; Allmen, *Vocabulary of the Bible,* 50–53. "Congregation" and "church" were hot button words in the Henrician debates of More and Tyndale, but the specific concerns of this debate had faded by 1611—and at any rate, they had little place in translations of the Old Testament. The 1611 translators discuss "church" and "congregation" in the "Translation to the Reader"; as Smith writes, "the scrupulositie of the Puritans [i.e., Tyndale], who leave the olde Ecclesiasticall words, [such as] *Congregation* instead of *Church*," but this refers to the Greek of the New Testament (KJV, 1611, B2 ᵛ).

3. On Spenser's relation to the Geneva Bible, see Shaheen, *Biblical References in* The Faerie Queene; Kearney, "Reformed Ventriloquism," 111–151; Nicholson, "Pastoral In Exile," 41–71, revised in *Uncommon Tongues*, 100–123.

4. On this topic, see Stillman, *Spenser's Elect England*.

5. Shaheen counted some 147 allusions to the Book of Revelation, and 105, or 68 percent, of these are in Book 1; *Biblical References in* The Faerie Queene, 215–217.

6. On Babylon in biblical scholarship, see Mandlebrot, "Bondage in Babylon," 469–497.

7. See Brownlee, *Biblical Readings*, 169–210.

8. From the note in Spenser, *Faerie Queene* (2013), on 152.

9. Groves, "England's Jerusalem in Shakespeare's Henriad," 88. This stems from the visions of John: "And I sawe a new heaven, & a new earth. . . . And I John saw the holie citie newe Jeru-

salem come downe from God out of heaven, prepared as a bride trimmed for her husband. And I heard a great voyce out of heaven, saying, Beholde, the Tabernacle of God is with men, and he wil dwel with them" (Revelation, 21:1–3). Groves cites Sharpe, *Reading Authority*, 59–69; Ball, *Great Expectation*; Richey, *Politics of Revelation*.

10. See *FQ* I.x.55–64, where Contemplation provides a vision of the "new Hierusalem."

11. Nohrnberg, *Analogy of* The Faerie Queene, 151.

12. For a discussion of this chronology, see the discussion of I.x.65 in Edumund Spenser, *The Faerie Queene* (2013), 136.

13. Two examples are Cummings' *Literary Culture of the Reformation*, and Shuger, *Renaissance Bible*.

14. Of course, Spenser's composition process arguably goes back still further; see Hadfield, *Spenser: A Life*, 74, 94, 98. An early composition date was hypothesized by Bennett, *Evolution of* The Faerie Queene, largely on the uncertain properties of Spenser's stylistic evolution.

15. Erasmus, *Annotations* (1516), 782: "Equidem video veteres theologos magis ornandae rei ravia hinc aducere testimonia quam ut rem seriam euincant." Backus, *Reformation Readings of the Apocalypse*, xii, and, on Erasmus, 3–6. The authenticity was also questioned by Dionysius of Alexandria and Eusebius of Caesarea, among others, but Erasmus was the first to restate this claim of inauthenticity in the Renaissance. This claim occurs in his note on Apoc. 22:12, expanded in 1522.

16. Milton, *Catholic and Reformed*, 108. Backus, *Reformation Readings of the Apocalypse*, 7–8; Firth, *Apocalyptic Tradition*, 8–9. Milton shows that "That this tendency persisted into the late Elizabethan period is attested by Arthur Dent. In the introduction to his *The Ruine of Rome*, Dent admitted that there were still in England some divines "both learned and godly . . . rare and reverend men for learning, & great variety of gifts" who preferred out of "modesty and humility" not to "meddle with this booke of the Revelations" (108).

17. *The obedie[n]ce of a Christen man and how Christe[n] rulers ought to governe*, Fol. 131. As Tyndale explains, "the literal sense" must "prove the allegory and bear it." Tyndale, *Obedience*, 159.

18. "To write a preface which would be at all coherent," Backus writes of Luther's 1530 preface, "Luther had to have recourse to allegory—the very thing he had reproached the book for." Backus, *Reformation Readings of the Apocalypse*, 9. The Reformer's conception of the Apocalypse was not in fact new; it had been used by the Donatist Tyconius in the fourth century. Backus, *Reformation Readings of the Apocalypse*, xiii.

19. This is in Wycliffe's *De Papa*, in *English Works*, 458–482; see Firth, *Apocalyptic Tradition*, 7.

20. Van der Noot, *Theatre for Worldlings*, fol. 49ʳ⁻ᵛ.

21. John Foxe, *Acts and Monumentes* (London, 1589), pp. 65–66.

22. Backus, *Reformation Readings of the Apocalypse*, xix, and the conclusion, 135–148, esp: "there was a great deal of unease in the Protestant commentaries on the Apocalypse between 1539 and 1584. . . . Although Erasmus' objections to the place of the Apocalypse in the canon could not be answered, it is plain that it was not just respect for the canon that made several commentators try their hand at interpreting what they saw as an extremely awkward book," 135.

23. Downame, *A Treatise Concerning Antichrist* (1603), sig. A2ᵛ; Fulke, *A Sermon Preached at Hampton Court* (1571), sig. Biiʳ; discussed in A. Milton, *Catholic and Reformed*, 98–100.

24. Richard Bernard, *A Key of Knowledge* (1617), B8ᵛ–C1ʳ; A. Milton, *Catholic and Reformed*, 102.

25. Gabriel Harvey wrote to Spenser: "I hearde once a Divine, preferre Saint Johns Revelation before al the veriest Maetaphysicall Visions, and jollyest conceited Dreames or Extasies, that ever were devised by one or other, howe admirable, or superexcellent they seemed otherwise to the worlde. And truly I am so confirmed in this opinion, that when I bethinke me of the verie nota-

blest, and moste wonderful Propheticall, or Poeticall Vision, that ever I read, or hearde, me see-meth the proportion is so unequall, that there hardly appeareth anye semblaunce of Comparison." Spenser, *Complete Works*, vol. 9, 276–277.

26. See Herbert, *Historical Catalogue*, 107–108, 121; Groves, "England's Jerusalem," 89.

27. Bruce Gordon, "Bible in Transition," 30; O'Banion, "Pastoral Use," 693–710.

28. *The New Testament of Jesus Christ* (1582), 715.

29. Except for an occasional historicist note explaining the conditions of the Roman Empire at the time of the New Testament, as in Mark 3:21.

30. Backus, *Reformation Readings of the Apocalypse*, xii.

31. Bale, *Image of Both Churches,* in Christmas, ed., *Select Works of John Bale*, 253. At this mo-ment, after Cromwell died and Henry VIII reversed many reforms, Bale went into exile. King, 'Bale, John (1495–1563),' *Oxford Dictionary of National Biography, Oxford University Press* (2004).

32. Broughton, *Petition to the King* (1611); Broughton, *Epistle to the Learned Nobility* (1597), 3; quoted in Jones, *Discovery of Hebrew in Tudor England*, 165.

33. Broughton, *Concent of Scripture* [London: For Gabriel Simson and William White?, 1590?], Folger STC 3851 copy 1, sig. A3^v. Christ "dyed the day that Satan murdered Adam in the begynning," G4^v.

34. The full title was *The Theatre Wherein be Represented as Well the Miseries & Calamities that Follow the Voluptuous Worldlings*; after this—illustrating the instability of belief despite the rhetoric—Van der Noot converted to Catholicism. The translations of both du Bellay and van der Noot are done in the same unrhymed style, which Spenser substantially revises, adding rhyme and du Bellay's missing poems, in the *Complaints*. See also Spenser, *Yale Edition of the Shorter Poems*, 461–463; and Stillman, "Spenser's Elect England," 1–4.

35. Van der Noot, *Le theatre anquel sont exposés* ([1568]), Di^r., See Hadfield, *Edmund Spenser*, 38–42; Foster, "Translator" 27–34; du Bellay, *Antiquitez de Rome*, translated by Spenser as *Ruines of Rome*, edited by Smith, 10–14; Melehy, "Spenser and Du Bellay," 415–438.

36. The Dutch version of Van der Noot's sonnets has words missing in the French version and subsequently in the English, which follows the French. Here is an English translation of the Dutch, rendered with the help of Jan van Dijkhuizen: "On a red-hued animal having seven heads, / And also ten horns full of blasphemous names, / I saw sitting a woman, lewd without being ashamed, / Decorated with pearl, purple, gold, to embellish her: / She held in her hand a chalice of gold / Full of horrors and the uncleanness of her whoredom / And on her forehead was the se-cret and dismal name / Of great Babylon. I saw this woman drunk / With the sacred blood of Jesus' good witnesses [martyrs] / An angel very strong I heard with loud voice / Call, fallen is Babylon (thus he said) / And from the heavens I heard another voice bow down / Saying, go out from her lest you will partake of / Her plagues and become my people, my good delight."

37. Satterthwaite, *Spenser, Ronsard, and Du Bellay*, 263.

38. As Richard Schell (among others) has suggested, Richard Mulcaster, headmaster of the Merchant Taylors' School, had "close connections with the Dutch community in London, [and] may have nominated him [Spenser] for the task"; Spenser, *Yale Edition of the Shorter Poems*, 461.

39. Van der Noot, *Theatre for Worldlings* (1569), sig. D.iii^v

40. *Den Bibel* (Antwerpen, 1556), Qiiii^r.

41. Nicholson, *Uncommon Tongues*, 108.

42. See Galbraith, "English' Black-Letter Type," 13–40.

43. *Breefe Catechisme so Necessarie and Easie* (London: Hugh Singleton, 1576).

44. Kearney, "Reformed Ventriloquism, 111–151; at 118, 134. See Norbrook, *Poetry and Politics*, 53–81; and King, *Spenser's Poetry*, 14–46.

45. Kearney, "Reformed Ventriloquism," 128.

46. Collinson, *Elizabethan Puritan Movement*, 165; Kearney, "Reformed Ventriloquism,"131. Another repackaging of the work of the Genevan exiles was Laurence Tomson's revised New Testament, based on the notes of Theodore Beza, in 1576. On Tomson, see Backus, "Laurence Tomson and Elizabethan Puritanism," 17–27; Kearney, "Reformed Ventriloquism," 149.

47. See Kearney's discussion, and Collinson, *Elizabethan Puritan Movement*, 159; Collinson, *Archbishop Grindal*, 219–232.

48. Lehmberg, "Archbishop Grindal," 142. Discussed in Kearney, "Reformed Ventriloquism," 140, 150–51. See also Hadfield, *Edmund Spenser*, 34; and Hughes, "Preaching, Homilies, and Prophesyings," 7–32.

49. Betteridge, "Bitter Notes," 59.

50. Kearney, "Reformed Ventriloquism,"132.

51. Collinson, *Elizabethan Puritan Movement*, 165.

52. Foster, "Gregory Martin's 'Holy *Latinate* Jerusalem (1582)," 130–149. See Fulton and Specland, "Elizabethan Catholic New Testament," 251–275.

53. *The New Testament of Jesus Christ, Translated Faithfully into English from the Authentical Latin* (1582), 700.

54. From the title page of Fulke's *Text of the Nevv Testament of Iesus Christ* (1589). For a concise summary of the exchange between Martin and Fulke, see Norton, *A History of the Bible as Literature* (2000), 49–52. See Fulton and Specland, "Elizabethan Catholic New Testament," 255–265. Bauckham, 'Fulke, William (1536/7—1589)', *Oxford Dictionary of National Biography*, Oxford University Press (2004).

55. On Spenser's seven years at Cambridge, see Hadfield, *Edmund Spenser*, 51–82. On William Fulke, see Richard Baukham's entry in the *Dictionary of National Biography*. See also Bauckham, *Tudor Apocalyps*e, esp. 321–340.

56. Hamilton, *Spenser Encyclopedia*, 535. Hadfield, *Edmund Spenser*, 67–68, 98.

57. *Defense of the Sincere and True Translations* (London, 1583), sig. ¶ᵛ.

58. Discussed at greater length in Fulton and Specland, "Elizabethan Catholic New Testament."

59. Catholics took advantage of this printing of their Bible, as is shown in the annotations of some readers; see Fulton and Specland, "Elizabethan Catholic New Testament," 264.

60. Fulke, *Text of the New Testament* (London, 1589), sig. A3ʳ. Folger STC 2888.

61. See Kearney, *Incarnate Text*, 119–123.

62. Quilligan, *Language of Allegory*, 36–37; Kearney, *Incarnate Text*, 121.

63. Summit, *Memory's Library*, 101–135.

64. Summit, *Memory's Library*, 105.

65. De Hamel, *Meetings with Remarkable Manuscripts*, 19.

66. [Bateman,] *Trauayled Pylgrime* (1569).

67. Prescott, "Spenser's Chivalric Restoration," at 169.

68. Summit, *Memory's Library*, 102.

69. Although it does not actually have gold leaf as other medieval manuscripts and Gospels did, it is likely to have had a gold binding in Spenser's time. De Hamel, *Meetings with Remarkable Manuscripts*, 42.

70. See Gless, "armor of God," Hamilton, ed., *Spenser Encyclopedia*.

71. Fulke, *Text of the New Testament* (1617), 879.

72. See the notes in Spenser, *Faerie Queene, Book 1*, Kaske, ed., 84.

73. Backus, *Reformation Readings*, xiv.

74. *The New Testament of Jesus Christ*, 720; 12:13.

75. Fulke, *Text of the New Testament* (1617), 877.

76. The Folger owns marked copies of Spenser, such as STC 23082 copy 3 (which has sententious phrases marked with inverted commas for commonplacing); STC 23082 copy 5 and STC 23082 copy 6. See Prescott, "Two copies of the 1596 *Faerie Queene*," 261–273; Dixon is discussed in Saunders, "New Light," 356–357; and van Es, "Life of John Dixon," 259–261; other studies include Fowler, "Oxford and London Marginalia," 416–419; Fowler and Leslie, "Drummond's Copy"; and Manning, "Notes and Marginalia," 225–227. For a fascinating early Catholic reader of Book 1 of *The Faerie Queene*, Anthony Copley, see Monta, *Fig for Fortune*; Christian, *Spenserian Allegory*, 2.

77. Orgel, "Margins of Truth," 91–107.

78. Quoted from Kearney, *Incarnate Text*, 85.

79. Quoted from Kearney, *Incarnate Text*, 86.

80. Erasmus, *Booke Called in Latyn Enchiridion* (1533), sig. Aiiii[r]. Erasmus showed concern for idolatry with the cross: "Though honerest the tree of the crosse, moche more folowe the mistery of the crosse," sig. Lii[r]. Wells, "Spenser's Christian Knight," 350–366.

81. Erasmus, *Booke Called in Latyn Enchiridion*, sig. Miii[v]–Miiii[r].

82. Kearney, *Incarnate Text*, 86.

83. Van Es, "Life of John Dixon," 259–260.

84. Hough, *First Commentary*, 1. Van Es points out that "the volume is no longer owned by Lord Bessborough," but is kept at Stansted Park, Rowlands Castle, Hampshire; 261.

85. The tally is "Church," 10; "Christ," 17; and "Antichrist," 6. Hough, *First Commentary*, 2–11.

86. See Kearney, *Incarnate Text*, 85; 113–115.

87. *The Bible* (London, 1578), Bodleian Library pressmark Bodleian Bib. Eng. 1577 d.I.

88. Saunders, "New Light," 356. Saunders cites Matthew 22:12 at *FQ* I.xii.36.

89. Hough, *First Commentary*, 5, in Saunders, "New Light," 356.

90. A. Milton, *Catholic and Reformed*, 111.

91. Dekker, *Whore of Babylon* (1607), sig. A1[r].

92. Shakespeare refers to Revelation, but not with obvious reference to its propagandistic use. Shaheen records 133 instances, though there is a good bit of redundancy in this tally, which also includes echoes and uncertain references; see Shaheen, *Biblical References in Shakespeare's Plays*, 824–826. There is also a strong possibility that Shakespeare drew on Bale's *Image of Both Churches*; see Junker, "Image of Both Theaters," 167–187. See Hamlin, *The Bible in Shakespeare*, 214–230; Streete, "Politics of Ethical Presentism," 405–431.

93. This is the note in the *Riverside Shakespeare*, second edition; as Shaheen also writes, "the majority of Shakespeare's audience would have associated the 'whore of Babylon' with the Roman Catholic Church"; *Biblical References in Shakespeare's Plays*, 458—true, yet the scene seems to ridicule this association.

6. *MEASURE FOR MEASURE* AND THE NEW KING

1. Barlow, *Svmme and Substance* (1604), 45.

2. Norton, *A Textual History*, 6.

3. Curtis, "Hampton Court Conference," 2. On the conference and its significance, see Tyacke, *Anti-Calvinists*, esp. 9–28; Tyacke, "Puritan Politicians," 21–44; Collinson, "Jacobean Religious Settlement," 27–51. For a discussion of the relationship between Shakespeare's play and the conference, see Hamilton, *Shakespeare and Politics*, 111–127.

4. Barlow, *Svmme and Substance* (1604), 46–47.

5. Barlow, *Svmme and Substance* (1604), 47. Of the latter example, there is corroboration in a manuscript account of the conference, which records that "his Majesty" went on to say that "some in Scotland upon that ground woold have had him in such sort have proceeded against his grandmother," showing again the degree to which political argument hangs on the "ground" provided even by a biblical gloss. From British Library Harleian MSS. 828, excerpted in Usher, *Reconstruction of the English Church*, vol. 2, 345; also Fuller, *The Church-History of Britain* (1655), book 10, 7–21.

6. The annotators' assessment derives from a relatively commonplace argument for passive disobedience based on Acts 5:29, which counsels that divine rather than human authority must be obeyed. In Geneva Bibles of 1560, 1578, 1582, 1602.

7. Collinson, "Monarchical Republic," 394–424; at 410–411; see Bowler, "An Axe or An Acte," 349–359.

8. From the Bishops' Bible, *The holi bible* (1569) STC 2105, fol 200; the note is not (pace Bowler) in the sparser pulpit edition of 1568. See Bowler, "An Axe or An Acte," 357.

9. Henry VIII, *Copy of the* Letters (1527), sig. A5ᵛ.

10. L. Lupton, *History of the Geneva Bible*, vol 5, 133; Greaves, "Traditionalism," 94.

11. Notes on disobedience and tyrants in Exodus 1 are in the original 1568 Bishops' folio (STC 2099), designed for the pulpit, as well as in quarto and octavo editions. Just below this is more language about tyranny: "God for his names sake wyl deliver his Churche from the affliction of tirants." STC 2114 (1575) also has a longer note on Exodus 1:21 that differs little from the notes in the 1568 and 1572 folios or the Geneva Bible.

12. 1575 Quarto (STC 2114); 1602 Folio (STC 2188).

13. Daniel Swift makes a strong case that Shakespeare was at the conference, but the evidence for this does not seem certain; see *Shakespeare's Common Prayer*, 1–15; see also Kernan, *Shakespeare, the King's Playwright*, 203–204.

14. See the facsimile of the Revels Account, in Schoenbaum, *Shakespeare: A Documentary Life*, 200–201; see also Bennett, Measure for Measure *as Royal Entertainment*, and Lever, "Date of *Measure for Measure*," 381–388.

15. Doelman, *King James*. Doelman shows how readers responded to *Basilikon Doron* and "attempted to use it to advise and direct James by quoting the book back to him" in Doelman, "King of Thine Own Heart," 1.

16. The engraving is cited in English by Harington in a manuscript of his epigrams, Folger MS V.a.249; Doelman, *King James*, 33. The biblical allusion is to Luke 23:42.

17. Harington, *Epigrapms of Sir John Harington*, 309. Written April 14, 1603. Scott-Warren, *Sir James Harington*, 204–206; Doelman, *King James*, 33–34.

18. On Drayton's poem and Jacobean political theology, see Hammill, *Mosaic Constitution*, 138–155. The king's political works were entered in the Stationers' Register on March 28 and April 3, 1603, respectively, when the King arrived in May; see Arber, ed., *Transcript of the Registers*, vol. 3, 93–94.

19. On the early modern drama and the liturgical calendar, see Lin, "Festivity," 212–229; Lin, "Witch in the Morris," 335–361; also, Chapman, "Whose Saint Crispin's Day Is It?" 1467–1494, and Chapman, "Marking Time."; for a discussion of the way in which Shakespeare's play "marries James's accession to the older liturgical conventions," see J. Lupton, *Citizen-Saints*, 152.

20. See Fulton, "Political Theology," 204–221.

21. Barnaby and Wry, "Authorized Versions," 1225–1254. For a broader discussion of *Measure for Measure* and Jacobean politics, see Goldberg, *James I*, 230–239.

22. See Fleck, "To Write of Him," 545–560.

23. Shakespeare also occasionally echoes the wording in the Bishops' Bible, which probably stems from hearing it read at church. See Fulton and Poole, "Popular Hermeneutics in Shakespeare's London," 3; Shaheen, *Biblical References in Shakespeare's Tragedies*, 24. Shaheen suggests that Shakespeare's work often echoes a 1582 edition; it is certainly misleading to use only the 1560 in reading Shakespeare, which has far fewer annotations.

24. Other facts do not fit neatly into this narrative: It was another 13 years after the Hampton Court conference until the printing of the Geneva Bible stopped, for reasons that remain unclear. Hill, *English Bible*, 58; and Betteridge, "The Bitter Notes," 44. In 1632 a man was imprisoned for importing Geneva Bibles. Gardiner, ed., *Reports of Cases*, 274.

25. Avis, "Moses and the Magistrate," 149–172. On parliamentary debates about Mosaic law, see Shuger, *Political Theologies*, 30–31. For further discussion of legalism and sexual crimes, see Lake and Questier, *Antichrist's Lewd Hat*, 627–629. The term "Puritan" was less defined; see Collinson, "A Comment," 483–488. Biblical legalism had a continued presence in Elizabethan England; the decalogue was ordered by Queen Elizabeth to be "fixed upon the wall over the . . . Communion board the Tables of God's precepts imprinted." Aston, *England's Iconoclasts*, 362. Lander, "Maimed Rites," 197.

26. Ellison, "*Measure for Measure* and the Executions of Catholics in 1604," 44–87.

27. Whitgift, *Works*, vol. 3, 576.

28. James I, *Basilikon Doron* (1603), A4^r.

29. Lewalski, "Biblical Allusion," 34.

30. Hunter, "Theology," 237.

31. See Noble, *Shakespeare's Biblical Knowledge*, 221–228; Shaheen, *Biblical References in Shakespeare's Plays*, 245–263. Schoenbaum notes yet another in Barnardine's reference to Ecclesiastes 5:11; see *William Shakespeare, A Compact Documentary Life*, 58.

32. Unless otherwise indicated, New Testament passages in this chapter are quoted from the useful facsimile of the 1602 edition, Sheppard, ed., *Geneva Bible*.

33. Calculated by checking the references in Shaheen, *Biblical References in Shakespeare's Plays*; see Fulton, "Political Theology," 208.

34. See Clark, "Measure for Measure," 659–680.

35. "Mercy" also appears most in *Measure for Measure*, as do "justice," "authority," and "substitute."

36. All references to *Measure for Measure* and other Shakespearean texts are G. Blakemore Evans, et al., *Riverside Shakespeare*. Readings of the original 1623 Folio text, where desirable for word choice or typography, are taken from the facsimile of *Mr. William Shakespeares Comedies, Histories, & Tragedies*, and indicated with "F" and the page number to the original. In this case, "measure" may be in italics because it is a quoted word, and "law" is frequently in upper case, giving some indication of its value.

37. Sommerville, *Thomas Hobbes*, 89.

38. *Rape of Lucrece, Riverside Shakespeare*, ll. 305,693, 888, 997.

39. For examples, see Whitgift, *Works*, vol. 3, 576; Jewel, *Works of John Jewel*, vol. 3, 170; Griffiths, ed., *Two Books of Homilies*, 100, 553; Bucer, *Melanchthon and Bucer*, 186.

40. James, *True Lawe of Free Monarchies* (London, 1603), B3^{r-v}.

41. James, *True Lawe of Free Monarchies* (London, 1603), C4^v–C5^r. James makes the very exception here of Acts 5:29 that would upset him in the Geneva note.

42. For a range of perspectives, see Kelley, "Ideas of Resistance before Elizabeth," 48–76.

43. For relevant uses of Romans 13, see *An Homilie against Disobedience and Wylfull Rebellion* (London, [1570]), B3^v, and Luther's way of reading Romans 13 as affirming Protestantism in *Works of Martin Luther*, vol. 2, 71.

44. *The New Testament of Jesus Christ* (1582), 415–416. For distinctions between Catholic and Protestant readings of Romans 13, see the refutations of Fulke, *The Text of the New Testament* (London, 1601; first edition, 1589), 478.

45. The sword from Romans 13:4 appears in the hands of the monarch on the title pages of official Tudor Bibles (Bishops' Bible, Coverdale Bible), and at the end of *An Homilie agaynst Disobedience and Wylful Rebellion*, 1570, and on Crispin van de Passe I's *Elizabeth I Memorial Portrait*, ca. 1603–1604. This combination of the sword and the Bible "epitomizes," as John King writes, "the effort to reinterpret medieval iconography." King, *Tudor Royal Iconography*, 54.

46. Latimer, *Selected Sermons of Hugh Latimer,* ed. Chester, 58, 101.

47. Tyndale, *Obedience of a Christian Man*, 156. For Luther's literal approach, see Hendrix, "Luther," 229–239. On Tyndale's literalism, see Simpson, *Burning to Read*, 111–118; 169. See also Harrison, *Bible, Protestantism*, 111, see 107–120. For a useful discussion of Calvin's sense of history and his literalism, see Muller, "Hermeneutic of Promise," 68–82.

48. Tyndale, *Work of William Tyndale*, ed. Duffield, 287.

49. Griffiths, ed., *Two Books of Homilies*, 107.

50. Lambert, *Shakespeare Documents*, 47. Heywood, a collaborator in *Sir Thomas More*, lists "Morrall" as a genre with "Tragedy, History, Comedy" in *Apology for Actors* (1612), F4^r, a4^r.

51. Coldewey, ed., *Early English Drama*, title, 45; line 3; subsequent references to *Everyman* are to the line numbers in this edition.

52. See for example, Spivack, *Shakespeare and the Allegory of Evil*; Bevington, *From Mankind to Marlowe*; and Dessen, "Homilies and Anomalies," 243–258. For an excellent general study of the relationship between medieval moralities and Protestant drama, see Watkins, "Moralities, Interludes and Protestant Drama," 767–792. And in respect to *Measure for Measure*, see Cox, *Shakespeare and the Dramaturgy of Power*, 155–162; and Winston, "'Craft Against Vice,'" 229–248.

53. Lake discusses the "synergistic collaboration between magistrate and minister" in *Measure for Measure* in Lake and Questier, *Antichrist's Lewd Hat*, 622–700.

54. Dugdale, *Time Triumphant Declaring in Briefe* (London, 1604), B1^v. The title is entered in the Stationers Register March 27, 1604. Lever, "Date of *Measure for Measure*," 384–386.

55. Tyacke reminds us that "Calvinism was the *de facto* religion of the Church of England under Queen Elizabeth and King James," and thus the standard view of "Calvinists and Puritans as one and the same" needs to be corrected. *Anti-Calvinists*, 7. On the endorsement of predestination in the 1590s, see 3; yet see also Lake, *Anglicans and Puritans*, 162–197.

56. For discussions of substitution in *Measure for Measure*, see for example Leggatt, "Substitution in *Measure for Measure*," 342–359, and Lezra, "Pirating Reading," 258; Goldberg, *James I and the Politics of Literature*, 232; Hamilton, *Shakespeare and the Politics*, 113–114. On the interplay between the adultery of the main characters and the prostitutes, see Knoppers, "(En)gendering Shame," 450–471.

57. Kernan, *Shakespeare, the King's Playwright*, xv, 168.

58. See Ayers in Jonson, *Sejanus, His Fall*, 16. On the date of the court production, see 9–10.

59. See Jonson, *Sejanus: His Fall*, 37; Shakespeare may have acted the role of Tiberius, following his reported preference for "Kingly parts"; Davies, *Scourge of Folly* (n.d.; Stationers' Register, Oct. 1610), Epigram 159, 76–7; quoted by Ayers in Jonson, *Sejanus: His Fall*, 44 n.103.

60. McMillin, *Elizabethan Theatre*, 74–95; Taylor, "Date and Auspices," 118–119. *Sir Thomas More* includes a morality-play-within-the-play (3.2.45–355). Fulton, "Political Theology," 204–221.

61. See Daniel, *Tragedy of Philotas*, 36–66.

62. Tyacke, *Anti-Calvinists*, 9. The lengthy discussion of predestination is recorded in Barlow, *Svmme and Substance* (1604), 24–30, 41–43.

63. Discussed in Lake, *Anglicans and Puritans*, 147–187.

64. Lake, *Anglicans and Puritans*, 196. In relation to Shakespeare, see Hunt, *Shakespeare's Religious Allusiveness*, 97–118.

65. Lever in Shakespeare, *Measure for Measure*, 14.

66. Shakespeare, *Complete Works*, 846 (1.2.114).

67. Cummings, *Literary Culture of the Reformation*, 175; on just God, see 177.

68. For a similar view, see Lake and Questier, *Antichrist's Lewd Hat*, 658. On this passage in connection with Othello and predestination at Hampton Court, see Hunt, *Shakespeare's Religious Allusiveness,* 100–101.

69. On the ethics of divine justice in Protestant theology, see Cummings, *Literary Culture of the Reformation*, 98; and on the problems of earthly justice under a Protestant God, see Simpson, *Burning to Read*, 163–164.

70. See for example, Calvin, *Institutes of the Christian Religion*, ed. McNeill, vol. 1, 336–338 (2.5.17); Calvin argues here against Erasmus in *De Libero Arbitrio*.

71. See Cartwright, *Confutation of the Rhemists Translation* (1658), 359; Fulke, *The Text of the New Testament* (1589), 253r; *The New Testament of Jesus Christ* (1589), 406.

72. Emphasis added. 1602 Geneva Bible.

73. *The New Testament of Jesus Christ* (1582), 412.

74. Doleman [pseudonym], *Conference* (1594/5), 236; see Tyacke, "Puritan Politicians," 32.

75. Lake points out that Hooker, at "a far cry from conventional Elizabethan denunciations," argued not merely that "people could be saved under popery," but that the "popish church was a part of the true church." *Anglicans and Puritans*, 156. For Hooker's ecumenical view in relation to Shakespeare, see Hunt, *Shakespeare's Religious Allusiveness*, 50, 118. On Shakespeare's antisectarianism, see Knapp, *Shakespeare's Tribe*, 50–55.

76. Fulke, *Text of the New Testament* (1589); Cartwright, *Confutation of the Rhemists Translation* (1618); George Wither, *View of the Marginal Notes* [1588].

77. Fulke, *Text of the New Testament* (1589), 256ᵛ.

78. Whitgift was also accused, by Fulke, at the time a staunch puritan, of being ecumenical about this central Calvinist doctrine: "He holdeth, that the doctrine of free will is not repugnant to salvation: and yet is yt a doctyne cleane contrary to free justification by Christe" [Fulke], *Examination of M. Doctor Whytgiftes Censures* (1575), 8.

79. Lake and Questier, *Antichrist's Lewd Hat*, 656–700.

80. Bradbrook, "Authority, Truth, and Justice," 385.

81. Bloom, *Shakespeare*, 363.

82. Tilley, *Dictionary of the Proverbs*, 452; and Wilson, ed., *Oxford Dictionary of English Proverbs*, 520.

83. Beyond clear Shakespearean uses, the phrase "measure for measure" itself appears in only one other English drama, a domestic tragedy heavily indebted to the allegorical tradition, *A*

Warning for Faire Women (1599). Because Shakespeare's company performed the play, there seems a possible connection. See Shaheen, "Echoes," 521–525.

84. *New Oxford Annotated Bible.* Luther, *Biblia das ist die gantze Heilige Schrifft Deudsch* (1534).

85. Eells, *Attitude of Martin Bucer*, 35; 211.

86. James I, *Basilikon Doron* (1603), 57.

87. This same misuse of the Golden Rule to justify vengeful reciprocity is illustrated in Shuger's account of Thomas Lupton's legalist Mosaic utopia, *Too Good to be True* (1581), a possible source for *Measure for Measure*. See Shuger, *Political Theologies*, 49.

88. For discussion of Angelo marked as a "precise" puritan, see Knapp, *Shakespeare's Tribe*, 51; Hamilton, *Shakespeare and the Politics*, 111–112, 116; and for the use of the term, see Lake, *Moderate Puritans*, 10.

89. Cartwright, *Helpes for the Discovery of the Truth* (1648), 7.

90. Calvin, *Institutes*, 4.20. 14, 16. See Avis, "Moses and the Magistrate,"164–165.

91. Whitgift, *Works of John Whitgift*, 3:552, 3:576.

92. Sommerville, *Politics and Ideology*, 15; see chapter 2.

93. Bucer, *Common Places of Martin Bucer*, 303; quoted in Avis, "Moses and the Magistrate," 160.

94. See Simpson *Burning to Read*, 142–183.

95. Hooker, *Laws of Ecclesiastical Polity*, vol. 1, Preface, 7.3. Hooker's desire to work beyond scripture and his doubts about predestination theology are confronted in *A Christian Letter of Certaine English Protestantes* (London, 1599), where the authors take issue with Hooker's use of scripture as "a supplement," 7.

96. More, *Dialogue Concerning Heresies Published in 1530* in *The Complete works of St. Thomas More*, vol. 6, part 1, 290.

97. For discussion of reason and scripture in Hooker, see Lake, *Anglicans and Puritans*, 145–154. For a reading of Hooker's politics, see Kirby, *Richard Hooker's Doctrine*, and Lake, *Anglicans and Puritans*, 197–213. As Lake argues, Hooker disagreed with the merger of "the minister and the magistrate," and suggested instead that the "right to rule came directly from men and only indirectly from God," 203.

98. Lake, *Anglicans and Puritans*, 153.

99. Dodds, *Exploiting Erasmus*, 111.

100. Donne, *Sermons*, vol. 7, 302.

101. Perkins, *Commentary on the Galatians*, 117. For Perkins' application of Mosaic law, even the death penalty for theft, see Avis, "Moses and the Magistrate,"168–169.

102. Wood, for example, writes of the "pronounced Catholic colour" of *Measure for Measure* in *Shakespeare*, 270. For a nuanced look at the Catholicism in the play, see Lake and Questier, *Antichrist's Lewd Hat*, 673–676.

103. Lake and Questier, *The Antichrist's Lewd Hat*, 622.

104. Fotherby, *Foure sermons* (1608), 52.

105. On Donne and Lancelot Andrewes's use of the two Bibles, see McCullough, "Andrewes and *Donne*," 67–88; Filmer is discussed and cited in Chapter 5, above.

106. For Milton's treatment of the KJV as the received text, see for example *Doctrine and Discipline of Divorce, Complete Prose Works*, vol. 2, 153–154.

107. The first edition is *The Holy Bible . . . With most profitable Annotations . . . which notes have never before been set forth with this new translation* (Amsterdam, 1642); see Herbert, *Historical Catalogue*, 189, 198.

108. Rosenblatt, "Milton, Anxiety, and the King James Bible," 184.

109. John Keats, Letter in Perkins, ed., *English Romantic Writers*, 1209.

7. MILTON'S BIBLE AND REVOLUTIONARY PSALM CULTURE

1. Norton, "English Bibles from *c.* 1520 to *c.* 1750," 332.

2. Barlow, *Svmme and Substance*, 46–47.

3. *Holy Bible* (London, 1612), sig. A7ʳ. The translators' neutrality here may shed light on Matthew Parker's laconic words in designing the Bishops' Bible in the 1560s, also in contrast to the Geneva Bible, that it should not "set downe any determinacion in places of controversie." This directive may be more neutral than has been surmised, drawing from the now obsolete sense of "controversy" as "difference of opinion, disagreement." *OED*, noun, 3. Parker, *Correspondence*, 336.

4. Miller, "Earliest Known Draft," esp. 215, 237, 242–243; on the relationships between the Geneva and King James Bibles more generally, see also Miller, "Better, as in the Geneva," 517–543.

5. *Holy Bible* (London, 1612), sig. A7ʳ.

6. Providing variant readings was a potentially controversial thing in itself, as the translators' mild defensiveness suggests. An important edition of the Vulgate produced in 1590 included a Papal Bull that explained its complete lack of marginalia, for even alternate readings encouraged the possibility of dissent and disagreement. Kaulen, *Geschicte Der Vulgata*, 450.

7. Brisman, *Milton's Poetry of Choice*, 1; see Woods, "Elective Poetics and Milton's Prose," 193–211; Herman points out that "or" is the eighth most common word in *Paradise Lost* in *Destabilizing Milton*, 43. On Milton's "calculated indeterminacies," see Martin, *Ruins of Allegory*, 22. See also Brljak, "Satanic 'or'."

8. See Kerrigan, Rumrich, and Fallon, eds., *Complete Poetry*, 294. Elijah is taken to Horeb; see note in NRSV, 455. The difference may result from two oral traditions that developed after the separation of the kingdoms, with "Horeb" according to the northern tradition of Israel, and "Sinai" in Judah.

9. *Bible and Holy Scriptures* (1560), and common in later editions.

10. Schwartz, "Citation, Authority," 227–240; Schwartz, *Remembering and Repeating*; MacCallum, "Milton and Figurative Interpretation," 62–81; Haskin, *Milton's Burden of Interpretation*, passim.

11. Radzinowicz, *Toward* Samson Agonistes, 188–226; Radzinowicz, *Milton's Epics and the Book of Psalms*.

12. Hamlin, *Psalm Culture*, 75.

13. Hamlin, *Psalm Culture*, 72.

14. Lawes, *Choice Psalmes Put into Musick* (1648), A3ʳ. Discussed in Spink, *Henry Lawes*, 17–18.

15. Bodleian Douce Bib. NT. Eng. 1625. Brassington, *Historic Bindings in the Bodleian Library*, 30. This embroidered binding is featured on the dust jacket of this book.

16. Guibbory, *Christian Identity*, 124–140, and for Charles I as David, see 20, 284, 291–294.

17. Radzinowicz, *Milton's Epics and the Book of Psalms*, 3.

18. See for example, Moore and Sherwood, "Biblical Studies 'after' Theory," 17. A useful summary of the rise and possible fall of the "historical-critical" method is Barton, ed., *Cambridge Companion to Biblical Interpretation*, 9–34; Biblical historicism holds as self-evident many of the truisms in literary historicism, with the concern being to "place texts in their historical context,

and to argue that we misunderstand them if we take them to mean something they could not have meant for their first readers," 10.

19. Killeen, *Political Bible*, 4.

20. Calvin, *Psalmes of David and Others* (1571), fol. 1.

21. These are Psalms 3–9, 11–32, 34–41, 51–65, 68–70, 86, 101, 103, 108–110; the 13 that give more detail about the life of David are 3, 7, 18, 34, 51, 52, 54, 56, 57, 59, 60, 63, 142; see also 30. Ridderbos and Craigie, "Psalms," 1032.

22. Knox, *Appelation*, fol. 79ʳ; the Geneva translation has "against the wicked." Psalm 94:16.

23. Calvin, *Psalmes of David and Others* (1571), fols. 68ᵛ–69ʳ.

24. Calvin, *Psalmes of David and Others* (1571), second part, fol. 69ᵛ.

25. For example at *Complete Prose Works*, vol. 3, 205, 208, and 211, the example used by Radzinowicz to illustrate Milton's adherence to a Davidic authorship: "And this is verify'd by David, himself a King, and likeliest to bee Author of the *Psalm* 94:20. which saith *Shall the throne of iniquity have fellowship with thee?*" But Milton suggests royal authorship here in order to subvert the royalist position; this moment more significantly reveals that Davidic authorship of the psalms is not a given for Milton, and that he is interested in identifying the non-Davidic context for other psalms.

26. *Eikonoklastes* (1649), 191. Milton quotes Charles in *Eikon Basilike*, 157. Charles seems to be discussing the general goal of the Westminster Assembly of Divines to reform the Catechism & Confessions of Faith, and the Psalms, though this is not mentioned; it is therefore unclear what psalm in particular Milton is accusing Charles of rewriting, though he cites the psalms throughout *Eikonoklastes*. This passage is discussed by Schwartz, "Political Inaccuracy," 81–82.

27. *Tenure of Kings and Magistrates* (1649), *CPW* vol. 3, 205.

28. Calvin, *Psalmes of David and Others* (1571), second part, fol. 73r.

29. *CPW* vol. 3, 248.

30. Calvin, *Psalmes of David and Others* 1571, second part, fol. 39ᵛ.

31. Hill, *Intellectual Origins*, 4. This presumption has supported a biblically annotated *Paradise Lost* using the 1560 notes; Milton, *Paradise Lost*, Stallard, ed. For analysis of Milton's use of the KJV, see Rosenblatt, "Milton, Anxiety," 181–201.

32. On Elizabeth's Bible, signed "Elizabeth Milton, 1664," but also containing her maiden name (so not inherited from Milton), see Fletcher, *Use of the Bible*, 21. Fletcher followed Charles Sumner in using the 1630 Geneva printing of the popular Junius-Tremellius-Beza edition containing Latin of Beza in the New Testament and the Latin translation of the Syriac of Tremellius in parallel columns, because of a shared mistaken use of the word *patientia* rather than *patentia* in Hebrews 4:13; see Fletcher, *Use of the Bible*, 51. Hale and Cullington consult a Geneva edition of Beza's New Testament of 1598, which had the Greek, the Vulgate, and Beza's Latin: *Iesu Christi Domini Nostri Nouum Testamentum, siue Nouum foedus* ([Geneva], 1598); see *Complete Works of John Milton*, Hale and Cullington, eds., vol. 8, xlvii–li; Brljak, "The Satanic 'or'," 413. See also Cullington, "Latin Words for 'Marriage'," 35 n. 16. Milton used a text that had the Latin of Beza in one column and the Tremellius's Latin translation of the Syriac in the other; he refers to the Syriac frequently.

33. Milton, *The Doctrine and Discipline of Divorce* (Second ed., 1644), 47.

34. Milton, *Poems* (1673), 143.

35. Poole, "*Vita di Dante*," 139–170. William Poole discovered the eighth book, Boccaccio's *Vita di Dante*, in the Bodleian in 2014, and in 2019, Jason Scott-Warren tentatively attributed the heavy markings in a copy of Shakespeare's First Folio in the Free Library of Philadelphia to Milton; for discussion of this Folio see Bourne, "*Vide Supplementum*," 195–233.

36. Milton refers to Erasmus, for example, in his discussion of the Johannine comma, in the Oxford *De Doctrina*, vol. 1, 149; see also comments like "in Hilary and Cyprian 'God' is not read here, just as it is not read in numerous other [church] fathers either, if Erasmus has any credibility"; 175.

37. See Hale's introduction to the *De Doctrina Christiana* in *The Complete Works of John Milton*, vol. 8, lx; also Milton's mention of the "recent version" of the Syriac, which seems to be the Latin translation in Brian Walton's *Biblia Sacra Polyglotta* (1655–1657); see also Fletcher, *Use of the Bible*, 87–88. Edward Phillips also reports Milton's training in multiple languages; see Darbishire, *Early Lives of Milton*, 31; Rosenblatt, "Milton, Anxiety," 184.

38. David Norton comments that translations "were convenient rather than authoritative: real authority lay with the originals, and many of his variations are corrections to conform with their readings." Norton, *History of the Bible as Literature* (1993), vol. 1, 298–299. Fletcher, *Use of the Bible*, 30.

39. Michael's words are drawn mostly from 2 Peter 1:5–7. Milton discusses love and charity, mostly around the key passage 1 Corinthians 13 in *De Doctrina Christiana* in the Oxford edition, vol. 2, 600–601. For discussion of this history, see Jenkins and Preston, *Biblical Scholarship and the Church*, 99–102, and Ferguson, "Faith in the Language," 97. The Geneva Bible, in contrast, upholds Tyndale's reading.

40. Rosenblatt, "Milton, Anxiety," 184. Selden, *Table Talk of John Selden*, 9. On Milton's Hebraic knowledge, see Einboden, "Towards a Judaic Milton," 135–150.

41. Fletcher, *Use of the Bible in Milton's Prose*, 94.

42. British Library MS Additional 32310, a quarto edition printed in 1612 (STC 2220). See Brown, "King James Bible," 271–287; Ng, "Milton's Maps," 428–442.

43. Parker, *Milton*, vol. 1, 10.

44. French, "Milton's Family Bible," 363–366; Patterson et al., *Works of John Milton*, vol. 18, 559–562; Campbell and Corns, *John Milton*, 388, n16.

45. On these engravings, see Norton, *King James Bible*, 117–120.

46. On Milton's collation, see W. Poole's remarkable recovery of Milton's reading of Boccaccio's *Vita di Dante*, 146.

47. Milton, *Works of John Milton*, vol. 18, Patterson et al., eds. 560–561. Brown, "King James Bible," 273–277.

48. W. Poole, "*Vita di Dante*," 148.

49. Fulton, *Historical Milton*, 44–47, 192, 215–217, 222.

50. *Joannis Miltonii Angli De doctrina christiana* (1825), 75; *Jesu Christi Domini nostri Novum Testamentum, sive Novum Foedus, cujus graeco contextui respondent interpretationes duae: una, Vetus: altera, Theodori Bezae. Ejusdem Th. Bezae annotationes* (Geneva, 1598), 95. Milton was probably looking at the edition of Beza's New Testament with Tremellius's facing Latin translation of the Syriac, and he would see the same wording.

51. As Fletcher writes in *Use of the Bible*, an "easily recognizable group of deviations from the text of the Authorized Version is formed by those quotations which display the influence of marginal readings," which "show a tendency to use them," 25. This is more recently discussed by Cullington in "Interpreting Milton's Deviations," 58–68.

52. Milton, *Treatise of Civil Power* (1659), 2.

53. Fulton, *Historical Milton*, 192, 222.

54. On the dating of *A Treatise of Civil Power*, I benefit from conversation with Jeffrey Miller, and from reading part of his forthcoming book, *Signifying Shadows*. Milton is addressing

a parliament that had just been convened in January, and the tract is entered in the Stationers' Register on 16 February; see Campbell and Corns, *John Milton*, 281.

55. Milton, *Treatise of Civil Power* (1659), 18; these are all passages that occur in similar arguments in the *De Doctrina Christiana*; see Oxford vol. 8, part 1, p. 323.

56. For a fascinating reading of their importance in the 1673 print context, see von Maltzahn, "Making use of the Jews," 57–82.

57. Masson, *Life of Milton*, vol. 1, 243; see Hunter, "Sources of Milton's Prosody," 125–144; Hunter, "Milton Translates the Psalms," 485–494. Radzinowicz, *Toward* Samson Agonistes, 198.

58. Hunter, "Milton Translates the Psalms," 492.

59. Dobranski, *Milton, Authorship, and the Book Trade*, 58; see discussion on 52, and for Milton's active role in the 1673 poems, see 154–178. The 1648 Psalms appear at the very end of the edition of English poems, just before the Latin poems which have a separate title page. Fletcher, ed., *Facsimile*, vol. 1, 445.

60. British Library MS. Lat. Misc. d. 77. See Achinstein, *Citizen Milton*, 6.

61. "John Milton" is listed among the composers in Sternhold and Hopkins, *The Whole booke of psalmes . . . Newly corrected and enlarged by Tho: Ravenscroft* (London, 1621), sig. A3ʳ. As Radzinowicz noted, Milton's father "set two anonymous psalm tunes" for Ravenscroft's collection "to serve as music for Psalms 5, 27, 55, 66, 102, and 138;" *Toward* Samson Agonistes, 192.

62. Gentles, *New Model Army*, 397.

63. Gardiner, *History of the Great Civil War*, vol. 3, 364–67.

64. Boddy sought to draw evidence from detractors of Milton who might have heard of his involvement. Pierre du Moulin, for example, claimed that "when the death of the King was in agitation amongst the conspirators, and most were shrinking from so huge a crime, the fiendish gallows-bird wrote for them, and shoved the waverers to the evil side." This is either an inaccuracy on the part of Pierre du Moulin, who inverted the sequence of *The Tenure of Kings* and the execution of Charles, or, as Boddy surmises, a reference to Milton's Psalms. Boddy, "Milton's Translation of Psalms 80–88." 1–9. On the background, see Brailsford, *Levellers and the English Revolution*, Hill, ed. One possible connection to the Army for Milton is the regicidal judge, John Bradshaw, who had been engaged as his lawyer in the case against Sir Robert Pye in 1647. Bradshaw, praised by Milton later in *Defensio Secunda*, continued to work with Milton after the regicide. See French, *Milton in the Chancery*, 113; Campbell and Corns, *Milton: Life, Work, and Thought*, 190–191.

65. *Mercurius Pragmaticus . . . from Tuesday April 25. to Tuesday, May 2.* (1648), E2ʳ.

66. Allen, *A Faithful Memorial of that Remarkable Meeting of Many Officers of the Army in England, at Windsor Castle, in the Year 1648*, 4–5.

67. See Crawford, "Charles Stuart, That Man of Blood," 41–61; Dzelzainis, "Antimonarchism in English Republicanism," 27–41, at 33; Thomas Corns, *Royal Image*, 87–88, 105. For discussion of this rhetoric, see Kelsey, "Death of Charles I," 727–30.

68. The date on the title page of Milton's *Poems* is 1645; it appears on January 2, 1646. See Campbell, *Milton Chronology*, 86.

69. Fulton, *Historical Milton*, 115–42; "Edward Phillips and the Manuscript of the 'Digression,'" 95–112.

70. Rous, *Booke of Psalmes* (1638), sig. A3v. On this controversy, see Norton, *History of the Bible as Literature* (1993), vol. 1, 286–87; Hill, *English Bible*, 359. Another competitor was William Barton, whose Book of Psalms in Metre was printed "by order of the parliament" in 1645, with "the approbation of more than fourty eminent Divines of the City, & most of them of the Assembly." Title page.

71. *Excellent Encouragements against Afflictions* (1647), sig. A1r (facing title page).

72. *Excellent Encouragements against Afflictions* (1647), sig. bb.

73. *Excellent Encouragements against Afflictions* (1647), sig. aa3r.

74. Sonnet 13 to Henry Lawes in "Feb.9.1645 [i.e. 1646]," which exists in three versions in the Trinity collection. The version of the poem in this volume bears the same title, "To my Friend Mr. Henry Lawes," as the first draft of the poem in the Trinity Manuscript, suggesting that the copy sent to Lawes derived from Milton's original. However, Milton's very first draft—and the one entitled "To my Friend . . ."—did not have the lines about the airs, suggesting that the occasion "on the publishing of his Aires" was added. When the airs appeared in 1653, Milton's nephews wrote commendatory verses, but Milton's own was not used. See Fletcher, *Facsimile*, vol. 1, 368, 445–447.

75. Lawes reads the biblical occasion of the original psalms as monarchical: "Your majestie knowes when the Regall Prophet first penn'd these Psalmes, he gave them to the Musitians to be set to tunes; and they humbly brought them to David the King. Besides, Mr. Sandys incribest his Translation to Your Sacred Majestie; so that this I offer is Your Majesties in all capacities, and doth not so properly come, as rebound back to Your Majestie. . . . The King of Heaven and Earth restore Your Majestie according to Your own righteous heart . . ." *Choice Psalmes put into Music* (1648), A3ᵛ. The sonnet is discussed in Fulton, *Historical Milton*, 24, 33; Fletcher, ed., *Facsimile*, vol. 1, 368; see Carey, ed. *Complete Shorter Poems*, 294.

76. Boddy, "Milton's Translation of Psalms 80–88," 1. Lawes's volume does not appear in the *Stationers' Register*, nor, it seems, does Sandys; there is on Feb. 17, 1648 a volume entitled *The Psalms of David Paraphrased*, by Robert Barker, who is a printer as well as a translator of the King James Bible, but he does not seem to have issued this in print.

77. *A Paraphrase upon the Divine Poems by George Sandys* (1648), "To the Prince," sig. A3ʳ.

78. Hill, *English Bible*, 381–382.

79. This is in Psalm 80, lines 37 and 40. In Line 60, Milton also retains the exact line of Rous's translation, suggesting that Milton's translations are participating in the debate.

80. Thomas Sternhold and John Hopkins, *The Whole Book of Psalmes* (1621), 42ᵛ.

81. "If any king because a king be unpunishable by . . . *Asaph Psalme* 83:11 prayes that Nobles and Princes of enemies may be used after former examples. And as this ranke of men is opposing Christ in the last times; so thare they by him and his people to be punished *Psal.* 2 *Psal* 110.5 the Lord at they right hand shall strike through (kings in the day of thy wrath *Psa.* 149.8.9." Rushworth, *An Abridgment of the Late Remonstrance of the Army* 1648, 8.

82. James I, *The True Lawe of Free Monarchies* (Edinburgh, 1603), B3ʳ.

83. *Great Britans Vote* (1648), 35. Dated in the Thomason copy as "March 13ᵗʰ 1647." Thomason E.431[26].

84. This becomes clear in the next line, 10:35, "If he called them gods, unto whom the word of God came, and the scripture cannot be broken." See the commentary in Hammond and Bush, eds., *New Testament and The Apocrypha*, 217–218.

85. Baldwin, "Milton and the Psalms," 461.

86. The significance of these distinctions are played out in *Paradise Lost*, in which Satan seems to misunderstand the problem of singularity in the special "Son of God," when all sons of God. See Satan's speech at 5.790: "Will ye submit your necks . . . ye will not, if I trust / To know ye right, or if ye know your selves / Natives and Sons of Heav'n possest before / By none, and if not equal all, yet free, / Equally free." (5.787–792). See also 5.863, 11.622.

87. Baldwin, "Milton and the Psalms," 457–463.

88. Tyndale, *Obedience*, 156. On the same page he explains that that which figurative language such as "allegory signifieth is ever the literal sense which thou must seek out diligently." for discussion of literalism and literature, see for example Luxon, *Literal Figures*, ix, 9, 80, passim; Brownlee, *Biblical Readings*, 10, 15, 173, passim.

89. Dante, *Literary Criticism*, 112–114.

90. Ames, *The Marrow of Sacred Divinity* (London, 1642), 170–171; see MacCallum, 69.

91. The thirtieth chapter of part 1 of Milton's treatise, and the thirty-fourth chapter of part 1 of Ames, *Medulla s.s. theologiae* (1629), 178.

92. *De Doctrina Christiana* (Oxford, 2012), vol. 8, part 2, 802–803.

93. Milton's method of reading is not, of course, unique to reformation readers. See Shuger, "Isaiah 63," 149–163. See also Lewalski, *Protestant Poetics*, 117–140.

94. Dante, *Literary Criticism*, 99.

95. *CPW* vol. 6, 589; see also *De Doctrina Christiana* (Oxford, 2012), vol. 8, part 2, 813. Milton refers again in this passage to Erasmus; the citation in the Yale edition is *Opera Omnia* (1705), vol. 6, 374.

96. *De Doctrina Christiana* (Oxford, 2012), vol. 8, part 2, 811; "Double" is Maurice Kelley's translation in the Yale version. See Forsyth, "Milton's Corrupt Bible," 212.

8. MILTON CONTRA TYNDALE

1. Sharpe, "Personal Rule of Charles I," 53.

2. Dawson, *John Knox*, 200. Kellar, *Scotland, England, and the Reformation*, 206–214.

3. Milton, *CPW* vol. 1, 827.

4. Rupp and Watson, eds., *Erasmus and Luther, Free Will and Salvation*, 244. Quoted in Rumrich, *Milton Unbound*, 150, n42.

5. For discussion of this problem in Protestant theology, see Cummings, *Literary Culture of the Reformation*, 98.

6. Milton, *CPW* vol. 1, 523–32. On Milton's reconception of the Reformation, see Loewenstein, "Milton and the Creaton of England's Long Reformation," passim.

7. Achinstein, "Law in This Matter to Himself," 174–199.

8. *CPW* vol. 2, 432.

9. Palmer, *Glasse of Gods Providence* (London, 1644), 57; see Lewalski, *Life of Milton*, 179; discussed in Loewenstein, *Author's Due*, 171–172.

10. *CPW* vol. 2, 242, 279, 282, 333, 340, and 279.

11. *CPW* vol. 2, 334.

12. *CPW* vol. 2, 665, 668, 588, 589, 602, 629, 715.

13. Milton, *Doctrine and Discipline of Divorce* (1643), 5; *CPW* vol. 2, 242.

14. *CPW* vol. 2, 431. The same argument is made in *Doctrine and Discipline of Divorce, CPW* vol. 2, 282.

15. *CPW* vol. 2, 350; see Rosenblatt, *Renaissance England's Chief Rabbi*, 5, 135–172; Shoulson, *Milton and the Rabbis*, 72.

16. *Tetrachordon*, in *CPW* vol. 2, 595. For discussion, see Tayler, "Milton's Grim Laughter," 76.

17. The quest for nonscriptural politics is flippantly voiced in the *Table-talk* of John Selden. Under the rubric "Human invention," he asks, "if we must admit nothing, but what we read in the Bible, what will become of parliament?"; Selden, *Table-talk*, 25.

18. *Areopagitica*, 17; *CPW* vol. 2, 526.

19. *CPW* vol. 6, 639.

20. *Samson Agonistes*, ll. 1372–1373, in Carey, ed., *Complete Shorter Poems*, 402.

21. Patterson et al., *Works of John Milton*, vol. 14, 83.

22. *A Discourse presented to those who seeke the reformation of the Church of England . . . with a short exposition upon some of Davids Psalmes, pertinent to these times of sedition* (London, 1642), 5. It is printed in Oxford in 1645.

23. Milton, *Areopagitica* (1644), 12; *CPW* vol. 2, 513–514.

24. *CPW* vol. 2, 224.

25. As the puritan Stephen Marshall wrote in 1640, "Take heed you understand it not as some [who] set up the rotten Dagon of mans free-will." *A Sermon Preached before the Honourable House of Commons* (London, 1640), in Jeffs, ed. *Fast Sermons*, vol. 1, 22–23. See Kahn, *Wayward Contracts*, 116. On Arminianism, see White, "Rise of Arminianism Reconsidered," 34. The Baptists also broke with Calvinism and adopted Arminianism. See Tyacke, "Rise of Puritanism," 31, and Hill, *Milton and the English Revolution*, 272–273. For a full account of Arminianism among puritan sectarians and others, see Wallace, Jr., *Puritans and Predestination*, 104–157. Discussed at greater length in Fulton, *Historical Milton*, 82–114.

26. Prynne, *Church of England's Old Antithesis* (London, 1629), sigs. A4v, c3v, quoted from Tyacke, "Arminianism and English Culture," 94. As Tyacke shows, "Englishmen labeled Arminian by their compatriots did usually espouse the cause of man's free will," 95. See also John Owen, *Theomachia Autexousiastike* (London, 1643). On Arminianism at this moment, see White, "Rise of Arminianism Reconsidered," 34.

27. See for example, *CPW* vol. 1, 533–534, 917. See Lewalski, *Life of Milton*, 139; Corns, "Milton, Roger Williams," 72–85, at 83. On Milton's early Arminianism, see Corns, "Milton's Antiprelatical Tracts," 39–48 and "Milton before 'Lycidas'," 23–36.

28. See the biography, Lamont, *Marginal Prynne*; "To the Christian Reader," in the margin of Prynne, *Histrio-Mastix* (1633), sig. **6ʳ. Milton terms Prynne "marginal P_____" in the Trinity manuscript version of "On the New Forcers of Conscience under the Long Parliament," but is amended to "baulk your ears" in the printed version. See Woodhouse and Bush, eds., *Variorum Commentary*, Part 2, 517. Milton, *Shorter Poems*, eds. Lewalski and Haan, 242, 505–507.

29. Prynne, *The Soveraigne Povver of Parliaments and Kingdomes. Wherein the Parliaments present necessary defensive warre against the Kings offensive malignant, popish forces; and subjects taking up defensive armes against their soveraigne* (1643).

30. The debate is captured in a pamphlet against a pamphlet against a pamplet by William Prynne himself: *PRYNNE The MEMBER reconciled to PRYNNE The BARRESTER. OR An Answer to a Scandalous Pamphlet, Intituled, PRYNNE against PRYNNE. Wherein is a cleare demonstration, That William Prynne, Vtter Barrester of Lincolnes Inne, in his Soveraigne Power of Parliaments and Kingdomes, is of the same Judgement with, and no wayes contradictory to William Prynne Esquire, A Member of the House of Commons in his MEMENTO* (London, 1649).

31. *The Soveraigne Povver of Parliaments and Kingdomes in Four Parts* (London, 1643), 105.

32. The title-pages of the first edition and second editions have the same wording here.

33. Erasmus, *Novum Testamentum Omne* (Basel: 1527), 338.

34. In the *Institution of Christian Religion*, Calvin translates Romans 13:3 with "magistratui"; Calvin, *Institutio Christianae Religionis* (Geneva, 1609), fol. 308ᵛ. (Book 4, chapter 20, 19).

35. The gloss "The revenge of unbridled government belongeth not to private men" appears also in the margin of this passage. Calvin, *The Institution of Christian Religion* (London, 1634), 748.

The translation and the marginalia is slightly different in older editions. The original is essentially the same, using "magistratus" in the sense distinct from the prince and the people. Calvin, *Institutio Christianae Religionis* (Geneva, 1609), fol. 311r. (Book 4, Chap. 20, 19). For a more detailed discussion of this passage, see Fulton, *Historical Milton*, 143–73, which informs the next few paragraphs.

36. Calvin, *Institutes*, vol. 2, 1512–1513, 1517.

37. Prynne, *Briefe Memento* (1649), 11; *IX queries upon the printed charge of the army against the XI. members and the papers thereto annexed*, 12; Romans 13 also appears equipped with capital letters to emphasize such phrases as "YE MUST NEEDS BE SUBJECT" and "DAMNATION" at the end of *A Plea for the Lords*, 68; Keeble and McDowell, introduction to Milton, *Vernacular Regicide and Republican Writings*, vol. 6, 153. Keeble and McDowell also point to Prynne's *Mr. Pryn's Last and Finall Declaration* (1649), 3; see 160, n. 401.

38. Milton, *Tenure* (1649), 1; *Vernacular Regicide and Republican Writings*, 151.

39. Milton, *Tenure* (1649), 8; *Vernacular Regicide and Republican Writings*, 155; Anon., *Certain Sermons*, 102.

40. Milton, *Tenure* (1649), 7; *Vernacular Regicide and Republican Writings*, 155.

41. Large numbers of allusions without citation as well as actual citations have escaped Harris Fletcher's otherwise helpful reference guide; yet see Fletcher, *Use of the Bible*, 98, 101 (his tally of *Tenure of Kings* has one instance, where there are dozens), 115, 156.

42. *CPW* vol. 6, 582. See Schwartz, "Milton on the Bible," 48.

43. *Tetrachordon* (1645), 8; *CPW* 2, 596. See his use of scriptural comparison in *CPW* 2, 262, 282, 431, 453; and his arguments from contradiction in *CPW* 2, 261, 461, 633, 640, 686; 689. See Forsyth, "Milton's Corrupt Bible," 212–213.

44. Milton, *Tenure* (1649), 15; *Vernacular Regicide and Republican Writings*, 160.

45. Milton, *Tenure* (1649), 15; *Vernacular Regicide and Republican Writings*, 160.

46. Here I disagree with my former reading in *Historical Milton*, 164, which I draw from.

47. Milton, *Tenure* (1649), 8–9; *Vernacular Regicide and Republican Writings*, 155–156, emphasis added.

48. Dzelzainis, ed., Milton, *Political Writings*, xvi. Dzelzainis also writes that Milton's method in 1649 "amounted to a decisive break with the Protestant tradition of voluntarism which held that whatsoever God commands is just simply because it is the will of God. For Milton the lawfulness of an action followed not from the expressed will of God, but from the fact that it was an intrinsically just and reasonable thing to do. What this implied was the possibility of forming correct ethical and moral judgements quite independently of any knowledge of revelation or scripture." Dzelzainis, *Political Writings*, xv.

49. Killeen discusses the use of Jehu in a section entitled "anointing regicide," in *Political Bible*, 167–178. There are examples provided by Hughes in *CPW* vol. 3, 215.

50. *Tenure* (1649), 21; *Vernacular Regicide and Republican Writings*, 163–164.

51. See Dzelzainis, *Political Writings*, xv; see Kahn's reading of Milton's hermeneutics in *Wayward Contracts*, 120–24.

52. Milton, *CPW* vol. 4, part 1, 381; his reading extends to 386.

53. James, *True Lawe of Free Monarchies* (1603), C4ᵛ–C5ʳ.

54. Milton, *CPW* vol. 4, part 1, 385.

55. Milton, *Vernacular Regicide and Republican Writings*, 9.

56. *Treatise of Civil Power* (1659), 24; *CPW* 7, 255.

57. *Treatise of Civil Power* (1659), 31; *CPW* 7, 252.

58. *Treatise of Civil Power* (1659), 44; *CPW* 7, 259.

CODA

1. Anon., *Vindiciae Contra Tyrannos* (Matthew Simmons, 1648). The Thomason indexer added a manuscript note: "This translation was the work of Mr. William Walker of Darnal near Sheffield, the person who cut off King Charles's head." According to Muddiman, for reasons explained in *The Trial of King Charles I*, 180–181, it was the brother of William, Henry Walker, who translated the *Vindiciae* and held the executioner's axe.

2. See for example Hadfield, *Shakespeare and Republicanism*, 32; see also Skinner, *Foundations of Modern Political Thought*, vol. 2, 338, where he identifies it as a watershed moment in early modern poltical thought, providing a "recognisably modern, secularized thesis."

3. Here I share the position taken by McLaren, "Rethinking Republicanism," 23–52. The author of the *Vindiciae* in fact excludes private individuals from "any form of resistance, except against tyrants without title." Brutus, the Celt, *Vindiciae, contra Tyrannos*, ed. Garnett, 60–61; McLaren, 27. As I have argued, Milton takes this argument one step further in *The Tenure of Kings and Magistrates*.

4. Schiller, *Roman Law*, 221; Gates, *Latin World-building*, 26; see also a commentary on Caesar, Sauveur, *C. Julii Caesaris Commentarii de Bello Gallico*, 65.

5. Habermas, *Legitimation Crisis*.

6. *The Diary of Samuel Pepys*, vol. 1, 158. I am grateful to Steven Zwicker drawing my attention to this.

7. Julie Zauzmer and Keith McMillan, "Sessions cites Bible Passage Used to Defend Slavery in Defense of Separating Immigrant Families," *Washington Post*, June 15, 2018; Antonin Scalia quoted Romans 13:1–5 in full when arguing for the legitimacy of capital punishment. "The core of [Paul's] message," he argues, "is that government . . . derives its moral authority from God. It is the 'minister of God' with powers to 'revenge,' to 'execute wrath,' including even wrath by the sword (which is unmistakably a reference to the death penalty)." Scalia, "God's Justice or Ours," 19.

8. As has been shown, Spenser follows the liturgical calendar for 1594. See Spenser, *Edmund Spenser's Amoretti and Epithalamium*, Larsen, ed., 3–20. See Prescott, "Thirsty Dear," 33–76. *Theatre wherein be represented . . . the voluptuous Worldlings* (London, 1569).

9. Milton, *Paradise Lost* (1667), lines 1–4.

10. On the four lines now cut from the opening of *The Aeneid*, see G. P. Goold, revised ed., Virgil, *Eclogues, Georgics, Aeneid 1-VI*, 261.

11. *Paradise Regain'd a Poem in IV Books: to which is added Samson Agonistes* (1671), ll. 1–4. These lines of the *Aeneid* are also echoed by Spenser at the beginning of the *Faerie Queene*. See Rogers, "Paradise Regained," 606.

12. As Aaron Pratt observes, "it might even be wrong to use the term 'paratext' with these books at all, at least insofar as 'para' implies a subordinate position in a hierarchy of value." Pratt, "Trouble with Translation," 35.

13. Dodds, "An Accidental Historian," 280, n27; Stillingfleet, *Several Conferences between a Romish Priest*, 119; Dodds, *Exploiting Erasmus*, xix. For a classic argument on Erasmus's role in Reformation England, see McConica, *English Humanists*.

14. Dodds, *Exploiting Erasmus*, 5. The requirement for clergy were those below the degree of a Bachelor of Divinity, 10. Dodds points out that by 1591, these injunctions were included in a list of articles that were no longer being enforced, 13.

15. On the legacy of Erasmus's *via media* rhetoric, see Dodds, *Exploiting Erasmus*, 37, 109, 171–178; passim.

16. Hooker, *Of the Laws of Ecclesiastical Polity*, vol. 1, Preface, 7.3. Hooker's desire to work beyond scripture and his doubts about predestination theology are confronted in *A Christian Letter of Certaine English Protestantes* (London, 1599), where the authors take issue with Hooker's use of scripture as "a supplement," 7.

17. *Discourse Presented* (London, 1642), 5.

18. Bucer, *Common Places of Martin Bucer*, 303; Avis, "Moses and the Magistrate," 13.

19. Tyndale, *Work of William Tyndale*, ed. Duffield, 287; *An Exposycyon vpon The V.Vi.Vii. Chapters of Mathewe* (1536), M3ᵛ.

20. Bucer, *De Regno Christi,* in *Melanchthon and Bucer*, 162.

21. Morison, *A Lamentation* (1536), sig. A3ʳ; quoted from Rex, "Crisis of Obedience," 883. See also R. Morison, *An Exhortation to Styre all Englvsche men* (1539), sig. B2ʳ.

22. Erasmus, *Novum Instrumentum Omne* (Basel, 1516), 550.

23. See Erasmus, *On Copia of Words and Ideas*, 68.

24. Gilby, *Admonition to England and Scotland* (Geneva, 1558), fol. 72ʳ.

25. Dodds, *Exploiting Erasmus*, xvi.

26. Dodds, *Exploiting Erasmus*, 204, 211.

27. Malvolio is called a puritan in *Twelfth Night* at 2.3.146; see Bevington's reading of this in context in "Debate about Shakespeare and Religion," 25–28.

28. See for example, Brownlee, *Biblical Readings and Literary Writings*.

29. For the Henrician and Edwardian periods, see Simpson, *Burning to Read*; King, *English Reformation Literature*; see also the essays on Tudor drama in Happé and Hüskin, eds., *Staging Scripture*; particularly Carpenter, "Reforming the Scriptures," 12–41.

30. Bucer, *Melanchthon and Bucer*, 175; *De Regno Christi* (1557), 2.

BIBLIOGRAPHY

BIBLICAL TEXTS CONSULTED, IN CHRONOLOGICAL ORDER

[The New Testament.] Translated by William Tyndale. [Cologne: Peter Quentell?], 1525.

The new Testame[n]t as it was written and caused to be writte[n] by them which herde yt. To whom also oure saveoure Christ Jesus commaunded that they shulde preach it vnto al creatures. [Worms: Peter Schöffer?, 1526]. Also available as *The New Testament: A Facsimile of the 1526 Edition.* Edited by David Daniell. London: British Library and Hendrickson, 2008.

The Psalter of Dauid in Englishe purely a[n]d faithfully tra[n]slated aftir the texte of Feline [ie., Martin Bucer]: euery Psalme hauynge his argument before, declarynge brefly thentente [and] substance of the wholl Psalme. Translated by George Joye. Emprinted at Argentine [i.e., Antwerp]: 1530. the. 16. daye of Ianuary by me Francis foxe [i.e., Martin de Keyser, 1530].

[The Pentateuch]. Translated by William Tyndale. Emprynted at Malborow in the lande of Hesse, by me Hans Luft. [Antwerp: Martin De Keyser and Joannes Grapheus], January 17, 1530.

Biblia das ist die gantze Heilige Schrifft Deudsch. Translated by Martin Luther. Frankfurt am Main: Röderberg-Verlag, 1983. Facsimile, originally published in 1534.

The newe Testament, dylygently corrected and compared with the Greke by Willyam Tindale. Antwerp: Marten Emperowr, 1534.

Tyndale's New Testament, translated from the Greek by William Tyndale in 1534. Edited by David Daniell. New Haven, CT: Yale University Press, 1989.

BIBLIA The Byble, that is, the holy Scrypture of the Olde and New Testament. Translated by Miles Coverdale. [Antwerp, Cologne or Marburg?: E. Cervicornus & J. Soter?], 1535.

The Byble, which is all the holy Scripture (The "Matthews Bible"). Printed for R. Grafton and E. Whitchurch of London, 1537.

The Most Sacred Bible, whiche is the holy scripture ("Taverner's Bible," a revision of Matthews). London: John Byddell for Thomas Barthlet, 1539.

The Byble in English, that is to say the content of all the holy scripture (The "Great Bible."). London: Grafton and Whitchurch, 1539.

The newe testament in englyshe, translated after the texte of Master Erasmus of Roterodame. London: Richard Grafton and Edward Whitchurch, 1540; STC 2846.

The Newe Testament yet once agayne corrected whearevunto is added an exhortacio to the same Erasmus Rot. [Antwerp: M. Crum?], 1542.

The Byble, that is to say all the holy Scripture. Edited by Edmund Becke. STC 2077. London: Day and Seres, 1549.

The Newe Testament in Englyshe and in Latin of Erasmus Translacion. Novvm Testamentvm Anglice et Latine. W. Powell: London, 1549.

The New Testament in Englishe after the Greeke Translation Annexed wyth the Translation of Erasmus in Latin. Printed by Thomas Gaultier for J. C., 1550.

The Byble, that is to say al the holy Scripture. Edited by Edmund Becke. STC 2088. London: Jhon [John] Day, 1551.

The new Testament of our Saviour Jesu Christ. Faithfully translated out of the Greke. Wyth the Notes and expositions of the darke places therein. (Jugge's popular revision of Tyndale with a portrait of Edward, printed through Elizabeth's reign.) London: Rycharde Jugge, 1552.

The Newe Testament of Our Lord Iesus Christ. Conferred diligently with the Greke, and best approued translations. Geneva: C. Badius, 1557.

La Bible, qui est Toute la saincte Escriture. Geneva: Nicholas Barbier and Thomas Courteau, 1559.

The Bible and Holy Scriptvres conteyened in the Olde and Newe Testament. Translated according to the Ebrue and Greke, and conferred the best translations in diuers langages. Geneva: Rouland Hall, 1560.

The Bible and Holy Scriptures conteyened in the Olde and Newe Testament. Geneva: [John Bodley], 1562.

La Bibia, che si chiama il Vecchio Testamento. [Geneva]: F. Durone, 1562.

The holie Bible conteynyng the olde Testament and the new. (Bishops' Bible). London: R. Jugge, 1568.

The holi bible (Bishops' Quarto Bible). London: R. Jugge, 1569.

The Bible, that is, the Holy Scriptures. STC 2119. London: Christopher Barker, 1577; Bodleian Library pressmark BOD Bib. Eng. 1577 d.1.

The Nevv Testament of Jesus Christ, Translated faithfully into English, out of the authentical Latin, according to the best corrected copies of the same, diligently conferred with the Greeke and other editions in divers languages. Translated by Gregory Martin. Rheims: John Fogny, 1582.

The Text of the Nevv Testament of Iesus Christ, translated out of the vulgar Latine by the papists of the traiterous seminarie at Rhemes. Edited and annotated by William Fulke. London: Christopher Barker, 1589.

Jesu Christi Domini nostri Novum Testamentum, sive Novum Foedus, cujus graeco contextui respondent interpretationes duae: una, Vetus: altera, Theodori Bezae. Ejusdem Th. Bezae annotationes. [Geneva]: Héritiers d'Eustache Vignon, 1598.

The Geneva Bible: The Annotated New Testament 1602 Edition. Edited by Gerald T. Sheppard. Cleveland: Pilgri m Press, 1989.

The Holie Bible faithfvlly translated into English, ovt of the avthentical Latin. Diligently conferred with the Hebrew, Greeke, and other Editions in diuers languages. Douay: Laurence Kellam, 1610. Reprinted in facsimile, edited by D. M. Rogers. London: Scolar Press, 1975.

The Holy Bible, Conteyning the Old Testament, and the New: Newly Translated out of the Originall tongues: & with the former Translations diligently compared and reuised, by his Maiesties speciall Commandement. London: Robert Barker, 1611.

The Holy Bible, Conteyning the Old Testament and the New. Quarto edition of the King James Bible owned by Milton; MS Additional 32310, STC 2220. London: Robert Barker, 1612.

Testamenti Veteris Biblia Sacra, sive Libri Canonici Priscae Ivdaeorum Ecclesiae a Deo Traditi, Latini recens ex Hebraeo facti, breuibusque; Scholiis illustrati ab Immanuele Tremellio, & Francisco Iunio. . . . Novi Testamenti libros ex sermone Syro ab eodem Tremellio, & ex Graeco a Theodoro Beza in Latinum versos. Geneva: sumptibus Matthaei Berjon, 1617.

Biblia Sacra polyglotta: complectentia textus originales, Hebraicum, cum Pentateucho Samaritano, Chaldaicum, Græcum; versionumque antiquarum, Samaritanæ, Græcæ lxxii. Interp., Chaldaicæ,

Syriacæ, Arabicæ, Æthipicæ, Persicæ, Vulg. Lat. quicquid comparari poterat. Edited by Brian Walton. London: T. Roycroft, 1655–1657.

The English Bible, The King James Version: The Old Testament. Edited by Herbert Marks. New York: Norton, 2012.

The New Oxford Annotated Bible, Edited by Bruce M. Metzger and Roland E. Murphy. New York: Oxford University Press, 1991 (New Revised Standard Version, or NRSV).

PRINTED BOOKS CITED

Anonymous. *Breefe catechisme so necessarie and easie to be learned euen of the symple sort.* London: Hugh Singleton, 1576.

———. *A Briefe treatise concerning the Burnynge of Bucer and Phagius, at Cambrydge, in the tyme of Quene Mary . . . wherein is expressed the fantasticall and tirannous dealynges of the Romishe Church.* London, 1562.

———. *Admonition to the parliament.* [Hamel Hempstead?], 1572.

———. *The Case of the Armie Truly stated.* London, 1647.

———. *Calendar of Patent Rolls, Edward VI. Vol III: 1549–1551.* London: Her Majesty's Stationery Office, 1939.

———. *Certain Sermons, or Homilies, Appointed to be Read in Churches.* London: The Prayer-Book and Homily Society, 1852.

———. *A Christian letter of certaine English protestants.* Middleburg, 1599.

———. *A Discourse presented to those who seeke the reformation of the Church of England . . . with a short exposition upon some of Davids Psalmes, pertinent to these times of sedition.* London, 1642.

———. *The forme of prayers and ministration of the sacraments . . . vsed in the Englishe congregation at Geneva and approved, by the famous and godly learned man, John Caluyn.* Geneva: John Crespin, 1556.

———. *Great Britans vote: or, God save King Charles. A treatise seasonably published this 27th. day of March, the happy inauguration of his sacred (though now dispised and imprisoned) Majesty. Wherein is proved by many plaine texts of Scripture, that the resisting, imprisoning, or deposing our King, under what specious pretenses soever couched, is not onely unlawfull but damnable.* London 1648.

———. *An homilie against disobedience and wylfull rebellion.* London, 1570.

———. *A necessary doctrine and erudition for any Christen man.* London, 1543.

———. *A Revindication of Psalme 105.15 touch not mine Anointed, &c.* London, 1643.

———. *The Soveraignty of kings, or, An absolute answer and confutation of that groundlesse vindication of Psalme 105.15.* London, 1642

———. *A Serious and faithful Representation of the Judgements of Ministers of the Gospell within the Province of London.* London, 1649.

———. *A Solemn Engagement of the Army.* London, 1647.

———. (but see "Brutus"), *Vindiciae Contra Tyrannos: Defense of Liberty against Tyrants.* London: Matthew Simmons and Robert Wilson, 1648.

Achinstein, Sharon. "'A Law in This Matter to Himself': Contextualizing Milton's Divorce Tracts." In Nicholas McDowell and Nigel Smith, eds., *The Oxford Handbook of Milton,* 174–199. Oxford: Oxford University Press, 2009.

———. *Citizen Milton: An Exhibition Celebrating the 400th Anniversary of the Birth of John Milton (1608–1674)*. Oxford: Bodleian Library, 2008.

———. "Medea's Dilemma: Politics and Passion in Milton's Divorce Tracts." In *Rethinking Historicism from Shakespeare to Milton*. Edited by Ann Baynes Coiro and Thomas Fulton, 181–208. Cambridge: Cambridge University Press, 2012.

———. "Texts in Conflict: The Press and the Civil War." In *The Cambridge Companion to Writing of the English Revolution*. Edited by N. H. Keeble, 50–68. Cambridge: Cambridge University Press, 2001.

Adams, Robert P. *The Better Part of Valor: More, Erasmus, Colet, and Vives, on Humanism, War, and Peace 1496–1535*. Seattle: University of Washington Press, 1962.

Ahl, Frederick M. *Lucan: An Introduction*. Ithaca, NY: Cornell University Press, 1976.

Alford, Stephen. *Kingship and Politics in the Reign of Edward VI*. Cambridge: Cambridge University Press, 2002.

Allen, Amanda Wrenn. *The Eucharistic Debate in Tudor England: Thomas Cranmer, Stephen Gardiner, and the English Reformation*. London: Rowman and Littlefield, 2018.

Allen, William. *A Faithful Memorial of that Remarkable Meeting of Many Officers of the Army in England, at Windsor Castle, in the Year 1648*. London, 1659.

Allmen, J. J. von. ed, *Vocabulary of the Bible*. London: Lutterworth Press, 1956.

Ames, William. *The Marrow of Sacred Divinity*. London, 1642.

Ames, William. *Medulla s.s. theologiae, ex sacris literis*. London, 1629.

Andersen, Jennifer, and Elizabeth Sauer, eds., *Books and Readers in Early Modern England*. Philadelphia: University of Pennsylvania Press, 2002.

Anderson, Christopher. *Annals of the English Bible*. London: William Pickering, 1845.

Anderson, Judith H. "Language and History in the Reformation: Cranmer, Gardiner, and the Words of Institution." *Renaissance Quarterly* 54, no. 1 (2001): 20–51.

Anglo, Sydney. "An Early Tudor Programme for Plays and Other Demonstrations against the Pope." *Journal of the Warburg and Courtauld Institutes* 20, no. 1/2 (1957): 176–179.

Arber, Edward, ed. *A Transcript of the Registers of the Company of Stationers of London, 1554–1640*. 5 vols. London: British Library, 1875–1877.

Arblaster, P., G. Juhász, and G. Latré, eds. *Tyndale's Testament*. Turnhout, Belgium: Brepols, 2002.

Aston, Margaret. *England's Iconoclasts*. Oxford: Clarendon Press, 1988.

Aubrey, John. *Brief Lives*. Edited by Richard Barber. Woodbridge, Suffolk, UK: Boydell Press, 1975.

Augustine, Aurelius of Hippo, Saint. *Later Works*. Translated and edited by John Burnaby. Philadelphia: Westminster Press, 1955.

———. *The Works of Aurelius Augustine*. Edited by Marcus Dods. Edinburgh: Murray and Gibb, 1877.

Austin, Kenneth. "'Epitome of the Old Testament, Mirror of God's Grace, and Complete Anatomy of Man': Immanuel Tremellius and the Psalms." In *Shaping the Bible in the Reformation,* edited by Bruce Gordon and Matthew McLean, 217–235.

———. *From Judaism to Calvinism: the Life and Writings of Immanuel Tremellius (c. 1510–1580)*. Aldershot, UK: Ashgate, 2007.

Avis, P. D. L. "Moses and the Magistrate: a Study in the Rise of Protestant Legalism." *Journal of Ecclesiastical History* 26, no. 2 (1975): 149–172.

Backus, Irena. "Laurence Tomson (1539–1608) and Elizabethan Puritanism." *Journal of Ecclesiastical History* 28, no. 1 (1977): 17–27.

———. *Reformation Readings of the Apocalypse: Geneva, Zurich, and Wittenberg.* Oxford: Oxford University Press, 2000.

———. "Renaissance Attitudes to New Testament Apocryphal Writings: Jacques Lefèvre d'Étaples and His Epigones." *Renaissance Quarterly* 51, no. 4 (1998): 1169–1198.

———. *The Reformed Roots of the English New Testament: The Influence of Theodore Beza on the English New Testament.* Pittsburgh: Pickwick Press, 1980.

Baldwin, Edward Chauncey. "Milton and the Psalms." *Modern Philology* 17, no. 8 (1919): 457–463.

Bale, John. *The Complete Plays of John Bale.* Edited by Peter Happé. 2 vols. Cambridge: Brewer, 1985.

———. *Image of Both Churches after the moste wonderful and heavenly Revelation of Saint John the Evangelist.* Antwerp, 1545.

———. *The Image of Both Churches.* London: Thomas East, ca. 1580.

———. *Select Works of John Bale.* Edited by Henry Christmas, Cambridge: Cambridge University Press, 1849.

Ball, B. W. *A Great Expectation: Eschatological Thought in English Protestantism to 1660.* Leiden: E. J. Brill, 1975.

Barlow, Claude, ed. *Epistolae Senecae ad Paulum et Pauli ad Senecam (Quae Vocantur).* Rome: American Academy in Rome, 1938.

Barlow, William. *The Svmme and Substance of the Conference.* London, 1604.

Barnaby, Andrew, and Joan Wry. "Authorized Versions: *Measure for Measure* and the Politics of Biblical Translation." *Renaissance Quarterly* 51, no. 4 (1998): 1225–1254.

Barton, John, ed. *The Cambridge Companion to Biblical Interpretation.* Cambridge University Press, 1998.

Baskerville, Edward J. *Chronological Bibliography of Propaganda and Polemic Published in English Between 1553 and 1558 from the Death of Edward VI to the Death of Mary I.* Philadelphia: American Philosophical Society, 1979.

[Bateman, Stephen.] *The Trauayled Pylgrime bringing newes from all partes of the worlde, such like scarce harde of before.* London, 1569.

Bauckham, Richard. *Tudor Apocalypse: Sixteenth Century Apocalypticism, Millennarianism, and the English Reformation.* Oxford: Sutton Courtenay Press, 1978.

Bennett, Josephine Waters. Measure for Measure *as Royal Entertainment.* New York: Columbia University Press, 1966.

———. *The Evolution of* The Faerie Queene. New York: Burt Franklin, 1960.

Bentley, Jerry H. "Biblical Philology and Christian Humanism: Lorenzo Valla and Erasmus as Scholars of the Gospels." *Sixteenth Century Journal* 8, no. 2 (1977): 8–28.

———. *Humanists and Holy Writ: New Testament Scholarship in the Renaissance.* Princeton, NJ: Princeton University Press, 1983.

Bernard, G. W. *Anne Boleyn: Fatal Attractions.* New Haven, CT: Yale University Press, 2010.

———. *The King's Reformation: Henry VIII and the Remaking of the English Church.* New Haven, CT: Yale University Press, 2005.

Bernard, Richard. *A key of knowledge for the opening of the secret mysteries of St Iohns mysticall Reuelation.* London: 1617.

Berry, Lloyd., ed. *The Geneva Bible: A Facsimile of the 1560 Edition.* Madison: University of Wisconsin Press, 1969.

Betteridge, Maurice S. "The Bitter Notes: The Geneva Bible and Its Annotations." *Sixteenth Century Journal* 14, no. 1 (1983): 41–62.

Bevington, David. *From Mankind to Marlowe*. Cambridge, MA: Harvard University Press, 1962.

———. "The Debate about Shakespeare and Religion." In *Shakespeare and Early Modern Religion*, edited by David Loewenstein and Michael Witmore, 23–39.

Beza, Theodore. *Ane answer made the fourth day of septembre a thousand fyue hundreth syxtie one*. Edinburgh, 1562.

———. *Master Bezaes sermons vpon the three chapters of the canticle of canticles*. London, 1587.

Bishop, J. David. *Seneca's Daggered Stylus: Political Code in the Tragedies*. Hain: Königstein, 1985.

Bishop, Tom. "Discontented Harmonies: Words against Words in Pomfret Castle." In *The Bible on the Shakespearean Stage: Cultures of Interpretation in Reformation England*, edited by Thomas Fulton and Kristen Poole, 103–117. Cambridge: Cambridge University Press, 2018.

Blayney, Peter. *The Stationers' Company and the Printers of London*, 2 vols. Cambridge: Cambridge University Press, 2013.

Bloom, Harold. *Shakespeare: The Invention of the Human*. New York: Riverhead Books, 1998.

Boddy, Margaret. "Milton's Translation of Psalms 80–88." *Modern Philology* 64, no. 1 (1966): 1–9.

Boehrer, Bruce. "Tyndale's *The Practyse of Prelates*: Reformation Doctrine and the Royal Supremacy." *Renaissance and Reformation* 10, no. 3 (1986): 257–276.

Bossy, John. "Moral Arithmetic: Seven Sins into Ten Commandments." In *Conscience and Casuistry in Early Modern Europe*, edited by Edmund Leites, 214–234. Cambridge: Cambridge University Press, 1988.

Bourne, Claire. "*Vide Supplementum*: Early Modern Collation as Play-Reading in the First Folio." In *Early Modern English Marginalia*. Edited by Katherine Acheson, 195–233. Routledge, 2019.

Bowler, Gerald. "'An Axe or An Acte': the Parliament of 1572 and Resistance Theory in Early Elizabethan England." *Canadian Journal of History* 19, no. 3 (1984): 349–359.

Bradbrook, M. C. "Authority, Truth, and Justice in *Measure for Measure*." *Review of English Studies* 17, no. 68 (1941): 385–399.

Bradshaw, Christopher. "David or Josiah? Old Testament Kings as Exemplars in Edwardian Religious Polemic." In *Protestant History and Identity*. Edited by Bruce Gordon, 2 vols. Aldershot, UK: Ashgate, 1996.

Brailsford, Henry N. *The Levellers and the English Revolution*. Edited by Christopher Hill. London: Cresset Press, 1961.

Bramhall, John. *The Serpent Salve, or, A Remedie for the Biting of an Aspe*. N.p., 1643.

Brassington, William Salt. *Historic Bindings in the Bodleian Library, Oxford*. London: Sampson Low, Marston, 1891.

Brewer J. S. and James Gairdner, eds. *Letters and Papers, Foreign and Domestic, of the Reign of Henry VIII*, 21 vols. London: Longman, Green & Roberts: 1862–1910.

Brisman, Leslie. *Milton's Poetry of Choice and Its Romantic Heirs*. Ithaca, NY: Cornell University Press, 1973.

Brljak, Vladimir. "The Satanic 'or': Milton and Protestant Anti-Allegorism." *Review of English Studies* 66, no. 275 (2015): 403–422.

Brooke, Robert Greville. *A Discovrse Opening the Natvre of that Episcopacie*. London, 1641.

Broughton, Hugh. *An Epistle to the Learned Nobility of England Touching Translating the Bible* (1597); facsimile reprint, Amsterdam: Theatrum Orbis Terrarum, 1977.

———. *A Petition to the King. For authority and allowance to expound the Apocalyps in Hebrew and Greek, to shew Iewes and Gentiles: that Rome in Çæsars and Pope, is therein still damned*. [Amsterdam: G. Thorp,] 1611.

———. *The Concent of Scripture* [London: For Gabriel Simson and William White?, 1590?]. (Folger STC 3851 copy 1.)

Brown, Cedric. "A King James Bible, Protestant Nationalism, and Boy Milton." In *Form and Reform in Renaissance England: Essays in Honor of Barbara Kiefer Lewalski*, edited by Amy Boesky and Mary Thomas Crane, 271–287. Newark: University of Delaware Press, 2000.

Brown, Francis. *A Hebrew and English Lexicon of the Old Testament.* Oxford: Clarendon Press, 1907; 1968.

Brownlee, Victoria. *Biblical Readings and Literary Writings in Early Modern England, 1558–1625.* Oxford: Oxford University Press, 2018.

Brutus, Stephanus Junius, the Celt, *Vindiciae, contra Tyrannos.* Edited and translated by George Garnett. Cambridge: Cambridge University Press, 1994.

Bucer, Martin. *Common Places of Martin Bucer.* Translated and edited by D. F. Wright. Abingdon: Sutton Courtenay Press, 1972.

———. *De regno Christi Iesu seruatoris nostri, libri II. Ad Eduardum VI Angliae regem, annis abhinc sex scripti.* Basel: Joannem Oporinum, 1557.

———. *De Regno Christi*, In *Melanchthon and Bucer.* Edited by Wilhelm Pauck. Philadelphia: Westminster Press, 1969.

———. *Martini Bvceri Scripta Anglicana fere omnia.* Basel: Peter Perna, 1577.

Bullinger, Heinrich. *The Decades of Henry Bullinger.* Edited by Thomas Harding. Cambridge: Cambridge University Press, 1896.

Burke, Peter. *The Renaissance Sense of the Past.* New York: St. Martin's Press, 1970.

Burnett, Amy Nelson. "Church Discipline and Moral Reformation in the Thought of Martin Bucer." *Sixteenth Century Journal* 22, no. 3 (1991): 438–456.

Calvin, John. *A Commentary upon the Prophecie of Isaiah.* London, 1609.

———. *Calvin: Institutes of the Christian Religion.* Edited by John T. McNeill and translated by Ford Lewis Battles. 2 vols. Philadelphia: Westminster Press, 1960.

———. *Commentarii in Isaiam.* Geneva, 1559.

———. *Commentarii in Isaiam prophetam.* Geneva, 1551.

———. *Commentary on Corinthians.* Translated by John Pringle. Edinburgh: Calvin Translation Society, 1848–1849, 2: 172.

———. *Institutio Christianae Religionis.* Geneva, 1609.

———. *Joannis Calvini Commentarii in Isaiam prophetam.* Geneva: Jean Crespin, 1551.

———. *The Institution of Christian Religion.* London, 1561.

———. *The Institution of Christian Religion, written in Latine by M. John Calvine.* Translated by Thomas Norton. London, 1587.

———. *The Institution of Christian Religion.* London, 1634.

———. *The Psalmes of David and others: with M. Iohn Calvins Commentaries.* Translated by Arthur Golding. London, 1571.

Campbell, Gordon. *A Milton Chronology.* New York: St. Martin's Press, 1997.

———. "Milton's *Index Theologicus* and Bellarmine's *Disputationes De Controversiis Christianae Fidei Adversus Huius Temporis Haereticos.*" *Milton Quarterly* 11, no. 1 (1977): 12–16.

Campbell, Gordon, and Thomas N. Corns. *John Milton: Life, Work, and Thought.* Oxford and New York: Oxford University Press, 2008.

Camporeale, Salvatore I. "Lorenzo Valla's 'Oratio' on the Pseudo-Donation of Constantine: Dissent and Innovation in Early Renaissance Humanism." *Journal of the History of Ideas* 57, no. 1 (1996): 9–26.

Carley, James. *The Books of King Henry VIII and His Wives*. London: British Library, 2004.

———. *The Libraries of King Henry VIII*. London: British Library, 2000.

Carpenter, Sarah. "Reforming the Scriptures: Biblical Drama after the Reformation," In *Staging Scripture: Biblical Drama 1350–1600*. Edited by Peter Happé and Wim Hüskin. Leiden and Boston: Brill, 2016.

Cartwright, Thomas. *A Confutation of the Rhemists Translation, Glosses and Annotations on the New Testament*. London, 1618.

[Cartwright, Thomas]. *A Directory of Church-government*. London, 1644 [1645].

Cartwright, Thomas. *Helpes for Discovery of the Truth in Point of Toleration*. London, 1648.

Cavendish, George. *The Life and Death of Cardinal Wolsey*. Edited by Richard Sylvester. London: Published for the Early English Text Society by the Oxford University Press, 1961.

Chapman, Alison. "Marking Time: Astrology, Almanacs, and English Protestantism." *Renaissance Quarterly* 60, no. 4 (2007): 1257–1290.

———. "Whose Saint Crispin's Day Is It?: Shoemaking, Holiday Making, and the Politics of Memory in Early Modern England." *Renaissance Quarterly* 54, no. 4 (2001): 1467–1494.

Charles I, King. *Eikon Basilike*. Jim Deams and Holly Faith Nelson, eds. Plymouth: Broadview Editions, 2006.

Charnaik, Warren. "Biblical Republicanism." *Prose Studies* 23, no. 1 (2000): 147–160.

Christian, Margaret. *Spenserian Allegory and Elizabethan Biblical Exegesis: A Context for* The Faerie Queene. Manchester, UK: Manchester University Press, 2016.

Christie-Miller, Ian. "Henry VIII and British Library, Royal MS. 2 A. XVI: Marginalia in King Henry's Psalter." *eBLJ* 8 (2015): 1–19. http://www.bl.uk/eblj/2015articles/article8.html.

Chomarat, Jacques. *Grammaire et Rhetorique chez Erasme*, 2 vols. Paris: Belles lettres, 1981.

Clark, Ira. "'Measure for Measure': Chiasmus, Justice, and Mercy." *Style* 35, no. 4 (2001): 659–680.

Coiro, Ann Baynes, and Thomas Fulton, "Old New Now." In *Rethinking Historicism from Shakespeare to Milton*, edited by Coiro and Fulton, 1–20. Cambridge: Cambridge University Press, 2012.

Coldewey, John C. ed. *Early English Drama: An Anthology*. New York: Garland, 1993.

Colet, John. *An Exposition of St. Paul's Epistle to the Romans*. Edited by J. H. Lupton. Ridgewood: Gregg Press, 1965.

Collins, John J. *Introduction to the Hebrew Bible*. Minneapolis: Fortress Press, 2018.

———. *The Dead Sea Scrolls: A Biography*. Princeton, NJ: Princeton University Press, 2013.

Collinson, Patrick. "A Comment: Concerning the Name Puritan." *Journal of Ecclesiastical History* 31, no. 4 (1980): 483–488

———. *Archbishop Grindal, 1519–1583: The Struggle for a Reformed Church*. London: Cape, 1979.

———. *Elizabethan Puritan Movement*. London: Methuen, 1982.

———. *Godly People: Essays on English Protestantism and Puritanism*. London: Hambledon Press, 1983.

———. "The Elizabethan Exclusion Crisis and the Elizabethan Polity." In *This England: Essays on the English Nation and Commonwealth in the Sixteenth Century*, 81–84. Manchester, UK: Manchester University Press, 2011.

———. "The Jacobean Religious Settlement: The Hampton Court Conference." In *Before The Civil War: Essays on Early Stuart Politics and Government*. Edited by Howard Tomlinson, 27–51. New York: St. Martin's Press, 1983.

———. "The Monarchical Republic of Queen Elizabeth." *Bulletin of the John Rylands University Library of Manchester* 69, no. 2 (1987): 394–424.

Collinson, Patrick, and Polly Ha, eds. *The Reception of Continental Reformation in Britain* Oxford: Oxford University Press for the British Academy, 2010.

Corns, Thomas N, ed. *A Companion to Milton.* Oxford: Wiley-Blackwell, 2001.

———, ed. *Complete Works of John Milton.* Oxford: Oxford University Press, 2012.

———. "John Milton, Roger Williams, and the Limits of Toleration." In Achinstein and Sauer, *Milton and Toleration*, 72–85.

———. "Milton before 'Lycidas.'" In *Milton and the Terms of Liberty.* Edited by Graham Parry and Joad Raymond, 23–36. Cambridge: D.S. Brewer, 2002.

———. "Milton's Antiprelatical Tracts and the Marginality of Doctrine." In *Milton and Heresy.* Edited by Stephen B. Dobranski and John Rumrich, 39–48. Cambridge: Cambridge University Press, 1998.

———, ed. *The Royal Image: Representations of Charles I.* Cambridge: Cambridge University Press, 1999.

Coverdale, Miles. *The Supplicacion: that the Nobles and Comons of Osteryke made lately by their Messaungers, vnto Kyng Ferdinandus, in the Cause of the Christen* [Antwerp: Printed by M. Crom, 1542?].

Cox, John. *Shakespeare and the Dramaturgy of Power.* Princeton: Princeton University Press, 1989.

Cox, Virginia. "Rhetoric and Humanism in Quattrocento Venice." *Renaissance Quarterly* 56, no. 3 (2003): 657–658.

Craig, Hardin. "The Geneva Bible as a Political Document." *Pacific Historical Review* 7, no. 1 (1938): 40–49.

Crane, Mary Thomas and Amy Boesky, eds. *Form and Reform in Renaissance England: Essays in Honor of Barbara Kiefer Lewalski.* Newark: University of Delaware Press, 2000.

Cranmer, Thomas. *An Aunsvvere by the Reuerend Father in God Thomas Archbyshop of Canterbury, primate of all England and metropolitane, vnto a craftie and sophisticall cauillation, deuised by Stephen Gardiner Doctour of Law.* London, 1580.

———. *Catechismus, that is to say, a shorte instruction into Christian religion for the synguler commoditie and profyte of childre[n] and yong people.* London, 1548.

———. *The Miscellaneous Writings and Letters of Thomas Cranmer, Archbishop of Canterbury,* in *The Works of Thomas Cranmer,* vol. 16. Edited by John Edmund Cox. Cambridge, The Parker Society, 1846.

———. *Writings of the Rev. Dr. Thomas Cranmer, Archbishop of Canterbury and Martyr, 1556.* London: The Religious Tract Society, n.d. [1830].

Crawford, Patricia. "Charles Stuart, That Man of Blood." *Journal of British Studies* 16, no. 2 (1977): 41–61.

Cressy, David. *Literacy and Social Order: Reading and Writing in Tudor and Stuart England.* Cambridge: Cambridge University Press, 1980.

Cross, Frank Moore. *The Ancient Library of Qumran and Modern Biblical Studies.* Sheffield: Sheffield Academic Press, 1995; first published 1958.

Crossett, J. "More and Seneca." *Philological Quarterly* 40 (1961): 577–580.

Cullington, J. Donald. "Interpreting Milton's Deviations from the Junius-Tremellius Old Testament in *De Doctrina Christiana.*" *Reformation* 19, no. 1 (2014): 58–68.

———. "The Latin Words for 'Marriage' in *De Doctrina Christiana* Book 1, Chapter 10." *Milton Quarterly* 44, no. 1 (2010): 23–37.

Cummings, Brian. *Mortal Thoughts: Secularity, & Identity in Shakespeare and Early Modern Culture.* Oxford: Oxford University Press, 2013.

———. "Protestant Allegory." *The Cambridge Companion to Allegory.* Edited by Rita Copeland and Peter T. Struck. Cambridge: Cambridge University Press, 2010, 177–190.

———. *The Literary Culture of the Reformation.* Oxford: Oxford University Press, 2002.

———. "William Tyndale and Erasmus on How to Read the Bible: A Newly Discovered Manuscript of the English Enchiridion." *Reformation* 23, no. 1 (2018): 29–52.

Cunningham, Andrew. *The Anatomical Renaissance: The Resurrection of the Anatomical Projects of the Ancients.* Aldershot, UK: Scolar Press, 1997.

Cunnington, J. Donald. "Identifying and Interpreting Milton's deviations from the Junius-Tremellius Old Testament in *De Doctrina Christiana.*" *Reformation* 19, no. 1 (2014): 58–68.

Curtis, Cathy. "'The Best State of the Commonwealth': Thomas More and Quentin Skinner." In *Rethinking the Foundations of Modern Political Thought.* Edited by Holly Hamilton-Bleakley, Annabel Brett, and James Tully, 93–112. Cambridge: Cambridge University Press, 2006.

Curtis, Mark H. "Hampton Court Conference and its Aftermath." *History* 46, no. 156 (1961): 1–16.

Cicero, Marcus Tullius. *Letter to Atticus (Ad Atticum).* 4 vols. Cambridge, MA: Harvard University Press, 2014.

Daniel, Samuel. *The Tragedy of Philotas.* Edited by Laurence Michel, New Haven, CT: Yale University Press, 1949.

Daniell, David. *The Bible in English: Its History and Influence.* New Haven, CT: Yale University Press, 2003.

———. *William Tyndale: A Biography.* New Haven, CT: Yale University Press, 1994.

Danner, Dan G. "Calvin and Puritanism: The Career of William Whittingham." In *Calviniana: Ideas and Influence of Jean Calvin.* Edited by Robert V. Schnucker. Kirksville, MO: Sixteenth Century Journal Publishers, 1988.

———. *Pilgrimage to Puritanism: History and Theology of the Marian Exiles at Geneva, 1555–1560.* New York: Peter Lang, 1999.

———. "The Contribution of the Geneva Bible of 1560 to the English Protestant Tradition." *Sixteenth Century Journal* 12, no. 3 (1981): 5–18.

Dante, Dante Alighieri. *Literary Criticism of Dante Alighieri.* Translated and edited by Robert S. Haller. Lincoln: University of Nebraska Press, 1973.

Darbishire, Helen. *The Early Lives of Milton.* 1932. Reprint, New York: Barnes and Noble, 1965.

Davies, H. S. "Sir John Cheke and the Translation of the Bible." *Essays and Studies by Members of the English Association,* new ser., 5 (1952), 1–12.

Davies, John. *The Scourge of Folly consisting of satyricall epigramms, and others in honor of many noble and worthy persons of our land.* London: 1611.

Davies, Michael. "Converting Henry: Truth, History, and Historical Faith in *Henry VIII.*" In *Shakespeare and Early Modern Religion.* Edited by David Loewenstein and Michael Witmore, 258–279. Cambridge: Cambridge University Press, 2015.

Dawson, J. *John Knox.* New Haven, CT: Yale University Press, 2015.

Dekker, Thomas. *The Whore of Babylon.* London, 1607.

Demaus, Robert. *William Tyndale, A Biography.* London: The Religious Tract Society, 1886.

Dent, Arthur. *The Ruine of Rome. Or, An Exposition vpon the whole Revelation.* London, 1603.

Dessen, Alan C. "Homilies and Anomalies: The Legacy of the Morality Play to the Age of Shakespeare." *Shakespeare Studies* 11 (1978): 243–258.

Devereux, E. J. "Some Lost Translations of Erasmus." *The Library,* 5th Series, 17 (1962): 255–259.

Dobranski, Stephen B. *Milton, Authorship, and the Book Trade.* Cambridge: Cambridge University Press, 1999.

Dodds, Gregory D. "An Accidental Historian: Erasmus and the English History of the Reformation." *Church History*, 82, no. 2 (2013): 273–292.

———. *Exploiting Erasmus: The Erasmian Legacy and Religious Change in Early Modern England.* Toronto: University of Toronto Press, 2009.

Doelman, James. "'A King of Thine Own Heart': The English Reception of King James VI and I's *Basilikon Doron*." *The Seventeenth Century* 9, no. 1 (1994): 1–9.

———. *King James and the Religious Culture of England.* Woodbridge, UK: Brewer, 2000.

Doleman, R. [pseudonym]. *A Conference about the Next Succession to the Crowne of Ingland.* Antwerp?, 1594[5].

Donne, John. *Sermons,* Edited by G. R. Potter and Evelyn Simpson, 10 vols. Berkeley and Los Angeles: University of California Press, 1953–1962.

Downame, George. *A Treatise Concerning Antichrist.* London, 1603

Duffield, Gervase. "The First Psalter Printed in English." *Churchman* 85, no. 4 (1971): 291–293.

Dugdale, Gilbert. *The Time Triumphant Declaring in briefe, the ariual of our soueraigne liedge Lord, King Iames into England.* London, 1604.

Dzelzainis, Martin. "Anti-monarchism in English Republicanism." In *Republicanism and Constitutionalism in Early Modern Europe: A Shared European Heritage.* Edited by Martin van Gelderen and Quentin Skinner. Cambridge: Cambridge University Press, 2005.

———, ed. *Milton: Political Writings.* Cambridge: Cambridge University Press, 1991.

Eden, Kathy. "Equity and the Origins of Renaissance Historicism: The Case for Erasmus." *Yale Journal of Law and the Humanities* 5, no. 1 (1993): 137–45.

———. *Hermeneutics and the Rhetorical Tradition: Chapters in the Ancient Legacy and Its Humanist Reception.* New Haven, CT: Yale University Press, 1997.

Edward VI, King. *King Edward the Sixth on the Supremacy.* Edited by Robert Potts. Cambridge: W. Metcalfe, 1874.

Eells, Hastings. *The Attitude of Martin Bucer toward the Bigamy of Philip of Hesse.* New Haven, CT: Yale University Press, 1924.

Einboden, Jeffrey. "Towards a Judaic Milton: translating *Samson Agonistes* into Hebrew." *Literature and Theology* 22, no. 2 (2008): 135–150.

Ellison, James. "*Measure for Measure* and the Executions of Catholics in 1604." *English Literary Renaissance* 33, no. 1 (2003): 44–87.

Elyot, Thomas. *The Boke Named the Gouernour.* London, 1531.

Emerson, Oliver F. "Legends of Cain, Especially in Old and Middle English." *PMLA* 21, no. 4 (1906): 831–929.

Erasmus, Desiderius. [*A booke called in latyn Enchiridion militis christiani, and in englysshe the manuell of the christen knyght.* London, 1533.

———. *An exhortation to the diligent studye of scripture.* Antwerp, 1529.

———. *Annotationes in Novum Instrumentum.* Basel: Froben, 1516.

———. *Desiderii Erasmi Roterodami Opera Omnia,* Edited by Jean Leclerc, Leiden, 1703–1706. 10 vols. (abbreviated as LB).

———. *Erasmus, Enchiridion Militis Christiani: An English Version.* Edited by Anne M. O'Donnell, Oxford: Oxford University Press, 1981.

———. *Erasmus on His Times, A Shortened Version of the 'Adages' of Erasmus.* Edited by Margaret Mann Phillips. Cambridge: Cambridge University Press, 1980, 1967.

———. *Novum Instrumentum Omne.* Basel: Froben, 1516.

———. *Novum Testamentum Omne.* Basel: Froben, 1519.

————. *Novum Testamentum Omne*. Basel: Froben, 1522.

————. *Novum Testamentum Omne*. Basel: Froben, 1527.

————. *Novum Testamentum Omne*. Basel: Froben, 1535.

————. *On Copia of Words and Ideas*. Translated by Donald B. King and H. David Rix. Milwaukee: Marquette University Press, 1999.

————. *Opera Omnia Des. Erasmi Roterodami* Amsterdam: Elsevier, 1969– (abbreviated as *ASD*).

————. *Opus Epistolarum Des. Erasmi Roterodami*. Edited by P. S. Allen. 11 vols. Oxford: Oxford University Press, 1906–1947.

————. *The Collected Works of Erasmus*. 86 vols. Toronto: University of Toronto Press, 1974– (abbreviated as *CWE*).

————. *The Education of a Christian Prince* with the *Panegyric for Archduke Philip of Austria*. Edited by Lisa Jardine. Cambridge: Cambridge University Press, 1997.

————. *The First Tome or Volume of the Paraphrase of Erasmus vpon the Newe Testament*. 1548.

————. *The Praise of Folly*. Translated and edited by Clarence H. Miller. New Haven, CT: Yale University Press, 1979.

————, and Martin Luther. *Free Will and Salvation*. Edited by E. Gordon Rupp and Philip Watson. Philadelphia, 1979.

Es, Bart van. "The Life of John Dixon, *The Faerie Queene*'s First Annotator." *Notes & Queries* 48, no. 3 (2001): 259–261.

Faulkner, John Alfred. "Luther and the Bigamous Marriage of Philip of Hesse." *The American Journal of Theology* 17, no. 2 (1913): 206–231.

Fehrenbach, R. J., and E. S. Leedham-Green. *Private Libraries in Renaissance England*. 7 vols. Binghamton: Medieval and Renaissance Texts and Studies, 1992– .

Felch, Susan M. "The Rhetoric of Biblical Authority: John Knox and the Question of Women." *The Sixteenth Century Journal* 26, no. 4 (1995): 805–822.

Felch, Susan M., and Clare Costley King'oo, "Reading Tyndale's *Obedience* in Whole and in Part." *Reformation* 21, no. 2 (2016): 86–111.

Ferguson, Jamie. "Faith in the Language: Biblical Authority and the Meaning of English in More-Tyndale Polemics." *Sixteenth Century Journal* 43, no. 4 (2012): 989–1011.

Filmer, Robert. *The Anarchy of a Limited or Mixed Monarchy*. [London], 1648.

Fink, David C. "'The Doers of the Law Will Be Justified': The Exegetical Origins of Martin Bucer's *Triplex Iustificatio*." *Journal of Theological Studies*, NS 58, no. 2 (2007): 485–524.

Firth, John. *A pistle to the Christen reader The Revelation of Antichrist*. At Malborow in the lande of Hesse [i.e., Antwerp], 1529.

Firth, Katharine Robbins. *The Apocalyptic Tradition in Reformation Britain 1530–1645*. Oxford: Oxford University Press, 1979.

Fleck, Andrew. "'To Write of Him and Pardon Crave': Negotiating Biblical Authority in Lanyer's *Salve Deus Rex Judaeorum*." *Journal of Medieval and Early Modern Studies* 47, no. 3 (2017): 545–60.

Fletcher, Harris. *The Use of the Bible in Milton's Prose*. New York: Gordon Press, 1972; first published 1929.

Flicker, Noam. *The Song of Songs in English Renaissance Literature: Kisses of their Mouths*. Cambridge: D. S. Brewer, 2000.

Forsyth, Neil. "Milton's Corrupt Bible," In *The Oxford Handbook of the Bible in Early Modern England, c. 1530–1700*. Edited by Kevin Killeen, Helen Smith, and Rachel Willie. Oxford: Oxford University Press, 2015.

Foster, Brett. "Gregory Martin's 'Holy *Latinate* Jerusalem': Roman English, Romanist values, and the *Rheims New Testament* (1582)." *Prose Studies*, 28, no. 2 (2006): 130–149.

Foster, Leonard. "The Translator of the 'Theatre for Worldlings,'" *English Studies*, 48 (1967): 27–34.

Fotherby, Martin. *Foure sermons, lately preached, by Martin Fotherby Doctor in Diuinity, and chaplain vnto the Kings Maiestie.* London, 1608.

Fox, Adam. "Religion and Popular Literate Culture in England." *Archiv für Reformationsgeschichte* 95, no. 1. (2004): 266–282.

Fox, Edward. *The determinations of the moste famous and mooste excellent vniuersities of Italy and Fraunce, that it is so vnlefull for a man to marie his brothers wyfe, that the pope hath no power to dispence therewith.* London, 1531.

Foxe, John. *An Abridgement of the Booke of Acts and Monumentes of the Church.* London, 1589.

———. *The First (Second) Volume of the Ecclesiasticall History, Contaynyng the Actes and Monumentes of Martyrs.* London, 1570 (a.k.a. *Acts and Monuments*).

Fowler, Alastair. "Oxford and London Marginalia to '*The Faerie Queene*,'" *Notes & Queries*, 206 (1961): 416–419.

Fowler, Alastair, and Michael Leslie, "Drummond's Copy of *The Faerie Queene*." *TLS* (July 17, 1981): 821–822.

French, J. Milton. *Milton in the Chancery: New Chapters in the Lives of the Poet and his Father,* New York: MLA, 1939.

———. "Milton's Family Bible." *PMLA* 53, no. 2 (1938): 363–366.

Frere, Walter Howard, and William Paul McClure Kennedy, eds., *Visitation Articles and Injunctions of the Period of the Reformation: 1536–1558.* London: Longmans, Green & Co., 1910.

Frye, Northrop. *The Great Code: The Bible and Literature.* Toronto: Academic Press Canada, 1982.

———. *Words with Power: Being a Second Study of "the Bible and Literature."* San Diego: Harcourt Brace Jovanovich, 1990.

Fulke, William. *Defense of the Sincere and True Translations of the Holie Scriptures in tho the English Tong.* London, 1583.

———. *An Examination of M. Doctor Whytgiftes Censures.* [London?], 1575.

———. *A Sermon Preached at Hampton Court on Sonday being the 12. day of Nouember, in the yeare of our Lord. 1570. VVherein is plainly proued Babylon to be Rome, both by Scriptures and doctors.* London: 1571.

Fuller, Thomas. *The Church-History of Britain; From the Birth of Jesus Christ unto the Year M. DC.XL.VIII.* London, 1655.

Fulton, Thomas. "English Bibles and their Readers, 1400–1700." *The Journal of Medieval and Early Modern Studies* 47, no. 3 (2017): 415–435.

———. "Edward Phillips and the Manuscript of the 'Digression,'" *Milton Studies* 48 (2008): 95–112.

———. "Toward a New Cultural History of the Geneva Bible," *The Journal of Medieval and Early Modern Studies* 47, no. 3 (2017): 487–516.

———. *Historical Milton: Manuscript, Print, and Political Culture in Revolutionary England.* Amherst: University of Massachusetts Press, 2010.

———. "Political Theology from the Pulpit and the Shakespearean Stage: *Sir Thomas More, Richard II*, and *Henry V.*" In *The Bible on the Shakespearean Stage: Cultures of Interpretation in Reformation England*, edited by Thomas Fulton and Kristen Poole, 204–221. Cambridge: Cambridge University Press, 2018.

———. "Sara J. van den Berg and W. Scott Howard, eds., *The Divorce Tracts of John Milton: Texts and Contexts*." *Milton Quarterly* 46, no. 3 (2012): 196–199.

Fulton, Thomas, and Kristen Poole. "Popular Hermeneutics in Shakespeare's London," In *The Bible on the Shakespearean Stage: Cultures of Interpretation in Reformation England*. Edited by Thomas Fulton and Kristen Poole, 1–16. Cambridge: Cambridge University Press, 2018.

Fulton, Thomas, and Jeremy Specland, "The Elizabethan Catholic New Testament and Its Readers." *Journal of Early Modern Christianity* 6, no. 2 (2019): 251–275.

Furniss, Tom. "Reading the Geneva Bible: Notes toward an English Revolution?" *Prose Studies* 31, no. 1 (2009): 1–21.

Galbraith, Steven K. "'English' Black-Letter Type and Spenser's *Shepheardes Calender*." *Spenser Studies* 23 (2008): 13–40.

Gardiner, Samuel R., ed., *Reports of Cases in the Courts of Star Chamber and Hight Commission*. Westminster: Printed for the Camden Society, 1886.

———. *History of the Great Civil War*. London: Longmans, Green, and Co.: 1891.

Gates, Charles O. *Latin World-building: Root Words with Their More Common Derivatives and Their Meanings Illustrated by Sentences Taken from Caesar and Cicero*. New York: D. Appleton and Company, 1887.

Gayangos, Pascual de, ed. *Calendar of Letters, Dispatches, and State Papers, relating to the Negotiations between England and Spain, preserved in the Archives at Simancas and Elsewhere*. London: Longman, Green, Longman, & Roberts [etc.] 1862–19. 13 vols.

Genette, Gérard. *Paratexts: Thresholds of Interpretation*. Translated by Jane Lewin. Cambridge: Cambridge University Press, 1997.

Gentles, Ian. *The New Model Army in England, Ireland and Scotland, 1645–1653*. Oxford: Blackwell, 1992.

Gilby, Anthony. *An Admonition to England and Scotland to call them to repentance*. Geneva, 1558.

———. *An ansvver to the deuillish detection of Stephane Gardiner, Bishoppe of Wynchester*. London, 1548.

———. *A Briefe Treatice of Election, and Reprobation*. London, 1575.

———. *A Commentarye vpon the Prophet Mycha*. London, 1551.

———. [*A Commentarye upon the Prophet Malaky*.] [London, 1553?]

Gilman, Ernest B. *Iconoclasm and Poetry in the English Reformation: Down Went Dagon*. Chicago: University of Chicago Press, 1986.

Ginsburg, Carlo. *History, Rhetoric, and Proof*. Hanover: University Press of New England, 1999.

Gleason, John B. *John Colet*. Berkeley: University of California Press, 1989.

Goldberg, Jonathan. *James I and the Politics of Literature*. Baltimore: Johns Hopkins University Press, 1983.

Goodman, Christopher. *How Superior Powers Oght to be Obeyd of their subjects: and Wherin they may lawfully by Gods Worde be disobeyed and resisted*. Geneva: John Crispin, 1558.

Gordon, Bruce. "Bibliander's Oration on Isaiah and Commentary on Natum." In *Shaping the Bible in the Reformation: Books, Scholars, and their Readers in the Sixteenth Century*. Edited by Gordon and Matthew McLean, 107–141. Leiden: Brill, 2012.

———. "The Authority of Antiquity: England and the Protestant Latin Bible." In *The Reception of Continental Reformation in Britain*, edited by Polly Ha and Patrick Collinson. Oxford: Oxford University Press for the British Academy, 2010.

———. "The Bible in Transition in the Age of Shakespeare: A European Perspective." In *The Bible on the Shakespearean Stage: Cultures of Interpretation in Reformation England*. Edited by Thomas Fulton and Kristen Poole, 17–32. Cambridge: Cambridge University Press, 2018.

———. "Fagius, Paul," *Oxford Dictionary of National Biography* (2004).

Grafton, Anthony. *Forgers and Critics: Creativity and Duplicity in Western Scholarship*. London: Collins and Brown, 1990.

———. "Some Early Citizens of the *Respublica Litterarum Sacrarum*: Christian Scholars and the Masora before 1550." *Reformation* 23, no. 1 (2018): 6–28.

Grafton, Anthony, and Lisa Jardine. "'Studied for Action': How Gabriel Harvey Read his Livy." *Past and Present* 129, no. 1 (1990): 30–78.

Greaves, Richard L. "The Nature and Intellectual Milieu of the Political Principals in the Geneva Bible Marginalia." *Journal of Church and State* 22, no. 2 (1980): 233–249.

———. "Traditionalism and the Seeds of Revolution in the Social Principles of the Geneva Bible." *Sixteenth Century Journal* 7, no. 1 (1976): 94–109.

Green, Ian. *The Christian's ABC*. Oxford: Oxford University Press, 1996.

Greenblatt, Stephen. *Renaissance Self-Fashioning from More to Shakespeare*. Chicago: University of Chicago Press, 1980.

Greschat, Martin. *Martin Bucer: A Reformer and His Times*. Translated by S. E. Buchwalter [translated from M. Greschat, *Martin Bucer: Ein Reformator und seine Zeit* (München, 1990)]. Louisville: Westminster John Knox Press, 2004.

Griffiths, John, ed., *The Two Books of Homilies Appointed to be Read in Churches*. Oxford: Oxford University Press, 1859.

Groves, Beatrice. "England's Jerusalem in Shakespeare's Henriad." In *The Bible on the Shakespearean Stage*. Edited by Thomas Fulton and Kristen Poole, 87–102. Cambridge: Cambridge University Press, 2018.

———. "Shakespeare's Sonnets and the Genevan Marginalia." *Essays in Criticism* 57, no. 2 (2007): 114–128.

Guibbory, Achsah. "Charles's Prayers, Idolatrous Images, and True Creation in Milton's *Eikonoklastes*." In *Of Poetry and Politics: New Essays on Milton and His World*. Edited by P. G. Stanwood, 283–294. Binghamton: Medieval and Renaissance Texts and Studies, 1995.

———. *Christian Identity, Jews, and Israel in Seventeenth-Century England*. Oxford: Oxford University Press, 2010.

Habermas, Jürgen. *Legitimation Crisis*. Translated by Thomas McCarthy. Boston: Beacon Press, 1975.

Hackel, Heidi Brayman, *Reading Material in Early Modern England: Print, Gender and Literacy*. Cambridge: Cambridge University Press, 2005.

Hadfield, Andrew. *Edmund Spenser: A Life*. Oxford: Oxford University Press, 2012.

———. *Shakespeare and Republicanism*. Cambridge and New York: Cambridge University Press, 2005.

Haigh, Christopher. *English Reformations: Religion, Politics and Society under the Tudors* Oxford: Oxford University Press, 1993.

Halkin, Lèon E. *Erasmus: A Critical Biography*. Translated by John Tonkin. Oxford: Blackwell, 1992.

Hall, Basil. "The Genevan Version of the English Bible: Its Aims and Achievements," In *The Bible, the Reformation, and the Church: Essays in Honour of James Atkinson*. Edited by W. P. Stephens, 124–149. Sheffield, South Yorkshire: Sheffield Academic Press, 1995.

Hankins, John. *Source and Meaning in Spenser's Allegory: A Study of* The Faerie Queene. Oxford: Clarendon Press, 1971.

Hamel, Christopher de. *Meetings with Remarkable Manuscripts.* London: Allen Lane, 2016.

Hamilton, A. C. *The Spenser Encyclopedia.* Toronto: University of Toronto Press, 1997.

Hamilton, Donna. *Shakespeare and the Politics of Protestant England.* Lexington: University of Kentucky Press, 1992.

Hamlin, Hannibal. *Psalm Culture and Early Modern English Literature.* Cambridge: Cambridge University Press, 2004.

———. *The Bible in Shakespeare.* Oxford: Oxford University Press, 2013.

Hammill, Graham. *The Mosaic Constitution: Political Theology and Imagination from Machiavelli to Milton.* Chicago: University of Chicago Press, 2012.

Hammill, Graham, and Julia Reinhard Lupton, eds. *Political Theology and Early Modernity* Chicago: University of Chicago Press, 2012.

Hammond, Gerald, and Austin Bush, eds. *The New Testament and The Apocrypha,* vol. two of *The English Bible.* New York: Norton, 2012.

Happé, Peter, and Wim Hüskin, eds. *Staging Scripture: Biblical Drama 1350–1600.* Leiden and Boston: Brill, 2016.

Hardie-Forsyth, Alexander. "Towards a Marginal History of Reading the Geneva Bible." *FORUM: University of Edinburgh Postgraduate Journal of Culture & the Arts* 23 (2016): 1–16.

Harding, J. D. "Authorial and Editorial Influence on Luxury Bookbinding Styles in Sixteenth-Century England." In *Tudor Books and Readers.* Edited by John N. King, 116–137. Cambridge: Cambridge University Press, 2010.

Harington, John. *The Epigrams of Sir John Harington.* Edited by Gerard Kilroy. New York: Routledge, 2016.

Harris, John W. "'Written in the Margent': Shakespeare's Metaphor of the Geneva Bible Marginal Notes." *Notes and Queries* 64, no. 2 (2017): 301–304.

Harrison, Peter. *The Bible, Protestantism, and the Rise of Natural Science.* Cambridge: Cambridge University Press, 1998.

Haskin, Dayton. *Milton's Burden of Interpretation.* Philadelphia: University of Pennsylvania Press, 1994.

Hattaway, Michael. "Marginalia By Henry VIII in His Copy of *The Bokes of Salomon.*" *Transactions of the Cambridge Bibliographical Society* 4, no. 2 (1965): 166–170.

Healey, Robert M. et al. "Waiting for Deborah: John Knox and Four Ruling Queens." *The Sixteenth Century Journal* 25, no. 2 (1994): 371–386.

Hendrix, Scott H. "Luther Against the Background of Biblical Interpretation." *Interpretation* 37, no. 3 (1983): 229–239.

Henry VIII, King. *A Copy of the Letters, wherin the most redouted [and] mighty pri[n]ce, our souerayne lorde kyng Henry the eight . . . made answere vnto a certayne letter of Martyn Luther, sente vnto him by the same* [London], 1527.

Herbert, A. S., T. H. Darlow and H. F. Moule. *Historical Catalogue of Printed Editions of the English Bible 1525–1961.* London: British and Foreign Bible Society, 1968.

Herman, Peter. *Destabilizing Milton:* Paradise Lost *and the Poetics of Incertitude.* New York: Palgrave McMillan, 2005.

Heywood, Thomas. *Apology for Actors.* 1612.

Hiatt, Alfred. *The Making of Medieval Forgeries: False Documents in Fifteenth-Century England.* London: British Library, 2003.

Hill, Christopher. *Antichrist in Seventeenth-Century England.* Oxford: Oxford University Press, 1971.

———. *Intellectual Origins of the English Revolution Revisited.* Oxford: Oxford University Press, 1997; first published in 1965.

———. *Milton and the English Revolution.* London: Faber and Faber, 1977.

———. *The English Bible and the Seventeenth-Century Revolution.* 1993. Reprint, New York: Penguin, 1994.

Hobbes, Thomas. *Behemoth: A History of the Causes of the Civil Wars of* England. In *Tracts of Mr. Thomas Hobbs of Malmsbury.* London, 1682.

———. *Leviathan.* Edited by Richard Tuck. Cambridge: Cambridge University Press, 1996.

Hobbes, Thomas. *The History of the Civil Wars of England* [*Behemoth*]. London, 1679.

Hoffmann, Manfred. *Rhetoric and Theology: The Hermeneutic of Erasmus.* Toronto: Toronto University Press, 1994.

Holinshed, Raphael. *The Third Volume of Chronicles, Beginning at Duke William the Norman* London, 1586.

Hooker, Richard. *Of the Laws of Ecclesiastical Polity.* Edited by Georges Edelen. 3 vols. Cambridge, MA: Harvard University Press, 1977.

Hope, Andrew. "The Antwerp Origins of the Coverdale Bible: Investigations from the 1884 Athenaeum Controversy to the Present Day." In *Tyndale's Testament.* Edited by Paul Arblaster, Gergely Juhász, and Guido Latré, 39–54. Turnhout: Brepols, 2002.

Höpfl, Harro, ed. *Luther and Calvin On Secular Authority.* Cambridge: Cambridge University Press, 1991.

Hough, Graham. *The First Commentary on the Faerie Queene: being an analysis of the annotations in Lord Bessborough's copy of the first edition of the Faerie Queene.* Privately printed, 1964.

Hughes, Philip Edgcumbe. "Preaching, Homilies, and Prophesyings in Sixteenth Century England." *The Churchman* 89, no. 1 (1975): 7–32.

Hunt, Maurice. *Shakespeare's Religious Allusiveness: Its Play and Tolerance.* Hampshire: Ashgate, 2004.

Hunter, G. K. "The Theology of Marlowe's *The Jew of Malta.*" *Journal of the Warburg and Courtauld Institutes* 27 (1964): 211–240.

Hunter, William B. "Milton Translates the Psalms." *Philological Quarterly* 40, no. 4 (1961): 485–494.

———. "The Sources of Milton's Prosody." *Philological Quarterly* 28 (1949): 125–144.

Jackson, W. A. ed. *Records of the Court of the Stationers' Company 1602 to 1640.* London: The Bibliographical Society, 1957.

Jeffs, Robin. ed. *Fast Sermons to Parliament.* 34 vols. London: Cornmarket Press, 1970–71.

James VI and I. *Basilikon Doron.* London, 1603.

———. *Political Writings.* Edited by Johann P. Sommerville. Cambridge: Cambridge University Press, 1994.

———. *True Lawe of Free Monarchies.* London, 1603.

Jardine, Lisa. *Erasmus, Man of Letters: The Construction of Charisma in Print.* Princeton, NJ: Princeton University Press, 1993.

Jardine, Lisa, and Anthony Grafton. "'Studied for Action': How Gabriel Harvey Read his Livy." *Past and Present* 129, no. 1 (November 1990): 30–78.

Jarrott, Catherine A. L. "Erasmus' Annotations and Colet's Commentaries on Paul: A Comparison of Some Theological Themes." In *Essays on the Works of Erasmus.* Edited by Richard L. DeMolen, 125–144. New Haven: Yale University Press, 1978.

———. "Erasmus' Biblical Humanism." *Studies in the Renaissance* 17 (1970): 351–382.

Jenkins, Allan K., and Patrick Preston. *Biblical Scholarship and the Church: A Sixteenth-Century Crisis of Authority*. Aldershot, UK: Ashgate, 2007.

Jewel, John. *The Works of John Jewel*. 4 vols. Cambridge: Cambridge University Press, 1849.

Johnson, Dale Walden. "Marginal at Best: John Knox's Contribution to the Geneva Bible, 1560." In *Adaptations of Calvinism in Reformation Europe: Essays in Honour of Brian G. Armstrong*. Edited by Mack P. Holt, 241–248. Aldershot, UK: Ashgate, 2007.

Jonge, H. J. de. "The Relationship of Erasmus' Translation of the New Testament to that of the Pauline Epistles by Lefèvre d'Étaples." In *Erasmus in English* 15 (1987–1988): 2–7.

Jonson, Ben. *Sejanus, His Fall*. Edited by Philip J. Ayers. Manchester: University of Manchester Press, 1990.

Juhàsz, Gergely. "Antwerp Bible translations in the King James Bible." In *The King James Bible after 400 Years: Literary, Linguistic, and Cultural Influences*, 110–112. Cambridge: Cambridge University Press, 2011.

———. *Translating Resurrection: The Debate between William Tyndale and George Joye and Its Historical and Theological Context*. Leiden: Brill, 2014.

Junker, William. "The Image of Both Theaters: Empire and Revelation in Shakespeare's *Antony and Cleopatra*." *Shakespeare Quarterly* 66, no. 2 (2015): 167–187.

Kahn, Victoria. *The Future of Illusion: Political Theology and Early Modern Texts*. Chicago: University of Chicago Press, 2013.

———. *Wayward Contracts: The Crisis of Political Obligation in England, 1640–1674*. Princeton, NJ: Princeton University Press, 2004.

Kampen, Kimberly van. "Do We Really Have the Translator's Notes for the 1560 Geneva Bible?" *Analytical and Enumerative Bibliography* 11, no. 4 (2000): 290–302.

Kastan, David Scott. *A Will to Believe: Shakespeare and Religion*. Oxford: Oxford University Press, 2014.

———. "'The Noyse of the New Bible': Reform and Reaction in Henrician England." In *Religion and Culture in Renaissance England*, 56–62. Cambridge: Cambridge University Press, 1997.

Kaufman, Peter Iver. *Augustinian Piety and Catholic Reform: Augustine, Colet, and Erasmus*. Macon, GA: Mercer University Press, 1982.

Kaulen, Franz. *Geschicte Der Vulgata*. Franz Kirchheim: Mainz, 1868.

Kearney, James. "Reformed Ventriloquism: *The Shepheardes Calender* and the Craft of Commentary." *Spenser Studies* 26 (2011): 111–151.

———. *The Incarnate Text: Imagining the Book in Reformation England*. Philadelphia: University of Pennsylvania Press, 2009.

Keeble, N. H., and Nicholas McDowell, eds. *The Complete Works of John Milton. Volume VI: Vernacular Regicide and Republican Tracts*. Oxford: Clarendon Press, 2011.

Kellar, Clare. *Scotland, England, and the Reformation, 1534–1561*. Oxford: Oxford University Press, 2003.

Kelley, Donald R. "Ideas of Resistance before Elizabeth." In *The Historical Renaissance*, edited by Heather Dubrow and Richard Strier, 48–76. Chicago: University of Chicago Press, 1988.

Kelsey, Sean. "The Death of Charles I," *Historical Journal* 45, no. 4 (2002): 727–754.

Kermode, Frank. *The Genesis of Secrecy: On the Interpretation of Narrative*. Cambridge, MA: Harvard University Press, 1979.

Kernan, Alvin. *Shakespeare, the King's Playwright: Theatre in the Stuart Court 1603–1613*. New Haven, CT: Yale University Press, 1995.

Killeen, Kevin. *The Political Bible in Early Modern England*. Cambridge: Cambridge University Press, 2017.

King, John. *English Reformation Literature: The Tudor Origins of the Protestant Tradition*. Princeton, NJ: Princeton University Press, 1982.

———. "Henry VIII as David: The Kings Image and Reformation politics." In *Rethinking the Henrician Era: Essays on Early Tudor Texts and Contexts*. Edited by Peter Herman, 78–92. Urbana: University of Illinois Press, 1994.

———. *Spenser's Poetry and the Reformation Tradition*. Princeton, NJ: Princeton University Press, 1990.

———. *Tudor Royal Iconography: Literature and Art in an Age of Religious Crisis*. Princeton, NJ: Princeton University Press, 1989.

King, John, and Aaron Pratt, "Bibles as Books: The Materiality of English Printed Bibles from the Tyndale New Testament to the King James Bible." In *The King James Bible after 400 Years: Literary, Linguistic, and Cultural Influences*. Edited by Hannibal Hamlin and Norman W. Jones, 61–99. Cambridge: Cambridge University Press, 2010.

King'oo, Clare Costley. *Miserere Mei: The Penitential Psalms in Late Medieval and Early Modern England*. Notre Dame: University of Notre Dame Press, 2012.

Kirby, W. J. Torrance. *Richard Hooker's Doctrine of the Royal Supremacy*. Leiden: Brill, 1990.

———. *The Zurich Connection and Tudor Political Theology*. Leiden: Brill, 2007.

Knapp, Jeffrey. *Shakespeare's Tribe: Church, Nation, and Theater in Renaissance England*. Chicago: Chicago University Press, 2002.

Knoppers, Laura Lunger. "(En)gendering Shame: *Measure for Measure* and the Spectacles of Power." *English Literary Renaissance* 23, no. 3 (1993): 450–471.

Knox, John. *The Appellation of John Knoxe from the cruell and most iniust sentence pronounced against him by the false bishoppes and clergie of Scotland*. Geneva, 1558.

———. *The Historie of the Reformation of the Church of Scotland Containing Five Books*. London, 1644.

Kroeker, Greta Grace. *Erasmus in the Footsteps of Paul: A Pauline Theologian*. Toronto: University of Toronto Press, 2011.

Kroon, Marijn de. "Martin Bucer and the Problem of Tolerance." *The Sixteenth Century Journal* 19, no. 2 (1988): 157–168.

Lake, Peter. *Anglicans and Puritans? Presbyterianism and English Conformist Thought from Whitgift to Hooker*. London: Unwin Hyman, 1988.

———. *Moderate Puritans and the Elizabethan Church*. Cambridge: Cambridge University Press, 1982.

Lake, Peter, and Michael Questier. *The Antichrist's Lewd Hat: Protestants, Papists and Players in Post-Reformation England*. New Haven, CT: Yale University Press, 2002.

Lambert, D. H. *Shakespeare Documents*. London: George Bell, 1904.

Lamont, William M. *Marginal Prynne, 1600–1669*. London: Routledge & K. Paul, 1963.

Lander, Jesse. "Maimed Rites and Whirling Words in *Hamlet*." In *The Bible on the Shakespearean Stage: Cultures of Interpretation in Reformation England*. Edited by Thomas Fulton and Kristen Poole, 188–203. Cambridge: Cambridge University Press, 2018.

Latimer, Hugh. *Selected Sermons of Hugh Latimer*. Edited by Allan G. Chester. Charlottesville: University Press of Virginia, 1968.

———. *The fyrste Sermon of Mayster Hughe Latimer, whiche he preached before the Kinges Maiest[y] wythin his graces palayce at Westminster*. M.D.XLIX. the. viii. of March. London, 1549.

Lausberg, Heinrich. *Handbook of Literary Rhetoric: A Foundation of Literary Study*. Edited by David E. Orton and R. Dean Anderson; translated by Matthew T. Bliss, Annemiek Jansen, and David E. Orton; and Foreword by George A. Kennedy. Leiden: Brill, 1998.

Lawes, Henry. *Choice Psalmes put into Music*. Printed by James Young, for Humphrey Moseley, 1648.

Lefèvre, Jacques. *Epistolae Viri Pauli Apostoli: cum Commentariis Preclarissimi Viri Jacobi Fabri Stapulen*. Paris, 1517.

Leggatt, Alexander. "Substitution in *Measure for Measure*." *Shakespeare Quarterly* 39, no. 3 (1988): 342–359.

Lehmberg, Stanford E. "Archbishop Grindal and the Prophesyings." *Historical Magazine of the Protestant Episcopal Church* 34, no. 2 (1965): 87–145.

Lesse, Nicolas. *The censure and judgement of the famous clark Erasmus of Roterodam; whyther dyvorcemente betwene man and wyfe stondeth with the lawe of god*. London, 1550.

Lever, J. W. "The Date of *Measure for Measure*." *Shakespeare Quarterly* 10, no. 3 (1959): 381–388.

Lewalski, Barbara. "Biblical Allusion and Allegory in *The Merchant of Venice*." In *Twentieth Century Interpretations of* The Merchant of Venice: *A Collection of Critical Essays*. Edited by Sylvan Barnet, 33–54. Englewood Cliffs, NJ: Prentice-Hall, 1970.

———. *Protestant Poetics and the Seventeenth-Century Religious Lyric*. Princeton, NJ: Princeton University Press, 1979.

———. *The Life of Milton: A Critical Biography*. Oxford and Malden, MA: Blackwell, 2000.

Lezra, Jacques. "Pirating Reading: The Appearance of History in *Measure for Measure*." *English Literary History* 56, no. 2 (1989): 255–292.

Lim, Walter S. H. *John Milton, Radical Politics, and Biblical Republicanism*. Newark: University of Delaware Press, 2006.

Lin, Erika T. "A Witch in the Morris: Hobbyhorse Tricks and Early Modern Erotic Transformations." In *The Oxford Handbook of Dance and Theater*, edited by Nadine George-Graves. Oxford and New York: Oxford University Press, 2015.

———. "Festivity." In *Early Modern Theatricality*, edited by Henry S. Turner, 212–229. New York: Oxford University Press, 2013.

Lock, Anne Vaughan. *The Collected Works of Anne Vaughan Lock*. Edited by Susan M. Felch. Tempe: Arizona Center for Medieval and Renaissance Studies, 1999.

Locke, John. *A Paraphrase and Notes on the Epistles of St Paul*. London, 1671.

Loewenstein, David. "Milton and the Creation of England's Long Reformation." *Reformation* 24, no. 2 (2019): 165–180.

Loewenstein, David, and James Grantham Turner, eds. *Politics, Poetics, and Hermeneutics in Milton's Prose*. Cambridge: Cambridge University Press, 1990.

Loewenstein, David, and Michael Witmore, eds., *Shakespeare and Early Modern Religion*. Cambridge: Cambridge University Press, 2015.

Loewenstein, Joseph. *The Author's Due: Printing and the Prehistory of Copyright*. Chicago: University of Chicago Press, 2002.

Luders, Alexander et al., eds. *The Statutes of the Realm* (1225–1713). 11 vols. London: G. Eyre and A. Strahan, 1810–1828.

Lugioyo, Brian. *Martin Bucer's Doctrine of Justification: Reformation Theology and Early Modern Irenicism*. Oxford: Oxford University Press, 2010.

Lupton, Julia Reinhard. *Citizen-Saints: Shakespeare and Political Theology*. Chicago: University of Chicago Press, 2005.

Lupton, Lewis. *History of the Geneva Bible*. 25 vols. London: Olive Tree, 1966–1994.

Luther, Martin. *Luther's Correspondence and Other Contemporary Letters.* 2 vols. Translated and edited by Preserved Smith. Philadelphia, 1913.

———. *Works of Martin Luther.* 6 vols. Edited by Henry Jacobs. Philadelphia: A. J. Holman, 1915.

Luxon, Thomas H. *Literal Figures: Puritan Allegory and the Reformation Crisis in Representation.* Chicago: University of Chicago Press, 1995.

MacCallum, Hugh. "Milton and Figurative Interpretation of the Bible." *The University of Toronto Quarterly* 35 (1962): 397–415; republished in *Milton and Questions of History*, edited by Feisal G. Mohamed and Mary Nyquist, 62–81. Toronto: University of Toronto Press, 2012.

MacCulloch, Diarmaid. *Thomas Cranmer: A Life.* New Haven: Yale University Press, 1996.

———. *Tudor Church Militant: Edward VI and the Protestant Reformation.* London: Penguin Press, 1999.

Mallette, Richard. *Spenser and the Discourses of Reformation England.* Lincoln: University of Nebraska Press, 1997.

Maltzahn, Nicholas von. "Making use of the Jews: Milton and Philosemitism." In *Milton and the Jews*, edited by Douglas Bush, 57–82. Cambridge: Cambridge University Press, 2008.

Manning, John. "Notes and Marginalia in Bishop Percy's Copy of Spenser's *Works* (1611)." *N&Q* 229 (1984): 225–227.

Marius, Richard. *Martin Luther: The Christian between God and Death.* Cambridge, MA: Harvard University Press, 1999.

Martin, Catherine Gimelli. *The Ruins of Allegory: Paradise Lost and the Metamorphosis of Epic Convention.* Durham, NC: Duke University Press, 1998.

Martin, Gregory. *Discoverie of the Manifold Corruptions of the Holy Scripture by the Heretikes of Our Daies.* Rheims: John Fogny, 1582.

Masson, David. *The Life of John Milton.* 7 vols. Cambridge and London: Macmillan, 1859–1894.

May, Steven W. "Anne Lock and Thomas Norton's *Meditation of a Penitent Sinner.*" *Modern Philology* 114, no. 4 (2017): 793–819.

McConica, James. *English Humanists and Reformation Politics under Henry VIII and Edward VI.* Oxford: Clarendon Press, 1965.

McCullough, Peter. "Andrewes and Donne: Using Bibles in the Age of Translation." In *Lambeth Palace Library Annual Review* (2011): 66–88.

McDermott, Ryan. "The Ordinary Gloss on Jonah." *PMLA* 128, no. 2 (2013): 424–438.

———. *Tropologies: Ethics and Invention in England, c. 1350–1600.* South Bend, IN: Notre Dame Press, 2016.

McDiarmid, John F. "The Defense of Tyndale, 1528–1533." *Shakespeare and Renaissance Association of West Virginia: Select Papers* 9 (1984): 56–68.

———. "*The Practice of Prelates*: Tyndale's Papal Narrative and Its German Model." *Reformation* 9, no. 1 (2004): 25–48.

McDonald, Grantley. *Biblical Criticism in Early Modern Europe: Erasmus, the Johannine Comma and Trinitarian Debate.* Cambridge: Cambridge University Press, 2016.

———. "Erasmus and the Johannine Comma (1 John 5: 7–8)." *The Bible Translator* 67 (2016): 42–55.

McDowell, Nicholas. *The English Radical Imagination: Culture, Religion, and Revolution, 1630–1660.* Oxford: Oxford University Press, 2003.

———. *The Tenure of Kings and Magistrates* in *The Complete Works of John Milton.* Volume VI: *Vernacular Regicide and Republican Tracts.* Edited by N. H. Keeble and Nicholas McDowell, Introduction by Nicholas McDowell. Oxford: Clarendon Press, 2011.

McDowell, Nicholas, and Nigel Smith, eds. *The Oxford Handbook of Milton*. Oxford: Oxford University Press, 2009.

McGrath, Alister. *In the Beginning: The Story of the King James Bible and How It Changed a Nation, a Language, and a Culture*. London: Hodder and Stoughton, 2011.

McLaren, Ann. "Rethinking Republicanism: *Vindiciae, Contra Tyrannos* in Context." *The Historical Journal* 49, no. 1 (2006): 23–52.

McMillin, Scott. *The Elizabethan Theatre and The Book of Sir Thomas More*. Ithaca, NY: Cornell University Press, 1987.

Melanchthon, Philip. *Historia de vita et actis Lutheri*. Witebergae: Johannis Lufft, 1549.

———. *A famous and godly history contaynyng the Lyues & Actes of three renowmed reformers of the Christian Church, Martine Luther*. Translated by Henry Bennet. London, 1561.

Melehy, Hassan. "Spenser and Du Bellay: Translation, Imitation, Ruin." *Comparative Literature Studies* 40, no. 4 (2003): 415–438.

Mandelbrote, Scott. "'Bondage in Babylon': The Bible, Freedom of Conscience, and Ideas of Civil Liberty in England, c. 1640–c. 1750." In *Hebraistik—Hermeneutik—Homiletik. Die Philologia Sacra im frühneuzeitlichen Bibelstudium*. Edited by C. Bultmann and L. Danneberg. Berlin: W. de Gruyter, 2011.

Metzger, Bruce M., and Bart D. Ehrman. *The Text of the New Testament: Its Transmission, Corruption, and Restoration*, 4th ed. Oxford: Oxford University Press, 2005.

Metzger, Bruce M., and Roland E. Murphy, eds. *The New Oxford Annotated Bible*. New York: Oxford University Press, 1991.

Miller, Jeffrey Alan. "'Better, as in the Geneva': The Role of the Geneva Bible in Drafting the King James Version." *Journal of Medieval and Early Modern Studies* 47, no. 3 (2017): 517–543.

———. "The Earliest Known Draft of the King James Bible: Samuel Ward's Draft of 1 Esdras and Wisdom 3–4." In *Labourers in the Vineyard of the Lord: Scholarship and the Making of the King James Version of the Bible*. Edited by Mordechai Feingold, 187–265. Leiden: Brill, 2018.

———. *Signifying Shadows: Early Modern Typology, Milton, and the Writer's Mind at Work*, forthcoming.

Milton, Anthony. *Catholic and Reformed: The Roman and Protestant Churches in English Protestant Thought, 1600–1640*. Cambridge: Cambridge University Press: 1995.

Milton, John. *Areopagitica*. London. 1644.

———. *Complete Prose Works of John Milton*. 8 vols. Edited by Don M. Wolfe et al. New Haven: Yale University Press, 1953–1982 (abbreviated as *CPW*).

———. *The Complete Poetry and Essential Prose of John Milton*, edited by William Kerrigan, John Rumrich, and Stephen M. Fallon. New York: Modern Library, 2007.

———. *Complete Shorter Poems*, second edition, edited by John Carey. London: Longman, 1997.

———. *De Doctrina Christiana*. In *The Complete Works of John Milton*, edited and translated by J. K. Hale and J. D. Cullington, vol 8, part 1. Oxford: Oxford University Press: 2012.

———. *The Divorce Tracts of John Milton: Texts and Contexts*. Edited by Sara J. van den Berg and W. Scott Howard. Pittsburg: Duquesne University Press, 2010.

———. *The Doctrine and Discipline of Divorce*. London, 1643.

———. *The Doctrine and Discipline of Divorce*. London, 1644.

———. *Eikonoklastes in Answer to a Book intitl'd Eikon basilike*. London: 1649.

———. *Epistolae Familiares*. London, 1674.

———. *Joannis Miltonii Angli De doctrina christiana*. Edited by C. R. Sumner. Cantabrigiae [Cambridge]: Typis Academicis, 1825.

————. *John Milton: Complete Poems and Major Prose*. Edited by Merritt Hughes. New York: Macmillan, 1957.

————. *John Milton's Complete Poetical Works Reproduced in Photographic Facsimile*. Edited by Harris Fletcher, 4 vols. Urbana: University of Illinois Press, 1943.

————. *Judgement of Martin Bucer, concerning Divorce*. London, 1644.

————. *Paradise Lost, The Biblically Annotated Edition*. Edited by Matthew Stallard. Macon: Mercer University Press, 2011.

————. *Poems, &c. upon Several Occasions*. London, 1673.

————. *The Shorter Poems*. Edited by Barbara Kiefer Lewalski and Estelle Haan. *The Complete Works of John Milton*, vol. 3. Oxford: Oxford University Press, 2012.

————. *Tetrachordon*. London, 1645.

————. *Treatise of Civil Power*. London, 1659.

————. *Vernacular Regicide and Republican Writings*. Edited by N. Keeble and N. McDowell. *The Complete Works of John Milton*, vol. 6. Oxford: Oxford University Press, 2013.

————. *The Works of John Milton*. 18 vols. Edited by Frank Allen Patterson et al. New York: Columbia University Press, 1931–1938.

Minnis, Alastair. *Medieval Theory of Authorship: Scholastic Literary Attitudes in the Later Middle Ages*. Philadelphia: University of Pennsylvania Press, 2011; revised ed; first edition 1984.

Molekamp, Femke. "Genevan Legacies: The Making of the English Geneva Bible." In *The Oxford Handbook of the Bible in Early Modern England, c. 1530–1700*. Edited by Kevin Killeen, Helen Smith, and Rachel Willie, 38–53. Oxford: Oxford University Press, 2015.

————. "Using a Collection to Discover Reading Practices: The British Library Geneva Bibles and a History of their Early Modern Readers." *eBLJ* 10 (2006): 1–13. http://www.bl.uk/eblj /2006articles/article10.html.

Monta, Susannah Brietz. *A Fig for Fortune by Anthony Copley: A Catholic Response to* The Faerie Queene. Manchester: Manchester University Press, 2016.

Montefusco, Lucia Calboli. "*Ductus* and *Color*: The Right Way to Compose a Suitable Speech." *Rhetorica* 21, no. 2 (2003): 113–132.

Monnas, Lisa. *Renaissance Velvets*. London: V&A Publishers, 2012.

Moore, S. D., and Y. Sherwood, "Biblical Studies 'after' Theory: Onwards Towards the Past. Part One: After 'after Theory', and Other Apocalyptic Conceits." *Biblical Interpretation* 18, no. 1 (2010): 1–27.

More, Thomas. *Correspondence of Thomas More*. Edited by E. Rogers. Princeton: Princeton University Press, 1947.

————. *The Complete Works of St. Thomas More*. Vol. 2, *Richard III*. Edited by Richard S. Sylvester. 16 vols. New Haven: Yale University Press, 1963.

————. *The Complete Works of St. Thomas More*. Vol. 3, part 2. *Latin Poems*. Edited by Clarence Miller, Leicester Bradner, Charles A. Lynch, and Revilo P. Oliver. New Haven: Yale University Press, 1984.

————. *The Complete Works of St. Thomas More*. Vol. 4, *Utopia*. Edited by Edward Surtz and J. H. Hexter. 16 vols. New Haven: Yale University Press, 1965.

————. *The co[n]futacyon of Tyndales answere made by syr Thomas More knyght lorde chau[n]cellour of Englonde*. London, 1532.

Morison, Richard. *A Lamentation in VVhiche is Shovved what Ruyne and destruction cometh of seditious rebellion*. London, 1536.

————. *An Exhortation to styrre all Englvsche men to the defence of theyr contreye*. London, 1539.

[Morison, Richard.] *A Remedy for Sedition vvherin are conteyned many thynges, concernyng the true and loyall obeysance.* London, 1536.

Mowat, Barbara A. "Shakespeare Reads the Geneva Bible." In *Shakespeare, the Bible, and the Form of the Book: Contested Scriptures.* Edited by Travis DeCook and Alan Galey, 25–39. New York: Routledge, 2012.

Mozley, J. F. *Coverdale and His Bibles.* London: Lutterworth Press, 1953.

Muddiman, J. G. *Trial of King Charles the First.* London: William Hodge, 1928.

Muller, Richard A. "The Hermeneutic of Promise and Fulfillment in Calvin's Exegesis of the Old Testament Prophecies of the Kingdom." In *The Bible in the Sixteenth Century.* Edited by David C. Steinmetz, 68–82. Durham, NC: Duke University Press, 1990.

Murphy, Virginia. "The Literature and Propaganda of Henry VIII's First Divorce." In *The Reign of Henry VIII: Politics, Policy and Piety.* Edited by D. MacCulloch. Houndmills, Basingstoke, Hampshire: Macmillan, 1995.

Nedham, Marchamont, *Mercurius Pragmaticus. . . . from Tuesday, April 25, to Tuesday, March 2. 1648.* Number 5. 1648.

Neidorf, Leonard. "Cain, Cam, Jutes, Giants, and the Textual Criticism of *Beowulf.*" *Studies in Philology* 112, no. 4 (2015): 599–632.

Nelson, Alan. *Monstrous Adversary: The Life of Edward de Vere, 17th Earl of Oxford.* Liverpool, UK: Liverpool University Press, 2003.

Nelson, Eric. *The Hebrew Republic: Jewish Sources and the Transformation of European Political Thought.* Cambridge, MA: Harvard University Press, 2010.

Ng, Morgan. "Milton's Maps." *Word & Image: A Journal of Verbal/Visual Enquiry* 29, no. 4 (2013): 428–442.

Nichols, John Gough, ed. *Narrative of the Days of the Reformation, Chiefly from the Manuscripts of John Foxe the Martyrologist.* London: Camden Society, 1859.

Nicholson, Adam. *God's Secretaries: The Making of the King James Bible.* New York: Harper Collins, 2009.

Nicholson, Catherine. "Pastoral in Exile: Spenser and the Poetics of English Alienation." *Spenser Studies: A Renaissance Poetry Annual* 23 (2008): 41–71.

———. *Uncommon Tongues: Eloquence and Eccentricity in the English Renaissance.* Philadelphia: University of Pennsylvania Press, 2014.

Noble, Richmond. *Shakespeare's Biblical Knowledge.* New York: Macmillan, 1935.

Nohrnberg, James. *The Analogy of* The Faerie Queene. Princeton, NJ: Princeton University Press, 1976.

Noot, Jan van der. *Le theatre anquel sont exposés & monstrés les inconueniens & miseres qui suiuent les mondains & vicieux* ([John Day: London, 1568]).

———. *Het theatre oft toon-neel.* London: John Day, 1568.

———. *A Theatre wherein be represented as wel the miseries & calamities that follow the voluptuous Worldlings.* London: Henry Bynneman, 1569.

Norbrook, David. *Poetry and Politics in the English Renaissance.* London: Routledge, 1984.

———. *Writing the English Republic.* Cambridge: Cambridge University Press, 1999.

Norton, David. "English Bibles from *c.* 1520 to *c.* 1750." In *The New Cambridge History of the Bible: From 1450 to 1750.* Edited by Euan Cameron, 305–344. Cambridge: Cambridge University Press, 2016.

———. *A History of the Bible as Literature.* 2 vols. Cambridge: Cambridge University Press, 1993.

———. *A History of the Bible as Literature*. Cambridge: Cambridge University Press, revised, 2000.

———. *The King James Bible: A Short History from Tyndale to Today*. Cambridge: Cambridge University Press, 2011.

———. *A Textual History of the King James Bible*. Cambridge: Cambridge University Press, 2005.

O'Banion, Patrick J. "The Pastoral Use of the Book of Revelation in Late-Tudor England." *Journal of Ecclesiastical History* 57, no. 4 (2006): 693–710.

Orgel, Stephen. "Margins of Truth." In *The Renaissance Text: Theory, Editing, Textuality*. Edited by Andrew Murphy, 91–107. Manchester: Manchester University Press, 2000.

Owen, John. *Theomachia Autexousiastike: or, A Display of Arminianisme*. London, 1643.

Palmer, Herbert. *The Glasse of Gods Providence towards his Faithfull Ones*. London, 1644.

Panizza, Letizia A. "Gasparino Barzizza's Commentaries." *Traditio* 33 (1977): 297–358.

Parker, Douglas H. "Religious Polemics and Two Sixteenth Century English Editions of Erasmus's *Enchiridion Militis Christiani*, 1545–1561." *Renaissance and Reformation* 9 no. 3 (1973): 94–107.

———. "The English *Enchiridion Militis Christiani* and Reformation Politics." *Erasmus in English* 5 (1972): 16–21.

———, ed. *William Royle's An Exhortation to the Diligent Studye of Scripture*. Toronto: Toronto University Press, 2000.

Parker, Matthew. *Correspondence of Matthew Parker*. Edited by John Bruce and Thomas Thomason Perowne. Cambridge: Cambridge University Press, 1853.

Parker, William Riley. *Milton: The Life*. 2nd ed. Revised and edited by Gordon Campbell. Oxford: Oxford University Press, 2003.

Patterson, Annabel. *Censorship and Interpretation: The Conditions of Writing and Reading in Early Modern England*. Madison: University of Wisconsin Press, 1984.

Pauck, Wilhelm. "Butzer and Calvin." *The Heritage of the Reformation*, rev. ed. 85–99. Oxford: Oxford University Press, 1968.

Payne, John B. "Erasmus and Lefèvre d'Étaples as Interpreters of Paul." *Archiv für Reformationsgeschichte* 65 (1974): 54–83.

———. "Erasmus: Interpreter of Romans." *Sixteenth Century Essays and Studies* 2 (1971): 1–35.

Peltonen, Markku. *Classical Humanism and Republicanism in English Political Thought 1570–1640*. Cambridge: Cambridge University Press, 1995.

Pepys, Samuel. *The Diary of Samuel Pepys*. Volume 1: 1660. Berkeley: University of California Press, 2000.

Perkins, David, ed. *English Romantic Writers*. New York: Harcourt Brace Jovanovich, 1967.

Perkins, William. *A Commentary on the Galatians*. A facsimile of the 1617 edition, first published in 1604. New York: Pilgrim, 1989.

Persius, Aulus Persius Flaccus. *Juvenal and Persius*, Loeb bilingual edition, translated by Susanna Morton Braund. Cambridge, MA: Harvard University Press, 1993.

Pettegree, Andrew. *Marian Protestantism: Six Studies*. Aldershot, UK: Scolar Press, 1996.

Phillips, Margaret Mann. *Erasmus on His Times: A Shortened Version of the 'Adages' of Erasmus*. Cambridge: Cambridge University Press, 1980, 1967.

Pierson, Thomas. *Excellent Encouragements against Afflictions, or, Expositions of Four Select Psalmes*. London, 1647.

Pohl, Benjamin, and Leah Tether. "Books Fit for a King: The Presentation Copies of Martin Bucer's *De regno Christi* (London, British Library, Royal MS. 8 B. VII) and Johannes

Sturm's *De periodis* Cambridge, Trinity College, II.12.21 and London, British Library, C.24.e.5)." *eBLJ* 7 (2015): 1–35.

Pollard, Alfred W. *Records of the English Bible: The Documents Relating to the Translation and Publication of the English Bible, 1525–1611*. Oxford: Oxford University Press, 1911.

Pollard, Alfred W., and G. R. Redgrave. *A Short-Title Catalogue of Books Printed in England, Scotland, & Ireland, and of English Books Printed Abroad, 1475–1640*. Oxford: Oxford University Press, 1991.

Poole, William. "John Milton and Giovanni Boccaccio's *Vita di Dante*." *Milton Quarterly* 48, no. 3 (2014): 139–170.

Pratt, Aaron. "The Trouble with Translation: Paratexts and England's Bestselling New Testament." In *The Bible on the Shakespearean Stage*. Edited by Thomas Fulton and Kristen Poole, 33–48. Cambridge: Cambridge University Press, 2018.

Prescott, Anne Lake. "Exploiting King Saul in Early Modern England: Good Uses for a Bad King." In *Religious Diversity and Early Modern English Texts: Catholic, Judaic, Feminist, and Secular Dimensions*. Edited by Arthur F. Marotti and Chanita Goodblatt, 178–194. Detroit: Wayne State University Press, 2013.

———. "Spenser's Chivalric Restoration: From Bateman's *Travayled Pylgrime* to Redcrosse Knight." *Studies in Philology* 86, no. 2 (1989): 166–197.

———. "The Thirsty Dear and the Lord of Life: Some Contexts for *Amoretti* 67–71." *Spenser Studies* 6 (1985): 33–76.

———. "Two copies of the 1596 *Faerie Queene*." *Spenser Studies* 23 (2008): 261–273.

Prynne, William. *A Briefe Memento to the present Unparliamentary Junto touching their present intentions and proceedings to Depose and Execute, CHARLES STEWART, their Lawfull KING*. London, 1649.

———. *Histrio-mastix, The Players Scourge*. London, 1633.

———. *Mr. Pryn's Last and Finall Declaration to the Commons of England*. London, 1649.

———. *A Plea for the Lords*. London, 1648.

———. *The Third part of the Soveraigne Povver of Parliaments and Kingdomes. Wherein the Parliaments present necessary defensive warre against the Kings offensive malignant, popish forces; and subjects taking up defensive armes against their soveraigne*. London, 1643.

———. *The Church of England's Old Antithesis to New Arminianisme*. London, 1629.

———. *Vindication of Psalme 105:15*. London, 1642.

Quilligan, Maureen. *The Language of Allegory: Defining the Genre*. Ithaca, NY: Cornell University Press, 1979.

Quintilian, Marcus Fabius. *Institutio Oratoria*. Edited and translated by Donald A Russel, Loeb bilingual edition, 5 vols. Cambridge, MA: Harvard University Press, 2001.

Rabil, Albert Jr. *Erasmus and the New Testament: The Mind of a Christian Humanist*. San Antonio: Trinity University Press, 1972.

Radzinowicz, Mary Ann. *Milton's Epics and the Book of Psalms*. Princeton, Princeton University Press, 1989.

———. *Toward* Samson Agonistes: *The Growth of Milton's Mind*. Princeton, NJ: Princeton University Press, 1978.

Rankin, Mark. "John Foxe and the Earliest Readers of William Tyndale's *The Practyse of Prelates* (1530)." *English Literary Renaissance* 46, no. 2 (2016): 157–192.

———. "The Royal Provenance and Tudor Courtly Reading of a Wycliffite Bible." *Journal of Medieval and Early Modern Studies* 47, no. 3 (2017): 587–597.

———. "Tyndale, Erasmus, and the Early English Reformation." *Erasmus Studies* 38, no. 2 (2018): 135–170.

Raschko, Mary. "Taking Apart the Wycliffite Bible: Patterns of Selective and Interpretive Reading." *Journal of Medieval and Early Modern Studies* 47, no. 3 (2017): 459–486.

Reeve, Anne, and M. A Screech, eds. *Annotations on the New Testament: Acts—Romans—I and II Corinthians.* Leiden: Brill, 1990.

———, eds. *Annotations on the New Testament: Galatians to the Apocalypse.* Leiden: Brill, 1993.

———, eds. *Annotations on the New Testament: The Gospels.* London: Duckworth, 1986.

Rex, Richard. "The Crisis of Obedience: God's Word and Henry's Reformation." *The Historical Journal* 39, no. 4 (1996): 863–894.

———. "The Earliest Use of Hebrew in Books Printed in England: Dating Some Works of Richard Pace and Robert Wakefield." *Transactions of the Cambridge Bibliographical Society* 9, no. 5 (1990): 517–525.

Richards, Judith M. "'To Promote a Woman to Beare Rule': Talking of Queens in Mid-Tudor England." *The Sixteenth Century Journal* 28, no. 1 (1997): 101–121.

Richardson, Anne. "Tyndale's Quarrel with Erasmus: A Chapter in the History of the English Reformation." *Fides et Historia* 25, no. 3 (1993): 46–65.

Richey, E. Gilman. *The Politics of Revelation in the English Renaissance.* Columbia: University of Missouri Press, 1998.

Ridderbos, Nicholas H., and Peter C. Craigie. "Psalms." In *The International Standard Bible Encyclopedia*, vol 3. Edited by Geoffrey W. Bromiley et al., 1029–1040. Grand Rapids: Eerdmans, 1986.

Robinson, Hastings, ed. *Original Letters Relative to the English Reformation.* Cambridge: Parker Society, 1846.

Rogers, John. "Paradise Regained and the Memory of *Paradise Lost*." In *The Oxford Handbook of Milton.* Edited by Nicholas McDowell and Nigel Smith, 589–612. Oxford: Oxford University Press, 2009.

Rosenblatt, Jason P. "Milton, Anxiety, and the King James Bible." In *The King James Bible after 400 Years.* Edited by Hamlin and Jones, 181–201. Cambridge: Cambridge University Press, 2011.

———. *Renaissance England's Chief Rabbi: John Selden.* Oxford: Oxford University Press, 2006.

Rous, Francis. *The Booke of Psalmes, in English Meeter.* Rotterdam, 1638.

Rummel, Erika. *Erasmus' Annotations on the New Testament.* Toronto: University of Toronto Press, 1986.

———. "God and Solecism: Erasmus as a Literary Critic of the Bible." *Erasmus of Rotterdam Society Yearbook* 7 (1987): 54–72.

———. "St. Paul in Plain Latin: Erasmus' Philological Annotations on 1 Corinthians." *Classical and Modern Literature* 7, no. 4 (1987): 309–318.

Rumrich, John. *Milton Unbound: Controversy and Reinterpretation.* Cambridge: Cambridge University Press, 1996.

Rupp, Gordon and Philip Watson, eds. *Luther and Erasmus: Free Will and Salvation.* Philadelphia: Westminster Press, 1969.

Rushworth, John. *An Abridgement of the late Remonstrance of the Army. VVith some Marginall Attestations, for the Better Understanding Rembrance, and Judgement of the People.* Decem. 27, 1648. London, 1648.

Ryrie, Alec, "Sampson, Thomas," *Dictionary of National Biography.*

Sandys, George. *A Paraphrase upon the Divine Poems by George Sandys.* London, 1648.

Satterthwaite, Alfred W. *Spenser, Ronsard, and Du Bellay: A Renaissance Comparison.* Princeton, NJ: Princeton University Press, 1960.

Saunders, Austen. "New Light on a Puzzling Annotation to Spenser's *Faerie Queene.*" *Notes and Queries* 57, no. 3 (2010): 356–357.

Sauveur, L. *C. Julii Caesaris Commentarii de Bello Gallico.* New York: Henry Holt, 1878.

Scalia, Antonin. "God's Justice or Ours." *First Things* 123 (May 2002): 17–21.

Scarisbrick, J. J. *Henry VIII.* New Haven, CT: Yale University Press, 1997; first published in 1968.

Schiller, Arthur A. *Roman Law: Mechanisms of Development.* New York: Mouton, 1978.

Schochet, Gordon, Fania Oz-Salzberger, and Meirav Jones, eds. *Political Hebraism: Judaic Sources in Early Modern Political Thought.* Jerusalem: Shalem Press, 2008.

Schoeck, R. J. "Erasmus in England, 1499–1517: Translatio Studii and the Studia Humanitatis." *Classical and Modern Literature* 7, no. 4 (1987): 269–283.

Schoenbaum, Samuel. *Shakespeare: A Documentary Life.* New York: Oxford University Press, 1975.

———. *William Shakespeare, A Compact Documentary Life.* Oxford: Oxford University Press, 1987.

Schwartz, Michael. "The Political Inaccuracy of Milton's Psalms 1–8 and 80–88." In *Reassembling Truth: Twenty-First-Century Milton.* Edited by Charles W. Durham and Kristin A. Pruitt, 79–94. Selinsgrove, PA: Susquehanna University Press, 2003.

Schwartz, Regina. "Citation, Authority and *De Doctrina Christiana.*" In *Politics, Poetics, and Hermeneutics in Milton's Prose,* edited by David Loewenstein and James Grantham Turner. Cambridge: Cambridge University Press, 1990.

———. "Milton on the Bible," In *A Companion to Milton,* edited by Thomas N. Corns. Oxford: Wiley-Blackwell, 2001.

———. *Remembering and Repeating: On Milton's Theology and Poetics.* Chicago: Chicago University Press, 1993.

Scribner, Bob. "Heterodoxy, Literacy, and Print in the Early German Reformation." In *Heresy and Literacy, 1000–1530.* Edited by Peter Biller and Anne Hudson, 255–278. Cambridge: Cambridge University Press, 1994.

Scott-Warren, Jason. *Sir James Harington and the Book as Gift.* Oxford: Oxford University Press, 2001.

Seebohm, Frederic. *The Oxford Reformers: John Colet, Erasmus, and Thomas More.* New York: Longmans, Green, and Co., 1913.

Selden, John. *Table-talk: being the discourses of John Selden, Esq.* London, 1689.

Selden, John. *The Table Talk of John Selden.* Edited by Samuel Harvey Reynolds. Oxford: Oxford University Press, 1892.

Seneca, Lucius Annaeus [Pseudo]. *Epistolae Senecae ad Paulum et Pauli ad Senecam (Quae Vocantur).* Rome: American Academy in Rome, 1938.

Seneca, Lucius Annaeus. *Senecae Opera.* Edited by Erasmus. Basel, 1515.

Seneca, Lucius Annaeus. *Tragedies.* Loeb ed., edited and translated by John G. Fitch. 2 vols. Cambridge, MA: Harvard University Press, 2004.

Shaheen, Naseeb. *Biblical References in Shakespeare's Plays.* Newark: University of Delaware Press, 1999.

———. *Biblical References in Shakespeare's Tragedies.* Newark: University of Delaware Press, 1987.

———. *Biblical References in* The Faerie Queene. Memphis: Memphis State University Press, 1976.

———. "Echoes of *A Warning for Faire Women* in Shakespeare's Plays." *Philological Quarterly* 62, no. 4 (1983): 521–525.

———. "Misconceptions about the Geneva Bible." *Studies in Bibliography* 37 (1984): 156–158.

Shakespeare, William. *The Complete Works*. Edited by Stanley Wells and Gary Taylor. Oxford: Clarendon Press, 2005.

———. *Measure for Measure*. Edited by J. W. Lever, London: Routledge, 1989.

———. "Mr. William Shakespeares Comedies, Histories, & Tragedies." In *The First Folio of Shakesepare*. Edited by Charlton Hinman. New York: Norton, 1968.

———. *Riverside Shakespeare*, 2nd ed. Edited by G. Blakemore Evans, et al. Boston: Houghton Mifflin, 1997.

Shakespeare, William, Anthony Munday, and others. *Sir Thomas More*. Edited by Vittorio Gabrieli and Giorgio Melchiori. Manchester: Manchester University Press, 1990.

Sharpe, Kevin. "'An Image Doting Rabble': The Failure of Republican Culture in Seventeenth-Century England." In *Refiguring Revolutions: Aesthetics and Politics from the English Revolution*, edited by Sharpe and Zwicker, 25–56. Berkeley: University of California Press, 1998.

———. *Reading Authority and Representing Rule in Early Modern England*. London: Bloomsbury, 2013.

———. *Reading Revolutions: The Politics of Reading in Early Modern England*. London: Yale University Press, 2000.

———. *Selling the Tudor Monarchy: Authority and Image in Sixteenth-Century England*. New Haven, CT: Yale University Press, 2009.

———. "The Personal Rule of Charles I." In *Before the English Civil War: Essays on Early Stuart Politics and Government*. Edited by Howard Tomlinson. New York: St. Martin's Press, 1983.

Sharpe, Kevin, and Steven N. Zwicker, eds. *Refiguring Revolutions: Aesthetics and Politics from the English Revolution*. Berkeley: University of California Press, 1998.

Sherman, William. *Used Books: Marking Readers in Renaissance England*. Philadelphia: University of Pennsylvania Press, 2008.

Shoulson, Jeffrey. *Milton and the Rabbis: Hebraism, Hellenism, and Christianity*. Columbia: Columbia University Press, 2001.

Shuger, Debora Kuller. "Isaiah 63 and the Literal Senses of Scripture." In *The Oxford Handbook of the Bible in Early Modern England, c. 1530–1700*. Edited by Kevin Killeen, Helen Smith, and Rachel Willie, 149–163. Oxford: Oxford University Press, 2015.

———. *Political Theologies in Shakespeare's England: The Sacred and the State in* Measure for Measure. New York: Palgrave, 2001.

———. *The Renaissance Bible: Scholarship, Sacrifice, and Subjectivity*. Berkeley: University of California Press, 1998.

Sider, Robert D. "Erasmus on the Epistle to the Romans: A 'Literary' Reading." In *Acta Conventus Neo-Latini Torontonensis*. Edited by Alexander Dalzell, Charles Fantazzi, and Richard J. Schoeck, 129–135. Binghamton: Medieval and Renaissance Texts and Studies, 1991.

Simpson, James. *Burning to Read: English Fundamentalism and Its Reformation Opponents*. Cambridge, MA: Harvard University Press, 2007.

———. *Permanent Revolution: The Reformation and the Illiberal Roots of Liberalism*. Cambridge, MA: Harvard University Press, 2019.

———. "Tyndale as Promoter of Figural Allegory and Figurative Language: A Brief Declaration of the Sacraments." *Archiv für das Studium der Neueren Sprachen und Literaturen* 245 (2008): 37–55.

Skinner, Quentin. *The Foundations of Modern Political Thought.* 2 vols. Cambridge: Cambridge University Press, 1975.

Slights, William W. E. "'Marginal Notes that spoile the Text': Scriptural Annotation in the English Renaissance." *Huntington Library Quarterly* 55, no. 2 (1992): 255–278.

———. "The Edifying Margins of Renaissance English Books." *Renaissance Quarterly* 42, no. 4 (1989): 682–716.

Smalley, Beryl. *The Study of the Bible in the Middle Ages.* South Bend, IN: Notre Dame Press, 1989; originally published 1940.

Smith, Helen, and Louise Wilson, eds. *Renaissance Paratexts.* Cambridge: Cambridge University Press, 2011.

Smith, Nigel, and Nicholas McDowell, eds. *The Oxford Handbook of Milton.* Oxford: Oxford University Press, 2009.

Sommerville, J. P. *Politics and Ideology in England, 1603–1640.* London and New York: Longman, 1986.

———. *Thomas Hobbes, Political Ideas in Historical Context.* London: Macmillan, 1992.

Somos, Mark. "*Mare Clausum, Leviathan,* and *Oceana*: Bible Criticism, Secularism and Imperialism in Seventeenth-Century English Political and Legal Thought." In *In the Name of God: The Bible in the Colonial Discourse of Empire.* Edited by C. L. Crouch and Jonathan Stökl, 85–132. Leiden: Brill, 2013.

Spenser, Edmund. *Edmund Spenser's Amoretti and Epithalamion: A Critical Edition.* Edited by Kenneth J. Larsen. Tempe, AZ: Medieval and Renaissance Texts and Studies, 1997.

———. *Faerie Queene, Book 1.* Edited by Carol V. Kaske. Indianapolis: Hacket, 2006.

———. *Joachim Du Bellay, Antiquitez de Rome, Translated by Edmund Spenser as Ruines of Rome.* Edited by Malcolm C. Smith. Binghamton: Medieval and Renaissance Texts and Studies, 1994.

———. *The Complete Works in Verse and Prose of Edmund Spenser.* 10 vols. Edited by Alexander B. Grosart. London: Printed for Private Circulation, 1882.

———. *The Faerie Queene.* Edited by A. C. Hamilton, with Hiroshi Yamashita and Toshiyuki Suzuki. London: Routledge, 2013.

———. *The Yale Edition of the Shorter Poems of Edmund Spenser.* Edited by William A. Oram, et al. New Haven, CT: Yale University Press, 1989.

Spink, Ian. *Henry Lawes: Cavalier Songwriter.* Oxford: Oxford University Press, 2000.

Spivack, Bernard. *Shakespeare and the Allegory of Evil.* New York: Columbia University Press, 1958.

Spufford, Margaret. "First Steps in Literacy: The Reading and Writing Experiences of the Humblest Spiritual Autobiographers." *Social History* 4, no. 3 (1979): 407–435.

———. "'I bought me a primer,' or, 'How godly were the multitude?': The Basic Religious Concepts of Those Who Could Read in the Seventeenth Century." In *The World of Rural Dissenters, 1520–1725.* Edited by Margaret Spufford, 72–85. Cambridge: Cambridge University Press, 1995.

Stallybrass, Peter. "Books and Scrolls: Navigating the Bible." In *Books and Readers in Early Modern England.* Edited by Jennifer Anderson and Elizabeth Sauer, 42–79. Philadelphia: University of Pennsylvania Press, 2002.

Starkey, David. *Six Wives: The Queens of Henry VIII*. New York: Harper, 2003.

Steele, Robert. *Tudor and Stuart Proclamations 1485–1714*. 2 vols. Oxford: Clarendon Press, 1910.

Steenbeek, Andrea. "The Conceptual Background of the Controversy between Erasmus and Lefèvre d'Étaples." In *Acta Conventus Neo-Latini Hafniensis: Proceedings of the Eighth International Congress of Neo-Latin Studies*, 935–945. Binghamton: Medieval and Renaissance Texts and Studies, 1994.

Steinmetz, David C. ed. *The Bible in the Sixteenth Century*. Durham, NC: Duke University Press, 1990.

Sternhold, Thomas. *The Whole booke of psalmes with the hymnes euangelicall, and songs spirituall, composed into 4. parts by sundry authors . . . Newly corrected and enlarged by Tho: Ravenscroft Bachelar of Musicke*. London, 1621.

Sternhold, Thomas and John Hopkins, *The Whole Book of Psalmes collected into English meeter, by Thomas Sternhold, Iohn Hopkins, and others, conferred with the Hebrew, with apt notes to sing them withall*. London, 1621.

Stillingfleet, Edward. *Several Conferences between a Romish Priest, a Fanatick Chaplain and a Divine of the Church of England concerning the Idolatry of the Church of Rome*. London, 1679.

Stillman, Carol. *Spenser's Elect England: Political and Apocalyptic Dimensions of* The Faerie Queene. Dissertation, University of Pennsylvania, 1979.

Stock, Raymond. *Complete Concordance to the Bible (Douay Version)*. London: B. Herder Book Co, 1953.

Streete, Adrian. "The Politics of Ethical Presentism: Appropriation, Spirituality, and the Case of *Antony and Cleopatra*." *Textual Practice* 22, no. 3 (2008): 405–431.

Struever, Nancy. *The Language of History in the Renaissance*. Princeton, NJ: Princeton University Press, 1970.

Styrpe, John. *Annals of the Reformation and the Establishment of Religion*. London: Thomas Edlin, 1725.

Summit, Jennifer. *Memory's Library: Medieval Books in Early Modern England*. Chicago: Chicago University Press, 2008.

Swift, Daniel. *Shakespeare's Common Prayer: The Book of Common Prayer and the Elizabethan Age*. Oxford: Oxford University Press, 2013.

Tadmor, Naomi. "The Social and Cultural Translation of the Hebrew Bible in Early Modern England: Reflections, Working Principles, and Examples." In *Early Modern Cultures of Translation*, edited by Karen Newman and Jane Tylus, 175–187. Philadelphia: University of Pennsylvania Press, 2015.

———. *The Social Universe of the English Bible: Scripture, Society, and Culture in Early Modern England*. Cambridge: Cambridge University Press, 2010.

Tayler, Edward W. "Milton's Grim Laughter and Second Choices." In *Poetry and Epistemology: Turning Points in the History of Poetic Knowledge*. Edited by Roland Hagenbuchle and Laura Skandera. Regensburg, Germany: F. Pustet, 1986.

Taylor, Gary. "The Date and Auspices of the Additions to *Sir Thomas More*." In Howard-Hill, *Shakespeare and Sir Thomas More: Essays on the Play and Its Shakespearian Interest*. Edited by T. H. Howard-Hill, 101–130. Cambridge: Cambridge University Press, 1989.

Thompson, C. R. *The Translations of Lucian by Erasmus and St. Thomas More*. Ithaca, NY: Vail-Ballou Press, 1940.

Tilley, Morris Palmer. *A Dictionary of the Proverbs in England*. Ann Arbor: University of Michigan Press, 1950.

Tov, Emanuel. "List of the Texts from the Judaean Desert." In *The Texts from the Judaean Desert.* Edited by Tov et al., 192–94. Oxford: Clarendon, 2002.

Tracy, James. *Holland under Habsburg Rule, 1506–1566: The Formation of a Body Politic.* Berkeley: University of California Press, 1990.

———. *The Politics of Erasmus.* Toronto: University of Toronto Press, 1978.

Trapp, J. B. *Erasmus, Colet and More: The Early Tudor Humanists and their Books.* London: British Library, 1991.

Tribble, Evelyn B. *Margins and Marginality: The Printed Page in Early Modern England.* Charlottesville: University Press of Virginia, 1993.

Tudor-Craig, Pamela. "Henry VIII and King David." In *Early Tudor England: Proceedings of the 1987 Harlaxton Symposium.* Edited by Daniel Williams. Woodbridge, Suffolk, UK: Boydell Press, 1989.

Tyacke, Nicholas. *Anti-Calvinists: The Rise of English Arminianism c. 1590–1640.* Oxford: Oxford University Press, 1990; first published 1987.

———. "Arminianism and English Culture." *Britain and the Netherlands* 7 (1981): 94–117.

———. "Puritan Politicians and King James VI and I, 1587–1604." In *Politics, Religion and Popularity in Early Stuart Britain.* Edited by Peter Lake, Richard Cust, and Thomas Cogswell, 21–44. Cambridge: Cambridge University Press, 2002.

———. "The 'Rise of Puritanism' and the Legalizing of Dissent, 1571–1719." In *From Persecution to Toleration.* Edited by O. Grell, J. Israel, and N. Tyacke, 17–50. Oxford: Oxford University Press, 1991.

Tyndale, William. *An Exposycyon vpon the V.Vi.Vii. Chapters of Mathewe which thre chapters are the keye and the dore of the scrypture, and the restoring agayne of Moses lawe corrupt by ye scrybes and pharysessigs.* 1536.

———. *A path way into the holy scripture* [London], [1536?].

———. *Expositions and Notes on Sundry Portions of Holy Scriptures Together with The Practice of Prelates.* Edited by Henry Walter. Cambridge: Cambridge University Press, 1849.

———. *The Obedience of a Christian Man* (1528). Edited by David Daniell. London: Penguin, 2000.

———. *The Work of William Tindale.* Edited by S. L. Greenslade. London: Blackie & Son, 1938.

———. *The practyse of Prelates. Whether the Kinges grace maye be separated from hys quene, because she was his brothers wyfe.* [Antwerp,] 1530.

———. *The Work of William Tyndale.* Edited by G. E. Duffield. Philadelphia: Fortress Press, 1965.

———. *The Whole Workes of W. Tyndall, Iohn Frith, and Doct. Barnes, Three Worthy Martyrs, and Principall Teachers of this Churche of England.* London, 1573.

Usher, Roland G. *The Reconstruction of the English Church.* 2 vols. New York and London: D. Appleton, 1910.

Valla, Lorenzo. *On the Donation of Constantine.* Translated by G. W. Bowersock. Cambridge, MA: Harvard University Press, 2008.

———. *Opera Omnia.* 2 vols. Turin: Bottega d'Erasmo, 1962.

———. *The Treatise of Lorenzo Valla on the Donation of Constantine, Text and Translation into English.* Edited by Christopher B Coleman. New Haven, CT: Yale University Press, 1922.

Velz, John W. "Shakespeare and the Geneva Bible: The Circumstances." In *Shakespeare, Marlowe, Jonson: New Directions in Biography.* Edited by Takashi Kozuka and J. R. Mulryne, 113–118. Aldershot, UK: Ashgate, 2006.

Vessey, Mark. "Basel 1514: Erasmus' Critical Turn." In *Basel 1516: Erasmus' Edition of the New Testament*. Edited by M. Wallraff, S. Menchi, and K. von Greyerz, 3–26. Tübingen: Mohr Siebeck, 2016.

Virgil. Publius Vergilius Maro. *Eclogues, Georgics, Aeneid I-VI*, revised ed. Edited by G. P. Goold. Cambridge, MA: Harvard University Press, 1999.

Walker, Greg. *Persuasive Fictions: Faction, Faith, and Political Culture in the Reign of Henry VIII*. Aldershot, UK: Scolar Press, 1996.

Walker, Greg. *Writing Under Tyranny: English Literature and the Henrician Reformation*. Oxford: Oxford University Press, 2005.

Wallace, Dewey D., Jr. *Puritans and Predestination: Grace in English Protestant Theology 1525–1695*. Chapel Hill: University of North Carolina Press, 1982.

Walsham, Alexandra. "Jewels for Gentlewomen: Religious Books as Artefacts in Late Medieval and Early Modern England." *Studies in Church History* 38 (2004): 123–142.

———. "Unclasping the Book? Post-Reformation English Catholicism and the Vernacular Bible." *Journal of British Studies* 42, no. 2 (April 2003): 141–166.

Walzer, Michael. *In God's Shadow: Politics in the Hebrew Bible*. New Haven, CT: Yale University Press, 2012.

Warner, J. Christopher. *Henry VIII's Divorce: Literature and the Politics of the Printing Press*. Woodbridge, Suffolk, UK: Boydell Press, 1998.

Watkins, John. "Moralities, Interludes and Protestant Drama." In *The Cambridge History of Medieval Literature*. Edited by David Wallace, 767–792. Cambridge: Cambridge University Press, 1999.

Weinfeld, Moshe. *Deuteronomy and the Deuteronomic School*. Oxford: Clarendon Press, 1972.

Wells, Robin Headlam. "Spenser's Christian Knight: Erasmisan Theology in *The Faerie Queene*, Book I." *Anglia* 97 (1979): 350–366.

Westbrook, Vivienne. *Long Travail and Great Paynes: A Politics of Reformation Revision*. Dordrecht, Netherlands: Kluwer Academic Publishers, 2001.

Willis, Jonathan. *The Reformation of the Decalogue: Religious Identity and the Ten Commandments in England, c. 1485–1625*. Cambridge: Cambridge University Press, 2017.

Whitaker, Richard E. and James E. Goehring, eds. *The Eerdmans Analytical Concordance to the Revised Standard Version of the Bible*. Grand Rapids: William B. Eerdmans, 1988.

White, Micheline. "The Psalms, War, and Royal Iconography: Katherine Parr's Psalms or Prayers (1544) and Henry VIII as David." *Renaissance Studies* 29, no. 4 (2015): 554–575.

White, Peter. "The Rise of Arminianism Reconsidered." *Past and Present* 101 (1983): 34–54.

Whitford, David M. "The Papal Antichrist: Martin Luther and the Underappreciated Influence of Lorenzo Valla." *Renaissance Quarterly* 61, no. 1 (2008): 26–52.

———. "Yielding to the Prejudices of his Times: Erasmus and Comma Johanneum." *Church History and Religious Culture* 95:1 (2015): 19–40.

Whitgift, John. *The Works of John Whitgift*. 3 vols. Edited by J. Ayre. Cambridge: Cambridge University Press, 1851–1853.

Wilkinson, Robert. "Immanuel Tremellius' 1569 Edition of the Syriac New Testament." *The Journal of Ecclesiastical History* 58 (2007), 9–25.

Williams, George Huntston. *The Radical Reformation*. Kirksville, MO: Sixteenth Century Journal, 1992.

Wilson, F. P. ed. *The Oxford Dictionary of English Proverbs*. Oxford: Oxford University Press, 1970.

Winston, Mathew. "'Craft against Vice': Morality Play Elements in *Measure for Measure*." *Shakespeare Studies* 14, no.1 (1981): 229–248.

Wither, George. *A View of the Marginal Notes of the Popish Testament*. London, [1588].

Wittreich, Joseph, Jr. *Visionary Poetics: Milton's Tradition and His Legacy*. San Marino, CA: Huntington Library, 1979.

Wood, Michael. *Shakespeare*. New York: Basic Books, 2003.

Woodhouse, A. S. P., and Douglas Bush, eds. *Variorum Commentary on the Poems of John Milton: The Minor English Poems*. New York: Columbia University Press, 1972.

Woods, Susanne. "Elective Poetics and Milton's Prose." In *Politics, Poetics and Hermeneutics in Milton's Prose*. Edited by David Loewenstein and James Grantham Turner, 193–211. Cambridge: Cambridge University Press, 1990.

Worden, Blair. "Toleration and the Cromwellian Protectorate." In *Persecution and Toleration: Papers Read at the Twenty-Second Summer Meeting and the Twenty-Third Winter Meeting of the Ecclesiastical History Society*. Edited by W. J. Sheils, 199–234. Oxford: B. Blackwell for the Ecclesiastical History Society, 1984.

Wyatt, George. *Extracts from the life of the Virtuous, Christian, and Renowned Queen Anne Boleigne*. In *The Life of Cardinal Wolsey by George Cavendish*. Edited by Samuel Weller Singer, 417–449. London: Davidson, 1827 [first published in 1641].

Wycliffe, John. *The English Works of Wyclif hitherto unprinted*. Edited by F. D. Matthew. London: Early English Text Society, by Trübner & Co., 1880. http://name.umdl.umich.edu /AEH6713.0001.001.

Zauzmer, Julie and Keith McMillan. "Sessions cites Bible Passage Used to Defend Slavery in Defense of Separating Immigrant Families," *Washington Post*, June 15, 2018.

Zwicker, Steven N. "Reading the Margins: Politics and the Habits of Appropriation." In *Refiguring Revolutions: Aesthetics and Politics from the English Revolution*. Edited by Sharpe and Zwicker, 101–115. Berkeley: University of California Press, 1998.

———. "What Every Literate Man once Knew." In *Owners, Annotators, and the Signs of Reading*. Edited by Robin Myers, Michael Harris, and Giles Mandelbrote, 75–90. London: British Library, 2005.

Zysk, Jay. "John 6, *Measure for Measure*, and the Complexities of the Literal Sense." In *The Bible on the Shakespearean Stage: Cultures of Interpretation in Reformation England*. Edited by Thomas Fulton and Kristen Poole, 51–68. Cambridge: Cambridge University Press, 2018.

BIBLICAL INDEX

Note: Terms and names can be found in the **General Index**.

HEBREW BIBLE/OLD TESTAMENT

Genesis 166–67, 237–38
   1:26 244
   1:30 209
   2:18 237–38
   3:16 .... 60, 108
   3:19 178–79
   6:4 .... 129, 280n69
   6:14 129
   9:6 222
   10:8 129
   12:9 143
   33:6 129–30
   38 68
Exodus 18, 55, 63, 90, 93, 102, 120, 179
   1:15 .... 175–76, 278n34
   1:19 .... 175–76, 278n34
   1:21 .... 278n34, 287n11
   1:22 129
   3:1 202
   14:13 120
   14:14 120
   20:12 .... 16, 54, 58, 60, 61–62, 64, 255
   21:12 .... 100, 102
   21:24 179
   22 91
   22:28 .... 91, 253
   31:14 104
   31:14–15 100
   33:19 188
   35:2 .... 100, 104
Leviticus 20, 52–53, 55, 66, 67, 69, 70, 71
   18:16 .... 66, 96
   20 68
   20:10 100
   20:21 .... 37, 66, 69
   24:15–16 100

24:16 104
24:17 100
Numbers 55
  15:30–36 104
  15:32–36 100
  15:40 101
  35:33 222
Deuteronomy 18, 20, 52–53, 55, 66, 67, 69–70, 86, 87, 88, 92–95, 100
  5:16 58
  9:21 202
  13:1–5 101
  13:1–10 104
  13:4–18 101
  13:5 ....100, 275n62
  13:6–10 100
  16:20 109
  17 ....59, 92, 94, 95, 101
  17:2–3 101
  17:2–5 ....100, 104, 275n62
  17:6 100
  17:8–12 100
  17:14 126
  17:14–15 ....59, 125
  17:14–20 91–92
  17:15 118
  17:18–19 250
  17:18–20 ....92, 93
  19 70
  19:11–13 100
  19:11–21 ....275n62
  19:16–21 100
  21:15 97
  21:18–21 ....100, 275n62
  22:13–28 ....275n62
  22:20–25 100
  22:21 100
  24:1 105
  24:1–2 237
  24:7 ....100, 275n62
  25 70
  25:5 ....69, 70
  31:26 93
  32:35 183
Joshua 82, 87, 88
  1:8 74–75
  8:34 88
  10:13 ....281–82n101
Judges
  8 221
1 Samuel 126, 128, 273n22
  8 95

2 Samuel 128, 273n22
  11:2–4 76
  16:7–8 222
1 Kings
  1:18 .... 280n70
  4:29 ....281–82n101
  4:32 ....281–82n101
  5:18 12
  11:41 ....281–82n101
  12:6–11 245
  22 77
2 Kings 86
  5:8 152
  9:7 246
  22:8 93
  23 86
  23:2–4 .... 86, 273n22
  23:25 86
1 Chronicles
  16:1–22 125
  16:22 .... 16, 124, 125
  23:21 ....277n28
  29:29 ....281–82n101
2 Chronicles
  15:16 175
  16:10 132–33
  23:21 ....277n28
Ezra
  4:[6] 260n26, 278n36
Nehemiah
  1:3 224–25
Job
  3:17 128
  6:23 128
  15:20 128
  27:13 128
Psalms 16, 22–23, 74, 76–77, 125–26, 128
  2:2 127
  20 ....77, 78
  27 .... 224, 295n61
  34:19 120
  42–49 206
  44:1 225
  50 206
  51 207
  52:1[53:1] 75–76
  54:3 128
  55 ....295n61
  63 77
  66 ....295n61
  68 76

73–83...206
80–88.......................................203, *210*, 219–39, *223, 228*, 236
81..226
81:14...226
82...218–19
82:1..227
82:6..227
82:6–7..227, 229
82:7..221
82:11..222
83..221, 226–27, *228*
83:1–2...226–27
83:11..221
83:12..227
84..206, 224
85..206, 224–25
87..206, 224
88..206, 222, *223*
94..132, 206, 207
94:16..293n22
94:20..207, 293n25
102..295n61
105..125
105:12–15..125
105:15.....................................16, 124–25, 255–56, 279n61
108–110..293n21
114..10–11, 230
114:1–2...230
117..221
137:1–6..206
Proverbs.......................74, 76, 80, *215, 216*, 221–22, 271n117
1:23...222
3:1–6...80
4:5..213, *216*
8:15...81
30:21,23...81, 209
Ecclesiastes...76
5:11..288n31
Song of Songs..14, 138
Isaiah....................128, 133, 136–38, 139, 267n31, 281n99, 281n100
2:7...136, 281n91
3:12...139
3:14...139
5...132, 138
5:1–7...135
5:5..132
5:17..138
8:1...136, 137, 281n96
8:2..281n96
13:11..128
37:20–38..130

49:24–25...128
49:25..128
Jeremiah 128, 132, 267n31
    10 .... 278–79n52
    15:21...128
Lamentations.....................132, 136, 141, 142, 267n31
    1:10 141–42
    3:37..13
    4:20...14, 134, 148
Ezekiel
    27:9 12
Daniel
    7:25 167
Hosea
    11.1...230
Amos
    8:14..156
Jonah 267n31
Habbakuk
    2:2 137

APOCRYPHA
  1 Esdras
    2:16 ....278n36
  Wisdom of Solomon.................................76, 138, 281n101
    12:14 .... 280n67
  Ecclesiasticus (Sirach)..76, 123
    14:13 ....124, 124
    40:24..123–24, 124
    49:3 98
  1 Maccabees
    1:25,36... 225
  2 Maccabees
    4:25 .... 128, 280n67
    7:27 ....128, 280n67

NEW TESTAMENT
  Matthew............................50, 51, 163, 237, 262n19, 272n6
    3:2 29
    5:31–32..237
    5:32...237
    5:38–42..179
    5:44 178–79
    14:7 29
    16:18 ....51, 152, 254, 278n39
    18:17 ....278n39
    19:24..13
    22:12 ....286n88
    26:28 163
  Mark
    3:21..284n29

4:24...179
10:25...260n32
10:30..118
Luke...192
6:31..179
6:36–38..191
7...218
7:30..218
18:25...260n32
23:42..176
John.. 11, 265n92
1:1..142
5:39..135
10:34,36..227–28
10:35..296n84
Acts..41
5:29...175, 287n6, 289n41
16:18..165
17...41
17:23–25..41
18...35
18:12–17...35
19:9..130
Romans..18, 30, 38, 263n29
1:11–12...38, 41
2:13...97
3:20...97
3:28..97, 193
5:19..251
9–11...190
9:15..190
9:15–17..179, 188, 191
9:16..188
11:6... 179, 190, 191
13:1..102
13:1–4...179, 180
13:1–5.. 300n7
13:1–6... 244
13:1–7.............................. 19, 20, 22, 30, 31, 32, 33, 34, 45, 46, 49, 53, 54, 55, 58, 60,
.... 61, 62, 63, 64, 65, 74, 81, 85, 86, 89, 98, 102, 103, 109, 176–77,
.... 178–79, 180, 181, 183, 186, 187, 194, 214, 216, 227, 232, 235, 237, 240,
.... 241, 242, 243, 244, 245, 246–47, 248, 249, 250, 268n53, 299n37
13:1,2,3..241
13:2...33, 244
13:3..118, 268n54, 298n34
13:3–5...186
13:4..181, 244, 289n45
13:4–6..85
13:5...33
13:7...33

13:7–8 33–34

15:6 .... 216–17, *218*

1 Corinthians 30, 108–9

6:9–20 ....278n51

7 237

7:11 237

11:18,19 218

13:13 164

14 160

14:2–5 152

14:34 108

2 Corinthians

3 15

3:6 15

Galatians

2:16–19 196

4 14

4:22 14

5:12 247

Ephesians

5:2–5 178

6:11–17 165

6:13–17 165

Colossians

4:6 42

2 Thessalonians

3:1 74–75

Hebrews

4:13 ....293n32

1 Peter 245

2:13 245

3:7 90

2 Peter

1:5–7 ....294n39

1 John 282–83n9

5 209

5:7 29

5:7–8 .... 209, 211, 266n10

Revelation (Apocalypse) 11, 11:23, 13–14, 18:4, 21, 22:12, 23, 67, 90, 109, 113, 118, 129–30,

.... 140, 142, 143–44, 145–46, 147–48, 149, 150–51, 152, 153, 156, 158–59, 162,

.... 164, 165–66, 168, 169, 171, 172, 173, 251, 256, 282n1, 282n5, 283n16, 286n92

2:8 172

2:9 153

2:20 133

2:24 ....277n23

6:12 166

9 154

9:1 153

11:2 166

12 .... 143, *150*, 154, 166, 167, 169, 171

12:1 ....149, 167
12:1–17 143
12:5 ....149, 167
12:6 170
12:6–7 167
12:9 .... 143, 149, 154, 167, 169
13:5 148
13:18 156
14:8 154
16:13 171
16:14 171
17 ....143, 147, 149, *151*, 154, 157, *158*
17:1–5 ....*158*, 269n66
17:3–6 173
17:16 149
18:2 157–58
18:6 149
18:24 119
20 169
20:2 166–67
21 ....144, 171
21:1–3 .... 282–83n9
21:2 165
21:10 165
21:10–11 145
21:10–21 145–46

GENERAL INDEX

Note: Page numbers in italic indicate figures and tables. A list of biblical texts can be found in the separate **Biblical Index**.

Adam (biblical figure), 142, 144, 211, 239, 251, *252*

Adnotationes in Novum Testamentum [*Annotations*] (Erasmus): biblical interpretations, 46, 129, 255, 262n15; Milton and, 209, 294n36; Peter as "rock" or pope allegory, 51; political rhetoric and historicism, 27, 33, 61, 235; publication of, 25, 27, 30, 262n15; Vulgate, 29

advisors/counselors, and ruler: biblical texts, 109, 139, 244–45; Edward VI, 97–99, 102, 109; Erasmus, 36, 38, 40, 45, 53; Henry VIII, 104, 193; humanists, 26–27, 35; James I/VI, 287n15; Luther, 104, 193; Paul and, 38, 42; *Utopia* (More), 25, 26

Ahl, Frederick M., 261n9

allegorical (typological) interpretation: biblical interpretation and, 10–11, 230; Geneva Bible annotations, 14; Jesus Christ, 11, 14; literalism and, 15, 48–50, 61–62, 90, 146–47, 183, 283n17, 297n88; *Measure for Measure* (Shakespeare), 183–84, 185, 186, 191, 197; medieval era Quadriga, 10–12, 133; Pauline obedience, 32–33, 263n33; Protestantism, 147, 164, 198; Revelation, 147–48, 166, 168, 172; Spenser, 13–14, 201

alternate readings, 2, 200, 201, 202, 226, 231, 292n6, 292n8

alternate readings, and Milton: *De Doctrina Christiana*, 230–31, 244–45, 297n93, 297nn95–96; King James Bible (Milton's 1612 copy), 199, 201–2, 208, 209, 216–19, *218*, 226, 292n7, 296n86; *Psalms*, 202, 208, 209, 222, 227, *228*, 228–29, 231. *See also* alternate readings

Ames, William, 230, 297n91

anachronistic reading: about, 13; Bale, 153; Colet, 27; Erasmus, 27; Geneva Bible annotations, 3, 127, 156; Hebrew Bible, 139; Matthew Bible, 86, 93; Valla, 24, 27

anagogical (spiritual) interpretation, 10–12, 63, 80–81, 133

Andrewes, Lancelot, 112

annotations: about, 2–3, 4, 12, 114, 253, 300n12; biblical interpretation and, 12, 15, 17, 127; Calvin, 115; cultural role of biblical texts, 4, 123–24, *124*; Douay-Rheims Catholic Bible (1582) annotations, 6–7, 146, 153; Henry VIII and, 56, 77, *78*, *79*, 80, 271n117; italicized words, 12, 120; Latin Bible (Bucer's translation/annotations), 84; monarch's written, 56, 71–72; readership and, 56, 77, *78*, *79*, 80, 123, 271n117, 278n52. *See also* Geneva Bible (1560) annotations; paratexts; *and specific Bibles*

annotations, and political role of biblical texts: about, 21–22; Geneva Bible (1560), 5, 21, 81, 110–11, 117, 124–25, 130, 175, 278n35, 279n61, 287n6; Hampton Court conference, 175, 287nn5–6. *See also* annotations

Antichrist analogy: Douay-Rheims Catholic Bible (1582), 167; *The Faerie Queene* (Spenser), 169, 170; Fulke, 167–68; Overall, 172–73

Antiochus IV Epiphanes, 205, 208

anti-prelaticals, 53, 106, 233, 235, 240

Apocalypse (Revelation). *See* Revelation (Apocalypse); Revelation (Apocalypse), and annotations

Apocrypha, 111, 128, 280n67

applied literalism: about, 17, 85, 194, 255–56;
Bucer, 96, 102, 255; Erasmus, 195, 255, 256;
Geneva Bible (1560) annotations, 135–36,
140; *Measure for Measure* (Shakespeare),
177, 180, 184, 190, 198; Mosaic Law, 20, 102;
political thought, 63, 80–81, 102, 180–81,
198; presentism, 140; Tyndale, 55, 60, 63, 65,
82, 102, 172, 195, 255; utilitarian reading
and, 82, 180–81. *See also* literalism
Armin, Robert, 185
armor/sword/Christian knight metaphor,
165–66, 168, 286n80
Arthur (prince), 53, 64, 67, 77, 80, 96, 123
Asa (biblical figure), 102, 132–33, 175
Augustine (saint), 15, 51, 163–64, 285n69

Babylon: as analogy, 143, 153, 154, 156, 157–58;
exile of Jews/Israelites, 14, 118, 119–20, 138,
141, 142, 162. *See also* Whore of Babylon
allegory
Backus, Irena, 36, 148, 283n18, 283n22
Bale, John: Antichrist analogy, 148; dragon
allegory, 149, *150*; Henry VIII, 82; *The Image
of Both Churches*, 90, 129–30, 140, 149, 150,
150, 161, 286n92; on John, 153; Pauline
obedience, 81; plays, 81, 82; as Protestant
exile, 115, 153, 234, 284n31; true church and,
149, 150; Whore of Babylon allegory,
149–50, *151*; woman clothed with sun
allegory, 149, 150, *150*
Barbier, Nicholas, 115, 134, 280n83, 281n91,
281n96, 281n99
Barker, Christopher, 160, 161
Barker, Robert, 296n76
Barlow, William, 174–75
Barton, William, 295n70
Bateman, Stephen, 164
Bathsheba (biblical figure), 76, 76–77
Becke, Edmund: about, 89–90, 101; biblical
production, 6, 9, 86, 89; Henrician Bibles,
90; Henry VIII and, 93, *94*; Matthew Bible
and, 86, 89–96, *94*, 109, 273n22
Bennet, Henry, 281n97, 283n14
Bennet, Josephine Waters, 283n14
Bentley, Jerry H., 262n19
Beowulf, 129, 280n69
Bernard, G. W., 66, 70
Beza, Theodore de: about, 147; Beza-Tomson
New Testament, 285n46; Beza-Tremellius
Bible, 213, 217, 293n32, 294n50; Junius-Beza
Bible, 208; Junius-Tremellius-Beza Bible,

293n32; Latin Bibles and, 208, 293n32;
Milton and, 230
biblical interpretation: figurative interpretation, 3, 15, 229; tropological interpretation,
10–12, 13, 14, 109, 133. *See also* allegorical
(typological) interpretation; biblical texts;
cultural role of biblical texts; literalism;
paratexts; political role of biblical texts
biblical legalism. *See* legalism; Mosaic Law
biblical production: about, 6–7, 8, 9–10, 90,
111, 174; court authorities and, 72, 270n103;
diglot editions, 6, 54, 161; Edward VI and,
6–7, 9, 54, 111, 161, 276–77n16; Henry VIII
and, 80, 111, 161; KJV, 6–7, 8, 9. *See also*
royal iconography; specific Bibles
biblical text, paratext, literature intersection,
5–6, 202, 251, *252*, 253, 256–57, 300n8.
See also paratexts
biblical text, paratext, politics intersection,
251, 254–55, 301n16. *See also* paratexts;
political role of biblical texts
biblical texts: about, 22–23; controversies and,
4; iconography, 7, 72, *73*, 74, *75*, 75–76.
See also biblical interpretation; translations/
translators; *specific Bible, and biblical figures*
Bishops' Bible(s): about, 6–7, 9, 111, 116, 135;
annotations, 113, 116–17, 175–76, 200,
278n34; Bishops' Bible (1569), 135, 175,
278n34, 287n8; Bishops' Bible (1572), 181,
182, 278n34, 287n11; Bishops' Bible (1575),
277n30, 278n34, 287n11; critiques, 116–17,
278n34, 292n4; Elizabethan England and,
9, 116, 181, *182*, 279n53; Geneva Bible (1560)
annotations, 113, 175–76, 278n34; Geneva
Bible translation/annotations and, 113,
175–76; obedience/disobedience, 287n11;
Parker, 7, 116–17, 292n4; Pauline obedience,
33; red velvet binding, 279n53; royal
iconography, 7, 181, *182*, 186, 260n19,
289n45; Shakespeare and, 288n23; Stuart
England, 117; "tyrant," 175–76, 278n34;
word of God, 175
Blayney, Peter, 270n102
Bloom, Harold, 191
Boddy, Margaret, 221, 295n64
Bodley, Thomas, 253–54
Boel, Cornelis, 213, *214*
Boleyn, Anne: dedication page in Coverdale
Bible, 72; Henry VIII and, 20, 57, 70, 71;
New Testament (Tyndale translation), 56,
267n35, 279n53; *The Obedience of a Christian*

Man (Tyndale) readership, 56–57, 267nn38–39; vernacular literature, 57, 268n41

Book of Common Prayer, 5, 85, 159, 160, 233

Book of Law: "BIBLIA" synecdoche, 86, *87*, 88; biblical production, 23; discovery of, 81, 86, 88, 93; divine right and ruler, 93, 103; Edwardian era and, 95, 109; Josiah and, 86, 93, 101; *sola scriptura*, 142; utopic politics and, 93

Bossy, John, 267n33

Bowler, Gerald, 287n8

Bradbrook, M. C., 191

Bradshaw, John, 295n64

Bramhall, John, 106

Broughton, Hugh, 154, *155*, 284n33

Brutus, Lucius Junius, 59, 268nn48–49

Bucer, Martin: about, 83–84, 106, 107, 147, 272n8; applied literalism, 96, 102, 255; biblical plays, 105–6; Book of Common Prayer, 5, 84; canon law, 101, 105, 106, 178, 235, 273n20; divine right and ruler, 102–4, 194; *The Education of a Christian Prince* (Erasmus) and, 98, 256; Edward VI, 97–99, 102, 109; Latin Bible translation/annotations, 84; legacy, 98, 106, 107, 108; legalism and, 89, 95, 103, 108, 238; literalism, 254, 255, 256; marriage law, 96, 99–100, 104, 105; *Martini Buceri Enarrationes Perpetuae*, 97; Milton and, 83–84, 96, 104, 235–36; Mosaic Law, 97, 99–100, 101–2, 104–5, 178, 194, 235, 255, 273n20, 274n50, 275n62; Pauline obedience, 97, 103–4; penal code, 100, 101–2; political theology, 101; printed copies, 97–98; Protestant nation, 89, 99, 234; Psalms (Joye translation), 267n31; Revelation debate, 146, 283n16; *Scripta Anglicana*, 98, 274n57; theo-politics, 83–84, 92, 99, 247; utopia/utopic literature, 98, 101, 105, 238. See also *De Regno Christi [On the Kingdom of Christ]* (Bucer)

Bullinger, Heinrich, 139, 147

Busleyden, Hieronymus van, 32

Calamy, Edmund, 203, 224

Calvin, John, and Calvinism: about, 147; annotations and, 115; Church of England and, 186, 191, 194, 206–7, 256, 289n55; Commentary on Isaiah, 137, 281n94, 281n99; deposition of ruler, 62, 118, 241–42, 268n54, 298nn34–35; disciplinary plan and,

99; divine right and ruler, 240; grace, 190, 191; *Institutes of the Christian Religion*, 130, 241–42, 268n54, 298n34; literalism, 3, 15–16, 256; Pauline obedience, 62, 244, 268n54; political thought, 244, 249; predestination, 186, 187, 188–89, 234–35, 290n78; psalms/psalm culture, 205, 206–7, 225; resistance, 130, 242, 244, 246; Revelation as inauthentic, 146; Saul and David, 208; translators, 115; tyrant, 62

camel proverb, 12–13, 260n32

Campbell, Gordon, 259n10

Campion, Edmund, 160–61

canon law: Bucer, 101, 105, 106, 178, 235, 273n20; Milton, 235, 272n15, 273n20

canon law versus Mosaic Law: bigamy and, 96–97; Bucer, 101, 105, 178, 235, 273n20; Cranmer and, 83, 85, 86, 88, 235, 272n15, 273n20; divorce of Henry VIII, 99, 193, 273n26; Edwardian era and, 178, 272n15; Gardiner, 273n20; Gilby, 273n20; Latimer, 85, 181, 183; Reformation, 85, 101, 181, 183

Capito, Wolfgang, 147

Cartwright, Thomas: biblical text annotations disputes, 190–91, 237; magistrate and Mosaic Law, 193–94; political role of biblical texts, 195, 233, 254

Catherine of Aragon (queen), 20, 55, 66, 67, 68, 96

Catholicism: anagogical (spiritual) interpretation, 63; biblical production and, 9–10; Council of Trent and, 45, 146; divine right and ruler, 74; English biblical production, 80; Erasmus and, 25, 45, 46, 49, 53–54, 146; free will, 189, 190, 290n70; grace, 190–91; humanists, 19, 24, 25, 59; *Measure for Measure* (Shakespeare), 197–98, 291n102; medieval Catholic reading, 15, 49–50, 236; Mosaic Law and, 197, 267n33; obedience and ruler, 161, 285n59; political role of biblical texts, 16; political thought, 115; Protestantism/Reformation versus, 53, 71, 148–49, 166; Revelation as authentic, 146; translations of biblical text, 9–10; true church versus, 143, 154; Tyndale and, 62–63; woman as ruler and, 131–32, 139. *See also* canon law; canon law versus Mosaic Law; Douay-Rheims Catholic Bible (1582); pope(s); Rome; Whore of Babylon allegory

Cecil, William, 116, 123

Cervicornus, Eucharius, 270n102

Chapman, George, 187
chapter and verse numbers: English Bibles, 28, 39, 124; Geneva Bible (1560), 21, 28, 39, 120, 124, 137; Geneva Bible New Testament (1557), 21, 28, 39; Latin Bibles, 28, 39; Milton, 171, 226, 251; New Testament(s), 278n45; Whittingham, 120
Chapuys, Eustice, 70, 71
Charles I (king): allies, 220; Davidic association, 203, 207, 293n26; divine right and ruler, 233, 235, 240–41; *Eikon basilike*, 207, 293n26; execution of, 208, 220, 221, 249, 295n64, 300n1; "Long Parliament," 211, 232–33, 298n28; opposition and deposition of, 207, 232, 249, 293nn25–26; *Psalms* (Milton), 207, 208, 220, 221, 222, 225, 227–28, *228*, 295n64; psalms/psalm culture, 203, *204*, 225, 293n26, 296n75; royal iconography, 203; Scotland and, 225, 232–33; trial, 207, 222, 235; Westminster Assembly of Divines, 203, 219, 224, 235, 293n26, 295n70; Westminster Assembly of Divines reforms, 293n26; *The Whole Booke of Psalmes* (Sternhold and Hopkins), 203, *204*
Charles II (king), 231, 235, 250
Cheke, John, 9, 58, 84, 85, 89, 272n15
Christianization, and Hebrew Bible, 127, 138, 139, 141, 282n2, 282n103. *See also* true church (church)
Christian knight/armor/sword metaphor, 165–66, 168, 286n80
Christie-Miller, Ian, 271n117
Church of England: Bucer's legacy and, 107; Calvinism, 186, 191, 194, 206–7, 256, 289n55; Erasmus's legacy, 44–47, 53–54, 266n6; King's Book, 56, 63–64, 68, 69, 88; nonconformists, 107, 186; obey parents and ruler, 63–64; Pauline obedience, 31, 248; predestination, 148, 186, 187. *See also* Reformation
Cicero, Marcus Tullius, 32, 263n33
Claudius (emperor), 19, 31, 247
Clement VII (pope), 67
Cole, Thomas, 115, 117
Cole, William, 278n38
Colet, John: about, 29, 30, 263n29; anachronistic reading, 27; contextualist historicism, 30; Erasmus's relationship with, 29–30, 40, 262n24, 263n29; historicism and, 25, 30, 31–33, 262n24, 263n33; magistrate and divine right, 30, 31–33; Pauline obedience,

3, 30, 31–34, 247; philological historicism, 29–30; political rhetoric and historicism, 30, 32, 33, 36, 45; political role of biblical texts, 34, 36; presentism, 32; rhetoric of praise/truth to power, 45; Suetonius texts, 31, 262n24; Vulgate and, 30
Collinson, Patrick, 83–84, 106, 107, 108, 117
"congregation" versus "church": Geneva Bible annotations, 117–18, 141–42, 143, 151, 152; Geneva Bible New Testament annotations, 117–18, 152; KJV, 141, 282n2; New Testament (Tyndale translation), 117–18, 151
Constantine (emperor), 24
Counter-Reformation, 19, 145, 160, 169, 267n33. *See also* Reformation
Courteau, Thomas, 115, 134, 280n83, 281n91, 281n96, 281n99
Coverdale, Miles: about, 10, 277n26; *The Books of Solomon*, 76, 80; *Enchiridion* (Erasmus) translation, 46; Geneva Bible translators, 277n26; Matthew Bible, 89, 90; Protestant as term of use, 272n2; writing and production of Coverdale Bible, 10, 74, 80
Coverdale Bible: annotations, 74; "BIBLIA" synecdoche, 86, *87*, 88; dedication page, 72; Holbein the Younger woodcut, 7, 9, 72, *73*, 74, 76, 86, *87*, 88, 181, 250; marrying one's brother's wife, 69, 70; Matthew Bible and, 89, 90; Mosaic Law, 82; royal iconography, 7, 9, 72, *73*, 74, 181, 270n105, 289n45; writing and production, 9, 10, 70, 72, 74, 80, 82, 270nn102–3
Cranach, Lucas, 147, 153, 154
Cranmer, Thomas: biblical production and, 7, 9, 84, 272n6; Book of Common Prayer, 159; canon law versus Mosaic Law, 83, 85, 86, 88, 235, 272n15, 273n20; *Catechism*, 7, 84, 86, *87*, 88–89, 93; divine right and ruler, 85, 234; divorce of Henry VIII, 270n97; Edward VI and Josiah, 85–86, 134; Erasmus's legacy, 46–47; Gardiner and, 88, 273n26; marrying one's brother's wife, 68; obey parents and ruler, 88–89; Protestant nation and, 89, 99; reason, 232, 233; Reformation program and, 83, 84, 96; royal iconography in Great Bible, 7; theo-politics, 92
Crispin, John, 122, 124, 280n78
Cromwell, Thomas: about, 261n51; biblical plays and, 81; biblical production and, 9, 270n103; English Civil Wars and, 221;

iconography in biblical texts, 7, 72, *73*; Tyndale and, 71, 270n99

Cullington, J. Donald, 293n32

cultural role of biblical texts: about, 1–3, 17, 194, 199; annotations, 4, 123–24, *124*; biblical production and, 10; Erasmus, 2, 17; Geneva Bible/annotations and, 1–2, 111, 112, 113, 123, 175, 177, 178, 259n2, 276n3, 288n23; James I/VI, 198; justice/mercy, 179, 193, 197, 291n87; *Measure for Measure* (Shakespeare), 193, 291n87; Renaissance, 4–5, 259n8, 259n10; spiritual mode of interpretation versus, 63; theo-political treatises and, 89, 108, 273n29; Tyndale and, 2, 9

Cummings, Brian, 27, 48–49, 188, 264n72

Daniel, Samuel, 187

Daniell, David, 57–58, 70

Danner, Dan G., 278n38

Dante Alighieri, 10–11, 229–30

David (biblical figure): adultery, 55, 76–77, 207; Bathsheba and, *76*, 76–77; Charles I association, 203, 207, 293n26; divine right and ruler, 102, 125, 126; harp iconography in biblical texts, 72, *73*, 74, *75*, 75–76; Henry VIII association, *75*, 75–76, *76*, 77, 80, 203; Jesus Christ and, 151–52; as king, *73*, 75, *75*, *77*, 82, 280n70; political role of biblical texts, 55; polygamy, 97; psalms and, 74, 203, 205, 207, 293n21; Saul and, 208; spiritual role of ruler, 99

Davies, Michael, 66

Day, John, 9, 89, *94*, *158*

Dead Sea Scrolls, 138, 281n100

Decalogue. *See* Ten Commandments (Decalogue)

De Doctrina Christiana (Milton): about, 4; alternate readings, 230–31, 244–45, 297n93, 297nn95–96; divine right and ruler, 217, 295n55; historicism, 235; Johannine comma, 294n36; literalism critique, 230, 297n91; "love" translation, 294n39; Pauline obedience, 15, 244; Picard and, 216, 218; Ten Commandments, 238–39

Dekker, Thomas, 173

Demaus, Robert, 67

Dent, Arthur, 283n16

deposition of ruler: army and, 242, 299n37; Calvinism, 62, 118, 241–42, 268n54, 298nn34–35; Charles I, 240–41, 298n28, 298n30; magistrates, 62, 118, 240–42,

268n54, 298nn34–35; Milton, 241, 242, 245, 247, 300n3; parliament and, 242, 299n37

De Regno Christi [*On the Kingdom of Christ*] (Bucer): about, 89, 254, 274n57; Erasmus and, 98, 256; marriage and divorce law, 105; More and, 98, 101, 254, 256; Mosaic Law, 99–100; Pauline obedience and, 103–4; political role of biblical texts, 5, 58, 96, 247, 273n29; presentation and printed, 97–98; printed copies, 107; Protestant exiles/nation and, 98, 99; translation by Milton, 105, 235, 237, 238; utopic Protestantism, 238

detorqueret (twisted) rhetorical procedure, 17, 41, 43, 45, 135, 255, 264n72

de Vere, Edward, 17th Earl of Oxford, 123, 126, 278n51, 279n53, 279n58

de Vere Geneva Bible (1570): about, 112; commonplace topics, 123–24, *124*; handwritten notes/marks, 123, 278–79n52, 279n57; readership/reader as translator, 1, 124, *216*; red velvet binding, *122*, 123

Diodati, Giovanni, 209

Dionysius of Alexandria, 283n15

disobedience/obedience. *See* obedience, and ruler; obedience/disobedience

divine right, and ruler: Book of Law, 93, 103; Bucer, 102–4, 194; Calvinism, 240; Catholicism, 74; Charles I, 233, 235, 240–41; Cranmer, 85, 234; Edward VI, 85, 91–92, 93, 234; Geneva Bible and, 91, 92, 125–26; Hebrew Bible, 91, 93, 102–3, 125–26, 228, 296n84; Henry VIII, 72; James I/VI, 180–81, 247, 289n41; KJV, 77, 91, 92–93, 103; Latimer, 85, 181, 183, 184, 234; magistrate, 30, 31–33, 91, 178–79, 180–81, 183, 186; Matthew Bible, 91–92; Milton, 61, 126, 214, 216, 217, 235, 247–48, 295n55, 300n3; Pauline obedience, 81, 85, 89, 103–4, 235, 240, 241, 247–48; presentism, 124–25, 134–35; royalists, 227–28, 296n84; sword of power and, 72, *73*, 74; Tudor era, 93; Tyndale, 59, 91, 102, 125

divorce, and Mosaic Law, 66, 96, 99, 105, 237, 273n26. *See also* divorce of Henry VIII

divorce/divorce tracts, and Milton: about, 222, 224, 232, 234–35; Bucer and, 96, 235; canon law, 236; *The Doctrine and Discipline of Divorce* (1643, 1644), 208–9, 236, 237, 239; literalism critique, 235, 236–37; Mosaic Law, 104, 105, 237; Paul and, 237; reason and, 237–38, 242, 246, 297n17. *See also* divorce, and Mosaic Law

divorce of Henry VIII: Bucer, 96; canon law
    versus Mosaic Law, 99, 193, 273n26;
    Cranmer, 270n97; Edwardian era, 53,
    266n23; Latimer, 70, 270n97; Luther, 104;
    marrying one's brother's wife, 66, 96; pope
    and, 71; Protestantism, 71, 270n97;
    Tyndale, 6, 52–53, 67, 70–71, 96; Wolsey,
    71, 270n97; writings against, 71, 270n99
Dixon, John, 141, 142, 144, 169, 170–72,
    286n84
Dobneck, Johann, 266n11
Dodds, Gregory, 46, 195, 254, 256, 265n92,
    300n14
Doleman, R. (pseud.), 287n13
Domitian (emperor), 153, 154
Donation of Constantine, 24, 27, 36
Donne, John, 196, 198, 259n2
Douay-Rheims Catholic Bible (1582): about,
    6–7; annotations, 6–7, 146, 153, 190–91;
    Antichrist analogy, 167; Bale, 148; biblical
    production, 160, 161, 285n59; "church,"
    161, 282n2; contextualist historicism, 181;
    dragon/devil/Satan allegory, 167; Foxe, 148;
    free will, 189, 190; Fulke, 162; Luther, 25,
    261n4; obedience and ruler, 161, 285n59;
    Revelation, 149, 156, 166; Tyndale, 65,
    269n66
Downame, George, 148–49
dragon/devil/Satan allegory: about, 143; Bale,
    149, 150; Douay-Rheims Catholic Bible
    (1582), 167; The Faerie Queene (Spenser),
    144, 145, 170, 171; Geneva Bible annota-
    tions, 167; Revelation, 154, 155, 166–67;
    true church and, 152
Du Bellay, Joachim, 157, 284n34
Duffield, Gervase, 71
Dugdale, Gilbert, 185
Duke of Saxony, George, 147
Du Moulin, Pierre, 295n64
Dzelzainis, Martin, 246, 299n48

ecumenism, 190, 191, 198, 254, 290n75, 290n78
Eden, Kathy, 263n38
The Education of a Christian Prince [Institutio
    Principis Christiani] (Erasmus): about, 6, 25,
    54–55, 89; biblical text, paratext, literature
    intersection, 5; De Regno Christi (Bucer)
    and, 98, 256; Henry VIII and, 35, 53;
    historicism, 19, 34–35, 46, 53, 263n38;
    magistrate/magistratus, 33–34, 61; tyrant,
    34–35

Edward VI (king), and Edwardian era:
    accession/reign of, 75, 80, 81, 84, 85;
    advisors/counselors, 97–99, 102, 109;
    biblical texts and, 250; Book of Common
    Prayer, 85; Book of Law and, 95, 109; Bucer
    and, 84–85, 97–99, 102, 109; canon law
    versus Mosaic Law, 101, 105, 178, 235,
    273n20; Commentary on Isaiah (Calvin),
    137, 281n94; death of, 272n14; divine right
    and ruler, 85, 91–92, 93, 234; divorce of
    Henry VIII and, 53, 266n23; Erasmus's
    legacy and, 46, 54, 254; Joshua and, 82;
    Josiah and, 14–15, 81, 85–86, 98, 101, 109,
    134–35, 148; legalism, 89, 93–96, 103, 108,
    272n15; legitimate lineage debate, 250;
    Matthew Bible and, 90, 93, 94; Milton and,
    84–85, 272nn14–15; Mosaic Law, 80, 82, 85,
    86, 89, 91, 93–96, 177, 178, 272n15; obey
    parents, 80; Pauline obedience, 20, 85;
    political literature, 85; Promised Land
    analogy, 75, 82, 95; Protestantism and, 84,
    85; Reformation and, 20, 84–85, 234,
    272n15; royal iconography, 84, 86, 87, 88;
    theo-politics and, 22, 90; translations and
    production of biblical texts, 6–7, 9, 54, 111,
    161, 276–77n16; Treasons Act in 1534,
    280n74; tutors, 80, 84, 85, 272n15, 273n17;
    Tyndale's legacy and, 54; utopic Protestant-
    ism, 81, 93
Elijah (biblical figure), 292n8
Elisha (biblical figure), 152
Elizabeth I (queen), and Elizabethan England:
    biblical production, 9, 276–77n16; Bishops'
    Bible, 9, 116, 181, 182, 279n53; Calvinism and
    Church of England, 289n55; Commentary
    on Isaiah (Calvin), 137, 281n94; ecumenism,
    190, 290n75; Erasmus's legacy and, 46, 254;
    The Faerie Queene (Spenser), 170–71;
    Geneva Bible, 1, 7, 111–13, 116, 117–18, 140,
    175, 250, 276–77n16; Grindal and, 160;
    legitimate lineage debate, 53, 70, 148, 250;
    literature, 257; liturgy and, 84; Mosaic
    Law, 288n25; New Testament (Tremellius
    translation), 272n3; New Testament
    (Tyndale translation), 84; obedience and
    ruler, 161, 285n59; obliquus ductus, 25;
    prayerbook, 278n43; presentism, 134, 170;
    Protestantism and, 119–20, 121, 170–71,
    278n43; royal iconography, 7, 181, 182,
    260n19, 289n45; second Temple and, 10,
    117, 278n36; theology and, 83, 84, 272n3;

Treasons Act in 1534, 280n74; tutors, 84; woman as ruler, 108–9, 132, 139; Zerubbabel and, 10, 117, 162. *See also* Tudor era

Elyot, Thomas, 53

Enchiridion militis Christiani [Handbook of the Christian Soldier] (Erasmus): about, 30, 44, 48–49; Coverdale translation, 46; Tyndale translation, 2, 5, 48–50, 168, 254, 266n10, 268n53

English Bible(s): about, 9, 81–82; biblical production, 7, 9–10, 84, 272n6; Catholicism and, 80; chapter and verse numbers, 28, 39, 124; cultural role of biblical texts, 3, 4; *La Bible* (Barbier and Courteau), 115, 134, 136, 137, 280n83, 281n96, 281n99; political role of biblical texts, 7, 220–22, 295n64; reception/indictments of, 2. *See also* *specific Bibles*

English Civil Wars: Geneva Bible (1560) and, 1, 2, 110, 111, 124–25, 140, 279n61; New Model Army, 220, 221, 241; political role of biblical texts, 220–21, 295n64; Pride and, 224, 241; *Psalms* (Milton), 220–21, 226–28, *228*, 295n64; Scotland, 220, 221, 233; Windsor Army meeting, 221, 222, *223*

English Protestantism. *See* Church of England

English Reformation. *See* Reformation

Erasmus: about, 29, 44; advisors/counselors, 36, 38, 40, 45, 53; anachronistic reading, 27; applied literalism, 195, 255, 256; biblical production and, *28*, 29, 30, 161; biblical text, paratext, literature intersection, 5, 253; Catholicism and, 25, 45, 46, 49, 53–54, 146; Christian knight/armor/sword metaphor, 168, 286n80; Colet's relationship with, 29–30, 40, 262n24, 263n29; collection of passages practices, 77; cultural role of biblical texts, 2, 17; *De Copia*, 35; *De Libero Arbitrio*, 46–47, 290n70; *detorqueret* (twisted) rhetorical procedure, 17, 41, 43, 45, 135, 255, 264n72; *emphasis* rhetorical procedures, 44, 265n83; *An Exhortation to the Diligent Study of Scripture*, 46; "flattery," 37, 38, 39, 40, 44, 49; free will, 29, 46, 50, 239, 290n70; *The Handsome Weapon of a Christian Knight* (1534), 2, 5, 48–50, 254, 268n53; Henrician court and, 53; Henry VIII's attributes, 35, 45, 265n85; Johannine Comma, 29, 209–10, 211, 294n36; Letters of Paul (Epistles), 3, *28*, 30; Luther and, 5, 41, 45, 46–47, 264n72; *Manuel of a Christen Knight* (1533), 5, 48–50, 168, 286n80; More's

epigram, 45; *Novum Testamentum* (1519), 25, 29, 42, 266n10; *Novum Testamentum* (1522), 29, 42, 50, 264n74, 266n10, 283n15; *Novum Testamentum* (1527), 29, 38–39, 42–43; *Novum Testamentum* (1535), 29, 42, 264n74; obedience, 54; *Oration on the Pursuit of Virtue*, 40; *Panegyric for Archduke Philip of Austria*, 25, 36–37, 38, 39–40, 44; panegyric genre and, 40, 44; *Paraclesis*, 5–6, 38, 46, 50; Pauline obedience, 19, 32–35, 53, 247–48; political power, 25, 34, 35, 36, 44, 45, 59, 268n48; *The Praise of Folly*, 43–45, 46; presentism, 43; *Ratio seu Methodus Verae Theologociae*, 46; reason, 233; rhetoric of praise, 37–45, 264n72, 264n74; Vulgate, 29, 33. See also *Adnotationes in Novum Testamentum* [*Annotations*] (Erasmus); *Enchiridion militis Christiani* [*Handbook of the Christian Soldier*] (Erasmus); *Novum Instrumentum Omne* [1516] (Erasmus)

Erasmus, and legacy: about, 45–47, 255–56; Cranmer, 46–47; Edwardian era, 46, 54, 254; Elizabethan England, 46, 254; Great Bible, 46; Milton, 22, 209, 230, 234, 235, 247–48, 294n36, 297n95; Reformation/Protestantism, 5–6, 45–47, 50, 53–54, 253–54, 265n87, 266n6; Tyndale, 48, 52, 54

Esau (biblical figure), 129–30

Esdras (biblical figure), 205

Estienne, Robert, 278n45

Eusebius of Caesarea, 283n15

evangelicalism, 80, 86, 91, 271n1, 272n2. *See also* Protestantism

Eve (biblical figure), 142, 144, 211, 239, 251, *252*

exile/persecution/stranger/defeatism: Elizabeth I and, 120, *121*, 278n43; Geneva Bible annotations, 7, 60, 81, 109, 114, 115–16, 118, 119, 278n36; Geneva Bible New Testament (1557), 118, 119, *119*, 170. *See also* Protestant exiles

Ezra (biblical figure), 205, 224–25

The Faerie Queene (Spenser): Antichrist analogy, 169, 170; biblical text, paratext, literature intersection, 5, 251, 253, 300n11; Christian knight/armor/sword metaphor, 165–66, 168, 286n80; composition process, 146, 283n14; Dixon's annotations, 141, 142–43, 144, 169, 170–72, 286n80; dragon/devil/Satan allegory, 144, 145, 170, 171; Elizabethan readers, 170–71; Hamilton's

The Faerie Queene (Spenser) (continued)
annotations, 171; Jesus Christ, 169, 171, 172,
288n86; medievalism, 163–64, 168, 170,
285n69; New Jerusalem, 144–45, 165; Paul
and, 164, 165; political role of biblical texts,
251, 253; Protestant nation allegory, 163, 164,
166, 170, 172; Stuart England era annotations, 168, 170; "testament," 162–63, 164–65;
true church, 145, 149, 151, 152, 169, 170–71,
288n86; tyranny, 166; Whore of Babylon
allegory, 143, 144, 149, 169, 170; woman
clothed with sun allegory, 145, 149, 166,
170–71; word of God, 145, 165

Fagius, Paul, 83, 84, 106, 107

Felch, Susan M., 57, 267n38

fifth commandment (obey parents), and ruler.
See obey parents (fifth commandment), and
ruler

Filmer, Robert, 130–31, 198, 200, 250

Fisher, John, 68

Fleck, Andrew, 177

Fletcher, Harris, 211, 213, 217, 293n32, 294n51,
299n41

Fletcher, John, *66*

Foxe, Edward, 270n97

Foxe, John: Antichrist analogy, 148; Calvin
translations, 115; Louth manuscript, 57;
Ninety-five Theses (Luther), 281n97;
presentism, 148, 158–59; royal iconography,
181; Tyndale and, 5, 6, 54

free will: Arminian doctrine, 239–40, 256,
298nn25–26; Catholicism, 189, 190, 290n70;
Erasmus, 29, 46, 50, 239, 290n70; Luther,
50, 189, 290n70; Milton, 242, 244, 245, 246;
Protestantism, 148, 239, 298n25; Whitgift,
290n78. *See also* reason

Froben, Johann, *28*, 29, 30

Frye, Northrop, 4

Fulke, William, 160–61, 162, 166, 167–68, 190,
290n78

Fuller, Thomas, 7, *8*, 9–10, 140

Gad (biblical figure), 281–82n101

Gardiner, Stephen, 88, 132, 271–72n1, 273n20,
273n26

Geneva Bible(s): alternate readings and
annotations, 200; biblical production, 117,
118, 159, 160, 177, 280n78, 288n24; Geneva
Bible (1578), 111, 160, 276–77n16, 287n6;
Geneva Bible (1582), 287n6, 288n23; Geneva
Bible (1588), 208; Geneva Bible (1602), 150,

190, 287n6; Geneva-Tomson Bible (1576),
62, 113, 118, 159, 160; magistrate/princes,
241; obedience/disobedience, 287n6; word
of God, 153, 175, 287n6. *See also* de Vere
Geneva Bible (1570); Geneva Bible (1560);
Geneva Bible (1560) annotations; Geneva
Bible (1560) annotations, and presentism;
Geneva Bible New Testament (1557) annotations; Geneva Bible New Testament(s)

Geneva, and biblical texts, 115

Geneva Bible (1560): about, 1, 7, 8, 9, 20–21,
109, 117; advisors/counselors, 109; biblical
interpretation, 12, 113–14; biblical production, 1, 6–7, 21, 28, 80, 81, 111, 113, 116, 117,
123, 198, 276–77n16, 278n38; Bucer's legacy
and, 108; chapter and verse numbers, 21, 28,
39, 120, 124, 137; controversies and, 292n4;
critiques, 2, 111, 116, 173; discipline, 99;
divine right and ruler, 91, 92, 125–26;
Elizabethan England, 1, 7, 111–13, 116,
117–18, 250, 276–77n16, 278n36; historicism
and, 12–13, 14, 15, 33, 113–14; italicized
words, 209; Jacobean England and, 1, 111,
112; James I/VI as reader/user, 2, 111, 112,
116, 175, 278n34; kings in biblical texts, 95;
KJV and, 111; "love" translation, 294n39;
marrying one's brother's wife, 69; Milton,
112–13, 208, 276n13; Mosaic Law, 108, 109;
Old Testament, 139, 141–42, 282n103; penal
code, 101; as people's Bible, 1–2, 111, 123,
174, 198, 259n2, 276n3, 276–77n16; political
role of biblical texts and, 116, 142, 206,
277n28, 293n22; *The Psalms of David*, 205;
revisions after death of Mary I, 117;
Scotland and, 112, 174; Tudor era and, 117.
See also Geneva Bible (1560) translators;
"tyrant," and Geneva Bible (1560)

Geneva Bible (1560) annotations: about, 2, 3,
113–15, 140, 175; allegorical interpretations,
14, 153; anachronistic reading, 3, 127, 156;
applied literalism and, 140; Bishops' Bible(s)
and, 113, 175–76, 278n34; "congregation"
versus "church," 117–18, 141–42, 143, 151, 152;
cultural role of biblical texts, 1–2, 111, 112,
113, 123, 175, 177, 259n2, 276n3; dragon/
devil/Satan allegory, 167; Elizabethan
context, 117–18, 139; English Civil Wars, 1,
2, 110, 111, 124–25, 140, 279n61; Erasmus's
annotations comparison, 39; exile/
persecution/stranger/defeatism, 7, 60, 81,
109, 114, 115–16, 118, 119, 278n36; "flattery,"

126, 129, 133; *Image of Both Churches* (Bale), 149, *150*, 150–51, *151*; James I/VI critique, 2, 116, 174, 175, 177, 287n5, 289n41; Jews/Israelites exiled to Babylon, 14, 118, 119–20, 138, 141, 142; Jezebel, 133; King James Bible and, 198, 291n107; literalism, 113–14, 140; magistrate/princes, 61, 118; obey parents and ruler, 64; *Paradise Lost* (Milton), 153, 276n13, 293n31; Paul and prophecy, 160; philological notes, 12–13, 120, 127; political role of biblical texts, 5, 21, 81, 110–11, 117, 124–25, 130, 175, 278n35, 279n61, 287n6; pope/papacy/papist, 127, 150, 153, 154, *155*, 156, 200–201; presentism and, 140; Protestant nation and, 112, 119–20, *121*, 133; *The Psalms of David*, 205; readership and, 123, 278n52; Rome, 119, *119*, 150, 153, 154, *155*, 156, 284n29; word of God, 160, 175, 176, 287n6

Geneva Bible (1560) annotations, and presentism: about, 2, 14, 15, 113–14, 118, 133, 140; admonition/prophetic admonition, 132–33, 139; anachronistic reading, 127; applied literalism and, 135–36, 140; Christianization in Hebrew Bible, 139, 141–42, 282n103; divine right, and ruler, 134–35; "door of the temple," 136–37, 281nn96–97, 281n99; magistrate and ruler, 139–40; reading practices, 114, 135–40; "tyrant," 130, 138, 139. *See also* Geneva Bible (1560) annotations

Geneva Bible New Testament (1557): biblical production, 28, 80, 113; chapter and verse numbers, 21, 28, 39; grace, 190–91; "rock" or papal allegory, 278n39; translators, 108, 115, 117, 120

Geneva Bible New Testament (1557) annotations: allegorical interpretation, 14; "congregation" versus "church," 117–18, 142, 143, 152; exile/persecution/stranger/defeatism, 118, 119, *119*, 170; exodus from Egypt, 120, *121*; italicized words, 108, 120; Pauline obedience, 33, 108, 118; Protestant nation, 118, 120, 133; woman as ruler, 108–9

Geneva Bible New Testament(s): Geneva-Tomson-Junius Bible, 113; Geneva-Tomson New Testament (1576), 62, 113, 118, 285n46. *See also* Geneva Bible New Testament (1557); Geneva Bible New Testament (1557) annotations

Geneva Bible (1560) translators: about, 107, 115, 275n82, 277n26; Calvin and, 115; Cole, 278n38; Cole, Thomas, 115, 117; Gilby, 64, 99, 114, 115, 117, 277n26, 278n38; Whittingham, 117, 277n26, 278n38. *See also* Geneva Bible (1560)

Geneva-Tomson-Junius Bible, 113

Geneva-Tomson New Testament (1576), 113, 118

German Reformation, 7, 83, 84, 96. *See also* Reformation

Gilby, Anthony: about, 131; *An Admonition to England and Scotland*, 110, 131, 132–33, 138; *Admonition to the Parliament* (Anonymous), 99, 107; canon law, 273n20; Geneva Bible translator/annotator, 64, 99, 114, 115, 117, 277n26, 278n38; obey parents and ruler, 64; presentism, 138, 140; prophetic admonitions, 132–33; reading practices, 135; resistance, 206, 207; "tyrant," 131, 132, 133, 139; woman as ruler, 139; writings lost during persecution, 114, 132, 138, 282n102

Gleason, John B., 262n24

glosses. *See* annotations; Geneva Bible (1560) annotations; paratexts; *and specific Bibles*

Goffe, William, 221, 222

Golden Rule, 179, 291n87

Golding, Arthur, 205

Goodman, Christopher, 108, 115, 131–32, 133, 280n78

Gordon, Bruce, 84, 272n6, 282n104

grace, 10–11, 127, 190–91

Grafton, Anthony, 135

Great Bible: biblical production, 7, 9, 80, 111, 276n15; Erasmus's legacy and, 46; Henry VIII, 7; preface, 233; royal iconography, 7; translations critique, 174; Tyndale's legacy, 80

Green, Ian, 273n23

Greenblatt, Stephen, 6, 268n47

Greschat, Martin, 272n6

Greville, Robert (Robert Greville Brooke), 106–7

Grey, Lady Jane, 81, 115

Grindal, Edmund, 107, 116, 159–60, 274n57, 277n30

Grotius, Hugo, 237

Groves, Beatrice, 144

Grynaeus, Simon, 96

Guibbory, Achsah, 203

Habermas, Jürgen, 250

Haddon, Walter, 106, 272n15

Hadfield, Andrew, 163, 164

Haigh, Christopher, 11, 80

Hale, John K., 293n32

Hamilton, A. C., 171

Hammill, Graham, 17–18, 267n30

Hampton Court conference: annotations and political role of biblical texts, 175, 287nn5–6; attendees, 176, 287n13; Geneva Bible annotations critique, 2, 116, 174, 177; predestination, 187; reports, 174–75, 287n5; translations critique, 174

Harington, John, 176, 286n16

Harvey, Gabriel, 135, 149, 283n25

Hebrew Bible (Old Testament): admonitions/prophetic admonitions, 132–33, 139, 282n104; advisors/counselors, 139, 244–45; alternate readings, 202, 292n8; annotations, 200–201; biblical history and, 137–38; Christianization and, 127, 138, 139, 141, 282n2, 282n103; divine right and ruler, 91, 93, 102–3, 125–26, 228, 296n84; historicism, 201; political role of biblical texts, 80–81; presentism, 138; translations of, 55, 261n31; true church and, 129–30, 139, 141, 144, 151–52. See also Pentateuch (Tyndale translation)

Hebrew language, 55, 84, 267n30. See also Hebrew Bible (Old Testament)

Henry VIII (king): Act of Supremacy in 1534, 54, 57, 131; advisors/counselors, 104, 193; annotations and readership, 56, 71–72, 77, 78, 79, 80, 271n117; attributes, 35, 45, 265n85; biblical production and, 7, 80, 111, 161; biblical texts and readership, 56, 66, 68–69, 72, 73, 74, 270n103, 270n105, 271n117; Boleyn and, 20, 57, 70, 71; Catherine of Aragon, 20, 55, 66, 67, 68, 96; childlessness or lack of heir, 66, 67, 68–69; Coverdale Bible, 9, 72, 73, 74; David association, 75, 75–76, 76, 77, 80, 203; divine right and ruler, 72; humanists, 55; Joshua and, 82; King's Book, 63–64, 68, 88; kingship passages, 77, 80; legitimate lineage debate, 53, 70, 250; Luther on gospel versus Mosaic Law, 193; marrying one's brother's wife, 66, 67, 68, 69, 70; New Testament (Tyndale translation) critique, 6, 51, 175; *The Obedience of a Christian Man* (Tyndale) and, 57, 71, 267n38, 267n39; obey parents and ruler,

63–65, 88; papal dispensation, 20, 67, 71; polygamy and, 96; Pope's authority, 52–53, 67, 68, 71–72, 85, 171; Reformation program and, 271–72n1; royal iconography, 7, 9, 72, 73, 270n105, 289n45; Supreme Head and Act of Supremacy in 1534, 64, 181; sword of power, 72, 73, 74; Treasons Act in 1534, 131; "tyrant," 131; vernacular literature, 57, 268n41

Herbert, A. S., 266n11, 276n3

Herman, Peter, 292n7

Heywood, Thomas, 289n50

Hezekiah (biblical figure), 99, 102

Hilkiah (biblical figure), 86, 88, 93, 101

Hill, Christopher, 2, 111, 208, 259n2, 276n3

historicism: about, 25; biblical texts, 205, 292n18; contextualist historicism, 12, 29, 30, 39, 181; Douay-Rheims Catholic Bible (1582), 181; Geneva Bible (1560), 12–13, 14, 15, 113–14; Hebrew Bible, 201; humanists and, 3, 19, 25, 31, 32, 49; literalism and, 49; Milton, 22, 228–29, 235, 247–48; Pauline obedience, 31–35, 263n33; political rhetoric and, 24, 25, 27, 33, 61, 235; psalms/psalm culture, 205, 206, 224–25, 228–29, 292n18; rhetorical procedures, 25–27, 45, 261n4. *See also* literary historicism; philological historicism; political rhetoric and historicism

historicism, and Erasmus: contextualist historicism, 12, 29, 39, 181; *The Education of a Christian Prince* (Erasmus), 19, 34–35, 46, 53, 263n38; literary historicism, 19, 27, 29, 34, 39; Milton, 22, 247–48; philological historicism, 27, 29–30, 50; political rhetoric and historicism, 25, 27, 33, 36, 44, 45, 61, 235, 247–48

Hobbes, Thomas: about, 110, 259n2; *Behemoth: A History of the Causes of the Civil Wars*, 1, 3, 110, 140; biblical texts, 198, 259n2, 276n1; cultural role of biblical texts, 4, 259n2; political role of biblical texts, 1, 2, 3; political thought, 58; on Protestant exiles and English Civil Wars, 1, 2, 110, 111, 140

Holbein, Hans, the Younger, 7, 9, 72, 73, 74, 76, 86, 87, 88, 181, 250

Hooker, Richard: cultural role of biblical texts, 1, 112; ecumenism, 190, 290n75; political role of biblical texts, 195, 233, 254–55, 256, 291n95, 301n16; predestination, 291n95, 301n16; reason, 237

Howard, Thomas, 3rd Duke of Norfolk, 271–72n1

Huldah (biblical figure), 86

humanists: advisors/counselors, 26–27, 35; biblical texts/interpretation, 27, 138; Catholicism, 19, 24, 25, 59; Henry VIII, 55; historicism and, 3, 19, 25, 31, 32, 49; rhetorical procedures, 25–26, 45. See also *specific humanists*

Hunter, G. K., 178

Hunton, Philip, 130

Hus, John, 147

iconography in biblical texts, 7, 72, *73*, 74, *75*, 75–76

Isaac, Jasper, 213, *214*

Isaiah (biblical figure), 128, 137, 139, 156, 282n104

Israelites/Jews. *See* Jews/Israelites

italicized words: annotations, 12, 120; Geneva Bible (1560), 209; Geneva Bible New Testament (1557) annotations, 108, 120; King James Bible (Milton's 1612 copy), 222, 226; KJV, 92–93, 209; *Psalms* (Milton), 209, *210*, 222, 228, *228*, 251

Jacob (biblical figure), 129–30

Jacobean England: biblical texts, 1, 111, 112, 116–17; liturgy and, 84; *obliquus ductus*, 25; poetry, 176, 287n18; political theology, 84, 187, 287n18

James I/VI (king of England/king of Scotland): advisors/counselors, 287n15; Calvinism, 289n55; Catholic heretics and, 178; Church of England, 289n55; cultural role of biblical texts, 198; divine right and ruler, 180–81, 247, 289n41; Geneva Bible annotations critique, 2, 116, 174, 175, 177, 287n5, 289n41; Geneva Bible readership, 2, 111, 112, 116, 175, 278n34; King's Men, 176, 187; legalism, 178; London arrival, 176, 185; Mary's execution, 117, 175, 278n35; Mosaic Law, 177–78, 193; obedience/disobedience and, 175, 247; plays as confrontational, 187; Solomon, 178; writings and political works, 176, 178, 193, 287n15, 287n18. *See also* Hampton Court conference; Jacobean England; King James Bible (KJV, Authorized Version)

Jardine, Lisa, 135

Jehoram (biblical figure), 246

Jehu (biblical figure), 246, 299n49

Jerome, 29, 36, 41, 51. *See also* Vulgate

Jesus Christ: allegorical interpretation, 11, 14, 143, 151–52; biblical plays and, 81; camel proverb, 12–13, 260n32; death in biblical texts, 154, 284n33; divine right and ruler, 134, 135; Eucharist and, 97, 163; *The Faerie Queene* (Spenser), 169, 171, 172, 288n86; Hebrew Bible Christianization and, 127, 139, 141, 282n103; historicism and, 12–13, 14, 15; Josiah and, 134, 280n83; political role of psalms, 206; rewards for persecuted, 118; "testament," 163; Trinitarian debate, 29, 209, 262n19

Jews/Israelites: bondage in Egypt analogy, 85, 181, 183, 278n34; Claudius and, 31; exiled to Babylon, 14, 118, 119–20, 138, 141, 142, 162; exodus from Egypt, 10–11, 75, 101, 120, *121*, 230; Mosaic Law, 69–70, 104

Jezebel (biblical figure), 133

Johannine Comma, 29, 209, 211, 262n19, 294n36

John (biblical figure), 90, 145, 146, 149, 152, 153, 157, 255, 292–93n9

Jonson, Ben, 144, 187, 290n59

Joshua (biblical figure), 75, 82, 88, 93, 94–95, 109

Josiah (biblical figure): advisors/counselors, 109; Book of Law, 86, 93, 101, 142; divine right and ruler, 102, 135; Edward VI and presentism, 14–15, 81, 85–86, 98, 101, 109, 134–35, 148; Hilkiah the priest and, 86, 88, 93, 101; Jesus Christ and, 134, 280n83; Mosaic Law and, 86, 103; reform and, 85–86; spiritual role of ruler, 99

Joye, George, 76, *76*, *78*, *79*, 84, 267n31

Judah (biblical figure), 67–68

Jugge, Richard, 84, *151*

Julius (pope), 67, 268n48

Junius, Francis: annotations, 153; *Apocalypsis*, 23, 150; Geneva-Tomson-Junius Bible, 113; Junius-Beza Bible, 208; Junius-Tremellius-Beza Bible, 293n32

justice/mercy: cultural role of biblical texts, 179, 193, 197, 291n87; *lex talionis* ("an eye for an eye"), 179, 191, 193; *Measure for Measure* (Shakespeare), 188–90, 191, 192–93, 196–97; "measure for measure" phrase, 191–93, 290n83; New Testament, 188–89, 191, 196; political role of biblical texts, 179, 188–89; royal iconography, 181, *182*, 186

Kahn, Victoria, 18
Kearney, James, 159, 160, 168
Keats, John, 199
Kermode, Frank, 4
Kethe, William, 132, 206, 207, 220
Killeen, Kevin, 15, 205, 299n49
King, John, 270n105, 276–77n16, 289n45
King James Bible (Milton's 1612 copy): about,
    22, 112–13, 124, 198, 226; alternate readings,
    199, 201–2, 208, 209, 216–19, *218*, 226,
    292n7, 296n86; biblical text, paratext,
    politics intersection, 251; chapter and verse
    numbers, 226, 251; divine right and ruler,
    214, 216; family history, *212*, 213; italicized
    words, 222, 226; "John," 222, *223*; obedi-
    ence/disobedience, 251, *252*, 253; Pauline
    obedience, *243*, 244; poetry, 218–19; prose
    and, 112–13, 208–9, 212, 213, 217, 294n51;
    readership/reader as translator, 211, *216*,
    216–17, 294nn38–39; reading marks, 213–14,
    215, 216, *243*, 244; "Windsor," 222, *223*
King James Bible (KJV, Authorized Version):
    about, 2, 198–99, 213, *214*; alternate
    readings, 2, 200, 201, 226, 292n6; annotations as sparse, 2, 6–7, 131, 174–75;
    biblical production, 6–7, *8*, 9, 177, 198;
    camel proverb, 13; "congregation," 141,
    282n2; controversies and, 201, 292n4;
    cross-references, 2, 200; divine right and
    ruler, 77, 91, 92–93; Geneva Bible and, 111;
    with Geneva Bible annotations, 198, 199,
    291n107; historicism and, 12, 13, 201;
    italicized words, 92–93, 209; margins,
    200–201, 216, 253, 294n51; "Or, anointed,"
    127; Pauline obedience, 33; philological
    notes, 2, 141, 200, 226; Revised Standard
    Version, 92–93, 128, 136; Spenser and, 168;
    Tyndale and, 141; "tyrant," 127–28, 130, 131,
    280n71; word of God, 296n84. *See also* King
    James Bible (Milton's 1612 copy)
King'oo, Clare Costley, 57, 267n38, 278n43
King's Book, 56, 63–64, 68, 69, 88
Knox, John: *Book of Discipline*, 233; Locke,
    Anne Vaughan and, 277n24; magistrate
    and presentism, 139; resistance, 115, 121, 132,
    133, 206, 207, 277n17, 293n22; "tyrant," 131,
    132, 133; woman as ruler, 131

La Bible, qui est Toute la saincte Escriture
    (Barbier and Courteau), 115, 134, 136, 137,
    280n83, 281n96, 281n99

Lake, Peter, 187, 191, 195, 198, 290n75
Lanyer, Aemilia, 1, 112, 117, 177
Łaski, Jan, 147
Latimer, Hugh: about, 83, 234; canon law
    versus Mosaic Law, 85, 181, 183; divine right
    and ruler, 85, 181, 183, 184, 234; divorce of
    Henry VIII, 70, 270n97; Hilkiah and, 86;
    sermons, 85, 86
Latin Bible(s): biblical production, 7, 28, 84,
    272n6; Bucer translation/annotations, 84;
    chapter and verse numbers, 28, 39; Erasmus
    New Testament, 5, 6, 26, 33, 50, 161; Milton,
    217. *See also* Vulgate
Latré, Guido, 270n102
Laud, William, 112, 177
Lawes, Henry, 203, 208, 220, 225, 296nn74–76
Lefèvre, Jacques, 25, 27, 36, 262n15,
    263n48
legalism: Edwardian era, 89, 93–96, 103, 108,
    238; literalism and, 177, 178; *Measure for
    Measure* (Shakespeare), 178, 179, 195–98,
    288n35; Milton, 238; Protestantism, 193, 194,
    197, 238; reason and, 239; Stuart England
    accession, 180
"legitimation": defined, 249–50; political legit-
    imacy, 53, 70, 132, 148, 249–50
Lever, J. W., 185
Lewalski, Barbara, 52, 178
lex talionis ("an eye for an eye"), 179, 191, 193.
    See also "measure for measure" phrase
literalism: about, 3, 10–11, 232, 254–57, 301n27;
    allegorical interpretation, 15, 48–50, 61–62,
    90, 146–47, 183, 283n17, 297n88; biblical
    texts and, 195, 230; Geneva Bible (1560),
    113–14, 140; historicism and, 49; legalism
    and, 177, 178; *Measure for Measure*
    (Shakespeare), 180, 181, 256, 301n27;
    medievalism and, 10–12, 49, 133, 297n88;
    Milton's critique, 16–17, 230, 235, 236–37,
    256, 297n91; political role of biblical texts,
    16, 85; Presbyterianism, 16, 183; presentism
    and, 56, 63, 135–36; *sola scriptura*, 195;
    utilitarian reading and, 56. *See also* applied
    literalism
literalism, and Tyndale: about, 3, 11, 13, 14, 15,
    16–17, 55, 195, 254; allegorical interpretation,
    15, 48–50, 61–62, 90, 146–47, 183, 283n17,
    297n88; applied literalism, 63, 82, 102, 172;
    medievalism versus, 49; *The Obedience of a
    Christian Man*, 48–49; Pentateuch (Tyndale
    translation), 20, 55. *See also* literalism

literary historicism: about, 292n18; Erasmus, 19, 27, 29, 34, 39; Paul, 35–36; political rhetoric/historicism, 25–26, 35–36, 263n46; Valla, 24–25, 27, 29; Vulgate, 29

literature: biblical texts and, 5–6, 202, 251, *252*, 253, 256–57, 300n8; vernacular literature, 57, 268n41. See also *specific literary works, and authors*

Locke, Anne Vaughan, 115, 277n24

Locke, John, 58, 120, 250

Loewenstein, David, 272n4, 272–73n15, 297n6

Louth, John, 57

Lupton, Julia Reinhard, 17–18, 261n5

Lupton, Thomas, 291n87

Luther, Martin: absolutism, 29; as advisor/counselor, 104, 193; Antichrist analogy, 25, 261n4; applied literalism, 63; Babylon allegory, 143; *Babylonian Captivity of the Church*, 142, 152; biblical interpretation, 15, 17; *detorqueret* (twisted) rhetorical procedure and, 41, 264n72; divorce of Henry VIII, 104; Erasmus and, 5, 41, 45, 46–47, 264n72; exiled Jews/church versus pope, 142; free will, 50, 189, 290n70; Indulgences, 29, 137, 262n19; Isaiah and, 156; Mosaic Law versus gospel, 97, 104, 106, 193, 197, 267n33, 274n50; New Testament (1522), 50, 143, 266n11; Ninety-Five Theses in 1517, 25, 137, 281n7, 281n97; obedience doctrine, 57; obey parents and ruler, 58; Philip of Hess and bigamy, 96, 274n43; political literature, 58; predestination, 188, 233; Revelation and, 146, 283n18; *Septembertestament*, 147, 153, 154; Tyndale and, 5; Whore of Babylon allegory, 147, 152, 153, 154; writings, 58, 147, 154

Maacah (biblical figure), 175

MacCulloch, Diarmaid, 83, 272n2

magistrate: Calvin, 62, 118, 241–42, 268n54, 298nn34–35; deposition of ruler, 62, 118, 240–42, 268n54, 298nn34–35; divine right, 30, 31–33, 91, 178–79, 180–81, 183, 186, 248; Mosaic Law, 105, 174, 178, 179, 193–94, 197; negative connotations, 33–34, 139; New Testament (Tyndale translation), *61*, 62, 183; obedience, 102, 107, 289n41; presentism, 109; princes, *61*, 62, 118, 183, 241; Protestant exiles and, 139; Stuart England, 183

Malet, Francis, 265n92

margins, and biblical texts, 12, 200–201, 216, 253, 294n51. *See also* annotations; Geneva Bible (1560) annotations; paratexts; *and specific Bibles*

Marian exiles. *See* Protestant exiles

Marlowe, Christopher, 178

marriage law: Bucer, 96, 99–100, 104, 105; Milton, 16; *Tetrachordon* (Milton), 84–85, 236, 237, 244, 272n15; Westminster Assembly of Divines, 235

marrying one's brother's wife: Coverdale Bible, 69, 70; Geneva Bible (1560), 69; Henry VIII, 66, 67, 68, 69, 70, 96; Mosaic Law, 66, 67, 69–70; Tyndale, 66, 67–68, 69, 70, 96; Vulgate, 69, 70; Wolsey, 66, 71. *See also* marriage law

Martin, Gregory, 160

Martyr, Peter, 83, 146, 147, 272n15, 283n16

Mary, Queen of Scots: *The Faerie Queene* (Spenser) *and*, 144; Howard and, 279n58; Jezebel and, 133; presentism, 148; trial/execution, 117, 133, 175, 278n35, 287n8; woman as ruler, 139

Mary I (queen, Mary Tudor): about, 67, 81, 117, 170, 171; accession/reign of, 81, 84, 115, 117; biblical production, 80; Jezebel comparison, 133; political role of biblical texts and, 7, 110–11, 138, 250; presentism and, 148; Protestants/Protestant nation and, 115, 118, 119, *119*, 120, 170; translation of Erasmus's work, 46, 265n92; "tyrant," 115, 119, *119*, 138, 139, 166, 170; woman as ruler, 108, 131–32, 139

Matthew Bible: about, 9, 89, 90; anachronistic reading, 86, 93; annotations, 86, 90–91, 273n22; Becke and, 86, 89–96, *94*, 109, 273n22; biblical production, 93, *94*, 273n78; Coverdale and, 89, 90; divine right and ruler, 91–92; Edward VI and, 90, 93, *94*; Joshua and, 94–95; legalism, 89, 93–96; magistrate and divine right, 91; Mosaic Law and, 91, 100–101; Rogers and, 89, 90; theo-politics, 90–91, 92–93; Tyndale and, 9, 89, 90, 273n31; word of God, 92

Maximilian I (emperor), 37, 44

McConica, James, 253–54

Measure for Measure (Shakespeare): about, 21–22, 173, 176; allegorical interpretation, 183–84, 185, 186, 191, 197; annotations and, 178, 190, 191, 288n31; applied literalism, 177, 180, 184, 190, 198; biblical text, paratext,

Measure for Measure (Shakespeare) (continued)
literature intersection, 5, 251; Catholicism
and, 197–98, 291n102; cultural role of
biblical texts, 193, 198, 291n87; ecumenism,
190, 191, 198; grace, 190, 191; justice/mercy,
188–90, 191, 192–93, 196–97; legalism, 178,
179, 195–98, 288n35; *lex talionis* ("an eye for
an eye"), 179, 191, 193; literalism, 180, 181,
256, 301n27; magistrate and divine right,
178–79, 186; "measure for measure" phrase,
191–92, 193, 256; medievalism, 173, 184–86,
191; Mosaic Law, 179–80, 196; political
theology, 178, 180, 181, 183–84, 185–86;
predestination, 186, 187–89, 190; Ten
Commandments, 179, 190, 195–96
"measure for measure" phrase, 191–92, 193,
256, 290n83. See also *lex talionis* ("an eye for
an eye"); *Measure for Measure* (Shakespeare)
medievalism: Catholic reading, 15, 49–50, 236;
Everyman (play), 184, 185, 186; *The Faerie
Queene* (Spenser), 163–64, 168, 170, 285n69;
Glossa Ordinaria, 114; literalism and, 10–12,
49, 133, 297n88; *Mankind* (play), 184, 185,
186; *Measure for Measure* (Shakespeare),
173, 184–86, 191; Quadriga, 10–12, 133;
St. Augustine Gospel and, 163–64, 285n69;
sword and, 289n45; true church and,
143–44, 168
Melanchthon, Philip, 96, 147, 281n97
Midas (king), 39, 45, 265n85
Middle Ages. *See* medievalism
Miller, Jeffrey Alan, 201
Milton, 5, 60, 220–21, 226–28, *228*
Milton, Elizabeth (Elizabeth Minshull), 208,
293n32
Milton, John (1562–1647), 221, 295n61
Milton, John (1608–1674): about, 22, 208, 213,
216, 234, 247–48, 293n32; anti-prelaticals
and, 233, 235; *Areopagitica*, 105, 106, 234–35,
236, 238, 239, 246; Beza and, 230; Beza-
Tremellius Bible, 212, 213, 217, 293n32,
294n50; biblical text, paratext, literature
intersection, 5; blindness, 202, 211, *212*, 213,
217; Bucer and, 83–84, 104; canon law, 235,
272n15, 273n20; Charles I and, 207, 225, 232
293nn25–26, 235; Commonplace Book, 4,
216, 218, 259n10; cultural role of biblical
texts, 4, 259n10; *Defensio Secunda*, 295n64;
deposition of ruler, 241, 242, 245, 247,
300n3; *De Regno Christi* (Bucer) translation,
105, 235, 237, 238; "Digression," 224; divine

right and ruler, 61, 126, 214, 216, 217, 235,
295n55, 300n3; Edward VI and, 84–85,
272nn14–15; *Eikonoklastes*, 200, 207,
272n14, 293n26; Erasmus's legacy, 22, 209,
230, 234, 235, 294n36, 297n95; free will, 242,
244, 245, 246; Geneva Bible(s), 112–13, 208,
276n13, 293n32, 294n50; "heresy," 218, 235,
238, 254; historicism and, 22, 228–29, 235;
"J.M.," *210*, 220; Johannine Comma,
209–10, 294n36; *The Judgement of Martin
Bucer concerning Divorce* address, 235–36;
Junius-Beza Bible, 208; Latin Bible, 217;
legalism, 238; literalism critique, 16–17, 230,
235, 236–37, 256, 297n91; marriage law, 16;
Moseley and, 224, 225; multilingual
scholarship, 209, 293n32, 294n37; music
and psalms, 208, 221; "On the Lord Gen.
Fairfax," 220–21, 222, 224; "On the New
Forcers of Conscience," 211, 298n28;
Paradise Regained, 206, 251, *252*, 253, 300n11;
parliamentary reform, 211, 232, 233, 235–36,
298n28; Pauline obedience, 15, 235, *243*,
246–47, 299n41; Picard and, *212*, 216, 217,
218, *218*, 222; *Poems*, 210, 211, 220, 228,
295n59, 295n68; poetry, 211, 218–19, 224,
225, 294n39; political role of biblical texts,
60, 202, 220–21, 226–28, *228*; predestination and, 234–35, 238; *Of Prelatical
Episcopacy*, 233; Presbyterianism, 106, 211,
233; presentism, 4, 5, 226–29, *228*; *Pro
Populo Anglicano Defensio* (*Defense of the
English People*), 218, 246–47; psalms and
authorship, 205, 207, 208, 293n25; reason,
233, 237–38, 239, 240, 242, 246, 297n17,
299n48; *The Reason of Church Government*,
233; Reformation and, 84–85, 107, 233–34,
247, 272n15, 276n13; *Of Reformation
touching Church-Discipline in England*, 107,
233, 234; Revelation debate, 283n16; *Samson
Agonistes*, 220, 239; Shakespeare's First Folio
markings, 209, 293n35; Sonnet 13 to Henry
Lawes, 220, 273n16, 296n74; Ten Commandments, 238–39; *Tetrachordon*, 84–85,
236, 237, 244–45, 272n15; *A Treatise of Civil
Power in Ecclesiastical Causes*, 217–18, 235,
247–48, 294n54; Trinitarian debate, 29,
209; Tyndale's literalism, 234, 235;
utopianism critique, 238. *See also* alternate
readings, and Milton; *De Doctrina
Christiana* (Milton); divorce/divorce tracts,
and Milton; King James Bible (Milton's

1612 copy); *Paradise Lost* (Milton); *Psalms* [1648 Psalms, Psalms 80–88] (Milton); *The Tenure of Kings and Magistrates* (Milton)
Minshull, Elizabeth (Elizabeth Milton), 208, 293n32
morality: Pentateuch (Tyndale translation), 97; plays, 184, 185, 187, 191, 289n50, 290n60; tropological interpretation, 10–12, 13, 14, 109, 133; universalist moralizing, 14, 109
More, Thomas: about, 30, 45; "congregation" versus "church," 282n2; epigram by Erasmus, 45; *History of Richard III*, 25, 45; "love" translation, 211; marrying one's brother's wife, 66; Peter as "rock" or pope allegory, 51; political rhetoric and historicism, 25, 26–27, 32, 40, 45, 261nn8–9; political role of biblical texts, 16; political thought, 59, 268n48; rhetorical procedures, 39, 45; Tyndale and, 48, 52. See also *Utopia* (More)
Morison, Richard, 64–65, 81, 105, 255
Mosaic Law: biblical plays and, 81; Bucer, 97, 99–100, 101–2, 104–5, 178, 194, 235, 255, 273n20, 274n50, 275n62; Catholicism, 197, 267n33; disobedience and, 100, 175; divorce/ divorce tracts and, 66, 96, 99, 105, 237, 273n26; Edwardian era, 89, 93–96, 177; Edward VI, 80, 82, 85, 86, 91, 272n15; Elizabethan England, 288n25; Geneva Bible (1560), 108, 109; James I/VI, 177–78; Jews, 69–70, 104; Josiah, 86, 103; King's Book, 56; literalism/applied literalism, 17, 20, 102; Luther on gospel versus, 97, 104, 106, 193, 197, 267n33, 274n50; magistrate and, 174, 178, 179, 193–94, 197; marrying one's brother's wife, 66, 67, 69–70; Matthew Bible and, 91, 100–101; *Measure for Measure* (Shakespeare), 179–80, 196; Paul, 19–20, 196, 197; penal code, 99–100, 101–2, 275n62; political role of biblical texts, 55, 194, 267n30; Promised Land and, 75, 82, 88, 95, 120; Protestantism, 55, 197; Reformation and, 89, 267n33; Shakespeare, 176, 177, 179–80; *sola scriptura*, 64, 97, 106, 194, 197; Tyndale, 54–55, 85, 99, 114, 194; woman as ruler, 108. *See also* canon law versus Mosaic Law; Ten Commandments (Decalogue)
Moseley, Humphrey, 224, 225
Moses (biblical figure), 18, 55, 82, 118
Mulcaster, Richard, 284n38

Munday, Anthony, *Sir Thomas More* (Shakespeare, Munday, and others), 187, 289n50, 290n60
music, and psalms, 56, 203, 208, 221, 225

Nathan (biblical figure), 281–82n101
A Necessary Doctrine (1543), 56, 77
Nedham, Marchamont, 221
Nehemiah (biblical figure), 102, 224–25
Nelson, Eric, 267n30
Nero (emperor), 19, 26, 30, 31, 35, 45, 154, 247
New Jerusalem, 144–45, 154, 156, 165, 282n9
New Testament (Jugge printer, 1552?), 84, *151*
New Testament (Luther translation), 50, 143, 266n11
New Testament (Tyndale translation): about, 5, 6, 20, 52, 84, 254; annotations, 50, 51, 52, 71–72, 117–18, 141, 266n11, 282n2; biblical production, 50–51, 84, 266n11; Boleyn and, 56, 267n35, 279n53; "congregation" versus "church," 51, 117–18, 141, 151, 282n2; critiques, 6, 21, 51–52, 175, 266n17; Erasmus's legacy and, 46, 54; *An Exhortation to the Diligent Study of Scripture* (Erasmus) in appendix, 46; "love" translation, 211, 294n39; magistrate/princes, *61*, 62, 183; Matthew Bible and, 89, 90; New Testament (Luther's translation), 50, 266n11; *The Obedience of a Christian Man* (Tyndale), 60–61, 62, 268n53; "presbyteros" translation, 211; royal iconography, 84
New Testament(s): biblical history and, 137; chapter and verse numbers, 278n45; justice/ mercy, 188–89, 191; political role of biblical texts, 80–81; reading practices, 230–31, 297nn95–96; royal iconography, 203; translations, 9, 34, 54, 84, 263n37. *See also specific New Testament translations*
New Testament(s), and Erasmus: Greek New Testament, 5, 50, 161; Latin Bible(s), 5, 6, 26, 33, 50, 161; New Testament (Tyndale translation), 46, 54; *The Paraphrases on the New Testament*, 30, 41, 46, 50, 254, 265nn92–93, 300n14; reading practices, 230. *See also* New Testament(s)
Nicholson, Adam, 127–28, 130, 131
Nicholson, Catherine, 159
Nicolson, James, 72, 74
nonconformists, 107, 108, 130, 131, 148, 183, 186
Norton, David, 294n38
Norton, Thomas, 241, 298n35

notes. *See* annotations; Geneva Bible (1560)
    annotations; paratexts; *and specific Bibles*
Novum Instrumentum Omne [1516] (Erasmus):
    about, 54; annotations and retranslation, 6,
    90; Bucer and, 84; Johannine Comma, 211;
    publication of, 25, *28*, 29, 30; Revelation as
    inauthentic, 146, 147, 152–53, 283n15,
    283n22; rhetoric of praise, 42, 264n74.
    See also under Erasmus

obedience, and ruler: Bale, 81; Bucer, 58;
    Milton, 62, 299n41; Tudor era, 54, 161,
    285n59; Tyndale, 57, 60–62, 64, 103, 268n41,
    268n43, 268n47, 268n53, 268n55. *See also*
    obey parents (fifth commandment), and
    ruler
obedience/disobedience: Bishops' Bible(s),
    287n11; Geneva Bible(s), 287n6; James I/VI,
    175, 247; King James Bible (Milton's 1612
    copy), 251, *252*, 253; Mosaic Law, 100, 175;
    Tyndale, 54, 58, 183, 244, 268n54, 289n45.
    See also obedience, and ruler; obey parents
    (fifth commandment), and ruler
The Obedience of a Christian Man (Tyndale):
    about, 52; allegorical interpretation and
    literalism, 90, 146–47, 283n17, 297n88;
    Boleyn's copy of, 56–57, 267nn38–39;
    critiques, 71; Henry VIII and, 57, 71,
    267n38, 267n39; literalism, 48–49; New
    Testament (Tyndale translation), 60–62, *61*,
    268n53; obedience and ruler, 57–58, 60, 62,
    61, 103, 268n53, 268n55; obedience/
    disobedience, 54, 58, 268n54; obey parents
    and ruler, 60, 62, 268n53; political
    literature, 58, 71, 270n99; political role of
    biblical texts, 57; preface, 50; print copies,
    71; rhetorical procedures, 6
obey parents (fifth commandment), and ruler:
    Bucer, 101–2, 255; Church of England,
    63–64; Geneva Bible annotations, 64;
    Gilby, 64; Henry VIII, 63–65, 88; Luther,
    58; Morison, 64–65, 255; penal code and,
    101–2; political role of biblical texts, 194; *sola
    scriptura*, 64; Tudor period, 64; Tyndale, 54,
    60, 62, 63, 64, 88, 183, 255, 268n53, 268n61.
    See also obedience, and ruler
Oecolampadius, Johannes, 146, 147
Old Testament (Hebrew Bible). *See* Hebrew
    Bible (Old Testament)
On the Donation of Constantine [*Declamatio*]
    (Valla), 24, 27, 36

Orgel, Stephen, 168
Overall, John, 172–73

Palmer, Robert, 235, 236
panegyric genre, 40, 44
Paradise Lost (Milton): alternate readings in
    Milton's KJV, 202, 292n7, 296n86; biblical
    text, paratext, literature intersection, 5, 251,
    252, 253, 300n11; chapter and verse numbers,
    171; Geneva Bible annotations, 153, 276n13,
    293n31; reason and, 238, 240; translation of
    biblical texts, 211, 294n39
paratexts: about, 253, 300n12; biblical text,
    paratext, literature intersection, 251, 253–55,
    300n8, 300n12; biblical text, paratext,
    politics intersection, 251, 254–55; black letter
    style, 111, 159, 160, 276–77n16; columns, 161,
    209, 293n32; diglot editions, 6, 54, 161; font,
    111, 159, 160, 222, 276–77n16; lowercase
    letters/punctuation marks, 120–21, 123; red/
    crimson/scarlet/purple velvet bindings, *122*,
    123, *204*, 273nn53–54. *See also* annotations;
    chapter and verse numbers; italicized words
Parker, Matthew: about, 159, 163; Bishops'
    Bible, 7, 116–17, 292n4; Bucer and, 106, 107;
    Fagius and, 106; St. Augustine Gospel and,
    163–64, 285n69
Parker, William Riley, 213
parliament/parliamentary reform: adultery
    laws, 177; Charles I deposition, 240–41,
    298n28, 298n30; deposition of ruler, 142,
    242, 299n37; divine right and ruler, 240–42,
    298nn34–35; "Long Parliament" period, 211,
    232–33, 298n28; Milton and, 211, 232, 233,
    235–36, 298n28; "Personal Rule" period,
    232; Pride's purge, 224
Patterson, Annabel, 25
Pauck, Wilhelm, 97, 274n50
Paul (apostle): about, 45; advisors/counselors,
    38, 42; allegorical interpretation, 15;
    anachronistic reading, 27; Christian
    knight/armor/sword metaphor, 165, 168,
    286n80; *detorqueret* (twisted) rhetorical
    procedure, 41, 43, 45, 255; *The Faerie Queene*
    (Spenser), 164, 165; "heresy," 218; histori-
    cism, 25, 27, 35–36; iconography in biblical
    texts, 72, *73*; justice/mercy, 188–89, 196;
    Letters of Paul (Epistles), 5, 23, 27, *28*, 30,
    36; literalism, 15–16, 255; literary historicism,
    35–36; Mosaic Law, 19–20, 196, 197;
    political rhetoric and historicism, 27, 35, 36;

political role of biblical texts, 18; predestination, 187–88; prophecy, 160; rhetoric of praise, 37, 38–44; Seneca's spurious correspondence with, 27, 35–36, 263n48; "testament," 164; true church, 152

Pauline obedience: about, 30; allegorical interpretation, 32–33, 263n33; Bucer and, 97; Calvinism, 62, 244, 268n54; Church of England, 31, 248; Colet, 30, 31–34, 247; divine right and ruler, 81, 85, 89, 103–4, 235, 240, 241, 247–48; Erasmus, 19, 32–35, 53, 247–48; Geneva Bible New Testament, 33, 108, 118; historicism and, 31–35, 263n33; KJV, 33; literalism, 31; Milton, 15, 235, 243, 246–47; Mosaic Law, 19–20; political thought, 249; Shakespeare, 244; Ten Commandments, 108; Tyndale, 30–31, 33, 60, 62, 61, 63, 85, 244, 268n53; United States laws, 250, 300n7

Pentateuch (Torah), 91. See also Hebrew Bible (Old Testament)

Pentateuch (Tyndale translation): about, 6, 52, 55, 267n31; annotations, 54–55, 67, 68, 69, 71–72; Bucer and, 97; divine right and ruler, 91, 125; literalism, 20, 55; marrying one's brother's wife, 66, 67–68, 69, 70; morality and, 97; obedience and ruler, 61; political role of biblical texts, 6, 20, 54, 97; political theology, 126; preface, 266n6

Perkins, William, 196

persecution. See exile/persecution/stranger/ defeatism

Persius (Aulus Persius Flaccus), 37–38

Peter (biblical figure), 27, 48, 51, 74, 152, 254, 278n39

Philip, Archduke of Austria, 36–37, 38, 39–40, 44

Philip II (king of Spain), 117, 118, 138, 166

Philip of Hess (prince), 96–97, 274n43

Philips, Katherine, 4

Phillips, Edward, 294n37

philological historicism, 12–13, 27, 29–30, 50

philological notes: Geneva Bible (1560) annotations, 12–13, 120, 127; KJV, 2, 141, 200, 226; Lefèvre, 27, 262n15; Psalms (Milton), 222, 226, 251; Valla, 27, 262n15

Picard, Jeremie, 212, 216, 217, 218, 218, 222

Pierson, Thomas, 224

Plato and Platonism, 44, 98, 99, 100, 105, 106, 238, 254

plays: biblical texts, 80–81, 82, 105–6, 176–77, 178; medievalism, 184, 185, 186; morality plays, 184, 185, 289n50, 290n60. See also Measure for Measure (Shakespeare); Shakespeare, William

poetry: Grindal and eclogues, 159–60; Milton, 211, 218–19, 224, 225, 294n39; Milton and Moseley collection, 224, 225; Poems (Milton), 210, 211, 220, 228, 295n59, 295n68; Whore of Babylon allegory, 157–59, 158, 284n36

Pole, Reginald, 66, 80

political legitimacy, 53, 70, 132, 249–50

political rhetoric and historicism: allegorical interpretation, 32–33, 263n33; Colet, 30, 32, 33, 36, 45; Erasmus, 25, 27, 33, 36, 44, 45, 61, 235, 247–48; literary historicism, 25–26, 35–36, 263n46; More, 25, 26–27, 32, 40, 45, 261nn8–9; obliquus ductus, 25, 26–27, 32, 40, 261nn8–9; truth to power, 25, 26, 27, 44, 45; Valla, 24–25, 27. See also historicism

political role of biblical texts: about, 2–3, 4–6, 17–18, 25, 80–81, 194; biblical production and, 7, 10; biblical text, paratext, politics intersection, 251, 254–55, 301n16; Hooker, 195, 233, 254–55, 256, 291n95, 301n16; Mary's trial/execution and, 117, 133, 175, 278n35, 287n8; sola scriptura, 59, 254–55

political role of biblical texts, and Spenser: about, 142; Complaints, 157, 284n34; The Faerie Queene, 5, 251, 253; The Shepheardes Calender, 156–57, 159, 161, 251; The Theatre for Worldings (Spenser translation), 145, 147, 157, 158, 251, 284n34, 284n38. See also political role of biblical texts

political role of biblical texts, and Tyndale: about, 51, 52, 53, 54–55, 72, 181, 254; The Obedience of a Christian Man (Tyndale), 57; Pentateuch (Tyndale translation), 6, 20, 54, 97; The Practice of Prelates (Tyndale), 6, 54, 57, 63, 67, 68, 69, 70, 71. See also political role of biblical texts; political role of biblical texts, and Spenser

political theology: about, 17–18; Bucer, 101; Jacobean England, 84, 187, 287n18; Measure for Measure (Shakespeare), 178, 180, 181, 183–84, 185–86; pope(s), 181, 183; Protestantism/Reformation, 18, 58–59, 178, 183, 186, 248; reason and, 233; Tyndale and, 18–19, 22, 126, 180, 194. See also political role of biblical texts political thought: applied literalism, 63, 80–81, 102, 180–81, 198; Calvinism, 244, 249; Catholicism, 115; Erasmus, 59, 268n48; Hobbes, 58; lineage debates, 53, 70, 250; Locke, John, 58; More, 59, 268n48; Pauline obedience, 249; Protestantism, 57–59, 115, 268n49; Tyndale and, 57–58; *Vindiciae Conta Tyrannos*, 249, 250, 268n49, 300nn1–3

Poole, Kristen, 12

Poole, William, 293n85

pope(s): as term of use, 48; annotations with pope/papacy/papist, 127, 150, 153, 154, *155*, 156, 200–201; bondage in Egypt analogy, 85, 181, 183, 278n34; dispensation for Henry VIII, 20, 67, 71; divorce of Henry VIII and, 71; Donation of Constantine, 24, 27, 36; exile in Babylon and, 142; historicism, 24, 25, 181; Peter as "rock" allegory, 48, 51, 74, 152, 254, 278n39; political theology, 181, 183; politics, 24, 25, 181; Reformation versus, 53, 71. *See also* Antichrist analogy; canon law; canon law versus Mosaic Law; Rome

The Practice of Prelates (Tyndale): divorce of Henry VIII, 52–53, 67, 70–71, 96; marrying one's brother's wife, 96; obey parents and ruler, 63; Pauline obedience, 63; political role of biblical texts, 6, 54, 57, 63, 67, 68, 69, 70, 71; print copies, 53, 266n23

Pratt, Aaron, 116, 267n27, 276–77n16, 300n12

predestination: Calvinism, 186, 187, 188–89, 234–35, 290n78; Hooker, 291n95, 301n16; Luther, 188, 233; *Measure for Measure* (Shakespeare), 186, 187–89, 190; Milton and, 234–35, 238; Paul, 187–88; Presbyterianism, 234–35; Protestantism, 148, 186, 187; reason and, 233; Whitgift, 290n78

Presbyterianism: Charles I's imprisonment, 225; English Civil Wars and, 220; free will, 239, 298n25; literalism, 16, 183, 232; literature, 99; Milton and, 106, 211; predestination and, 234–35; "presbyteros" translation, 211; psalms/psalm culture, 225

Prescott, Anne Lake, 164

presentism: about, 3, 4, 13, 17, 56, 133–34, 135–36, 138–39, 140; applied literalism and, 135–36, 140; Bale, 153; Colet, 32; divine right and ruler, 124–25, 134, 135; Elizabethan England, 134, 170; Erasmus, 43; exiled Jews/church versus pope and, 142; Gilby, 138, 140; literalism and, 56, 63; Milton, 4, 5, 226–29, *228*; New Jerusalem, 144, 282n9;

psalms/psalm culture, 206–7, 224–25, 226; Revelation, 147–48, 166, 168, 172; true church and, 144; "tyrant," 131; utility and, 136, 213. *See also* Geneva Bible (1560) annotations, and presentism

Pride, Thomas, 224, 241

princes/magistrate, *61*, 62, 118, 183, 241

Promised Land analogy, 75, 82, 88, 95, 120

Protestant exiles: about, 115, 116, 234; biblical texts and, 9–10, 81, 140; Bucer legacy, 98, 106, 107, 108, 234; Coverdale Bible production, 72, 270nn102–3; *De Regno Christi* (Bucer), 98; Elizabethan England, 118; English Civil Wars and, 1, 2, 110, 111, 140; Geneva Bible New Testament (1557), 118, 119, *119*, 170; psalms, 205, 206; resistance, 115, 121, 132, 133, 206, 207, 277n17, 293n22. *See also* Protestant nation

Protestantism: as term of use, 83, 272n2; allegorical interpretations, 147, 164, 198; biblical interpretation, 11, 16; biblical production, 1, 7, 9–10, 72, 74, 270nn102–3; Catholicism versus, 148–49, 166; cultural history of, 19, 261n51; divorce of Henry VIII and, 71, 270n97; Edward VI and, 84, 85; Elizabeth I and, 119–20, *121*, 170–71, 278n43; Erasmus and, 5–6, 45–47, 50, 53–54, 253–54, 265n87, 266n6; evangelical as term of use, 272n2; free will, 148, 239, 298n25; legalism, 193, 194, 197, 238; literalism, 3, 16–17; Mosaic Law and, 55, 197; political theology, 178, 183, 186, 248; political thought, 57–59, 115, 268n49; predestination, 148, 186; *sola fida*, 148, 188; utopic politics, 81, 93, 238. *See also* Protestant exiles; Reformation; *sola scriptura*; true church (church)

Protestant nation: allegorical interpretation, 163, 164, 166; Bucer, 89, 99, 234; Cranmer, 89, 99; Elizabeth I, 119–20, *121*; *The Faerie Queene* (Spenser), 163, 164, 166, 170, 172; Geneva Bible annotations, 112, 119–20, *121*, 133; Geneva Bible New Testament annotations, 118, 120, 133. *See also* Protestantism; Reformation

Prynne, William, 240, 241, 242, 279n61, 298n28, 299n37

Psalms [1648 Psalms, Psalms 80–88] (Milton): about, 22, 219–20, 236; alternate readings, 202, 208, 209, 222, 227, *228*, 228–29, 231; biblical text, paratext, literature intersection, 5, 211, 219, 253; chapter and verse numbers, 222, 251; Charles I, 208, 220, 221, 222, 227–28, *228*, 295n64; commentaries, 203; historicism, 228–29; initials J.M., *210*, 220; italicized words, 209, *210*, 222, 228, *228*, 251; literature and biblical texts, 202; music and, 221; philological notes, 222, 226, 251; *Poems* (Milton), 210, 211, 220, 228, 295n59, 295n68; political role of biblical texts, 202, 220–21, 226–28, *228*, 295n64; presentism, 226–29, *228*; psalms/psalm culture, 203, 207, 224, 295n70; Sternhold and Hopkins, 208, 222, 225, 226; translations, 202, 208, 211, 219, 225–26, 296n79; Windsor Army meeting, 221, 222, *223*

psalms/psalm culture: about, 203; alternate readings, 231; authorship, 74, 203, 205, 206, 208, 293n18; Calvin, 205, 206–7, 225; David and, 74, 203, 205, 207, 293n21; historicism, 205, 206, 224–25, 228–29, 292n18; Jesus Christ, 206; music and, 56, 203, 208, 221, 225; political role of biblical texts, 224, 295n70; Presbyterianism, 225; presentism, 206–7, 224–25, 226; *Psalms* (Milton), 203, 207, 224, 295n70; psalter(s), 74, 136, 203, *204*, 271n117; royalists, 203, *204*, 205, 207, 225, 293n26, 296n75; *The Tenure of Kings and Magistrates* (Milton), 207; Tudor era, 205; Westminster Assembly of Divines, 203, 219, 224, 235, 293n26. See also *Psalms* [1648 Psalms, Psalms 80–88] (Milton)

psalter(s), 74, 136, 203, *204*, 271n117. *See also* psalms/psalm culture

Pullian, John, 277n26

Quadriga, 10–12, 133

Quintilian, Marcus Fabius, 26, 40, 44, 45, 265n83

Radzinowicz, Mary Ann, 202, 203, 207, 293n25, 295n61

Rankin, Mark, 67, 71, 266n10

Ravencroft, Thomas, 221, 295n61

reading practices, 17, 18–19. *See also* alternate readings; anachronistic reading; applied literalism; biblical interpretation; literalism; utilitarian reading

reason: Cranmer, 232, 233; Erasmus, 233; Hooker, 237; legalism and, 239; Milton, 233, 237–38, 239, 240, 242, 246, 297n17, 299n48; *Paradise Lost* (Milton), 238, 240; political

theology, 233; predestination, 233; *sola scriptura* versus, 59, 233. *See also* free will

red/crimson/scarlet/purple velvet bindings, 122, 123, *204*, 273nn53–54

Reformation: admonitions/prophetic admonitions, 132–33, 139, 282n104; biblical texts and interpretation, 11, 134, 145; canon law versus Mosaic Law, 11, 85, 101, 181, 183; Counter-Reformation, 19, 145, 160, 169, 267n33; Cranmer and, 83, 84, 96; Edward VI, 20, 84–85, 234, 272n15; Erasmus and, 5–6, 45–47, 50, 53–54, 253–54, 265n87, 266n6; German reformers and, 7, 83, 84, 96; Henry VIII and, 271–72n1; history of, 234; liturgy, 56, 84; Milton and, 84–85, 107, 233–34, 247, 272n15, 276n13; Mosaic Law and, 89, 267n33; papacy versus, 53, 71; political literature, 58; political theology, 18, 58–59; polygamy and, 96–97; predestination, 189; Scotland, 110, 139–40, 233; *sola scriptura* and, 135; theologians and, 83–84, 272n3. *See also* Church of England; Protestant exiles; Protestantism; Protestant nation

Rehoboam (biblical figure), 244–45

Renaissance, 4–5, 17, 259n8, 259n10

resistance: Calvinism, 130, 242, 244, 246; Protestant exiles, 115, 121, 132, 133, 206, 207, 277n17, 293n22; *Vindiciae Conta Tyrannos*, 300n3

Revelation (Apocalypse): authentic/inauthentic text debate, 145–47, 152–53, 283nn15–18, 283n22, 283n25; *The Theatre for Worldings* (Spenser translation), 145, 147, 157, *158*, 251, 284n34, 284n38

Revelation (Apocalypse), and annotations: allegorical interpretation and presentism, 147–48, 166, 168, 172; Antichrist analogy, 149, 156, 166; Babylon analogy, 154, 156, 157–58; dragon/devil/Satan allegory, 154, *155*, 166–67; pope/papacy/papist, 150, 153, 156; Protestantism versus Catholicism, 148–49, 166, 171; Rome, 119, *119*, 150, 153, 154; Shakespeare, 173, 286n92; true church, 152; woman clothed with sun allegory, 167, 170. *See also* Revelation (Apocalypse); Whore of Babylon allegory

Rex, Richard, 57, 63

Reynolds, John, 174

Rheims Catholic Bible. *See* Douay-Rheims Catholic Bible (1582)

rhetorical procedures: allegorical interpretation, 32–33, 263n33; *emphasis*, 26, 44,
265n83; historicism, 25–27, 261n4;
humanists, 25–26, 45; rhetoric of praise,
37–45, 264n72, 264n74; *telum occultum*, 26,
40. *See also* political rhetoric and historicism
Richardson, Anne, 50
Ridley, Nicholas, 90
Rogers, John, 89, 90
Rome: annotations, 119, *119*, 150, 153, 154, *155*,
284n29; Babylon analogy, 143, 153, 154, 156,
157–58. *See also* pope(s)
Rosenblatt, Jason P., 211, 222
Rous, Francis, 224, 225, 296n79
royal iconography: Bishops' Bible(s), 7, 181,
182, 186, 260n19, 289n45; Charles I/David,
203, 207; Edward VI, 84, 86, *87*, 88; Great
Bible, 7; justice/mercy, 181, *182*, 186; New
Testament(s), 203; Tudor era, 7, 9, 72, *73*,
74, 181, *182*, 270n105, 289n45. *See also*
political role of biblical texts
royalists: divine right and ruler, 227–28,
296n84; psalms/psalm culture, 203, *204*,
205, 207, 225, 293n26, 296n75
royal readership: biblical texts, 56, 66, 68–69,
72, *73*, 74, 270n103, 270n105, 271n117; *The
Obedience of a Christian Man* (Tyndale),
56–57, 71, 267nn38–39; Vulgate, *75*, 75–76
ruler: biblical texts and, 20, 59, 82, 95, 123;
Jesus Christ and, 134, 135; kingship
passages, 77, 80; political legitimacy, 132,
249, 250; spirituality and, 99; woman as
ruler, 108–9, 131–32, 139. *See also* advisors/
counselors, and ruler; deposition of ruler;
divine right, and ruler; magistrate;
obedience, and ruler; *and specific ruler*;
obey parents (fifth commandment), and
ruler
Rummel, Erika, 263n37

Salmasius, Claudius, 246–47
Sampson, Thomas, 107, 275n82
Samson (biblical figure), 239
Samuel (biblical figure), 59, 95
Sandys, Edwin, 107, 175, 197
Sandys, George, 203, 208, 225, 296nn75–76
Saul (biblical figure), 59, 77, 82, 95, 126, 128,
208
Saunders, Austen, 171–72
Scalia, Antonin, 250, 300n7
Scarisbrick, J. J., 66

Schell, Richard, 284n38
Schmitt, Carl, 18, 58
Scotland: Charles I and, 225, 232–33; English
Civil Wars, 220, 221, 233; Geneva Bible, 112,
174; political role of biblical texts and, 131,
132, 287n5; Reformation, 110, 139–40, 233
Second Temple, 10, 117, 205, 278n36
Selden, John, 199, 211, 237, 297n17
Seneca (Roman philosopher), 26–27, 35–36,
45, 263n48
Seres, William, 89
Seymour, Jane (queen), 72
Shaheen, Naseeb, 282n5, 286nn92–93, 288n93
Shakespeare, William: biblical plays, 176–77,
178; Bishops' Bible and, 288n23; Geneva
Bible/annotations and, 1, 112, 177, 178,
288n23; Hampton Court conference,
287n13; *Henry V*, 173, 176–77; *Henry VI,
Part 3*, 192; *Henry VIII* (Shakespeare and
Fletcher), 66; justice/mercy theme, 189–90,
191, 192–93; *King Lear*, 118–19; King's Men,
187; "measure for measure" phrase, 191–93,
290n83; *The Merchant of Venice*, 176, 178,
179; *Midsummer Night's Dream*, 173;
morality plays, 184, 185, 191; Mosaic Law,
176, 177, 179–80; Pauline obedience, 244;
Rape of Lucrece, 180; Revelation, 173,
286n92; *Richard III*, 124–25, 192; *Sejanus,
His Fall* (Jonson) and, 187, 290n59;
Shakespeare's First Folio, 209, 293n35; *Sir
Thomas More* (Shakespeare, Munday, and
others), 187, 289n50, 290n60; Whore of
Babylon allegory, 173, 286n93. See also
Measure for Measure (Shakespeare)
Sharpe, Kevin, 72
Sheppard, Gerald T., 270n102
Shuger, Debora Kuller, 18, 49, 99, 291n87
Simmons, Matthew, 249
Simpson, James, 16, 195, 272n2
Sir Thomas More (Shakespeare, Munday, and
others), 187, 289n50, 290n60
Skinner, Quentin, 300n2
Smith, Miles, 201, 282n2
social role of biblical texts. *See* cultural role of
biblical texts
sola fida, 148, 188
sola scriptura: biblical interpretation, 16, 135,
136–37; Book of Law, 142; literalism and,
195; Mosaic Law and, 64, 97, 106, 194, 197;
political role of biblical texts, 59, 254–55;
reason versus, 59, 233

Solomon (biblical figure): *The Books of Solomon* (Coverdale), 76, 80; divine right and ruler, 102; Henry VIII and, 77, 80; James I/VI, 178; as king, 102, 280n70; psalter/proverbs, 74, 136, 271n117; succession and, 280n70; Temple of Solomon, 12, 81, 205, 208

Sommers, William, *75*, 75–76

Soter, Johannes, 270n102

Spenser, Edmund: about, 21, 160–61; allegorical interpretation, 13–14, 201; *Amoretti*, 251, 300n8; biblical text, paratext, literature intersection, 253, 300n8; cultural role of biblical texts, 1, 112, 199. See also *The Faerie Queene* (Spenser); political role of biblical texts, and Spenser

spiritual (anagogical) interpretation, 10–12, 63, 80–81, 133

spiritual versus, 63

Spufford, Margaret, 259n8

Sternhold and Hopkins, *The Whole Booke of Psalmes*, 56, 203, *204*, 208, 222, 225, 226

Stillingfleet, Edward, 254

stranger. See exile/persecution/stranger/defeatism

Stuart England: accession and legalism, 180; Bishops' Bible, 117; *The Faerie Queene* (Spenser) annotations, 168, 170; Geneva Bible and, 113; literature, 257; magistrate and divine right, 180–81, 183; Milton, 229, 240; nonconformists, 108, 130, 131, 148, 183; presentism, 125; psalms, 203, 227; royalist psalms/psalm culture, 203. See also James I/VI (king of England/king of Scotland)

Suetonius (Roman historian), 31, 262n24

Summit, Jennifer, 163

Sumner, Charles, 293n32

Swift, Daniel, 287n13

sword: Christian knight/armor/sword metaphor, 165–66, 168, 286n80; divine right and, 72, *73*, 74; medievalism, 289n45; royal iconography, 72, *73*, 74, 181, *182*, 289n45; Tyndale and, 60, *61*, 63, 65

Sylvester I (pope), 24

Tadmor, Naomi, 3

Tamar (biblical figure), 67–68

Tasso, Torquato, 144

Taverner's Bible, 269n84

Temples, 10, 12, 81, 117, 205, 208, 278n36

Ten Commandments (Decalogue): *Catechism* (Cranmer), 88–89; King's Book, 56, 64; *Measure for Measure* (Shakespeare), 179, 190, 195–96; Milton, 238–39; Pauline obedience, 108; Tudor era, 55–56; Tyndale, 194. See also Mosaic Law; obey parents (fifth commandment), and ruler

The Tenure of Kings and Magistrates (Milton): about, 222, 224, 235, 295n64; deposition of ruler, 241, 242, 245, 300n3; initials J.M., 220; obedience and ruler, 62, 299n41; parliament/parliamentary reform, 240; psalms/psalm culture and royalists, 207

The Theatre for Worldings (Spenser translation), 145, 147, 157, *158*, 251, 284n34, 284n38

theo-politics: Bucer, 83–84, 92, 99, 247; *Catechism* (Cranmer), 7, 84, 86, *87*, 88–89, 93; Edwardian era and, 22, 90; Matthew Bible and, 90–91, 92–93; Milton, 22, 247–48

Tomson, Laurence: Geneva-Tomson-Junius Bible, 113; Geneva-Tomson New Testament (1576), 61, 113, 118, 285n46

Torah (Pentateuch), 91. See also Hebrew Bible (Old Testament)

translations/translators: about, 29, 34, 263n37; de Vere Geneva Bible (1570) readers, 1, 124, *216*; King James Bible (Milton's 1612 copy) reader, 211, *216*, 216–17, 294nn38–39. See also *specific Bibles, translations, and translators*

Treasons Act in 1534, 131, 280n74

Tremellius, Immanuel, 83, 107, 212–13, 217, 272n3, 293n32, 294n50

Trinitarian debate, 29, 209, 211, 262n19, 294n36

tropological (moral) interpretation, 10–12, 13, 14, 109, 133

true church (church): Bale and, 149, 150; Catholicism versus, 143, 154; "congregation" versus "church," 51, 117–18, 141, 282n2; Douay-Rheims Catholic Bible (1582), 161, 282n2; dragon/devil/Satan allegory and, 152; exiled Jews/church and pope, 142; *The Faerie Queene* (Spenser), 145, 149, 151, 152, 169, 288n86; Hebrew Bible, 129–30, 139, 141–42, 151–52; Jesus Christ allegory and, 143, 151–52; medievalism and, 143–44, 168; New Jerusalem; presentism, 144; Whore of Babylon allegory, 152. See also Protestantism

Tudor-Craig, Pamela, 77, 80, 271n117
Tudor era: annotations, 2; divine right and
    ruler, 93; Geneva Bible (1560), 117;
    magistrate and divine right, 180, 183;
    Mosaic Law, 55–56; obedience and ruler, 54,
    61, 161, 285n59; obey parents and ruler, 64;
    political role of biblical texts, 18; psalms/
    psalm culture, 205; royal iconography, 7, 9,
    72, 73, 74, 181, 182, 270n105, 289n45;
    translations of biblical texts, 2, 54, 112, 113.
    See also Elizabeth I (queen), and Elizabe-
    than England
Tunstall, Cuthbert, 51, 266n6
twisted (detorqueret) rhetorical procedure, 17,
    41, 43, 45, 135, 255, 264n72
Tyacke, Nicholas, 289n55, 298n26
Tyconius, 253n18
Tyndale, William: about, 9, 10, 20, 22, 80;
    anagogical interpretation, 63; Antichrist
    analogy, 65, 269n66; applied literalism, 55,
    60, 63, 65, 82, 102, 172, 195, 255; biblical
    production and, 6–7, 9, 50–51, 266n11;
    camel proverb, 13; Catholicism and, 62–63;
    Catholic medievalism, 49–50; critiques, 80,
    266n17; Cromwell and, 71, 270n99; cultural
    role of biblical texts, 2, 9; divine right and
    ruler, 59, 102, 125; divorce of Henry VIII, 6,
    52–53, 67; Enchiridion (Erasmus) transla-
    tion, 2, 5, 48–50, 168, 254, 266n10, 268n53;
    Erasmus and, 45–46, 48, 50, 53, 54, 266n6;
    An Exposition upon the Fifth, Sixth, and
    Seventh Chapters of Matthew, 6, 52, 63,
    268n61; Glossa Ordinaria, 114; Hebrew
    Bible translation, 6, 52, 55, 61, 66, 67, 89,
    90, 125, 126, 267n31, 273n31; Henry VIII
    and, 51; heresy and, 48, 80; historicism, 13;
    An Homilie against Disobedience, 183, 244,
    289n45; KJV and, 141; legacy of, 54, 80, 82,
    253; Luther and, 5, 50, 266n11; Matthew
    Bible, 9, 89, 90, 273n31; More and, 48, 52;
    Mosaic Law, 54–55, 85, 99, 114, 194;
    obedience and ruler, 54, 57, 60–61, 64, 183,
    268n41, 268n43, 268n47, 268n53, 268n55;
    obey parents and ruler, 54, 60–61, 62, 63,
    64, 88, 255, 268n53, 268n61; Pauline
    obedience, 30–31, 33, 60–62, 63, 85, 244,
    268n53; Peter as "rock" or pope allegory, 48,
    51, 152; political theology, 18–19, 22, 126,
    180, 194; political thought, 57–58; Pope's
    authority, 48, 51, 52–53, 54, 58, 62, 65, 70,
    71–72; reason versus sola scriptura, 59, 233;

    Revelation as inauthentic, 146–47, 152–53;
    royal iconography, 7; scandalous texts, 6,
    52, 54, 90; sword of power and, 60, 61, 63,
    65; Ten Commandments, 194; translations
    of biblical texts, 211, 267n31, 294n39;
    vernacular literature, 57, 268n41; Vulgate,
    33; The Whole Workes of W. Tyndall, 266n23;
    Whore of Babylon allegory, 269n66.
    See also literalism, and Tyndale; New
    Testament (Tyndale translation); The
    Obedience of a Christian Man (Tyndale);
    Pentateuch (Tyndale translation); The
    Practice of Prelates (Tyndale)
"tyrant," and Geneva Bible (1560): annotations
    reception and history, 114, 115–16, 124–25,
    126, 277n28, 278n34, 279n61; "giants," 129,
    280n69; kings, 129, 280n70; number of
    occurrences, 127–28, 280n67; presentism,
    130, 138; text and notes lexical differences,
    128–33; word of God, 176. See also "tyrant"/
    tyrant
"tyrant"/tyrant: biblical texts, 103; Bishops'
    Bible(s), 175–76, 278n34; Calvin, 61;
    Erasmus, 34–35; KJV, 128, 131, 280n71;
    Mary I, 115, 119, 119, 138, 139, 166, 170;
    Persius, 37; Philip II, 138, 166; Quintilian,
    26; woman as ruler, 131–32

Udall, Nicholas, 46, 254
United States laws, 250, 300n7
universalist moralizing, 14, 109
utilitarian reading, 17, 56, 82, 136, 180–81, 213
utopia: Book of Law, 93; Bucer, 98, 101, 105,
    238; critique, 238; literature, 98; Plato, 105,
    106; Protestantism, 81, 93, 238
Utopia (More): advisors/counselors, 25, 26;
    Bucer and, 98, 101, 254, 256; Epigram 198,
    59, 268n48; literalism, 256; Mosaic Law, 20;
    political rhetoric and historicism and, 25,
    26; publication and uses, 25, 29; Seneca, 35

Valla, Lorenzo, 24–25, 27, 29, 36, 262n15,
    262n19
van der Noot, Jan, 157–59, 158, 284n34,
    284n36
van Dijkhuizen, Jan, 284n36
Vaughan, Stephen, 71, 270n99
Vermigli, Peter Martyr, 83, 146, 147, 272n15
Vindiciae Conta Tyrannos, 249, 250, 268n49,
    300nn1–3
Virgil, Aeneid, 251, 253, 300n11

Vulgate: authentic/inauthentic text, 45; camel proverb, 13; historicism and, 13, 24, 30; Johannine Comma, 29, 209–10, 211, 262n19; Lefèvre and, 27; literary historicism, 29; magistrate/princes, 61, 241; marrying one's brother's wife, 69, 70; Papal Bull on annotations, 292n6; Pauline obedience, 32, 33; royal readership and, *75*, 75–76; translations, 29; Valla and, 24. *See also* Jerome

Wakefield, Robert, 68
Walker, Greg, 72, 74, 131
Walker, William, 300n1
Walker, William Henry, 300n1
Walton, Brian, 209, 211, 294n37
Walzer, Michael, 93, 261n51
Westminster Assembly of Divines, 203, 219, 224, 235, 293n26, 295n70
White, Micheline, 271n117
Whitford, David M., 261n4
Whitgift, John: about, 107; Bucer's legacy, 107; cultural role of biblical texts, 1, 112; magistrate and Mosaic Law, 174, 178, 179, 193, 194, 197; predestination, 290n78
Whittingham, William: chapter and verse numbers, 120; Geneva Bible translators, 108, 115, 117, 120, 277n26, 278n38; Goodman and, 131–32; political role of biblical texts, 5, 208; "tyrant," 133
The Whole Booke of Psalmes (Sternhold and Hopkins), 56, 203, *204*, 208, 222, 225, 226
Whore of Babylon allegory: *Concent of Scripture* (Broughton), 154, *155*; Cranach's illustration, 147, 153, 154; *The Faerie Queene* (Spenser), 143, 144, 149, 169, 170; Geneva Bible New Testament (1577) annotations,
119, *119*, 152; *Image of Both Churches* (Bale), 149–50, *151*, 161–62; presentism, 158–59; Protestant exiles and, 119, *119*, 170; *Septembertestament* (Luther), 147, 153, 154; Shakespeare, 173, 286n93; Tyndale and, 269n66; van der Noot's poetry, 157–59, *158*, 284n36; *Whore of Babylon* (Dekker), 172; Wycliffe, 147. *See also* Babylon
Whytchurch, Edward, *76*, *78*, *79*, 271n117
Willis, Jonathan, 55–56
Wither, George, 190
Wolsey, Cardinal Thomas, 52, 57, 66, 71, 74, 267n39, 270n97
woman as ruler, 108–9, 131–32, 139. See also *specific ruler*
woman clothed with sun allegory: *The Faerie Queene* (Spenser), 145, 149, 166, 170–71; *Image of Both Churches* (Bale), 149, 150, *150*; New Testament (Luther translation), 143; Revelation annotations, 167, 170; Tyndale and, 269n66; *Whore of Babylon* (Dekker), 172; Wycliffe, 283n19
Worden, Blair, 18
word of God: Bishops' Bible(s), 175; Coverdale Bible, 74; *The Faerie Queene* (Spenser), 145, 165; Geneva Bible(s), 153, 160, 175, 176, 287n6; KJV, 296n84; Matthew Bible, 92
Wyatt, George, 57, 76–77, 267n39
Wycliffe, John, 13, 144, 147, 148, 168, 234, 283n19
Wycliffite Bible, 51

Young, John, 161

Zedekiah (biblical figure), 14, 134–35
Zerubbabel (biblical figure), 10, 117, 162
Zwingli, Ulrich, 97, 146, 147, 278n52

ACKNOWLEDGMENTS

Much of the research and writing of this book occurred during a year of leave in 2015–2016 at the Folger Shakespeare Library that was funded by the National Endowment for the Humanities. I am grateful for the invaluable conversations I had there with the community of visiting and long-term scholars, curators, and librarians, including Jan van Dijkhuizen, Nicholas Hardy, Chris Highley, John King, Kathleen Lynch, Scott Mandelbrote, Kirsten Macfarlane, Alan Nelson, Jason Powell, Owen Williams, Michael Witmore, Betsy Walsh, Alexandra Walsham, Heather Wolfe, and Steven Zwicker. At the Folger, I managed to persuade Jerry Singerman to be interested in publishing this book, and I've been grateful for his kind support and advice over the several years it took to complete it.

The project began long before that happy year at the Folger, and I have many people and institutions to thank for their help along the way. For the first chapter on Erasmus I owe thanks to audiences who heard and responded to various versions presented at the CUNY Graduate Center, the Renaissance Society of America, and the Princeton University Renaissance Colloquium, and for the advice of readers over the years from Miriam Diller, Kathy Eden, Judith Rice Henderson, Michael Masiello, Lawrence Manley, the late Richard Marius, Kirsten Tranter, Lee Wandel, and anonymous readers at Cambridge University Press, which published a different version of this article in Thomas Fulton and Ann Baynes Coiro, eds., *Rethinking Historicism from Shakespeare to Milton*, 2012 as "The Politics of Renaissance Historicism: Valla, Erasmus, Colet, and More." The chapter on Tyndale received extremely helpful comments from Mark Rankin, Clare Costley King'oo, and Micheline White. Chapter 4, on the Geneva Bible, received help from many early readers, including Michael Cornett, editor of the *Journal of Medieval and Early Modern Studies*, which published an earlier version ("Toward a New Cultural History of the Geneva Bible") in 2017. I thank Michael for his editorial acumen and dogged persistence. Other readers include Clare Costley King'oo, Jacqueline Miller, Annabel Patterson, Brian

Pietras, Kristen Poole (to whom I have many scholarly debts), Debora Shuger (who discovered debts to Calvin among many other vital points), Jeremy Specland (who advised me concerning the Geneva Bible's French sources and in many other crucial ways), and Henry Turner. Noam Flicker helped with Hebrew and Stacy Klein helped with Old English. Various parts of this chapter were presented to helpful audiences at the Renaissance Society of America in Berlin, the Folger Shakespeare Library, and the Rutgers Medieval-Renaissance Colloquium. Aaron Pratt also advised me with this and other chapters. For the Spenser chapter, I received valuable feedback from Melissa Schultheis and from audience members at the International Congress on Medieval Studies—Robert Stillman in particular. The chapter on *Measure for Measure* appeared in a much earlier version in 2010 as "Shakespeare's *Everyman*: *Measure for Measure* and English Fundamentalism" in the *Journal of Medieval and Early Modern Studies*, and I would like to thank an insightful anonymous reader for that publication, Emily Bartels, Sarah Beckwith, Ann Baynes Coiro, Brian Cummings, Erika Lin, Ray Lurie, James Kearney, Molly Murray, James Simpson, Kirsten Tranter, Susanne Wofford, and audiences at Columbia University and at the Shakespeare Association of America. The chapter on Milton's psalms started as a paper given in Tokyo at the International Milton Symposium in 2013, and I am very grateful for early audiences there (particularly Gordon Campbell, Tom Corns, and John Hale), and at various other venues, including the Renaissance Society of America in Chicago; a longer version was read by members of the Northeast Milton Seminar, whose comments were particularly helpful, with special thanks to Achsah Guibbory, Nicholas von Maltzahn, James Nohrnberg, Jeffrey Miller, and Gordon Teskey. At one of these occasions I received considerable advice about psalms from Hannibal Hamlin. This chapter also benefited greatly from audiences at the Catholic University of America, particularly Tobias Gregory, and Georgetown University, where I received helpful feedback from Daniel Shore, David Norbrook, and Jason Rosenblatt, and years later from audiences at Johns Hopkins University, with special thanks to Sharon Achinstein, Earle Havens, and David Norbrook. The final chapter on Milton benefited from discussions at the International Milton Symposium in Strasbourg, especially with David Loewenstein and Catherine Gimelli Martin.

A book that has taken this long to write has accrued more debts than I can enumerate, especially from Rutgers University. A long list of Rutgers faculty, undergraduates, and graduate students should certainly be added if there were space, as I could not have written it without the kind support of my colleagues and students. Rutgers also provided invaluable sabbatical leaves essential for research and time to attend courses at the Yale Divinity School, where I was able to study the Hebrew Bible with Robert Wilson and have more instructive conversations with Bruce Gordon. Two anonymous readers for the press offered sustained criticism that I hope I have been able to address fully; I am, at any rate, deeply indebted for their care and erudition. I am also grateful for the indexing work of J. Naomi Linzer. Finally, my family has played a crucial role. Jessica Brantley has read every page and offered endless words of advice and support over the years, and I am deeply grateful for her conversation and companionship. My mother, Peg Fulton, may have started all of this when long ago (as a humanities editor at Harvard University Press) she brought home a copy of Frank Kermode's *Genesis of Secrecy* for her puzzled teenager to read. She has read every page with extraordinary acumen and insight, and has been an invaluable interlocutor on the subject of biblical interpretation over the years. My family has been a source of constant support, encouragement, and humor, and I would like to thank Chandler Fulton, Elaine Lai Fulton, Margot Robert, Paul Robert, Kaysh Shinn, William Fulton, Gillian, Lucie, Gabriel, David, and James.